CONTENTS

CONTENTS

THE PITCH...

For almost as long as I can remember, movies were always important, an event, like church, the only difference being that the queue to get in to see *Jungle Book* was a fair bit longer. But movies took you out of yourself, made you belong to something, a quasi-religious experience if you like. Which is why, today, whenever I go to the cinema, I spend the first minutes of every movie worrying in case the audience is going to talk all the way through it.

This book has something to do with all that but it really exists for one reason only – to increase your enjoyment of the movies.

If you want a thoroughly exhaustive reference work, put this back on the shelf now. If you want a film buff's guide to cinema as an art form, sorry. Or if you want a list of the cast and crew on every film, best go elsewhere, there are certain websites we'd recommend.

But if you want several hundred socking good reasons to visit your local rep house, watch a late-night rarity on TV or splash out on that DVD movie you've been promising yourself, you'll find them in here. There are no dull films in this book. Mad films, yes. Great films, certainly. Films that provoke fierce disputes as to whether they're well cool or, well, crap: you bet.

So if your ambition is to spend even more of your life watching films than you already do, this should serve you well. Now go. Use it wisely. And may the hairs on the back of your neck stand on end at least once.

Paul Simpson

PART ONE

WHAT MAKES A MOVIE CULT?
THE HISTORY, THE DIRECTORS, THE STARS
THE BASICS

CULT MOVIES

A cult has been described as any cause, person or object admired by a minority – a definition which comes awfully close to embracing Jerry Lewis' later work. But without cults in general (and cult films in particular) what a grey old world this would be.

There are almost as many different definitions of what makes a cult movie as there are cults in the world today. The movies, where one man's masterpiece is always liable to be someone else's *Howard The Duck*, is a world where no opinion is final and deciding what makes a film 'cult' can be as intellectually arbitrary an exercise as deciding whether a film is 'good' or 'bad'. There is also a considerable difference between the films we watch over and over again and the films which are mentioned in critics' lists of greatest ever movies: the gap between the films we admire and the films we love, however irrationally. (For a selection of actors' and directors' favourite films turn to p16.)

The *Concise Oxford Dictionary* defines 'cult' as:

1) a system of religious worship especially as expressed in ritual
2) a devotion or homage to a person or thing
3) a popular fashion especially followed by a specific section of society
4) denoting a person or thing popularised in this way.

The dictionary, in its linguistic wisdom, assigns the last definition to a cult figure or cult film. In cinematic terms, the word 'cult' has often been applied to films starring 50ft women on a mission of personal revenge, killer tomatoes, or an entire western town populated by midgets. Sometimes this has been extended to include movies that are either 'so bad they're good' (the clichéd example of this genre being any work by the 'world's worst director' Ed Wood) or are the objects of a quasi-religious worship (*Star Wars*).

The word 'cult' also implies some kind of secrecy, a knowledge hidden from the masses. So a cult film may be the preserve of a few (eg *Where's Poppa?*, the comedy where George Segal's brother, dressed in a gorilla costume, is implicated in the gang rape of a policeman in drag) or have depths missed by the casual viewer (while many of us have never wondered what was in Marsellus' case in *Pulp Fiction*, for others it is a celluloid Holy Grail).

THE CULT OF CASABLANCA

Umberto Eco, author of *The Name Of The Rose* (which became a cult book and, to a lesser extent, a cult film) identifies *Casablanca* as a cult movie. This sounds ludicrous as *Casablanca* is one of the most famous films of all time. But Eco goes on to say that: "The work… must provide a completely furnished world so that its fans can quote characters and episodes as if they were aspects of the fan's

STANTON'S LAW

One of the unwritten laws of the film business used to be that Harry Dean Stanton had never appeared in a bad movie. It was a law broken by *Man Trouble* (1992) and *Playback* (1995), but Stanton, by dint of a career in which as a supporting actor he has specialised in what one critic described as "wolf-faced loners", has appeared in more than enough classics for the general principle to still stand.

Repo Man, Paris, Texas, Wild At Heart, The Straight Story, Wise Blood and *The Missouri Breaks* are all to his credit. His performance holds *Paris, Texas* together in a way no mere star (not even the 1980s edition of Jack Nicholson) could have done. Who else could shout: "Repo man is always intense!" with the same insane conviction? Somehow, at the end of *The Straight Story*, when Richard Farnsworth has ridden 300 miles on that lawnmower, it is inconceivable that his estranged brother could be anyone but Harry Dean Stanton. So for these and other reasons too numerous to list, respect.

Harry Dean Stanton. Always immense

private sectarian world, a world about which one can make up quizzes and play trivia games so that the adepts of the sect recognise through each other a shared expertise."

By this definition, *Casablanca* is a cult movie, as is *Pulp Fiction*, just as, in the adjacent kingdom of the small screen, *Monty Python* is still a cult in that people (mostly men) still go around saying "it has ceased to be" and nudging each other hilariously in the ribs. For the purposes of this book, we have taken Eco's definition and added a few other criteria of our own.

Any movie mentioned here should therefore:

1) inspire people to go around quoting it to each other or generally inspire an unreasonable amount of devotion long after the fickle masses have forgotten the movie's existence

2) be good but under-appreciated, possibly because in a marketing machine increasingly built on stars and event movies, they were just too different to be guaranteed a long residence at a cinema near you

3) be an undiscovered gem, possibly because it's foreign or went straight to video in this country

4) be so bad it really is worth watching

5) be compelling for some other reason – the script may stink but there's a song, a stunt or something that makes it all worthwhile

6) be a mainstream film which nonetheless has that indefinable something we can only describe as 'juice'

7) not be *Police Academy 2-7*.

The only thing to add to that is that we have made a conscious effort to include as many different actors, directors, genres and countries as possible. That's because we we think it's possible to enjoy *The Battleship Potemkin* and the moment *Springtime For Hitler* breaks into "Don't be foolish, be a smarty, come and join the Nazi party", to feel a great and irrational exhilaration when you hear John Belushi chant: "Toga! Toga! Toga!", or cheer as an outraged John Wayne thunders into battle shouting: "Fill your hands, you son of a bitch!"

"Was it over when the Germans bombed Pearl Harbor?"

Anyway, enough already...

MAKING MOVIES

This account of the movie industry's rise, fall and rise again focuses on the likes of Ed Wood, urban myths about suicidal munchkins and the chaos theory of filmmaking.

The clash between artistic integrity and commercialism, almost as old as the movies themselves and a major point of contention for many producers, is sent up beautifully in *Sullivan's Travels*, where director John L Sullivan wants to produce a prestige message picture about social conditions called *O Brother Where Art Thou?* but ends up debating the issue with studio executives Hadrian and Lebrand.

Sullivan: I want this picture to be a commentary on modern conditions, stark realism, the problems that confront the average man.

Lebrand: But with a little sex in it.

Sullivan: A little, but I don't want to stress it. I want this picture to be a document. I want to hold a mirror up to life. I want this to be a picture of dignity, a true canvas of the suffering of humanity.

Lebrand: But with a little sex in it.

Sullivan: With a little sex in it.

Hadrian: What about a nice musical?

Hollywood is often accused of crassness, but money rules in most film industries: why else would the French pass a law that Gérard Depardieu must feature in 40 per cent of all that country's films?

Dorothy and friends take a break to figure out where they're up to in *Dark Side Of The Moon*

Sadly, no one has pursued Sullivan's goal of making an important message musical about social conditions "with a little sex in it". That said, *The Howling: New Moon Rising* (1995), a film about line-dancing, a werewolf and a detective, is a valiant bid to straddle all those genres.

THE 1920s: THE SOUND AND SILENCE

The movie business really kicks off with DW Griffith's great, big, racist epic *Birth Of A Nation* in 1916. Hollywood wasn't yet the film industry's epicentre and the greatest director of the time was probably Sergei Eisenstein. Another historical epic, 1925's *Ben-Hur*, directed by Fred Niblo, marked a sad movie first. This is the first film where an extra was reportedly killed on set, in one of the naval battles. When William Wyler remade *Ben-Hur* in 1959 (he'd been 2nd unit director on Niblo's version) the rumour spread that the double for Stephen Boyd had been killed in the chariot scene. It's hard to prove a negative, so neither rumour will ever be completely scotched.

The era of the director-king came to a close as the studios created the 'star' system – most stars being more malleable and less intelligent than their directors. The coming of sound also allowed the studios to cull a few stars such as John Gilbert. Mind you, Asa Yoelson, aka Al Jolson, who said: "You ain't heard nothing yet" in *The Jazz Singer* (1927), didn't last long. The film was a sensation but made $1.5m less than the now forgotten *The Singing Fool*.

Archetypal hero: The Latin lover
Strangest sub-genre: Melodramas about the evils of wood alcohol
Underrated classic: *Pandora's Box*
The actor's actor: John Barrymore
The decade in a phrase: "You ain't heard nothing yet"

THE 1930s: GANGSTERS, MONSTERS, MUSICALS

The screens were bursting with gangsters and monsters (Dracula, Frankenstein, King Kong) and a plethora of musicals so numerous and so bad they almost murdered the genre. The decade began and ended with a John Wayne western – *The Big Trail* (a flop) and *Stagecoach* (a hit). The Duke's reign over the Hollywood western would only end with his death in 1976.

The box-office smash was *Gone With The Wind*, its success proving writer William Goldman's theory that in Hollywood no one knows anything. MGM had turned it down, with Irving Thalberg telling his boss: "Forget it, Louis. No Civil War picture ever made a nickel."

The cult film of this decade is *The Wizard Of Oz*, subject of another 'extra' death riddle. Fans insist that at one point you can see a munchkin hanging himself out there on the horizon, past the Yellow Brick Road. Various accounts of this scene are posted on the Web but read more than a handful of them and all you'll discover is the wisdom of the old Russian proverb: "He lies like an eyewitness."

Archetypal hero: The all-American democrat (Clark Gable)
Strangest sub-genre: German 'mountain' films
Underrated classic: *Fury*
The actor's actor: Spencer Tracy, Greta Garbo
The decade in a phrase: "To die, to be really dead, that must be glorious"

THE 1940s: THE GOLDEN AGE

The decade when the movie industry produced more masterpieces than you'll find hanging in most major art galleries kicked off in fine style with *Casablanca*, *Citizen Kane*, *His Girl Friday* and *The Maltese Falcon*, and rattled on almost as impressively with such differing gems as *Les Enfants Du Paradis*, *Notorious* and *It's A Wonderful Life*.

Screwball comedy was one of the brighter innovations of the late-1930s and (even though it's a remake of *The Front Page) His Girl Friday* is a supreme example of the genre. The speed of Cary Grant and Rosalind Russell's dialogue delivery has been clocked at 240 words per minute – so fast that when Grant says: "The last person to say that to me was Archie Leach, just before he cut his throat," it takes you a while to recall that Archie Leach is Grant's real name.

Casablanca is a chaos theory masterpiece, shot in sequence because the script wasn't ready, so Ingrid Bergman never knew whether she'd walk away with Humphrey Bogart or Paul Henreid at the end of the film. *Citizen Kane*, in contrast, was a considered masterpiece making use of rich shadows and the deep-focus cinematography developed by Orson Welles' cameraman Greg Toland. But, like Capra's *It's A Wonderful Life*, it left the public cold.

But the 1940s greatest legacy may lie in the creation of a genre called 'film noir'. The exact nature (and origin) of the genre is still debated but writer Paul Duncan summed it up best when he said "a lucky day for a resident of noirland was when you didn't get killed".

Archetypal hero: The private eye
Strangest sub-genre: Indonesian Zorro movies
Underrated classic: *Les Enfants Du Paradis*
The actor's actor: Bette Davis
The decade in a phrase: "Here's looking at you, kid"

THE 1950s: AN AMERICAN TRAGEDY

The studio system was already reeling from the double blows of having to change the contracts it gave to stars and selling off its cinemas, when TV came along... Hollywood was convinced that the way to fight TV was with wider screens (Cinemascope, etc), bigger spectacles and shallower pictures. But at the same time sci-fi evolved into a truly subversive genre where movies like *The Incredible Shrinking Man* could raise the then unfashionable concerns about the H-bomb, fallout and social and sexual repression.

The emergence of Federico Fellini, Ingmar Bergman and Akira Kurosawa, and the return of Luis Buñuel made the 1950s less monotonous, but it took Marlon Brando and James Dean to wake Hollywood up and inspire French auteurs like Jean-Luc Godard.

Thank God for Alfred Hitchcock who, in making three great films (*Rear Window*, *Vertigo* and *North By Northwest*) in five years, surpassed what many directors achieve in a lifetime. At the other extreme was Ed Wood: while Hitch was filming his works of genius, Ed was making *Girl Gang Terrorists* and *The Night The Banshee Cried*.

Archetypal hero: The white collar expert (doctor, shrink, scientist, lawyer)
Strangest sub-genre: Argentinian sexploitation movies, heavily censored
Underrated classic: *Kiss Me, Deadly*
The actor's actor: Marlon Brando
The decade in a phrase: "I could have been a contender""

THE 1960s: IF YOU CAN'T REMEMBER THEM...

As the decade opened, the studios were floating wrecks and the movie stars were less glamorous than the occupants of the White House. All of which made this a fascinating cinematic decade, where the moviegoer was presented with more choice than a child at a Woolworths' pick'n'mix counter. You want epics? Try *Cleopatra*. Westerns? You can have traditional (*The Magnificent Seven*), ironic (*El Dorado*) or violent (delivered fresh from Italy). If you want weird films by people who weren't in their heads while they made them, try the Monkees/Jack Nicholson/Bob Rafelson collaboration *Head*. And if you just want macho fantasy, there's always James Bond.

The filming of *Rosemary's Baby* marked the rise of another genre of urban movie legend: the cursed movie. The rumours, this time, have more substance to them than munchkin suicides: the composer Krzysztof Komeda died from a clot in the brain, producer William Castle was rushed into hospital with uraemic poisoning, and Sharon Tate, wife of director Roman Polanski, would later be Charles Manson's most famous victim. Castle had to undergo surgery and when he came round is reported to have shrieked: "Rosemary, for God's sake, drop that knife!"

The name Coleman Francis won't mean much to most movie buffs, but his films make Ed Wood's worst work seem like Stanley Kubrick. One of his efforts, *The Beast Of Yucca Flats*, was bound to struggle after the soundtrack was accidentally erased. Francis wrote the narration himself and takes the credit for lines like: "Boys from the city. Not yet caught up in the whirlwind of progress. Feed soda pop to the thirsty pigs." He ended the decade in a part billed as 'Rotund drunk' in *Beyond The Valley Of The Dolls*. And the biggest box office stars of the turbulent, rebellious, swinging Sixties? Come on down, Doris Day and John Wayne.

Archetypal hero: James Bond
Strangest sub-genre: Filipino 'blood island' movies
Underrated classic: *The Lion In Winter*
The actor's actor: Dustin Hoffman
The decade in a phrase: "The name's Bond. James Bond"

THE 1970s: THE FALL AND RISE

By now, people had stopped trying to change the world and were busy trying to change their sex life instead. So the 1970s began with porn chic. The major studios, meanwhile, were bankrupt and obviously not thinking too clearly. In 1976, Disney and MCA would sue Sony, unsuccessfully claiming that video recorders infringed copyright. Just as well really, because in 1988 video sales of *ET* would reach $150m, more than Indiana Jones' first adventure took at the box office in 1981.

Hollywood spent the decade alternating between disaster epics like *Earthquake* (which prompted a *Time Out* reviewer to note "Any movie in which Charlton Heston dies in a sewer is alright with me") and quirkier films like *Taxi Driver*, *Network* and *Two Lane Blacktop*. Director power made a comeback, with the rapid rise of hot auteurs like Coppola, Scorsese, Bogdanovich, Altman, De Palma, Friedkin and Spielberg, several of whom crashed and burned just as fast.

Comedy took a grosser turn with *Where's Poppa?* starring Ruth Gordon as Segal's senile mum and a scene where George Segal's lover says her ex used to poo in the bed during lovemaking, all some 20 years ahead of the Farrelly brothers' best/worst efforts. But the cult comedian was Woody Allen: this was when he made all his 'early, funny' films, all of which were a welcome relief when so many other movies smacked of 'post-Watergate disillusionment'.

Archetypal hero: Sensitive, gorgeous, slim, weakling (Robert Redford)
Strangest sub-genre: Turkish vampire movies
Underrated classic: *The Conversation*
The actor's actor: Jack Nicholson
The decade in a phrase: "A long time ago, in a galaxy far, far away"

THE 1980s: GREED IS GOOD

A great decade for sci-fi fans with two more instalments of *Star Wars*, *Aliens* and *L'Uomo Puma*, an Italian budget film about a man who is given a medallion which turns him into a puma man. The only way to convey the film's full flavour is to give you a snatch of dialogue:
Jane Dobson: Have you ever made love in the air?
Professor Tony Farms: How else would you make little puma men? How else indeed? But it was also the decade when Gordon Gekko announced "Greed is good" in *Wall Street*. Producer Don Simpson

took him literally and invented the 'high concept' movie, which simply means a movie that can be pitched in 30 seconds. Altman sends this up in *The Player* (1992) when one of the on-screen writers says his film is "not unlike *Ghost* meets *Manchurian Candidate*." Thus Simpson and Jerry Bruckheimer would give us such profitable eye candy as *Top Gun*. By the decade's end, the high concept monster was eating everything in sight. As of 1989, the tally for franchises was: *Back To The Future* 2, *Friday The Thirteenth* 8, *James Bond* 17, *Rocky* 4, *Star Trek* 4. But it wasn't all bad: there was a certain fascination in watching William Shatner's rug develop a character of its own as it went star trekkin' across the universe.

Archetypal hero: The wisecracking all-action hero
Strangest sub-genre: Hindi horror
Underrated classic: *Brazil*
The actor's actor: Robert De Niro, Meryl Streep
The decade in a phrase: "I had a farm in Africa"

THE NERVOUS 1990s

As the 1990s are barely gone, it's too soon to say whether a French critic (and it is always a French critic) will acclaim Adrian Lyne's *Indecent Proposal* as a misunderstood classic. If there's anything positive to come out of the 1990s as a decade of film, it is probably the ease with which a much wider range of films found an audience. In America, this was thanks, partly, to directors like Quentin Tarantino, the Coen brothers and John Woo.

Disappointingly, even bad movies in the 1990s were made with a cheerless technical proficiency. A slight exception to this rule is *Troll 2*, directed by a man called Joe D'Amato but who sometimes bills himself as Sarah Asproon, James Burke, Drago Floyd, Chana Lee Sun or Aristide Massacesi. Such a fine array of aliases promised a long and gorgeously bad career as a director but he turned to high concept porn movies like *Gangland Bangers* which did exactly what it said on the box. Then, in 1999, he died of a heart attack.

Archetypal hero: The virtuous loner
Strangest sub-genre: Japanese high-school horror movies
Underrated classic: *Fight Club*
The actor's actor: Kevin Spacey
The decade in a phrase: "A royale with cheese"

MY FAVOURITE FILM IS...

GILLIAN ANDERSON

"Truffaut's film about his childhood – *The 400 Blows* (*Les Quatre Cents Coups*) – because it's absolutely brilliant. My childhood in Crouch End wasn't anything like that."

KATE BLANCHETT

"I love Krzysztof Kieslowski's *Three Colours: Blue* because it is so enigmatic."

JIM CARREY

"Jimmy Stewart in *Harvey* or *Mr Smith Goes To Washington*."

PETER CATTANEO (director of *The Full Monty*)

"My best film is *On The Waterfront*. It is so inspiring for a young director and still when I go to Hollywood and I walk past the Oscar for the film I feel thrilled."

JULIE CHRISTIE

"*Three Kings* (see p435) and *Galaxy Quest* because it always makes me howl."

JOAN COLLINS

"*The Fabulous Baker Boys* – amazing love story with a grown-up plot and fabulous performances."

JOHNNY DEPP

"*Day Of The Locust*, because I'm obsessed by the 1920s and 1930s in Hollywood."

EDWARD FOX

"It would have to be John Ford's *The Informer* or *La Grande Illusion*."

BRIDGET FONDA

"I've been attracted to horror films since I was 11 and one of my favourites is Sam Raimi's *Evil Dead 2*. It's his most outrageous."

GIANCARLO GIANNINI

"*Seven Beauties*, the Lina Wertmüller film made in 1976, which got four Oscar nominations. It's about a World War II survivor who was a sort of Punchinello in the concentration camps."

TERRY GILLIAM

"Fellini's *8 1/2* because it is seminal to my age group of filmmakers."

NICHOLAS HYTNER (director of *The Madness Of King George*)

"*The Band Wagon*, the most entertaining of all backstage musicals. Wonderful performances, terrific choreography by Michael Kidd, and brilliantly directed by Vincente Minnelli."

ANGELINA JOLIE

"I think everybody has a certain Disney movie that says something about them. *Dumbo* was always laughed at for the things that were strange about him. Eventually he was proud of them."

BEN KINGSLEY

"I was very moved by Wim Wenders' *Wings Of Desire*. For me it was a series of beautifully balanced equations and centres around man, woman, life and death. It's a gorgeous film."

BERT KWOUK

"*Twelve Angry Men* because it has 12 stars. That's my favourite acting, ensemble acting."

MIRIAM MARGOYLES
"*Les Enfants Du Paradis*, because it is morally ambivalent, sexy, full of wonderful performances and a picture of the actor's life that is still true and painful."

JULIANNE MOORE
"I love *Shampoo*, which has such wonderful performances and seems so casual, haphazard and unimportant as you're watching it. It's kind of slippery."

Joan says the Bakers are ab fab

BRAD PITT
"*Hud* with Paul Newman. That made me tear up a little. It's sort of depressing but wonderful."

CHRISTINA RICCI
"*Who's Afraid Of Virginia Woolf?* mainly for the love scene in the car when Liz Taylor laughs."

MEG RYAN
"*Splendor In The Grass*. I cry for no reason at all, even at ads, but there are scenes in this, when Warren Beatty and Natalie Wood fall into adolescent love, that gets me going every time."

KEVIN SPACEY
"*The Lady Eve*, because the double entendres and innuendos are far more sexy and sophisticated than anything seen today on-screen."

ALISON STEADMAN
"*Pather Panchali*. It's so moving. There's a scene where the girl takes her brother out for a long walk, but you don't know where. Eventually you realise they're going to see a train, and then this massive train rolls by and they're standing there and it's like a trip out, an experience for them."

JULIET STEVENSON
"*Happiness*. I am astonished such a film, with a complete absence of any feel-good factor, could come out of America. It is bleak, passionate, and brilliantly observed, written and performed."

DENZEL WASHINGTON
"*PT 109* with Cliff Robertson. There is this really cool guy who had to swim off an island, tread water all night and wait for a boat to come." [Editor's note: The "really cool guy", Denzel, is JFK.]

RAY WINSTONE
"*They Shoot Horses, Don't They?* For an hour-and-a-half you are watching people dance. At the end of the film Jane Fonda pulls a gun out and says to Michael Sarrazin: 'Shoot me.' And he shoots her. The policeman asks him: 'Why did you do it, son?' And he says: 'They shoot horses, don't they?' And I went: 'Yessss!' This director [Sydney Pollack] had bored me for an hour-and-a-half but that one line still has the hairs on the back of my neck stand up on end."

SIGOURNEY WEAVER
"Hitchcock's *Notorious*, starring Cary Grant and Ingrid Bergman, because it is so sexy and suspenseful, while always being romantic and emotional."

DIRECTING MOVIES

"I'm a film director." Sounds impressive. What is it about the title that implies such creativity, glamour, power and, for the very lucky few, an astoundingly healthy bank balance?

MR. HITCHCOCK

In the very early days, there were no directors, just cameramen. The moving pictures themselves were the draw, so the nickelodeons showed footage of people doing everyday things. As film's popularity grew, the exhibitors realised they had to keep people coming back, and demanded a high turnover of filmed stories, new ones every week. The Dream Factory began production, and the early film directors were not much more than factory foremen, hired by studio heads to be in charge of the set, keep things moving and deliver new films as fast as possible.

Films started out as a rough scenario, which the director would flesh out as he went along, usually filming scenes in the order they appeared in the story. Gradually, as the public's taste became more sophisticated and the stories became more complex, directors started using written scripts which could be broken down and filmed more efficiently (all the scenes taking place in one location being shot together, for example), and this became the overwhelming model of production throughout the film industry.

Directors began to be associated with certain genres of film.

Mack Sennett, who made 322 films, was a successful comedy director who created the Keystone Kops and gave Charlie Chaplin his break in Hollywood. More serious subjects and spectacular epics were tackled by directors like DW Griffith and Cecil B DeMille.

In the early 1920s there was an influx of European directors to Hollywood (the lure of Tinseltown was as strong then as it is today). Many, like Paul Leni, Ludwig Berger and Victor Sjöström, made a few films and departed, appalled by the assembly-line approach, although their attention to lighting, decor and cinematography left a lasting impression on American filmmaking. But some European directors flourished: Ernst Lubitsch stayed in Hollywood and made some of the best sophisticated comedies of the late 1930s and 1940s, such as *Ninotchka* and *The Shop Around The Corner*.

ART IN EUROPE; IN HOLLYWOOD, SHOWBIZ

Meanwhile, back in Europe, directors were exploring film as a personal art form, influenced by artists from other disciplines. Expressionism was reflected in films like *The Cabinet Of Dr Caligari* (Robert Wiene) and *Metropolis* (Fritz Lang). The Surrealists Salvador Dali and Luis Buñuel collaborated on the weird-fest *Un Chien Andalou*, featuring eyeballs sliced with razor blades and grand pianos containing dead donkeys.

There was no such pretension in Hollywood. Bums on seats were what they wanted, and directors were judged mostly by box office. The studio system, whereby actors and directors were under strict contract to make films for their studio alone, ruled Hollywood, making it efficient but above all productive. Harry Cohn, head of Columbia in Hollywood's golden age, hired and fired directors at will and referred to his employees as "a lot of other pricks". He was also given to spying on his directors using hidden microphones.

Under this system, Hollywood produced an astounding number of entirely forgettable films, but a few directors broke through the assembly-line approach and put a personal stamp on their movies. Busby Berkeley flourished with his all-singing, all-dancing musical extravaganzas, while Mervyn LeRoy made gritty, violent films such as *Little Caesar* and *I Am A Fugitive From A Chain Gang*.

Another influx of European talent, fleeing Fascism, included directors like Billy Wilder and Fred Zinnemann, and it's ironic that

Man with a Klan: Griffith used the KKK to boost *Birth Of A Nation*

so many of the films that America considers to be the epitome of its own cinema style (*Some Like It Hot, High Noon, White Christmas*) were made by immigrants. Frank Capra, director of small town America classics like *It's A Wonderful Life,* was Sicilian by birth.

Television was a watershed for film directors. Technological advances helped directors like John Huston and Joseph L Mankiewicz to make widescreen westerns and epics, but neither these films nor the glorious technicolour musicals such as those directed by Vincente Minnelli (so popular in the late 1940s) could shore up the film industry.

Gradually, the studios lost their iron grip, and directors became the driving force behind a movie, especially since there were now film schools where they could learn to take themselves very, very seriously. Stars liked to work with directors they knew would make them look good, and directors began to gain their own power to negotiate for creative control and a share of the box-office take.

All-American storyteller, Frank Capra – actually from Sicily

By the 1970s, the most successful directors were making deeply personal films about subjects like Vietnam, but only 10 years later, the 'event movie', spawned in the wake of George Lucas' *Star Wars*, led big studios and many directors back to the formulaic churn-'em-out approach. This time the films were aimed at kids, with John Hughes (*Ferris Bueller's Day Off, The Breakfast Club*) making some of the best teen movies, while teen horror films such as Wes Craven's *Nightmare* series and overblown action/adventure flicks came into their own, the jokes getting ever lamer and the body count ever higher.

THE SIGNATURE

John Ford If a doomed character is playing poker, there will be a close-up of their cards (the ace of spades, another ace and two eights), the same hand Wild Bill Hickock held when he was murdered. At any funeral, the mourners usually sing *Shall We Gather At The River*.

Orson Welles Liked to shoot characters from below, so had to build ceilings onto his sets, especially in *Citizen Kane*, so we wouldn't see the top of the scenery flats.

Alfred Hitchcock The most famous directorial quirk is Hitchcock's habit of using himself as an extra. One blink-and-you-miss-him appearance is as a butler in the songwriter's flat in *Rear Window*.

Less famous is Martin Scorsese's habit of casting his parents: one or both appear in *The Age Of Innocence*, *The Color Of Money*, *Goodfellas*, *King Of Comedy* and *Mean Streets*.

Ernst Lubitsch Mary Pickford called him "a director of doors, not people", alluding to his love of lingering door shots to hint at the naughtiness he was not allowed to show going on behind them.

John Landis Often has a director in his films. Or seven. *Into The Night* has a raft of director cameos from, among others, Amy Heckerling, Don Siegel, David Cronenberg, Jim Henson, Roger Vadim, Jonathan Demme and Lawrence Kasdan.

Inevitably, directors who wanted greater control over their films had to look for backing outside the traditional studio setup. This led to the birth of a now-thriving independent film sector. Female directors like Kathryn Bigelow and Susan Seidelman got a foot in the door, and Spike Lee led the way for young black directors like John Singleton to make films that more accurately reflected the racial make-up of 20th-century America. These days, it's independent directors who garner the lion's share of critical acclaim.

YOU'RE A FILM DIRECTOR. WHAT DOES THAT MEAN?

So what does a film director actually do in the run-up to you parting with hard cash for a cinema ticket, a bucket of popcorn and a vat of Diet Coke? And no, it's not just about sitting in a folding chair with his name on it. While Steven Spielberg's experience of directing a multi-million-dollar blockbuster may be very different from that of Joe film student who has a borrowed a camera and his mum to make sandwiches, their actual responsibilities throughout the various phases of production are pretty much the same.

Even if the script is ready when the director is hired by a producer

UNDER THE INFLUENCE

Pity the poor directors. Each one wants to do something with his films that nobody has ever seen. Sadly, pretty much everything has been done already and they are often reduced to 'paying tribute' to directors past.

John Ford, director of such western classics as *The Searchers* and an influence on many directors today, was heavily influenced by Thomas Ince, a director from Hollywood's early days who established many of the genre's dramatic conventions and its sharp, deep-focus photography. Similarly, the Coen brothers' trademark zany style and complex plotting owe a lot to 1940s director Preston Sturges, who loved absurdly complex stories involving large casts of eccentrics.

Spotting these influences and even, in some cases, duplicates of whole scenes, is a great parlour game. Did Martin Scorsese mean the long single take of Ray Liotta in *Goodfellas* as a tribute to Orson Welles' opening shot in *Touch Of Evil*? In *Educating Rita*, did Lewis Gilbert mean to lift a shot straight out of *Dr Zhivago*?

Deliberate or not, directors will raid other directors' work as long as there's celluloid to fill. But please don't call it stealing – call it a subtle "homage".

Preston Sturges sees the Coens in his future

or gets involved with the film, most directors will continue to work with the writer to bring the script up to the kind of film he thinks it should be. Often (in Hollywood) the director has a fight with the writer and gets him replaced. During this time, casting begins and the director will oversee that process, usually helped by a casting director.

If a big star is to be involved, any script rewrite may be tailored to that star's persona and even include some of their suggestions. The rest of the senior crew members are approved by the director, who might want his favourite director of photography or production designer as part of the team. Once everyone is happy with the script, or at least not too unhappy with it, and the studio (or whoever is putting up the cash) is happy with the team, the project gets the green light.

Pre-production then starts in earnest, and the director oversees every aspect, from locations to lighting to make-up. On a big shoot the director will have minions to do his bidding. But on a low-budget movie, he will do most of it himself.

Once the camera starts to roll, things get really tedious. Generally, a director will first rehearse with actors and crew.

Then everyone stands around while the lighting and camera crews set up what the director has asked for. This is usually when the star is able to use that immortal line: "I'll be in my trailer," as they are usually replaced by stand-ins for the boring bits.

TIME FOR THE DIRECTOR'S CUT...

Scenes are usually shot over and over again, until all the technical crew are happy and the director is happy with the performances from his actors. The director also decides which takes are good enough to be printed by the lab. Throughout filming, 'rushes', the prints of the previous days' filming, are sent over for the director to view. Often, his editor will already have started assembling a very rough cut of the film to speed up the post-production process. Once shooting is finished, the director will work closely with his editing team, and any special effects team, to create the finished film.

If the director is very powerful, his cut will be the final cut. More likely, the producer and the studio will get involved and if they're not happy with the director's cut (usually because it's too long)

AUTEUR THEORY

The popular view that film directors are creative geniuses with something astounding to say to the world through their films owes a lot to an essay by François Truffaut, *Une Certaine Tendance Du Cinéma*, which appeared in a 1954 edition of *Cahiers Du Cinéma*, the bible of intellectual film students.

Although Truffaut's essay was more an attack on the staleness of the French film industry, through various interpretations and subsequent mis-translations the theory emerged that great cinema is created by great directors who were the sole authors of their films and who have a uniquely personal vision and style which can be immediately recognised in any of their movies. This theory became fashionable in film circles, and many

Gauloises were smoked as critics debated which directors deserved the title 'great'.

Applying this theory to Hollywood films had its problems. Critics tended to champion the work of directors who famously battled with the studios and tried to make films over which they had total control. So Orson Welles was a great favourite with the *Cahiers* folk. But this theory ignores the work of many talented directors. Michael Curtiz, a senior contract director at Warner Bros, never made a wave in his life, but his films include *The Adventures of Robin Hood*, *Mildred Pierce*, and *Casablanca*, all with his trademark detailed visual style. Since the Auteur Theory also rates thematic consistency in a director's work, Curtiz loses out on that front too.

The director and the star. But did Quentin re-invent John or did Travolta's genius create the myth of Tarantino?

they'll force him to change it. This is where you get stories about whole scenes that end up on the cutting room floor, like the one in *Notting Hill* that was in the trailer, but not in the finished film, or like the Kevin Costner character who was cut from *The Big Chill*, with only a shot of his wrists left on screen.

The production team may even return to shoot a new ending. Rows between directors and producers at this point can be spectacular. One director stole the print of the film from the editing room when he heard the producer was to exercise his right to make cuts. The film was found hidden in a bathroom having been driven around Los Angeles in the trunk of the director's car.

UN FILM DE...

The director's last job is to promote his film. While Spielberg will have the right to approve his film's poster and publicity materials (and in this way he's rather like Joe film student, who has the same right, because he's probably designing and handing out his own leaflets at the Moose Jaw Independent Film Festival), most directors won't have much say in how the studio markets their work. They'll just turn up at press junkets and try to explain their life's vision in under five minutes using words of one syllable.

In the making of almost every film these same processes take place, but not always in the same order. Some directors initiate their own film projects and are not hired by a producer. Some films are cast before a word of the script is written. Some scripts (such as *Gladiator*) are still unfinished when the film is being made. Some films are shot to fit in with special effects, rather than vice versa. But no matter how it gets put together, the director has to oversee and make decisions about every creative element of a film.

THE DIRECTORS CUT

A book 10 times the size of this could be entirely devoted to a discussion of which directors were all-time greats, but space and your valuable reading time means that we are only able to offer a brief taste of a few of the directors whose films are included in our review section.

WOODY ALLEN

A New Yorker to the bone, Allen developed his very personal brand of talky, neurotic humour as a stand-up comic. Zany hits like *Bananas* gave way to more introspective and some would say less entertaining films, but more recent offerings like *Mighty Aphrodite* are a joy.

ROBERT ALTMAN

It's hard to imagine this maverick director helming episodes of *Bonanza*, but after making his first feature, *The Delinquents*, that's what he did. Luckily, he escaped and broke into the top rank with *M*A*S*H* in 1970, pioneering one of his most recognisable techniques which was to record sound in a way that allowed actors to speak over each other's lines in a far more naturalistic style than had been heard before. Altman's best films, like *Nashville*, *McCabe And Mrs Miller* and *Short Cuts*, feature large casts and wandering narratives, and he likes to use shallow focus to pick his protagonists out of seemingly endless crowds.

LINDSAY ANDERSON

Iconoclastic British director with a passion for socially conscious filmmaking and a distaste for Hollywood – except for John Ford, about whom he wrote a successful biography. *This Sporting Life*, a tense study of a couple's affair in 1960s Yorkshire, embodies his concerns with human desires repressed by convention. His loose trilogy *If...*, *O Lucky Man!* and *Britannia Hospital*, all set around the character of Mick Travis (Malcolm McDowell) became increasingly farcical, but Anderson's disgust with all things bourgeois shines throughout.

JOEL AND ETHAN COEN

Although Ethan is credited as producer and Joel as director, the Coen brothers work very closely on all aspects of making their films. They draw deeply on classic Hollywood cinema, but make the genres their own with stylish scripts and inspired performances. Their first three films all refer heavily to established genres – *Blood Simple* to film noir, *Raising Arizona* to madcap comedy and *Miller's Crossing* to gangster films, but each one is far more than just an homage to filmmakers of the past.

Try as he might, Marty could never get Bobby to take him south of the river

FRANCIS FORD COPPOLA

Like so many of today's top directors, Coppola made low-budget schlock for Roger Corman, but quickly progressed to sumptuous epics with a trademark attention to detail, such as *The*

Godfather and *Apocalypse Now*. Coppola has won five Oscars, but some of his films (such as *One From The Heart* and *The Cotton Club*) have been spectacular box-office flops.

DAVID CRONENBERG

He started out as a purely horror director with films like *They Came From Within*, before moving on to more mainstream subjects, often with a horrific edge. Exploding heads (*Scanners*), TV sets with human entrails (*Videodrome*) and a sexual fetish for car accidents (*Crash*) may sound like gimmicks but Cronenberg's movies always transcend the horror.

FEDERICO FELLINI

His best movies were canvases on which he painted sprawling casts of grotesques engaged in stories of love, creativity and satire. His distinctive imagination led to the adjective 'Felliniesque' being used to describe any eccentric and colourful film moments.

STANLEY KUBRICK

It's rare that a single filmmaker is responsible for such diverse masterpieces as *Spartacus*, *Dr Strangelove* and *2001: A Space Odyssey*, but Kubrick's cinematic genius was never limited to a single genre. Controversial stories like *Lolita* and *A Clockwork Orange* were given a stunning visual gloss without compromising the impact of their subject matter, and although his output was never prolific, it is consistently interesting and provocative.

SPIKE LEE

Lee's technical brilliance is matched by his often in-your-face approach to telling things the way he sees them. Whether an early comedy like *She's Gotta Have It* or one of his more serious later films like *Malcolm X*, Lee's films are characterised by sharp observation, great performances, and a penchant for tackling the uncomfortable issue of racism in all its forms.

DAVID LYNCH

Just when everyone thought brilliant but weird films like *Eraserhead*, *Wild At Heart* and *Lost Highway* were the only kind of film Lynch was interested in making, along came *The Straight Story*, one of the most touching and direct films of recent years.

OLIVER STONE

If there's a conspiracy theory out there, Stone will have made a film about it, whether it's *JFK*, *Salvador* or his Vietnam trilogy: *Platoon*, *Born On The Fourth Of July* and *Heaven And Earth*. His style is to wake up the audience with fast cutting, huge changes of pace and vibrant performances extracted from, if rumours are to be believed, terrified actors. No matter what he does to get the films made, he pulls no punches in getting his stories across.

ORSON WELLES

Despite making only a handful of films on his own terms, Welles looms large over filmmaking history as the director who still claims the title of best feature debut. *Citizen Kane*, made when Welles was only 26, revealed an extraordinary cinematic gift and directors all over the world have adopted Welles' use of eye-popping camera angles, deep focus, sound devices and montage. *The Magnificent Ambersons* and *Touch Of Evil* are also visionary films.

THE ACTORS

Movies were supposed to be a director's medium. So how did actors hijack them, stop being the industry's version of highly paid mules and become 'stars'? Thereby hangs a tale as tortuous as any movie plot.

In the 1920s, a Russian filmmaker called Lev Kuleshov with a mischievous sense of humour (and possibly too much time on his hands) did an experiment. He cut together a close-up of an actor with three other shots: a bowl of soup, a child playing with a toy bear and a woman in a coffin. The audiences raved about the actor's subtlety: how he shifted from pensive contemplation of the soup, to mild joy as he watched the child and to deep sorrow as he stared at the coffin. Only Kuleshov and his pupil knew that they used the exact same shot in all three sequences. (Presumably the later films of Sylvester Stallone are a continuation of Kuleshov's fine work.)

This experiment, one of the most famous in film history, seems to prove a couple of things which don't, today, really need proving. First, that you don't have to act to impress moviegoers. The movie business's most durable star is John Wayne (voted one of the 10 top stars a record 23 times in the industry's annual polls), an actor universally held to be playing himself. This isn't quite fair to the Duke: he hated horses with a rare loathing and, one of his stunt men said, left to his own devices sat about as easily in the saddle as a bag of walnuts. Second, that our need to identify with the human face on the screen is far deeper than we care to admit.

Movies weren't supposed to have stars at all. Until 1910 producers and directors didn't even namecheck their actors, fearing that to do so would only invite demands for higher wages (at that

BESS FLOWERS

THAT EXTRA INGREDIENT

Bess Flowers has appeared in some of the 20th century's seminal movies: *Vertigo*, *Around The World In 80 Days*, *Mr Deeds Goes To Town* and *Singing In The Rain*, to name but four. In a 41-year movie career she appeared in at least 387 films. She is, of course, the über-extra, so dedicated to her craft that in 1935 alone she appeared in 23 films.

Born in Sherman, Texas in 1898, she made her debut as Mrs Nesbit in *The Silent Partner* in 1923. And here, in a way, you could argue her career peaked, because for the next 386 or so films she was lucky if her character had anything as significant as a name. Indeed, her contribution to such classics as *Calamity Jane* and *The Manchurian Candidate* is uncredited.

Her roles do have a certain monotonous similarity. She was 'a well-wisher' in *All About Eve*, the 'woman with poodle' in *Rear Window* while in the Lubitsch/Garbo classic comedy *Ninotchka* she is identified only as a 'gossip'.

She was married to Cullen Tate, Cecil B DeMille's assistant director, although he didn't use her on *The Ten Commandments*. Not that Bess would have minded: she had an uncredited part in that year's winner of the Best Picture Oscar, *Around The World In 80 Days*.

In all, she appeared in five films which won that most coveted of Oscars but may be best remembered for her work in seven movies with the Three Stooges, for Stooges fans have voted her (through the magic of the Internet) the best actor to appear in a Stooges movie.

time, a movie actor might be lucky to earn five bucks a day). And, as film was still a disreputable medium, the actors happily agreed.

But three events would change actors' subordinate position for good. In 1910 movie mogul Carl Laemmle began billing an actress with the wonderfully assonant name of Florence Lawrence by name. Laemmle's profits boomed, Lawrence became the "Queen of the Screen", and other studios followed suit. In the 1920s, studios began to build a star system, realising that actors could be used to sell tickets even if the movie was awful and could be used to raise money as if they were real estate assets. Then in 1944, the unlikeliest of rebels, Olivia de Havilland, won a test case which declared the standard studio contract illegal. The star/studio relationship changed forever with that decision, although it would take the collapse of the studios to make that finally clear.

Among the many rights that these contracts had given the studios was the ability to change an actor's name and to add time onto the end of a contract if a performer was suspended. There was also a 'morals clause', always a useful disciplinary tool in an industry where Mrs Patrick Campbell's dictum (do what you want in the bedroom as long as you don't do it in the street and frighten the horses) was as close as you got to an ethical code.

Hang-dog actor Peter Coyote (the nasty prosecutor in *Jagged Edge*) once divided stars into

"Bess Flowers' gossip has given this comedy something extra"

two types: a few "transformers" who people will pay to see as anything, and a vast array of "archetypes" who will sell tickets as long as they are doing what the audience sees as their thing. The distinction is already apparent in the 1920s with John Barrymore (until booze consigned him to cue cards) able to appeal as Don Juan, Dr Jekyll or Sherlock Holmes. Most of the rest of his peers simply defined (or slotted into) archetypes which still exist today.

The sex goddess. Clara Bow was the "It" Girl (nobody asked what the "it" was). Like her successors (Jean Harlow and Marilyn Monroe), she would be the subject of unsavoury rumours about her private life (for example, the recurring charge that she once had sex with an entire college football team), the whiff of scandal often leading to the sweet smell of success at the box office. Garbo (like Chaplin, famous enough to be known just by her surname) started her career as a fallen woman and only shook off the temptress mantle for a rare comedy, *Ninotchka*. For Monroe, the sexual image only added to her confusion about herself. All the candle-in-the-wind sentimentality has made it easy to underestimate her but as director Billy Wilder admitted, "You would think it's not that difficult to make another Monroe; it should be easy – a blonde, a small girl with a sweet face, my God there should be thousands of them."

The screen lover. Rudolf Valentino's combination of exoticism and eroticism seemed peculiarly threatening in a society still trying

"You'd think it'd be easy to make another Monroe" – wishful thinking from Billy Wilder

to sort out the roles of the sexes after the disruption caused by World War I. Valentino solved the problem by dying. But the studios took note: Clark Gable, the first great sex symbol of the talkies, would be an all-American package, who would sidestep resentment of the kind which had prompted some men to interrupt screenings of Valentino movies by laughing out loud in the cinema. Gable's successors, with the possible exception of Robert Redford, would usually find it necessary to stress their macho credentials.

America's sweetheart. Mary Pickford, Shirley Temple Judy Garland, Doris Day (Suzie Creamcheese as friends call her) in laughing acknowledgement of her virginal onscreen persona) would each in their way be suffocated by this stereotype.

The all-action hero. Douglas Fairbanks (Pickford's significant other) was the first and, some critics insist, the best in a macho genre which would embrace such performers as Errol Flynn, Steve McQueen, Arnold Schwarzenegger and (in more monotonous form) Jean-Claude Van Damme and Sylvester Stallone. In a parallel celluloid universe, William S Hart and Tom Mix took the action hero out West and made him seem to symbolise something deeper, more eternal – a stereotype that would be perfected by John Wayne. Stars like Jimmy Cagney, Humphrey Bogart, and Clint Eastwood have risen by adding varying degrees of violence to this persona.

The clown. Chaplin's tramp is the most famous, but in the 1930s Will Rogers (a Cherokee Indian who once said: "If stupidity got us into this mess, why can't it get us out?") made comedies which touched on such issues as lynching and farms being repossessed. He died in a plane crash in 1935 and is now forgotten.

In his wake would come Jerry Lewis, Woody Allen and Eddie Murphy, but few would have the longevity of Chaplin.

The actor. Not all stars were chosen for their looks. With Bette Davis, the appeal would be at least partly due to the succession of defiant heroines she played, but also because of her obvious acting gifts. Acting with a capital A really began in the 1950s with the Method, a theory about acting which, whatever else it did, gave actors a certain intellectual legitimacy. Not that Noel Coward agreed. He once told a Method-ist: "My dear boy, forget about the motivation. Just say the lines and don't trip over the furniture." The Method was mainly a guy thing and helped ensure that stars like James Dean got much more of the emotional limelight in films than their predecessors.

For all our nostalgia for a golden age, today is, in many ways, the most intriguing time to watch movies. Travis Bickle, Randle Patrick McMurphy, Lester Burnham – these are not roles which, in the old Hollywood, would have sealed the stardom of De Niro, Nicholson and Kevin Spacey.

DUSTIN HOFFMAN'S GUIDE TO ACTING

Producers, Hollywood insurance brokers, and not to mention his wife, are no doubt counting themselves lucky that the king of 'Method' acting, Dustin Hoffman, didn't canvas for the role of astronaut Jim Lovell in *Apollo 13*. Accounting for the few million dollars spent on having him sent into outer space would be difficult even for a numbers genius. Not that we're saying Dustin can go a little too far in the name of art.

MIDNIGHT COWBOY
To make a limp more realistic put pebbles in one of your shoes so you won't swap limping legs and appear on a bloopers show. And to get that consummate dying cough, put so much effort into it that you retch up your lunch.

LITTLE BIG MAN
If you're ever playing a character 87 years older than yourself, in order to get that raspy, on-your-death-bed-yet-the-epitome-of-wisdom voice just right, scream at the top of your lungs in your dressing room for an hour before filming begins.

MARATHON MAN
To convincingly play a character who has stayed up all night, stay up all night. Ignore any pithy comments from co-stars (Laurence Olivier) about it being easier to try acting.

TOOTSIE
Always remain in character, even if it means conducting conversations with close friends (Jon Voight) while in drag.

HOOK
Don't chop your hand off. (Let's not go Method mad.) Do base your portrayal on late great Terry Thomas.

To get his smile right, Dustin spent days slightly amused

IS THAT YOU, LEON?
My Official Wife is an unremarkable 1914 movie about a woman on the run from the Russian police who plots to kill the Tsar. Unremarkable except for the fact that, in an uncredited role as a nihilist, is a young Russian called Leon Trotsky who, just four years later, would be part of the Bolshevik regime which would, indeed, execute the Tsar and (probably) his immediate family.

Strangely, in his memoirs, *My Life*, the future leader of the Russian revolution and enemy of Stalin doesn't dwell on his movie career. (He also appeared, again uncredited, in another spy melodrama *Battle Cry Of Peace* and *The Kiss Of Hate*, starring Ethel Barrymore.) Instead, Trotsky scoffs: "In Norway, journalists had me working as a codfish cleaner and in New York the newspapers had me engaged in any number of occupations, each more fantastic than the last. My only profession in New York was that of a revolutionary socialist."

It wouldn't really have sounded as good if he'd added "and film extra".

But star power has given the lie to the old cliché that the studio system wrecked actors' careers through artistic ignorance and crass commercialism. Stars have, after all, not been much more successful at picking parts than the studios.

James Caan, in one magnificent four-year streak, would turn down *One Flew Over The Cuckoo's Nest*, *Superman* and *Kramer vs Kramer*. To do what? To play in *The Killer Elite*, *Gone With The West* and *Harvey And Walter Go To New York*. If this had been a deliberate strategy to seek obscurity, it could hardly have been more effective. Montgomery Clift had a similar run in the 1950s, turning down the male leads in *Sunset Boulevard*, *East Of Eden*, *On The Waterfront* and *Somebody Up There Likes Me*. Mind you, we must be grateful to whatever mysterious force prevented OJ Simpson from playing *The Terminator*.

Typecasting is subtler these days but it's imposed by the audience who, all things being equal, would prefer to see Jack grinning like a shark, Spacey playing a charismatic sleazeball and Julia Roberts co-starring in every movie she does with either Richard Gere or Hugh Grant, with Albert Finney as her decent, if irascible, boss.

It's a common complaint of actors that people confuse them with their roles. Cary Grant made light of it: when told everybody would like to be Cary Grant, he famously replied: "So would I." Most actors' roles play off our knowledge of their real lives. Why else is Nicholson so often a philanderer? Is it coincidence Brando so often plays a hefty, paranoid, recluse since he became a, well, hefty, paranoid, recluse?

John Updike once observed that celebrity is a mask which eats into the face. The realisation that you are being observed, studied, cannot not have an effect on you. Just as adoration unbalances, as when Geena Davis groaned that Stephen Hawking, the author of *A Brief History Of Time*, had not replied to her letter explaining just how she could help him refute Heisenberg's Uncertainty Principle.

We think of stars as unique, but in industrial terms they can't be. If Tom Hanks can't team up with

Clint shows the unique firing in two directions at once style which has made him such an action hero

Meg Ryan in a romantic comedy, some other heir to Cary Grant's mantle must step in. So, while stars' uniqueness is constantly stressed, the choice between them can be like choosing between different flavours of the same toothpaste. Which may explain why, although we remember actors with staying power, the more striking fact is how transient most acting careers are.

This is one reason we don't remember Florence Lawrence, who helped start all this. She formed her own studio in 1914, injured her back and after two unsuccessful comebacks and years of misery, killed herself in 1938. Her fate was to become wearily familiar though her method was original: she ate a fatal amount of ant paste.

Stars' names live on but, like Rita Hayworth, their vogue may be brief. In the case of Margarita Carmen Cansino (her real name), she was a star at 21 and a has-been by the time she was 30, when she appeared in her husband Orson Welles' *The Lady From Shanghai* (a movie in which no character is actually from Shanghai – Welles invented the title to con Columbia's boss Harry Cohn into financing it.) The film was a poisoned chalice: a misogynistic film noir with a tangled plot that alluded to her real-life relationship with Welles, it was the last movie she made that was worthy of her.

For many actors, success can be defined as delaying failure. The most perfect female movie star, Joan Crawford, lived the role to the hilt, replying to all her fan mail personally. But she ended her days sitting in front of the TV, nursing a bottle of vodka and shouting "Joan Crawford you really stink!" at reruns of her old films.

A STAR REALLY IS BORN

Most of us enter this world with three things: a mother, a father and a birth certificate. Jack Nicholson arrived with none of these things. The official proof of his birth is lost somewhere in New Jersey officialdom, the identity of his father is still in dispute and the woman he thought was his mother was actually his sister. (The woman he thought was his grandmother was actually his mum.)

Nicholson may have been lucky. As dysfunctional as his family seems from outside, he was (by all accounts) smothered with love. Even a casual inspection of star biographies reveals a certain monotonous (and depressing) similarity: one psychologist estimates that up to a third of stars have suffered parental rejection as a child.

The classic star combo is the absent or weak father and a domineering or smothering mother. Lucille Ball, Charles Chaplin, Cher, Douglas Fairbanks, Jodie Foster, Greta Garbo, Samuel L Jackson, Demi Moore, Eddie Murphy, Gary Oldman and Julia Roberts all fall into this pattern.

Variations on the theme include: James Dean (mother died of cancer when he was nine); Clark Gable (mother died when he was six months old); Cary Grant (mum disappeared when he was nine – to a seaside resort, he was told, but actually to a mental home, and he didn't see her again until he was in his 20s); Sophia Loren (born illegitimate); Marilyn Monroe (mother abandoned her to an orphanage when she was nine); and Meg Ryan (hasn't spoken to her mother since she was 15 when her mum quit the Ryan household to become an actress). So if you're reading this and you're not already a movie star, it's probably something else you can blame on your parents – but only if they're still together.

PART TWO

FROM A BOUT DE SOUFFLE
TO ZOLTAN, HOUND OF DRACULA

THE FILMS

ACTION & ADVENTURE

The scene: a typical snowy winter's day in Chicago. It's quiet, too quiet in fact. If you had a suspicious mind, a cop's mind, you'd think something was about to happen. And you'd be right. When disaster strikes, only one man keeps his head (while others, often literally, are losing theirs). Armed only with a flow of wisecracks and a magically white T-shirt, can this lone hero save the world?

"MY NAME IS INIGO MONTOYA, YOU KILLED MY FATHER, PREPARE TO DIE!"
Inigo Montoya, The Princess Bride

Sound familiar? Sound like a fast and furious shoot 'em up you may have seen recently? Towards the end of the 1970s the term action/adventure film took on a whole new meaning. An audience's appetite for action had previously been sated with a dusty western, a Charlton Heston epic or an America-against-the-world war movie. For good old-fashioned adventure you might head for an Errol Flynn/Basil Rathbone swashbuckler, but action-for-action's-sake films came into their own with Spielberg's *Jaws* (1975) and Lucas' *Star Wars* (1977).

From then on, if you couldn't write the plot of a movie on the back of a business card, it was too complicated. And the ideal action blockbuster should aim to be around 100 minutes (*First Blood*, 90 minutes, *Beverly Hills Cop*, 99 minutes, *Top Gun*, 110 minutes). Beyond this and people would start worrying about whether they'd switched the oven off. Besides, as Alfred Hitchcock put it: "The length of a film should be directly related to the endurance of the human bladder."

The basic elements of the action film are rip-offs of every other cinematic genre. Take the gunfights of a western, the explosions of a war film, the car chases of the quintessential crime thriller, add a slice of comedy, a romantic love interest and you've got yourself a Mel Gibson blockbuster.

Classic action leads are usually male (Sigourney's an occasional exception), from the wrong side of the tracks, taking on a particular mission as part of their job, but also because it holds deep personal meaning for them. Indiana Jones can't bear to see an archaeological artefact fall into the wrong (often Nazi) hands, while Axel Foley (*Beverly Hills Cop*) is chasing the killers of his best friend. If emotional involvement isn't a factor, there's always greed (Michael Douglas as a treasure seeking soldier of fortune in *Romancing the Stone*).

Once you've got your tried and tested plot, your overpaid star and your checklist of set pieces, there's only one final element to take care of: a cheesily addictive soundtrack, preferably with a hit single. The definitive example being *Take My Breath Away*, used to promote first *Top Gun* (1986) and later, French cars. Now you have all the necessary ingredients, feel free to read on.

Thrills Pimpernel style: the frills are thrilling, as for action, there's the Sicilian Canal-Sokolsky Attack, 3...Bd7

ADVENTURAS DE ROBINSON CRUSOE 1954

Director Luis Buñuel *Cast* Dan O'Herlihy, Felipe de Alba, Jaime Fernandez

This simple telling of the Robinson Crusoe tale displays little of Buñuel's usual flamboyant surrealistic flair. But the additions he made (with blacklisted writer Hugo Butler, who had to amend the script by night so as not to arouse the suspicions of O'Herlihy) are memorable: Crusoe's furious reaction when Man Friday finds and puts on a dress and his fevered dream of scrubbing a pig while being lectured by his father. Irish star O'Herlihy was nominated for an Oscar for his stirring, unsentimental portrayal of Crusoe, with strong support from de Alba. The colour in some scenes now looks a bit washed out, but the film is still one of the most original reworkings of Daniel Defoe's classic adventure story. Most moving of all is the scene where Crusoe, mad from loneliness, goes to the valley of echoes and shouts the 23rd Psalm to himself as the valley echoes back "The Lord is my shepherd; I shall not want".

THE AFRICAN QUEEN 1951

Director John Huston *Cast* Humphrey Bogart, Katharine Hepburn, Robert Morley

John Huston's jungle adventure (which he insisted he shot on location in the Congo – more chance of shooting an elephant there) sees Humphrey Bogart's hard-nosed, gin-swilling riverboat captain Charlie Allnut meeting his match in the form of prissy missionary Rose Sayer (Katharine Hepburn). You wonder how the film might have changed if the makers had stuck with their original plan to cast David Niven as the male lead. The couple fend off both the advances of a German army and the perils of the jungle itself, making their hazardous way down an East African river in Charlie's clapped-out steamer *African Queen* and falling for each other in the process. It might sound far-fetched, but this is a beautifully moving, romantic adventure story. See Clint Eastwood's *White Hunter, Black Heart* for an unsettling account of the making of the film.

AGUIRRE: WRATH OF GOD 1972
Director Werner Herzog *Cast* Klaus Kinski, Alejandro Repulles, Cecilia Rivera

> "WELL, I AIN'T SORRY FOR YOU NO MORE – YA CRAZY, PSALM-SINGING, SKINNY OLD MAID!"
> Charlie Allnut, The African Queen

Although the opening credits attribute this tale of Spanish conquistadors heading off in search of the cities of gold to an actual diary written by monk Gaspar de Carvajal, Herzog now admits that he invented this to give his tale more credibility. What is most startling about this story, shot on location in the Amazonian jungles, is the director's attention to detail. The opening shot pans down from the spectacular scenery of the group in the Andes, to detail the character of each figure and their place in the tale. Although star Kinski rarely displayed much discrimination when choosing his roles, his best work often came from collaborations with the equally intense Herzog.

BEAU GESTE 1939
Director William A Wellman *Cast* Gary Cooper, Ray Milland, Brian Donlevy

This remake of the 1926 silent original starring Ronald Colman succeeds in heightening the excitement of PC Wren's classic tale of heroism. Cooper is the eldest of three brothers from a well-to-do British family who run off and join the French foreign legion to avoid scandal back home. The brothers get a rough ride from the sadistic legion leader, Donlevy. Donlevy's character was originally called Lejeune, but to avoid offending the French, he became a Russian called Markoff. Visually stunning, the rousing Wellman version is the best of the bunch, although the 1966 Marty Feldman rendition, *The Last Remake of Beau Geste*, is worth a look for comic value.

BEVERLY HILLS COP 1984
Director Martin Brest *Cast* Eddie Murphy, Judge Reinhold

The forerunner of a million action comedies, *Beverly Hills Cop* (summed up as simply as it was probably pitched in the first place) sees Axel Foley (Eddie Murphy) as the tough, foul-mouthed cop from the wrong side of town heading to the land of beautiful people to hunt down the killer of his friend. Judge Reinhold and John Ashton play the bad cop, good cop sidekicks, but, despite the laughs, the action is the key feature. *Beverly Hills Cop* remains the highest-grossing R rated film. For full enjoyment steer clear of trimmed-for-TV versions.

CAPTAIN BLOOD 1935

Director Michael Curtiz *Cast* Errol Flynn, Olivia de Havilland, Lionel Atwill, Basil Rathbone

Warner Bros' original choice to play physician-turned-pirate Rafael Sabatini was Robert Donat, but when he failed to turn up at the start of shooting, an unknown Australian called Errol Flynn was hired. The film also marked the first appearance of the Flynn, de Havilland and Rathbone trio, who went on to star in a string of similar swashbucklers. Here Flynn is forced to change careers and become the pirate Captain Blood (although he already seems a dab hand at the old sword fighting and other swashbuckling activities) to save himself and England. Although rescue adventure stories of this kind spawned imitations, often with Flynn reprising the same role, *Captain Blood* stands out as Flynn's first starring role, one which cemented him in Hollywood history. Youthful, dashing and with a constant glint in his eye. A star was born, and an ego hideously inflated.

DIE HARD 1988

Director John McTiernan *Cast* Bruce Willis, Alan Rickman, Bonnie Bedelia

As Willis stars in his first, and best, stint as a lone man against the odds, you can tell just how far along you are in the story by the state of his T-shirt: white for low body count, steel grey for treble figures. The plot for what remains one of the best modern action flicks is a simple one: a cop from out of town is thrown into a dangerous situation where he is the only man who can save not just a bunch of hostages, but more importantly his wife.

KING CANUTT

THE STUNT MAN

One man staged the chariot race in Ben-Hur, taught John Wayne how to ride a horse, talk and fight on film, and also controlled the horses when they were getting a bit skittish as Atlanta burned in *Gone With The Wind*. His name? Yakima Canutt. Hollywood's most influential stuntman, Canutt was born in Penewawa Creek in Washington state (despite the name and the birthplace he was of European descent) in 1896. He took the name Yakima because that was where he first became famous as a rodeo rider just after World War 1. After a rodeo in Los Angeles, he met Tom Mix and got work as an extra on one of his films. He never, as they say in Hollywood, looked back.

His influence on Wayne was immense: "I spent weeks studying the way Yakima Canutt walked and talked," said Wayne. "He was a real cowhand. I noticed the angrier he got, the lower his voice, the slower the tempo. I try to say my lines low and strong and slow, the way Yak did." As a fake cowboy, Wayne was smart enough to learn from a real one. Canutt worked with John Ford but was too independent to survive the director's sets for long.

Not that he missed out, working on *Gone With The Wind* and *Ben-Hur* where, as 2nd unit director, he spent two years planning, organizing and choreo-graphing the most famous chariot race in film history with his son Joe doubling for Heston in the long shots. That was probably his finest hour. He died in 1986.

All the action clichés are present – non-American baddies (German in this case), an overweight, black, doughnut-eating cop as Willis' CB sidekick, and an intermittent stream of wisecracks interspersed with hard-boiled violence. Where *Die Hard* stands above its rivals is in the quality of its acting, particularly from Alan Rickman as the ultimate suave yet lethal terrorist, Hans Gruber. Don't settle for any imitations.

FIRST BLOOD 1982

Director Ted Kotcheff *Cast* Sylvester Stallone, Richard Crenna

The lasting image of John Rambo is of a muscle-bound man in full militia battledress, complete with blood-red headband and M-16 strapped to his side, doing his best impression of a mumbling Rocky Balboa. Rambo movies, however, don't degenerate into complete cliché-ridden schlock until Roman numerals have been added to the title (eg "God would have mercy, John Rambo won't" – the tagline for *Rambo III*). This first Rambo story finds the former Green Beret and Vietnam veteran (struggling to readjust to normal peace-time society) searching for his only surviving comrade, but drifting into the wrong town. No holds barred blood-and-guts action engulf the screen from here on, with Stallone overcoming bigotry and his own demons. Sigmund Freud might have read something into the fact that the knife he wields gets bigger in each film but we certainly won't. Not to Mr Stallone's face anyway.

LINDA HAMILTON

The climax to the cult classic *The Terminator* sees heroine Sarah Connor (Linda Hamilton) driving off into the sunset in search of a place to hide so she can prepare for future battles with Skynet Terminators. Seven years later, a radically transformed Sarah returns to our screens. Seemingly, our heroine thought that if wimpish Michael Biehn was as good a defence as she was going to get from her future rulers, she'd better learn to look after herself. Complete with rippling muscles, an artillery of weapons and a barrage of dubious biker allies to help her, did she really need Arnold and his clunking size 10s to confuse the situation? Up

until this point women's roles in action and adventure films had usually been that of screaming damsels in distress. (See Olivia de Havilland as Maid Marion or that irritating screecher Kate Capshaw – aka Mrs Spielberg – in *Indiana Jones And The Temple of Doom*.) But from *T2* on, actresses were demanding more brawn in their roles. Given that extra bit of encouragement to get down the gym by Hamilton's example, women were heading for a different kind of action. Cue gun-toting *Thelma & Louise*, or Rene Russo who kick-boxed her way into Mel Gibson's affections in *Lethal Weapon 3 & 4*. Thanks, Linda.

G.I. JANE 1997

Director **Ridley Scott** *Cast* **Demi Moore, Viggo Mortensen, Anne Bancroft**

With such a distinct lack of female action heroes, everyone involved with *G.I. Jane* must have thought they were on to a sure-fire winner. *Private Benjamin* without the comedy or the ditzy blonde, Demi (with bulging biceps and shaven head) completes a gruelling course and is chosen as the first woman to train to be a Navy SEAL. If they'd left it at that, the reviews would have been a lot more favourable and Moore's plummet into obscurity wouldn't have started so early. But the plot turns from one woman against the odds to America against The Enemy. Any feminists hoping to see a strong female lead should stay clear as Moore simply does her best impression of her (now ex) husband Bruce Willis. Those who just want to improve their one-arm press-ups should definitely check this out.

GUNGA DIN 1939

Director **George Stevens** *Cast* **Cary Grant, Victor McLaglen, Douglas Fairbanks Jnr**

You can always rely on Rudyard Kipling for a rousing adventure tale (see *The Man Who Would Be King* for further proof). In *Gunga Din*, which is based on a Kipling poem, three soldiers based in British India must overcome the savage Thuggee cult and find the gold Indian temple. Somewhere between a Three Musketeers film and Indiana Jones (Spielberg featured the same Indian cult in *Indiana Jones and the Temple of Doom*), the swashbuckling action is enhanced through the relationship of our four heroes, with Grant on top comedic form and Fairbanks as the romantic lead. No doubt Hollywood shortly give it the makeover treatment with George Clooney and his band of merry bachelors in the lead roles.

> **"THEY DREW FIRST BLOOD, NOT ME. THEY DREW FIRST BLOOD"**
> John Rambo, First Blood

HARD BOILED 1992 LASHOU SHENTAN

Director **John Woo** *Cast* **Chow Yun-Fat, Tony Leung Chiu Wai, Philip Chan, Teresa Mo**

American producers certainly made the action film into the monster that it is today, but in the 1990s Hong Kong enjoyed its own cinematic resurgence with directors, led by John Woo (see also Johnny To and Yonfan), adding a harder edge to the action. Although Woo claims violence makes him sick ("I get pretty upset. And I'd bring that to the screen. Let's beat him harder, let's hit him with more bullets"), you wouldn't guess it from looking at his movies. The *Hard Boiled* plot is standard action fare, very similar to *Beverly Hills Cop*: dedicated cop (Yun-Fat) seeks out the killers of his partner with the aid of an undercover agent. The action, however, is slick and choreographed, featuring what have become Woo trademarks (the Mexican stand-off between adversaries, two-handed gun action, slow motion and freeze-frame shots) and the comedy is blacker than the usual wisecracks. One of the best action films of the last decade, but stick to the original Cantonese version.

HERCULES 1957 LE FATICHE DI ERCOLE

Director **Pietro Francisci** *Cast* **Steve Reeves, Sylva Koscina, Fabrizio Mioni**

> **"NOW YOU'RE ALL UNDER ARREST. HER MAJESTY'S VERY TOUCHY ABOUT HAVING HER SUBJECTS STRANGLED"**
> Archibald Cutter, Gunga Din

Who would have thought a former Mr Universe (Steve Reeves) would help to create an entire new cinematic genre? Prior to the release of this 1957 version of the labours of Hercules (Nemean lion, Erymanthian boar et al), Italy was churning out a modest 10 costume epics a year. Between 1960 and 1964, however, the number increased to more than 150. Admittedly the standard of Hercules movies diminished somewhat. Hercules was no longer seen out on adventures with Jason and his Argonauts – he was up against Genghis Khan, the Incas, or Spanish pirates, and in 1974 he was battling against the perils of the biggest and baddest of cities, the Big Apple. Such absurdities probably came down to the need to appeal to American audiences, hence the import of American 'stars' Broderick Crawford, Bob Mathias (Olympic decathlon champion) and Jayne Mansfield. *Hercules* is the original, but the alternative lavish spectacles in the same vein include *Hercules Unchained*, *Goliath and the Barbarians (Il Terrore dei Barbari)* and *Dual of the Titans (Romolo e Remo)*.

HIGHLANDER 1986

Director **Russell Mulcahy** *Cast* **Christopher Lambert, Sean Connery**

You have to wonder if the language coach for *Highlander* ever worked again after you have listened to Lambert's non-specific hodgepodge of an accent and Connery's Spanish/Scottish brogue. Although the dubious accents and Queen's stirring *It's A Kind Of Magic* theme song dominate the memory, the original (by Hollywood standards) plot and fast camera action from pop-video director Mulcahy make an electrifying action adventure film out of this tale of an immortal warrior learning swordsmanship, battling through time to confront his power-hungry enemy in (where else?) modern-day New York. It's not without its clichés (evil guy kidnaps good guy's girl, good guy saves girl) but the acting – even from Lambert who has not been as good since – and the glorious, rugged scenery (particularly those parts shot in Scotland), help make *Highlander* cult. Lambert says "It's a kind of magic" just before he goes off to the final battle, just to ensure you buy the album.

LETHAL WEAPON 1987

Director Richard Donner *Cast* Mel Gibson, Danny Glover,
Gary Busey

Suicidal cop Martin Riggs (Gibson) is partnered with steady
family man Roger Murtaugh (Glover). Together they head off
after drug lord and murderer Mr Joshua (Busey, armed with
fierce bleach job). With so many poor imitations since, it's hard
not to see the *Lethal Weapon* series as simply another loud, brash
cop film, but the fact there are so many take-offs is just proof
that this is a classic. Gibson is at his best as the crazed Vietnam
vet who doesn't play by the book and Glover has the straight-
man routine to a tee. It's also worth noting that
originals such as this kept a hard edge to the
violence, warranting an 18 certificate, a rarity now
that an 18 rating is seen as a box-office killer.
Classic scene: the final battle between Mr Joshua
and Riggs. Both men did their own stunts and took
up martial arts to make this a cult fighting scene.

THE MAN WHO WOULD BE KING 1975

Director John Huston *Cast* Sean Connery,
Michael Caine, Christopher Plummer, Saeed Jaffrey

Huston believed the most important part of his job
was casting, and Connery and Caine are perfectly
cast as British soldiers in India, conning the local

**"I don't mind the woods, it's the
Jewish miracle man I'm scared of"**

people into believing Connery is a god. Originally,
Huston had envisaged Gable and Bogart, and then Redford and
Newman as our heroes, but neither pairing would have been
able to provide the story with the 'Englishness' it needs. Fine
support is provided by Saeed Jaffrey and (among others) a 103-
year-old Karroom Ben Bouih in his first and only screen
appearance, as the high-priest Kafu-Selim.

MUTINY ON THE BOUNTY 1935

Director Frank Lloyd *Cast* Charles Laughton, Clark Gable,
Franchot Tone

Lloyd had thought of playing Captain Bligh himself. In the end,
the closest he got to it was to have Charles Laughton model his
character's black beetly eyebrows on the director's. Laughton
dominates the film but Gable won the Oscar. He may have
deserved it because Laughton played Bligh as someone who
could not look his colleagues straight in the eye. A sound piece
of characterisation but nevertheless one which played hell with
Gable's attempts to match his eyelines. The sea played even
greater hell with Laughton's stomach. As Dustin Hoffman says
of this film, the scariest thing about it is that Laughton's Bligh is

THE DIRECTORS

JOHN WOO
(Hard Boiled, Hard Target, Face/Off, MI:2)
Hong Kong's premier film talent is now building up a body of work in the US. He even managed to make Jean-Claude Van Damme look like more than a long-haired buffoon throwing his legs about (not easy). Trademarks: balletic fight sequences, motorbikes, doves in flight and two-handed gun play.

MICHAEL BAY
(Bad Boys, The Rock, Armageddon, Pearl Harbor)
Bay might still have been only a relative newcomer, but it was his *Bad Boys* that cemented Will Smith as the new multi-million dollar action hero. Trademarks include intense slow motion shots of his characters, usually just before all hell breaks loose. It was also his decision to kill Bruce Willis in *Armageddon*.

TONY SCOTT
(Top Gun, Beverly Hills Cop II, Days of Thunder, Revenge, Last Boy Scout, Enemy of the State)
So committed to action he turned down *Beautiful Girls* (1996) because he felt he couldn't do justice to a film with such a strong emphasis on character and dialogue. Trademarks include a heavy use of smoke and light breaking through windows.

RIDLEY SCOTT
(Black Rain, Gladiator, Thelma & Louise, G.I. Jane)
Brother of Tony (above). Trademarks include stunning visuals (the landscape in *Thelma & Louise, 1492* in its entirety) and strong female leads.

easily the smartest person on the ship. Look out for a cameo from James Cagney, who happened to be passing the location and told director Lloyd that he was looking to earn a bit of extra cash and would be happy to help.

THE PRINCESS BRIDE 1987
Director Rob Reiner Cast Cary Elwes, Robin Wright, Mandy Patinkin, Chris Sarandon, Andre the Giant
In true fairytale fashion, the opening sequence sees a grandfather (Peter Falk) reading his bedridden grandson a bedtime story. The tale is a classic one of love and adventure with duelling and fighting, monsters and giants, captures and escapes, and – spoiler alert! – happy endings. Buttercup (Wright, pre-Penn hyphenation) and Westley (Elwes) fall in love, only for Westley to be lost at sea. Buttercup is seized by the wicked Prince Humperdinck (Sarandon) as his bride-to-be, and so ensues a fantastical journey with rhyming giants, an embittered (and Jewish) miracle man ("You rush a miracle man, you get rotten miracles") and a swordsman extraordinaire ("My name is Iñigo Montoya. You killed my father, prepare to die"). Scripted by William Goldman from his own original novel, the film's humour is sharp, appealing to children and adults alike, with Reiner proving he can do more than coax Meg Ryan to orgasmic climax.

THE PRISONER OF ZENDA 1937
Director John Cromwell Cast Ronald Colman, Madeleine Carroll, David Niven, C Aubrey Smith
This lavish costume adventure sees Colman taking on the dual role of King Rudolf V and his distant cousin, who stands in for the king to save the country from his evil half-brother, the Duke of Strelsau (Raymond Massey). This is the best by far of six versions (avoid the 1979 Peter Sellers effort as if it were a biblical plague. Or worse, a live national lottery draw). Dashing support is provided by both David Niven and Douglas Fairbanks Jr in his scene-stealing performance as villainous Rupert of Hentzau. The tagline of "the most thrilling swordfight ever filmed" probably holds true today. Without

consulting his director, producer David Selznick had additional footage shot by WS Van Dyke and George Cukor, as he wasn't happy with Cromwell's work. Restless entrepreneur/auteur Selznick would later replace his *Gone with the Wind* director Cukor with Victor Fleming and later, Sam Wood.

RAIDERS OF THE LOST ARK 1981
Director Steven Spielberg Cast Harrison Ford, Karen Allen

Only the Midas touch of Spielberg and Lucas (who wrote the story; future director Lawrence Kasdan helped out too) could create a contemporary adventure story in which the main protagonist is an archaeologist. But with Ford in the title role (Indiana is named after George Lucas' dog), this is a classic adventure yarn, with a rugged if bumbling hero ("I'm making this up as I go along"), evil adversaries in Hitler's Nazis, and events in far-off lands. Only the modern-day visual effects set this apart from something Michael Curtiz might have directed. There are enough references to previous Spielberg and Lucas classics for film fanatics to have a field day (eg the hieroglyphics in the Well of Souls include engravings of R2-D2 and C-3P0).

ROMANCING THE STONE 1984
Director Robert Zemeckis Cast Michael Douglas, Kathleen Turner, Danny DeVito, Zack Norman

Michael Douglas is caddish adventurer Jack Coltan (such a classically heroic name), embroiling spinster romantic novelist Joan Wilder (Turner) in a quest for riches, while she is only out to save her sister. The two stars are perfectly cast in what was seen as an Indiana Jones adventure for an older generation, their sparring wit and jibes interspersed with the more slapstick humour of comic villains DeVito and Norman. Douglas, Turner and DeVito went on to make a sequel (*The Jewel of the Nile*) and the black comedy *The War of the Roses* (see p109).

"HE DOESN'T
PUNISH MEN
FOR DISCIPLINE.
HE LIKES TO SEE
MEN CRAWL"
Fletcher Christian, Mutiny On The Bounty

THE SCARLET PIMPERNEL 1934
Director Harold Young Cast Leslie Howard, Merle Oberon, Raymond Massey

"They seek him here, they seek him there, the Frenchies seek him everywhere. Is he in Heaven? Is he in Hell? That damned elusive Pimpernel." Although he will forever be remembered (to his own disgust) as Ashley Wilkes in *Gone with the Wind*, here Howard is the perfect incarnation of the foppish British aristocrat Sir Percy Blakeney, leading a double life in 18th-century France. Howard started acting as therapy for shell shock, but when World War II began, he quit to devote his time to the war effort, dying in 1943 when his plane was shot down.

THE THREE MUSKETEERS 1973

Director Richard Lester *Cast* Oliver Reed, Raquel Welch, Richard Chamberlain, Michael York, Frank Finlay

Lester's tongue-in-cheek version of the classic Alexandre Dumas tale was originally slated as a film venture for The Beatles. (Lester had directed them in *A Hard Day's Night* and *Help*.) Fortunately for us, the film became an unlikely star vehicle for Oliver Reed, who nearly died when he was stabbed in the throat during a duel sequence. The sequel (*The Four Musketeers*) was filmed at the same time as this original, but the actors believed all the scenes were part of one film. The actors successfully sued Lester but the damages didn't amount to what they would have each been paid for two productions. Amazingly, most of the cast were still prepared to film a third in the series, *The Return of the Musketeers*, with Lester in 1990.

> **"NOT GODS, ENGLISHMEN, WHICH IS THE NEXT BEST THING"**
> Peachy Carnehan,
> The Man Who Would Be King

THUNDERBOLT AND LIGHTFOOT 1974

Director Michael Cimino *Cast* Clint Eastwood, Jeff Bridges

This, director Cimino's debut four years before his much-lauded *The Deer Hunter*, sees Eastwood as a wise, older thief out to retrieve the loot from a previous robbery. Bridges, in a scene-stealing performance, is the good-natured yet wild drifter who becomes embroiled in the adventure and pupil to Eastwood's tutor. Although the two have yet to team up again, *Thunderbolt and Lightfoot* has all the elements of an excellent buddy movie. The film is also notable for an early appearance by Gary Busey as Curly; Busey would go on to make a healthy living starring in almost every Hollywood action film thereafter (*Lethal Weapon*, *Predator 2*, *Point Break*, *Under Siege* and *Drop Zone*).

VANISHING POINT 1971

Director Richard Sarafian *Cast* Barry Newman, Cleavon Little

Cross an ex-cop with an ex-race car driver and you get a man who, when put behind the wheel of a 1970 Dodge Challenger R/T, just has to drive as fast as he can, ignoring a growing fleet of cops on his tail. Obviously we eventually discover the deep and meaningful reasons behind the reckless behaviour of our driver Kowalski (Newman), but *Vanishing Point* – complete with the mysterious guiding light of blind DJ Super Soul (Little) – is a surreal interpretation of the ultimate car chase. The chases, as exciting as any in more recent action films, are interspersed with esoteric scenes of gay hitchhikers and naked motorcyclists. Charlotte Rampling originally appeared as one of those whom Kowalski met along the way but her scenes were cut. Avoid the 1997 remake with Jason Priestly in the DJ role – need we say more? But Walter Hill's *The Driver* (1978) offers similar thrills.

ALCOHOL

The film industry is full of boozers. The celebrated antics of drunken films stars like Errol Flynn, Dean Martin and Sid James are the stuff of movie legend. But on film it's often a different story. America's puritanical roots have historically demanded that drinking to excess be punished by breakdown, death, or, worst of all, rehab. Thankfully, drunks on film can now be interesting, even likeable characters, despite their fondness for the cocktail hour.

BARFLY 1987

Director Barbet Schroeder *Cast* Mickey Rourke, Faye Dunaway

An underrated gem with Rourke and Dunaway turning in two of their best performances. Henry, a poet and drinker, meets Wanda, a woman who hangs out in bars waiting for men to buy her drinks. Both have become so enmeshed in the world of seedy bars and all-night drinking dives that when someone publishes Henry's poetry, he is unable to seize the chance of acclaim and a new life. *Barfly* manages to be painfully sad yet still retains a genuine sense of humour, it's a real shame this didn't do better in the cinemas.

THE BUTCHER BOY 1997

Director Neil Jordan *Cast* Stephen Rea, Eamon Owens, Fiona Shaw

Films featuring stereotypical violent, drunken Irishmen are almost a sub-genre of their own, but this one is a lot more interesting than most. The instability of Francie's (Owens) home life with his alcoholic father and suicidal mother leads to his own gradual descent into madness, culminating in increasingly bizarre acts of destruction and gore. That these things are being done by an angel-faced 12-year-old makes the story all the more fantastical. What humour the film contains is blacker than black, and some of the more stomach-turning moments edge it into the realms of horror, but it remains a compelling and hugely original piece of work throughout.

When drunk, Elwood liked to go to fairs and win toy furry animals

47

DAYS OF WINE AND ROSES 1962
Director **Blake Edwards** *Cast* **Jack Lemmon, Lee Remick**

A young couple who seem to have it all find themselves sinking deeper and deeper into alcoholism. This may sound like a moralizing TV movie, and was in fact based on John Frankenheimer's 1958 TV drama of the same name, but Lemmon and Remick's performances are too good, and the observations too painfully sharp, for that to be the case.

DUMBO 1941
Director **Ben Sharpsteen**

No, we're not suggesting Mrs Jumbo got so depressed being locked up that she hit the sauce – just that *Dumbo* contains one of the best drunk sequences on film. *Pink Elephants On Parade*, the musical number following Dumbo's brush with the bottle, is an extraordinarily inventive piece of psychedelic animation that has delighted and terrified kids and adults for 60 years.

HARVEY 1950
Director **Henry Koster** *Cast* **James Stewart, Josephine Hull**

A woman attempts to have her heavy-drinking brother certified when he insists he is accompanied everywhere by a 6ft white rabbit called Harvey. The film, an adaptation of Mary Chase's Pulitzer Prize-winning play, sometimes seems static, but that's more than compensated for by the wonderful dialogue. Stewart's character, Elwood P Dowd, is a gentle, hopeful, good-natured alcoholic, something very rarely seen in a Hollywood film, and this performance is one of his best. Interestingly, you never actually see Stewart having a drink in the film.

THE LOST WEEKEND 1945
Director **Billy Wilder** *Cast* **Ray Milland, Jane Wyman**

This searing drama has lost little of its impact for modern audiences. Milland plays a young writer, briefly on the wagon, who falls off it and goes on a spectacular four-day bender. Ironically, he feels that drinking improves his writing, yet ultimately it will destroy both him and his creativity. The scene of Milland lugging his typewriter around to find an open pawn shop emphasises the futility of his situation, and details like his variety of booze hiding places have entered the popular consciousness as representing the way all alcoholics behave.

MY FAVOURITE YEAR 1982
Director **Richard Benjamin** *Cast* **Peter O'Toole, Mark Linn-Baker**

A young TV writer gets the job of babysitting his childhood idol, a famously inebriated aging movie star called Alan Swann

> **"THIS IS THE WAY I LOOK WHEN I'M SOBER. IT'S ENOUGH TO MAKE A PERSON DRINK"**
>
> Kirsten Arnesen Clay, Days Of Wine And Roses

(based on Errol Flynn) when he is due to appear on a live TV show in the 1950s. The brutish star of the show, *King Kaiser* (based on Sid Caesar – look it up), is also under fire from a union boss unhappy about Kaiser's on-air impressions of him. Great scenes include O'Toole using a firehose to abseil down the side of the building, and the final farcical fight scene broadcast live to millions.

MY NAME IS JOE 1998
Director Ken Loach *Cast* Peter Mullan, Louise Goodall

The plot could have been lifted straight from Hollywood – a recovering alcoholic endangers his relationship with a nurse when he gets involved with a drugs deal in order to help a friend in trouble – but since this is directed by Loach in his characteristically angry and brutally honest style, the result could not be more different. Mullan deservedly won a Best Actor award at Cannes for his performance as a man walking a very fine line between right and wrong. Painful and grim, this is not one to watch when you're feeling a bit down. However, the atmosphere Loach creates makes it absorbing viewing.

NIL BY MOUTH 1997
Director Gary Oldman *Cast* Ray Winstone, Kathy Burke

Oldman's directorial debut, which he also wrote, is uncompromising in its portrayal of a family living under the pressures of poverty, drugs and alcohol. Terrifying and claustrophobic, the film's most harrowing scene is probably where a drunken Winstone phones round friends and family trying to find Burke after he has given her a savage beating. The film is presented as a story to watch, not as a lesson to be learned or a set of people to judge. Take from it what you will.

THE SOUND OF ONE HAND CLAPPING 1998
Director Richard Flanagan *Cast* Kerry Fox, Kristof Kaczmarek

There aren't many films set in Tasmania, which is a shame as the setting and coastal scenery are amazing. The story is told in flashback when a young woman returns to her home in Hobart

LUSH LIFE

LEAVING LAS VEGAS

One of the best (and saddest) performances of drunkenness on film has to be Nicolas Cage in the 1995 Mike Figgis film *Leaving Las Vegas*. Thankfully, Cage didn't attempt method acting and try to drink himself to death in preparation for the role. But he did go to Ireland so he could experience "some essence, some soul, in the land of great writers and drinkers". He also videotaped himself drinking gin and talking to the camera to study the slurs in his speech while intoxicated, and he attended Alcoholics Anonymous meetings, of which there are a lot in Hollywood, to see the effect drinking can have on people's lives. Cage was also apparently inspired by Albert Finney's performance in *Under The Volcano*. Since he never met the writer of the original novel *Leaving Las Vegas* (John O'Brien committed

suicide two weeks after selling the film rights), Cage was able to create the character of Ben from scratch, and the results won him an Oscar, a Golden Globe and the Screen Actors Guild award.

UIP; Initial Productions/Lumiere Pictures; Warner

after a 20-year absence. She left when her father beat her in a rage, and now finds him a lonely alcoholic. She recalls the struggles the family faced when they first settled in Tasmania after leaving Slovenia, and although that may sound dull, it's actually a terrific story of people surviving in a wilderness.

UNDER THE VOLCANO 1984

Director John Huston *Cast* Albert Finney, Jacqueline Bisset

An in-depth study of a drunk. What action there is takes place over the course of a single day, as Finney's ex-consul (he has been stripped of official duties) struggles to remain coherent and able to communicate with his wife (Bisset) and half-brother (Anthony Andrews). Unusually for a screen alcoholic, the consul's family is supportive but there is nothing they can do to help him. The fact that Finney knows he is doomed, his sad intelligence clear in every scene, makes this even more moving.

> "MOST MEN LIVE LIVES OF QUIET DESPERATION. I CAN'T TAKE QUIET DESPERATION"
>
> Don Birnam, The Lost Weekend

WHISKY GALORE 1948

Director Alexander MacKendrick *Cast* Basil Radford, Gordon Jackson

Wonderful comedy based on the real story of the shipwreck of the *SS Politician*, which was carrying a cargo of whisky. When 50,000 bottles of Scotch wash up on a small Hebridean island, bereft of whisky due to the war, the locals and customs and excise officer are soon at loggerheads. The usual Ealing brand of farce and skulduggery follows, but sparkling performances and great dialogue lift the film. The last case of drink from the real shipwreck was auctioned in 1993 for £12,012.

WHO'S AFRAID OF VIRGINIA WOOLF 1966

Director Mike Nichols *Cast* Elizabeth Taylor, Richard Burton

This film, based on Edward Albee's play, is about the mother of all awkward evenings. George and Martha, a middle-aged history professor and his wife, entertain Nick and Honey, newcomers to campus. The sociable atmosphere quickly deteriorates into a vicious, drunken slanging match between the older couple, using the younger couple as their foils. It was a milestone in cinema permissiveness, especially in swearing, and is compelling to watch, even if only to wonder if this is what it was like at home chez Burton and Taylor. A breathtaking performance by Taylor reminds you just how good she could be and she won her second Oscar for the role. In fact, the whole cast was Oscar-nominated (Sandy Dennis also won), a feat shared only by *Sleuth*.

"Didn't I tell you not to give her that second glass of sherry?"

ANIMALS

Animals of both the heartwarming and menacing kind have always played a supporting role in movies. But some, notably Rin Tin Tin, got more fan mail (30,000 letters in a week) than human stars did at the same studios. Their enduring appeal to the industry is not that hard to explain: animal movies are normally cheap to make and every so often a shaggy dog story (or a shaggy dog story involving any other kind of animal, such as a pig or a bull) will strike box-office gold.

A PRIVATE FUNCTION 1985
Director Malcolm Mowbray *Cast* Michael Palin,
Maggie Smith, Denholm Elliott
With more top British actors than you'll find at a BAFTA awards ceremony and a script by Alan Bennett, it's hard to see how this satire of pigs, sausages and social climbing in rationing-era small-town England could fail. Smith carries the film as Joyce Chilvers. Palin is suitably bland as her pig-napping husband, although he does get to come home and announce that a customer's ingrown toenail "seems to have turned the corner". The film has a cruel streak wider than the streaks of bacon in the butcher's shop but loses momentum after the pig's famous diarrhoea scene. After that it's best just to sit back and watch Smith declare: "It's not pork, it's power."

ATTACK OF THE CRAB MONSTERS 1957
Director Roger Corman *Cast* Richard Garland, Pamela Duncan
Giant crabs, which live on a diet consisting mainly of human brains (whose intelligence they then absorb), try to kill scientists stranded on a shrinking atoll. It's typical Roger Corman fare, with the script containing more good ideas than he had the budget to explore. More vigilant viewers may notice that the

51

crabs have wheels and legs. These monster crabs can also talk, one telling a potential victim: "So you have wounded me! I must grow a new claw, well and good, for I can do it in a day, but will you grow new lives when I have taken yours from you?"

BABE 1995

Director **Chris Noonan** *Cast* **Christine Cavanaugh, James Cromwell**
This heartwarming tale of a pig who becomes a champion sheepdog (sorry, didn't mean to spoil the suspense) is even more impressive when you realise that the producers had to use 48 different infant pigs to play Babe because young pigs grow faster than Topsy. If you like this but would like it even more if it had fewer special effects and more sloppy country music, try *Gordy* (1995). For those who like pig movies with a little more point, *Babe: Pig In The City* is much darker but then it is directed by George Miller who made his name on *Mad Max*.

THE BIRDS 1963

Director **Alfred Hitchcock** *Cast* **Tippi Hedren, Rod Taylor**
Sadly, Hitch's plan to film a scene showing the Golden Gate bridge encrusted with homicidal birds was scuppered by the cost. Because the movie never explains why the birds turn

BEE MOVIES

THE BEARS AND THE BEES
Even though it's just six minutes long, this Disney short about a big bear, some cubs and a beehive still feels a little light on plot.

THE BEES
South American killer bees smuggled into the US inadvertently get grandiose ideas about ruling the world. Only two Johns (Carradine and Saxon) can stop them.

THE DEADLY BEES
Pop singer goes to remote tropical island to film a video, collapses of exhaustion (or perhaps because actress Susannah Leigh has finally been shown the script) and tries to recover with the help of two bee farmers. Everything is going swimmingly until one day that buzzing noise suddenly gets louder and louder and then...

THE SWARM
The bees in this movie are more virulent than the Australian brown box jellyfish. Some of them really were. The bees on set were supposed to have had their stings removed but the de-stingers missed quite a few and every so often a scene would be interrupted with frantic cries of "There's a hot one!"

WAX
Subtitled "The discovery of television among the bees", this 1992 movie is just your run-of-the-mill fare. A programmer and part-time Mesopotamian beekeeper has a hole drilled in his head by his bees who, being of a profoundly curious turn of mind, decide to fill the hole they've made with a TV set. After that, it goes a bit weird. Stars William S Burroughs and Clyde Tombaugh, the scientist who discovered Pluto.

vicious, critics have devised all kinds of theories including the suggestion that the film is a disguised western (with the birds as Indians) or an allegory about sexual repression (the first attack prevents a couple from getting together). Hedren spent days with birds attached to her dress by nylon threads to film the famous attack scene and had to be taken to hospital after one of her winged co-stars cut her face. Hitchcock, who by now needed repressing himself, gave Hedren's daughter Melanie Griffith a doll

that resembled her mother in an ornate wooden box which the young girl assumed was meant to be a coffin. Still, it's hard not to marvel at the wizardry involved: the film took three years to make, consisting of 1360 shots (including 370 trick shots) and that last tortuous scene was compiled from 32 pieces of film.

Zoltan has the most distinctive eyes on celluloid since Paul Newman's. His teeth are pretty effective too – throat-ripping is, as you might expect, both a hobby and a lifestyle choice for the hound of Dracula

THE BRAVE ONE 1956

Director Irving Rapper *Cast* Rodolfo Hoyos Jnr, Michel Ray

This movie comes to you courtesy of the Communist witch-hunt of the late 1940s. Writer Dalton Trumbo (who would later pen the script for *Spartacus*) fled across the Mexican border where, with another exiled chum Hugo Butler, he went to see a bullfight. Trumbo didn't enjoy the entertainment very much but was moved enough by what he saw to write this film about a boy who raises a bull and tries to save it from its inevitable gory end. It was filmed in Mexico and Trumbo was credited pseudonymously as Robert Rich. His contribution became one of Hollywood's worst-kept secrets when the fictitious Rich was nominated for (and won) an Oscar for best original story in 1957. The statuette was finally collected 18 years later.

DIGBY 1973

Director Joseph McGrath *Cast* Jim Dale, Spike Milligan

The ultimate shaggy dog story was marketed with the slogan "The Biggest Howl Ever Unleashed!" and is a timely warning of what can happen if your sheepdog happens to eat a bowl of a secret liquid growth formula called Project X by mistake. Pity the FX are so dire, but *Digby* has a certain wayward charm, especially when compared to the infamous *Beethoven* movies which were about as indistinguishable as cans of dog food.

"I THINK SEXUAL INTERCOURSE IS IN ORDER, GILBERT"
Joyce Chilvers, A Private Function

LASSIE COME HOME 1943

Director Fred M Wilcox Cast Pal, Roddy McDowall, Elizabeth Taylor

Lassie was one of Hollywood's first gender benders – a bitch played by a male dog called Pal who had to wear a patch over his genitalia. You probably know the drill: loyal dog walks length and breadth of land to be reunited with her old master. Good as Pal is, (s)he is slightly overshadowed by the young Liz Taylor, who on one occasion was sent back to the dressing room to have her false eyelashes removed, only for the director to realise that they were genuine. Co-writer Hugo Butler later fled to Mexico to evade the McCarthy era witchhunt, but viewers looking for subliminal subversive messages will be disappointed. If you're looking for cheap laughs, try *Lassie's Adventures in the Gold Rush* (1951) – easily the worst in the series, say aficionados.

NIGHT OF THE LEPUS 1973

Director William F Claxton Cast Rory Calhoun, Stuart Whitman

A sci-fi/horror/thriller which doesn't thrill or scare the viewer and whose sci-fi credentials begin and end with the fact that it features DeForest Kelley – Dr McCoy in *Star Trek* (Janet Leigh and Robert Hardy also 'star'). It's rabbit life as neither Jim, Bones nor anyone else knows it, as giant mutant bunnies terrorize Arizona causing such mayhem that the National Guard have to be called in. "How many times will terror strike?" asked the posters for this movie. Answer: Not very often. As rabbits go, these ones are about as menacing as Bambi's friend Thumper. But be warned: you may find yourself drawn into the whole ludicrous spectacle against your will.

PIRANHA II: THE SPAWNING 1981

Director James Cameron Cast Tricia O'Neil, Steve Marachuk

In 1978, Joe Dante directed *Piranha* – about genetically mutated piranha terrorizing a holiday resort – playing it for laughs as a Roger Corman homage. Three years later a young tyro called James Cameron directed this sequel/copy, which he always calls "without doubt, the greatest flying piranha movie ever made". But what's on screen is less interesting than what happened off it.

KING KONG

GORILLA WARFARE

King Kong is not just a movie about a giant gorilla's relationship with a beautiful woman. (For that try Ed Wood's *The Bride And The Beast*.) No, the ape is… a symbol of the beastly side of Fay Wray's significant other's subconscious; a misunderstood Christ figure; a symbol of the oppressed black man fighting white America; or a radical taking on Wall Street. If you've ever wondered why you never heard a gorilla roar like King Kong, it may be because the noise is an amalgam of a lion's and a tiger's roar, run backwards.

Long live the King

UIP, Vic, RKO

Cameron was thrown off the film by producer Ovidio G Assonitis but broke into the editing room in a desperate bid to cut his own footage, only to be apprehended and ejected.

THE RETURN OF RIN TIN TIN 1947

Director Max Nosseck *Cast* Rinty III, Robert Blake

In the late 1940s, Hollywood movies were full of returning war heroes but few were fêted as much as Rinty III, grandson of the original Rin Tin Tin dog which, in the 1920s, had saved Warner Brothers from bankruptcy. Rinty III was a sergeant in the US Army's K-9 corps and won a Purple Heart which made him a more genuine war hero than Ronald Reagan or John Wayne. He came back in this 1947 movie, billed as "the most human heart-warming movie in years". For a Rin Tin Tin caper of a slightly different breed, try *Won Ton Ton, The Dog Who Saved Hollywood* (1976) which had an amazing cast and might have been a satire if it hadn't been directed by Michael Winner.

TARANTULA 1955

Director Jack Arnold *Cast* John Agar, Mara Corday, Leo G Carroll

Eighteen years before Arizona came under vicious and unprovoked attack from mutant rabbits, it was terrorized by a 100ft-tall tarantula fed on a special nutrient formula which, alas, remains as much of a mystery as the real recipe for Coke. It's all the fault of a scientist of course (Leo G Carroll – Mr Waverly from *The Man From UNCLE*) and his crazed assistant. Ultimately, the only way to defeat the aggressive arachnid is to call on the services of a young jet pilot (played by Clint Eastwood) and some napalm. You get a bigger budget version of this kind of thrill in *Arachnophobia* but this is funnier.

ZOLTAN, HOUND OF DRACULA 1978

Director Albert Band *Cast* Michael Pataki, José Ferrer

Risibly renamed *Dracula's Dog* in the US, this is an ideal movie to watch in that very special interval between coming in from the pub after a few too many and actually falling asleep. The added bonus is that if you do wake up after an hour, the plot won't have moved on. It tries to democratize the Draculas, introducing the viewer to an American branch led by a man with the very unTransylvanian name of Mike. Dog and master are woken from their grave by some bumbling Russian soldiers and set out for America in the erroneous belief that this will boost their movie's box office takings. Zoltan's bark may not be worse than his bite, but it's certainly more irritating. Among the vast cast are José Ferrer as an inspector and an actor called Roger Pancake, an escapee from *The Cat From Outer Space*.

> **"HUMAN PREY OF GIANT GORILLA ON HER WEDDING NIGHT"**
> Tagline, The Bride And The Beast

If you've seen a peanut stand and heard a rubber band, watched a needle that winked its eye or even seen an elephant fly, you'll know the magic of the animated movie. Anything is possible – even jive-talking crows (infinitely preferable to jive-talking Gibb brothers).

Early animations were based on newspaper strips like *Gertie The Dinosaur*. The first full-length animated feature, *The Adventures Of Prince Achmed* (1927), has silhouettes re-telling the Arabian Nights against hand-tinted backgrounds.

Mickey Mouse was the first to synchronize sound and pictures in *Steamboat Willy* (1928). But it was *Snow White* (1937) that impressed as the first full-length, full-blown animation, and it's still a stunning piece of work. In parts of the UK, children under the age of 16 had to be accompanied by an adult, so scary was the Wicked Queen deemed to be. But since then the idea of animation for adults has vanished in a miasma of straight-to-video pap like *The Land Before Time VII*.

It took the Japanese to breathe new life into the genre, creating anime, based on their adult comic books or mangas. Suddenly sex and ultraviolence were in. Influences rattled across the Pacific, and the anime epic *Ghost In The Shell* will give you an idea where *The Matrix* came from, while *The Matrix* in turn inspired Princess Fiona's kickboxing in *Shrek*. The wild card is Nick Park, master of the stop-frame animated plasticine model (claymation) whose half-hour Wallace and Gromit films are classics but whose 90-minute *Chicken Run* isn't.

Today battle lines are drawn up between Disney and anime. While Disney believed in simplicity of story mixed with complex animation, the Japanese way is to weave complex storylines into a simplistic animated style. Broadly, if you like beautiful pictures and good jokes, Disney's your man; if you want a searing indictment of the human condition but don't mind if the pictures jerk a bit, you should be turning Japanese.

AKIRA 1988
Director **Katsuhiro Otomo** *Cast* **Mitsuo Iwata, Nozomu Sasaki**
Not just a film, more a philosophy. Tokyo was destroyed by a psychic blast from Akira (the most advanced form of human

being) which started World War III. By 2019, when the film is set, Neo Tokyo has risen from its ashes and a collection of ESPers (people with extra sensory perception), teenagers, soldiers, drug addicts and politicians struggle for control of Akira. One child, Tetsuo, develops his ESP and nearly destroys everything. A classic slice of Japanese anime, it's very bloody and violent but visually astonishing. Most of the film takes place at night, so the animators had to create a new range of dark colours, rather than relying on standard blue tones. Akira is an abbreviated version of a 37-volume manga comic book. Fans say it all starts to make sense after the seventh viewing.

ALICE 1987

Director Jan Svankmajer Cast Kristina Kohoutová

You know the story, but in the hands of the Czech master of the surreal, Svankmajer, it becomes a strange, terrifying nightmare. The film combines stop-frame animation (invented in 1910 by Ladislaw Starewicz), puppetry and live action, and creates a world of intense malevolence. The white rabbit is constantly splitting open, losing his stuffing and sewing himself back together. Large lumps of raw meat crawl around, skulls of dead birds come to life and peck their way out of their eggs. In homage to that other great master of stop-frame animation, Ray Harryhausen, Svankmajer has the white rabbit leading an army of animated skeletons identical to those in *Jason and the Argonauts*. The ending is far from Lewis Carroll's pastoral idyll but it's probably best not to say more.

FANTASIA 1940

Directors James Algar, Samuel Armstrong, Ford Beebe, Norm Ferguson, Jim Handley, T Hee, Wilfred Jackson, Hamilton Luske, Bill Roberts, Paul Satterfield

A musical collaboration with the conductor Leopold Stokowski, *Fantasia* still looks grand, bold and imaginative today. Eight pieces of music are set to cartoons, encompassing the evolution of life on Earth, plus a few cute dancing Chinese mushrooms. Using a metronome timed to the animation speed of 24 frames per second, the

> "SO TELL ME, EDDIE, IS THAT A RABBIT IN YOUR POCKET OR ARE YOU JUST PLEASED TO SEE ME?"
> Dolores, Who Framed Roger Rabbit

A great buddy movie even if one buddy is a wascally wabbit

animation was timed to fit the music perfectly. Killjoy Leonard Bernstein even had to tell his students not to think of Disney's dancing centaurs when listening to Beethoven's *Pastoral Symphony*. The film moved Mickey Mouse on, though: for the first time his eyes had whites, instead of just being black circles. Walt Disney said he never got over the failure of *Fantasia* and that it loomed like a shadow over his whole life. Some failure…

> **"I'M JUST SCARED I'LL COME HOME ONE DAY AND FIND YOU SCREWING THE TOASTER"**
> Gloria, Heavy Metal

FRITZ THE CAT 1972

Director Ralph Bakshi *Cast* Skip Hinnant, Rosetta LeNoire

The first (officially) X-rated cartoon. A cat wanders through college life in the 1960s trying to do as many drugs and have as much sex as possible. Filled with unlikely and unholy couplings of cats and birds, aardvarks and zebras, the (now dated) film deals with racism, sexism, unemployment and the sense of waste that crippled America's disaffected youth. It's most remarkable for its portrayal of black people – always seen as vast, shiny black, jive-talking crows (imagine the crows in Dumbo recreated with the benefit of Malcolm X and LSD).

HEAVY METAL 1981

Director Gerald Potterton *Cast* John Candy, Harold Ramis

Good and evil, swords and sorcerers, sex and toasters, plus lots of very, very loud music. *Heavy Metal* may have limited appeal yet it broke new ground as the first film to introduce anime (the Japanese style of exotic and erotic, highly stylized flamboyant cartoons) to the West. It was based on a magazine of the same name, itself spawned by a French magazine called *Metal Hurlant* (Screaming Metal). Six stories are tied loosely together by the presence of Loch-nar, not an obscure Scottish dram but a small, round, green embodiment of all evil. Music is provided by Black Sabbath, Grand Funk Railroad, Blue Oyster Cult and Nazareth, plus other, even hairier, bands. But however futuristic the film, its creators used a multiplane camera to enhance the animation – a technique unused since Disney's *Pinocchio*.

THE JUNGLE BOOK 1967

Director Wolfgang Reitherman *Cast* Phil Harris, George Sanders, Louis Prima

Indian boy gets lost in the jungle and is brought up by wolves, befriended by bears, hunted by snakes and tigers, and learns that his true place is among men. Or more specifically among pretty Indian girls. But it has the best characters, most memorable songs (for the right

reasons) and the best jokes of any Disney film – sadly Walt died before it was finished. The star is Baloo the bear, the voice of Phil Harris doing near-approximation to John Wayne, while for King Louie (the swinging ape), Louis Prima (an Italian) makes a good stab at sounding like Satchmo. Myth to be dispelled: the Beatles didn't really do the voices for the vultures – they *were* booked, but Walt thought they'd only be a flash in the pan.

"Take that, you calorie-laden, piece of spiced sugar and flour!"

MY NEIGHBOUR TOTORO 1988

Director **Hayao Miyazaki** *Cast* **Hitoshi Takagi, Noriko Hidaka**

Miyazaki is sometimes called Japan's Disney, which does a disservice to both, but *Totoro* is about as far from the blood-spattered manga-style of Japanese animation as you can get. Charming, adorable and uncynical, it's the ultimate kiddie film. Two girls, Mei and Satsuki, move to the country with their father: there they are befriended by magical creatures called Totoro and have lots of enchanting adventures. The film caused raised eyebrows in the West because of a scene where the girls share a bath with the father – perfectly acceptable in Tokyo, very dodgy in Texas. Miyazaki was a great Hitchcock fan, and the girls' wait at the bus stop owes a debt to *North by Northwest*.

SHREK 2001

Directors **Andrew Adamson, Vicky Jenson** *Cast* **Mike Myers, Eddie Murphy, Cameron Diaz**

A loveable but grumpy ogre, Shrek (originally voiced by Chris Farley, who died mid-production), agrees to rescue a beautiful princess from a fire-breathing dragon, accompanied by a motormouth donkey. A host of other familiar and well-loved fairytale characters make brief cameos in a very modern, post-modernist way, and it all ends happily ever after. Apart from its desire to create more lifelike humans than the old, hand-drawn animations – these characters are computer-generated in such detail that each individual hair moves in the breeze – there are loads of good anti-Disney in-jokes. When Princess Fiona starts singing to a little bluebird à la Snow White, she hits a high note and the bird explodes. Jeffrey Katzenberg, one of DreamWorks' co-founders, is ex-Disney, and clearly delighted to be out.

TOY STORY 1995

Director John Lasseter *Cast* Tom Hanks, Tim Allen

Woody is a toy cowboy whose world is rocked when a new toy, Buzz Lightyear (who thinks he's a real astronaut) enters the playroom. But the two rivals are united by threats to other toys, a toy-torturer called Sid and love of their owner, Andy. Heroically, Disney and Pixar didn't rely on technological wizardry for this first computer-generated film. Instead a great plot, witty script and inspired casting (John Ratzenberger, the mail man from *Cheers*, as Hamm the piggy bank) all make it a serious classic. Favourite background joke: Andy's house is being sold by a company called Virtual Realty. Favourite obscure fact: Andy's car numberplate is A113 – the number of the classroom where animator John Lasseter learned his craft. Favourite big question: if Buzz doesn't know he's a toy, why does he pretend to be one when humans are around?

> **"NOW YOU'RE KING OF THE MOUNTAIN, BUT IT'S ALL GARBAGE!"**
> Shotara Kaneda, Akira

WHO FRAMED ROGER RABBIT 1988

Director Robert Zemeckis *Cast* Bob Hoskins, Kathleen Turner

Set in a very film-noir LA in 1947, *Roger Rabbit* is the most successful mix of live action and animation yet achieved. It's a complex plot of crosses and double-crosses, hidden identities and a million in-jokes that only three concurrent childhoods spent watching cartoons would allow you to get. Behind it all it's a satire on American treatment of black people as second-class citizens way back in 1947. Cartoons and people interact flawlessly – it's all done with padding, mirrors and hydraulics, so when in the film Roger pops out of Eddie Valiant's (Bob Hoskins) jacket, in the real world the jacket was filled with compressed-air inflated balloons to create a Roger-shaped bump. And, to bring the cartoons into our world, they were 3D and threw shadows. Even more impressively, it's the first film in which Disney and Warner characters meet: Donald Duck and Daffy Duck both play pianos in the Ink and Paint Club.

ARTS

In the mid-19th century, the invention of photography put painters in fear for their wallets. But painting survived, and this new-fangled photography business (and its successor, moving pictures) became a larger canvas for creative types to play with.

F ilm may have begun as crowd-pleasing novelty (the French magician Georges Méliès' trick film *The Man With The Rubber Head* (1902) being one mind-expanding example) but after World War I modern artists took a serious interest in films. Artists like Richter, animator Oskar Fischinger and painter/photographer Man Ray experimented with abstract forms on film. But none of this was enough to convince cynics that these were more than conjuring tricks.

What this new movement desperately needed was a film to capture the imagination of the world. They got it. In 1929 Luis Buñuel and Salvador Dali released the most famous avant-garde film of all time, *Un Chien Andalou*, whose success (and the riots by outraged right-wingers at the screening of Buñuel and Dali's second creative collaboration *L'Age d'Or*) finally announced that the art movie had truly arrived.

On the other side of the Atlantic, a post-Depression breed of young filmmakers absorbed the powerful, provocative imagery of *Un Chien Andalou* and *L'Age d'Or*. In 1943 a couple from California (Maya Deren and Alexander Hammid) took the cinema of dreaming to its next level. Instead of using shock tactics, their *Meshes Of The Afternoon* tried to replicate the act of dreaming with Deren as the central character. The film manages to convince its audience that they are playing an active role in her dream, making it a worthy successor to *L'Age d'Or*.

But the underground film really came of age in America in the 1960s, spearheaded by Jack Smith, Harry Smith, Stan Brakhage and, most famously, Andy Warhol (whose early silents replaced, temporarily, what he'd been doing as a painter). Less well known but equally influential was Jack Smith, whose shakily shot *Flaming Creatures* rocked the establishment with scenes of disrobed queens at play and influenced a generation of American underground filmmakers. Most famous of these is John Waters, whose *Pink Flamingos* ignored Hollywood's

Vicomte De Noailles

L'Age d'Or caused riots on its first public showing because of its vicious attack on the church, the middle class and the fact that some of its characters just threw their litter out onto the streets

rules by making stars out of "disgusting ugly freaks".

Although the art movie has now moved into the mainstream (*Blue Velvet* being one example), the urge to push cinema over the edge – taking its audience with it – will always be with us.

BLOW JOB 1963
Director Andy Warhol

Pop art guru Andy Warhol's decision to temporarily abandon painting to concentrate on filmmaking resulted in a series of silent portrait films that were the cinematic equivalent of his silk-screened canvases. The most controversial of these was *Blow Job*, a 35-minute study of ecstasy and boredom where, despite its title, the only part of the anonymous recipient's anatomy the audience saw was his face. Despite this tease, Warhol was saying much about physical presence (as well as the unseen fellator, a camera is present), facial expression, voyeurism, and that most pornography on film is more mechanical in its manufacture than sensual.

EARLY ABSTRACTIONS: FILMS NO 1–10 1939–56
Director Harry Smith

Harry Smith was an admirer of Aleister Crowley's magical works. He was also interested in alchemy, folklore and collecting records of American folk music, a selection of which he released as three compilations on the Folkways label. Smith's other main interest was abstract animation, and the series of films he made are playful moving paintings to which, at a later date, he eccentrically added a soundtrack of Beatles songs. The results are akin to Oskar Fischinger's equally abstract animation sequence set to JS Bach's *Toccata and Fugue* which opens *Fantasia* (1940). Smith would later pay his respects to Fischinger with his animated short film *Film No 5 Circular Tensions: Homage To Oskar Fischinger* (1950).

THE FLICKER 1965
Director Tony Conrad

Conrad provided the soundtrack for Jack Smith's *Flaming Creatures* and was a member of the Theatre Of Eternal Music with La Monte Young, Marion Zazeela and John Cale. While working with the group he made *The Flicker*, an experimental film made up of 47 different patterns of black-and-white frame combinations which took Conrad two days to film and seven months to edit. When released it came with this warning: "The producer, distributor and exhibitors waive all liability for physical or mental injury possibly caused by the motion picture *The Flicker*. Since this film may induce epileptic seizures or produce mild symptoms of shock treatment in certain persons, you are cautioned to remain in the theater only at your own risk. A physician should be in attendance." Those who did not suffer a fit were treated to a mind-nudging experience where non-existent colours began to appear and, towards the end, a feeling of inner peace. Conrad followed this stroboscopic masterpiece with *The Eye Of Count Flickerstein* (1966).

L'AGE D'OR 1930

Director Luis Buñuel *Cast* Gaston Modat, Lya Lys

Like its predecessor *Un Chien Andalou*, *L'Age d'Or* was co-written by Dali and Buñuel, and contains dreamlike scenes that are the very essence of surrealism. Both films probe beyond the limitations of reality to produce images which are by turns hilarious, deeply disturbing or sexual, but *L'Age d'Or* – a scathing attack on the church (bishops turn into skeletons), the establishment and middle-class morality – introduced themes he would develop later. Dali's trademarks (ants, rotting donkeys, pianos, statues coming to life) are liberally scattered throughout both films, but it is Buñuel's masterful direction which nudges the viewer's subconscious into accepting the shifts in time, the cascade of bizarre imagery and, best of all, those scenes in which reality is only slightly blurred. Buñuel would embellish this technique in films such as *Exterminating Angel* (1962) and *Discreet Charm Of The Bourgeoisie* (1972).

UN CHIEN ANDALOU 1929

Director Luis Buñuel *Cast* Simone Mareuil, Pierre Batcheff

The creative collaboration between Spanish filmmaker Luis Buñuel and Spanish surrealist painter Salvador Dali produced two astonishing films, the other being *L'Age d'Or* (1930). The first of the two, this opens with what remains one of cinema's most extreme scenes. A man smoking a cigarette (Buñuel) is gazing up at the full moon whilst sharpening a cut-throat razor. He then opens the eye of his seated female companion and, as a cloud passes over the moon, slices her eyeball with his razor. Despite later assurances that it was, in fact, a slaughtered calf's eyeball which had been slashed, the effect upon the viewer remains one of horror and disbelief.

"WE WILL PLUNGE IT RIGHT INTO THE HEART OF WITTY, ELEGANT AND INTELLECTUALIZED PARIS WITH ALL THE WEIGHT OF AN IBERIAN DAGGER"

Salvador Dali on Un Chien Andalou

B MOVIES

Your mouth feels like the Sahara desert, there are thumb marks at the base of your neck and in the back of your mind there's a suspicion that something awful happened last night if only you could remember the specifics... don't worry, you're just trapped in a B movie. Normal service will be resumed after 80 or 85 minutes.

Movie moguls had assumed their business was recession-proof, but by 1933 weekly cinema audiences had slumped by 50 million in three years. In response, MGM and RKO devised the value-for-money double bill and the B movie was born. In the American South, Bs could be bigger draws than A pictures, especially if the A was a sophisticated comedy/romance by a director like Ernst Lubitsch.

For studios, B movies had one big advantage over A pictures: they never made a loss. They didn't make much (maybe $10,000 profit on an $80,000 budget) but they were a reliable revenue stream. Each studio had a B unit and new studios set up on what was known as 'Poverty Row' just to make second features. (In Britain studios like Butchers and Danzigers served the same need.) Some great directors and stars started in Bs (William Wyler and George Stevens; Robert Mitchum and Rock Hudson) but the striking fact is that most remained poor man's versions of the directors or stars they hoped to emulate.

At the bottom of the B movie business, real life could often seem indistinguishable from the weirder plots immortalized on screen. Ed Wood Jr was a gloriously eccentric crossdresser (who confronted that very issue in *Glen Or Glenda?*) but other lives were just as strange or desperate. Barbara Payton had once co-starred with Cagney but in 1951 she was the object of a fistfight on her front lawn between her present and future husbands, Franchot Tone and Tom Neal. In 1953 and on the skids, Hollywood's baddest blonde made *Bad Blonde* (its irresistible slogan "They called me BAD – spelled M-E-N"). A few years later she was arrested for prostitution and passing bad cheques. She staged a mini-comeback with a tell-all memoir *I Am Not Ashamed*. The films may have been cheap to make but for the actors who starred in them failure could be horribly expensive.

In the 1950s, TV killed the old second feature while the likes of Roger Corman were making low-budget films for a teen audience ignored by the big studios. These films provided a testing ground for talents like Jack Nicholson and directors like Bogdanovich, Coppola, Scorsese, and Cameron (all of whom worked with Corman).

Bs could compete on fairly equal terms in genres like film noir, crime, thrillers and westerns, where story, a simple (often claustrophobic) setting and dialogue would disguise the lack of budget or stars. (The dialogue in *The Narrow Margin* is as good as in many wisecracking main features of its day.) B sci-fis were risky: despite the director's efforts, lack of cash for effects could consign them to kitschdom. B musicals could be as charmless as they were tuneless (*Pete Kelly's Blues* is an honourable exception).

"People say I've got a very distinctive walk, but I'm just trying to keep my gut in"

The best Bs outclassed the very films they were made to support. Edmond O'Brien's first line in the noir classic *D.O.A* (1950), "I want to report a murder – mine," is still one of the finest opening gambits in cinema history.

BLONDE ICE 1949
Director Jack Bernhard *Cast* Leslie Brooks, Robert Paige

Brooks is chillingly, beautifully believable as the columnist who discovers just how much fun it can be to murder people and read all about it your very own newspaper afterwards. Good as this B noir is, it didn't do much for either of the leading players' careers: this was Brooks' last film and in a few years time Paige would be doing beer commercials.

DETOUR 1945
Director Edgar Ulmer *Cast* Tom Neal, Ann Savage

Justly famous for the last line where Neal, as he climbs into the police car, says: "At any time, fate or some mysterious force can put the finger on you for no good reason at all." This may be the closest Hollywood came to existentialism in the 1940s. (The Camus quote which bears comparison is: "At any street corner the absurd may strike a man in the face.") The absurdest aspect of this film was the budget: like all of Ulmer's B movies this tale of an innocent hitchhiker who gets embroiled in crime was shot in just six days. The famous line is heavily ironic given that Neal would later shoot his wife to death in a jealous rage.

FEAR IN THE NIGHT 1947
Director Maxwell Shane *Cast* Paul Kelly, DeForest Kelley

A classic noir premise: man wakes up after having a nightmare that he killed someone and then finds thumb marks on his own throat. Throw in a sinister hypnotist (is there any other kind?) played by Robert Emmett Keane, and you have the ingredients for a cracking mystery which also marked Kelley's screen debut.

FIVE CAME BACK 1939
Director John Farrow *Cast* Chester Morris, Lucille Ball, Wendy Barrie

The all-star disaster movie starts here. Except all the stars are either B favourites (like Morris and John Carradine) or on their way to better things (Ball) and the budget wouldn't stretch to paying for Charlton Heston's limo. A plane crashes in the Amazonian jungle and the dozen survivors know there's only enough fuel to carry five people. Meanwhile, a nearby tribe is making plans to shrink heads... Farrow remade this film badly but this version is decently done and feels far more real than it ought to, given the jungle's obviously artificial nature. Dalton Trumbo and Nathanael West worked on the script.

FORTY GUNS 1957
Director Samuel Fuller *Cast* Barbara Stanwyck, Barry Sullivan

A TERRIFYING TALE OF SLUTS AND BOLTS.

FRANKENHOOKER

18

WHERE SEX CAN COST YOU AN ARM AND A LEG...

Beverly reminded him of every woman he'd ever met

Fuller had to tone down the climax of this strange, dark movie. The studio wouldn't accept that when Stanwyck's crazed brother uses her as a shield, the cop (Sullivan) would just shoot through her. Pity, because that would have been entirely in keeping with what had gone before. Stanwyck is more hard-boiled than ever as the Amazonian baroness of Tombstone Territory with her own ranch and ranch hands (who are also, it is heavily implied, her sex slaves).

FRANKENHOOKER 1990
Director Frank Henenlotter *Cast* James Lorinz, Beverly Bonner

It's out of the period but if any movie of the last 20 years has 'B' stamped all over it, this has. Brain transplants being old hat after 1962's seminal *The Brain That Wouldn't Die*, this takes things a step further. When a medical student's girlfriend is killed in a lawnmower accident (hey, it happens to all of us), he (Lorinz) tries to make himself a new one, assembled from only the finest body parts. Done in the worst possible taste, this happily twisted film is only for the serious connoisseur of movies where the

B stands for Baaaad. The party where the prostitutes' bodies explode must be unique in the annals of cinema (we hope).

GONKS GO BEAT 1965

Director **Robert Hartford-Davis** *Cast* **Kenneth Connor, Lulu**

Hartford-Davis made one truly notable film (*The Sandwich Man*) and one archaeological curiosity: this genre-straddling sci-fi/comedy/musical variation on *Romeo And Juliet*. An alien visits earth to settle a dispute between the two great houses: one loves rock, the other loves ballads. Solomon wasn't around to solve this bitter debate so Connor must do his best. Lulu sings and Ginger Baker plays the drums in a prison cell. Don't ask.

THE B DETECTIVES

BULLDOG DRUMMOND The British crime-solver was never better than when Ronald Colman played him in *Bulldog Drummond Strikes Back* (1934). But the formula had enough appeal for the studios to make 22 more films in the series including two attempts to turn Bulldog into a Bond rival in the 1960s, with Richard Johnson starring.

CHARLIE CHAN Swede Warner Oland played the world's most famous Chinese detective in 15 films between 1931 and 1938. He died of a drink-related illness and he was replaced by Sidney Toler and Roland Winters. But nobody could deliver the clinching line, "You are murderer!" like Oland. (This was normally sufficient for the killer to break down and confess.) Oland's last Chan film mutated into *Mr Moto's Gamble*, with Peter Lorre as another Oriental detective. Chan was so successful that Monogram persuaded Boris Karloff to play Chinese gumshoe Mr Wong.

FALCON *The Saint*, but from another studio. Both roles were played by George Sanders and when Sanders tired of the *Falcon* his brother Tom Conway took over for nine more instalments. There were 15 films in all including one, *Falcon Takes Over*, loosely based on Raymond Chandler's *Farewell My Lovely*.

HILDEGARDE WITHERS Men didn't have crime solving all their own way, *The Penguin Pool Murders* were cleared up by Withers (no relation to Googie), played by Edna May Oliver. One Hildegarde film is noteworthy just for its title: *The Plot Thickens*.

SAINT Leslie Charteris' novels have provided roles and halo for Sanders, Roger Moore and Val Kilmer. Sanders was the best film Saint although German-born actor Felix Martens played Templar in a 1960 French version.

SHERLOCK HOLMES Basil Rathbone and Nigel Bruce made 14 films as Holmes and Watson between 1939 and 1946. Among the many subsequent actors to play Conan Doyle's opium-smoking sleuth and his faithful dog, sorry, doc are: Christopher Lee, Michael Caine and Ben Kingsley; John Cleese and Arthur Lowe and, unlikeliest of all, George C Scott and Joanne Woodward in the homage/spoof *They Might Be Giants* (1971).

WHISTLER A weird tune is whistled by an unseen voice who then proceeds to intone: "I am the whistler and I know many things. For I walk by night. I know the tales of men and women who have stepped into the shadows." Richard Dix stepped into the shadows in seven out of the eight films as the whistling do-gooder. Quite a feat for a character who, as the series opens, has just paid a man to pay a man to kill him because he doesn't have the guts to commit suicide. Oddly he hasn't also lost the nerve to whistle.

JAIL BAIT 1954

Director Edward D Wood Jr *Cast* Lyle Talbot, Dolores Fuller

A rare foray by Wood into crime movies, this is prized for startling dialogue, a neat plot twist and for Wood's thrifty genius in borrowing the score from *Mesa Of Lost Women*, one of the worst horror films of all-time (even though, by some oversight, Wood hadn't made it). The best exchange may be where the cop turns to the plastic surgeon's daughter and says: "Carrying a gun can be a dangerous business," to which she replies: "So can building a skyscraper." The surgeon's son and a crook rob a theatre, shooting a night watchman fatally and injuring a woman by mistake. The crook kills his accomplice, who wants to surrender. He then goes to the surgeon and tells him to give him a new face or he'll never see his son alive again. Sadly the evil genius' plan of hiding the son's corpse in the closet backfires. Realising his boy is dead, the surgeon turns the villain into the spitting image of his son. Top that.

MACHINE GUN KELLY 1958

Director Roger Corman *Cast* Charles Bronson, Susan Cabot

Bronson got this role by default after a squabble over two other actors (one of whom was screenwriter R Wright Campbell's brother) but he grabs his chance. The silent opening robbery

---

THE B KILLER

Fame fame fatal fame, as Morrissey sang. Well, B movie fame seems even more fatal than real fame judging from these lives

TOM CONWAY The Falcon star lost his struggle with the bottle and was found destitute in a flophouse in Venice, California. A national appeal for funds followed but by 1967, he was in hospital. At least he died happy: he fled the ward with $200 and his ex-sister-in-law Zsa Zsa Gabor gave him and was found dead in his girlfriend's bed.

WILLIAM HUDSON Cirrhosis claimed the 1950s B movie actor when he was just 49. By then he had not appeared in a film for 12 years and must have realized his best shot for celluloid immortality was probably *Attack Of the 50ft Woman*.

CHESTER MORRIS Star of the Boston Blackie series about a safecracker in the 1940s, Morris was found dead at the age of 69 of a drug overdose.

SONNY TUFTS Son of a banker, became Paramount B comedy star but from 1949 to 1951 he was found drunk on a sidewalk, accused by two men of biting them and jailed for drunkenness at his wife's behest. He died of pneumonia in 1970, aged 58, after appearing in just two films in the last 12 years of his life.

LUPE VELEZ The Mexican spitfire was as famous for her offscreen affairs as her explosive screen presence in a series of 1930s Bs. After her stormy marriage to Johnny Weissmuller ended in 1938, she had flings with Gary Cooper and a young actor called Harold Rammond. She was pregnant with Rammond's child when, despairing of reviving her career and finding a man to marry her, she took an overdose of Seconal. She was just 36.

sequence is well done, thanks partly to *High Noon* cameraman Floyd Crosby. Cabot deserves a special lifetime achievement Oscar for consistent overacting

MY NAME IS JULIA ROSS 1945

Director Joseph H Lewis *Cast* Nina Foch, Dame May Whitty, George Macready

What do you do when you go to your new company as a secretary in London and wake

up with a headache in a stately pile in Cornwall, apparently married to a man who is rather too fond of icepicks and knives? That is the problem facing Foch in this efficient and pacy (it only takes 65 minutes to tell the story) British B chiller; the source for Arthur Penn's *Dead Of Winter*.

Carmen Miranda substitute Ann Savage gets a break from her role as second best supporting actress supporting a bowl of fruit, in *Detour*. From here on in, it was ciggies and come hither looks

THE NARROW MARGIN 1952

Director Richard Fleischer *Cast* Charles McGraw, Marie Windsor

McGraw's cynical cop tells his charge (a witness in a mob trial, beautifully played by Windsor): "You make me sick to my stomach," to which she replies: "Well, use your own sink." When budget is scarce (and you've got a whole 13 days to get the film in the can), more directors should do what Fleischer does: focus on a specific, claustrophobic locale (the train taking witness and cop to the trial) and the dialogue.

ROUGHSHOD 1949

Director Mark Robson *Cast* Robert Sterling, Claude Jarman Jr, Gloria Grahame

Robson's career later disappeared into the mainstream vapidity of *The Inn Of The Sixth Happiness* but this is an unusual western with Jarman and Sterling as two brothers who find a quartet of stranded saloon dames and are confronted by violent ex-cons (as opposed to pacifist ex-cons). Within two years of this release, Grahame would be starring opposite Bogart.

THE TALL T 1957

Director Budd Boetticher *Cast* Randolph Scott, Richard Boone, Maureen O'Sullivan

As Randolph Scott is in danger of being known chiefly as the man who may or may not have slept with Cary Grant, it seems appropriate to pay tribute to this fine B western which earned Scott overdue recognition. Sadly for those hoping to avoid gay sub-texts when discussing Scott, Boetticher would later insist that Boone's villain was physically attracted to Scott's hero. The picture (one of three fine Boetticher/Scott collaborations in the

1950s) must have influenced Mann's *Man of the West* (starring Jimmy Stewart): the similarities in plot are too frequent for coincidence. The story, scripted from an Elmore Leonard novel by Burt Kennedy, is an old standby. Scott has to undermine the solidarity of the outlaw band which holds him and O'Sullivan prisoner. But in these capable hands, it becomes an understated fable about the nature of American progress.

WHEN STRANGERS MARRY 1944

Director William Castle *Cast* Robert Mitchum, Kim Hunter, Dean Jagger

Mitchum's screen debut is a very fine B movie indeed, one of the best ever. Castle, not famed for his subtlety, shows that he can build suspense slowly, in a tale of a small-town girl who finds out her hubby may be a murderer. Didn't do quite well enough to inspire a sequel 'When Cousins Marry'.

THE WOMAN THEY ALMOST LYNCHED 1953

Director Allan Dwan *Cast* John Lund, Joan Leslie, Audrey Totter

The title rather gives the plot away in this Civil War period drama starring Leslie as a woman who learns how to use a gun. Leslie, who had left Warners after being typecast as a virginal good girl, quit acting in the 1950s to raise kids. This performance suggests that this was some loss to movies.

X 1963 THE MAN WITH X RAY EYES

Director Roger Corman *Cast* Ray Milland, Diana Van der Vlis, Harold Stone

This may just be Corman's best film. As great B sci-fi movies go, its only serious rival is probably *The Incredible Shrinking Man* (1957). Much of the film's power comes through Milland's searing portrayal of a decent man who acquires a gift which, ultimately, he can't cope with. Corman chucks in the idea that Milland can now see God and the images of his eyes staring out of the screen, almost begging to be torn out, are incredibly haunting. If you like this, Jack Arnold's *Shrinking Man* should appeal.

FROM A TO B

A STARS & THEIR B VERSIONS

JOHN BARRYMORE/WARREN WILLIAM
William may have been a "poor man's John Barrymore" but he was the first actor to play Perry Mason on film. He also took over the Philo Vance role from Bill Powell. But his real expertise was at playing charming cads.

CLARK GABLE/JOHN CARROLL
Carroll was a Gable clone who came closest to the King's roles as the lead in *Congo Maisie*, a budget remake of Gable's *Red Dust* with Jean Harlow wannabe Ann Sothern.

JOHN GARFIELD/DANE CLARK
Warners bought Clark and tried to make him the next John Garfield, a rival which became even larger when Garfield fell foul of the witch hunt and worried and drank himself to death. Garfield's death did not, however, benefit Clark, who was seen as too much of a copy to be a true star.

JEAN HARLOW/TOBY WING
Toby was a platinum blond who showed more stamina than the original, who died of uremic poisoning in 1937 when she was just 26. Wing never quite made it as a top star – in the big pictures she always had a supporting or minor role (even if her performances did catch the eye).

CARMEN MIRANDA/ANN SAVAGE
Such was the demand for actresses who could perform while supporting a bowl of fruit in the 1940s that poor old Carmen couldn't keep up. So Ann Savage made her name in *Two Señoritas from Chicago*. But she broke out to become a cigarette-

BANNED

Censors, governments and directors have all tried to ban movies. Grace Kelly and Peter Sellers have the rare distinction of having all their movies banned in different countries for completely different reasons. Sometimes, the ban is just more grist to a movie's PR mill. Sometimes, though, the censorship can be more insidious, meaning that controversial films like *The Last Temptation Of Christ* can just be bloody hard to find at your local video shop. And then there are those films, devoid of any artistic merit (and often starring a buxom former member of the SS called Ilsa) which can only be defended on the theoretical grounds of free speech.

BLOODSUCKING FREAKS 1978
Director Joel M Reed Cast Seamus O'Brien, Viju Krem

Are you into "home-style brain surgery!", "human dart boards" or "dental hijinks!" (with or without the exclamation marks)? Then this is the film for you. The synopsis almost says it all: "Sardu is into the theatre of the macabre. Sardu is into S&M. Sardu likes to kill people in public and make them think it's fake." We've all had party guests like that. All this may explain why Women Against Pornography campaigned, successfully, to ban this in the US. Reed's other contributions to movie history? *Blood Bath* and *GI Executioner*. Nuff said.

A CLOCKWORK ORANGE 1972
Director Stanley Kubrick Cast Malcolm McDowell, Patrick Magee, Michael Bates

The funniest thing about this much-analyzed film is that so many of the actors ended up in *Last Of the Summer Wine, May To December* and, well, *Coronation Street,* where actor John Savident has achieved lasting fame as butcher Fred Elliott. Kubrick himself withdrew the film after all the stories that real

> "THIS WOULD MAKE YOU READY FOR A BIT OF THE OLD ULTRAVIOLENCE"
>
> Alex, A Clockwork Orange

criminals had felt inspired to copy the crimes committed by McDowell and his gang – which seems doubly ironic when one of the messages of this savage satire is that you can't escape the law of karma. Kubrick does change the emphasis of Burgess' novel, often in ways that seem misogynistic, and was accused of creating "intellectual pornography". The furore is, in part, a tribute to the film's disturbing power.

ILSA, SHE WOLF OF THE SS 1974

Director **Don Edmonds** *Cast* **Dyanne Thorne, Gregory Knoph**

When people fondly recall the 1970s, they normally talk of hot pants, glam rock and *Saturday Night Fever*. Relatively few of us dwell lovingly on the decade's sleaziest contribution to cinematic history, the Nazi sexploitation film. *Ilsa* is as good (ie bad) a specimen of this genre as any. Ilsa wants to prove that women can stand more pain than men so she decides to do some experiments. From the people who brought you *Bummer!* and *Larceny*, both of which apply to this movie. This spawned

VERBOTEN!

You just never know how movies are going to affect a country's film censors…

ABBOTT AND COSTELLO MEET FRANKENSTEIN
Banned in Finland – as was *Abbott and Costello Meet Dr Jekyll and Mr Hyde*. The fact that *Bulldog Drummond Strikes Back* was also banned would seem to suggest that the Finns just happened to have a very squeamish board of film censors.

THE ADVENTURES OF BARRY McKENZIE
This Barry Humphries comedy upset the New Zealand censor. He said he'd approve it with just one cut "from beginning to end".

This was one of two Abbott and Costello films to be banned in Finland. Lucky Finns

CATCH-22
Banned by Portuguese censors worried about the damage the glimpse of a naked Yossarian in a tree might do to the national psyche.

LIFE OF BRIAN
Banned in Norway and Runnymede and marketed in Sweden as: "The film that is so funny it was banned in Norway."

MICKEY MOUSE
Banned in Romania in 1935 because the authorities feared he would scare children. How prescient they were.

MONKEY BUSINESS
The Marx Brothers' comedy was banned in Ireland because censors feared it would encourage anarchic tendencies.

PINK FLAMINGO
John Waters' exercise in poor taste was deemed in too poor taste to be screened in Australia, the land which gave us Rolf Harris, Frank Ifield and Barry McKenzie. Maybe they were just trying to fix the competition.

SCHINDLER'S LIST
Banned in Malaysia for being pro-Jewish.

two sequels (*Harem Keeper of the Oil Sheikhs* and *The Tigress of Siberia*). The Norwegians banned *Ilsa* on the not unreasonable grounds that having been invaded by the Nazis, they'd already suffered enough without being forced to watch this nonsense. The Sheikh sequel is dafter and less gratuitously offensive.

I SPIT ON YOUR GRAVE
1978
Director Meir Zarchi
Cast Camille Keaton, Eron Tabor

This came out at the height of the media pandemic about snuff movies. The idea that actors (especially women) were being routinely killed to make movies spread faster than that urban myth about the thieves who shoved other people's toothbrushes up their bottoms. And in the midst of this came *I Spit On Your Grave*, also known as *Day Of The Woman* in a pathetic bid to give it some feminist credentials. The plot, about a woman who is horribly raped and wreaks murderous revenge, could be described as an updated Jacobean revenge tragedy if it had any of the things you normally associate with that genre: dialogue, characters or an intellectual rationale less spurious than seeing how many grisly scenes you can get past the censor. In the end, it was banned in the UK and many other places. If you haven't seen it, you haven't missed too much. Keaton, who married into the Garland/Luft showbiz dynasty, would appear as 'Girl in the toilet' in her next film.

THE MILLIONAIRESS 1960
Director Anthony Asquith Cast Peter Sellers, Sophia Loren

Hard to believe anyone could object to this comedy (except, perhaps, on the grounds that it isn't as funny as it thinks it is) but King Bavendra, the Eton-educated monarch of Nepal, decided that Sellers' Indian doctor was too close to him in both manner and appearance. And being king he decided the only appropriate response to this slight on his royal honour was to ban all Peter Sellers films. On the downside, this did mean his loyal subjects missed out on *Dr Strangelove* but they also avoided such flim-flammery as *There's A Girl In My Soup* and *The Bobo* in which he played a matador who'd rather chase girls than bulls. Grace Kelly's movies were banned in Monaco on the

Peeping Tom, a critic suggested, should be flushed down a sewer. Others wanted to know what sewers had ever done to him

> "DO YOU KNOW WHAT THE MOST FRIGHTENING THING IN THE WORLD IS? IT'S FEAR"
>
> Mark Lewis, Peeping Tom

★★★★

IT'S ONLY WORDS

Clark Gable wasn't the first man to say "damn" on screen. Here is our list of linguistic breakthroughs.

BASTARD

Another first for the British film-making industry: first heard on celluloid in *The Blue Lamp* (1950).

BLOODY

First heard in *Pygmalion* (1938).

DAMNED

First uttered (in the phrase "Well, I'll be damned") by Emma Dunn in *Blessed Event* (1932).

FUCK

First used by Marianne Faithfull in Michael Winner's *I'll Never Forget What's His Name* (1967). Also used by critics at the movie's preview. Later heard 206 times in Brian de Palma's *Scarface* and 254 times in *Reservoir Dogs*.

SHIT

Made its big screen debut in Truman Capote's film *In Cold Blood* (1967). Thanks Tru.

PEEPING TOM 1960

Director Michael Powell *Cast* Carl Boehm, Anna Massey, Moira Shearer

"The only really satisfactory way to dispose of *Peeping Tom* would be to shovel it up and flush it swiftly down the nearest sewer. Even then the stench would remain." That was a not untypical reaction when Powell's film about a serial killer who films his victims as he kills them was first released. The critical savaging, and the film's subsequent withdrawal and then re-release in a butchered version, almost ended Powell's career as he was deemed unbankable in the British movie business. The question today is: how good is the film? Answer: very good indeed. Powell makes the audience confront their own voyeurism when watching this film, which is why even today, when we've had more serial killer exploitation flicks than serial killers, this can still shock. There is no get-out for the viewer: we are invited to sympathize with the mad, abused hero even as we despise him.

THE TRIP 1967

Director Roger Corman *Cast* Peter Fonda, Bruce Dern, Susan Strasberg

Jack Nicholson wrote this film about an advertising director who tries to get in touch with his inner self through LSD. This may have been the Swinging Sixties but the British censors still huffed and harrumphed and decided it was nothing but an advert for the benefits of acid. A stupid decision but not an entirely stupid thought: Nicholson's script was based on experience and Corman, in preparation for the role, spent seven hours face down in the mud in Big Sur after taking the drug.

Don't show this to Norwegians and people in Runnymede

not unreasonable grounds that it was demeaning for the principality's princess to be seen dialling M for misogyny in a Hitchcock film.

BLOCKBUSTERS

Until the late 1970s the idea of a film making the kind of profit which could repay the debt of a Third World nation was unheard of. Then *Jaws* and *Star Wars* amassed a billion dollars between them. Movies would never be quite the same again. Neither would we.

There are two kinds of blockbuster: those manufactured to be the biggest of the biggest and those which just catch fire with the mass audience. *Jurassic Park* was always destined to be a blockbuster. Just as, in the 1980s, any Schwarzenegger, Stallone or Murphy vehicle that didn't make more than $100m at the box office was considered a flop. Now the stakes are higher – less than $200m and someone has to take the rap.

In 1990, before their release, *Dick Tracy*, *The Godfather III* and *Days of Thunder* were all vying for top box office spot. So their makers thought. But they were beaten by an obnoxious kid (*Home Alone*), a prostitute looking for her prince charming (*Pretty Woman*) and a dead man saving his girlfriend (*Ghost*).

ALIEN 1979
Director Ridley Scott *Cast* Sigourney Weaver, Tom Skerritt, Veronica Cartwright, John Hurt

Ripley (Weaver) remains the one true female action star in a universe dominated by male caricatures. Odd that, because the role was originally written for a man and Veronica Cartwright (who plays Lambert in this film) was the first female choice. The film grossed over $60m in the US alone and the sequels are still going strong (we're up to number four, although they have stopped numbering them, opting for *Alien Resurrection* instead). The tale of a space ship responding to an SOS and inadvertently letting an alien on board was inspired by the 1958 budget sci-fi flick, *It! The Terror From Beyond Space*.

THE BIG PARADE 1925
Director King Vidor *Cast* John Gilbert, Renée Adorée

Depending on the true gross of *Birth Of A Nation*, Vidor's *The Big Parade* may be the highest grossing silent film of all time, with worldwide rentals in excess of $22m. Gilbert is the idle son of a wealthy businessman who joins the army at the start of World War I and falls for French girl Melisande (Adorée). Vidor's talent shines, but it was Gilbert, poised to become the

> **"HERE'S TO SWIMMIN' WITH LONG-LEGGED WIMMIN"**
> Quint, Jaws

biggest male silent star with Valentino's death a year later, who lights up the screen. Shame he didn't have the voice for talkies.

THE BIRTH OF A NATION 1915

Director DW Griffith Cast Lillian Gish, Mae Marsh, Henry B Walthall
Griffith's masterpiece never grossed anywhere near the $50m once claimed, the actual sum falling between *Variety*'s quote of $5m and Griffith's own quote of $10m. The film remains a landmark epic however, telling the dramatic tale of two families during the American Civil War and featuring such historical events as the rise of the Klan (director John Ford claimed he was one of the klansmen) and Lincoln's assassination. Griffith visualized the entire film in his mind, making no notes and no script, with actors ad-libbing throughout, and the memorable epic battle scenes shot in a single day. The film's pro-Klan attitudes make it uncomfortable viewing today; klansmen in full robes were used to publicize the Los Angeles première.

> **"I SAID NO CAMELS! THAT'S FIVE CAMELS! CAN'T YOU COUNT?"**
>
> Indiana Jones, The Last Crusade

THE BODYGUARD 1992

Director Mick Jackson Cast Kevin Costner, Whitney Houston
Despite dull star performances (the film was written for Diana Ross and Steve McQueen) this grossed over $400m. Costner is hired to protect a pop diva (Houston) from her fans. You can guess the rest. Success was sealed by Whitney's shoulder-shaking rendition of Dolly Parton's *I Will Always Love You*.

CLEOPATRA 1963

Director Joseph L Mankiewicz Cast Elizabeth Taylor, Richard Burton, Rex Harrison, Roddy McDowall
This epic tale of love on the Nile was supposed to star Joan

WHAT IS AN EVENT MOVIE?

A favourite term among film critics, there are actually three kinds of event movie.

THE ONE WITH AN ACTUAL EVENT
You don't need to have a passing interest in history to know what happens in *Titanic* or *Pearl Harbor*, but what a spectacle! Or in the latter case: what spectacle?

THE ONE WHERE IT'S ALL IN THE TAGLINE
Ghostbusters: "They're here to save the world."

Independence Day: "Earth. Take a good look. It could be your last."
Men In Black: "Protecting the earth from the scum of the universe."

THE ONE WHERE IT'S ALL IN THE NAME
Fans of *Batman, Dick Tracy, Superman* and particularly the *Star Wars* sequels no doubt had the date of the advance screening pencilled in on their calendars and their tickets bought a month in advance.

Don't worry kids, it's not a real dinosaur, it's just an allegory for America's involvement in the Vietnam war

Collins and Peter Finch. But first Taylor and then Burton became available, triggering the greatest love affair the movies had seen since Joan Crawford looked in a mirror. The film itself is a rather bloodless spectacle, as if 'le scandale' (as Burton dubbed it) had drained all the energy out of cast and crew. Recut so badly the person doing it must have been wearing metal gloves, it's a hard film to judge. Costing $270m to make (at today's prices), it was the biggest grosser of the year and didn't, despite all the stories, bankrupt Fox.

CONFESSIONS OF A WINDOW CLEANER 1974

Director Val Guest *Cast* Robin Askwith, Antony Booth, Sheila White

Frightening as it may sound, this, the first *Confessions* film, was the biggest box office draw in Britain in 1974. Askwith stars as Timmy, a window cleaner whose female customers demand a hands-on service. Cherie Blair's dad Antony Booth also appears. And he has the nerve to accuse Tone of selling out.

CROCODILE DUNDEE 1986

Director Peter Faiman *Cast* Paul Hogan, Linda Kozlowski

This unique blend of amiable comedy and advert for the Australian tourist board became the highest grossing film not to come from Hollywood. The feel-good movie of 1986 had reporter Sue Charlton (Kozlowski) flying to Australia to

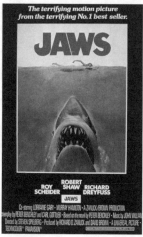

The terrifying motion picture from the terrifying No.1 best seller.

JAWS

ROY SCHEIDER   ROBERT SHAW   RICHARD DREYFUSS

JAWS

Co-starring LORRAINE GARY · MURRAY HAMILTON · A ZANUCK/BROWN PRODUCTION
screenplay by PETER BENCHLEY and CARL GOTTLIEB · Based on the novel by PETER BENCHLEY · Music by JOHN WILLIAMS
Directed by STEVEN SPIELBERG · Produced by RICHARD D. ZANUCK and DAVID BROWN · A UNIVERSAL PICTURE
TECHNICOLOR® PANAVISION®

Jaws: Even more terrifying than Crocodile Dundee in Los Angeles. Almost

interview crocodile-conquering Mick Dundee (Hogan). He's such a character he returns to New York with her where he shows off his enormous knife (more Freudian symbolism?) and treads on folk in the nicest possible way. The original had more charm than it is now given credit for. Unlike the sequels.

DUEL IN THE SUN 1946
Director King Vidor Cast Jennifer Jones, Gregory Peck, Joseph Cotten
Producer David O Selznick went into a funk after he had made *Gone With The Wind*, fearing that he could never top it. But seven years later he had a go. He miscast his then mistress Jennifer Jones (the pair wed in 1949) as Pearl Chevez who, after her family are killed, heads to distant relatives in Texas where she meets hostility and lust. Peck was just as miscast as unruly suitor Lewt. But with a cast including Lillian Gish and Joseph Cotten, and the nickname 'Lust in the dust', the film survived critical scorn to become a huge success. The film boasts great scenery and an unusual ending (for Hollywood) but Scarlett and Rhett it ain't. Selznick would finally end up trying to top them in 1957.

FATAL ATTRACTION 1987
Director Adrian Lyne Cast Michael Douglas, Glenn Close
Although pipped to the post as the highest grosser of 1987 by *Beverly Hills Cop 2*, it was Adrian Lyne's tale of infidelity which captured the public's imagination. Based on the British short film *Diversion*, it features Douglas as happily married Dan who has a weekend fling with publisher Alex (Close). She banked on more than a fling, however, and terrorizes Douglas and wife (Anne Archer) with constant phone calls, acid attacks and threats to tie them up and make them listen to Dean Friedman records. Originally, the film was to end with Alex's suicide and Dan's arrest for her murder but audiences weren't happy. Reshoots helped the film gross in excess of $300m.

GHOSTBUSTERS 1984
Director Ivan Reitman Cast Dan Aykroyd, Bill Murray, Sigourney Weaver, Harold Ramis, Rick Moranis
Just the mention of the film's title will have men of a certain age and mental disposition assuming a funny stance and saying

"Who ya gonna call?" in a phoney American accent. But then this did become the sixth highest grossing film of all time. An amusing yarn about paranormal investigators, it's well cast, with Murray especially funny as the cynical Venkman more concerned with the damsel in distress than the cause of distress. The original cast was supposed to be Eddie Murphy, John Candy (ugh!) and John Belushi.

> **"I'VE GOT HUNDREDS OF PEOPLE DYING TO ABUSE ME"**
> Dr Peter Venkman, Ghostbusters

INDIANA JONES AND THE LAST CRUSADE 1989
Director **Steven Spielberg** *Cast* **Harrison Ford, Sean Connery**
The third installment in the Indiana chronicles, with Connery and Ford as father-and-son archaeologists, was the most commercially successful. With dad missing, Indiana tries to rescue him and is embroiled in pa's quest for the holy grail. The film has become cult for a slew of errors and anachronisms (why, for example, are two passengers in the airship lounge reading newspapers dated 1918 if the film is set in 1938?).

JAWS 1975
Director **Steven Spielberg** *Cast* **Roy Scheider, Robert Shaw, Richard Dreyfuss, Carl Gottlieb, Lorraine Gary**
The first film in history to break the $100m mark in North America. The plot is pure 1950s sci-fi, with a shark terrorizing sleepy Amity Island. The unlikely trio of crusty sailor (Shaw), police chief (Scheider) and bumbling scientist (Dreyfuss) spoil the shark's fun. Although Bruce, as Spielberg dubbed the shark,

WHEN LESS IS MORE...

Media studies students in *Scream 2* quibbled as to whether a sequel is ever better than the original. With the exception of the *Godfather Part II*, the theory of diminishing returns normally applies (critically if not financially).

SPEED 1994 & SPEED 2: CRUISE CONTROL 1997
Complete with tough-guy heartthrob, damsel in distress and a variety of speeding modes of transport, *Speed* was a blast. Take away the hero and replace him with a B-list star, keep the girl but move the action to a slower-than-a-tortoise cruise liner and you've got all the ingredients of a recipe for disaster. It isn't even an *Under Siege 2*.

ATTACK OF THE KILLER TOMATOES 1978 & KILLER TOMATOES EAT FRANCE 1991
Originally a spoof on the classic 50s B movie with fierce vegetables corrupting politicians and housewives through their Bloody Marys. A 'so bad it's good' film, but it's never a good idea to do a sequel to a one-joke movie.

LETHAL WEAPON 1987 & LETHAL WEAPON 4 1998
The original remains the ultimate buddy action film with the wisecracking duo up against the odds. By the fourth instalment they're both moaning they're too old, with wild man Riggs (Gibson) heading into domestic bliss and the bad guys better than our heroes. Zzzzzzz.

can look a bit plastic 25 years on, this is still a thrilling horror. In 1993, Spielberg would make "Jaws with claws" *Jurassic Park*, also genuinely scary. (How can a glass of water make your heart jump?) Buried in here somewhere may be a message about Vietnam (see p429). The film's success is even more amazing when you realize that Spielberg only saw the dinosaur footage on a shaky black and white screen in Poland, where he was busy making his next film, *Schindler's List*.

LES VISITEURS 1993
Director **Jean-Marie Poiré** *Cast* **Christian Clavier, Jean Reno**
France's biggest domestic hit at the time, this was remade for American audiences in 2001 with Reno reprising his role as knight Godefroy, who along with his faithful squire (Clavier, who also co-wrote the script) is transported into the future. The bumbling pair aim to go back in time to change history but end up in the 20th century, not the 12th. After that the action resembles a Benny Hill sketch with the pair battling with cars, stealing food and learning to cope with modern life. The same team made the imaginatively titled *Operation Corned Beef*.

SIBERIADE 1979 SIBIRIADA
Director **Andrei Konchalovsky** *Cast* **Natalya Andreychenko, Sergei Shakurov**

While American films ruled the world, Russian audiences were fed a steady stream of home-grown talent alongside third-rate Indian films and little-known productions from the developing world. But when Konchalovsky released this epic family saga, some 80 million people flocked to movie houses to see the film. It focuses on the lives of two families, one rich and one poor, and their stories from the start of the century, through the revolution, World War II and on into the 1960s.

SNOW WHITE AND THE SEVEN DWARFS 1937
Director **David Hand**
Dubbed 'Disney's Folly' before its release, this became a licence to print money. The tale of a jealous queen, beautiful stepdaughter and seven dwarfs might not have been as successful if the creators had stuck with their original plans to call the dwarfs Blabby, Biggy, Hotsy, Hoppy, Nifty, Shifty and Jumpy.

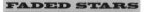

FADED STARS

ROY SCHEIDER
Starring in not only the biggest film of 1977, but the film which helped launch a whole new sub-genre, still the man can't get any better work than the three sequels and a supporting role in *Marathon Man*.

BILL PULLMAN
You know the face but you can't quite place the name. Everyman actor Pullman must come up against this all the time, despite starring in *Casper* and *Sleepless In Seattle*, not to mention playing the President in the sure-fire hit *Independence Day*. What does the man have to do to get noticed!

BILL PAXTON
Face-in-the-crowd Paxton can list *Terminator, Commando, Aliens, True Lies, Twister* and the biggest of them all, *Titanic*, on his impressive resumé. Yet can you remember what he looks like?

BUDDY FILMS

You could argue that Cervantes wrote the blueprint for the buddy movie with *Don Quixote*. But the original emphasis on the quirky relationship of two mismatched characters (usually of the same sex) has changed as the 'buddy act' became a compulsory part of every action potboiler. The twists on that central relationship have become increasingly desperate. You almost feel sorry for James Belushi – forced to relate to a German shepherd dog in *K9* (the real indignity: the dog's character is better defined than his) – but then you stop and think how rich that film must have made him.

BAISE-MOI 2000 RAPE ME
Director Virginie Despentes Cast Raffaela Anderson, Karen Lancaume
In America, the PR for this said it made *Thelma And Louise* look like a Merchany-Ivory film. For once, a PR person got it half right. Despentes' debut as a director doesn't flinch from its dark comedy, finding humour in the fact that the homicidal duo Manu (Anderson) and Nadine (Lancaume) shoot one man because he used a condom (at least it's original). Their violence is provoked because one of them has been raped, and they go on a spree which *Thelma And Louise* suggested but never delivered. You may be overwhelmed by the cumulative brutality.

A BETTER TOMORROW 1986
Director John Woo Cast Chow Yun-Fat, Ti Lung, Leslie Cheung
The most famous scene in this movie is the dinner-table assassination by Chow Yun-Fat wearing, somewhat implausibly given the Hong Kong setting, a trenchcoat. But the action sequences are just trappings; at the heart of the film is the relationship between two brothers: one a gangster (Ti Lung) and the other a cop (Cheung). This film made Woo's reputation outside Hong Kong and yielded an all-action sequel.

> **"A SUICIDE TELEGRAM? WHO SENDS A SUICIDE TELEGRAM?"**
> Murray, The Odd Couple

BECKET 1964
Director Peter Glenville Cast Richard Burton, Peter O'Toole
Even in the movies, buddies can fall out. And very occasionally, even in the movies, they don't make it up again. Burton (as the

turbulent priest Becket) and O'Toole (as Henry II) combine to marvellous effect here, O'Toole, in his co-star's fantastic description, looking like "a beautiful emaciated secretary bird". Check the scene where Henry puts the ring on Becket's finger: it took endless retakes because the actors had been on a two-and-a-half day binge and it was (in Burton's words) "like trying to thread a needle wearing boxing gloves".

BUTCH CASSIDY AND THE SUNDANCE KID 1969

Director **George Roy Hill** *Cast* **Paul Newman, Robert Redford**

Newman liked to say of this film: "It's a love affair between two men, the girl is really incidental." Katharine Ross' incidental status is confirmed in a famously unchivalrous scene where Sundance (Redford), told that Butch (Newman) is flirting with his girl, waves a tired hand and says: "Take her". The tale of outlaws who wisecrack all the way across the West and then down to Bolivia isn't really popular with western aficionados, probably because the backdrop is incidental too. This is just an excuse for writer William Goldman's witticisms and for the male leads to spark off each other, which they do beautifully. All of which makes it even more astonishing to recall the trouble the studio had casting this. Among the other

PARTNERS

ABBOTT AND COSTELLO

The archetypal short-and-fat meets tall-and-thin duo were incredibly popular in the 1940s. But Costello (the tall one) had some interesting pals: mobster Frank Costello (no relation) was a childhood friend and Joe Bozzo, head of the New Jersey mafia, was his daughter's godfather. *Abbott And Costello Meet The Mob* might have been funnier than *Abbott And Costello Meet The Mummy* – but maybe not.

HEPBURN AND TRACY

The only duo in this list who cross the gender divide. Hepburn was once dubbed box office poison, partly because she lacked certain qualities prized by the superficial male. Her on-screen chemistry with Tracy was all about the conflict between two very different intelligences. *Adam's Rib* (1949) may be their best outing but most are worth watching

HOPE AND CROSBY

The Road To Utopia (1946) was probably their finest 90 minutes. But any duo who can sit on a camel and sing "Like Webster's dictionary, we're Morocco bound" are alright by us.

MARTIN AND LEWIS

Long before Ben and Jerry, there was Dino and Jerry. Lewis was considered a comic genius by the French and some (not all) members of his own family. Dino was a *serenfreghista*, an old Italian word meaning "one who can't give a fuck". *Artists And Models* (1955) isn't bad but it did have Dorothy Malone, Shirley MacLaine and Anita Ekberg in the cast.

TURNER AND HOOCH

Hanks and his canine were better than Belushi and the German shepherd dog. And they quit while they were ahead. Just. On both counts.

possible line-ups: Newman and Presley, Newman and Brando, and Redford and McQueen. One reason the final duo work so well is because Newman ignored studio hacks who complained his co-star was getting too many close ups.

Redford, Ross and Newman watch as the director tests a German shepherd dog called K9 for the sequel

48 HOURS 1982
Director Walter Hill Cast Nick Nolte, Eddie Murphy
Another divine casting accident. It could have starred Stallone, Burt Reynolds (then the biggest box office draw in the US) or Richard Pryor. But it ended up at Paramount, which had Nolte on contract but nothing for him to do. Hill signed to direct. His then girlfriend Hildy Gottlieb was a talent agent representing a certain up-and-coming black comedian. Nolte stars as the cop who borrows Murphy from jail for 48 hours to find a criminal. The film has most of the action movie clichés, although in fairness they weren't clichés when it was made. Worth watching, if only for the scene where Murphy intimidates a bar full of rednecks.

MIDNIGHT RUN 1988
Director Martin Brest Cast Robert De Niro, Charles Grodin
Let's be heretical and suggest this may be more compelling evidence of De Niro's acting genius than any of his gangsters. Playing a bondsman who finds an accountant (Grodin) who has skimmed the mob, cuffs him, and takes him back to LA, he has the guts to let the laughs arise from the character, lifting what could have been a formula film out of the rut. Grodin, possibly relieved to have a co-star who isn't a dog called Beethoven, holds his own as the duo are pursued by the mob, the FBI and another bounty hunter. Grodin still has real scars on his wrists from wearing the cuffs in this film.

NATIONAL LAMPOON'S ANIMAL HOUSE 1978
Director John Landis Cast Tim Matheson, John Belushi, Peter Riegert, John Vernon
Buddy movies don't have to be about two buddies. A buddy movie can be any film where one sex (usually the male sex) is relishing its camaraderie while the other (usually female) are

> **"WHO DELIVERED THE MEDICAL SCHOOL CADAVERS TO THE ALUMNI DINNER?"**
> Dean Wormer, National Lampoon's Animal House

"I'm willing to trade good looks for a certain morally casual attitude"

confined to the margins. Indeed, you could say that *JFK*, where a woman only appears occasionally to nag Kevin Costner away from doing what he'd like to do with the boys (namely solve the Kennedy assassination), is a buddy film. In *Animal House*, Landis has assembled all kinds of buddies: tall and handsome (Matheson), charismatically obese (Belushi) or just obese (Stephen Furst as Kent Dorfman). And set them in mortal combat with the anally retentive crypto-Nazis who run the Dean's favourite fraternity. Sophisticated it isn't (food fight, anyone?), but if you don't like it at all, you may have to confront the fact that you simply don't have a sense of humour.

THE ODD COUPLE 1968
Director Gene Saks *Cast* Walter Matthau, Jack Lemmon

In the popular imagination, Lemmon and Matthau seemed to spend their closing years eternally appearing in movies together. They did co-star in nine films (not counting *JFK*) but this, about two friends who become flatmates, is the most enduring. They had sharpened their repartee a year earlier in Wilder's *The Fortune Cookie* (Matthau just beat Jackie Gleason to play the ambulance-chasing lawyer). Neither actor could waste lines like: "You leave little notes on my pillow, 'We're all out of cornflakes, F. U.' It took me three hours to figure out F. U. was Felix Unger." Lemmon improved on Neil Simon's play by giving his character something the writer often failed to create, a sense of genuine human emotion and melancholy.

OF MICE AND MEN 1939
Director Lewis Milestone *Cast* Lon Chaney Jr, Burgess Meredith

Steinbeck's novel is here translated pretty faithfully to the screen, with Chaney magnificent as the none-too-bright migrant farm worker whose fondness for small furry things will be the undoing of him and his friend George (Meredith). Although Steinbeck's story, in Milestone's capable hands, is about the emptiness of the American dream, the relationship between the two central characters has obvious similarities to that between the brothers in Barry Levinson's 1988 classic *Rain Man*. The Hoffman-Cruise collaboration, though, gives the story a more optimistic spin, with the autistic brother forcing Cruise to re-evaluate his life. But it's not cheesily done, and both stars deserve credit for bringing such material to the screen in the face of studio indifference.

BUDGET

For movie budgets, like so much else in life, size doesn't always matter. With any budget of the kind James Cameron has become accustomed to comes pressure and scrutiny. Sometimes, the best films really can be made by someone who believes so strongly in their movie they're prepared to have drugs tested on them to raise cash. But then some budget films just serve to remind you that no money, no craft and no imagination are a very deadly combination.

THE ANGRY RED PLANET 1959
Director Ib Melchior *Cast* Gerald Mohr, Nora Hayden, Les Tremayne, Jack Kruschen

The sci-fi movie that invented the 'Cinemagic' process. As is so often the case in Hollywood, Cinemagic was an inspired response to an order to cut the budget midway through production. To reduce costs the movie was to be released in black and white but some of the sequences on Mars came out double exposed, giving the film a shimmering quality which, when dyed purple, became Cinemagic. Folk on the red planet don't like being probed by humans, hence the anger of the title and cue the appearance of incredible monsters. Incredible in the sense that that 40-foot alien is actually a 15-inch high combination of rat, crab, spider and bat. Not bad for a movie filmed in nine days for just $200,000.

> "HEY, DID YOU KNOW THE FAKE BLOOD IS MINT FLAVOURED?"
> Bert, Starving Artists

BLAIR WITCH PROJECT 1999
Directors Daniel Myrick, Eduardo Sànchez *Cast* Heather Donahue, Michael C Williams, Joshua Leonard

A small budget is no guarantee of virtue, just as a big budget does not always signify that a movie will fall victim to cinematic elephantiasis. Would this project have garnered anywhere near as much attention if it had been released by a major Hollywood studio and not launched through a clever guerrilla marketing campaign over the Internet? The movie does put a very chilling spin on the "if you go down to the woods today…" line but by the time *Blair Witch 3* comes out in 2002, this series will be just something else we can blame the Internet for.

EL MARIACHI 1992

Director Robert Rodriguez *Cast* Carlos Gallardo,
Consuelo Gomez, Peter Marquardt

Initially made for just $7,000 (the director raised $3,000 by
volunteering to be a human lab rat for a new cholesterol-
reducing drug), this is a triumph of hope over the laws of movie
making. Many of the guns in this film are water pistols, others
were borrowed from the police. The plot is simplicity itself:
a mariachi (a travelling guitar player) strolls into town, dressed
in black and carrying a guitar case. A killer arrives the same day
in the same outfit. It sounds predictable but Rodriguez has
fashioned fabulous entertainment using amateur actors (some
cast members were just passers-by) and very little money.

> "IT IS VERY
> HARD TO
> GET LOST
> IN AMERICA
> THESE DAYS"
>
> Heather, The Blair Witch Project

ETAT DES LIEUX 1995

Director Jean François Richet *Cast* Patrick Dell'Isola, Marc de
Jonge, Stéphane Ferrara, François Dyrek

This black and white French realist inner city drama was made
out of the money Richet won by gambling his dole money in
casinos over eight months. Angry and gritty, it is a powerful, if
uncomfortable, film. Richet is part of 'un cinema de banlieu',
a shift in France from costume dramas to the contemporary feel
many French New Wave films had in the 1950s.

FOUR WEDDINGS AND A FUNERAL 1994

Director Mike Newell *Cast* Hugh Grant, Andie MacDowell

This may be one of the biggest grossing British films of all-time
($260m taken at the worldwide box office) but the budget
wouldn't cover the cost of taking the cast to Scotland to film
a Scottish wedding. Indeed, for that scene the extras had to
bring their own suits. During filming Grant was convinced the
movie would be terrible but it did well
enough for MacDowell to be asked to
sell anti-ageing cream.

HOLLYWOOD SHUFFLE 1987

Director Robert Townsend
Cast Townsend, Anne-Marie Johnson,
Helen Martin, Starletta DuPois

The story behind this movie is often
presented as another triumphant
showbiz against-all-odds tale. This is
partly true. Black actor Robert
Townsend, despairing of finding the
right part in a Hollywood film, decides
to make his own for less than

If you go down to the woods today, you're in for a
big surprise. *Blair Witch 3,4,5* are being shot there

$100,000. The film, about a young man who wants to become an actor and dreams of the day when Rambo will be black, is very funny indeed. The only trouble with this scenario is the next Spike Lee didn't become the next Spike Lee at all. The movie industry laughed, patted Townsend on the head and forgot almost all about him.

PERMANENT VACATION 1982

Director **Jim Jarmusch** *Cast* **Chris Parker, Leila Gastil, Maria Duval, John Lurie**

Jarmusch made this, his first film, with the help of his old film school teacher Nicholas Ray. It's intriguing to see how, even when he was 28, Jarmusch was already playing with the idea of someone who doesn't belong. In this case, the perpetual tourist who justifies the title is a Charlie Parker fan who walks the streets of New York having various encounters. Jarmusch's later films have more charm, but then it's hard to be charming when you've got a budget of just $12,000.

RAT PFINK A BOO BOO 1965

Director **Ray Dennis Steckler** *Cast* **Ron Haydock, Carolyn Brandt, Titus Moede**

Unusual name for a film you might 'pfink'. The title is down to a, well, boo boo by the designer who left out the 'nd' of the 'and' which was supposed to be the third word of the title and the director didn't have the budget to correct the error. Still the 'A' gives the film, about a crime fighting duo called Rat Pfink and Boo Boo (who, as the dialogue says, "have only one weakness – bullets") a misleading air of continental sophistication. It's hard to criticize a film which has a narrator called Dan Danger and a cast member called Romeo Barrymore but this is only for agoraphobics.

STARVING ARTISTS 1997

Director **Allan Piper** *Cast* **Allan Piper, Sandi Carroll, Joe Smith, Bess Wohl**

Everybody who helped fund this movie (even if they only gave $1) has their name in it somewhere. And, says Piper, the only woman who complained didn't like the fact that her name appeared on a porn mag. Almost psychotically eager to please, this movie offers you satire (about starving artists), slapstick, puns galore and if none of that tickles your funny bone, how about a barrelful of monkeys?

TOO MUCH BUDGET

A BRIDGE TOO FAR 1977
Overblown, overlong war epic with a dazzling array of stars parachuted in for a specific scene or emotion. Olivier is hired to look tragic, Redford to look decisive. Not a casting strategy, but an admission by the director that he's failed to keep our interest.

THE KLANSMAN 1974
This cost $5m in 1974 yet the best performance in the film comes from… OJ Simpson. Scary. Lee Marvin and Richard Burton co-starred, although there is a rumour that they were so drunk throughout that when they were reintroduced at a Hollywood party, they couldn't remember meeting each other.

SHEENA 1984
This cost $26m to make although Columbia must have wondered where the money had been spent after the director's attempt to pass a made-up horse off as a zebra. Starring Bond girl Tanya Roberts this was a camp Tarzan-like tale which took less than $3m.

BUSINESS

Only the French have the guts to make a thriller about the banking system. When Hollywood makes movies about business they either worship the individual, even when it's a reigning lizard like Gordon Gekko, or denigrate the faceless nameless corporation. The British can, at least, offer that devastating satire of modern industrial life, *Carry On At Your Convenience*. Only joking, we do of course mean the marvellous *The Man In The White Suit*.

ANGLAR, FINNS DOM? 1961
Director Lars-Magnus Lindgren Cast Jarl Kulle, Christina Schollin

Given that Sweden's contribution to comedy is usually held to be roughly on a par with Switzerland's contribution to the history of naval warfare, this little gem comes as something of a surprise. Jan Froman (Kulle) decides he wants to become the boss of his local bank but having few qualifications and less clout, he's obliged to start out as janitor. He falls in love with a married woman and starts trading in shares and property. In 1961, this achieved notoriety for its seaside love scenes, held to be very startling at the time, and this fuss rather obscured the quality of the rest of the film.

THE DEVIL AND MISS JONES 1941
Director Sam Wood Cast Jean Arthur, Charles Coburn

Department store owner (Coburn) goes undercover to track down union agitators (led by Arthur as Miss Jones) at his company but is soon won over to their demands. Sounds a bit trite, but this comedy is one of the last products of the liberal optimism which pervaded Hollywood after the New Deal. Wood's direction lives up to his surname. But then he would later form the Motion Picture Association for the Preservation of American Ideals (with a name like that you know those ideals didn't include free speech). He would have felt more at home with Peter Sellers' portrayal of the socialist shop steward Fred Kite in *I'm All Right Jack* (although he wouldn't have appreciated the Boulting brothers' satire of the upper classes).

THE FOOL 1990

Director Christine Edzard *Cast* Derek Jacobi, Cyril Cusack,
Maria Aitken, Miranda Richardson

Bear with this film. What it lacks in narrative drive, it makes up
for in the performance of its stellar British cast and in the scene
where Jacobi, playing a man who is really a clerk but has
conned society into thinking he is the infinitely wealthy Sir
John, turns on the upper classes and rips them to pieces.
Edzard had previously directed *Little Dorrit* and the same care
for detail is evident here. A marvel.

THE FOUNTAINHEAD 1949

Director King Vidor *Cast* Gary Cooper, Patricia Neal

Gary Cooper is the first film superman, but in the
Nietzschean sense rather than in the underpants-
flaunting sense. Here he stars as a visionary
architect who defends "the individual against the
collective", sees his new building designs vindicated
and still manages to meet an heiress whose chat-up
lines include: "I'll cook, I'll wash, I'll scrub the
floor." Good as Cooper and Neal are (their torrid
affair began on set), it's hard not to be reminded
of those Nazi 'mountain' movies, where the lone
blonde hero triumphs over the Alpine heights.

RKO/Frank Ross, Norman Krasna

GLENGARRY GLEN ROSS 1992

Director James Foley *Cast* Al Pacino, Jack Lemmon,
Alec Baldwin, Ed Harris

David Mamet's play never stops looking like a play
but it's hard to complain about a movie where
employees who get third prize in the monthly sales
contest are told their reward is to be fired. Lemmon

**"Some firms sing the company
song. We like to play sardines"**

once said this was the best cast he'd ever worked with and the
overall level of thespianry is so high that even Baldwin rises to
the occasion in the role of a nauseating motivator, a part
created for him. While filming, the movie was known to the cast
as 'Death of a fuckin' salesman'.

THE INSIDER 1999

Director Michael Mann *Cast* Al Pacino, Russell Crowe,
Christopher Plummer

Halfway into this film you might find yourself praying for it to
end. Not because you're bored – Mann's real-life drama about
an employee who blows the whistle on the tobacco industry and
the legal and journalistic shenanigans which ensue is too well
made for that. No, you might just feel you can't bear to see

Jeffrey Wigand (the informer played by Crowe) take any more punishment. Ultimately, Crowe and Plummer steal the film from Pacino who, good as he is, is on familiar territory. But Crowe's performance is a thing of rare subtlety and truth.

L'ARGENT DES AUTRES 1978

Director **Christian de Chalonge** Cast **Jean-Louis Trintignant, Catherine Deneuve, Claude Brasseur**

Bank worker Henri Rainier (Trintignant) is blamed when his bank's loan to a big investor goes awry. The bank tries to cover this up but news soon leaks and Rainier is blamed and sacked. Chalonge directs an intriguing political-financial thriller known in English as *Other People's Money*, not to be confused with the less convincing Danny DeVito film of the same name.

THE MAN IN THE GRAY FLANNEL SUIT 1956

Director **Nunnally Johnson** Cast **Gregory Peck, Jennifer Jones**

Gregory Peck has always seemed like a decent, slightly idealized version of how America would like to see itself. The same heightened normality which made his Captain Ahab so hard to accept works for him here, as a Madison Avenue ad-man who has to choose career or family. At least he thinks he does, and picks family, but with typical Hollywood fudge he suddenly inherits a huge chunk of land. Watch out for DeForest Kelley (*Star Trek*'s Dr McCoy) as the Army doc who gets to say: "This man's dead, Captain." Spooky, eh? *Executive Suite* (1956) is a more right-wing version of the above which chastises wife June Allyson for daring to interfere with her husband's inalienable right to push the envelope in sofa design.

Edward R Pressman/American Entertainment

"Hey Bud, did you know there are more than 300 different species in the Gekkonidae lizard family?"

THE MARRIAGE OF MARIA BRAUN 1978

Director **Rainer Werner Fassbinder** Cast **Hanna Schygulla, Klaus Löwitsch**

Fassbinder took a fatal overdose three years after this film was made. He was just 37. The main character Braun (played wonderfully by Schygulla) inadvertently (plot spoiler alert!) kills herself at the end having, in Fassbinder's view, committed emotional suicide long ago. This isn't a film about business as such, but it shows how an entire country, in its urge to forget an unforgettable past, became a corporate enterprise. The 'economic miracle' is a personal disaster for Braun's lover (the boss of the textile firm where she works), and finally for Braun, a Thatcherite heroine before Thatcherism had been invented.

MODERN TIMES 1936

Director Charles Chaplin *Cast* Chaplin, Paulette Goddard

One of the more enduring movie clichés is that Chaplin should have stuck to being a clown and not tried to make message pictures. *Modern Times*, a picture which sends up capitalism and automation something rotten and gets his message across while still making you laugh, exposes that for the utter balderdash it is. The film is memorably and anachronistically silent – Chaplin sings in gibberish and the only other spoken voices are from the machines which enslave the workers. The film was banned as Communist propaganda in Germany and Italy. Indeed, the Nazis so hated it that Josef Goebbels would 'persuade' René Clair to sue over the similarities between this film and his *A Nous La Liberté*. Clair dropped the suit as soon as he could.

TIN MEN 1987

Director Barry Levinson *Cast* Richard Dreyfuss, Danny DeVito, Barbara Hershey

Two aluminium salesmen feud after a prang in this comedy set in 1950s Baltimore. The feud, in a classic example of what shrinks call transference, is an outlet for frustrations about things they can't change: a commission investigating high pressure sales techniques, the IRS, and the mysterious success of *Bonanza*, a show with a 50-year-old dad and three 47-year-old sons. The film peters out but the journey is so enjoyable the absence of any apparent destination doesn't matter.

WALL STREET 1987

Director Oliver Stone *Cast* Charlie Sheen, Michael Douglas, Martin Sheen

Douglas scuppers the 'auteur' theory. Although Stone wrote and directed a scathing attack on the system which allows asset strippers like Douglas' character Gordon Gekko, named after a family of lizards, to flourish, his star's evil genius is so magnetic he takes over. The Sheens do their best, especially Charlie as the trader who wants to know the answer to the question: "How much is enough?" When this film was made, such predators seemed to have had their day. Today, with a mantra like "Greed is good", Gekko wouldn't be in jail, he'd be helping Dubya carve up Alaska for his oily chums.

> **"THEY SAY IT WAS SO HOT TODAY GROWN MEN WERE WALKING UP TO COPS ON STREET CORNERS BEGGING THEM TO SHOOT"**
> Roma, Glengarry Glen Ross

CHICK FLICKS

Women no longer rule the box office. The raft of melodramas, mysteries and romances with strong female leads has waned since the 1930s and 1940s, when stars like Bette Davis, Joan Crawford and Katharine Hepburn were huge draws. The lack of good roles for women is bemoaned by actresses across the world, but nowhere more so than in Hollywood, where bouncy young girls who trot along behind the hero are still woefully familiar. A good chick flick could be a tissue-soaking romance, a witty comedy, or an uplifting 'I Am Woman, Hear Me Roar' drama, as long as it has women's stories, interests and concerns at heart.

ALICE DOESN'T LIVE HERE ANYMORE 1974

Director Martin Scorsese Cast Ellyn Burstyn, Kris Kristofferson

When Alice Hyatt's husband dies in an accident, she decides to sell the house and, with 12-year-old son in tow, realize a lifetime dream of becoming a singer. Along the way she meets some creeps, some new friends and a gentle, available farmer who just might be Mr Right. Diane Ladd plays Flo, a waitress with an astounding repertoire of curses and if you look closely, you'll see a young Laura Dern (Ladd's daughter) eating an ice cream at the diner. The film got both criticism and plaudits from the feminist lobby, but whatever your views, the humour and pathos make this a great film for when you're in need of a lift.

ALL ABOUT EVE 1950

Director Joseph Mankiewicz
Cast Bette Davis, Ann Baxter

Backstabbing bitchery and catty one-liners make this a must-see. Davis plays Margot Channing, a Broadway legend whose star is on the wane, and Baxter is Eve Harrington, an ingénue who manipulates her position as Davis' assistant to steal her lover and her limelight. Davis' immortal line: "Fasten your seatbelts, it's going to be a bumpy night," is delivered deadpan, only hinting at the turmoil going on inside. (Ironically, years

Jasmin and Brenda run the best café in Bagdad but there's a gulf between them

Mainline/Pelemele/Pro-ject;

later, Davis was to star in the TV series *Hotel* but became ill and was replaced by Baxter.) The film's effect is summed up by Thelma Ritter as the wardrobe woman: "What a story! Everything but the bloodhounds snappin' at her rear end."

BAGDAD CAFE 1988 OUT OF ROSENHEIM

Director **Percy Adlon** *Cast* **Marianne Sägebrecht, CCH Pounder**
Jasmine, a large German housewife (Sägebrecht), is left in the desert by her husband after an argument. She ends up living and working at a lonely truck stop and strikes up an unlikely friendship with Brenda, the free-thinking black café owner (Pounder). As Jasmine teaches Brenda about running the café with efficiency and cleanliness, Brenda reciprocates by helping her to become unbuttoned both physically and emotionally. Background characters (including Jack Palance as a former Hollywood set painter) help create an offbeat, charming film with real emotional depth, that avoids becoming overly cutesy.

> **"WHAT I CAN'T UNDERSTAND IS HOW YOU CAN HIT SOMEONE SIX TIMES BY ACCIDENT"**
> Ed Crouch, Fried Green Tomatoes

DIRTY DANCING 1987

Director **Emile Ardolino** *Cast* **Patrick Swayze, Jennifer Grey**
Inexplicably delightful pile of old tosh about a young girl coming of age. Despite the hammy acting, overchoreographed dance numbers and a ludicrously contrived plot, this is a chick flick of the highest order. Is the heroine shy but brave deep down? Yup. Is the hero a cool-dude bad boy who would never be likely to notice her? Yup. When they finally start dancing together, does she earn his respect and love? Yup. And is the sex great? Apparently, although the film is too coy to show us much, despite all the pelvic grinding in the dance numbers.

FRIED GREEN TOMATOES 1991

Director **Jon Avnet** *Cast* **Kathy Bates, Jessica Tandy, Mary Stuart Masterson, Mary-Louise Parker**
In this screen adaptation of her own novel by the fabulously named Fannie Flagg, dowdy, downtrodden Evelyn (Bates) meets Miz Threadgoode (Tandy) during a visit to an old people's home. They strike up a friendship, and Miz Threadgoode spins tales of the complex, intimate friendship between two very different women (Masterson and Parker) who ran the Whistlestop Café in 1930s Alabama. As the stories unfold, so does Evelyn's repressed life; she becomes more assertive with her couch-potato husband and has a hilariously satisfying run-in with two parking-space-stealing teenage girls. It's hard to know which is more entertaining, the flashbacks or the modern story. Either way, the tales of love, loyalty, murder and discreet same-sex attraction make for a rich, fulfilling film.

THE GROUP 1966
Director **Sidney Lumet** *Cast* **Candice Bergen, Joan Hackett**
The entwined stories of a group of eight friends from an upper-class girls' school who graduate in 1933. Following their lives and loves, high and lows, up to the outbreak of World War 2, the film deals with marriage, divorce, motherhood, alcoholism, mental illness, abortion and a host of other issues that would have been taboo at the time. Great performances from the cast (look out for a pre-*Dallas* Larry Hagman) make this a gripping and often painful journey in the days before feminism.

MURIEL'S WEDDING 1994
Director **PJ Hogan** *Cast* **Toni Collette, Rachel Griffiths**
Overweight and rejected by her trendy friends, Muriel Heslop spends her days being ridiculed by her father, listening to Abba songs and dreaming of the day someone will want to marry her. It's an old premise – sad case trying to get a life – but it's handled with such passion, hilarity, pathos and flair that you can't help but root for Muriel every step of the way. The farcical sex scene at the flat she shares with her trashy, fabulous friend Rhonda is one of the funniest you're likely to come across and the actual wedding is the most glorious piece of over-the-top wish fulfilment on film. You'll be miming to *Waterloo* in no time.

THE RED SHOES 1948
Directors **Michael Powell, Emeric Pressburger** *Cast* **Moira Shearer, Anton Walbrook, Marius Goring**
Based very loosely on the Hans Christian Andersen tale of the wicked shoemaker who forces a young girl to dance to death. Shearer plays Victoria Page, a talented young dancer torn between her brilliant but controlling dance master, Boris (Walbrook), and her penniless composer lover, Julian (Goring). With fabulous dancing from a huge corps de ballet, Oscar-

IT'S RAINING MEN

DINER 1982
Launched Mickey Rourke, Kevin Bacon, Paul Reiser and Steve Guttenberg.
THE OUTSIDERS 1983
Jam-packed with testosterone and the brat pack at their youngest/greasiest. Matt Dillon, Tom Cruise, Rob Lowe, Emilio Estevez, Patrick Swayze, C Thomas Howell and Ralph Macchio. How much would this cast cost to assemble today? Quite a bit, methinks.

THE BOUNTY 1984
Anthony Hopkins, Daniel Day Lewis, Mel Gibson and Liam Neeson star, with Neil Morrissey, John Sessions and Dexter Fletcher for those who like their men less macho.
ANOTHER COUNTRY 1984
Rupert Everett (before we knew he was gay), Colin Firth (before he was Mr Darcy), Cary Elwes (before he vanished from films), and a slew of well-spoken, pale young boys.

winning art direction (Hein Heckroth made over 600 sketches for the central ballet sequence alone) and gorgeous technicolour photography from Jack Cardiff, it's a British film classic.

SHIRLEY VALENTINE 1989
Director Lewis Gilbert
Cast Pauline Collins, Tom Conti

A middle-aged, neglected housewife leaves her family for a holiday in Greece with her friend. A funny and touching story of mid-life awakening, it's saved from sappiness by Collins' sap-busting asides to camera. When Conti, alluring

Women on the edge have been known to get violent urges for other people's soft drinks

despite his Zorba moustache and ludicrous accent, makes a gallant comment about her stretchmarks, she turns to the audience and says: "Aren't men full of shit?" Julia McKenzie, Joanna Lumley and Alison Steadman are on great form too.

THE WOMEN 1939
Director George Cukor *Cast* Norma Shearer, Joan Crawford

There are over 130 roles in this movie, and each one is played by a woman, in an entirely male-free film by director Cukor. Even the dogs and horses used were female, and similarly the art on the set walls was devoid of male imagery. This is not, however, a story of female solidarity in a man-free utopia. Far from it. You'd be hard-pushed to find a more vicious and catty bunch. Shearer plays the classy good wife who loses her husband to trashy homewrecker Crawford. Rosalind Russell, Joan Fontaine and Paulette Goddard also feature, with Anita Loos' sparkling script shining in every scene.

WOMEN ON THE VERGE OF A NERVOUS BREAKDOWN 1988 MUJERES AL BORDE DE UN ATAQUE DE NERVIOS
Director Pedro Almodóvar *Cast* Carmen Maura, Antonio Banderas

Delicious farce about a philandering husband whose worlds collide one day when his wife's, his ex-lover's and his new lover's paths all cross. The brightly coloured sets and over-the-top fashions all add to the sense of ludicrous unreality, Almodóvar catches the spirit of sexual unbuttoning in post-Franco Spain exactly, and even with subtitles, the frantic humour and energy comes across in buckets. Banderas is almost unrecognisable in this, but it was the movie that set him on the road to international stardom.

> **"HELLO, I'M THE MOTHER OF THE NOTORIOUS CROSSROADS KILLER. WHEN MY SON COMES HOME AFTER ONE OF HIS FAMOUS CRIMES, HIS CLOTHES ARE JUST FILTHY"**
> Pepa, Women On The Verge Of A Nervous Breakdown

CIRCUS

Where would films be without the circus? There was, after all, no better excuse to put men in tights on screen. And if the action was getting a little slow, you could always throw in a faulty trapeze to liven things up. Failing that, send in the clowns to make 'em laugh or cry with fear. Yes, folks, step this way, for the greatest show on earth!

THE CIRCUS 1928

Director Charles Chaplin Cast Chaplin, Merna Kennedy, Allan Garcia

Circus comedies that really make you laugh are few and far between. Even the Marx Brothers' *At The Circus* is about as funny as having a bucket of water poured over you. So when Chaplin takes his tramp into the circus you fear the worst. This may be no *City Lights* or *Modern Times* but Chaplin does at least have a few decent jokes as he falls in love with a bareback rider and joins her circus. The finale is especially funny and something of a feat of professionalism as two-thirds of the way through filming, the star/producer/writer/director/composer had a nervous breakdown.

"I'VE SURVIVED VIETNAM, I CAN SURVIVE THIS BULLSHIT!"
Curtis Mooney, Killer Klowns From Outer Space

CIRCUS OF HORRORS 1960

Director Sidney Hayes Cast Anton Diffring, Erika Ronberg, Donald Pleasence

"Spectacular towering terror! One man's lust made men into beasts, stripped women of their souls!" Cecil B DeMille, eat your heart out. A mad plastic surgeon (Diffring) and his accomplices flee Britain and murder their way into control of a run-down French circus. Diffring plays the kind of doctor who makes you wish you had an apple in the house. After 10 years of enhancing the physogs of thieves and prostitutes, he has to resort to extreme measures when the circus' star performers express a wish to do something else. Look out for the future R2-D2 Kenny Baker as a dwarf. If you like circus films that chill the blood, try *Berserk!*, a post-*Baby Jane* Joan Crawford schlock-horror with La Joan supported by Diana Dors and Robert Hardy.

FREAKS 1932

Director Tod Browning *Cast* Wallace Ford, Olga Baclanova, Leila Hyams, Roscoe Ates, Harry Earles, Johnny Eck, Prince Randian, Zip and Pip

MGM pulled this masterpiece from the screens soon after its release, happier to lose $164,000 on the movie it had commissioned to be "more horrifying than *Dracula*" than face the wrath of various guardians of public morality. MGM boss Louis B Mayer had already insisted that the studio's famous logo would not be on the film which, coupled with the film's rapid withdrawal, has set conspiracy theorists wondering: could it be that Mayer recognized that the circus master's relation to its 'freak' performers was an allegory of the studio's relationship to its star performers? Or that the cigar-smoking dwarf Hans, who deluded himself into thinking beautiful women would love him for himself (and not his wealth), may or may not have been a representation of the diminutive, cigar-smoking and powerful Mayer? The advertising campaign for this film wasn't exactly sensitive either (one choice slogan was: "Can a full grown woman truly love a midget?"). In many respects, the most remarkable thing about this film is that it ever got made. The cast's presence in the MGM canteen during filming was a matter of studio-wide controversy and Browning was plagued during filming by a recurring dream that two of the cast kept interrupting scenes by dragging a cow through a door backwards. On top of all these 'offences', the film's dialogue was pretty racy for its day.

The Trouble With Girls is that they will keep getting their heels stuck in strange places

I CLOWNS 1971

Director Federico Fellini *Cast* Federico Fellini, Anita Ekberg, Scotti the Clown

Deserves to be cherished if only for the scene in which Fellini sits down for one of those profound discussions of his art with a journalist and, just as he launches into a deeply pretentious answer, a bucket of water falls on his head, to be followed only seconds later by another bucket on his questioner's head. The world of clowns and circuses had intrigued the director ever since he ran away from boarding school to join a circus. This enclosed, apparently jovial but also slightly sinister world, was the setting for one of his finest early works, *La Strada*, starring Anthony Quinn as a malevolent strongman.

KILLER KLOWNS FROM OUTER SPACE 1988

Director Stephen Chiodo *Cast* Grant Cramer, Suzanne Snyder,
John Allen Nelson, John Vernon

A cult favourite which ended Chiodo's career as a director –
nine years later he was making the creatures for a *Power Rangers*
movie. It was a sad fate for someone who directed and co-wrote
(with his brothers Charles and Edward) this bizarre little film
about aliens who invade a small Californian town and,
disguised as clowns, wreak havoc. It's hard not to like a movie
with a lead character called Mike Tobacco who utters lines like:
"It was a space ship. And there was these things, these killer
clowns, and they shot popcorn at us!" This may be the film
which inspired Jack Handey, of *Saturday Night Live*, to say:
"To me, clowns aren't funny. In fact, they're kind of scary. I've
wondered where this started and I think it goes back to the time
I went to the circus and a clown killed my dad."

> "THEN RANG THE
> BELLS BOTH LOUD
> AND DEEP. GOD IS
> NOT DEAD NOR
> DOTH HE SLEEP"
> Mr Dark, Something Wicked This Way Comes

SOMETHING WICKED THIS WAY COMES 1983

Director Jack Clayton *Cast* Jonathan Pryce, Jason Robards

With the possible exception of the *Hunchback Of Notre Dame*,
this may just be the darkest movie Disney has ever made. The
circus comes to small-town America but the ringmaster (Pryce
as Mr Dark) is a smiling demon who is soon engaged in mortal
combat with the town librarian (Robards). Based on the Ray
Bradbury novel, this is for adults, older children and those who
don't know the meaning of the word squeamish. The scene with
the skeleton and the merry-go-round is terrifically terrifying.

THE TROUBLE WITH GIRLS 1969

Director Peter Tewkesbury *Cast* Elvis Presley, Marilyn Mason

Perhaps because manager Colonel Tom Parker used to manage
a circus, the big top was seldom far away when Elvis was on
celluloid. (Thankfully the Colonel never went as far as including
his most successful circus act: a troupe of 'dancing' chickens on
a hot plate.) Here the King stars as the manager of a chautauqua,
an American phenomenon of the 1920s – a kind of cross
between a circus and a travelling university, albeit one where the
lectures were likely to be about cannibalism and French cuisine.
This had three things that most Elvis films conspicuously
lacked: a plot (and get this, one substantial enough to include
a murder), a fine cast (including Vincent Price and John
Carradine) and something for Elvis to do (save his troupe from
bankruptcy). Some of the familiar absurdities remain and the
drunk scene should have been cut significantly but Elvis,
resplendent in white suit and sideburns, never looked more
relaxed as an actor. A picture of considerable quiet charm.

COMEDIES

How do you like your comedy? Black? Dry? Sexy? Screwball? Sadly, you can't bottle humour, but at least you can preserve it for all time on celluloid and there are plenty of comic geniuses who have. So go on, have a laugh. Alright, don't then, have it your way.

ANIMAL CRACKERS 1930
Director Victor Heerman *Cast* Groucho, Harpo, Chico, Zeppo

The Marx Brothers' second film was the last of their Broadway shows to be turned into a movie. It was also unseen from 1930 until 1974 due to a dispute over copyright. The film was finally re-released following a campaign headed by Groucho with the backing of students across America. Like most Marx Brothers films, the plot and supporting characters are superfluous really. Groucho plays the famous explorer, Captain Spaulding, who shoots elephants in his pyjamas and is guest of honour at a society party when a valuable painting is stolen. The brothers try to help, but actually hinder its recovery. Classic lines include the gag about the charge for falling down a manhole. Just a cover charge.

ANNIE HALL 1977
Director Woody Allen *Cast* Woody Allen, Diane Keaton

Semi-autobiographical (Allen and Keaton were lovers who split up and Keaton's real name is Diane 'Annie' Hall), this is Allen's finest, if not cinema's best romantic comedy of all time. Realistic romance rather than sickly sweet, we watch people meet, fall in love and then fall out of it. Full of snappy one-liners and Allen's usual peppering of insights into love, sex, death, New York and the meaning of life, the film features early sightings of Sigourney Weaver, Beverley D'Angelo and Jeff Goldblum. This is Allen's first film where the characters actually have adult emotions. The cocaine sneezing scene was an accident, great joke though it is.

Society demanded success but all they could offer was failure

99

THE APARTMENT 1960

Director Billy Wilder *Cast* Jack Lemmon, Shirley MacLaine

Perfect and deeply satisfying comedy drama about an ambitious young executive who curries favour with his seniors by lending them his apartment for their extra-marital trysts. His collusion becomes a problem when he falls for his manager's latest mistress. Lemmon is at the peak of his 'everyman' persona – amoral and cringing to begin with, but growing a backbone with every passing scene – while MacLaine is perfect as the elevator girl with an utter lack of self-esteem. Stuffed full of great dialogue and delightful detail (Lemmon straining his spaghetti through a tennis racket is as good a representation of bachelordom as you'll find), it was the last black-and-white film to win a Best Picture Oscar until *Schindler's List* came along.

A SHOT IN THE DARK 1964

Director Blake Edwards *Cast* Peter Sellers, George Sanders, Elke Sommer

Released just three months after its predecessor *The Pink Panther*, this was originally written for a detective team which had Peter Sellers opposite Walter Matthau. When Sellers threatened to quit, *Panther* director Edwards came in, totally rewriting the script into an Inspector Clouseau vehicle. Sanders' chauffeur is murdered with the beautiful Sommers as the prime suspect.

Jake and Elwood Blues: they're on a mission from God, believe it or not

The bumbling Clouseau falls for her and refuses to believe she is capable of such acts, despite the escalating body count and the evidence pointing to her. The film features some of the best-ever Clouseau moments, (such as the nudist colony scene). Supporting characters Herbert Lom, as the inspector's despairing boss ("Give me 10 men like Clouseau and I could destroy the world"), Graham Stark as his long-suffering assistant Hercule, and Burt Kwouk as Kato, all hold their own against one of cinema's most hilarious creations.

BILLY LIAR 1963

Director John Schlesinger *Cast* Tom Courtenay, Julie Christie

Billy Fisher is an ambitious, but chronically lazy, young man who escapes the dullness of his life by constructing elaborate fantasies with himself as the hero of every one. His real life, however, is a disaster: he messes up at work, becomes engaged to two women and his family is falling apart. Then he meets Liz, a free spirit who might hold the key to escape that he is looking for. The excellent supporting cast, including Leonard

Rossiter and Rodney Bewes, gives the film a rich, natural detail that contrasts superbly with Schlesinger's freewheeling fantasy sequences. It's a perfect tale of an everyman who lacks the strength to change his own life.

BLUES BROTHERS 1980
Director *John Landis* Cast *Dan Aykroyd, John Belushi*
Worth watching if, like us, you're the kind of saddo who goes "Hang on, is that..." because the odds are in this picture (which has cameos from James Brown, Ray Charles, Aretha Franklin, Spielberg, Twiggy, Joe Walsh and the director) the answer is almost certainly "yes". The tale of two blues brothers on a mission to raise money for the Catholic home where they were raised didn't do well on release because the world was still worshipping the false musical god of disco. But it's become one of those films where aficionados will, on the slightest pretext, quote almost the whole script. Landis' finest 132 minutes.

BRINGING UP BABY 1938
Director *Howard Hawks* Cast *Cary Grant, Katharine Hepburn*
We have the audiences of 1938 to blame for this being Hepburn's only screwball comedy. Loosely based on a newspaper story relating to Hepburn's own affair with John Ford during the making of *Mary Of Scotland*, the film bombed on its release, leading to director Hawks getting fired from his next production and Hepburn being forced to buy out her RKO contract. She plays Susan, a madcap heiress who sets her sights on Grant, a bumbling buffoon of a paleontologist. The film contains all the stable ingredients of the screwball genre: implausible situations, contrary animals (Hepburn's pet leopard, Baby, for one) pratfalls, confusion... The two leads are sublime, particularly Grant who modelled his role on Harold Lloyd. Grant hated cats so Hepburn ended up doing most of the scenes with Baby.

CARRY ON UP THE KHYBER 1968
Director *Gerald Thomas* Cast *Sid James, Kenneth Williams, Charles Hawtrey, Bernard Bresslaw, Joan Sims, Roy Castle*
A historically insignificant movie (although probably no more inaccurate than Mel Gibson's *The Patriot*), this is a genuinely funny send-up of the British Empire, the nation's psychotic need to keep a stiff upper lip and what Scots may or may not wear under their kilts. Like *Carry On Cleo*, this is a good spoof of the kind of history we used to learn by rote in school. Bresslaw had to reshoot the scene where he shouts "Fakir off", putting a longer pause between the words to please the censor.

> **"YOU KNOW I LOVE LISTENING TO YOU TALK. I HATE LIVING WITH YOU BUT YOUR CONVERSATION IS FIRST RATE"**
> Elliot, The Goodbye Girl

THE CASTLE 1997

Director Rob Sitch Cast Michael Caton, Anne Tenney, Eric Bana

It's rumoured that so tight was the budget on this ripping comedy, shooting was cut from 20 to 11 days because the producers couldn't afford to feed cast and crew. The fact that it was picked up by Miramax boss Harvey Weinstein for $6m is testament to director Sitch's talent. Mind you, the film's success owes a lot to the cast's hilarious portrayal of bluecollar-ites refusing to give in to corporate ball-busters as the Kerrigan family fight to stop the family home being swallowed up by an airport. So charming are the characters and sharp the script, that you can forgive the slightly dodgy production values.

> "I DON'T LIKE TO READ ABOUT MOVIES. THEY'RE SO VIOLENT"
> Beverly, Serial Mom

CHOPPER 2000

Director Andrew Dominik Cast Eric Bana, Simon Lyndon

Extraordinarily accomplished blacker-than-black comedy by first-time writer/director Dominik, featuring a captivating performance by top Aussie comedian Bana in his first major film role as notorious criminal, Mark 'Chopper' Read. The story, told in flashback, follows Read from fit, fast and furious fighter in prison to an enraged, overweight paranoid on the outside – and then back to prison as a media celebrity. Though technically not a biopic, it's impossible to distinguish the fictional character from the real thing. Bana's portrayal of this eloquent, complex crook who asks "are you alright" of someone he's just shot in the head is utterly enthralling but never glorifies his atrocities. Gruesomely shocking, funny and tragic.

FLETCH 1985

Director Michael Ritchie Cast Chevy Chase, Joe Don Baker, George Wendt

Chase, the epitome of laid-back Los Angeles cool, is perfect as wise-cracking investigative reporter Irwin Fletch. While disguised as a beach bum, he is approached by a wealthy cancer-ridden man with a proposition to help him commit suicide. Fletch decides to open his own investigation, which leads to drug-dealing, the police and an expensive piece of land in Utah. Chase gets to crack some hilarious one-liners, act cool and show us his talents as an impersonator. Even non-Chase-fans will have trouble holding their sides together in this one.

THE GOODBYE GIRL 1977

Director Herbert Ross Cast Marsha Mason, Richard Dreyfuss

A single mother discovers her boyfriend has left her when the actor to whom he has sub-let their apartment arrives to claim his space. An uneasy sharing arrangement gives way to blossoming romance in Neil Simon's perfect script. Dreyfuss won a Best Actor Oscar for his role as the meditating health freak trapped in the worst production of *Richard III* ever, and Quinn Cummings manages the role of Mason's 10-year-old daughter with great style, never descending into Hollywood cutesiness.

KIND HEARTS AND CORONETS 1949
Director Robert Hamer *Cast* Dennis Price, Alec Guinness
One of the first truly black comedies, with a wonderful, heartless wit at its core and a neat twist at the end. Dennis Price plays Louis Mazzini, a young man whose mother was rejected by her aristocratic family when she ran off with an opera singer. On discovering that he is ninth in line to a dukedom, Louis sets about murdering the members of the D'Ascoyne family one by one. Alec Guinness plays all eight of them, including Lady Agatha, and it's his performances, along with Joan Greenwood's seductive minx Sybilla, which raise this to classic status.

LA REGLE DU JEU 1939
Director Jean Renoir *Cast* Nora Gregor, Marcel Dalio
Renoir's follow-up to the hugely successful *La Bete Humaine* failed to live up to expectations on its release. His big-budget (five million francs) comic satire on the peculiarities of French society was actually booed at its Paris premiere. The film fared no better internationally, or in its new re-edited form, and it was 20 years till it received the critical acclaim it deserved. The central relationship of the film involves a gung-ho pilot and his lover, a married French aristocrat. An unusual combination of poignant drama and farcical humour.

MATINEE 1993
Director Joe Dante *Cast* John Goodman, Cathy Moriarty, Simon Fenton
William Castle's finest movie. Pity he didn't make it or appear in it. He is, instead, the thinly disguised role model for John Goodman's flamboyant film director Lawrence Woolsey, who comes in to Key West – just as the Cuban missile crisis breaks – to promote a film called *Mant,* about a man who mutates into an ant. Goodman is still vastly underrated by almost everyone except the Coen brothers and their fans but he is superb here,

Stan and Ollie flex their muscles ready for another hard day's piano shifting. Stan, as the creative genius, insisted he got paid twice as much as his partner. But with films like *The Music Box* he's worth the money

helped by Cathy Moriarty's portrayal of his big, blonde girlfriend who dons a nurse's uniform and makes the kids sign 'medical consent' forms promising not to sue if they suffer medical trauma from the shock of seeing the mutated ant.

MONTY PYTHON'S LIFE OF BRIAN 1979

Director Terry Jones *Cast* Graham Chapman, John Cleese, Terry Gilliam, Eric Idle, Terry Jones, Michael Palin

We have George Harrison to thank for making this classic happen after EMI balked at the blasphemy in the final script. Harrison's Handmade Films was created because he felt it was the only chance to save this film. Originally titled *Jesus Christ: Lust For Glory*, it shows the Three Wise Men searching the desert for the Messiah, mistakenly ending up at the manger of Brian Cohen. Harrison was supposed to have a scene as a waiter who couldn't find a table for 13 in his restaurant for the last supper. (The crew also shot as many of the scenes as they could on the same locations as Zeffirelli's *Jesus Of Nazareth* to sharpen the satire.) If you're not devout in any way, this is Python's finest. Great cameos and great one-liners such as "He's not the Messiah. He's a very naughty boy!"

THE MUSIC BOX 1932

Director James Parrott *Cast* Stan Laurel, Oliver Hardy

Regarded by Stan Laurel as the best of his 99 collaborations with Oliver Hardy, *The Music Box* not only demonstrates the expertise of the pair's impeccable timing, but the darkness behind their comedy. They live in a world where nursemaids, professors, horses and electric sockets are united in a vast comic conspiracy against them. Cynics have criticized the film for endless repetition of one gag, as Stan and Ollie are relentless in their efforts to get a piano up 131 steps, but this is really sublime comedy with Laurel's pseudo-malapropisms (he accuses the cop of "bounding over your steps") some surrealist touches, an astonishing dance and a nod to another movie with famous steps in it, *Battleship Potemkin*.

MY LITTLE CHICKADEE 1940

Director Edward Cline *Cast* WC Fields, Mae West

Fields is a con man, West is, well, West and there's a bandit, a cowpoke and a goat. And anything else the stars dreamed up. Dick Foran, who plays the cowpoke, has a real sparkle in his eye throughout, maybe because he was being paid by the week and, by the simple ruse of telling each star that the other was rewriting their lines, prolonged the film by provoking endless script rewrites. He also helped make the film as funny as it is.

NINOTCHKA 1939
Director Ernst Lubitsch *Cast* Greta Garbo, Melvyn Douglas

In Garbo's penultimate film you do in fact see her laugh, but
not for the first time as MGM insisted. Garbo shines as the
humourless Russian envoy sent in pursuit of three comrades to
find out what is delaying their mission. In a role which is almost
a send up of her own onscreen persona, she meets and falls in
love with a dashing count, Douglas, who does indeed make her
laugh. Great performances all-round, aided by a witty script
(which Billy Wilder had a hand in), and Lubitsch's direction.
The scene in which Garbo pretends to be drunk had to be shot
last because she was, as the director said, "the most inhibited
person I have ever worked with". At the test screening, a
member of the audience wrote on his preview card: "I
laughed so hard I peed in my girlfriend's hand." Censors
in Bulgaria, Estonia, France, Italy and Lithuania weren't
as amused: it was banned for making fun of Communism.

NURSE BETTY 2000
Director Neil LaBute *Cast* Renee Zellweger, Morgan Freeman,
Chris Rock

After directing the strikingly original dramas *In The
Company Of Men* and *Your Friends & Neighbours*, director
LaBute turned his hand to comedy of the darkest kind.
Zellweger is Betty, a sweet, innocent waitress whose only
escape to happiness is the half-hour when her favourite soap
opera is on TV. Freeman is a hitman on his final job before he
retires to Florida (where else?), the final job being Betty's
bullying husband, a car salesman and spare-time drug dealer.
Dry, witty comedy (Betty goes into shock and off to Hollywood
to find her dream soap doctor) is mingled with Freeman and
Rock's sparring double act. One minute you're laughing out
loud, the next stunned to see someone being scalped.

Garbo liked
Ninotchka so much
she ran around the
hills of Hollywood
after each day's
shooting shouting her
character's key line
"Why?" over and over

PASSPORT TO PIMLICO 1949
Director Henry Cornelius *Cast* Stanley Holloway, Sydney Tafler,
Hermione Baddeley, Margaret Rutherford, Michael Hordern

Wonderfully funny and good-natured movie in which the
Pimlico locals find themselves living on foreign territory and, as
such, are free of post-war rationing restrictions. Holloway and
Margaret Rutherford turn in typically terrific performances.
The film was inspired by the story that, during the war,
Princess Juliana of the Netherlands was exiled in Canada and
was about to give birth. In order that her baby be heir to the
Dutch throne, the Canadian Government declared the room in
which she was to give birth to be a territory of the Netherlands.

SERIAL MOM 1994
Director **John Waters** *Cast* **Kathleen Turner, Sam Waterston, Ricki Lake, Matthew Lillard**

Taking a pop at those films that help turn mass-murderers into a media frenzy, this is the tale of a whiter than white, suburban middle-class family, whose mom just happens to be a serial killer. Turner is astounding as Beverly Sutphin, beaming wife of a perfect husband (Waterston) and mother to the two best-behaved teenagers imaginable (Lake and Lillard). She is also a killer who strikes down those she feels are unjust towards her family – such as boyfriends who stand her daughter up or little old ladies who fail to rewind their video cassettes. Allegedly based on some relationship to real events, *Serial Mom* remains a nasty yet hilarious piece of kitsch.

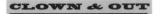

CLOWN & OUT

When did Steve Martin stop being funny? The mysterious process by which one of the big screen's most promising comics became about as humorous as an enema is still debated. But let's retrace his steps.

THE JERK
The story of a naïve idiot who believes his white skin is a transitionary device before he turns black like the rest of his family. Absurd, yet original and hilarious fun.

ALL OF ME
A comic tour de force of a performance by Martin as the poor lawyer whose body is inhabited by the spirit of Lily Tomlin. Riotous comedy, possibly Martin's best.

ROXANNE
Could America's version of *Cyrano De Bergerac* be more sickly-sweet? Humorous but formulaic, like a Tom Hanks and Meg Ryan film without the winsome twosome.

FATHER OF THE BRIDE
There never has been (and never will be) another Spencer Tracy, so why embarrass yourself Steve?

SGT BILKO
Audiences all across the world are losing the will to live.

BOWFINGER
The comeback begins?

SLEEPER 1973
Director **Woody Allen** *Cast* **Woody Allen, Diane Keaton**

One of Allen's funniest early films, this sci-fi spoof was filmed in 50 days for $2m, with futuristic costumes designed by none other than Joel Schumacher. Allen plays a 20th-century man who has been frozen for 200 years. He wakes in a world where there is no sex (hence the need for the orgasmatron) and America is ruled by a dictator's nose. He discovers a field of giant fruit and the world of film is treated to the best banana skin sight gag ever. Completely and utterly daft, it remains the best spoof of the futuristic genre. From the same vintage Allen, *Bananas* is, in part, a media satire ahead of its time and very funny. Watch out for Sylvester Stallone as a hood.

SOME LIKE IT HOT 1959
Director **Billy Wilder** *Cast* **Marilyn Monroe, Jack Lemmon, Tony Curtis**

Although Monroe's contract stipulated that all her films be shot in colour, director Wilder eventually persuaded her they needed to shoot in black and white as the make-up worn by Lemmon and Curtis

Avco/Springtime/Crossbow; Universal; MGM; Guild/Savoy/Polar; RKO

made them look green. This was the end of his easy ride with the siren (she went so far as comparing Wilder to Hitler; it did take her 47 or 59 takes to say one simple line). But she still carries the film as Sugar Kane, the alluring member of the all-girl band which Lemmon and Curtis join in drag to hide from the mob. Lemmon, in a role offered to Sinatra, keeps the zany momentum going, seemingly relishing his drag character, while Curtis' concern about being seen as effeminate was perfect for his straight man role. Well-known for basing the voice of his oil industry heir on Cary Grant, he reportedly based his body language as Josephine on Grace Kelly.

Kathleen Turner as Beverley Sutphin, sewing and serial killing a speciality

SON OF PALEFACE 1952
Director Frank Tashlin Cast Bob Hope, Jane Russell, Roy Rogers
Hope reprises a favourite role as a cowardly dude, here playing the son of the original Paleface, in search of his father's missing gold. Russell is the sassy leader of a gang of bandits on the run from marshal Rogers and his ever-faithful Trigger. Rogers' send-up of his screen persona, along with all the usual Western clichés, makes the movie superior to its predecessor, but it is Trigger who steals the film when he shares a bed with Hope.

THE STRONG MAN 1926
Director Frank Capra Cast Harry Langdon, Priscilla Bonner
Forgotten silent comedian Langdon was never better than as the Capra-esque immigrant who comes to America, saves the blind heroine and becomes a cop. Langdon's character is a precursor of the heroes of 1930s Capracorn but the credit for this tour de farce must partly go to Langdon, whose inspired clowning, especially in the scene where he unknowingly carries his unconscious beloved backwards up a stepladder, makes this seem surprisingly fresh for a silent comedy.

THAT SINKING FEELING 1979
Director Bill Forsyth Cast Robert Buchanan, Billy Greenlees
Bill Forsyth, who *was* the Scottish film industry in the early 1980s, made his feature debut with this surreal comedy about Glasgow teenagers who decide there's money in stainless-steel sinks. A bizarre plan to dress up as women and raid a sink warehouse is hatched, and the film just gets weirder and more wonderful from there. The characters are a delight, a

"REAL DIAMONDS! THEY MUST BE WORTH THEIR WEIGHT IN GOLD!"
Sugar Kane, Some Like It Hot

All you need to make great comedy: love, leopard, and a missing dinosaur bone

well-observed group trying to be angsty and nihilist but failing miserably, and the comatose van driver and canalside chase sequence are particular joys. There are moments when even a Brit might struggle to catch all the dialogue, but if you liked the wandering penguin in *Gregory's Girl*, you'll love this.

THIS IS SPINAL TAP 1984
Director Rob Reiner *Cast* Michael McKean, Christopher Guest, Harry Shearer

A monumental mockumentary which suggests that Rob inherited comic genes from old man Carl and, ironically, influenced more serious rock biopics like Oliver Stone's *The Doors*. The lead actors and director were given $10,000 to write a script and make a 20-minute film to convince investors. Lucky they got the go-ahead because this is one of the most dead-on satires ever. Rock, especially this kind of pompous heavy rock, still hasn't recovered from this skewering. The name of the album (*Smell My Glove*), their hit (*Lick My Love Pump*), even the cold sores, are so right it's scary.

THE TWELVE CHAIRS 1970
Director Mel Brooks *Cast* Ron Moody, Frank Langella, Dom DeLuise

This is Brooks' follow-up to his classic comedy *The Producers*. Moody is a former Russian aristocrat who discovers from his dying mother that she has sewn the family jewels into the lining of one of the dining-room chairs. The chairs, however, are no longer in the dining room but have been scattered throughout the country. Moody teams up with Langella in search of the chair full of riches, with the town priest (who is also aware of the bounty) hot on their heels. The farcical treasure hunt allows Brooks' heroes to meet a variety of oddball characters. A worthy follow-up to his acclaimed debut which reminds you that the director could also be a comic writer of genuine subtlety.

> "MY BRAIN! IT'S MY SECOND FAVOURITE ORGAN"
> Miles Monroe, Sleeper

TWO WAY STRETCH 1960
Director Robert Day *Cast* Peter Sellers, Bernard Cribbins

British comedy gem, about a prison inmate who has only a few days left to serve when he decides to break out for a once-in-a-lifetime diamond heist – then break back in to finish his sentence with a watertight alibi. With a raft of delightful supporting actors – Wilfrid Hyde-White as affable master-of-crime Soapy Stevens (posing as a vicar), Irene Handl as accomplice Cribbins' crooked 'mum' and Lionel Jeffries as Crout, the new warder out to make life difficult – the film romps along, full of terrific one-liners and the farcical situations that British comedy handles so well. Sellers is a marvel as the wide-boy gang leader who plays the system for all it's worth: good to see him acting before he settled for the easy caricature of Clouseau.

THE WAR OF THE ROSES 1989
Director Danny DeVito Cast Kathleen Turner, Michael Douglas

This noir comedy reunited three cast members from the *Romancing The Stone* sagas but with DeVito behind the lens and a script (by Michael Leeson) blacker than a deck of cards with all the hearts and diamonds removed. Douglas (DeVito's old roommate) and Turner are the thoroughly unlikeable couple for whom the term "messy divorce" is a cosmic understatement. No celluloid battle of the sexes has had the guts to be this mean and, at times, it goes beyond funny. But there are some wonderful scenes such as the one where Douglas puts an added ingredient into the fish dish Turner is serving to her VIP guests. Not to be missed, it isn't every Hollywood film which convinces you there's a realistic chance that the pet dog will be served as paté.

WHERE'S POPPA? 1970
Director Carl Reiner Cast George Segal, Ruth Gordon

An acquired taste, this film is the ultimate Jewish momma joke. Segal plays a successful lawyer whose love life is hampered by living with his occasionally senile mother (Gordon). When he does finally meet the woman of his dreams (the nurse he has hired for his mother), Gordon continues to obstruct his happiness, but Segal has promised his dying father never to have her put into a nursing home. From here we see Segal plotting the death of his mother, with much of the humour derived from his absurd methods (like dressing as King Kong to scare her). Gordon, at her maddest as the seemingly indestructible old woman, is supplemented by a wealth of equally eccentric characters, like the brother-in-law who has a pact with Central Park muggers. A fast-moving black comedy and probably Reiner's best film, it also features his son and future director, Rob Reiner.

IMPROV

ANNIE HALL
The movie which went on to become one of the finest romantic comedies of all time was, until it reached the edit suite, a murder mystery called *Anhedonia* (a psychological term for inability to experience pleasure). When Allen studied the film he decided the love story played better than the actual plot. So he re-edited, focusing on his and Keaton's relationship. It wasn't until 1993 that the pair made the film Allen originally planned, *Manhattan Murder Mystery*.

SOME LIKE IT HOT
Billy Wilder's classic film is justly famed for its final scene when Osgood Fielding III, hearing that Lemmon's drag character Daphne is a man, says: "Well, nobody's perfect." The line was written the night before shooting when Monroe became too ill to go on, forcing Wilder to switch the focus of the finale from Curtis and Monroe to Lemmon and Brown. Truly scary thought: Wilder first wanted to cast Danny Kaye and Bob Hope in the Lemmon/Curtis roles.

COPS

As long as there have been movie criminals, the cop has been there to pursue them. They come in all guises. There's the self-absorbed loner, living only for his next job. There's the maverick who'll throw away the rulebook if it gets the job done. Or there's the bad apple, as bent as a $9 bill. And let's not forget the everyday, doughnut-eating cops who play second fiddle, only to find themselves on the receiving end of the first stray bullet. It's a dirty job…

BULLITT 1968

Director Peter Yates *Cast* Steve McQueen, Robert Vaughn, Jacqueline Bisset

A forerunner to *Dirty Harry*, *Bullitt* is McQueen's finest hour, with Yates' slick, visually enthralling direction paired with sparse dialogue and jazzy soundtrack – the perfect complement to McQueen's ice-cold portrayal of a police officer devoted to duty and little else. Despite a well thought-out plot involving corruption, murder and the mob, the film's most enduring sequence is still the famous (and much imitated) car chase in San Francisco. Each car in the scenes notched up speeds of over 110mph, with one 10-minute scene taking three weeks to shoot. One has fond visions of Yates directing Cliff Richard in *Summer Holiday* – he must have been dying to film a scene where the double-decker bus took on allcomers after rounding a corner on two wheels…

COP LAND 1997

Director James Mangold *Cast* Sylvester Stallone, Robert De Niro, Harvey Keitel, Ray Liotta

And the award for best actor goes to… Sylvester Stallone. No joke. Muttering muscles won the prestigious award at the Stockholm film festival (not quite the Oscars, but still). Stallone did a De Niro, gaining 40lbs to add more realism to his portrayal of a small town sheriff working in Garrison, the town where the 'proper' cops of the big city, New York, live. Investigating the murder of two youths, his findings lead to corruption in the town and the police force. Don't get overly excited about Stallone's performance; it's good, but Hollywood can get overenthusiastic when actors suffer, or eat, for their art.

DIRTY HARRY 1971

Director Don Siegel *Cast* Clint Eastwood, Harry Guardino, Andrew Robinson

One of the coolest personae on celluloid, Eastwood's maverick cop Harry Callahan gave a new cred to the police force. Suddenly it wasn't simply about toeing the line and playing by the book: it was about fighting crime at all costs, the end justifying the means. Although Eastwood was the last in a long line of stars to be offered the role (behind such unlikely choices as Frank Sinatra, who would have played Harry if he hadn't injured his hand, and John Wayne), Eastwood made the role his. The film also features one of the screen's greatest psycho killers, portrayed by second-choice Robinson (Audie Murphy was originally offered the role but died in a plane crash before filming). A staunch pacifist in real life (firearms experts worked with him for a week before they could get him to stop flinching when he fired a gun), Robinson received a death threat after the film was released. For a dry run in a cowboy hat for both star and director, see *Coogan's Bluff*.

> **"WHEN A NAKED MAN IS CHASING A WOMAN THROUGH AN ALLEY WITH A BUTCHER KNIFE AND A HARD-ON, I FIGURE HE'S NOT COLLECTING FOR THE RED CROSS"**
>
> Harry Callahan, Dirty Harry

FARGO 1996

Director Joel Coen *Cast* Frances McDormand, William H Macy

Despite the claim on the opening credits, *Fargo* may not be based on a true story. Based on reality maybe, with the Coens creating a perfect portrayal of small-town America. Here the action centres on Brainerd, Minnesota, where everyone has a Scandinavian edge to their accents and says things like: "You're darn tootin'." McDormand is Marge, chief of police at Brainerd – efficient and pregnant, and as far away from a clichéd movie cop as possible. There is never any doubt she will uncover two-bit schemer Macy's lies and his bungled plot to have his wife kidnapped and steal the ransom. The film also features Coen regular Steve Buscemi, who dies in almost every Coen film, his remains gradually shrinking. Here we only see half a leg.

THE FRENCH CONNECTION 1971

Director William Friedkin *Cast* Gene Hackman, Fernando Rey, Roy Scheider

This film was based on a 1962 real-life drugs

Kim goes mattress surfing with two Aussie ex-soap stars in LA

It's so cold in Fargo that just because someone's stiff it doesn't necessarily mean they're dead

seizure by maverick cop Eddie Egan and partner Sonny Grosso. Director Friedkin won an Oscar for his semi-documentary style filming: the movie contains non-staged stunts during the famous car chase sequence. Although the New York streets were due to be cordoned off, a number of civilians only just managed to get out of the way of the speeding cars. The scene with the mother and her baby in the pram wasn't staged, and the woman ended up suffering from severe shock. The movie ended up scooping five Oscars.

HANA-BI 1997

Director Takeshi Kitano *Cast* Takeshi Kitano, Kayoko Kishimoto

An intriguing examination of the troubles facing a Japanese cop. Actor, writer and director Kitano uses the power of silence and facial expressions (or lack of them – the actor was recovering from a motorbike crash) to display the inner angst of the main character, Nisha. Constantly oscillating between agony (his wife is dying of leukemia and his partner is wheelchair-bound) and ecstasy (as when, in childlike manner, he plays with a kite with his wife), his quiet moments are normally interrupted by sudden, startling violence. Wanting to spend more time with his missus, Nisha turns to a life of crime, robbing a bank in order to fund a farewell trip with his wife. This plot thread is interspersed with frantic action sequences making this one of the more thoughtful police movies.

HEAT 1995

Director Michael Mann *Cast* Al Pacino, Robert De Niro, Val Kilmer, Tom Sizemore, Jon Voight, Natalie Portman

"A guy once told me: 'Do not have any attachments, do not have anything in your life you are not willing to walk out on in 30 seconds flat if you spot the heat around the corner.'" Spoken by master thief Neil McCauley (De Niro), the sentiment sums up the lives of both himself and cop Vincent Hanna (Pacino). Hanna puts his heart and soul into his job at the expense of his family life, while McCauley is continually pulling off that one last job. This is one of the best cops-and-robbers films, thanks to impressive acting from both the leading men and their respective crews and women, an intelligent script based on director Mann's own television movie *LA Takedown*, and his own fast and furious direction. Hanna is the 1990s Dirty Harry.

> **"WENDELL, I'D LIKE FULL AND DOCILE CO-OPERATION ON EVERY TOPIC"**
> Dudley Smith, LA Confidential

LA CONFIDENTIAL 1997

Director **Curtis Hanson** *Cast* **Russell Crowe, Guy Pearce, Kevin Spacey, Kim Basinger**

Part of writer James Ellroy's LA trilogy, *LA Confidential* is set against the seedy backdrop of 1950s LA, homing in on a corrupt police force and the Hollywood sleaze of *Hush-Hush* magazine ("Hush hush, very confidential and definitely on the QT"). Three very different detectives find themselves investigating strands of one big corruption scandal, each representing the choices facing every young rookie entering the force: Pearce as the righteous golden boy, Crowe the brutish yet moralistic brawn, and Spacey out for a quick buck and a slice of stardom until his conscience gets the better of him. The film uses the decade for atmosphere rather than as a strictly accurate period piece, and the cast are as excellent as the script, the real standout being James Cromwell who plays crooked Irish cop Dudley Smith – a man with an icepick where most of us have a heart.

THE MAN ON THE ROOF 1976

Director **Bo Widerburg** *Cast* **Carl-Gustaf Lindstedt, Sven Wollter**

Swedish director Widerburg mixes social commentary with action in this film which is absorbing both as an examination of police work and as straightforward suspense. When a cop is killed, the officers investigating the murder discover him to have been a particularly violent and brutal policeman, and realize that one of his victims is more than likely responsible for the murder. Either way, this killer isn't content with retribution against one man – he's going after the entire police force. Violent yet thought-provoking.

THE ONION FIELD 1979

Director **Harold Becker** *Cast* **John Savage, James Woods, Ted Danson**

Writer Wambaugh was so angered by the mess Robert Aldrich made of his first novel *The Choirboys*, that for *The Onion Field* he retained complete control over the script. Wambaugh's screenplay is gritty yet realistic (as you might expect from a former LAPD cop), and deals with a real-life 1963 case when two cops were kidnapped by small-time criminals – one was killed and one (played by Savage) left to cope with the psychological trauma of the event and being seen as a coward for surviving. Thrilling performances by

PARTNERS

COPS IN PAIRS

Most parts of the movie cops' world are so tough that they go around in pairs. And they're obliged to work as closely as possible with a cop whose ethnic origin, religion, politics and approach to personal hygiene is as different as possible to their own. But it's amazing how adversity can forge a deep and meaningful relationship between even the worst of enemies.

SIDNEY POITIER, ROD STEIGER, IN THE HEAT OF THE NIGHT
The contrast in style between a black cop and a white, Southern small-town sheriff was controversial in 1967. Illinois stood in for Mississippi to avoid a backlash.

EDDIE MURPHY, NICK NOLTE, 48 HRS
Not actually white cop, black cop since Murphy plays an ex-con opposite gruff, bigoted Nolte. The pair work the cop-crook, white-black angle to great comic and action effect.

ANTHONY QUINN, YAPHET KOTTO, ACROSS 110TH STREET
An unusual pairing of Quinn and Kotto (a distant relative of Queen Victoria) in Harlem. Quinn's the captain, but Kotto's royal blood gives him the upper hand.

Sophie was nabbed by the French police for stealing a crimping iron

Woods and Savage marked their cards for future stardom, with Danson making his big-screen debut.

POLICE 1985
Director Maurice Pialat *Cast* Gérard Depardieu, Sophie Marceau

The truly wonderful thing about French movies of this ilk is the way corruption among cops is accepted alongside other such inevitabilities as wet English summers and infidelity. In a US film, Depardieu's corruption would either be the plot for the entire movie or be explained, in flashback, with reference to some pivotal event. But Depardieu just gets on with the business of staying alive, trying to protect his new lover from Tunisian gangsters who would like their two million francs back please, and sorting out a few criminals. Pialat gives it a documentary feel while Depardieu is at his most playful, brutish and charismatic. A fine work by director and star, even if it takes one turn too many.

SERPICO 1973
Director Sidney Lumet *Cast* Al Pacino, John Randolph, Jack Kehoe

Pacino is outstanding in this fictionalized account of the real career of Serpico, a cop who has nothing to fear except... his colleagues. A black sheep (and possibly a righteous pain in the ass) thanks to his 'hippie' appearance and his refusal to take bribes throughout his NYPD career, Serpico finally informed on the entire corrupt squad. Fair enough: this was the kind of police station where a superior complained: "Who can trust a cop who don't take money?" Director Lumet tackled police corruption again in the impressive *Prince Of The City* (1981).

STRAY DOG 1949
Director Akira Kurosawa *Cast* Toshiro Mifune, Keiko Awaji

Kurosawa's own interpretation of the classic American film noir offers an insight into the Japanese underworld. Mifune stars (almost inevitably) as a young homicide detective who has his pistol stolen while on a bus. Frantic and ashamed, he finds the gun has been stolen not by a simple pickpocket but by a killer, and sets out to catch the criminal with the help of a wise, older colleague. Although nowhere near as ground-breaking as *Rashomon*, *Stray Dog* has a gritty edge to it, shot in the more rundown areas of Tokyo to capture the Japanese equivalent of the poetry of the gutter. The steamy hot summer backdrop matches Mifune's emotional temperature perfectly.

COURTROOM

The law is home to some of the cinema's favourite stereotypes: the idealistic young lawyer, the blinkered old judge, the cynical (often drunken) ageing lawyer dragged unwillingly into one final combat with the forces of evil. In films like *Dirty Harry*, the court is a place where psychopaths escape justice on a technicality. But at their best, films like *To Kill A Mockingbird* tap into our fondest fantasy: that although injustice may win the odd skirmish, good men like Atticus Finch will be on hand to make sure it doesn't win the war.

THE ACCUSED 1988

Director Jonathan Kaplan *Cast* Kelly McGillis, Jodie Foster

One reason this film seems so real is its deliberate echoes of the famous case of the woman who was raped on a pool table in a bar in New Bedford, Massachusetts. Kaplan has a clear and unwavering eye for the realities of the legal system as it deals with rape – in particular, the speed with which the victim becomes the suspect. Foster deserved her Oscar for her performance as the victim with a past which does not bear more than cursory examination. Debate still swirls about the inclusion of the gang rape scene which some see as confronting the audience with the reality of the crime (and the equal responsibility of those who stood by and watched) and others see as sheer sexploitation. You decide.

> **"PUNISHMENT TO FIT THE CRIME DOESN'T WORK. WE NEED UNJUST PUNISHMENT!"**
> Judge Fleming, And Justice For All

ADAM'S RIB 1949

Director George Cukor *Cast* Spencer Tracy, Katharine Hepburn

The best of the nine films Hepburn and Tracy made together takes the battle of the sexes and multiplies it with a battle in the courtroom as the co-stars (and off-screen lovers) play lawyers on different sides of an attempted murder case. But the real star of the film is Judy Holliday as the woman on trial for shooting her adulterous husband. There is a theory that her role in this film was part of a conspiracy between Cukor, Hepburn and Garson Kanin (who co-wrote the script) to convince Columbia to give Holliday the lead part in *Born Yesterday*. She got the role but probably wasn't as effective as she is in this, which, considering the quality of her co-stars, is praise indeed.

ANATOMY OF A MURDER 1959

Director **Otto Preminger** *Cast* **James Stewart, Lee Remick**

If the judge in this picture strikes you as a bit too goofy to be a real judge, you would (of course) be very wrong. He is Joseph Welch, a real judge famous for representing the Army against Joe McCarthy in the hearings which brought the Red-baiting Senator down. Welch's dialogue here isn't up to his famous line which destroyed McCarthy: "Have you no sense of decency, sir, at long last?" But the rest of the script crackles, especially when Stewart, as the country lawyer defending a man accused of murdering his wife's rapist, exchanges barbs with George C Scott. Jimmy gets most of the best lines ("There's only one thing more devious than a Philadelphia lawyer, and that's an Irish lawyer") but Scott almost steals the movie.

AND JUSTICE FOR ALL 1979

Director **Norman Jewison** *Cast* **Al Pacino, Jack Warden**

Although one of the most memorable scenes sees Pacino as lawyer Arthur Kirkland screaming, "You're out of order! This whole trial is out of order!", this is more a tale of morality and ethics than courtroom shenanigans. Arthur Kirkland has been ordered to defend his most hated judge, Judge Fleming (John Forsythe), in a rape trial. To make matters worse, Fleming has already admitted his guilt. The behind-the-scenes glimpses of courtroom life are as fascinating as the main story, particularly insane, suicidal Judge Rayford (Warden) being allowed to continue serving on the bench despite his eccentricities. The film features an impressive debut by Christine Lahti as Kirkland's girlfriend. We assume the role involved a lot of box hopping on the part of the vertically challenged Pacino opposite a 5ft 11in Lahti.

"Ladies and gentlemen, we are gathered here today to determine the murderer of an innocent mockingbird"

CLOSE UP 1990 NEMA-YE NAZDIK

Director **Abbas Kiarostami**
Cast **Hossain Sabzian, Mohsen Makhmalbaf**

An Iranian printer's assistant, Hossain Sabzian impersonated his favourite film director to feel important but was arrested when his hoax was exposed and tried for fraud (as the fake director, he obtained money from a family who thought he would shoot a film in their house). The real trial, which Kiarostami got permission to film, is shown here. (The scenes showing Sabzian's hoax are the only re-enactments.) The movie erases the line between real life and films both for the audience and the participants who play themselves. *Close Up* is so full of ideas and themes that it's not a film you can digest on a single viewing.

INHERIT THE WIND 1960

Director **Stanley Kramer** *Cast* **Spencer Tracy, Fredric March**
"People who believe in a literal interpretation of the miracles of the Bible, and especially the biblical account of creation, are portrayed in an outrageously uncomplimentary way." Thanks to the Missouri Association for Creation for that warning. This fictional account of the famous trial of the teacher who found himself in court for the 'crime' of teaching Darwin's theory of evolution is, as the TV movies put it, "based on a true story". March and Tracy duel to good effect as the lawyers on either side of the case but the film ultimately cops out by casting cynical journalist (Gene Kelly) as the real villain of the piece.

Kafka's *The Trial*, as filmed by the genius that was Orson, seems to have almost as much to do with Orson W as Josef K

PRIMAL FEAR 1996

Director **Gregory Hoblit** *Cast* **Richard Gere, Laura Linney**
This sadly underrated legal courtroom thriller is dominated by Gere's performance as a public defender whose conscience, if he has one, is untroubled by such quaint legal concepts as guilt and innocence. Gere's lawyer is only defending the suspect known to the media as 'the butcher boy' because he (Gere) craves publicity and this trial, about the murder of an archbishop, will briefly satisfy that craving. Because it's a Hollywood thriller there are plenty of plot twists which eventually take over what should have been an absorbing character piece, but the real pleasure here is watching Gere strutting his stuff in the courtroom.

> "WHY GAMBLE
> WITH MONEY
> WHEN YOU
> CAN GAMBLE
> WITH PEOPLE'S
> LIVES?"
> Martin Vail, Primal Fear

A SHORT FILM ABOUT KILLING 1988

Director **Krzysztof Kieslowski** *Cast* **Miroslawa Baka, Krzysztof Globisz**
Actually the title could have had an 's' on the end. The clumsy (and protracted) murder of a taxi driver by a young punk is followed by the brutal and protracted execution of the aforementioned punk. Kieslowski doesn't try to explore the murderer's motivations but that only adds to its power. You've read those reviews about movies being the emotional equivalent of going through a meat grinder. In this case, it's true.

TO KILL A MOCKINGBIRD 1962

Director **Robert Mulligan** *Cast* **Gregory Peck, Mary Badham**

Robert Duvall spent six weeks in the sun and dyed his hair blond for his often-heard, seldom-seen portrayal of Boo Radley. It was the beginning of his long, slow climb into the big league. Peck didn't have to go to such extremes as lawyer Atticus Finch, called on to defend a black man accused of rape in the American South – the part fitted him about as snugly as his character's waistcoat. Underrated because of its very decency, the film has more breadth than it's given credit for: the scene where the children are attacked on their way home from the pageant is genuinely scary. Mulligan had something of a gift for directing children and the scenes of childhood play and mischief actually seem real and devoid of sentimentality.

THE TRIAL 1962 LE PROCES

Director **Orson Welles** *Cast* **Anthony Perkins, Jeanne Moreau**

Welles once maintained this film (based on Kafka's book) "was much closer to my own feelings about everything than any other picture I've ever made." True? Probably. Welles suffered from recurring nightmares of guilt and imprisonment and this film is very like a nightmare, with Perkins as Josef K trapped in it. Welles played on his suspicion of Perkins' homosexuality, showing three sexy women (Moreau, Romy Schneider and Elsa Martinelli) all failing to seduce K/Perkins, and suggesting another reason why K/Perkins might live in such a state of fear. Roger Ebert suggests this film is an allegory of Welles' own career. After *Kane*, he too was pursued by beautiful woman but doomed to wander in search of benefactors, never sure of the crime for which he had been condemned.

CHOP THIS

COURTROOM SATIRE AND WALT DISNEY

Many filmmakers have tried to satirize the legal system, but has anyone summed up its alarming mixture of pomposity and caprice better than Clyde Geronimi and Wilfred Jackson? Clyde and Wilf were the directors of Disney's version of Lewis Carroll's *Alice In Wonderland*. The closing courtroom scene, where the king/judge is unable to stop the Queen trampling over such niceties as hearing evidence before proceeding swiftly to the verdict, hovers somewhere between Bambi and Kafka. Since the film was made, "Off with their heads" has become a penal policy.

THE VERDICT 1982

Director **Sidney Lumet** *Cast* **Paul Newman, Charlotte Rampling, James Mason**

Lumet apparently took Newman to one side and said that, although things were going smoothly, he didn't think the actor was hitting the emotional depth that was in David Mamet's script. What was required, Lumet suggested, was some sense of personal revelation in his performance as alcoholic failed lawyer Frank Galvin. "On Monday, Paul came into rehearsal and sparks flew," recalls Lumet. The script and the performances by all three of the film's stars make this so compelling that you even forgive (plot spoiler imminent!) the jury ignoring legal technicality to side with justice and Newman.

UIP: Pairs Europe/Ficit/Hisa

CRIME

Crime pays, as Woody Allen once put it, the hours are good and you travel a lot. (The box office takings aren't bad either.) For those filmmakers for whom plot is just a variable area of land, crime movies come with a ready made story: criminal breaks law, law breaks criminal.

The very first feature film was about a bunch of crimes. *The Story Of The Kelly Gang*, made in 1906, was the story of Australia's baddest bushranger, Ned Kelly, the first of many charismatic villains whose notoriety would sell cinema tickets.

Even without a star criminal, the world's movie industries have never been at a loss for an excuse to make a film about crime. Historically, there were certain differences in emphasis. In Britain, plots generally surrounded the crimes of titled people living in opulent settings, wealthy heiresses kidnapped, murdered or seduced for their fortunes or, if they were lucky, robbed by a gentleman thief like Raffles. In America, with a more organized form of crime emerging, the typical movie criminal was a streetwise gangster snarling like Jimmy Cagney.

Stereotypes change and genres veer in and out of fashion but movies about gangsters, heists, cops and robbers have become dominant since the 1970s when America lost its faith in one great institution (the presidency) and developed a crush on another (the mafia). The focus has since shifted again to loners like Travis Bickle or to the senseless violence as art form shtick of Oliver Stone's *Natural Born Killers*. But then for filmmakers, criminals have always made natural born movie heroes.

> **"KILLERS KILL, SQUEALERS SQUEAL"**
> Michel Poiccard, À Bout De Souffle

THE ANDERSON TAPES 1971
Director Sidney Lumet Cast Sean Connery, Dyan Cannon, Martin Balsam

Based on a Laurence Sanders novel that was written entirely in wiretap transcripts, which director Lumet, not always successfully, attempts to recreate in the film. Connery is Duke, recently released from prison. He shacks up with old girlfriend Cannon in her swish apartment, where he recruits his old crew (including Christopher Walken, in his movie debut) to rob the entire apartment block. What they don't realize is that several law enforcement agencies and the mob have the building under surveillance. A lighter foray into territory covered by Coppola's contemporary work *The Conversation*, this is fast paced and builds to an effective climax. Connery is good, although the role wasn't exactly a stretch. Balsam's turn as the stereotypical camp member of the crew is frankly bizarre. Quincy Jones' jazz-funk score is one of those you'll love or hate.

ROBBED!

The heist has always been a key feature of crime films whether as the robbery in a cops and robbers saga, or as one of the numerous crimes featured in your average gangster flick. But during the 1960s in particular, the heist movie became a genre all of its own. Although French film *Du Rififi Chez Les Hommes* is often seen as the granddaddy of the caper movie, as with many other genres it was Hollywood which took the genre to new heights. Both *Gambit* and *The Hot Rock* combined the heist with the buddy movie, the former a simple yet fun caper with Michael Caine and Shirley MacLaine plotting to steal a priceless statue, and the latter with George Segal persuading brother-in-law Redford to lead a bunch of bungling crims on one last heist. Redford's teaming with Paul Newman in *The Sting* must be the ultimate caper film, with the pair pulling the ultimate sting, conning the mob as well as the Feds.

BADLANDS 1973
Director Terence Malick Cast Martin Sheen, Sissy Spacek

One of the most stunning debuts by any director, Malick's own script, based loosely on the Starkweather-Fugate killing spree of the fifties, unusually never passes judgement on the two young killers. Sheen is a James Dean lookalike and garbage collector Kit who goes on the run with his girlfriend (Spacek) after he kills her father for disapproving of their relationship. The pair leave a trail of seemingly random yet brutal killings in their wake. The lack of sensationalism is aided by Malick and cinematographer Tak Fujimoto's golden hues of colour and Spacek's flat monotone narration. Malick gives himself a cameo as the visitor of the mansion owner taken hostage by Sheen and Spacek.

BIG BAD MAMA 1974
Director Steve Carver Cast Angie Dickinson, William Shatner, Tom Skerritt

In Roger Corman's take on the Bonnie and Clyde heists of the Depression, Dickinson and her equally sparsely clad teenage daughters travel through rural America bootlegging, robbing and picking up men, under the premise that if the likes of Ford and Capone can have it all, why can't they. Shatner and Skerritt play the lovers, the only fault with this comic crime drama being too many shots of Shatner's hairy legs. Avoid the unnecessary sequel, released in 1987.

BLACK GOD, WHITE DEVIL 1964 DEUS E O DIABO NA TERRA DO SOL
Director Glauber Rocha Cast Othon Bastos, Geraldo Del Rey, Mauricio do Valle

Director Rocha's first major film offers a fictionalized account of the real life last days of banditry in Brazil. Valle is hired gunman Antonio (the main character in the

sequel *Antonio Das Mortes*).
Here, however, the plot focuses
on Manuel (Del Rey) and his
descent into crime, joining
Antonio's sworn enemy Corisco
(Bastos). Although you need to
know the real life story to really
get this, it works both as an
interesting crime drama and as
a slice of Brazilian life. The
sequel in 1969 went on to win
Rocha the best director award at
the Cannes film festival.

Margaret Lockwood in a rare scene from *The Wicked
Lady* where the US censors approved of her neckline

BOXCAR BERTHA 1972
Director Martin Scorsese *Cast*
Barbara Hershey, David Carradine
Hired by Corman to direct a
sequel to *Bloody Mama*, *Boxcar Bertha*, Scorsese's second full-
length film, became a feature in its own right. Loosely based on
the memoirs of Bertha Thompson, Hershey is Bertha who, after
the death of her father, sets out on the road, linking up with
union leader Carradine and his band of robbers. Joining the
gang they rob train bosses, sending part of the haul back to the
unions, and are chased by a particularly sadistic lawman. Like
its inspiration *Bonnie & Clyde*, the film ends with a violent
shootout. Those hoping for typical Scorsese moments may be a
tad disappointed, although he does include two characters
named Michael Powell and Emeric Pressburger, two of his key
influences, and Hershey's hairstyle is modelled on Dorothy's in
The Wizard Of Oz. The film is notorious for Hershey and
Carradine's sex scenes, which the pair still insist were real. But
then Corman had told his protégé: "Read the script. Rewrite it.
But remember you must have some nudity every 15 pages."

DE VIERDE MAN 1983
Director Paul Verhoeven *Cast* Jeroen Krabbé, Renée Soutendijk
Verhoeven's final film before Hollywood recognized his talent
for persuading actresses to strip, is a surprisingly intriguing
work. Krabbé plays a bisexual writer who meets hairdresser
Soutendijk at one of his lectures. The pair strike up a rapport,
however Krabbé is more interested in the woman's lover,
Herman. Straightforward so far, from here Krabbé's character
begins to have visions, possibly warning him about his
relationship with a woman who has had three husbands, all of
whom died mysteriously. Is he or Herman the next target of this

femme fatale? Or indeed, is she is a fatale at all? A gothic crime thriller with plenty of Verhoeven's usual eroticism.

D.O.A 1950

Director Rudolph Maté *Cast* Edmond O'Brien, Pamela Britton

Frequently remade, *D.O.A* offers a more unusual twist to the traditional tale of murder, with O'Brien as mild-mannered accountant Frank, turning up at the police station to report his own murder. Deciding to have one last weekend of fun before he settles down with his fiancée, O'Brien awakens fatally poisoned. With only a week left to live, he sets out to find his killer. O'Brien gives the performance of his career in this most twisted and original noir. Avoid all remakes, this is the master.

> "THIS FILM IS DEDICATED TO ALL THE BEAUTIFUL WOMEN IN THE WORLD WHO HAVE SHOT THEIR HUSBANDS FULL OF HOLES"
>
> Roxie Hart

DOG DAY AFTERNOON 1975

Director Sidney Lumet *Cast* Al Pacino, John Cazale, Chris Sarandon

Warner/Pressman/Williams/Badlands; Columbia/Cannon.

Pacino and Cazale star as Sonny and Sal, holding up a bank to pay for Sonny's lover's (Sarandon in his debut film) sex-change operation. What should be a simple heist turns into a media frenzy with the hapless pair holed up with the bank clerks and customers while the media delve into their private lives and humiliate the inept police force. As with Lumet's debut movie *12 Angry Men*, the combination of oppressive surrounding, heat and the clever absence of any musical score, gives the film its claustrophobic feel. What could have ended up just another crime drama becomes a more personal piece, thanks to brilliant performances by Pacino (note the phone conversation he has with Sarandon) and Penny Allen as one of the frazzled bank staff. Cazale is just as good, reminding you of what a loss his early death (from bone cancer) in 1979 really was.

"And you, sir, do not have what it takes to join the Self-Preservation Society"

GUN CRAZY 1949

Director Joseph H Lewis
Cast Peggy Cummins, John Dall

An early forerunner to 1970s classics such as *Badlands* and *The Getaway*, Dall is gun-crazed Bart Tare. Sharp-shooting carnival performer Annie (unknown Welsh actress

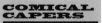

Cummins) is perfect for him and the pair marry. Annie, however, is your classic film noir femme fatale, leading the love-lorn Bart into a life of crime, sticking up banks to improve their (actually, her) financial situation. Lewis, a respected B movie director, was used to making the most out of limited budgets. The bargain casting of two unknowns suits the film, as does Lewis' technique of single-shot scenes. The script is credited to MacKinlay Kantor and Milliard Kaufman, but Kaufman was merely a front for blacklisted writer Dalton Trumbo.

IDIOT BOX 1996

Director David Caesar Cast Ben Mendelsohn, Jeremy Sims

Corrosive crime caper about two unemployed bums who spend their days kicking car alarms off in car parks, swigging beer and watching the 'idiot box' – from which they get the idea of pulling off a heist. But on the other side of town an infinitely more adept crook who robs banks to fund his girlfriend's drug habit is casing the same joint. Caesar's careering plotline is carried by clever camera work intercut with growling grunge music and frequently punctuated by a cheerfully insistent four-letter dialogue. But it's Mendelsohn and Sims as the adrenalin-fuelled meathead and his slightly less addled mate who really top the whole thing off. Fast, furious and above all very funny.

THE ITALIAN JOB 1969

Director Peter Collinson Cast Michael Caine, Noel Coward

The ultimate British caper movie of the 1960s (and Coward's last film) about a gang with gold bullion on their mind was scuppered, in Caine's eyes, by the marketing campaign centring on a poster of a naked woman sitting next to a gangster with a machine gun. The cliffhanging ending, with the gang's bus poised precariously on a precipice, was designed to leave scope for a sequel. Caine's idea was that the gang should turn the engine on, use up the petrol and drive the lightened bus to freedom. Don't worry Michael, there's still time.

JACKIE BROWN 1997

Director Quentin Tarantino Cast Pam Grier, Samuel L Jackson, Robert Forster, Michael Keaton

For Tarantino's third film he chose to adapt Elmore Leonard's novel *Rum Punch*, which has as convoluted a

COMICAL CAPERS

David Niven's 1940 comic adventure, *Raffles*, could have been a much quirkier film if F Scott Fitzgerald had not been fired after a few days. Hired by producer Samuel Goldwyn, he was supposed to revamp the dialogue of the film which stars Niven as a master cricketer -cum-jewel thief. After a matter of days however, he was fired on the basis of dialogue such as that featured in this never filmed love scene between Niven and Olivia de Havilland:

Raffles: Smile!
Gwen: (pressing closer… smiles)
Raffles: Wider!
Gwen: (smiles more widely)
Raffles: I'm going to ask you a very important question.
Gwen: (expectantly): Oh! Darling!
Raffles: Tell me… who is your dentist?

plot as he himself could have written. Grier plays Jackie Brown (a homage to her 1970s character Foxy Brown) supplementing her air stewardess wage by bringing in laundered money for her boss, Ordell (Jackson). Rumbled, she begins to play the situation just to stay alive and out of jail. On reading the novel Tarantino failed to realize the main character was white and went ahead writing the script with Grier in mind (she auditioned for a role in *Pulp Fiction* and Tarantino had promised her a role in his next film). All the characters are smart, from Ordell to bail bondsman Max (Forster, in his best role) and none of the key characters, including FBI agent Keaton as Ray Nicholet (he played the same character in *Out Of Sight*), are there merely to help the story along, each featuring in their own brilliant, quintessential Tarantino scenes. Grier shines through.

> "YOU STUPID BITCH? MICKEY, THAT'S WHAT MY FATHER USED TO CALL ME. I THOUGHT YOU'D BE A LITTLE MORE CREATIVE THAN THAT"
>
> Mallory, Natural Born Killers

KILLING OF A CHINESE BOOKIE 1976

Director *John Cassavetes* Cast *Ben Gazzara, Timothy Carey, Seymour Cassel*

Cassavetes' sombre pace and unique use of colour throughout the film sets it apart from your average thriller. Cassavetes regular Gazzara is Cosmo, owner of the Crazy Horse West topless club, with a passion for gambling. After losing money to the mob, they are willing to wave his marker if he kills another mobster, a Chinese bookie. Cassavetes chooses to set aside the usual gangster clichés, focusing on Cosmo and his loyalties to his club and extended family of dancers, intertwined with gambling, murder and double-crossing thrills. One of Cassavetes' best.

THE LADYKILLERS 1955

Director *Alexander Mackendrick* Cast *Alec Guinness, Peter Sellers, Herbert Lom, Cecil Parker*

A gang of thieves lodge with an old lady while planning a heist. When she stumbles on their plans, they decide to kill her, but she proves to be more resilient than they expect. In a classic story of twists and turns and everything going wrong, Peter Sellers appears to be just starting his metamorphosis into bumbling Inspector Clouseau and the other actors are all having the time of their lives. The scene where they are trying to help Mrs Wilberforce feed medicine to her parrot, General Gordon, should make you weep with laughter.

MR RELIABLE 1996

Director *Nadia Tass* Cast *Colin Friels, Jacqueline McKenzie*

In 1968, as the world was rocked by the Tet offensive in Vietnam, riots in Paris and the assassinations of Martin Luther

King and Robert Kennedy – the only dramatic event that happened in Australia involved one Wally Mellish and an eight-day 'hostage' drama in New South Wales. Friels is hilarious as the hapless larrikin who pulls a gun on cops questioning him about some stolen Jaguar hood ornaments. On glimpsing Mellish's girlfriend Beryl (McKenzie) and baby, the police assume that he's holding them hostage. It takes some time for Mellish to realize that an entire SWAT team are lurking outside but he quickly turns the situation to his advantage. As does virtually the entire population of NSW. Within hours Mellish's garden is inundated with locals, TV crews, anti-Vietnam protesters and various hotdog sellers. In America this would be an odd-ball drama where the lovable rogue is blasted to smithereens. But this was Australia in the 1960s and director Tass uses a certain 'artistic licence' and some dry humour to emphasize those relatively innocent times populated by characters today found mostly in fiction.

Starring in one of Jim Jarmusch's cinematic prose poems about America isn't all it's cracked up to be

MYSTERY TRAIN 1990

Director Jim Jarmusch *Cast* Masatoshi Nagase, Youki Kudoh, Screamin' Jay Hawkins, Cinqué Lee, Nicoletta Braschi, Elizabeth Bracco, Joe Strummer, Rick Aviles, Steve Buscemi

Hard to describe the crime in this three-into-one-must-go film without giving it all away. This tells three apparently unrelated stories (all based in Memphis) of a pair of Japanese tourists, a young Italian widow and a gang which rob a liquor store. Uniting all three stories are a gunshot and Elvis, either as a ghost or the singer of the ghostly *Blue Moon* which is playing on almost every radio anybody listens to. It's an odd film in which crime provides some kind of resolution and is a constant threat (as when the widow has to pay a wacko, who tells her the story of Graceland's hitchhiking ghost, just to leave her alone).

NATURAL BORN KILLERS 1994

Director Oliver Stone *Cast* Woody Harrelson, Juliette Lewis, Robert Downey Jr, Tommy Lee Jones

Although based on a Tarantino story, subsequent changes made by Stone have led Tarantino to all but disown the film. This is

Stone's satire on the media frenzy engulfing America, with Harrelson and Lewis as Mickey and Mallory, young, ruthless killers whose main priority on their killing spree is that they take all the credit. Initially banned, the film holds the record for the largest number of cuts and reshots needed on a film to secure an R-rating (150). Stone cut in several scenes from other films, including *Midnight Express* and *Scarface*, and splashed lurid colours across the screen, particularly blood red and green to suggest the sickness of the killers' minds. Not as clever as Stone would like it to be, this is still enthralling, if over-hyped. Downey stands out as a talk show lowlife.

NO WAY OUT 1987

Director Roger Donaldson *Cast* Kevin Costner, Gene Hackman, Sean Young

> "I CAN BREATHE AND I CAN MOVE BUT I'M NOT ALIVE BECAUSE I TOOK THAT POISON AND NOTHING CAN SAVE ME"
>
> Frank Bigelow, D.O.A

Remember Sean Young? She lights up the screen in this excellent thriller, reminding you how great she was before she started leaving voodoo dolls on her ex's doorstep and guesting on talk shows in a Catwoman costume claiming Michelle Pfeiffer had stolen her role. In this, she's the lover of Hackman and Costner. As the career Navy man assigned to Hackman (the secretary of state for defence), Costner stays firmly in neutral leaving us guessing as the plot twists, turns and eventually eats itself.(Hackman kills Young, Costner is witness, suspect and in charge of the investigation.) Donaldson's rare genius is to make a thriller with an ingenious plot without sacrificing too much of his characters' credibility and Costner is much more effective when he's not playing the straight hero.

OUT OF SIGHT 1998

Director Steven Soderbergh *Cast* George Clooney, Jennifer Lopez

"Is this your first time being robbed? You're doing great." This is how the suave Clooney as Jack Foley robs banks. Based on another Elmore Leonard novel, *Out Of Sight* has a plot as complex as *Pulp Fiction* with the action flitting between past, further past and present. But it's Leonard's colourful characters that propel the film, notably the buddy relationship between Jack and, er, Buddy (Ving Rhames), and Jack and FBI agent Lopez. The film also features a cameo by Samuel L Jackson and 500 convicts from Glades penitentiary.

PARADISE LOST: THE CHILD MURDERS AT ROBIN HOOD HILLS 1996

Directors Joe Berlinger, Bruce Sinofsky

In this documentary three teenagers are accused of killing three young children supposedly through their involvement in

Paramount/Oakhurst; Samuel Goldwyn; Palace/JVC;

Satanism. But there is no real evidence against them apart from a statement by one of the group who has learning difficulties and later says the confession was forced. As the film progresses, interviews with the victims' parents, police and locals show that the teenagers have really been singled out because they are the town's black sheep. They are interested in the occult, listen to heavy metal and wear black. That, in the heartland of America's Bible Belt, is enough to get them convicted. The fact that one of the accused is called Damien adds a ludicrous, chilling twist. The film is compelling and terrifying.

Some people become murderers, some have homicide thrust upon them and some, like our Mickey here, are born killers

POINT BLANK 1967

Director John Boorman *Cast* Lee Marvin, Angie Dickinson

Recently remade as the Mel Gibson vehicle *Payback*, this was ignored on its initial release but marks a turning point in American cinema in the 1960s even if Boorman is English. The film opens with Walker (Marvin) shot and left for dead. But he recovers to try and exact revenge on his double-crossing wife and mob-connected partner. Marvin's quiet brutishness dominates what is (at times) a very arty film – he had actor John Vernon in tears after a fight scene between the two.

RESERVOIR DOGS 1992

Director Quentin Tarantino *Cast* Harvey Keitel, Tim Roth, Michael Madsen, Steve Buscemi, Lawrence Tierney, Chris Penn

Make no mistake, *Dogs* is not a gangster film but out and out heist fun. They've got the suits, the unexplainable nicknames and ruthless boss Joe (1940s tough guy Tierney) keeping it in the family with son Nice Guy Eddie (Penn). What they don't got is loyalty. These guys are purely out for the money and in Mr Blond's case, the thrill of killing, although he is the only character who doesn't kill anyone (severe maiming doesn't count). Tarantino had planned to have friends playing the roles until actress Lorraine Bracco (Keitel's wife at the time) passed the script on to Keitel who signed up immediately, helping to raise cash and the film's profile. The role of Mr Blue eventually went to Eddie Bunker, a convicted armed robber who was once on the FBI's Ten Most Wanted list.

ROXIE HART 1942

Director *William Wellman* Cast *Ginger Rogers, Adolphe Menjou, George Chandler*

Rogers escaped from her dancing partner long enough to dazzle as the dancer who claims to be a murderess to grab some headlines in a story based on the play *Chicago* which would be turned into the eponymous Bob Fosse musical. Wellman doesn't do quite as well as Howard Hawks might with this material but it still zings and Rogers plays with real zest.

TARGETS 1968

Director *Peter Bogdanovich* Cast *Tim O'Kelly, Boris Karloff*

A forerunner to *Natural Born Killers* in terms of subject, Bogdanovich's first feature centres on Karloff, pretty much playing himself, as a horror movie star determined to retire as he feels his films can't possibly compete with the escalating violence in society. Running parallel to this is Bobby Thompson (O'Kelly) on a killing spree, which, though unexplained, proves Karloff's theory. Bogdanovich has a cameo as a writer in the film-within-a-film. The film works as a social commentary, a thrilling piece of horror and is full of homages to films of significance to the director and the star. And O'Kelly is the first of many natural born killers. "I don't know what's happening to me," he complains at one point to his wife, "I get funny ideas."

SECRETS

So what actually is the eerie glowing light from Marsellus Wallace's briefcase in *Pulp Fiction*? Tarantino says he couldn't think what to put in the case and decided to leave it up to the audience. And here's what they've come up with:

MARSELLUS' SOUL

Combined with the plaster on the back of Wallace's neck, Jules reciting Ezekiel 25:17 speech and his and Vincent's brush with divine intervention, Marsellus Wallace's soul is the most popular and interesting theory. But does the fact that the combination is 666, geddit, mean Marsellus is the devil?

SATCHEL OF DIAMONDS FROM RESERVOIR DOGS

Tarantino is famed for linking characters and events from his movies with one another and what did happen to the diamonds?

ELVIS GOLD SUIT

As worn by Val Kilmer as the ghost of Elvis in *True Romance*, which Tarantino scripted. Our Quent appeared in *The Golden Girls* as an Elvis impersonator and in the original script for *Pulp*, Vince is asked to confirm he's an "Elvis man" and not a "Beatles man" – which he does.

GOLD BULLION

It's yellow, it could glow under the right lighting, and it's a pretty impressive stash. **Other suggestions**: the stash from the car in *Repo Man*, an Oscar, a birthday cake , a Royale with cheese.

THE THIN BLUE LINE 1988

Director **Errol Morris**

In 1976 Dallas policeman Robert Wood was shot dead on duty. Drifter Randall Adams was convicted and served 11 years until Morris made this documentary after investigating the case for over two years. He discovered that the main testimony against Adams was flawed and after the screening of *The Thin Blue Line*, Adams' case was reopened. Far more than a documentary, the film features a slightly surreal restaging of Officer Wood's death, and Morris is clearly a man who is interested in more than just what people say, as his camera highlights quirks and reactions to great effect. Add all this to Philip Glass' hypnotic soundtrack and the film becomes a masterpiece of true-life storytelling.

THOMAS CROWN AFFAIR 1999

Director **John McTiernan** *Cast* **Pierce Brosnan, Rene Russo, Denis Leary**

The 1968 film was chiefly famous for the chess scene, the song *The Windmills Of Your Mind* and irritating split screen. In the remake, Brosnan is Crown, a bored billionaire who gets his kicks from staging elaborate art robberies. Russo is the maverick insurance investigator, prone to late nights and drinking bizarre concoctions. The dance of seduction is interchangeable with the game of cat and mouse. Action director McTiernan keeps the momentum going throughout with brilliant set pieces, particularly the two heist sequences. Brosnan does his best Bond impersonation even if he can't wear the tux (the Bond contract states he cannot wear a tux in any other film). Although the plot is the same as the 1968 film, in mood this is more a Cary Grant comedy thriller.

> "HE'S VERY LUCKY WITH THE WEATHER. MUST BE DEPRESSING TO BE HANGED ON A DAMP DAY"
> Lord Kingsclere, The Wicked Lady

THE WICKED LADY 1945

Director **Leslie Arliss** *Cast* **Margaret Lockwood, James Mason**

Lockwood, a bored noblewoman in the time of Charles II, escapes at night to commit highway robbery as a way of spicing up her life. Considered daring at the time and some scenes were reshot for US audiences because the women's gowns were deemed too low-cut, *The Wicked Lady* is mostly interesting now because of the sparks that fly between Lockwood and Mason, who plays the real highwayman, Captain Jackson. The film was the most successful of the Gainsborough costume dramas, and paved the way for Mason to make his name in Hollywood. Lockwood's fan mail soared too but her film career would almost draw to a close within a decade. The Michael Winner remake deserves to be roundly shunned.

CUT

Films can be cut to placate censors, in a row between directors and studio, or simply so they can be re-released as 'the director's cut'. Can't wait for the critical re-evaluation of *Pearl Harbor*.

CALIGULA 1980

Director Tinto Brass *Cast* Malcolm McDowell, Teresa Ann Savoy, John Gielgud, Helen Mirren, Peter O'Toole

For all the furore surrounding this movie, the end product is less entertaining than the documentary *The Making Of Caligula*, which is included on the DVD re-release, and nowhere near as strange as the real emperor's four-year reign. The chaos surrounding this film, *Penthouse* publisher Bob Guccione's bid to prove that porn really is an art form, can be seen from the credits (which say it is "adapted" from Gore Vidal's screenplay) and from the plethora of versions. The original unrated version lasts 156 minutes, an R-rated cut on video is 41 minutes shorter (minus most of the sex scenes), a 210-minute version was shown at Cannes while the original UK cinema version lasted 150 minutes. Confused? You will be because two completely different versions are now available on laserdisc and DVD. Guccione says the new DVD version will change the way people think about movies. But it won't change the way most of us feel about this particular movie or the acting.

> "LET THEM HATE ME, SO LONG AS THEY FEAR ME!"
> Caligula

THE CRYING GAME 1992

Director Neil Jordan *Cast* Forest Whitaker, Miranda Richardson, Stephen Rea

If you haven't seen this and don't know the final twist, look away now. This is an effective mystery about a black British soldier abducted by the IRA and held hostage, based on Frank O'Connor's story. Viewers in Japan must have found the film even more puzzling than most because the scene in which the supporting actress turns out to be a supporting actor was cut.

THE DRAUGHTSMAN'S CONTRACT 1982

Director Peter Greenaway *Cast* Anthony Higgins, Janet Suzman, Anne Louise Lambert

Alan Parker once described this as "a load of posturing poo poo", so who knows what he would have made of Greenaway's original four-hour cut, which he aimed to release (with added out-takes) as *The Hedgecutters*. The version released in the UK was a brisk 103 minutes and, thankfully, did not include a scene where one of the characters in this 17th-century comedy/drama uses a cellphone. The contract of the title, between a draughtsman who is hired to draw an estate and the mistress of that estate, is both less straightforward and darker than it appears. In this instance, the director's cut is likely to be awaited with bated breath only by Greenaway.

HAKUCHI 1951

Director Akira Kurosawa *Cast* Minoru Chiaki, Chieko Higashiyama
Kurosawa takes Dostoevky's *The Idiot* and transplants it to Japan in what was supposed to be a two-part film running a grand 265 minutes, but was cut to just two-and-three-quarter hours for release. The story (about a prince and his friend in love with the same woman) isn't that easy to follow but then nobody reads the Russian novelist for his plots. The film's rather stately progress is interrupted by sudden flashes of brilliance and is preferable to the 1960 faithful Russian version.

THE MAGNIFICENT AMBERSONS 1942

Director Orson Welles *Cast* Joseph Cotton, Dolores Costello
This was the film of which Orson Welles justly said: "The studio are cutting my movie with a lawnmower." Not satisfied with slashing 50 minutes off Welles' original film, RKO also tacked on a happy ending. This rather sorry saga is cited as the definitive tale of Hollywood's crass commercialism triumphing over artistic integrity and genius. The truth isn't that simple. Welles' best biographer, David Thomson, suggests Welles abandoned his film by preferring to chase carnival girls in Rio than come back to RKO and fight for it. That said, the 88-minute studio version is enough to suggest this could have been Welles' second greatest film after *Kane*. And there are scenes which suggest a greater emotional depth than its predecessor, possibly because the story of a child who destroys his family struck a guilty chord. For Welles, it was the start of death by a thousand cuts.

The real Caligula made his horse an emperor. The film *Caligula* had a horse as an extra and scriptwriter

DISASTER

The disaster movie gives the hungry audience the lot. Action, drama, special effects and romance in varying quantities (and qualities). You can even throw in some sci-fi for added spice. It's a perfect formula. And something worse can always happen for the sequel. No wait, that something worse *is* the sequel...

AIRPORT '77 1977

Director Jerry Jameson *Cast* Jack Lemmon, Lee Grant

By far the best of the 'Airport' series, which kicked off the disaster genre in 1970 with *Airport* (the suicide bomber), followed up with sequels in 1975 (the one most famously parodied in *Airplane!*), this one in 1977 and a final murder mission in 1979. *Airport '77* is a triple whammy – a hijacking, a smash with an oil rig and finally a crash landing in the Bermuda Triangle. As genre king Irwin Allen said: "The bigger the tragedy, the bigger the audience." You can't go wrong with this much disaster in one flick. Comes complete with the obligatory veteran George Kennedy as Joe Patroni. Kennedy is in all the *Airports* as well as *Earthquake* and *Sonic Boom*, a little known disaster spoof short in which he co-stars with Ricky Nelson and Keith Moon.

ALIVE 1993

Director Frank Marshall *Cast* Ethan Hawke, Vincent Spano

This true life story of South American rugby players who have to resort to cannibalism to survive in the Andes after a plane crash, was originally told in *Survive*, released in 1976, four years after the actual event. The survivors endure three months of the most appalling conditions, though in *Alive* it's hard not to think that Ethan and co look surprisingly plump. The scenery and photography is good, and all the action is narrated by one of the survivors, who is actually an uncredited John Malkovich. Watch the earlier *Survive*, a low-budget Mexican production which Paramount turned into a box office hit, if you like your action a bit more authentic (the actors are all South American for starters). *Alive*, twice as long as its predecessor, is better if you want to wallow in the general air of glumness for a bit longer.

AVALANCHE 1978

Director Corey Allen *Cast* Mia Farrow, Rock Hudson

'Six million tons of icy terror!' With a tagline like this and a title that sets the scene, all you have to do is wait for the worst. If you can ignore the Styrofoam overload interspersed with aged, scratchy footage of real avalanches, you'll find all the tension and action a great disaster movie needs. It's only a modest 90 minutes long, but the avalanche doesn't fall until an hour in.

DEEP IMPACT 1998

Director Mimi Leder *Credit* Morgan Freeman, Robert Duvall, Téa Leoni

It's the big moral dilemma: if a comet's on its way to destroy the earth and 800,000 lucky souls are going to be picked from a lottery to survive, should the draw be presented by Dale Winton or Regis Philbin? Morgan Freeman exudes a dilapidated moral authority as the celluloid president. The drama is deepened by the ethical dilemma, setting it aside from the action-driven *Armageddon* which is based on the same space collision premise. *Deep Impact* might lack a bit technically, and does push the boundaries of credibility (warning: if a comet does pass overhead you won't be able to watch it without being burnt to a crisp), but it has a certain emotional depth and if you miss the disaster movies of the 1970s, you'll enjoy this.

> **"IT'S LIKE COMMUNION – FROM THEIR DEATH, WE LIVE"**
> A survivor, *Alive*

EARTHQUAKE 1974

Director Mark Robson *Cast* Charlton Heston, Ava Gardner

Like all good disaster movies, *Earthquake* begins with a rundown of the characters so you can decide who will be DBTA (Dead By Third Act). There are the usual wives, widows and mistresses, a hot-tempered cop and a psychotic shop owner. *Earthquake* won the Oscar for best sound as the first of only four Universal productions to be presented in 'Sensurround', four special, low-frequency, bass speakers powerful enough to crack the plaster at some cinemas. There are some good goofs – the dead man raising his head out of the water for a breath, and the cows who stay upright in the overturned truck because the model was nailed that way. Look out for Walter Matthau as a drunk – he's credited by his real name, Walter Matuschanskayasky.

NIPPON CHINBOTSU 1973

Directors Andrew Meyer, Shiro Moritani *Cast* Hiroshi Fujioka, Lorne Greene

It's all hands on board as the US and UK come to the rescue of a Japan that is being destroyed by nature. Volcanoes, hurricanes and earthquakes send the citizens running for shelter before the ultimate tsunami threatens to sink the country. The film was released in two versions – this uncut and subtitled original, and the cut and dubbed American version featuring less of the action and more of Lorne Greene, known simultaneously as *Submersion of Japan*, *Japan Sinks* and *Tidal Wave*.

THE OMEGA CODE 1999

Director Robert Marcarelli *Cast* Casper Van Dien, Michael York

Blame the proximity of the millennium for apocalyptic visions like this. *The Omega Code*, an independent film from a cable TV religious broadcaster, is based on the *Book Of Revelation*, and pits goody Van Dien against baddy York, each after the Bible codes which reveal the secrets of the earth – past, present and future. Despite being shown in only 305 US theatres, it grossed $2.4m on its first weekend after being backed by churches and religious zealots. One Oklahoma CEO reportedly purchased 1,000 tickets to give to his employees, while another LA woman gave 1,600 tickets to youth groups.

THE POSEIDON ADVENTURE 1972

Director Ronald Neame *Cast* Gene Hackman, Ernest Borgnine

The Neptune of all disaster movies, *The Poseidon Adventure* sees a huge tidal wave upset the plans, and the luxury liner, of New Year's Eve partygoers. As the liner capsizes and sinks to the bottom of the ocean, cop Borgnine and priest Hackman compete for leadership of the survivors on their odyssey through fire and water and for the overacting honours. Hackman has the juiciest part: he gets to tell Stella Stevens to take her top off and Pamela Sue Martin to get rid of her skirt. Oh to be a priest. No fan can miss this, though you can safely skip the sequel, *Beyond The Poseidon Adventure* (1979), which provides an alternative ending (two rival salvage parties turn up looking for loot) but features none of the original cast or characters. And if you're wondering why a Greek ship would be decked out with Egyptian murals, it's because the décor was left over from the set of Mankiewicz's *Cleopatra*, nine years earlier.

THE QUIET EARTH 1985

Director Geoff Murphy *Cast* Bruno Lawrence, Alison Routledge

"Zac Hobson, July 5th. One – there has been a malfunction in Project Flashlight. Two – it seems I am the last man left on Earth..." Scientist Zac thinks (wrongly) that he's the sole survivor of the apocalypse in this end-of-the-world saga. This New Zealand production tackles the thought every kid has – but when we've ransacked the toy shop and stuffed ourselves silly with ice cream, what would we really do if we found ourselves utterly alone in the world? When the film opens the disaster has already occurred. This is more of a thoughtful, post-apocalyptic film, rather than a straight 'will they make it?' disaster flick. The ending leaves you trying to work out for yourself what really happened, which you'll either love or hate.

SAN FRANCISCO 1936
Director WS Van Dyke
Cast Clark Gable, Jeanette MacDonald, Spencer Tracy
Love story set just before the

When Time Ran Out had some big names in. They don't come much bigger than Gayle Kananiokalapontigay

big San Francisco earthquake, following the divine retribution theme familiar in later disaster films. Gable plays gambling drinker Blackie who hires MacDonald as a singer in his aptly named Paradise Club. Rumour has it that Gable (who had already won one Oscar) was not keen on playing second fiddle to MacDonald's singing lead and only agreed to star after the film was rewritten to give him more scenes. He reputedly turned up for love scenes stinking of garlic to show he wasn't entirely appeased, so MacDonald's swooning after their first kiss isn't entirely an act.

TITANIC 1997
Director James Cameron *Cast* Leonardo DiCaprio, Kate Winslet
The lure of the Titanic has proved too strong for producers to resist. The first film appeared in Italy only three years after the fateful maiden voyage of 1912 and the story has remained captivating ever since – Joseph Goebbels even planned to use the German 1943 film as Nazi propaganda. James Cameron's version has to come top of the heap though, not least for his visual flair and dedication to historical accuracy. The ship's décor was supervised by some of the original furnishing companies, and many of the paintings are authentic – including Picasso's *The Guitar Player*, which was flown in from Paris. Even the young boy with his father whom Jack passes by in his search for Rose on the first-class deck is taken from a photo which escaped the Titanic when it docked briefly in Ireland. Full marks to Kate as well – only a true pro would spit in the face of Billy Zane rather than opt for the scripted hairpin jab.

THE TOWERING INFERNO 1974

Directors Irwin Allen, John Guillerman *Cast* Steve McQueen, Paul Newman, Faye Dunaway

Short circuits on opening night of his record-breaking tall building leave architect Newman fretting about his wiring and leaves the rest of the party in the hands of head fireman McQueen. One of the biggest films of the 1970s and the first mega-budget blockbuster, it featured an all-star cast, with, among others, Fred Astaire, William Holden, Richard Chamberlain and OJ Simpson. McQueen insisted that he and Newman have the same billing, the same number of lines and that all his dialogue be rewritten with as few S and Z sounds as possible (he had trouble pronouncing them). The film draws on two books – hence the two climaxes (the lifeline rescue and the exploding water tanks) and its length (nearly three hours).

TWISTER 1996

Director Jan De Bont *Cast* Helen Hunt, Bill Paxton

Two researchers heading for a messy divorce join a team of stormchasers trying to get inside the world's most violent tornadoes. Director Jan De Bont (*Speed*) keeps the whole thing moving at a fast pace, creating a highly entertaining, big-budget movie. Warner Brothers even used the soon-to-be-demolished downtown of Wakita, Oklahoma, ripping down the buildings and smashing them to pieces before paying for the clean-up. Legend has it that the screening of *Twister* at a Canadian drive-in was interrupted by a tornado tearing the screen down – during the scene in the movie where the same thing happens at the drive-in viewing of *The Shining*. Sadly this isn't quite true. A tornado did rip through a drive-in south of Ontario, but it was a few hours before the film was due to be shown.

YOU BEAST!

Disaster movies aren't always natural – there may be a monster with a motive:

The Legend Of Boggy Creek (1972)
Return To Boggy Creek (1977)
The Barbaric Beast Of Boggy Creek (1985)
Behemoth The Sea Monster (1959)
The Boogens (1981)
The Crater Lake Monster (1977)
The Creature Wasn't Nice (1981)
Curucu, Beast Of The Amazon (1956)
Serpiente de Mar (1984)
Sora No Daikaijū Radon (1956)
Tremors (1990)
Them (1954)
Skeeter (1993)

WHEN TIME RAN OUT 1980

Director James Goldstone *Cast* Paul Newman, Jacqueline Bisset, William Holden

There are disaster movies and there are disastrous movies. This is one of the latter. A desperate bid to cash in on a formula which had passed its sell-by date, by a director who would go on to helm a TV movie about Charles and Di and from a producer (Irwin Allen) whose contract ran out with this film. (Newman and Holden's excuse was similar: they were contractually obliged to appear in one more Irwin Allen film.) The talented cast look lost, ashamed and fearful for their careers.

DOCTORS

On celluloid, doctors can be good, bad or merely hilarious. They can be the knight in the shining surgical smock (Ronald Colman in *Arrowsmith*), powerless but trustworthy (*Awakenings*) or the butt of countless comedies which have had their funny bone surgically removed. Occasionally, in films like *M*A*S*H*, we glimpse their darker side. Even then they fare better than dentists, who usually fall into three film genres: the bad, the very bad and the ugly.

AKAHIGE 1965

Director Akira Kurosawa *Cast* Toshiro Mifune, Yuzo Kayama

Kurosawa's last film starring Mifune (they fell out on set) and one of the director's lesser-known works. The tale of a medical intern coming to realize the wisdom of his tutor, an old doctor known as 'Red beard' (Mifune), it clocks in at three hours. This marked the end of Kurosawa's first great period – he would spend the next decade out of fashion which, coupled with the absence of any *Ran*-style spectacles, may explain why it still languishes in obscurity.

You can see why *Awakenings* never caught on: DeNiro isn't playing a mobster and Williams is underplaying

AWAKENINGS 1990

Director Penny Marshall *Cast* Robert De Niro, Robin Williams

This is that rarest of cinematic beasts, a De Niro movie which remains criminally underrated. Based on the experiences of Dr Oliver Sacks, author of *The Man Who Mistook His Wife For A Hat*, this is a poignant drama about a doctor (Williams) who brings patients out of their comas but is forced (plot spoiler alert) to watch as they slip back into a living death. Williams underplays brilliantly and De Niro is magnificent, his time spent watching Sacks and his patients put to moving effect.

BRITANNIA HOSPITAL 1982

Director Lindsay Anderson *Cast* Leonard Rossiter, Graham Crowden, Joan Plowright, Malcolm McDowell

A royal visit to a symbolically named hospital to open a wing where amazing, if sinister, experiments are being conducted, coincides with a reporter arriving to shoot a documentary, a protest against the hospital's decision to treat an African dictator, and industrial unrest. Anderson's hospital as a society metaphor isn't exactly subtle and although the fine cast includes almost every British actor of note (and Mark Hamill), they can't prevent the dialogue sounding like rhetoric at times. The last in Anderson's trilogy about Britain, this is an honourable failure.

M*A*S*H 1970

Director Robert Altman *Cast* Donald Sutherland, Elliott Gould, Sally Kellerman

This is an easy film to misunderstand. The third biggest box office success of 1970 (after *Love Story* and *Airport*), *M*A*S*H* is often seen as an anti-war comedy but it's really anti-authority. Although the antics of rebel surgeons Hawkeye and Trapper John are set in Korea, audiences often see this as an attack on what was then going on in Vietnam. The theme tune (*Suicide Is Painless*) was then going on in Vietnam. The theme tune (*Suicide Is Painless*) was blacker and bleaker than anything in the witty script. You didn't have to hate the war to enjoy this film, you just had to sympathize with the pre-*Animal House* guys in their continual struggle to have as much fun as possible, often at the expense of Major Frank Burns (Robert Duvall) and Hotlips (Kellerman). The film wouldn't have been anywhere near as effective without Altman's frantic cutting and overlapping dialogue. Not that the actors recognized this at the time: they rebelled on set saying Altman, the 18th choice to direct this film, would ruin their careers.

> "WERE YOU ON THIS RELIGIOUS KICK AT HOME OR DID YOU CRACK UP HERE?"
>
> Hawkeye Pierce, M*A*S*H

THE MEN 1950

Director Fred Zinnemann *Cast* Marlon Brando, Teresa Wright, Everett Sloane

Usually remembered as Brando's promising debut, this is also notable for a far more trivial reason: it is the first time DeForest Kelley (Dr McCoy in *Star Trek*) plays a doctor. To Brando's disappointment, the film, about paralyzed war veterans, was given a more hopeful ending than was originally planned. Coming out the same year as the Korean war started, and as the witch hunt (which would force writer Carl Foreman into exile after he'd teamed up with Zinnemann on *High Noon*) gathered macabre momentum, this film still dared to go beyond the usual cardboard celluloid heroics. (Note also the scientist lecturing on paraplegia in

"Can anyone say which part of the body this is?" M*A*S*H medicine

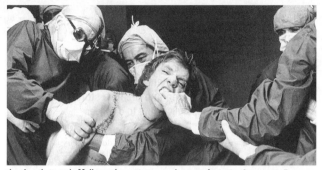

the chapel, an early Hollywood comment on science as the new religion.) Since this film, playing a paraplegic has become a rite of passage for actors needing a chance to flex their acting muscles. Jon Voight was Oscar-winning as the disabled vet in *Coming Home* (1978) while Tom Cruise was wheelchair-bound in Oliver Stone's *Born On The Fourth Of July*.

Seems not all Britannia Hospital's patients are that keen on the prospect of a royal visit

MERCI LA VIE 1991
Director Bertrand Blier *Cast* Charlotte Gainsbourg, Anouk Grinberg, Gérard Depardieu

It is hard to forget any film which begins with a scene of a beaten woman in a bridal outfit in a supermarket trolley with a seagull on her head, being pushed down an empty road by a girl she has just met. Released the same year as *Thelma And Louise,* this is a road movie on the road to nowhere. Depardieu appears as the appropriately named Dr Worms who, for reasons we can only guess at, is using Gainsbourg in a medical experiment which involves her sleeping with as many local men as possible to see how many of them get venereal disease and even (it is hinted) the HIV virus. Clearly they have a rather different view of the Hippocratic Oath in France. Even though his character is madder than all the hatmakers in Paris, Depardieu is horribly convincing; an odd role in an odd film.

AAAARRGH

Three dentists you wouldn't want to go anywhere near your teeth

JOEL FABIANI REUBEN REUBEN
Takes revenge on drunken poet for having an affair with his wife by removing the wrong teeth, forcing his patient to use falsies.

STEVE MARTIN LITTLE SHOP OF HORRORS
Orin Scrivello DDS became a dentist mainly because his first choice as employer, the Nazi Party, had disbanded.

LAURENCE OLIVIER MARATHON MAN
If you're ever in the chair, with cold metal pressing into your mouth, and the man in white asks: "Is it safe?" just kick him in the balls and run.

Columbia/TriStar; TCF/Aspen; EMI/Film and General/NFFC

DOCUMENTARIES

Documentaries, oh yawn. Who wants to pay to sit and watch real life when movies are supposed to be about escaping all that? In fact, feature-length documentaries can be among the most dramatic, shocking, uplifting and creative stories to reach the screens – as you are hopefully about to discover.

What definitely makes documentary features worth seeing is that often, the stories are so outrageous that an audience would never accept them as fiction. As is so often said, you couldn't make this stuff up. Characters so grotesque even Fellini would reject them, endings so fairytale that Meg Ryan would sneer, and political and legal conspiracies so tortuous that Oliver Stone would come out of the cinema shouting: "I told you so!"

The recent proliferation of good compact digital cameras has enabled documentary makers to produce their work faster and more cheaply than ever. This may mean more trash is produced, but it does mean filmmakers who are truly passionate about their subject can buy affordable equipment and don't have to wait years for funding. With any luck, this means that a few more films like the ones below will be coming our way soon.

> "SOME PEOPLE JUST DON'T LIKE TO CELEBRATE HUMAN TRAGEDY ON VACATION"
> Michael Moore, Roger And Me

BUENA VISTA SOCIAL CLUB 1999
Director Wim Wenders

Cuba was once the easy-living playground of the rich and famous, and had bars and clubs full of musicians playing the best Latin jazz. Since Castro came to power in 1959, those musicians have kept making music, but very few outside Cuba have heard it. Wenders' film follows Ry Cooder to Cuba as he meets the cream of Cuba's music scene, some of them now over 90. Every interviewee has an amazing story; one was playing on the street for money at the age of five, another was drafted into a band from his job as a shoeshine boy. The musicians, old men who make such stunning music, capture the heart.

COMMON THREADS: STORIES FROM THE QUILT 1989
Director Robert Epstein *Cast* Jeffrey Friedman

One of the most touching phenomenon to emerge from the Aids epidemic is the Aids Memorial Quilt, a vast blanket comprising thousands of individual panels, each made to commemorate the life and death of an Aids victim. Common Threads follows the stories of five of these panels – a former Olympic athlete, an 11-year-old haemophiliac, a retired Navy commander, a campaigning gay writer and a drug addict. Statistics about Aids are too huge to grasp but this brings it down to an entirely human level.

Michael Moore estimates the size of the pizza eaten (but not paid for) by Reagan

CRUMB 1994

Director Terry Zwigoff

Think your family is dysfunctional? Think again: you have nothing on the Crumbs.

Robert Crumb, creator of Fritz the Cat, is a legend among fans of underground comics and this film asks what inspires Crumb. Zwigoff gets some astoundingly intimate interviews with Crumb, his deranged mum and tortured brothers Max and Charles, all of whom see Crumb's creativity as a product of his home life. Like Crumb's work, the documentary is politically incorrect, hilarious and disturbing. As he says: "Perhaps they should just take away my pencils and lock me away."

GARLIC IS AS GOOD AS TEN MOTHERS 1980

Directors Les Blank, Maureen Gosling

Filmed at various San Francisco restaurants as well as the Gilroy Garlic Festival, this is a gentle celebration of the many uses for garlic, including ice cream. It's also a fun study of the inhabitants of Berkeley in the late 1970s, their preoccupations (other than garlic) and attitudes. Werner Herzog, director of *Fitzcarraldo*, appears and bet Blank he would never finish the film. After Blank made his feature, they made a short showing Herzog losing the bet called *Werner Herzog Eats His Shoe*.

GIRL GONE BAD 2000

Director Louis Yansen

Ride along with Dusty Switzer, an Apache biker chick and single mother, ex-convict and ex-go-go dancer, as she journeys through the extraordinary world of female bikers. Whether they're Dykes on Bikes or Biker Babes, all these women share a common love of speed, freedom and the smell of petrol. There are some fantastic stories here, from the LAPD officer who wants to be a motorcycle sergeant, to the family law practitioner who just can't help but go wild at weekends. One of the best lines in the film is delivered by a non-biker to her recalcitrant child: "If you don't behave, I'll let the biker lady babysit you."

Warner/Dog Eat Dog ; Revillon Freres

Nanook posing for Robert J Flaherty's camera;
his snowmobile is just out of shot to the left

HOOP DREAMS 1994
Director **Steve James**
Cast **Arthur Agee, William Gates**

Ambitious film spanning five years in the lives of two basketball hopefuls from inner city Chicago. In the cut-throat world of US sports, both boys make it into an elite high school which produced one of their idols, NBA star Isiah Thomas, but have trouble with grades and their home lives. Their longing to escape and become NBA stars is palpable, making their struggles more poignant. Amazingly *Hoop Dreams* was not even nominated for a best documentary feature Oscar. A key moment comes when one mum asks: "Do you all wonder sometimes how I am living? How my children survive and they're living? It's enough to really make people want to lash out and hurt somebody."

THE LIFE AND TIMES OF ROSIE THE RIVETER 1980
Director **Connie Field**

The title is taken from the World War II propaganda character who urged women to do their best for the war effort, and this film features interviews with five women from across America, all of whom heeded their country's call and became metal workers, either in shipyards or munitions factories. Intercut with footage of the war, plus hilarious propaganda films of the time, there are some fascinating revelations by the articulate and inspiring Wanita, Gladys, Lynn, Lola and Margaret. The final section shows how tough wartime women were encouraged to become docile housewives again when men returned to claim their jobs. During the war, magazines promoted recipes that took minutes to cook; afterwards, they advocated spending all day making hubby's evening meal.

NANOOK OF THE NORTH 1922
Director **Robert J Flaherty**

A year in the life of an Eskimo, or Inuit as they are now known, may not seem like the most riveting subject. After all, how much snow can an audience take? Luckily, Flaherty was a very skilled filmmaker, way ahead of his time, and the film is a classic, though not for all the reasons you might think. Flaherty wanted to make a genuine anthropological study but he knew the power of creating an image, and as he followed Nanook and family hunting and trading, many events were staged for the film. Instead of being a simple soul, untouched by the outside world, it later emerged that Nanook even owned a snowmobile. It is still worth watching, as many of the techniques (including faking the evidence) are still part of documentary making today.

NIGHT MAIL 1936

Directors Harry Watt, Basil Wright

Short film of the poem by WH Auden, set over real footage of the night mail train on a journey from London to Edinburgh. The music was written by Benjamin Britten, and the rhythm of the poem fits perfectly with the shots of the speeding train, and post sorters on the night shift. A terrific evocation of how things used to be. They really don't make them like this anymore.

OLYMPIA 1 1938

Director Leni Riefenstahl

Riefenstahl, a personal friend of Hitler, was commissioned by him to make this film of the 1936 Berlin Olympics. A chunk of Nazi propaganda, with swastikas and pictures of Hitler outnumbering Olympic flags, this is also an extraordinary piece of filmmaking. Not that this excuses some of the content, as well as the lack of footage of black US sprinter Jesse Owens who won four gold medals in the track events. If you can't sit through the whole thing (it's over three-and-a-half hours long), watch the opening ceremony – Riefenstahl's camera lingers over the bodies of the athletes, creating cinematic gods out of ordinary men, and her unusual angles and cutting techniques perfectly convey the hysterical atmosphere of the Games.

ROGER AND ME 1989

Director Michael Moore

Michael Moore, journalist turned giant-killer, takes on General Motors to try and make the corporation understand what they did to the town of Flint, Michigan, when they closed their plant there and made 40,000 people redundant. As he tries to get an interview with Roger Smith, president of GM, Moore takes the audience on a tour of the devastation to people's lives in Flint, showing the boarded-up shops and the attempts to bring new industry to the area. Despite the depressing story, the film is breathtakingly funny, with priceless scenes like a discussion of Autoworld (a theme park that was built to bring tourists to Flint and where they could see a replica of what downtown looked like before all the stores closed), or Ronald Reagan eating pizza with the unemployed and forgetting to pay for it.

"ONE GOES OUT THE DOOR, ANOTHER COMES IN THE DOOR. THAT'S WHAT THIS IS ALL ABOUT"
Gene Pingatore, Hoop Dreams

SHOAH 1985

Director Claude Lanzmann

Shoah means chaos or annihilation in Hebrew, and this is an extraordinary nine-hour documentary chronicling the chaos and annihilation of the Holocaust. What is particularly fascinating, and what sets it apart from similar documentaries, is that there is no stock footage, no newsreels of the liberation of the camps or of the war. It is simply the testimony of people, mostly Germans and Poles, who worked in the camps or saw what happened. There are few interviews with survivors; to understand how such a thing could have happened, Lanzmann talks to the perpetrators, ordinary people caught up in something horrific. Interspersed with the interviews is footage of the camps today, steam trains in the Polish countryside and rolling meadows, under which Hitler's victims lie buried. An incredibly moving and, at times, shattering film.

> **"I WANT TO DO FUR PANTS, BUT IF I DO THEM, I WILL BE STONED OFF OF FIFTH AVENUE"**
> Isaac Mizrahi, Unzipped

THEREMIN: AN ELECTRONIC ODYSSEY 1993

Director Steven M Martin

Fans of 1950s sci-fi will be very familiar with the music of the Theremin, others may have heard it only as the eerie riff in the Beach Boys' *Good Vibrations*. This extraordinary instrument was invented by Leon Theremin, a Russian scientist whose life story reads like the plot of one of the more ludicrous B movies. Theremin was the toast of New York in the 1920s, conducting electronic symphonies, while he dabbled with inventing colour television and other ahead-of-their-time devices. He was then kidnapped by the KGB, imprisoned and forced to work in surveillance for 60 years. Martin chronicles his forgotten life as well as the fortunes of the instrument (the basis for the Moog synthesizer). Interviews with spaced-out rockers like Todd Rungren add to the offbeat atmosphere.

UNZIPPED 1995

Director Douglas Keeve

Hilarious look at the creation of a catwalk show, following New York designer Isaac Mizrahi as he puts together his Autumn 1994 collection. Superficial, bitchy, glamorous, Mizrahi's world is chock full of spangles and superstars, with small appearances by Kate Moss, Naomi Campbell, Sandra Bernhard, Carla Bruni and Linda Evangelista. His collection is inspired in part by *Nanook Of The North* (see page 142), Mary Tyler Moore and advice from a ouija board that suggests he go for a Hitchcock dominatrix look. Surprisingly, the resulting collection is pretty cool; equally surprisingly, Mizrahi himself comes across as having his feet somewhere not too far from the ground.

DRAMA

The Greeks didn't think they'd seen a cracking drama until incest had been committed, several cast members had died and the tragic hero had ripped his own eyes out. The movies aren't usually quite that harrowing – unless you're watching a TV movie based on a true story starring Kirstie Alley or a former Charlie's Angel.

ALFIE 1966

Director Lewis Gilbert *Cast* Michael Caine, Shelley Winters, Julia Foster, Jane Asher

Womanizing Alfie, who thinks getting tied down would be worse than death, gradually realizes that his happy-go-lucky life is not as rosy as it seems. Millicent Martin, Alfie Bass, Graham Stark and the rest of the 1960s cast round out a story filled with humour and pathos. A shocking scene for the time features Denholm Elliott as a seedy abortionist. The film was a radio play, a stage play and a novel before it reached the screen, and this is apparent in Caine's direct addresses to the audience, explaining his actions and complaining about his lot.

AMERICAN BEAUTY 1999

Director Sam Mendes *Cast* Kevin Spacey, Annette Bening, Thora Birch, Wes Bentley

"I'll be dead in a year. In a way, I'm dead already." The essence of Mendes' film debut is summed up by Spacey in the opening monologue of the movie. As Lester Burnham, Spacey is unloved by his daughter, resented by his wife and ignored at work, leading him to realize, in true mid-life crisis style, that he has wasted the past 20 years of his life. From here the crisis takes hold of his actions, developing an infatuation with his daughter's friend, buying drugs from the boy next door and working in a burger joint – basically reliving his youth. Each of the characters experience their own brand of crisis, however, with events coming to a head one stormy night. *Beauty* is a rare Hollywood success considering it focuses on the darker side of American suburbia. The direction, screenplay and every performance is top notch, and we can be thankful Mendes dropped the original succinct ending of (spoiler alert) Bentley's and Birch's arrest for Spacey's murder, for a more open finale.

> **"I DIDN'T LOSE IT. IT'S NOT LIKE, 'WHOOPS! WHERE DID MY JOB GO?' I QUIT"**
> Lester Burnham, American Beauty

THE BEGUILED 1971

Director **Don Siegel** *Cast* **Clint Eastwood, Geraldine Page, Elizabeth Hartman**

This may just be Eastwood's best film. Certainly Siegel insists that it's his. Yet it took less than $1m at the US box office. Clint's fans clearly weren't interested in seeing him suffer in this psychosexual drama set in a Southern girls' school, and the rest of the world hadn't caught on to the idea that he could act, not just grunt. One of many Clint films in which he's threatened by actual or metaphorical castration by women. Analyze that.

> **"YOU KNOW MY FEELINGS ABOUT ARMING MORONS: YOU ARM ONE, YOU'VE GOT TO ARM THEM ALL, OTHERWISE IT WOULDN'T BE GOOD SPORT"**
>
> Judge Flatt, Nobody's Fool

THE BICYCLE THIEF 1948

Director **Vittorio De Sica** *Cast* **Lamberto Maggiorani, Enzo Staiola**

Producer David O Selznick was such an admirer of De Sica's work he offered to fund this film. All the director had to do was cast Cary Grant as the father whose bicycle is stolen and spends the rest of the film, accompanied by his son, in search of this bike without which he can't do his flyposting job. De Sica turned down Selznick's kind offer. Just as well, because a few volts of star power would have destroyed the balance of a piece cast entirely with amateur actors. Maggiorani and Staiola give performances of guileless simplicity as father and son. Their only cheer is in a restaurant where they feast on wine and bread. This film is now slightly out of fashion but watch it and be astounded by its freshness. As the father says: "You live and suffer."

THE CHANT OF JIMMIE BLACKSMITH 1978

Director **Fred Schepisi** *Cast* **Tommy Lewis, Freddy Reynolds**

Schepisi's brilliant transposition of Thomas Keneally's novel follows the plight of mixed race Aborigine Jimmie (Lewis), who, though educated, honest and hardworking, is constantly mistreated by his white bosses. Marrying a white girl in the mistaken belief that it will endear him to the Caucasian population, Jimmie finds himself ostracized by both the white folk and by his own people, and wages war on his oppressors. The extreme violence may seem over-zealous but it merely mirrors the fate of Jimmie's ancestors and of the Tasmanian Aborigines who were wiped out in horrific 'emu parades'. A serious indictment of racism, it's as relevant today as it was in 1978.

Maggiorani (right) as the dad in *Bicycle Thief*, a role Cary Grant was mooted for

THE CONFORMIST 1970

Director **Bernardo Bertolucci** *Cast* **Jean-Louis Trintignant, Stefania Sandrelli**

Bertolucci's first US hit follows the lifelong quest

of a member of the Italian Fascist party to lead a normal life. Upper-class Trintignant feels closed off from the rest of the world, reviling his dope-addict mother and insane father, and feeling his molestation by the family chauffeur has cut him apart from society. Dedicated to leading an average life, complete with a mediocre wife, he agrees to become the faceless assassin of his old professor to gain full acceptance by the Fascists. An intriguing examination of one man's need to belong.

Just your typical couple: she's a neurotic wife having an affair with a real estate mogul; he works in a fast food joint, is the object of a neighbour's homosexual lust and, to be pedantic, also happens to be dead

CUTTER'S WAY 1981

Director Ivan Passer *Cast* Jeff Bridges, John Heard

Probably the best film about a one-eyed, one-legged, one-armed, alcoholic Vietnam war veteran ever made. This may also be the best example of a clutch of films which, from the late 1970s to the early 1980s, focused on the socially corrosive aftermath of the Vietnam war. Cutter (he who has one of most things he should have two of) becomes obsessed by his friend's claim that oil tycoon JJ Cord is behind the recent murder of a hitchhiker. A quirky, disjointed film about moral responsibility, the need for heroes and the arrogance of the powerful.

DELIVERANCE 1972

Director John Boorman *Cast* Jon Voight, Burt Reynolds, Ned Beatty

Before Reynolds specialized in banal comedies manufactured to feed his own race-car obsession, he emerged as a fine actor in this adaptation of American poet James Dickey's novel. He is the leader of a group of four businessmen, getting back to nature by canoeing down the perilous Chatooga river. The film quickly turns into a psychological nightmare, with the locals presenting more of a threat than nature. An impressive, if disturbing debut by Beatty is matched by Reynolds and Voight. Remarkable, really, given that they had taken on roles which Marlon Brando and Henry Fonda had turned down because of the danger involved. And, to keep production costs low, they each performed all their own stunts (including Voight's cliff-climbing scene) without being insured.

THE DEVILS 1971

Director Ken Russell *Cast* Vanessa Redgrave, Oliver Reed

In what Reed described as his best performance ever, he plays the priest of a small 17th-century French town that is needed by Cardinal Richelieu and King Louis XIII if they are to exert complete control over the country. They therefore plot to destroy him through a devil-possessed nunnery and a sexually rampant hunchback nun (Redgrave). Russell's flamboyant style sits perfectly with the hallucinatory material, based on Aldous Huxley's novel *The Devils Of Loudon*. One of the most censored films ever, it was banned in Italy with Reed and Redgrave threatened with imprisonment if they ever set foot there. Look out for *Mother Joan Of The Angels* (1961), the Polish film inspired by the same subject.

THE EFFECT OF GAMMA RAYS ON MAN-IN-THE-MOON MARIGOLDS 1972

Director **Paul Newman** *Cast* **Joanne Woodward, Nell Potts**

Adapted from the Pulitzer-Prize-winning novel by Paul Zindel, *Marigolds* is a Tennessee-Williams-style drama focusing on the lives of an eccentric mum and her chalk-and-cheese daughters. Woodward is fantastic as mother Beatrice (she scooped the best actress award at Cannes), a middle-aged widow struggling to cope with modern life and looking for a solution in the classified ads. But it's Potts (Woodward and Newman's real-life daughter in her only screen performance) who steals the film as Matilda, the introverted daughter who focuses her life on her schoolwork and her animals. With skilful direction, Newman avoids turning this into an over-sentimentalized chick flick. Just.

FIGHT CLUB 1999

Director **David Fincher** *Cast* **Edward Norton, Brad Pitt, Helena Bonham Carter**

Fight Club is one of those films where you think you know what's going on until the very last reel and you realize you were completely off the mark. In a story adapted from Chuck Palahniuk's novel (Fincher gave the film a completely different ending, which Palahniuk preferred to his own), Norton is a bored, repressed, white-collar salesman whose meeting with Pitt and Carter – and the blowing-up of his apartment with all his possessions – changes his life. From here on we are in fight-club territory with the two men, and eventually a whole band of repressed males, getting their kicks from beating one another up. Stylishly directed by Fincher, *Fight Club* is a mesmerizing ride through contemporary culture fuelled by the performances of Pitt, Norton, Carter and a fantastic turn by Meatloaf.

FIVE EASY PIECES 1970

Director **Bob Rafelson** *Cast* **Jack Nicholson, Karen Black**

The second of six films that saw maverick director Rafelson teaming up with the equally off-the-wall Nicholson. Playing a man on the run – not from the law but from himself – Nicholson works as an oilrig labourer, lives with a Tammy-Wynette-obsessed waitress (Black), and generally lives so mundane an existence you know there must be a secret. But it's not until he suddenly jumps into the back of a truck during a traffic jam and begins to play the piano, that we realize that he stems from a wealthy family of musicians, a family he has chosen to escape. When he hears his dad has had a stroke, he decides to revisit

Nicholson excels in *Five Easy Pieces* as the pianist on the run from a family who will keep asking him to play *Chopsticks*

his family and we see two very different worlds collide. *Five Easy Pieces* was a landmark film of the 1970s, the epitome of a new kind of cinema, but it is the performances (by Nicholson and by Black, Susan Anspach and Lois Smith) which make this a must-see. One of the most influential films of its decade.

THE GRIFTERS 1990
Director Stephen Frears *Cast* Anjelica Huston, John Cusack, Annette Bening

While most cinema-goers were getting their crime kicks watching *Goodfellas*, they were missing out on one of the coolest films of the 1990s. Unlike most crime dramas where women play second fiddle to men, here Huston and Bening are given the show as two con women. Huston works the racetrack for the mob, while Bening uses her allure as a decoy for big-time operators. Both are leagues ahead of the nickel-and-dime grifters (con men) like Huston's son (Cusack). He is the pawn, the bone of contention between mother and girlfriend. Based on a 1950s novel by Jim Thompson, this colourful 1990s film noir with Huston a class act as a woman in control. The opening narration is by Martin Scorsese, producer of the film.

> "WE WERE SELLING RICH WOMEN THEIR OWN FAT ASSES BACK TO THEM"
> Narrator, Fight Club

THE INFORMER 1935
Director John Ford *Cast* Victor McLaglen, Heather Angel

McLaglen won an Oscar for this, although Ford ungraciously insisted that it was only because he got him drunk the night before a vital trial scene so the actor would seem properly disordered. This is not to be taken as gospel: Ford liked disparaging his actors, even John Wayne. McLaglen, hungover or not, is impressive as the IRA informer consumed by guilt. The film is a tad pretentious but still worth seeing.

INSOMNIA 1997

Director Erik Skjoldbjaerg *Cast* Stellan Skarsgard, Sverre Anker Ousdal

Now being remade by Christopher Nolan (*Memento*) with Al Pacino in the starring role, this original is a very recent and very strong debut from Norwegian director Skjoldbjaerg. *Insomnia* is an enticing psychological study of how people perceive themselves in society. Skarsgard is a cop who, on the trail of a killer, accidentally shoots his partner rather than the murderer. This is more of a character study than a police procedural, with Skarsgard (who first received international acclaim in *Breaking The Waves*) as the anguished cop for whom the real killer becomes nothing more than a shadow of his own torment.

> "THE ONLY PERFORMANCE THAT MAKES IT ALL THE WAY IS THE ONE THAT ACHIEVES MADNESS. AM I RIGHT?"
>
> Turner, Performance

LAST YEAR AT MARIENBAD 1961

Director Alain Resnais *Cast* Delphine Seyrig, Giorgio Albertazzi

If you're an impatient audience member, or have been brought up on movies where the answers always appear, this is not the movie for you. Nothing is certain and nothing is resolved in this tale of three people staying at a luxury hotel – a beautiful young woman (A), a stranger/previous lover (X) and a friend/husband/ authority figure (M). X claims to have had an affair with A the previous year at Marienbad – or did, but was it there, and was it then? A claims she can't remember, but is this true? The film is one huge question, annoying at times, but stick with it.

THE LOCKET 1946

Director John Brahm *Cast* Laraine Day, Brian Aherne, Robert Mitchum

Brahm's follow-up to *Hangover Square* offers a twist to the classic film noir. Day is the femme fatale of the film, set to marry until her ex-husband, Aherne, turns up and spins her fiancée a picture of her as a kleptomaniac and habitual liar. The story is told using the now famed flashback within a flashback within a flashback, but Brahm keeps a tight hold on the action, his stylistic talents never losing sight of the plot and the finale.

NOBODY'S FOOL 1994

Director Robert Benton *Cast* Paul Newman, Jessica Tandy, Bruce Willis, Melanie Griffith

In Don 'Sully' Sullivan, Newman created one of his least known but indelible cinematic characters – sharp-witted, laid back and a lovable sixty-something rogue. Nothing really major happens in Benton's adaptation of Richard Russo's novel but the performances of Newman – and indeed the entire cast, including Willis and Griffith – hold the audience's attention so much that there is a rare sense of regret when it ends. Simply the tale of one man and the changes forced upon him. Simple, yet enchanting.

PERFORMANCE 1970
Directors Donald Cammell, Nicolas Roeg
Cast James Fox, Mick Jagger

Fox is a violent gangster who relishes his work to the degree that he kills blindly and must go into hiding to escape those seeking retribution. Hiding out in Notting Hill, his landlord is Jagger, an ageing rock star (how true to life!) and a recluse, troubled by the loss of his creative powers. Jagger begins to see Fox as the source of rekindling his creativity, tormenting him with drug-induced mind games. Off-set Jagger and Cammell were said to be attempting the same effect in real life on Fox, deconstructing his ego to the point where he did indeed withdraw from society and acting for much of the 1970s. The film was in fact shot in essentially two separate parts, one side gangster film, the other very much sex, drugs and rock'n'roll, with the actors knowing only their half of the story.

PIXOTE 1981
Director Hector Babenco
Cast Fernando Ramos Da Silva, Jorge Juliao

Prior to his international hit, *Kiss Of The Spiderwoman*, director Babenco tackled the more disturbing topic of kids surviving poverty in the Third World. Here, Da Silva gives a haunting performance as a 10-year-old street kid who, having escaped from a brutal reform school, takes to a life of prostitution, drug-dealing and murder. Graphic and realistic, *Pixote* is hard to watch, partly because of the disturbing

TENNESSEE WILLIAMS

Sometimes, films and people can mark a turning point in a genre. In drama the plays of Tennessee Williams are a good example. In the 1950s, Williams' plays, with their psychoanalytical undertones, were a ripe new source of material for a Hollywood in thrall to Method-ism. The best include:

BABY DOLL 1956
Williams' least ambitious play, but probably the most impressive film interpretation. Minus blockbuster names, Karl Malden and Eli Wallach fight it out over Malden's nymphet wife (Carroll Baker). Unlikely to appear controversial today, this was pulled from cinemas and branded as immoral.

CAT ON A HOT TIN ROOF 1958
Not one of Williams' favourites: he told a queue of moviegoers: "This movie will set the industry back 50 years. Go home." But it has all the Tennessee trappings: star Paul Newman, southern setting and the usual themes (greed, lust, frustration and impotence). But the homosexual sub-plot fell foul of studio and censors.

NIGHT OF THE IGUANA 1964
Elizabeth Taylor had starred in two Tennessee flicks, now it was Richard Burton's turn with Liz on set to keep an eye on co-stars Ava Gardner and Sue Lyon. Playing a defrocked priest would become Burton's default mode.

A STREETCAR NAMED DESIRE 1951
Marlon Brando is the physical incarnation of brutal Stanley Kowalski, the tormentor of his sister-in-law Blanche (Vivien Leigh). Criticized for casting an unstable actress as an unstable Southern belle, this is still one of the best Williams screen adaptations.

Newman lights up *Nobody's Fool*, a fine film which failed to light up the box office

performances, and Babenco's direction, which never lapses into sentimentality. Da Silva was shot in his house by Brazilian police when he was just 19, a tragic event which makes the film's point.

QUEEN CHRISTINA 1933

Director Rouben Mamoulian
Cast Greta Garbo, John Gilbert

To MGM's Swedish historical adviser, a cross little chap called Colonel Einhornung, this picture was "a gross insult to Swedish history and royalty and Swedish womankind". The rest of the world remembers two scenes in particular. First and foremost there's the end, where Christina (Garbo) gazes vacantly at the viewer as her ship sails her into royal exile (to make sure her expression was correct, Mamoulian told her: "Think of nothing"). And then there's the scene where she moves around the room touching objects that remind her of her lover – a triumph. The story of the cross-dressing 17th-century Queen of Sweden who abandoned her throne and country when she was just 28, fits Garbo's own retirement so perfectly that you can't help but suspect that this is where she got the idea from.

THE SERVANT 1963

Director Joseph Losey *Cast* Dirk Bogarde, James Fox, Sarah Miles

In this early screenplay by Harold Pinter, Fox is a rich young gentleman who has recently acquired a townhouse and a man-servant, Bogarde. Fox's girlfriend warns him about Bogarde's character, but it's the experienced valet who assumes control, bringing in his own fiancée (pretending to be his sister) to seduce Fox to get rid of the girlfriend. A series of mind games and a battle of wills ensues, with Fox becoming enslaved to his own servant. Bogarde is suitably menacing, while Fox, in only his second film, is perfect as the prissy upper-class toff.

SUDDENLY LAST SUMMER 1959

Director Joseph L Mankiewicz *Cast* Elizabeth Taylor, Katharine Hepburn, Montgomery Clift

This is scary in a way many horror films aren't because the sense of evil springs from the characters. A homosexual youth (Clift) uses the beauty of his sister (Taylor) to lure boys to a beach but ends up devoured by them. Hepburn, a New Orleans grand dame of the 1930s, is chilling as the mother who wants Taylor to have a lobotomy to hide her son's shame. Tennessee

Williams, who wrote the play, had objected to Taylor's casting but changed his mind after seeing her give her character's speech where her mind clears. After five takes, Taylor was sobbing in the dressing room and the director told the crew they would make a fresh start tomorrow. "Fresh start my ass," said Taylor and got the whole agonizing speech in one take.

THE SUM OF US 1994
Directors **Kevin Dowling, Geoff Burton** *Cast* **Russell Crowe, Jack Thompson**

While Hollywood was congratulating itself for the mainstream success of the gay-sympathetic *Philadelphia*, first-time directors Dowling and Burton had already gone several steps further in portraying homosexual characters in a realistic, non-sensationalist way. Their big-screen adaptation of David Stevens' off-Broadway smash is a gay-themed, father-and-son story that has the distinction of being accessible to both your average modern-day family and the non-straight community. Crowe is superb as the macho-gay son looking for love, and Thompson is at his career best as his ultra-liberal widowed dad, Harry, whose open-minded attitude destroys both their budding romances and leads to tragedy. The transition from hilarious to heart-wrenching and back again is seamless with clever camera-asides enhancing the comedy value. But it's Stevens' stunning script and the palpable chemistry between the two leads that makes this underseen movie so memorable.

> **"DIDN'T YOU NOTICE THE POWERFUL AND OBNOXIOUS ODOUR OF MENDACITY IN THIS ROOM?"**
> Big Daddy, Cat On A Hot Tin Roof

MARLON VS MERYL

If you're looking to become one of the few distinguished luminaries residing in Hollywood, or at least stand a greater chance of filling that display cabinet you bought to house 13½-inch gold-plated naked men, you need to do one of two things. You can either specialize in playing disabled characters, (Hoffman as autistic, Pacino as a blind colonel) or you could pull a Streep and tour the accents of the world. Not even Marlon Brando can beat Meryl when it comes to getting his tongue around those vowels, and he doesn't always get it quite right.

MARLON
English – *Mutiny On The Bounty, Raoni, Queimada!* (aka *Burn!*)

French/Nebraskan – *Desiree*
German – *Morituri, The Young Lions*
Italian-American – *The Godfather, The Freshman*
Mexican – *Viva Zapata*
Shakespearean/Nebraskan – *Julius Caesar*
Spanish – *Christopher Columbus: The Discovery*

MERYL
Australian – *Cry In The Dark*
English – *French Lieutenant's Woman, Plenty*
Irish – *Dancing In Lughnasa*
Italian – *Bridges Of Madison County*
Polish – *Sophie's Choice*
South African – *Out Of Africa*
South American – *The House Of Spirits*

SUNRISE 1927

Director FW Murnau *Cast* George O'Brien, Janet Gaynor

Nothing to do with the Rolf Harris song, this silent masterpiece from German director Murnau was released days before the first talkie film (*The Jazz Singer*) and was overshadowed by the emergence of a new era in film. It did, however, amass critical acclaim, just missing out in the first-ever Academy Awards for Best Picture (*Wings* won it), but scooping Best Unique & Artistic Picture (an award which was scrapped the following year). A farmer falls for a city girl's wiles and plots to murder his wife, but when he tries to kill her realizes how much in fact he loves her. Poignant and enticing, this is often cited as the greatest silent film ever. The moving camera influenced such later works as Ford's *The Informer* and Welles' *Kane*. This was an expensive flop but the light is astonishing and the temptation of the sinful city is brilliantly evoked.

> "YOU KNOW, THE WORST AIN'T SO BAD WHEN IT FINALLY HAPPENS. NOT HALF AS BAD AS YOU FIGURE IT'LL BE BEFORE IT'S HAPPENED"
> Bob Curtin, Treasure Of The Sierra Madre

THREE COLOURS: BLUE 1993

Director Krzysztof Kieslowski *Cast* Juliette Binoche, Benoit Regent

This was the first instalment of Polish director Kieslowski's contemporary trilogy based on the colours of the French national flag (blue symbolizing liberty, white for equality and red for fraternity). Binoche plays a young woman whose husband, a famous composer, and daughter die in a car crash at the start of the film. The theme of liberty manifests itself in how Binoche chooses to rebuild her life. We see her cutting her ties with her previous existence, moving to the heart of Paris and living her life as an anonymous entity. She finds, however, that she cannot escape from either her previous life or the memories of her husband, whose music constantly plays in her head. Binoche is excellent in what is essentially a one-woman vehicle – quiet yet emotionally charged. This and the subsequent *Red* and *White* parts are now seen as Kieslowski's best works and examples of his great skill and genius.

THE TREASURE OF THE SIERRA MADRE 1948

Director John Huston *Cast* Humphrey Bogart, Walter Huston, Tim Holt

This was a box-office flop when it was first released – the public wanted the reluctant-hero Bogart of *Casablanca*, not the repugnant, mumbling gold-prospector found here. Today, however, both critics and audiences regard *Sierra Madre* as Bogie's finest performance, and he receives sterling support from Huston as the old prospector who knows the damage that lust for gold can do to a man, and Holt as the straightforward, if naïve, young thing. The mismatched group find gold and in turn lose it, with Bogart's Fred C Dobbs losing both his mind and his life in the process. The film is let down somewhat when it becomes obvious that the location shots are studio-based, although this does add to the oppressive feeling of the film. *Sierra Madre* won awards for both John and Walter Huston, who became the first father-and-son winning team.

WALKABOUT 1971
Director Nicolas Roeg *Cast* Jenny Agutter, Lucien John, David Gumpilil

Made in the days when people shot real films, as opposed to blockbusters, Roeg's masterpiece is still as jaw-dropping as it must have been in the 1970s. Part travelogue, part coming-of-age fable, it's also an examination of what happens when modern society collides with nature – played out through the tale of two schoolkids stranded in the Outback who meet an aboriginal man-child on 'walkabout'. As brother and sister roam through the bush, their enigmatic guide leads them not only to 'civilisation' but also to self-realisation, although Agutter's plummy 14-year-old won't admit this. To help create an eerie, otherworldly feel, Roeg preferred clever cinematic techniques over dialogue, intercutting freeze-frame and zoom shots of beady-eyed lizards and slithering scorpions. The result is often terrifying as well as visually stunning. The ideal that respect for nature can free us from the evils of the modern world seems so seventies man, but this is still a beautiful, erotic and mesmerizing movie.

The image which launched the marketing for *Suddenly Last Summer* somehow didn't help convince moviegoers that Taylor's character was an innocent abroad

A WOMAN UNDER THE INFLUENCE 1974
Director John Cassavetes *Cast* Peter Falk, Gena Rowlands

Between his stints as the popular detective Columbo, Falk made several notable films with his friend John Cassavetes. *A Woman Under The Influence* is their finest collaboration. Falk is a construction worker trying to cope with his mentally unstable wife (Rowlands) and three children, while ignoring his own bizarre behaviour. He comes to believe he must have Rowlands committed but the family, despite her previous unruly behaviour, are left bereft by her exit. It's moving stuff, even if Rowlands' performance is OTT at times. America's Library of Congress lists this as a national treasure: they're right.

Before 1960, very few films were made about or even referred to drugs. In the notorious 1927 Hays Code, filmmakers are warned not to show "the illegal traffic in drugs" and to be wary if showing the use of drugs. Since the 1960s, drug-taking on film has become far more visible, with several movies made about little else. Moviemakers wishing to be taken seriously are always drawn to illegal activities, so if cannabis gets legalized, it may cease to appear on a big screen near you. Whatever your drug of choice, you can always find a film to match it. Or you could just say no.

DRUGSTORE COWBOY 1989

Director Gus Van Sant *Cast* Matt Dillon, Kelly Lynch

In far and away the best performance of his career, Dillon plays a pharmacy-robbing dope fiend who leads his band of junkie highwaymen around the Pacific Northwest, returning home only to shoot up the spoils of their crimes. Peppered with black humour and some lovingly filmed sequences of the paraphernalia and rituals of drug-taking, this is not one for needle-phobes. Van Sant simply shows the junkie lifestyle the way it probably is – depressing and bleak with a few good times thrown in – and leaves the audience to make their own moral judgment about these characters. The story is based on the autobiographical novel by James Fogle who, at the time of the film's release, had spent an impressive (if that's the right word) 35 of his 53 years in prison on drugs-related charges.

EASY RIDER 1969

Director Dennis Hopper *Cast* Peter Fonda, Dennis Hopper, Jack Nicholson

Probably the most famous stoner movie of all time – even the rock soundtrack is awash with references to joints and getting high. Two bikers ride through the American West in search of freedom, meeting a raft of oddball characters along the way and finding little to celebrate in the American Dream. Drugs feature throughout, with an inspired acid trip scene which also features Toni Basil, later a perky pop one-hit wonder with

Mickey. The cinematography is absolutely stunning and the performances are superb, and even if the film feels a little dated now, it is still well worth seeing and trying to appreciate just how radical it was in its time.

GO 1999

Director Doug Liman *Cast* Sarah Polley, Katie Holmes, Scott Wolf, Jay Mohr

A drugs deal told from three different points of view is the basis for this hectic, convoluted and (in parts) screamingly funny saga of a girl who reckons that selling drugs might just solve her rent problems and duly kicks off a chain of extraordinary events on Christmas Eve in Los Angeles. The Las Vegas sequences turn out slightly dull in comparison, but the sequence of two gay soap stars helping the police after they have been caught with drugs is a blast, as is the scene where a very stoned and paranoid customer is convinced the drug dealer's cat is talking to him. The film has been unfairly compared to *Pulp Fiction*, due to the overlapping stories, but it's a very different kind of movie, far less stylized and telling stories about believable characters in bizarre situations.

HUMAN TRAFFIC 1999

Director Justin Kerrigan *Cast* John Simm, Lorraine Pilkington

Jip thinks he's impotent, Lulu thinks men are rubbish, Koop thinks Nina is cheating on him and so on. Five friends sort out their lives through a haze of Ecstasy over one weekend on the Cardiff club scene. It's slightly disappointing, with not much of a plot leading up to a conveniently neat ending, but it's notable for the accuracy of the club scenes, full of shiny happy people dancing like loons, looking like idiots and loving it.

THE MAN WITH THE GOLDEN ARM 1955

Director Otto Preminger *Cast* Frank Sinatra, Eleanor Parker

Shocking in its time, the film tells the story of Frankie Machine, a heroin addict returning from prison to find himself locked into a loveless marriage with a crippled wife, unable to leave her for his understanding lover, Kim Novak. Parts of the film have dated now, but Preminger's noirish photography and Sinatra's performance (an absolute revelation if you've only ever seen him in musicals) make it worth seeing, if for no other reason than to get a glimpse of real American life in the 1950s that's about something well beyond Doris Day and apple pie. Jazz fans will love the Elmer Bernstein soundtrack. Samples from Sinatra's dialogue were used in the US indie band Ministry's single *Just One Fix*.

> "THEY TALK TO YA ABOUT INDIVIDUAL FREEDOM. BUT THEY SEE A FREE INDIVIDUAL, IT'S GONNA SCARE 'EM"
>
> George Hanson, Easy Rider

MARIHUANA 1935

Director **Dwain Esper** *Cast* **Harley Wood, Gloria Browne**

The fact that this is also known as *Marihuana, The Weed With Roots In Hell*, will give you an idea of the film's attitude to an illicit spliff. A reporter goes undercover to investigate a dope ring when a bunch of teenagers become addicted to marijuana after just a single toke. As a direct result, an innocent summer becomes awash with drowning, alcoholism, heroin addiction, kidnapping, pregnancy and death. But of course! Gloriously inept performances and terrible direction make this a classic among B movies, although the tag line: "Weird orgies! Wild parties! Unleashed passions!" hints that Esper (who had made a film about an addicted doctor called *Narcotic* in 1933) may have been considerably more interested in exploitation than social responsibility. For more along the same lines, see *Reefer Madness* (1936) in which a high-school principal warns students' parents about a couple called Mae and Jack who entice good kids to their apartment and turn them into reefer addicts leading, in one case, to life in a mental hospital. Incredibly, this film is on DVD in a trilogy with the equally astoundingly bad *Cocaine Fiends* and *Sex Madness*.

NAKED LUNCH 1991

Director **David Cronenberg** *Cast* **Peter Weller, Judy Davis**

Cronenberg's fantasy masterpiece interweaves various parts of writer William S Burroughs' bizarre novel with episodes

from his real-life experiences. Bill Lee (Weller) accidentally shoots his own wife and is embroiled in dodgy dealing in a shadowy port called Interzone. Then his typewriter morphs into a giant cockroach. Viewers who are unfamiliar with Burroughs' work are quite likely to feel utterly lost in this film, and even reading the original novel is unlikely to throw a great deal of light on the subject. Best just to accept the film as a discussion about drug-induced creativity and destruction, rather than a coherent story of a man's life. Be warned though – while watching this, you may start to suspect that someone has slipped something in your popcorn.

"I've got enough money in my hand to keep us in lighter fuel, alcohol and drugs for at least an hour"

PULP FICTION 1994

Director **Quentin Tarantino** *Cast* **John Travolta, Uma Thurman, Bruce Willis, Samuel L Jackson**

Lashings of sharp dialogue, offbeat characters and horrific violence punctuate four intertwining stories about small-time thieves, drug-dealers and hitmen, spread over the few days surrounding a supposedly fixed boxing match. But it's the drug-taking scenes that stick in the mind most. A fetishistic sequence of John Travolta shooting up heroin is closely followed by Uma Thurman's spectacular overdose and her subsequent recovery thanks to a dealer (Eric Stoltz) with a syringe of adrenaline. Many directors have since tried to copy the black humour but have only succeeded in making gross films. If you're a real buff, repeated viewings will reveal that the famously film-literate Tarantino has included a tribute to Howard Hawks, plus character names and snippets of dialogue from *Saturday Night Fever*, *On The Waterfront*, *Psycho* and *Charley Varrick*.

> **"WHY DO WE FEEL IT'S NECESSARY TO YAK ABOUT BULLSHIT IN ORDER TO BECOME COMFORTABLE?"**
> Mia, Pulp Fiction

TRAFFIC 2000

Director **Steven Soderbergh** *Cast* **Michael Douglas, Catherine Zeta-Jones, Benicio Del Toro**

A conservative politician with a heroin-addict daughter spearheads an anti-drugs campaign; a wife tries to help her dealer husband's business; DEA agents protect a witness against the dealer, and a corrupt Mexican cop fights with his conscience. This gung-ho, war-on-drugs film gets a stylish twist from Soderbergh's clever direction and the use of different film stocks and colourizing techniques. Douglas (in a part written for Harrison Ford) and Zeta-Jones are surprisingly good, but Del Toro steals every scene, well deserving his Oscar.

TRAINSPOTTING 1996

Director **Danny Boyle** *Cast* **Ewan McGregor, Johnny Lee Miller, Robert Carlyle**

Fresh from their success with *Shallow Grave*, the same team turned its attention to Irvine Welsh's drug-crazed novel about addicts in Edinburgh and did a pretty terrific job. John Hodge's script is shocking, funny, terrifying and heartbreaking, creating the junkie's junkie movie where even the minor characters light up the screen. Ewan Bremner as the hopelessly stupid Spud gets most of the funniest moments, while Carlyle's psychopath Begbie is responsible for a number of moments of terror. For a film with such horrifying and explicit scenes of taking drugs and going cold turkey, it has a surprisingly upbeat ending – although you may not come away feeling that taking heroin is the wisest lifestyle choice you could make.

UP IN SMOKE 1978

Director **Lou Adler** *Cast Cheech Marin, Tommy Chong*

The first and best of Cheech and Chong's good-natured movies about their eternal quest for the best grass. Here they head across to Mexico, where they agree to drive a highly suspect van back to the US. That's about it really: just a long, hilarious road movie about meeting weirdos and getting high, with cameos from Stacy Keach and Tom Skerritt and inspired silliness that will get you laughing as if you'd indulged in one of the boy's monster joints – "mostly Maui wowie but also part Labrador".

WITHNAIL AND I 1987

Director **Bruce Robinson** *Cast Richard E Grant, Paul McGann*

Although accurate, to describe *Withnail And I* as a story about two 1960s unemployed actors who share a disastrous holiday in the country, does nothing to convey the achingly brilliant performances, script and direction of one of the funniest British movies of all time. It was not a huge success when it first came out, but has since been re-evaluated, partly due to the inspired supporting role of Uncle Monty, played with treacherous pathos by Richard Griffiths. It would be hard to pinpoint which substance comes in for the most abuse (alcohol and lighter fluid feature, among others) but it's the scene with Danny the drug-dealer (Ralph Brown), rolling his multi-Rizla super-spliff, The Camberwell Carrot, that most people remember.

IT'S A WRAP!

PERSONAL BEST 1982

By the time he got around to directing this dull tale of lesbian athletes training for the Olympics, Robert Towne (best known for his outstanding script for *Chinatown*) had something of a cocaine habit. His editor on the film described him as "ol' write-a-line, snort-a-line Robert Towne" and complained that the budget on the film had more than doubled because Towne spent most days in the steam room snorting coke with Mariel Hemingway.

DAYS OF THUNDER 1990

Don Simpson's movies were party central with drugs freely available in the producer's office. No doubt squeaky-clean Tom Cruise abstained, but the rest of the cast and crew just got on with the fun. As director Tony Scott put it: "There was a wrap every Friday." A few years later, Simpson's doctor was found dead from an overdose. A year after that, Simpson died "from natural causes".

SWEET SMELL OF SUCCESS 1957

After problems with the screenplay, Burt Lancaster's production company eventually hired left-wing playwright Clifford Odets. Odets wrote the whole script on Benzedrine, delivering the pages on the morning of shooting by shoving them under his hotel room door.

RETURN OF THE JEDI 1983

By this time the life of a Hollywood princess, let alone an intergalactic one, had got to Carrie Fisher. She was addicted to Percadin and floated through the film hardly noticing what was going on. But she kicked the habit, as detailed in her autobiographical novel *Postcards From The Edge*.

DUBBED

Movies get dubbed for all sorts of reasons. Because the leading players in your musical can't sing (*West Side Story*), because the Americans won't understand your accents (*The Full Monty*, *Gregory's Girl*) or just to enable another country to enjoy the subtle interplay of your characters. That's the intention anyway. But dubbed movies often come with the kind of time delay you used to get on transatlantic telephone calls. Not that subtitled films are necessarily any better: as anyone who has watched a subtitled Bollywood film knows, subtitling will often reduce dialogue to a horrible pidgin language – Esperanto for morons.

BAREFOOT IN THE PARK 1967

Director Gene Saks *Cast* Robert Redford, Jane Fonda, Charles Boyer, Mildred Natwick

This wafer-thin Neil Simon comedy, enjoyably underplayed by Redford (if not always by Fonda), seems just good clean fun. Why then was the dialogue changed in France? Because the newlyweds' apartment, whose fifth-floor location is the subject of a long-running gag, wasn't high enough for the French. Their country is, after all, positively littered with old multi-storey houses without elevators, so five flights of stairs didn't seem especially arduous. So the apartment was moved four floors higher, to the ninth floor, so the French could enjoy the joke. Thankfully they didn't redub the movie's best line. When Fonda says she's going to get a dog to guard her and take for a walk, Redford sneers: "A dog? That's a laugh. One look at those stairs and he'll go straight for her throat."

> **"I TRIED TO KILL MYSELF TODAY. I TOOK A MOUTHFUL OF CORNFLAKES AND MILK AND HELD MY MOUTH SHUT"**
> Ronnie, That Sinking Feeling

CHARADE 1963

Director Stanley Donen *Cast* Cary Grant, Audrey Hepburn

JFK's assassination on 22 November 1963 was such an unprecedented event that it sent Hollywood into a moral panic. Eager to ensure that all releases were in the best possible taste, the studios scanned scripts for anything which might offend a grieving nation. In this pleasant comedy-thriller, Hepburn says at one point: "We could be assassinated." Sure enough, when the film was released, "assassinated" had become "eliminated". A similar sensitivity affected *Dr Strangelove* where, when discussing a survival kit, a character said: "You can have a pretty good weekend in Dallas with that stuff." "Vegas" had been overdubbed for "Dallas" by the time the film reached the cinemas.

THE DAM BUSTERS 1954

Director Michael Anderson *Cast* Michael Redgrave, Ursula Jeans, Richard Todd

Afraid that this British bouncing-bomb movie would bomb at the US box office, the studio spiced up the film by inserting more battle scenes. Warner Bros soon had to pull most of them when they realized they had used the wrong planes (Flying Fortresses, whereas the RAF used Lancasters). Todd played the bouncemeister Guy Gibson but his dog gave Warners another problem – it was called "Nigger". This was hastily redubbed as "Trigger" for the US, although the Morse code in the ops room still spelt out the original name. This typically British tale had another unavoidable inaccuracy: the bombs that bounced were actually the wrong shape; even as late as 1954 the shape of the real bombs was still an official secret.

"His name's Martin Guerre – guerre as in French for war... and he's back from the war, bit of a giveaway if you ask me"

MOGAMBO 1953

Director John Ford
Cast Clark Gable, Ava Gardner, Grace Kelly

If this film proved anything (apart from the fact that, as a fiftysomething, Gable was now far too old to wear shorts and hope to still be considered a sex symbol) it was that the Spanish censors had some strange ideas when it came to morality. Gable's adulterous affair with Kelly's character was more than the censors could stand so they changed the dialogue in the dubbed version, so that they weren't committing adultery – but incest instead.

THE RETURN OF MARTIN GUERRE 1982

Director Daniel Vigne *Cast* Gérard Depardieu, Nathalie Baye, Bernard-Pierre Donnadieu, Roger Planchon

This is the original from which sprang *Sommersby* (starring Richard Gere and Jodie Foster). Outside France, the audience's enjoyment of this mystery of identity in 16th-century France was marred by a dubbing exercise which was to the art of dubbing what Paul McCartney is to modern poetry. Thankfully the subtitled version has now been released.

TO HAVE AND HAVE NOT 1944

Director Howard Hawks *Cast* Humphrey Bogart, Lauren Bacall

This film owes its existence to a bet. Ernest Hemingway bet Hawks that he couldn't make a film out of his worst piece of work, this very short story. Hawks proved him wrong and discovered Bacall in the process. He persuaded her to change her voice but then wished he hadn't. He wanted to dub her singing, but her voice was so low that no female singer sounded convincing. Eventually Hawks asked Andy Williams to sing her parts. Opinion differs as to which voice Hawks used in the final version: Bacall's or Williams'. Dubbing singing parts was par for the course at the time: in *West Side Story* the voices of Tony, Maria and Rita were all dubbed.

> ## "I'M HARD TO GET, STEVE. ALL YOU HAVE TO DO IS ASK ME"
> Marie Browning, To Have And Have Not

YOSEI GORASU 1962

Director Ishiro Honda *Cast* Akira Kubo, Tatsuro Tamba

Well before *Armageddon*, the idea of a meteor wiping out the human race had already had a deep impact on the Japanese, possibly because of what had fallen out of the sky on them in 1945. This film has a unique (and scientifically credible) twist: because the giant lump of rock is 6,000 times the size of Earth, the scientists decide it'd be easier to move our planet out of the meteor's path. In the original, Antarctica is subject to a giant walrus attack but in the American dubbed version you merely see the rocket ship firing at the ground. Academics and serious students of film are still debating whether, as the ship flies away, you can see the bloodied walrus corpse on the ground. The real mystery, though, is why whoever was dubbing this decided that while they were doing that, they'd just excise a walrus. What, one wonders, had walruses ever done to them?

PARDON?

The following have all had their voices dubbed because it was suspected Americans would not understand them.

MEL GIBSON (in *Mad Max*)
PAUL LUKAS (in *The Wolf Of Wall Street*)
THE CAST OF GREGORY'S GIRL
THE CAST OF THAT SINKING FEELING
THE CAST OF TRAINSPOTTING (some of the dialogue was also rewritten to include Americanisms)

German actor Emil Janning was about to be dubbed out of *The Patriot* (1928) until he took legal action. Rupert Everett suffered in reverse – director Francesco Rosi was so stunned by his attempt at a Latin accent in *Cronaca Di Una Morte Annunciata* that he had his voice dubbed out of the film.

Palace/Marcel Dassault/SFP

EPICS

Epic movies normally contain one or more of the following: blood, sand, sandals, ancient costumes, ambitious set pieces, and a belief (not always shared by the audience) that a moral lesson is being imparted. Today, directors lack the divine certainty of a Cecil B. DeMille and the epic has been reinvented as *Lethal Weapon* in period costume, bigger spectacles and with better special effects.

As Victor Mature liked to tell friends, "I can't act and I've got 64 pictures to prove it"

BEN-HUR 1959
Director William Wyler *Cast* Charlton Heston, Jack Hawkins, Stephen Boyd

"I swore I would never do another epic period picture again. Then I read a script. The leading role was perfect for me – Ben-Hur!" You can imagine Kirk Douglas' disappointment when Wyler told him he wanted him as the baddie, Messala. Douglas said he wasn't interested in playing a "one-note baddie" and Boyd got the job, turning Messala into a two-note baddie in a film that saved MGM from bankruptcy. But apart from the chariot race, was this tale of a Jewish prince who is enslaved and challenges his old enemy really good enough to win 11 Oscars? Revisionists suggest that at 212 minutes it sags somewhat, that the music grates after a while and the story doesn't always make sense. But if it isn't great art, it is (mostly) great fun. Gore Vidal, who contributed to the script, famously suggested a previous homosexual relationship between Messala and Ben-Hur. Wyler thought this a good idea but told Vidal to mention it only to Boyd and not to Heston because Chuck would never agree to play his character that way. One reason the chariot race was so great was Wyler shot 263ft of film for every foot he kept in. Enjoy.

BRAVEHEART 1995
Director Mel Gibson *Cast* Mel Gibson, Sophie Marceau, Patrick McGoohan

This stirring biopic of William Wallace would be in the historical section if there was more than a trace of historical accuracy in it. To avoid endless debates about its factual errors, it's best just to call it an epic and admit the fact that it stirs the blood, even if you're English. The battle scenes are well shot – thousands of men, horses and equipment marshalled to vivid effect. And don't let the 13th-century setting fool you: this is Mel as the all-action hero set very firmly in the mould of Mad Max, albeit with a few more (anachronistic) speeches about freedom.

IL COLOSSO DI RHODI 1961
Director **Sergio Leone** *Cast* **Rory Calhoun, Lea Massari, Georges Marchal**

Leone started shooting this film without a script and decided it would be fun to treat this epic ironically – without telling the studio. But he soon became absorbed in the (for their day) grisly and realistic torture scenes – one reason this film was such a box office hit. In his toga, Calhoun looks as if he's perpetually wondering when he can put his trousers back on, but Leone gives this story of a slave revolt in ancient Rhodes enough touches of brilliance to make you forget the script. This film finally convinced him he didn't want to film any more 'peplum', the word French critics used to describe these ancient adventure films.

THE CONQUEROR 1956
Director **Dick Powell** *Cast* **John Wayne, Susan Hayward**

Wayne, *Time* magazine declared, "portrays the great conqueror [Genghis Khan] as a cross between a square-shootin' sheriff and a Mongolian idiot". The star himself would shudder if anyone mentioned this film in his presence. His audacious decision to play Khan as a gunfighter did not, after all, pay off, just as a hairstyle based on the three pigtails worn by Hayward failed to take the fashion world by storm. The real pity of this film is that it was shot in Nevada in a location contaminated by nuclear fallout: Wayne, Hayward and more than 100 other members of the cast and crew subsequently died of cancer and tumours. Omar Sharif would be slightly more convincing than

El Cid had Sophia, Charlton and a beach scene to make Frankie Avalon jealous

the Duke in the same role in 1965. Sai Fu and Mai Lisi directed a Mongolian version of the same life in *Genghis Khan* (1998) which is probably the best of the three.

EL CID 1961
Director Anthony Mann *Cast* Charlton Heston, Sophia Loren

Mann has become a cult director since he died, which may explain the rising reputation of this epic set in medieval Spain. Scorsese has described this as "one of the greatest epic films ever made" and waxes lyrical about Mann's composition, use of space and graceful camera work. The film takes its tale of the rise of Rodrigo Diaz very seriously and there's a fair bit of speechifying. But the plot is, as David Thomson says, very similar to the Westerns that Mann directed: a man's honour has to be vindicated by trial of arms. Heston and Loren give depth to roles which could have reeked of cardboard. And the end is a wondrous piece of heroic optimism, of a kind no director would dare propose today.

EXCALIBUR 1981
Director John Boorman *Cast* Nigel Terry, Nicol Williamson, Helen Mirren, Nicholas Clay

Worth watching out for camera and crew in this film, especially when Lancelot and Guinevere are making out in the forest. Such minor misdemeanours apart, this is a cracking retelling of the Arthurian legend, with fight scenes which actually look arduous. (One cameraman had a nervous breakdown trying to film the opening battle sequence.) Mirren and Williamson hated each other from a previous engagement so their scenes as Morgana and Merlin have a certain edge. By contrast, Michael Winner's *Sir Gawain And The Green Knight* is often cited as one of the worst films ever made about the medieval era.

GLADIATOR 2000
Director Ridley Scott *Cast* Russell Crowe, Joaquin Phoenix, Derek Jacobi, Richard Harris, Oliver Reed, Connie Nielsen

Blood and sandals are back! Although some carpers described Scott's epic as "*Mortal Kombat* with dialogue", Crowe's gruff charisma and Scott's direction make it pointless to resist. There are even a few in-jokes. Lucius is given two horses called

Argento and Scarto – in other words, Silver and Scout, the same names as the horses of the Lone Ranger and Tonto. The story, about gladiator Maximus who goes *mano a mano* with the Roman emperor Commodus, isn't the most original in movie history but it's decently told and the combat scenes are a grisly spectacle well staged. And Reed, who died during filming, reminds you that when he took time off from drunken appearances on chat shows, he could still act.

KAGEMUSHA 1980

Director Akira Kurosawa *Cast* Tatsuya Nakadai, Tsutomo Yamazaki, Kenichi Hagiwara, Kata Yui, Shuji Otaki

Kurosawa had to rely on the sponsorship of George Lucas and Francis Ford Coppola to make this film. (The budget, $6m, puny by Hollywood standards, was a bit steep for Japanese studios.) If not quite up to the standard of *Ran*, this is fine work. He conveys both the sweep of events in the clan wars of 16th-century Japan and shows how the conflict affects individual lives. This dual focus does slow the film but the battle scenes are gloriously done and the warlords' intrigues are of almost Shakespearian subtlety.

KING RICHARD AND THE CRUSADERS 1954

Director David Butler *Cast* Rex Harrison, Virginia Mayo, George Sanders

Sanders is sadly best remembered as the star who killed himself

INTOLERANCE

BIRTH OF A GENRE

Intolerance, made in 1916, is still the most ambitious epic ever attempted in Hollywood. DW Griffith saw the film partly as a rebuke to those who had condemned his earlier film *Birth Of A Nation* for racism. So he set out to make a film showing the effects of intolerance. The film expanded from one story (*The Mother And The Law*) set in ancient Babylon to four parallel stories: the Babylonian epic, a modern tale of a young boy who cheats the gallows, and three historic stories set in Christ's Judea and 16th-century France. Trying to save the film in the editing suite, Griffith decided to cross-cut from one story to another. Although *Intolerance* was soon dubbed "the greatest

motion picture of all time", the cross-cutting was not popular (in Mexico, the film was rearranged into four separate parts), one critic groaning: "One was fearful lest Belshazzar be run over by an automobile." Still, the film did decent box office (until America entered World War I and its message of peace and goodwill seemed inappropriate) but it cost $485,000 to make ($7.7m in today's terms) and couldn't help but lose money. No one, though, has ever made a movie so epic in scale, ambition or daring. No other director, not even DeMille, would have been arrogant enough to tell four stories from utterly different epochs in one film. Nobody has done it since. Maybe Spielberg should take up the challenge.

because he was bored. That was 18 years after this movie so it can't really be to blame, although he must be the only celluloid King Richard to be addressed as Dick Plantagenet. The comic book derived from this saga did better than the movie, possibly because the characterisations in the comic were more subtle. Still, Laurence Harvey debuts as a Scottish knight who delivers his dialogue so loudly he sounds as if he's trying to order a drink at last orders in a Glasgow pub. Harrison plays Saladin as inscrutable, ie as Charlie Chan.

LAND OF THE PHARAOHS 1955
Director Howard Hawks *Cast* Jack Hawkins, Joan Collins

If you find Hawkins' pharaoh a) dull and b) unconvincing, Hawks' comment on the making of this film may help explain why. "Faulkner said: 'I don't know how a pharaoh talks – is it all right if I write him like a Kentucky colonel?' And [Harry] Kurnitz [dialogue writer] said: 'I can't do it like a Kentucky colonel, but I could do it as though it were King Lear.'" So what you see onscreen is Kentucky colonel crossed with King Lear, rewritten by Hawks and plonked down in Egypt in 3000 BC. But you do get a good look at Joan Collins' midriff.

> "THAT'S ALL YOU EVER THINK OF, DICK PLANTAGENET! YOU BURNER! YOU PILLAGER!"
> Lady Edith, King Richard And The Crusades

SIGN OF THE CROSS 1932
Director Cecil B DeMille *Cast* Fredric March, Elissa Landi, Claudette Colbert, Charles Laughton

This biblical epic does, at least, suggest just how kinky DeMille's movies might have been without the Hays Code. Made just before the Code was sanctified, this Christian-Roman saga stars Laughton as an OTT (but clearly homosexual) Nero and allows Colbert to show her nipples (you have to look very closely) and invite one of her servants into her bath, presumably for a spot of lesbian lovemaking. Re-released in 1944 with the steamier scenes cut, this is now available in its original ludicrous, compelling form. Some of us are born tone deaf; DeMille (this film proves) was just deaf to bad dialogue.

TESEO CONTRO IL MINOTAURO 1961
Director Silvio Amadio *Cast* Bob Mathias, Rosanna Schiaffino, Alberto Lupo

"See the captive maidens sacrificed to the minotaur monster! See the goddess of the sea rise from the depths to claim her mortal lover! See the ranging revolt of the Cretans! See the yawning pit of terror where the dogs howl for victims! See man and monster battle to death!" The poster says it all really. After a build-up like that, the movie itself could only ever be an anti-climax. Which, alas, it was.

EROTICA

Sexual chemistry has sold so many films. But the elements of that chemistry keep changing. In *Red Dust*, Clark Gable ordering Jean Harlow to take his boots off gave audiences an erotic charge. In the 1980s, it took Mickey Rourke, some fruit and a submissive Kim Basinger. Eroticism on celluloid takes many forms, partly because every filmmaker has their very own sexual chemistry set.

AI NO CORRIDA 1976
Director Nagisa Oshima *Cast* Tatsuya Fuji, Eiko Matsuda

This tale of obsessive sex between an innkeeper and a servant was seized by US customs in the year of its release, hit by an obscenity charge in Japan and only came to British cinemas in 1991. The appeal may pale if your passion for onscreen passion doesn't match the director's but this is no porn film. For once, the sex really is vital to the development of the central characters as it takes over their lives until, finally, violence has its say.

BETTY BLUE 1986 37.2° LE MATIN
Director Jean-Jacques Beineix *Cast* Béatrice Dalle, Jean-Hughes Anglade

A film about madness, romantic obsession or Beatrice Dalle's boobs? Beineix never seems sure and nor are we. The only certain thing here is that the costume designer was overpaid. The sex starts straightaway as artist (Anglade) and Dalle are shown sideways on a bed under a picture of Mona Lisa. If the sex begins to pale, there are some fine (ie daft) typing scenes and ever more frequent signs that our Betty's a bit of a nutter. Best just to admire the panache.

BODY HEAT 1981
Director Lawrence Kasdan *Cast* Kathleen Turner, William Hurt

The most famous line in this film comes when Turner tells Hurt: "You're not too smart, are you? I like that in a man." This is *Double Indemnity* with more sex: Turner has an affair with

Betty Blue may pout for France but she can't type for toffee

Hurt and decides her husband must die. It is rare for a woman to be allowed to be this sexually confident and manipulative onscreen and Turner relishes the opportunity, making us believe poor old Hurt is so besotted he will do anything she says. His only protest is to tell her: "You shouldn't wear that body."

EXTASE 1932

Director Gustav Machaty *Cast* Hedy Lamarr, Aribert Mog

This is not the first movie to show an actress totally nude on screen. (That honour belongs to Audrey Munson who starred in the buff in the 1915 silent *Inspiration*.) This probably is (because this is one of those 'firsts' which will always be open to debate) the first film in which the sex act is depicted on screen. In the crucial scene, Lamarr acts with a passion inspired by the fact that the director had just stuck a pin in her backside.

LAST TANGO IN PARIS 1972

Director Bernardo Bertolucci *Cast* Marlon Brando, Maria Schneider

Brando's dresser noted one day: "Something's going on here; he's taking this seriously." And indeed Brando was. Perhaps rejuvenated by the work he had just done on *The Godfather*, he delivers an autobiographical performance of intensity and depth. His quality may be down to something as mundane as the fact that, so chaotic was this film, he was not reading his lines from cue cards. The sex seems more incidental today, though it might not had Bertolucci kept to his plan to show intercourse. (Brando persuaded him not to.) The hype with which it was greeted (Pauline Kael suggested it would usher in

LA GIGGIOLINA

ARE LA CICCIOLINA'S FILMS WORTH WATCHING?

Her stage name means 'Cuddles', her cinematic trademark is to wear a pink dress cut low enough to show one breast, and she was famously elected to the Italian Parliament for the Radical party, even though she was born (as Ilona Staller) in Budapest. These facts about the most famous porn actress in Italy (and possibly the world) are well known. What isn't so well known, however, is whether the films which have made her a star are any good or even watchable. The cognoscenti, to use a long Italian word, say her best movie is *Cicciolina E Moana Ai Mondali* (or *Sexy World Cup*). The plot sees her and her partner-in-crime (Moana Pozzi) on a mission to help Italy win the 1990 World Cup by shagging the German, Dutch and Argentinian squads into fatigue. For all of the lasses' sterling work, it is porno veteran Ron Jeremy who steals the film as Maradona, doing a brilliant impersonation of the famous film of the player doing his stretch routines. The film was released in 1990 after the Italian team had proved the central point – they weren't good enough to win the World Cup on their own, even on home soil. Sadly none of Cuddles' other films match this for originality, plot or action (ie the footage of the 1982 World Cup used in the film).

a new age of cinema, Italian novelist Alberto Moravia claimed it was based on Freudian symbolism) is best forgotten so the movie can be watched for itself. Whatever else, it is a star vehicle for Brando, as a man who seeks to obliterate his wife's suicide with an affair with a young Parisienne. He does not disappoint.

In *Last Tango In Paris*, Maria Schneider plays a woman who never tired of hearing the speaking clock say "At the third stroke..."

9½ WEEKS 1986
Director Adrian Lyne *Cast* Mickey Rourke, Kim Basinger
A success du scandale although opinions differ about the nature of the scandal. For some, it's the absence of a back story or any clue as to why Basinger should be so obsessed by the sleazeball Rourke and so willing, up to a point, to play his strange games. Ultimately Basinger draws the line and the film's defenders say this proves this isn't just another sexploitation movie. Others may agree with the heroine when she says early on in the proceedings: "I don't like this any more, I want to go home."

THE OUTLAW 1943
Director Howard Hughes *Cast* Jane Russell, Thomas Mitchell, Jack Buetel, Walter Huston
Russell's breasts are really incidental to this retelling of the Billy the Kid saga. Incidental to everyone, that is, except director/producer Howard Hughes. The billionaire had seen a photo of Russell when she was just a chiropodist's assistant and, engineer that he was, he designed a special cantilever bra for her to wear in this film with the same dedication with which he'd sit down and design a new plane. But Russell, with a mind as sound as her body, refused to wear it – and to become Hughes' mistress.

MAE WEST

MAE THE FORCE BE...

Tony Curtis said the famous Mae West walk was down to her shoes. Or, to be precise, the six-inch platforms she had fixed to them to raise her height, so she could only walk, literally, one foot at a time. The story is entirely plausible. Here is a woman whose Broadway play *Sex* so enraged the authorities in 1926 that she spent 10 days in jail on an obscenity charge. It's often forgotten that she wrote most of her films too, including lines like: "I wasn't always rich. No, there was a time I didn't know where my next husband was coming from." Her two Paramount films of the early 1930s, *She Done Him Wrong* and *I'm No Angel*, were so laden with innuendo they speeded up the arrival of the Hays Code. After that she was never quite the same, retiring from films in 1943. By then she was already a legend, a woman after whom lifejackets were named and whose photo session as the Statue of Liberty was renamed the Statue of Libido.

RED DUST 1932

Director Victor Fleming *Cast* Clark Gable, Jean Harlow

The old gag about the 't' in Harlow being silent is testament to the fact that she looked like a sex goddess who enjoyed sex. The scandal which almost shut down this film and could have killed her career (her husband committed suicide leaving an ambiguous note) only added to that aura. She would have no finer onscreen partner than Gable, although like her, he hated the sex symbol tag. This film of lust and love triangles on a Malaysian plantation broke many of the rules about the presentation of adultery on screen. Indeed when the story was remade in 1935 and set in the China Seas, the new Hays Code would force the studio to tone it down.

THE SEVEN YEAR ITCH 1955

Director Billy Wilder *Cast* Marilyn Monroe, Tom Ewell

When you watch this enjoyable farce, remember that this is the film which ended Monroe's marriage to baseball legend Joe Di Maggio. The famous scene where she stands over a grating and her dress billows around her hips was shot while Di Maggio watched, uneasily, from the sidelines and a New York crowd shouted: "Higher! Higher!" While Monroe thought it was funny, her husband took a rather dimmer view. But then the whole film goes out of its way to emphasize Monroe's sexual availability (if only the hitherto-faithful husband next door Tom Ewell can find the magic formula) in ways which few hubbies would like. Monroe makes this work because, underneath the sexual magnetism, she still exudes an astonishing innocence.

THE SHEIK 1921

Director George Melford *Cast* Rudolph Valentino, Agnes Ayres

"QUO VADIS BABY?"
Paul, Last Tango In Paris

One of Valentino's bit parts on his road to stardom was as a 'New Type Heavy'. Here he played a 'New Type Lover' to such devastating effect that no other male film star has had such an impact on women. In part, it was because he had learned from all those minor roles as gangsters and lounge lizards, bringing some of that menace to his role as the good/bad hero in this film. In *The Sheik*, in particular, he was a glamorous, foreign, obscure object of desire, an erotic charge strengthened by the not-so-subtle hint of rape in the air. Today, his eye-popping acting style seems so alien that his appeal seems mysterious, but he was the original (and greatest) lover on the silver screen.

FANTASY

There is no fantasy more seductive to the American mind (and, by extension, to Hollywood) than a second chance at life. This is the emotional root of such differing fantasies as *Field Of Dreams* and the eerie Rock Hudson/John Frankenheimer collaboration *Seconds*. Yet some fantasy films are just excuses to scare us with witches and wizards. Not that there's anything wrong with that...

ALICE 1990
Director Woody Allen *Cast* Mia Farrow, Joe Mantegna, William Hurt
To say *Alice* is a modern take on Lewis Carroll's fable would be a slur on the originality of Allen's Oscar-nominated screenplay. Alice (Farrow) lives a sheltered Manhattan life cut off from all suffering in her apartment with bland husband (Hurt) and two children. This Alice doesn't have a looking glass but uses Chinese herbs to become invisible, travel with the ghost of a past boyfriend (a literally transparent Alec Baldwin) and meet her own muse (Bernadette Peters). Allen's funniest film since *Radio Days*.

AMAZING MR BLUNDEN 1972
Director Lionel Jeffries *Cast* Laurence Naismith, James Villiers
Based on Antonia Barber's novel *The Ghosts*, this follow-up to actor-turned-director Jeffries' debut *The Railway Children* is a charming fantasy with a hint of danger. A widowed mum and two young children act as housekeepers at a derelict mansion which, like all such movie mansions, is said to be haunted, with the kids meeting the previous tenants and ghostly orphans Sara and George. The children escort the ghostly pair back in time to rewrite history. The film has all the standard elements of a haunted house movie (derelict buildings, inquisitive children and even magic potions) while Diana Dors is amusing as the housekeeper/mother-in-law in on the plot to kill the children.

> **"YOU HAVE A GOOD PERSONALITY AND YOU KNOW SWEATERS"**
> Joe Tate, Alice

THE BISHOP'S WIFE 1947
Director Henry Koster *Cast* Cary Grant, Loretta Young, David Niven
In the wake of such whimsical fantasy box office draws as *Here Comes Mr Jordan*, it was Grant's turn to put on wings and right wrongs. Descending from heaven at the request of Bishop

Brougham (Niven), Dudley is keener to help the bishop save his marriage than his parish church. Grant was to play Niven's role as the cleric seeking help from above but the stars swapped roles, with Grant deemed better suited to the role of a debonair angel. Director Koster replaced the sacked William A Seiter who'd finished the film but not to the satisfaction of producer Samuel Goldwyn Jr, who ordered a total reshoot. Koster was then nearly fired for failing to shoot stars Young and Grant's 'best' sides as specified. Goldwyn settled the row by threatening to halve their salaries if he only got half of their faces.

> "THERE ARE THREE THINGS IN THIS WORLD YOU NEED RESPECT FOR. ALL KINDS OF LIFE, A NICE BOWEL MOVEMENT ON A REGULAR BASIS, AND A NAVY BLAZER"
>
> Parry, The Fisher King

BRAZIL 1985

Director Terry Gilliam *Cast* Jonathan Pryce, Robert De Niro, Katherine Helmond, Kim Greist, Bob Hoskins

A bleak yet humorous take on the future. Sam (Pryce) feels suppressed in a world of technology and bureaucracy, and dreams of flying off with his dream girl Jill (Greist) whom he has never met. Gilliam's experience directing this film was almost as nightmarish as the story of Sam. He fought with Universal Studios' chairman Sid Sheinberg (as documented in the book *The Battle Of Brazil*) with Sheinberg insisting on an upbeat ending, first shown in the US TV version. Gilliam was also unhappy with Kim Greist's performance as Jill (he'd wanted Ellen Barkin for the role after seeing screen tests by her, Greist, Jamie Lee Curtis, Kelly McGillis and even Madonna). So he cut several of her scenes which Sheinberg added to his studio version, referred to as 'Love Conquers All'.

Like R Kelly, Sam believed he could fly. As with R Kelly, the rest of the world weren't convinced

CHINESE GHOST STORY 1987
SINNUI YAUMAN

Director Ching Siu-Tung *Cast* Leslie Cheung, Michelle Li, Wu Ma

The first tale in a trilogy sees tax collector Ning Tsai-Shen arriving in the small town where he must do his work. His presence unappreciated, he seeks refuge in the haunted Lan Ro temple. There he meets the ghost of a young woman, Nieh Hsiao-Tsing, whose curse in life is to lure young men to their death. The fun doesn't stop there as a hideous tree spirit goes around sucking the yang from people and a Taoist swordsman appears. The action sequences, not to mention the soul-sucking demon, make this one of the better more recent ghost stories – terrain revisited in two sequels (1990 and 1991), the last with the (presumably) Sting-influenced words *Do Do Do* added to its title. Star Cheung made his name in John Woo films.

CITY OF THE LOST CHILDREN 1995
Directors Marc Caro, Jean-Pierre Jeunet *Cast* Ron Perlman, Daniel Emilfork, Judith Vittet, Dominique Pinon

There's a brain in a tank on an island in a harbour. It's uncle to five identical guys who are giving it a birthday party which is broken up by another guy who has no sense of humour, can't cry or feel and has to kidnap kids and connect them to his thought-stealing equipment because he needs innocent dreams to prolong his life. But the kids are scared so they only have nightmares. Then a circus strongman (a child in a man's body) arrives with an orphan to find the kids. This orgy of sick jokes, startling images and twisted ideas makes *12 Monkeys* look like Enid Blyton.

FIELD OF DREAMS 1989
Director Phil Alden Robinson *Cast* Kevin Costner, Amy Madigan, Ray Liotta, James Earl Jones

"It's okay, honey. I... I was just talking to the cornfield." Although one of the most fantastical elements of the film must be the fact that his wife didn't laugh him into a sanatorium or the divorce courts at least, *Field of Dreams* remains one of the most unusual tales of second chances and lost dreams. Inexperienced farmer Ray (Costner in his favoured role as everyman) hears voices in his cornfield telling him: "If you build it, he will come." 'He' is Shoeless Joe Jackson, a White Sox baseball player who became known as one of the ten 'Black Sox' for throwing the World Series in 1919. Spurred on by both his love for baseball and his own lost dreams, Ray turns his field into a baseball pitch and Joe Jackson and the other players do indeed come. In WP Kinsella's novel (on which this is based) Ray enlisted the help of reclusive author JD Salinger. However Salinger was so incensed when the novel was published that a fictitious writer, Terence Mann (Jones), was created to avoid legal action.

THE FISHER KING 1991
Director Terry Gilliam *Cast* Robin Williams, Jeff Bridges, Mercedes Ruehl, Amanda Plummer

It's easy to spot the key Gilliam moments (the terrifying ghost horseman for example). This is fantasy cemented

WICKED! WITCHES

**1 MARGARET HAMILTON
THE WIZARD OF OZ**
Frank Morgan as the wizard may have had an entire movie named after him, but no-one could stir nightmares in a child like the Witch of the West.

**2 ANJELICA HUSTON
THE WITCHES**
Roald Dahl's creation is more than enough to give anyone the willies. Or maybe that's just Anjelica.

3 THE WITCHES OF EASTWICK
Just can't pick the best from such a fantastic bunch, all a match for Nicholson's Devil.

**4 KIM NOVAK
BELL, BOOK & CANDLE**
What better way to use your powers than to charm men?

**5 BETTE MIDLER
HOCUS POCUS**
Even when not playing a witch Ms Midler is known to cackle.

in the real world and therefore far tamer than his *Munchausen*. Jack (Bridges) was a radio talk DJ who, after a listener goes on a killing spree in a restaurant, falls into alcoholic-fuelled despair, supported only by his long-suffering partner (Ruehl). Williams, a homeless man, rescues him from muggers. Bridges begins to help Williams' mad quest for the Holy Grail, believing that it could cleanse his own soul. Encompassing many elements (the search for the Holy Grail, demons both real and imaginary, despair, loneliness and love), this is a touching, exhilarating and frightening tale, aided by fantastic performances from Bridges, Ruehl and Plummer in particular, and Williams in a role where his naturally manic character is allowed to shine without taking over the film.

GROUNDHOG DAY 1993

Director **Harold Ramis** *Cast* **Bill Murray, Andie MacDowell**

Murray is at his sardonic best as Phil Connors, an egotistical weatherman who feels he is too big a celebrity to cover the Groundhog Day celebrations in the Gobbler's Knob (it really exists) for the fourth year in succession. His cynicism leads him to be seemingly doomed to re-live the same day for the rest of his life. Ramis manages to repeat the essential action elements while covering almost every scenario imaginable. Phil swings from confusion to milking his new found immortality (seducing women, breaking laws) till he finally realises he will only escape the "same-old same-old" cycle – and persuade his producer Rita (MacDowell) to love him – if he mends his ways. Although many actors would fall into a pit of cheese and corn, Murray keeps the bone-dry wit coming till it almost feels like you've seen Capra crossed with Woody Allen.

IF... 1968

Director **Lindsay Anderson** *Cast* **Malcolm McDowell, David Wood, Richard Warwick**

A scathing view of a year in a bizarre archetypal English public school, where the boys rebel against the establishment in spectacular fashion. Very much a movie of its time, with jarring cutting and swaps from colour to sepia, *If...* still has a frantic appeal, and the sociopathic performance by the then-unknown McDowell is mesmerising. Its original title of *Crusaders* was an ironic nod to the Kipling poem of the same name which celebrates a true Englishman's fortitude and restraint. With its beatings, machine gun battles and surreal, twisted scenes of violence and anarchy, this educational establishment could not be further from Kipling's ideal.

Put this man in charge of the new Wembley stadium. Now

JASON & THE ARGONAUTS 1963

Director Don Chaffey *Cast* Todd Armstrong, Nancy Kovack

Todd Armstrong stars as fleece-hunting Jason aided (and hindered) by a seafaring crew and squabbling gods (including Honor Blackman as Hera). But stop-motion animator Ray Harryhausen, who worked on many fables of this kind, is the real star. The final battle of the skeletons is his meisterwork. Three minutes on screen, four and a half months in the making, this gladiatorial contest between seven skeletons and three men still has a certain grandeur.

LA BELLE ET LA BETE 1946
BEAUTY AND THE BEAST

Director Jean Cocteau

Cast Jean Marais, Josette Day

The persistent aroma of Christmas-tree air freshener finally got to repo man Estevez

Writer, director, poet, playwright, artist and set designer, Jean Cocteau used all his skills on this classic fairy tale, often cited as one of the greatest films ever. Starring his favourite actor and long-time companion Marais as the beast, this was only Cocteau's second film, following a 15-year break since his directing debut with the short *The Blood Of A Poet*. During filming, Cocteau was in hospital with the skin condition impetigo and wrote in his diary: "I look at myself in the mirror... it's awful. The pain is now a torture so horrible I am ashamed of ever showing myself." Like director, like beast.

> **"NEVER INTERRUPT A MURDERER, MADAM"**
> Professor Oliver Lindenbrook,
> Journey To The Centre Of The Earth

LE BALLON ROUGE 1956

Director Albert Lamorisse *Cast* Pascal Lamorisse, Georges Sellier, Vladimir Popov

Winner of the best screenplay Oscar in 1957, Lamorisse's dialogue-free script tells the simple tale of a lonely boy who comes across a bewitching red balloon and travels with it through the Belleville district of Paris. Lamorisse's son, Pascal, stars here as he does in the sequel, *Le Voyage En Ballon* (*Stowaway In The Sky*). The film now has added poignancy as Belleville was razed in the 1960s.

LOST HORIZON 1937

Director Frank Capra *Cast* Ronald Colman, Jane Wyatt, Edward Everett Horton

Colman and his fellow passengers end up in the mystical world of Shangri-La, somewhere in the Himalayas. There,

HOME HINTS

Moving house is always stressful especially if you have unwelcome guests like...

THE MAITLANDS

Just because Barbara and Adam Maitland are dead they don't see why they should move out of their New England house, not even when it's bought by yuppies. Determined to stay on, they even call on Beetlejuice who, judging by his suits, must be a spirit of the 1970s.

BODIES IN THE WALL

Cavity insulation is usually a bonus but not, as happened in *The Frighteners*, when the walls are insulated with corpses.

POLTERGEISTS

Never mind spirits in the walls or even the television set, these little fiends can suck your house into a black hole, thereby severely affecting its resale value.

peace, good health and longevity rule and Colman is torn between returning to 'civilisation' and staying in tranquility. That indecision matched Colman's own dithering over the film: he only finally decided when Capra lined up Brian Aherne as a stand-in. Sam Jaffe, meanwhile, only got to play the 200-year-old lama after a series of wizened actors hired by Capra died. The preview audience thought the film was hilarious (partly because they only knew the director for his comedies) and Capra panicked. Convinced he'd made a stinker, he cut the first two reels and created a classic.

MERLIN'S SHOP OF MYSTICAL WONDERS
1996

Director Kenneth J Berton *Cast* Ernest Borgnine, George Milan

Borgnine is a granddad (and former screenwriter) who tells his grandson horror stories about Merlin, a shop and a toy monkey that kills things every time it clashes its toy cymbals. Berton, who wrote, directed and produced this, hasn't made a film since. Funny that.

REPO MAN 1984

Director Alex Cox *Cast* Harry Dean Stanton, Emilio Estevez

Cox's most original film is a fantastic conflation of every budget sci-fi theme: a dystopian lawless future, a government conspiracy, aliens and atomic power.

Otto (Estevez in his first and best starring role) is a disaffected youth who meets a car repossession man (Stanton in the funniest performance of his career) and is persuaded to join the agency. In mortal danger as a repo man, he is soon caught up in the hysteria surrounding a mysterious 1964 Chevy and its glowing deadly cargo. Cox adds to this already unusual brew the finer details that define any cult film. Many characters are named after kinds of beer, all the cars have Christmas tree air fresheners (very sinister if you've seen *Se7en*) and all the cars turn the opposite way from the one they're indicating.

THE SEVEN FACES OF DR LAO 1964

Director George Pal *Cast* Tony Randall, Barbara Eden

Based on Charles Finney's 1935 cult novel, *The Circus Of Dr Lao*, the mysterious Dr Lao (Randall) arrives at a turn-of-the-century western town and, with his magical circus, mesmerises the townsfolk and confronts them with their own prejudices and foibles. Randall, presumably on parole from Doris Day and

Rock Hudson, plays each of the circus characters, but is hardly recognisable beneath William Tuttle's Oscar-winning make-up. Pal's last film also stars Eden in her pre-*I Dream of Jeannie* days.

THE SEVENTH SEAL 1957
DET SJUNDE INSEGLET
Director Ingmar Bergman
Cast Gunnar Bjornstrand, Bengt Ekerot, Nils Poppe, Max von Sydow

She fled the dream-stealing baddie in City of Lost Children and ran into the arms of a gorgeous goodie

Even if you've never seen an Ingmar Bergman film, you may know the *Bill And Ted* spoof of Death. A knight (von Sydow) and his squire return home from the Crusades only to meet Death (Ekerot). The final scene with death and his followers dancing away was actually acted out by a group of technicians and tourists left on set as the actors had all left. The studio originally rejected the script because it was too dour. In the most sinister coincidence of all, Ekerot died shortly after playing Death in this film.

TRULY, MADLY, DEEPLY 1991
Director Anthony Minghella *Cast* Juliet Stevenson, Alan Rickman
When Jamie dies he leaves an ache in Nina's life she is unable to mend. She misses him so much she even thinks she hears him speaking to her. When it turns out she was right and he's come back, she is happy to escape from the world and stay with him. But when he starts bringing friends home, problems arise. Stevenson and Rickman are perfect lovers who could have been together forever, if one of them wasn't dead, and the rest of the cast, especially Michael Maloney and Bill Paterson, provide exactly the right atmosphere of eccentricity with a touch of fantasy. Funny and touching, it's a bittersweet meditation about making a choice between looking backwards and moving on.

> "IF ANYTHING IS IMPERFECT IN THIS IMPERFECT WORLD, LOVE IS MOST PERFECT IN ITS PERFECT IMPERFECTION"
> Jons, The Seventh Seal

XANADU 1980
Director Robert Greenwald *Cast* Olivia Newton-John, Gene Kelly
This can only have been made because a Hollywood executive had a fetish about seeing Newton-John on roller skates. Olivia plays Greek muse Kira, whose role in life is to inspire men on Earth to achieve (pity she didn't inspire the director). With Kelly's help, she persuades musician Sonny (Michael Beck) to build a roller rink. It is a rare privilege to see a star light the blue touch paper and watch their career explode on camera, and this is worth catching for that reason alone. *Grease* had made her a movie star. After this, she couldn't get a leading role in Greece.

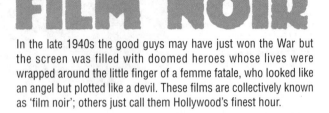

FILM NOIR

In the late 1940s the good guys may have just won the War but the screen was filled with doomed heroes whose lives were wrapped around the little finger of a femme fatale, who looked like an angel but plotted like a devil. These films are collectively known as 'film noir'; others just call them Hollywood's finest hour.

Among movie genres, film noir is one of a kind. For a start, the term 'film noir' (French for 'black film') was first used in 1946 by a French critic, years after many films now described as classics of the genre (*Double Indemnity, Stranger On The Third Floor*) had already been made.

The first book devoted to noir appeared (again in France) in 1955, by which time America had almost stopped making these films. It is a genre, defined by critics, imposed partially retrospectively on a body of films made between 1940 and 1960. (You will find a checklist of noir 'symptoms' on page 183.) Noir is a look, a feeling (of uncertainty, cynicism and of being trapped) which often turns into paranoia, a theme (usually crime or corruption) and a tone far removed from the corporate optimism which typified most Hollywood films in the war years. Certain personnel recur in front of and behind the camera: Robert Mitchum, Barbara Stanwyck, Humphrey Bogart, Peter Lorre, Billy Wilder, Fritz Lang, cameraman John Alton and hard-boiled crime writers like Raymond Chandler.

The classic age of noir probably lasted from 1944 to 1955. Several small technical developments had made it possible. Sound had made shooting by night and on location – two staples of the silent movies – difficult in the 1930s but by the 1940s filmmakers had overcome these problems. Indeed, many of the great silent movie cameramen were used on noir films.

New lightweight cameras, used by many of Hollywood's best directors to make war documentaries, smoothed the way for new camera techniques. The distinctive look of many B movie noirs owed much to the fact that the dark shadows disguised the lack of a set, often the first victim of budget cuts as Hollywood adjusted to the loss of its European markets.

The sociological explanation for noir is probably best summed up by Abraham Polonsky, who wrote and directed

> **"IT WAS HIS STORY AGAINST MINE BUT, OF COURSE, I TOLD MY STORY BETTER"**
> Dixon Steele, In A Lonely Place

Forces Of Evil, when he said: "An extraordinary, horrible war. Concentration camps, slaughter, atomic bombs, people killed for nothing. That can make anybody a little pessimistic."

America seemed triumphant, yet the victory was bittersweet. Women were reluctant to give up their new freedom and retreat to the home and many veterans found peace hard to adjust to. In many noir films the woman has the upper hand. It is tempting to see this as a reflection of these changes but the truth may be more mundane: director Howard Hawks just thought that it was sexier if women did the chasing in his films.

But Hawks' *The Big Sleep* is not, purists will tell you, true noir. In one sense they are right: Bogart's Marlowe is always in control. The archetypal noir hero soon realises that whatever situation he's become embroiled in has slipped out of his control and, as in *Out Of The Past*, the cost of fixing things may be death. Not heroic death as in the war films but futile, lonely death. Doomed these 'heroes' may be, but they still have the best lines. As Mitchum tells Jane Greer in *Out Of The Past*: "You're like a leaf the wind blows from one gutter to another."

THE BIG COMBO 1955
Director Joseph H Lewis Cast Cornel Wilde, Richard Conte
The title doesn't refer to a jumbo-sized platter but, perhaps, to the combination of forces ranged against Wilde, a cop obsessed with bringing down mobster Conte but also in love with the crime boss's moll (played by Jean Wallace, Wilde's off-screen wife). This film is full of strange moments that don't fit into the formula, such as the homo-erotic banter between two of the gangster's hoodlums (one played by Lee Van Cleef). Or the scene where Conte kisses Wallace on the face and neck and disappears out of shot, the implication being his kisses have just travelled southwards. Even the unusually happy ending can't obscure the fact that this film has its mind fixed very firmly in the gutter.

BLUEBEARD 1944
Director Edgar G Ulmer
Cast John Carradine, Jean Parker
Ulmer was in exile in PRC, a studio on Hollywood's Poverty

If it wasn't the plot confusing the actors in *Laura*, it was the complicated casting process going on off-screen

"You see these fingers, dear hearts? These fingers have veins that run straight to the soul of man. The right hand, the hand of love"

Row, when he made this. So he couldn't afford Boris Karloff as the serial killer, painter and puppet master in 19th-century Paris and was forced to make do with Carradine, who described this as his favourite performance. The budget shows at times but Ulmer manages to bring some distinction to what could easily have been a routine movie. For example, Carradine stages a puppet performance of *Faust* for one of his potential female victims in a scene that is both appropriate to his character and genuinely creepy. To see how bad this could have been, just see the Richard Burton remake.

DOUBLE INDEMNITY 1944

Director Billy Wilder *Cast* Fred MacMurray, Barbara Stanwyck, Edward G Robinson

Even in a movie industry increasingly content to pillage its own past for future profit, *Double Indemnity* has been largely left alone, sacrosanct apart from *Body Heat,* and a Mr Magoo spoof (*Trouble Indemnity*). Wilder gets (and deserves) most of the credit for this classic yarn of a woman who persuades her lover/insurance salesman to murder her husband. But spare some praise for Stanwyck – she had to wear a wig (which the studio boss complained made her look like George Washington) and look as sleazy as possible in order to, as she put it, "go into an out-and-out cold-blooded killer." She was genuinely worried. Wilder asked her if she was an actress or a mouse. The answer's right there on the screen.

FORCE OF EVIL 1948

Director Abraham Polonsky *Cast* John Garfield, Thomas Gomez
The only film Polonsky directed before he was blacklisted, this

has some similarities with his 'comeback' western *Tell Them Willie Boy Is Here*. The latter has more genuine humour but both take themselves a little too seriously. That said, Garfield is fantastic as a mob chief's lawyer who has a cash register where his heart ought to be. Polonsky gave cinematographer George Barnes a book of Edward Hopper paintings to show how he wanted the film to look and Barnes did his best. Beau Bridges makes an uncredited debut at the ripe old age of seven.

> **"WE DIDN'T NEED DIALOGUE, WE HAD FACES!"**
> Norma Desmond, Sunset Boulevard

HANGOVER SQUARE 1945

Director John Brahm Cast Laird Cregar, Linda Darnell

If Cregar seems incredibly realistic as the British composer increasingly exhausted by his own madness, it's probably because he lost 100lbs on a crash diet so he could play the lead. As he was normally as svelte as a nightclub bouncer, this wasn't a good idea and he died, at 28, from a heart attack before the film was released. This was something of a pity because he is superb as the composer who turns to homicide whenever life gets too noisy and is hopelessly in love with the wrong woman (Darnell). George Sanders is droll as the investigating doctor.

HIGH SIERRA 1941

Director Raoul Walsh Cast Humphrey Bogart, Ida Lupino

Roy 'Mad Dog' Earle was just the first of four cracking roles turned down by George Raft in the 1940s (the others were in *Treasure Of The Sierra Madre*, *Casablanca* and *Double Indemnity*, and any one of them would have been better than any film Raft actually appeared in – with the honourable exception of *Some Like It Hot*). But Raft's loss was Bogart's gain in this elegiac gangster heist movie. The nobly named hero is the tragic centre of a film which implies that his kind are now obsolete. It isn't 100 per cent noir but it marks the beginning of Bogart as an icon and his future director, John Huston, worked on the script.

IN A LONELY PLACE 1950

Director Nicholas Ray Cast Humphrey Bogart, Gloria Grahame

Ray takes the ambiguity inherent in many noir films and runs with it in this film, using Bogart as a frustrated screenwriter who may or may not have murdered a waitress. Grahame gives Bogart an

BLACK LIST

Film buffs could argue about what constitutes a true film noir for almost as long as it would take you to watch all the movies in this genre. But this list of classic noir symptoms may help your diagnosis.

1 Dark, shadowy, contrasty images, sometimes colour but usually black and white.
2 Cynical, tough, disillusioned but likeable characters.
3 A male hero with a moral dilemma or danger to overcome.
4 A sexy femme fatale.
5 A distinctively world-weary tone, often provided by one-liners and voice narration.
6 Flashbacks.
7 No happy ending.

To simplify grossly, the essence of noir is, to quote Private Fraser from *Dad's Army*: "We're all doomed."

alibi because she likes his face although when Bogie tries to kiss her she objects: "I said I liked it; I didn't say I wanted to kiss it." Grahame was married to Ray and it's hard not to inspect this for parallels to their marriage which would end two years later. This may be as close as we get to the real Bogie onscreen. Grahame came in when Warners refused to lend Bacall and had to sign a contract which forbade her from influencing her husband director in a "feminine fashion".

THE KILLING 1956
Director Stanley Kubrick *Cast* Sterling Hayden, Marie Windsor, Vince Edwards, Coleen Gray

This study of a racetrack heist made Kubrick's name. Hayden leads well as the criminal mastermind. For once, it's not the robbery that goes wrong but the aftermath where the selection of suitcase to carry the money becomes critical. In its use of multiple flashbacks, the film anticipates *Reservoir Dogs*. Blacklisted Jim Thompson wrote the dialogue. Windsor is definitive as the treacherous temptress.

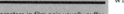

DOUBLE INDIGNITY

Characters in film noir usually suffer. But not perhaps quite as much as Raymond Chandler suffered when he co-wrote the script for *Double Indemnity* with Billy Wilder. Sharing an office with Wilder, Chandler quit the film saying he wouldn't return until his demands were met. The main ones were:

1 "Mr Wilder is at no time to swish under Mr Chandler's nose or to point in his direction the [his] thin, leather-handled malacca cane."

2 "Mr Wilder is not to give Mr Chandler orders of an arbitrary or personal nature such as 'Ray, will you shut that door please?'"

Chandler also objected to Wilder's constant chatter on the phone to the young girls he was sleeping with and added: "I can't work with a man who wears a hat in the office. I feel he is about to leave momentarily." Wilder found it hard working with a pipe-smoking ex-alcoholic. He had the consolation of knowing he had driven Chandler back to bourbon.

LA BETE HUMAINE 1938
Director Jean Renoir *Cast* Jean Gabin, Simone Simon

Film noir owes much to French films like this, part of a movement critics have dubbed poetic realism. Lang would remake this story as *Human Desire* in 1954 with Ford in the Gabin role as an engineer who has fits of uncontrollable violence against women and is soon embroiled in a plot to kill his lover's husband. Renoir wrote the script from the Emile Zola novel and this is one of those films you'll enjoy more if you read the book first. Another Renoir film from this period, *La Chienne*, was remade as the classic 1945 noir *Scarlet Street*.

LAURA 1944
Director Otto Preminger *Cast* Gene Tierney, Dana Andrews, Clifton Webb

This film emerged from what, even in the licensed lunacy that was Hollywood in the 1940s, was an exceptional degree of chaos. Preminger, called in to replace the first (sacked) director, was still banned from the Fox lot by boss Darryl F Zanuck when this film started shooting. Jennifer Jones turned Tierney's part down. Zanuck refused to cast Webb until a special screen test was made and then tried to change the ending. Set against such intrigue and

subterfuge, the film seems simplicity itself. Andrews is the detective falling for the girl whose murder he is investigating (but who turns out not to be murdered at all). Webb shines as a villainous columnist (Preminger hated journalists, so this was a petty act of revenge) but he had a breakdown afterwards and was sent into therapy. He recovered, but the only noticeable change, Tierney said, "was to make him rude to his mother".

> "I knew it was a mistake to beat my pimp to death with the heel of my shoe"

LEAVE HER TO HEAVEN 1945
Director **John M Stahl** *Cast* **Gene Tierney, Cornel Wilde**

If anyone ever tells you a true film noir has to be in black and white, tie them to an armchair and force them to watch this. Shot in glorious Oscar-winning technicolour, this film uses the beautiful backdrop of fabulous homes to change the formula and turn up the volume on the melodrama. Tierney is chiefly remembered today for her beauty but she shows rare talent here as the woman who loves people so much she kills them, especially when she flings herself down a staircase to kill her unborn child. The film sheds plausibility and Vincent Price overacts, but you will be mesmerised by Tierney.

> "YOU SAY TO YOURSELF, 'HOW HOT CAN IT GET?' THEN, IN ACAPULCO YOU FIND OUT"
>
> Jeff Bailey, Out Of The Past

THE MAN WITH MY FACE 1951
Director **Edward Montagne** *Cast* **Barry Nelson**

Nelson's dual role as the businessman whose life is taken over by a lookalike was a step up from that in his last film, where he played the voice over the loudspeaker in *Command Decision*

(1948). One of several dual-identity films (see also *Dark Mirror* with Olivia de Havilland), this doesn't quite live up to its premise, possibly because the director and writer would later find their natural environment on *The Phil Silvers Show*.

THE NAKED KISS 1964

Director Samuel Fuller *Cast* Constance Towers, Anthony Eisley

Fuller may be about as subtle as a tactical nuclear strike on occasion but he has an undeniable knack for telling images. The scene that opens this film, where the hooker beats her pimp to a pulp with the heel of her shoe and is revealed to be bald, is one of his most notorious. But this tale of a woman who was sexually abused as a child (a daring theme in 1964) and gives up prostitution to seek redemption in a small town, has many more such moments, including the scene where she stuffs money into the mouth of the local brothel-keeper.

NIGHT OF THE HUNTER 1955

Director Charles Laughton *Cast* Robert Mitchum, Lillian Gish

"MY WHOLE BODY'S JUST A QUIVERIN' WITH CLEANLINESS!"

Willa Harper, Night Of The Hunter

As Laughton himself liked to say, he had a face like an elephant's backside, so it's odd that he didn't go behind the camera more often – especially as Mitchum always said he was the best director he'd ever worked with. Laughton may, though, have been depressed by the commercial and critical failure of this film which, almost inevitably (given its storyline about a psychotic preacher who pesters two kids to find out where their dad has hidden his loot from a robbery), was banned in Finland. Gish's casting is just one of many nods by Laughton to DW Griffith. Nobody has ever played a psychopath with the charisma and complete confidence of Mitchum. Laughton apparently warned him: "The character you are about to play is a complete shit." To which Mitchum replied: "Present."

OUT OF THE PAST 1947

Director Jacques Tourneur *Cast* Robert Mitchum, Jane Greer, Kirk Douglas

One of the surprises of this film, for those who haven't seen it, is the way that Mitchum, at the age of 32, is already so completely and gloriously Mitchum. Tourneur's complex noir, in which Mitchum plays a private eye sent by gambler Kirk Douglas to find his runaway dame but inevitably falls in love with her instead, plays beautifully on the ambiguity that marked the star's best films. Douglas is excellent as the gambler and chief villain, playing him as a sinister businessman. Greer, after failing to live up to her advance billing as the kind of dame who would (in Raymond Chandler's words) make a bishop kick a hole through a stained glass window, is slipperiness personified as she switches between good and evil, often between lines. The voiceover narration does, at times, lapse into Chandler parody but otherwise this is a true classic.

SHADOW OF A DOUBT 1943

Director **Alfred Hitchcock** *Cast* **Teresa Wright, Joseph Cotten**

The ambiguous blend of good and evil so suited Hitchcock that many of his films could have been mentioned here. (His other classic noirs include *Notorious* and *The Wrong Man*, a fine tale about a family wrecked by police procedure.) In this film, Wright plays a bored young girl called Charlie who invites her uncle Charlie (Cotten) to visit but soon discovers that he is a murderer. The film is full of pairs (both obvious and subtle): the two Charlies, the two detectives, the two suspects, even the two conversations about murder techniques and the double brandy Charlie orders in the Till Two bar. This is said to be Hitchcock's favourite film possibly because he worked some of the details of his early life into the script including a rare (for him) glimpse of a benevolent screen mum called Emma (the director's own mother Emma was very ill when he made this).

MAXIMUM BOB

Noir would have been a much whiter shade of grey without Robert Mitchum. His only rival as a noir leading man was Humphrey Bogart but with Bogie, from *Casablanca* onwards, the decency within that hard-boiled exterior was often slightly too visible. With Mitchum, as he stared out at the world from under those heavy lids, there was a genuine sense of moral neutrality.

Like that other vastly underrated actor Cary Grant, Mitchum had an extraordinary ability to step out of the normal Hollywood categories of good and bad. While Grant could appear to be both good and bad at the same time in films like *Notorious* and *Suspicion*, Mitchum always seemed to be somewhere in the grey middle. His real life only reinforced this impression, especially when he was jailed for using marijuana in 1949.

Even his rare public utterances sound like lines of noir dialogue. When asked about some of the wilder stories about his private life, he told the press: "They're all true. Make up some more if you want to."

His work from this period is an easy way to get to know the genre: *The Locket* (1947), *Out Of The Past* (1947), *The Big Steal* (1949), *Angel Face* (1952), *Where Danger Lives* (1950), *Night Of The Hunter* (1955) and the western *Blood On The Moon* (1948).

With Mitchum, grey was the new black

187

THE STRANGER 1946

Director Orson Welles *Cast* Edward G Robinson, Loretta Young,
Orson Welles, Billy House

One of the odder ironies of film noir was the way it turned
Robinson from a gangster into a good guy. Here he is the dogged
detective who tracks Welles' war criminal in disguise to a small
town in Connecticut. This is Welles being a good boy, delivering
a film that is under budget and conventional enough to be a
commercial success. His biographer David Thomson suggests
that it might have been better if Robinson had taken Welles' role
and, as the director originally wanted, Agnes Moorehead had
played the detective. Welles reckoned it was "my worst film".
Sorry, Orson: *Mr Arkadin* was much, much worse.

> **"HE'S CHANGED**
> **SOME. BEING**
> **BURIED IN**
> **THE EARTH**
> **DOES THAT"**
> Mr Potter, The Stranger

STRANGER ON THE THIRD FLOOR 1940

Director Boris Ingster *Cast* Peter Lorre, John McGuire

One of a handful of American movies made at the very birth of
film noir. McGuire plays a reporter who testifies to convict a man
of murder but then begins to have doubts about the man's guilt.
The use of three flashbacks, the expressionistic photographic
style, the inversion that sees the hero put in jail and the
remarkable nightmare sequence – all mark this out as true noir.

SUNSET BOULEVARD 1950

Director Billy Wilder *Cast* William Holden, Gloria Swanson,
Erich von Stroheim

Wilder's classic movie straddles many genres. Film writer
Richard Corliss calls it "the definitive Hollywood horror movie"
but it can also be watched as a straight satire of the movie
industry and/or the greatest film noir. The film could have been
even darker in tone: it originally opened with Holden as one of
a number of talking corpses, narrating the story from the
morgue. Yet the film as we know it now is mordant enough with
Holden vacillating charismatically between the right and the
wrong woman, only in this instance the wrong woman is a silent
movie actress (Swanson). The pairing of Holden and Swanson
was fortuitous: it could have been Brando and Mae West or
Montgomery Clift and Mary Pickford. America's sweetheart
in exile turned the part down because the story was vulgar. She
was right, of course, but it is also one of the most compelling
movies ever to come out of Hollywood.

SWEET SMELL OF SUCCESS 1957

Director Alexander Mackendrick *Cast* Tony Curtis, Burt Lancaster

Burt Lancaster has never been more chilling than as the
megalomaniac newspaper columnist JJ Hunsecker, loosely

based on the real life of Walter Winchell, a legend of American journalism and a man of such massive ego that he called his daughter Walda (after himself). Lancaster wants Curtis, a press agent called Sidney Falco, to break up his sister's romance with a jazz musician. Written by Clifford Odets and Ernest Lehman, this is as (verbally and emotionally) nasty as noir gets, certainly far nastier than anything Mackendrick, whose previous films include *The Ladykillers* and *The Man In The White Suit*, had done. The film's deadly accuracy is suggested by the fact that even today, showbiz PRs still talk of "going into Sidney Falco mode".

TOUCH OF EVIL 1958

Director Orson Welles *Cast* Orson Welles, Charlton Heston
Orson Welles is Hank Quinlan, a corrupt cop who asks Marlene Dietrich to read his future. "You're all used up, you haven't got any," she tells him – but you don't need to be Mystic Meg to see that. By then he is almost friendless, pursued by his old sidekick and by do-gooding Mexican lawyer Heston. But the plot is almost incidental in this study of corruption and menace in a small border town. The scene where Janet Leigh retreats up her hotel bed while a gang prepare to pump her with what the viewer thinks is heroin sticks in the memory. Ironies abound on and off-screen. Heston insisted that Welles direct but Welles' character takes over the movie, which is peculiarly ironic as the focus on Quinlan unbalances the film and underlines the fact that as an actor Welles is not on top form here. Quinlan is too much of a monster, and Heston's lawyer is more convincing.

YOU ONLY LIVE ONCE 1937

Director Fritz Lang *Cast* Sylvia Sidney, Henry Fonda
Fonda is impressive as the ex-con who tries to go straight but fails. Even more impressive is Lang's grasp of the Hollywood idiom only three years after he'd arrived from Nazi Germany without understanding or speaking a word of English. He had fled to the US after Josef Goebbels had offered him a senior role in the German film industry. Lang had declined, saying he had Jewish grandparents, to which Goebbels replied: "We'll decide who's Jewish." This was his second American film, one of a pair he made at the end of the 1930s about society's outcasts (the other is *You And Me*). His genius as a director was blighted only by the fact that, Fonda says, he refused to treat actors as human beings.

WHOSE NOIR?

Film noir is probably the cinema's finest international co-production. The term is obviously French and was applied by French critics to the hard-boiled school of American crime fiction written by James M Cain and Dashiell Hammett. But its distinctive visual techniques, especially the high contrast black and white look, were borrowed from German expressionist movies like Fritz Lang's *M* and whose themes were often based on French poetic realist films of the 1930s like *Rue Sans Nom* (1933). John Alton, the cameraman who created the chiaroscuro look of Anthony Mann's three great noir films, was born in Hungary. Most noir directors were from central or eastern Europe: Michael Curtiz, Fritz Lang, Otto Preminger, Edgar Ulmer, Billy Wilder were from the old Austria-Hungarian empire while Robert Siodmak was from Germany. Given what was happening to their old homeland in the 1940s, it's not hard to understand noir's peculiar combination of cynicism, fatalism and pessimism.

FILMS OF THE BOOK

The film of the book is usually, whatever its flaws, at least a step up from the book of the film. And for every book brought to the screen in a manner that suggests the adaptors would struggle to write a synopsis of a Janet and John story, there are many books whose flaws, concealed by a conspiracy between the author and the reader's imagination, become horribly apparent on screen.

A SOLDIER'S DAUGHTER NEVER CRIES 1998

Director James Ivory *Cast* Kris Kristofferson, Barbara Hershey

James Jones' novels have provided the source for at least two very good movies (*From Here To Eternity* and *The Thin Red Line*) but here it's his life that is the inspiration for a film. Essentially the story of an American ex-pat family who move to Paris and then on again to North Carolina, this is based on the semi-autobiographical novel by Jones' daughter and as such is a departure for Ivory, Ismail Merchant and Ruth Prawer Jhabvala, whose more usual line is adapting novels by EM Forster or, failing that, Henry James. They do these well enough (although some critics, notably David Thomson, dismiss them as *Masterpiece Theatre*), but *A Soldier's Daughter* is an underrated gem, much helped by strong performances from the two leads.

> DO YOU KNOW WHAT LIES AT THE BOTTOM OF THE MAINSTREAM? MEDIOCRITY
>
> Alfred, Death In Venice

THE BETSY 1978

Director Daniel Petrie *Cast* Laurence Olivier, Robert Duvall, Katharine Ross, Tommy Lee Jones, Lesley-Anne Down

Olivier's attempt to speak like an American tycoon is so grotesque that his accent, as writer Joe Quinlan says, "takes the film prisoner, making it impossible to concentrate on anything else." Such a diversionary tactic might, of course, have been deliberate. He may have realised that fans of Harold Robbins (on whose novel the movie is based), wondering when his character was going to live up to the promise implied in his surname (Hardeman), might console themselves for the absence of raunch by gazing at the beauteous Down. For a film of a mass-market bestseller that truly lives down to expectations, try *The Stud* (1978) from the Collins (Jackie and Joan) stable with Oliver Tobias, lots of smut, a *Crossroads* refugee and a cameo appearance by the boxer John Conteh.

DEATH IN VENICE 1971

Director Luchino Visconti *Cast* Dirk Bogarde, Mark Burns

A work of genius or an extra large helping of Venetian ham? Visconti's film tends to be underrated by those who overrate the Thomas Mann book it was based on – it is not, to be frank, one of the author's major works. The writer in the original is here portrayed as a composer – loosely based on Mahler, whose music adds much to the film's operatic effect – who goes to Venice to die of consumption (and/or melancholy) and becomes obsessed with a beautiful young boy. Slow-moving, over-the-top, even camp at times, the film has enough scenes of breathtaking beauty to be worth viewing.

THE GREAT GATSBY 1974

Director Jack Clayton *Cast* Robert Redford, Mia Farrow, Bruce Dern

A curious film. Francis Ford Coppola was supposed to write the script but elected instead to incorporate as much of F Scott Fitzgerald's original prose as he could while still getting credit for the screenplay, and Clayton is credited as the director on a movie that has no real direction. Although the film finally sinks under the weight of its own fidelity to its source, Redford's Gatsby may come as close as

Dirk's contemplative consumptive certainly put the death into Venice

any actor can to personifying the contradictions embodied by Fitzgerald's greatest character.

Best of all, Redford's smile, the all-American smile as it was called in his earlier film *The Way We Were*, almost lives up to Fitzgerald's description of Gatsby's smile. Fans of the book will love this, but others may find it slow.

LORD OF THE FLIES 1963

Director Peter Brook *Cast* James Aubrey, Tom Chapin, Roger Elwin, Tom Gaman

William Golding's book, about a group of boys stranded on an island who descend into savagery, has haunted and/or bored generations of British schoolchildren. Here the director takes an amateur cast of boys and sticks to the book's chilling premise. This was remade and relocated in a 1990 version which somehow made the horror seem less authentic.

OBLOMOV 1979

Director **Nikita Mikhalkov** *Cast* Oleg Tabakov, Yuri Bogatyryov, Yelena Solovey

A 19th-century novel about a Russian bloke who can't quite see why he should ever get out of bed is not the obvious source for a fine movie, but you'll go a long way to find a richer portrait of lovable human sloth. The contrast between Oblomov and his friend Stoltz (thrusting and dynamic but ultimately unlikeable) is wonderfully drawn. A good key to the Russian character.

PETULIA 1968

Director **Richard Lester** *Cast* Julie Christie, George C Scott

John Haase's novel *Me And The Arch Kook Petulia* is the source for this modern American tragedy, virtually ignored when it was released but now seen as Lester's finest work. Set in San Francisco in the mid-1960s (ie right in the spiritual heart of the 1960s), this tale of a recently divorced doctor's relationship with an unhappily married nut, Petulia (Christie), becomes an indictment of an entire society. On a television set somewhere

A MAN FOR ALL OCCASIONS

One screenwriter bestrides all genres like a colossus. No, not Joe Eszterhas. Nor William Goldman. But William Shakespeare. Okay, he died 374 years before the moving image was ever shown but his work spans horror, westerns, musicals and film noir. The only thing preventing him from getting a Lifetime Achievement Oscar is that he is, in fact, already dead and not, like most winners, retired or partially dead. His breadth of work is so vast, the only surprise is that none of his characters have met Abbott and Costello.

COMEDY: THE TAMING OF THE SHREW
Zeffirelli/Taylor/Burton could have formed a Bermuda Triangle into which the spirit of the play disappeared. Instead they combined to produce a movie that is a good deal of unpretentious fun.

CRIME: JOE MACBETH
The king as a gangster in a British 1955 revamp with Sid James and the wonderfully named Minerva Pious in the cast.

EPIC: HENRY V
Okay, so one of the Agincourt corpses winks but otherwise Kenneth Branagh's *Henry V* is a movie of rare distinction, a different film to Olivier's version.

EROTICA: THE SECRET SEX LIVES OF ROMEO AND JULIET
This late 1960s porn romp was banned in Finland but not, alas, anywhere else.

FILM NOIR: MACBETH
Welles brings a noirish sense of dreamlike darkness to this hastily assembled yet stunning rendering of the Scottish play.

HORROR: TITUS ANDRONICUS
Severed hands, rape, inadvertent cannibalism, gratuitous violence – the play

in the background, the Vietnam war is continually blaring, a constant reminder of what American violence is doing to the world. And the relationships between the characters are unusually believable. Christie gives a more effective performance than she would for her future beau, Warren Beatty.

SHANE 1953

Director **George Stevens** *Cast* **Alan Ladd, Jean Arthur, Van Heflin**

Stevens spent days making sure the clouds were in the right place for this film's funeral scene, yet nobody has been able to read anything into that sky. Because this film (based on a Jack Schaefer novel) is so familiar, such puzzling details are often overlooked. Ladd is resplendent as the ghostly buckskinned stranger who rides into the valley, gets drawn into the conflict between the homesteaders (the Starrett family in particular) and rancher Stryker, and becomes a father figure to the Starretts' boy. But if this were all the film were about, it would have dated by now, as even *High Noon* has. We never really know why Shane chooses to help fight this battle. We do know that, because of his feelings for little Joe's mum (Jean Arthur), he must either die in a duel with a hired gunman (Wilson, played by Jack Palance) or ride off into the sunset. As a friend of Joe Starrett and idol to his son, Shane cannot honourably

> **"A GUN IS AS GOOD OR BAD AS THE PERSON USING IT. REMEMBER THAT"**
> Shane, Shane

had all of these and more. The young bard's attempt to outgore his rival Christopher Marlowe is improved in *Titus* (1999) with Anthony Hopkins in the title role.

MUSICAL: KISS ME KATE

The Taming Of The Shrew set to music with Kathryn Grayson and Howard Keel. Will's other great stabs at the genre include *West Side Story*.

POLITICS: RICHARD III

Ian McKellen dazzles as the first camp monster of popular entertainment in this reworking set in a 1930s fascist Britain.

ROMANCE: ROMEO AND JULIET

Olivia Hussey and Leonard Whiting convince as the archetypal star-crossed lovers (unlike Leslie Howard and Norma Shearer) because they're the right age. Probably the most popular Shakespearean romance after *Shakespeare In Love*. For a successful

updating (and transplant) try *China Girl* (1987) in which the lovers are an Italian boy and a Chinese girl.

SCI-FI: FORBIDDEN PLANET

Walter Pidgeon as Prospero, the monster as Caliban and Anne Francis as Miranda, as the Bard takes a rare trip into outer space.

WAR: RAN

King Lear and seriously bloody battles – probably the best Kurosawa take on the Bard although it 's almost impossible to decide between this and, say, *Kumonosu Jo* (1957), his retelling of *Macbeth*.

WESTERN: QUELLA SPORCA STORIA NEL WEST

Little-known late 1960s spaghetti western which turns the Bard's Danish prince into a gunslinger. Also known under its American title, *Johnny Hamlet*.

Warner/Alfa

193

resolve his feelings for Joe's wife – just as he cannot honourably resolve the fight with Starrett to decide who gets to challenge Wilson, finally resorting to knocking his friend out with a gun. This is an epic, sometimes self-consciously mythic, western which is far less straightforward than it appears.

THE THIRD MAN 1949

Director Carol Reed *Cast* Joseph Cotten, Trevor Howard, Orson Welles

Graham Greene's work often translates well to the big screen but this film far surpasses the story on which it is based. Is it Welles' performance as the racketeer Harry Lime? Maybe. He had a cold and he hated the smell of the sewers, so Reed rewrote the script and even used his hands, instead of Welles', to reach for the sewer grate. Then there was the score – according to rumour just a tune Reed found Anton Karas banging out on his zither in a café. And Welles' good relationship with Cotten, who had already played under Welles' direction in *Citizen Kane* and *The Magnificent Ambersons*. And then there's that speech about the Swiss, democracy and the cuckoo clock (Welles' idea). It may just be that Welles can't help but endear Lime to us thus, reinforcing the very qualities (moral ambiguity, betrayed friendships) which are essential parts of Greeneland.

TOM JONES 1963

Director Tony Richardson *Cast* Albert Finney, Susannah York, David Warner

Playwright John Osborne's adaptation of Henry Fielding's novel is a hectic and hilarious romp through the social mores of 18th-century England. Finney is a young foundling being raised by Squire Allworthy and in love with neighbour Squire Western's daughter. A jealous cousin and Tom's own inability to resist other women conspire to keep then apart. Richardson uses various cinematic devices like undercranking and obvious wipes and dissolves to set a comic pace for the film and John Addison's superb score catches the mood precisely.

WIDE SARGASSO SEA 1992

Director John Duigan *Cast* Karina Lombard, Nathaniel Parker

Jean Rhys's prequel to *Jane Eyre* is translated wonderfully by this Australian director, who doesn't flinch from the erotic charge the story (essentially how Mrs Rochester lost her grip on reality) has to carry to work. It was rewarded with a 17 rating in the US, which killed its box office chances. Proof that not all such adaptations have to be as impeccably mannered as the Ivory/Merchant/Jhabvala collaborations.

FOOD

Amazing as it may sound, food and films have always had a special relationship. From popping your cherry to a custard pie in the face (or an apple pie on 'Mr Torpedo Area'), food can sum up all those key moments in life that words just can't live up to.

CHOCOLAT 2000

Director Lasse Hallstrom Cast Juliette Binoche, Lena Olin, Johnny Depp, Judi Dench, Alfred Molina
Chocolat sees independent single mother, Vianne (Binoche), moving into a quaint rural town and setting up a chocolate shop across the road from the town church, with the small-minded townsfolk setting out to ruin her business. Vianne's chocolates manage to re-unite families, induce love and empower the downtrodden members of the town. It's a sublime and magical piece of cinema. Also worth the price of a rental is Alfonso Arau's *Like Water For Chocolate*, an adaptation of his then-wife's

A tray of Ferrero Rocher usually cured the leading lady's histrionics

(Laura Esquivel) tale of family life and social upheaval in Mexico over a 40-year period. The dishes come to represent milestones in the lives of the three sisters and their tyrannical mother, with central character Tita (Lumi Cavazos) destined to serve her family and focus her love, hopes and sadness into her culinary creations.

THE COOK, THE THIEF, HIS WIFE & HER LOVER 1989

Director Peter Greenaway Cast Richard Bohringer, Michael Gambon, Helen Mirren, Tim Roth
The food featured in Peter Greenaway's tale of love, greed and revenge is often overshadowed by the sumptuous sets, Gaultier costumes and Gambon's portrayal of unrelenting evil, but the scene of gangster Spica (Gambon) about to tuck into the naked, cooked man laid out before him remains an everlasting image. In terms of plot, the title pretty much sums it up, with the action always surrounded by the creations of the chef (Bohringer). *The Cook* was originally given an X certificate, but distributor Miramax released it without a rating. In case you were wondering, the dog poo was actually chocolate mousse.

> "A PIE IN THE FACE HAS NO EQUAL IN SLAPSTICK COMEDY. IT CAN REDUCE DIGNITY TO NOTHING IN SECONDS"
> Mack Sennett

GRUB'S UP!

TASTY MORSELS

Since the very first custard pie was pushed into a face in Fatty Arbuckle's *A Noise From The Deep*, classic moments in cinema's history have often contained food.

APPLE PIE

Jason Biggs gets friendly with his mum's home-made apple pie in *American Pie*.

BURGERS

Immortalised by John Travolta and Samuel L Jackson in *Pulp Fiction*, the humble burger had never been so cool.

CUSTARD PIES

The mother of all custard-pie fights – in Laurel & Hardy's *Battle Of The Century* – involved 3,000 pies being thrown, splattered and pelted.

DIM SUM

Robin Williams and Amanda Plummer wrestling with their elusive dim sum in *The Fisher King* is one of the great romantic warts-and-all scenes.

GRAPEFRUIT

Cagney rinsed Mae Clarke's face with one in *Public Enemy*. Should have run a B&B.

TOAST

Jack Nicholson in *Five Easy Pieces* started a trend for asking for our food exactly how we want it.

DELICATESSEN 1991

Directors Marc Caro, Jean-Pierre Jeunet *Cast* Dominique Pinon, Marie-Laure Dougnac, Karin Viard

This grisly tale of a landlord-cum-killer feeding his tenants the odd-job men in tasty meals is an entertaining comedic look at cannibalism. It's supplemented by a clutch of bizarre tenants, including an old man who's turned his cellar abode into a swamp home for frogs and snails, and you can't help but like each character for what they are. Despite the grotesque plot, it's a cult classic.

EAT DRINK MAN WOMAN 1994 YIN SHI NAN NU

Director Ang Lee *Cast* Sihung Lung, Yu-Wen Wang, Chien-lien Wu, Kuei-Mei Yang

Like director Lee's previous work *The Wedding Banquet*, this is a tale of love, relationships and traditions played out beneath the metaphor of food. A Taipei master chef tries to communicate his feelings for his three daughters through his ritual Sunday banquets. Rating this film by the food alone, *Eat Drink* ranks alongside the most delectable chocolates of *Chocolat*. Excellent.

TAMPOPO 1986

Director Juzo Itami *Cast* Tsutomu Yamazaki, Nobuko Miyamoto, Koji Yakusho

Tampopo (Miyamoto) is a widowed noodle chef whose night in shining armour is the trucker Goro (Yamazaki), who walks into town and teaches her to become the very best noodle chef possible. Food isn't simply a metaphor for something else in this film, it *is* the film. It envelopes the lives of every protagonist, from the gangster who misses sex and food to the finicky old lady who is driving a shopkeeper insane with her testing of his wares. This original comic-satire was an early foray into directing by Itami, and one of his less offensive pieces.

WHO IS KILLING THE GREAT CHEFS OF EUROPE? 1978

Director Ted Kotcheff *Cast* George Segal, Jacqueline Bisset, Robert Morley, Philippe Noiret

If you like ridiculous plots and brain-dead humour, you'll like this. One by one the greatest culinary masters of Europe are being bumped off, each in the manner in which they specialise in preparing food. Marginal mystery ensues with good performances by Morley and, as amazing as it sounds, Bisset. Different to say the least.

FOOTBALL

Years from now, your children will ask "Did it happen?" and you will be able to tell them "Yes, it did." There really was a film where Bobby Moore, Pele and Michael Caine played on the same team, Sylvester Stallone was in goal, and with half of the Ipswich Town first team, they won the War and escaped from occupied France in a crowd, wearing Adidas parkas, platform shoes and bri-nylon.

O nly in a football film could traditional staples like plot, convincing characterisation and plausibility get not so much ignored as flouted with breathtaking nonchalance. Consider *When Saturday Comes*. Local lad battles for a place in the first team and goes on to score the winner for Sheffield United against Manchester United late in extra time. Feasible? Hmmn. Hard to decide who looks less convincing in these films: the footballers or the actors pretending to be players. It's hard not to imagine Ian McShane sat in his trailer wondering where it all went wrong on the set of *Yesterday's Hero* (especially as McShane was briefly on Manchester United's books).

ALL STARS 1997
Director **Jean van der Velde** *Cast* **Antonie Kamerling**
Van der Velde directed and co-wrote this comedy about the mid-life crises facing the members of a Dutch football team about to play their 500th game. This likeable comedy-drama formed the basis of a Dutch TV series and of a Belgian remake, *Team Spirit,* which was described as "too typically Belgian" to appeal to the world market. The Dutch original was very popular at the Northwest Film Centre in Portland, Oregon.

THE ARSENAL STADIUM MYSTERY 1939
Director **Thorold Dickinson** *Cast* **Leslie Banks, Greta Gynt**
With Britain on the brink of war, the tonic the nation needed was a bizarre thriller in which the Arsenal team and Leslie Banks try to work out who's murdered one of the opposition. The film has tremendous curiosity value. The players play themselves, clad in some appropriately vast shorts and sporting enough Brylcreem to keep Denis Compton in flannels for the rest of his

> "MASS SUICIDE IS THE MOST EXHAUSTING PRACTICE ONE CAN ENGAGE IN. NEXT TO SOCCER"
> Loki, Dogma

life, and there are some atmospheric shots of the Highbury of yesteryear. While you're marvelling that this enjoyable film was ever made, don't forget to work out whodunnit.

ESCAPE TO VICTORY 1981
Director *John Huston* Cast *Sylvester Stallone, Michael Caine, Pele, Bobby Moore*

It's hard to work out what is more surprising. The fact that this film stars an eclectic combination of First Division footballers and character actors, or the fact that it was directed by John Huston. Either way, it's truly fantastic. A team comprising POWs raises a football team to play the Germans. Given the chance to escape at half time, they stick around, put a few past them and escape anyway. Honour is satisfied, and even the German manager (Max von Sydow, who else?) goes all dewy-eyed at the end. It's only mildly less laughable than a conspicuously overweight Michael Caine pretending to be an ex-international, a character so obviously modelled on his pal Bobby Moore that the England skipper should have got royalties. Legend has it that Pele's famous overhead kick was filmed in one take. Moore sent over a perfectly weighted cross, and Pele hit it first time. Pure brilliance.

> **"WHERE DO
> I STAND FOR
> CORNER KICKS?"**
> Robert Hatch, Escape to Victory

GARRINCHA 1962
Director *Joaquim Pedro De Andrade* Cast *Garrincha*

Made when the bandy-legged Brazilian (Garrincha overcame polio to become a professional footballer) was at his peak, this documentary contains some of the finest footballing footage known to man. In the 1958 World Cup he had been kept on the bench because the team psychiatrist insisted he was retarded but he came on against the Russians and the film of him keeping the ball away from five Russian players is even more mesmerising than Pele's free kick in *Victory*. When this film, which tells the amazing tale of his rise from poverty and sickness, was made he had just won the World Cup almost single-handedly for his country. This film is even more poignant because Garrincha would never be this good again, drinking and whoring himself to an untimely death in 1982.

THE GOALKEEPER'S FEAR OF THE PENALTY 1971
Director *Wim Wenders* Cast *Arthur Brauss, Kai Fischer*

A film that makes a tenuous entry into the football film canon by virtue of the fact that its main character is a goalkeeper. But the dilemmas of Shilts and Pat Jennings are not for Arthur Brauss. Nobody attempts to bring off a bubble perm. Nobody faces that tricky Jag/Bentley decision. This is a 'goalkeeping' movie of a much darker hue. Goalkeeper Bloch (Brauss) walks off the pitch and roams downtown Vienna and commits a murder for reasons that are never explained. Directed by Wenders, later to win fame with *Wings of Desire* and *Paris, Texas*, *Goalkeeper* is a disorientating and disconcerting masterpiece.

L'ARBITRO 1974

Director Luigi Filippo D'Amico
Cast Joan Collins,
Lando Buzzanca

An Italian comedy of manners

Allied POWs celebrate after the Russian linesman confirms, to German disgust, the ball was over the line

about a referee who can't concentrate on what's happening on the pitch because he's too busy thinking about what's happening in his bedroom. Understandable enough, because Joan Collins is happening in his bedroom. Also known as *Playing The Field* (nudge, nudge), this was one of several forays into sport by the director: he also made the even less well-known *Il Presidente del Borgorosso Football Club* (1970) and *Amore E Ginnastica* (1973). Still, even these are slightly less bizarre than *La Vida Sigue Igual* (1969), which stars former goalkeeper Julio Iglesias as a football-playing troubadour.

YESTERDAY'S HERO 1979

Director Neil Leifer Cast Ian McShane, Adam Faith

Before Ian McShane toured the antique shops of East Anglia looking for bargains, he was a proper actor. Really. Despite this, it's hard not to see his character in *Yesterday's Hero* as an alcoholic Lovejoy in unflattering nylon shorts. The reason why he's yesterday's hero is that he's a boozer, a maverick whose sublime skills are undermined by a defiant spirit that refuses to bow down, unless it's to be violently sick after the odd pint or 14. Naturally, he makes a glorious cup-final comeback from the bar – sorry, bench – and proves himself to be an all-round good egg. You find yourself watching in grim fascination as the whole thing unfolds like an accident in slow motion. Look at the credits, and it's easy to see why. Jackie Collins wrote the script, which explains a lot, John Motson provides the commentary and both Adam Faith and Paul Nicholas co-star with McShane. Weep as you realise that this line-up will never again be assembled on the silver screen. You wonder what McShane's dad, who used to be a scout for Manchester United, made of this.

GANGSTER

Goodfellas, Martin Scorsese's tour-de-force gangster epic, is based on the real-life hopes, dreams and actions of the genuine article. This isn't fiction. He wanted to be the guy in the suit with the gleaming shoes, the slicked back hair, the wad of neatly folded notes in his gold money clip, packing a pistol and always looking over his shoulder, keeping his friends close and his enemies closer, never getting high on your own supply. Oops, wrong film.

Although the people who write to *Points Of View* may believe that our love of onscreen violence is proof that society is decaying, we've been intrigued by rat-a-tat-tat movies almost since cinema began. The opening shot of DW Griffith's *The Musketeers Of Pig Alley* (1912) shows banknotes being passed from criminal to cop, one of the first such scenes on film. The title harks back to those heroes whose 'one for all and all for one' code of honour was romanticised to represent the mafia 'family' code in films such as *The Godfather*.

The gangster genre came into its own in the late 1920s with stories literally ripped from the newspaper headlines. Josef von Sternberg's *Underworld* (1927) is often cited as the first fully fledged gangster film. Written by former reporter Ben Hecht, the film's protagonist 'Bull' Weed is a bank robber who wants to build a criminal empire. The tale echoes the story of Al Capone whose rise, crimes (especially the St Valentine's Day massacre) and imprisonment inspired several films, either loosely (*Little Caesar*) or directly (*The Untouchables*).

The classic formula included such ingredients as the villainous hero, a gangster's moll, nightclubs, newspaper hounds and a tragic 'crime doesn't pay' ending. In the 1930s directors such as Mervyn LeRoy and Howard Hawks served up tales of egotism, violence, and, er, morality often based on real life, but it was the portrayal of gangsters by Jimmy Cagney, Edward G Robinson, Paul Muni and a young Bogart which made the genre so popular.

After the FBI gunned down John Dillinger (he was leaving a theatre having just watched the

Brando with cotton wool in his cheeks, in the ultimate gangster family saga

Gable gangster drama *Manhattan Melodrama*), the interest moved from law-breaker to law enforcer. Cagney and Robinson even switched sides, in *G Men* and *Bullets Or Ballots* respectively.

The 1950s saw another shift with the focus back on crime bosses, partly because they were again in the headlines as the Senate investigated them. In 1932 *Scarface* had merely alluded to Capone, but studios tackled these subjects more openly with such films as *Machine-Gun Kelly* (1958) and *Al Capone* (1959). Less biographical but still focused on character were *The Enforcer* (1951), *Murder Inc* (1960) and *New York Confidential* (1955), inspired by the Murder Inc syndicate. Having explored every variation, including kiddie gangsters (*Dead End Kids*), musicals with kiddie gangsters (*Bugsy Malone*) and comedy (*The Whole Town's Talking*), Hollywood went back to basics. *The Godfather*, its sequels and me-toos revived mobster chic.

> "DO I ICE HER? DO I MARRY HER? WHICH ONE A DESE?"
> Charley Patanna, Prizzi's Honour

Since *Casino* was released in 1995, filmmakers have seemed to be running a little low on material. The classic gangster film may even become a retro genre as the real life source for films like *Goodfellas* dries up. John Gotti is the one mob boss to have captured the media's attention in recent decades, but the 'Dapper Don' was famed more for his clothes than his crimes. Maybe *Traffic* points some kind of way ahead. Maybe not.

ANGELS WITH DIRTY FACES 1938

Director Michael Curtiz *Cast* James Cagney, Pat O'Brien, Humphrey Bogart, Ann Sheridan

Despite a plethora of gangster films in the 1930s, Curtiz's Oscar-nominated tale became a landmark in cinema history. Cementing the reputations of its three main protagonists, it is also a definitive example of the Warner Bros studio style: dim lighting, shadow-play and simple sets. Such minimalism is warranted here, as *Angels* is as much social commentary as gangster film. Cagney as Rocky heads back to the old neighbourhood where he becomes a local hero to the Dead End Kids. Childhood pal Jerry (O'Brien) persuades him to re-evaluate his life choices, the final scene showing Cagney seemingly turning coward when faced with the electric chair in order to save the kids from the same fate. The public got slightly agitated over the fact that Cagney never needed to reload his gun. So from here on in Cagney insisted he never be seen shooting more than six rounds without reloading.

BLACK CAESAR 1973

Director Larry Cohen *Cast* Fred Williamson, Gloria Hendry, Art Lund, D'Urville Martin

This charts the murderous misadventures of Tommy Gibbs

(Williamson) from shoeshine boy to mafia boss. His achievements are obviously all the more impressive as he manages to infiltrate the Italian mob despite being black. Although it's interesting to watch a Harlem version of the classic 1930s gangster film, you can't help thinking that the bloodbaths are there merely to titillate us. But then this is essentially a blaxploitation movie with a mob twist.

BOB LE FLAMBEUR 1955 BOB THE GAMBLER
Director **Jean-Pierre Melville** *Cast* **Isabelle Corey, Daniel Cauchy, Roger Duchesne**

Reportedly we have to thank an astute film archivist for discovering this little gem in the back of a safe. Bob is at the top of the mob hierarchy, living in Paris feeding his gambling habit. When his dosh runs out, Bob arranges a heist on a casino – complete with a crew, a plan and a traitor – that looks set to be a disaster. Shot in black and white, the direction by Melville (he took this name out of respect for the writer Herman Melville) is stylish and fluid. But *Bob* remains one of his lighter films compared to classics such as *Le Samourai*. In a comedy of manners, Bob struts around in his trenchcoat and fedora looking every bit the criminal, but is the epitome of honour and loyalty where his friends are concerned. Enjoyable stuff.

BONNIE & CLYDE 1967
Director **Arthur Penn** *Cast* **Warren Beatty, Faye Dunaway**

Despite Warner Bros giving the film only a limited release and

THE DEFINITIVE MOVIES

THE MAFIA
THE GODFATHER TRILOGY
1972-1990
Although director Francis Ford Coppola and writer Mario Puzo were at pains never to refer to the mafia, *The Godfather* saga remains the definitive mafia movie. This is organised crime headed by Brando's Don, and then his son Michael, who is drawn into joining the family business, sacrificing his moral beliefs.

THE YAKUZA
THE YAKUZA 1975
Although Sydney Pollack's film is an American take on the classic Japanese genre, Paul Schrader's debut script works well as a comparison to America's own gangster genre.

Robert Mitchum heads back to Japan in search of his friend's kidnapped daughter, and becomes involved with the Japanese mafia, the Yakuza. It is co-writer Leonard Schrader who provides the in-depth knowledge of the Japanese culture which comes alive on screen.

THE TRIADS
JIANG HU LONG HU MEN 1987
Released in the US as *Flaming Brothers*, and directed by Tung Cho Cheung, this is a tale of two brothers, one a triad member who wants to keep the organisation from drugs and gun-running, the other an ex-member who has gone legit. Unusually for a gangster movie, there are a lot of gay undertones, plus more bullets than in De Palma's *Scarface*.

its critical slaughtering at the hands of *New York Times* critic Bosley Crowther (he later changed his review and subsequently left the newspaper), the film became an unprecedented success with the public and created (or so it seemed at the time) a new Hollywood. The old Hollywood wasn't that impressed: studio boss Jack Warner, after a private screening, scolded Beatty about its length: "This is a three-piss picture." The tale of a 1920s gang of bank robbers led by Clyde Barrow and Bonnie Parker is essentially a film about reacting against the establishment, a kind of *Rebel Without a Cause* but with a gun. Although *Splendor In The Grass* had been a hit for Beatty in 1961, *Clyde* made him, and was a turning point in the careers of Faye Dunaway and Gene Hackman. Funnily enough, Beatty had originally wanted to cast Bob Dylan as the "runtish" Clyde but was encouraged to star himself. Penn wanted the final scene where a bit of Clyde's head is blown away by a bullet to remind viewers of the assassination of JFK.

"How many times have I got to tell you? You were only supposed to blow the bleedin' doors off"

BORSALINO 1970

Director *Jacques Deray* Cast *Jean-Paul Belmondo, Alain Delon, Michel Bouquet*

François (Belmondo) and Roch (Delon) are two small-time crooks just making their way in the Marseilles crime world in the 1930s. What begins as simple race-fixing and running errands for the local mob bosses rapidly turns more serious as the two decide to go into business for themselves. Claude

"COLIN NEVER HURT A FLY. WELL, ONLY WHEN IT WAS NECESSARY"
Harold, The Long Good Friday

'I ALWAYS TELL THE TRUTH, EVEN WHEN I LIE'
Tony Montana, Scarface

Bolling's delightful score, the nods to masters like Howard Hawks, and the sparkling performances of the stars make this a very entertaining, if sometimes bloody, pastiche. Followed in 1974 by the slightly less engaging *Borsalino & Co*.

BRIGHTON ROCK 1947

Director John Boulting *Cast* Richard Attenborough, Carol Marsh, Hermione Baddeley

Richard Attenborough gives his finest performance as babyfaced gang-leader Pinkie who, after murdering a rival racketeer, spirals out of control. Although author Graham Greene applauded Attenborough's chilling portrayal, the film, one of Britain's best film noirs, is marred by Greene's decision to give his screenplay an overly optimistic ending, with which Boulting went OTT. This aside, *Brighton Rock*, known rather reductively in the US as *Young Scarface*, remains a bleak, perfectly crafted slice of gang life. In the fine supporting cast is William Hartnell, the first Dr Who.

CARLITO'S WAY 1993

Director Brian De Palma *Cast* Al Pacino, Sean Penn, Penelope Ann Miller, John Leguizamo

"Sorry boys, all the stitches in the world can't sew me back together again." De Palma's most recent crime tale opens with Puerto Rican ex-con Carlito Brigante's retrospective view of what went wrong. Although the film is working to the tried and tested formula of a reformed gangster looking to get out, Carlito's pride and reputation draw him back in. If you ignore his Puerto Rican accent, Pacino gives a measured performance as someone who wants to better himself but knows he is fated not to lead a 'normal' life. But a barely recognisable Penn steals the movie as a sneaky, coke-fuelled lawyer. De Palma is back to his best, painting a glossy but pacy tale of gang life, and the mad scheme to rescue a criminal from a prison barge is a fine set piece. Deeply trivial fact: Carlito's nightclub El Paraiso shares its name with Tony Montana's taco stand in the De Palma/Pacino *Scarface*.

GET CARTER 1971

Director Mike Hodges *Cast* Michael Caine, Ian Hendry, Britt Ekland

Cool, unrelenting and vicious, Jack Carter returns to Newcastle to find those responsible for killing his brother and falls into a world of corruption, seedy pornography and murder. Although Ted Lewis' original work was set in an unnamed steel town, Newcastle-upon-Tyne provides a suitably gritty backdrop for the action (every southerner knows it's grim up north).

Twenty years on, the coolness with which Jack dishes out violence remains far more disturbing than any slasher film, and anticipates the measured violence of the following year's *The Godfather*. Playwright John Osborne is surprisingly effective as the crime boss. Caine didn't get to know him well: "He seemed to be someone who didn't like many other people, so I kept out of his way in case I was one of them." Sly Stallone's American remake has all the narrative coherence of *Thomas And The Magic Railroad*.

GLORIA 1980
Director John Cassavetes *Cast* Gena Rowlands, Julie Carmen, John Adames

Although the idea of teaming tough-talking gangsters with smart-mouthed kids isn't exactly new territory, the casting of Gena Rowlands (the late director's wife) as the tough-talking gangster's moll is what carries the film. A family is wiped out by the mob for giving information to the FBI, with only the seven-year-old son surviving. Gloria (Rowlands) is the former gangster's girl living next door who begrudgingly looks after the kid. From here a cat-and-mouse chase ensues, with Gloria and her street smarts trying to save the kid and herself. Cassavetes gives the film a suitably smoky feel but it is devoid of some of his usual touches and Rowlands' Oscar-nominated turn drives the film. Avoid the 1999 Sharon Stone remake.

GOODFELLAS 1989
Director Martin Scorsese *Cast* Ray Liotta, Robert De Niro, Joe Pesci, Lorraine Bracco

The scene of Henry Hill (Liotta) swaggering through the Copacabana club with girlfriend Karen (Bracco) and heading for the best seats in the house, complete with a special dedication by crooner Bobby Vinton, sums up perfectly why Henry has always wanted to be a gangster, and why good Jewish girl Karen is willing to believe his "I'm in construction" line. Scorsese's tale of the rise and fall of real-life mobster Hill is a whirlwind adventure. This is the mafia at its most seductive: the cars, the houses, the respect and the dangerous, whether in the persona of De Niro's paranoid mentor or the out-and-out mindless violence of Pesci's Tommy. Worryingly, it was Pesci himself who wrote and directed the "How the fuck am I funny?

He's short, he's round, he's always beating people to the ground, that's Jimmy Cagney in *White Heat*. That's the trouble with a Napoleon complex, you end up riddled with bullets and cackling "Top o' the world" madly

What the fuck is so funny about me?" scene, and he can take credit for most of the 246 times the f-word was used in the film. *Goodfellas* is sublime Scorsese, with a rousing soundtrack, frantic sequences (see Henry pursued by the helicopter) and a supporting cast that looks as if it has come straight to the set from San Quentin. The swearing obviously didn't put off Ma and Pa Scorsese, as they both have cameos in the film.

LITTLE CAESAR 1930

Director **Mervyn LeRoy** *Cast* **Edward G Robinson, Douglas Fairbanks Jr, Glenda Farrell**

Based on WR Burnett's debut novel (he later wrote such classics as *High Sierra*), *Little Caesar* is a variation on the life and crimes of Al Capone, with Robinson thrillingly vicious as gangster Rico. The opening credits labour the point that if you live by the gun, you die by it, but the gangster life still looks glamorous. As often happens, some of the film's power comes from the lack of budget: the cheap sets give the film a wonderfully sleazy air, making it seem more realistic than it probably was. Robinson's machine-gun-pace delivery still packs a punch. Producer Wallis had tried to convince Robinson to take a small part but he

MOBSTERS OR LOBSTERS?

Next time you whinge about De Niro as a Don, just remember who could have been playing a mafia boss

BERNARD CRIBBINS
NERVOUS O'TOOLE

Not even Mr Magoo would mistake cuddly Cribbins for a gangster on this performance in *The Wrong Arm Of The Law*.

DUSTIN HOFFMAN
DUTCH SCHULTZ

Schultz was described by his friends (most of them now swimming with the fishes) as an enigma, and he remains so to Hoffman throughout *Billy Bathgate*, possibly because he couldn't quite get into the role unless he started dishing out cement shoes in real life.

GENE KELLY
JOHNNY COLUMBO

One of the more creative casting decisions to come out of Hollywood. Gene 'sparkly eyes' Kelly as a violent gangster in *The Black Hand*? We think not.

STEVE MARTIN
VINCENT 'VINNIE' ANTONELLI

The early 1990s saw a whole slew of comic gangster films including *My Cousin Vinny*, Stallone's *Oscar*, etc. Whereas Joe Pesci offered us a comic rendition of his *Goodfellas* Tommy De Vito, in *My Blue Heaven* Martin gives us a one-joke gangster stereotype complete with shiny suits, Queens drawl and spats shoes.

THE ENTIRE CAST MOBSTERS

There's no denying Christian Slater can do a fantastic impersonation of Jack Nicholson, but Lucky Luciano he ain't. Then there's *Who's The Boss?* teen heartthrob Richard Grieco as the mighty Bugsy Siegel. Grieco returned to TV movie hell soon after.

refused flat out, saying he would only play Rico. Wallis thought he was bluffing but the next day the actor burst into his office in trenchcoat and hat and started delivering Rico's lines in such a manner that the producer realised he had no choice.

THE LONG GOOD FRIDAY 1980
Director John MacKenzie *Cast* Bob Hoskins, Helen Mirren, Dave King John (where is he now?) MacKenzie's tale of self-made mob boss Hoskins is as much an analysis of the social and political mood of the 1980s as a modern gangster film. Hoskins is a cockney geezer infused with inflated ideas of turning the London Docklands into the new Manhattan. With backing from New York, Harold's dream is nearly realised until some unknown rival starts knocking off his associates and bombing his businesses. Like Cagney before him, Hoskins proves it's the short, round ones you've got to watch, giving a suitably terrifying performance as a man on the verge. Mirren is perfectly cast as his moll Victoria, but even more shocking than Pierce Brosnan's appearance as an IRA man, is Derek Thompson (nurse Charlie in *Casualty*) as gang member Jeff.

MEAN STREETS 1973
Director Martin Scorsese *Cast* Harvey Keitel, Robert De Niro
"You don't make up for your sins in church. You do it in the streets." Charlie (Keitel) and Johnny (De Niro) are two young hoods establishing themselves in the New York mafia. Charlie, quiet, thoughtful and guilt-ridden, runs errands for his uncle, while Johnny is the embodiment of gangster glory. It's less polished than his later work, but many of Scorsese's trademarks are evident, notably the use of music in the memorable, much copied, scene of Charlie strutting through his friend's bar to the sound of Mick Jagger blaring *Jumpin' Jack Flash*. Although not exactly autobiographical, *Mean Streets* stems from a childhood where, in Scorsese's neighbourhood, you entered the mob or the priesthood. Thankfully for us, Scorsese entered neither. Be thankful also that Scorsese, who wrote 27 drafts of the script before anyone bought it, didn't accept Roger Corman's offer to finance it if he made it as a *Shaft* me-too with an all-black cast.

NEW JACK CITY 1991
Director Mario Van Peebles *Cast* Wesley Snipes, Ice-T, Judd Nelson, Bill Nunn, Michael Michele
Although gangster Nino Brown (Snipes) is modelled on Al Pacino's *Scarface*, the gangland world which Nino presides over is a complete reversal to that of the traditional mob. Here the mob is young, trigger-happy and displays no code of honour,

> **"YOU SHOOT ME IN A DREAM, YOU BETTER WAKE UP AND APOLOGISE"**
> Mr White, Reservoir Dogs

thus making it more susceptible to infiltration, in this case by ex-cops Appleton (Ice T, surprisingly good for a rap star) and Peretti (Nelson brought back from the dead, aka The Curse Of The Teen Movie). Although *New Jack* is an interesting re-take on the ambitious boss turns megalomaniac, the plot often spirals out of control with just too many characters to get to grips with. Although a case of could-have-been-better, Peebles makes an impressive stab at such a popular genre, creating a grim and suitably menacing feel to the movie, and employing music to help keep up the movie's pace.

ONCE UPON A TIME IN AMERICA 1984
Director **Sergio Leone** *Cast* **Robert De Niro, James Woods, Elizabeth McGovern, Treat Williams**
Sergio Leone's final film as director has never yet been released in its entirety. Noodles (De Niro) and Max (Woods) are childhood friends who rise in the Jewish mafia but whose friendship turns to betrayal. An attempt to edit the film into chronological sequence proved disastrous. Leone himself edited the 225-minute version, and it is only in this print that you come to realise how the characters relate to one another and the importance that time, seen through the use of flashbacks, has on the narrative and those involved. Beautifully photographed, the streets of New York almost resemble the dusty plains of Leone's *Fistful of Dollars*. Like that film, this can be brutal, especially the rape scene with Noodles and Deborah (McGovern). You'll need a padded seat to watch it all through.

PETE KELLY'S BLUES 1955
Director **Jack Webb** *Cast* **Jack Webb, Janet Leigh, Edmond O'Brien**
Pete Kelly (Jack Webb) and his band of jazz musicians come under threat from the local Kansas City mob and once their drummer has been killed, Pete allows the mob to take over the band. Although it can be hard at times to separate Pete from Jack's alter ego Joe *Dragnet* Friday, the music and the cast are impressive, with appearances from Peggy Lee, Ella Fitzgerald and Jayne Mansfield in her first screen role.

SALVATORE GIULIANO 1962
Director **Francesco Rosi** *Cast* **Frank Wolff, Salvo Randone, Federico Zardi**
The infamous Sicilian bandit Giuliano remains an enigma, with director Rosi preferring to stick to the few facts known rather than create his own dramatic interpretation of events. With its use of black-and-white photography, the film has a documentary feel to it. Although the Christopher Lambert film

Il Siciliano told the same story, Rosi's interpretation is probably the more stirring and actually prompted the Italian authorities to investigate the mob. The film, which brought Rosi international fame, is often regarded as his best work, with Frank Wolff almost as impressive as Giuliano's cousin.

SCARFACE 1932

Director Howard Hawks, Richard Rosson *Cast* Paul Muni, Ann Dvorak, George Raft

Al Capone liked this disguised story of his life so much he is supposed to have had his own copy. Muni starred as Tony Camonte, former bagman to an old-style gang leader, who sets out to rule the (mob) world. Despite the film's credits stating, "This picture is an indictment of gang rule in America and of the callous indifference of the government", censors wouldn't endorse it. Reshoots showing Tony arrested, convicted and hanged failed to persuade them, so Hawks eventually stuck to the original. The film also marks the arrival of George Raft as a coin-tossing henchman. Raft would play a slew of gangster roles, aided by his personal association with real-life mobsters like Bugsy Siegel, and rumours that he himself was a 'made' man. Although the 1983 Al Pacino/De Palma remake lacks originality, Pacino is suitably menacing as coke-fuelled, self-made boss Tony Montana – don't worry, it was icing sugar they were bathing their nostrils in. The scene where Montana, surrounded, his arm in a sling, waves his gun at his enemies and certain death is one of the most glamorous, romantic images of the doomed gangster on celluloid.

SONATINE 1993

Director Takeshi Kitano
Cast Beat Takeshi, Aya Kokumai, Tetsu Watanabe

Although this was only director Kitano's third film (he acts under the alias Beat Takeshi), few directors have managed to add such a novel slant to the gangster/yakuza film. Murakawa (Takeshi) is weary of his life as a yakuza, tired of the constant fear, and wants to

Donnie Brasco: Even gangsters drink to forget about it

THE MOLLS

A powerful man often has a good woman behind him pulling the strings, and the mob is no exception.

MICHELLE PFEIFFER
MARRIED TO THE MOB

A raven-haired Pfeiffer (as Angela de Marco) brings down mafia suitor Tony 'The Tiger' Russo, played by diminutive Dean Stockwell. Pfeiffer also impressed as Mrs Scarface in the Brian De Palma remake.

JUDITH ANDERSON SLADE
LADY SCARFACE

Not strictly speaking a moll: the entire Chicago police department assumes notorious gangster, Slade, to be a man. However, the scarred-faced boss is obviously a woman. A groundbreaking idea even now.

JEAN HARLOW
THE PUBLIC ENEMY

Fortunately for Harlow (who plays Gwen Allen) it wasn't the original platinum blonde who had a grapefruit squashed into her face by James Cagney. Harlow remains the definitive gangster's moll.

get out. But before he can do so he is asked to settle a dispute between warring factions. It becomes clear this is a set-up and he heads back into the yakuza world, seeking revenge. Kitano isn't afraid to display violence but it's not gratuitous and the set pieces are beautifully filmed. Indeed they're even more chilling for not being overdone (especially in the scene where a gambler gets chucked in the sea for not paying protection). And it's good to see a film where the gangster isn't enthralled by the shoot 'em ups but is deadened and depressed by them, as if he'd half welcome a fatally wrong outcome.

THE UNTOUCHABLES 1987

Director Brian De Palma *Cast* Kevin Costner, Sean Connery, Andy Garcia, Robert De Niro

Although this version features Al Capone (De Niro) rather than just alluding to the crime boss and tax evader, the film focuses on straight-laced, naïve law enforcer Eliot Ness (Costner playing himself) and his band of doomed sidekicks. De Niro put his all into the role, gaining weight, undergoing hours in make-up and even going so far as to track down the real Capone's tailor to have identical clothing made for the shoot. Despite its status now as a seasonal television release, the infamous climax shot in Chicago Union station is still best viewed on the big screen.

WHITE HEAT 1949

Director Raoul Walsh *Cast* James Cagney, Virginia Mayo

Cagney may never have said "You dirty rat!" on celluloid but he does say "Made it, Ma! Top of the world!" in this. In the convoluted way of Hollywood, the film started life as a police thriller, mutating when Cagney, who needed cash for his production company, signed on. Helped by veteran director Walsh, Cagney makes ruthless gang-leader Cody one of his most brutal and mesmerising villains. The scenes emphasising Cody's unnatural affection for his ma (when he's calmed lying in her lap or when he goes berserk in prison after being told of her death) are compelling if OTT, but then Cagney plays this as if he were a Universal monster. This was his last great gangster part. Maybe that's why he's so reluctant to die in the end; poor old Edmond O'Brien (the film's 'official' hero) has to keep pumping bullets in him, asking: "What's keeping him up?"

GAY

In 1927, Hollywood's first self-regulating code said: "The following shall not appear in motion pictures, irrespective of the manner in which they are treated: ...any inference of sexual perversity." Ruthlessly applied, this clause could have ended the careers of Marlene Dietrich, Anthony Perkins and Cecil B DeMille. Times and (most) attitudes have changed, though even today many actors are still at the mercy of professional "outers" and gossip columnists.

Even today, many gay and lesbian actors are scared to reveal their sexuality because the public might reject them. It's hardly surprising when you consider how gay people have been portrayed on screen. They have been killers (John Dall and Farley Granger in *Rope*), rapists (Bill McKinney and Herbert 'Cowboy' Coward in *Deliverance*) and even vampires (Catherine Deneuve in *The Hunger*), ie anything that might have been the product of a perverse, tortured lifestyle. So until the 1970s, most gay, or implied gay, characters came to a nasty end. Suicide was preferred, although being beaten to death like Sebastian in *Suddenly, Last Summer* was also an option.

Gradually filmmakers have fought against these stereotypes and there is now a thriving gay cinema full of stories of gays and lesbians who want the same things heterosexual characters want: love, relationships, adventure and fun. From fey characters like Peter Lorre's Joel Cairo in *The Maltese Falcon*, to Quentin Tarantino in *Sleep With Me* discussing the homo-erotic undercurrents of *Top Gun*, tracing the progression of gay characters and themes in the movies can be both hilarious and depressing, but also turns up a few filmic gems.

"ALWAYS KNOW WHERE I AM BY THE WAY THE ROAD LOOKS"
Mike Walters, My Own Private Idaho

ANDERS ALS DIE ANDEREN 1919
Director Richard Oswald *Cast* Conrad Veidt, Leo Connard
A rich man falls prey to a blackmailer when he makes advances to a stranger at a men-only dance. Way ahead of its time and a product of the German expressionist cinema, this silent film deals frankly and sympathetically with a gay relationship. Not surprisingly, almost every copy was destroyed when the Nazis came to power. Thankfully a fragmented print was rediscovered

in the 1970s and restored. It was years before Hollywood would show the same kind of maturity towards the subject.

ANOTHER COUNTRY 1984

Director Marek Kanievska Cast Rupert Everett, Colin Firth

Julian Mitchell's play, brought to the big screen, is a speculative exploration of the effect that public school life in the 1930s may have had on the willingness of Guy Burgess and Donald Maclean to spy for the USSR. Everett plays Guy Bennett, a louche, posturing teen, hopelessly in love with Cary Elwes' blonde beauty. Although homosexuality is rife at the school, it is ignored as it is assumed that the boys will grow out of it. When Everett declares it to be the way he is, he is shunned by his housemates, bringing him ever closer to Firth's left-wing intellectual – "the queer and the commie" as he puts it. The film is soaked in a dreamy nostalgia, despite some harrowing scenes, and the cast of young men and boys is shamelessly lingered over. Only the deeply crap make-up used to transform Everett into an old man breaks the spell.

THE BITTER TEARS OF PETRA VON KANT 1972

Director Rainer Werner Fassbinder Cast Margit Carstensen, Hanna Schygulla, Katrin Schaake

Talky, static and set in a single apartment, this is still a classic Fassbinder study of lesbianism and how women relate to each other. Petra (Carstensen) is a successful fashion designer, arrogant and tough, and unspeakably rude to her assistant. She begins a love affair with a young model (Schygulla), and her life begins to unravel. Fassbinder uses his setting, an absurdly ornate bedroom, full of mannequins and fabric, to convey the prison of Petra's mind, and composes numerous clever shots using mirrors, sheer fabric and the bars of the bed to enclose her further. The meticulous camera work is the perfect foil for the story of erotic power and sexual cruelty which unfolds.

"HE COULD LEAVE
MARKS ON ME
ANY TIME. I'D
BRING THE STICK"

Lt Kitty Lawrence, I Was A Male War Bride

THE BOYS IN THE BAND 1970

Director William Friedkin Cast Kenneth Nelson, Frederick Combs

Mart Crowley's play about a homosexual birthday party made it to the big screen as one of the first movies where gay characters were allowed to discuss openly the fact that they were gay. Not that these men are exactly happy with their lot – in fact the evening progresses to a drunken slanging match about how much they hate themselves – but it is a landmark in gay cinema in that no one dies or commits suicide, and that the implication is, despite the bitchery, that these men will always be there for each other. The fact that "same sex activity" was still illegal in several states when the film was released makes it even more intriguing.

THE CELLULOID CLOSET 1995

Directors Robert Epstein, Jeffrey Friedman *Cast* Lily Tomlin, Tom Hanks

A fascinating and sometimes hilarious documentary

Camp heaven: trapezes, tights, palm-reading and Tony and Burt

(narrated by Tomlin) tracing the development of gay characters and themes throughout Hollywood's history. Terrific interviews with performers, filmmakers and camp icons like Harvey Fierstein and Quentin Crisp are intercut with footage of all sorts of movie characters you wouldn't think were gay at first glance. The film was to feature biopics that straightened the sexual leanings of the likes of Alexander the Great, Hans Christian Andersen and Michelangelo, but the filmmakers refused to release the clips, proving homophobia still flourishes in parts of Hollywood. Epstein's documentary *The Times Of Harvey Milk*, about the life and assassination of San Francisco's first openly gay city councillor, is a sobering companion piece.

THE CHILDREN'S HOUR 1961

Director William Wyler *Cast* Audrey Hepburn, Shirley MacLaine

In 1936 Wyler made *These Three*, a discreet version of Lillian Hellman's play, with the references to lesbians removed because of the Hays Code. By 1961 he could return to the same material and make this overt version of the story of two teachers accused of lesbianism by a spiteful pupil. Groundbreaking in its time, and worth watching if you're in the mood for melodrama, but this is Hollywood at its clumsiest. Since the word "lesbian" is never spoken, the (incorrect) accusation that the women are lovers is handled with coy distaste, and there is no interest in why all the parents remove their children from school, just the implication that these are things nice people do not discuss. There is certainly sympathy for MacLaine's character in an excellent performance, but it just doesn't stop her from coming to the obligatory sticky end.

DESERT HEARTS 1985

Director **Donna Deitch** *Cast* **Helen Shaver, Patricia Charbonneau**

> "HE REACHED IN AND PUT A STRING OF LIGHTS AROUND MY HEART"
> Frances, Desert Hearts

Set in divorce-happy Nevada in the 1950s, the story follows an English literature professor, Vivian, who comes to a ranch to end her marriage but is increasingly drawn to the ranch-owner's daughter, Cay, a young and liberated lesbian. Not the most riveting of premises, but this is a refreshingly simple love story, which refuses to get bogged down in endless should-they, shouldn't-they. The desert settings, emphasising the freedom of Cay's way of life versus Vivian's buttoned-up attitude, are sumptuous, and the soundtrack, featuring the plaintive vocals of Elvis, Patsy Cline and Kitty Wells, suits perfectly.

MY BEAUTIFUL LAUNDRETTE 1985

Director **Stephen Frears** *Cast* **Daniel Day Lewis, Gordon Warnecke**

An ambitious young Asian negotiates local white thugs and the pressures of his family to open a glamorous launderette, helped by a childhood friend who becomes his lover. Hanif Kureishi has never written better than this story of Thatcherite ambition existing alongside a convention-flouting romance. Frears' direction often tips into a heightened reality that fits perfectly with the OTT interior of the revamped launderette. The relationship between Omar (Warnecke) and Johnny (Day Lewis) is believable and touching, despite their differences, and the whole story is a tribute to individuality and resilience.

MY OWN PRIVATE IDAHO 1991

Director **Gus Van Sant** *Cast* **River Phoenix, Keanu Reeves**

Mike (Phoenix) and Scott (Reeves) are rent boys in downtown Portland, Oregon. Mike is a narcoleptic, and Scott just happens to be the bi-sexual son of the town's mayor, slumming it with

deadbeat street characters. The story wanders into an offbeat reworking of Shakespeare's *Henry IV* which doesn't quite succeed, but the relationship between the two young men is the heart of the film. Touching and vulnerable, Mike is looking for someone who will love him and he thinks he has found that person in Scott, but Scott isn't so sure. Mike's dreamy detachment, reflecting his rootless life as well as his sleeping sickness, keeps him from feeling things too strongly, but his longing for love is palpable. The beautifully shot scenes on the road and by the campfire are

Emerging teen idols test drive their iconic look in *My Own Private Idaho*

stunning, both visually and emotionally, and Van Sant gets one of the best (and sadly, last) performances out of River Phoenix.

OUTRAGEOUS! 1977

Director Richard Benner *Cast* Craig Russell, Hollis McLaren

A drag queen shares a flat with a pregnant schizophrenic in this outstanding low-budget, pre-Aids, gay lifestyle story. Craig Russell was a female impersonator of awesome talent, morphing easily and completely into screen divas like Tallulah Bankhead, Bette Davis and Mae West, and here he uses his gift to punctuate a simple, but moving story about getting a break in show business and the people who help him along the way. The relationship between Russell and McClaren is a joy to watch, as these two are far from the dysfunctional pair that some viewers might expect.

TORCH SONG TRILOGY 1988

Director Paul Bogart *Cast* Harvey Fierstein, Anne Bancroft, Matthew Broderick

A glorious celebration of family life, drag queen style. Fierstein adapted his successful play for the big screen, and it's a touching, funny, sometimes sad but ultimately uplifting study of what it is like to be a camp gay man who simply wants what others have in life: love, success and a family who care. Arnold Becker (Fierstein) is a female impersonator always hoping to meet Mr Right. The early part deals with his love life, and then terrific scenes with Bancroft delve into the mother/son relationship. Humane and engaging: if anything can further the cause of gay cinema, this can.

CAMP CLASSICS

Many films that have nothing to do with gay lives, with no gay characters or themes, are adopted by the gay community as camp classics. It could be because of a single scene, or a character's outfit, or that the whole film is so trashy even the most macho gay men bow down in awe. Or it could feature Judy Garland in any way, no matter how marginal. Whatever the reason, here are a handful.

CALAMITY JANE (1953)
Doris Day in buckskins singing "Once I Had A Secret Love". What more can you want?

I WAS A MALE WAR BRIDE (1949)
If the title wasn't enough to ensure instant camp classic status, Cary Grant's turn in drag certainly is.

JOHNNY GUITAR (1954)
Joan Crawford, a gay icon of immense proportions, gets butch in the Wild West. Check out the cat fight between her and Emma Small, where the burly cowboys all stand around looking at their feet.

SHOWGIRLS (1995)
Possibly one of the worst scripted and acted films ever made, but celebrated for its high camp Las Vegas bitchery, not to mention the abundance of sequins, tassels and tasteless dance numbers.

TRAPEZE (1954)
Burt Lancaster and Tony Curtis chase the elusive "triple" in tights while Gina Lollobrigida pouts.

United Artists/Hecht-Lancaster; New Line

GODZILLA

If you thought mutant was a term of abuse, meet the king of monsters, the nuclear-fuelled amphibian from a bygone age who can vanquish smog monsters, robot monkeys and MechaGodzilla.

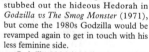

Godzilla (aka Gojira), the cinematic creation of Japan's Toho Studios, is a 400ft tall, amphibious tyrannosaurus mutant from the mesozoic period, brought to life by poisonous radiation fallout from nuclear weapon-testing. The radioactive energy from these atomic explosions kept Godzilla growing, as well as giving him the ability to spew nuclear fire.

The big G's debut was in *Gojira* (1954) where he terrorised and demolished Tokyo, thus warning the civilised world that tampering with forces beyond its control was a Very Bad Idea. (Gojira was the name of one of the workmen at Toho.) Retitled *Godzilla King Of The Monsters* in the US, this grim apocalyptic message was Americanized, but not dumbed down, by the insertion of a performance by Raymond Burr. Godzilla's debut was meant to be a one-off but giant-monster-lovers took him to their hearts, prompting many sequels involving Godzilla battling for supremacy against another (or several) gigantic formidable mutation(s), with Tokyo, Osaka or a nearby metropolis as the panic-stricken arena for their deadly combat.

In the 1960s the original baleful Godzilla was replaced with a greener, consumer-friendly version. In this guise Godzilla stubbed out the hideous Hedorah in *Godzilla vs The Smog Monster* (1971), but come the 1980s Godzilla would be revamped again to get in touch with his less feminine side.

Godzilla 1984 (1984) was a stylish remake of the original some 30 years on, complete with a second appearance by Burr. A welcome return to form, it enabled Godzilla to pull himself up to his full height without having to battle against increasingly dubious monsters. But this time, Godzilla's mood was more psychotic and the special effects were much more convincing. Although

Toho

The rubber suited rumble in the jungle: King Kong won this one, but only on points

Godzilla vs The Destroyer was to be his final bow, he returned more lethal than ever in *Godzilla 2000* (1999), as Toho tried to ensure the "King of the Movie Monsters" retains his crown.

GODZILLA VS THE DESTROYER 1995

Director Takao Okawara *Cast* Takuro Tatsumi, Megumi Odaka

Godzilla 1984 heralded in a new era for Toho's creation, inspiring a slew of Godzilla movies. But for their grand finale, Toho decided to kill off their biggest star by having him meet both Destroyer (a giant alien mantis creature) and his death by internal nuclear meltdown. Before burning up, however, the red-hot Godzilla avenges the supposed death of his son Minya with a blast of death ray. Destroyer goes down, but so does Godzilla in a blaze of glory. Although Godzilla has since arisen (in *Godzilla 2000*), this beautifully photographed, cleverly scripted and ingeniously staged film is the best of the new batch.

KING KONG VS GODZILLA 1963 (US 1964)

Director Ishiro Honda *Cast* Tadao Takeshima, Yu Fujiki

Director (US) Thomas Montgomery *Cast* Michael Keith, James Yogi, Harry Holcombe

Originally King Kong creator Willis O'Brien wanted to pit his giant gorilla against (somewhat improbably) Frankenstein's monster. That evolved into this rubber-suited rumble in the jungle where the mighty US ape clashes with Japan's finest flamethrower. Entire cities are flattened, Mount Fuji is threatened, a giant octopus is wrestled into submission and, after a furious underwater struggle, Kong swims away victorious into the sunset. Toho's Kong returned in *King Kong Escapes* (1967) where he meets MechaKong, a robot monkey controlled by the sinister Dr Who. We kid you not.

MONSTER ZERO 1965

Director Ishiro Honda *Cast* Nick Adams, Akira Takarada

Aka *Invasion Of The Astro Monsters*, this nonsensical film allowed Toho to introduce Ghidorah (here called Monster Zero) to a younger audience. The action takes place on nearby Planet X, where two astronauts find the planet is being constantly buzzed by the fearsome Ghidorah. The Earthlings agree to loan Godzilla and Rodan to Planet X to help, only to find that the aliens are in full control of Ghidorah and that this is nothing but a dastardly plot to use all three monsters to rob Earth of its water supply. In the end Planet X gets trashed, Japan falls again, Godzilla and Rodan return as heroes, Godzilla dances a celebratory highland fling (a pose now immortalised as an action model kit in Japan) and normality returns.

> "WHAT HAS HAPPENED HERE WAS CAUSED BY A FORCE WHICH, UP UNTIL A FEW DAYS AGO, WAS ENTIRELY BEYOND THE SCOPE OF MAN'S IMAGINATION"
>
> Steve Martin, Godzilla King Of The Monsters

HISTORICAL

Sam Goldwyn once asked a writer to do a script about the kidnapping of Charles Lindbergh's baby. The family couldn't, he said, be called Lindbergh. Nor, obviously, could the film include a baby. Or, come to think of it, a kidnapping. The film was never made but it says something about Hollywood's take on history.

CHE! 1969

Director *Richard Fleischer* Cast *Omar Sharif, Jack Palance*

You have to watch this if only to see Jack Palance play Castro with a voice borrowed from Marlon Brando, make-up on loan from Madame Tussaud's and a fake nose borrowed every day from the German make-up man on set. But this film's attractions don't end there. Fleischer, not an untalented director, decided to avoid the obvious political problems (it was only seven years since the world had almost been annihilated over Cuba) and focus on Guevara as a "handsome, sexy guy". Hence the casting of Sharif, Hollywood's favourite foreign leading man, who had in this decade already played a Russian doctor, a good Nazi, a Mongol emperor and an Austrian prince. The only way to endure lines like, "The peasant is like a wild flower in the forest, and the revolutionary like a bee. Neither can survive or propagate without the other", was to read them like the talented bridge player Sharif is.

DANTON 1982

Director *Andrzej Wajda* Cast *Gérard Depardieu, Wojciech Pszoniak*

Difficult to go wrong with a film which a) stars Gérard Depardieu as one of his nation's greatest historical figures and b) is about a man who, just before he was guillotined, told his executioner: "Show them my head. It will be worth it." Good as it is, it does plod in places. For a romantic view of 1789, it's hard to top Ronald Colman in *A Tale Of Two Cities* (1935).

> **"IN A WORLD WHERE CARPENTERS GET RESURRECTED, EVERYTHING IS POSSIBLE"**
> Eleanor of Aquitaine,
> The Lion In Winter

FIRE OVER ENGLAND 1937

Director *William K Howard* Cast *Laurence Olivier, Vivian Leigh, Flora Robson, Leslie Banks*

Wonderful, romantic, gung-ho piece of English patriotic fervour. The Armada is on its way and Queen Elizabeth sends Ingolby (Olivier) to fight, leaving his beloved Cynthia (Leigh) behind. The battle scene may have been filmed in a small wash tub, but it's the on-screen romance (also blossoming off-screen at the time) with its cut-glass accents and fervent pledges of eternal love that make this such a joy. Look out for a small uncredited appearance by a very young James Mason.

IVAN THE TERRIBLE 1945/58
Director *Sergei M Eisenstein*
Cast *Nikolai Cherkassov, Ludmila Tselikovskaya, Serafima Burman*

Never one to be swayed by conventional wisdom, Josef Stalin had decided by the end of the 1930s that Tsar Ivan The Terrible was due for rehabilitation. This was partly because he wanted to unite his subjects around "Mother Russia" as war neared and partly, perhaps, because he felt some kinship with a ruler chiefly known for mass murder. So he suggested that Eisenstein should make a film about him. The director researched his subject for two years, sketching every scene. Part one was premiered in 1945 and got a good review from you know who. Relieved, the director collapsed and as he lay in

hospital, Stalin got a sneak preview of part two, which he didn't like. Eisenstein died in 1948 and his *Terrible* sequel wasn't shown in public until 1958. The parallels between Ivan and Stalin are bitterly obvious in part two. But both films are alternately slow-moving and startling, unlike almost anything else you'll see.

THE LAST EMPEROR 1987
Director *Bernardo Bertolucci*
Cast *John Lone, Joan Chen, Peter O'Toole*

This ought to be called *The Lost Emperor* because Pu Yi, the last crowned monarch in Chinese history, all but disappears in the

Danton's style of oratory was later used by televangelists to solicit credit card donations

spectacle of this film. O'Toole, who seems to rouse himself for epics like these, is magnificent as the boy's tutor. The scenes of Pu Yi's childhood are fabulously surreal but the story fragments after that as Pu Yi becomes irrelevant to his nation and his century. But you stay hooked, right up to the audacious end where he visits, as a tourist, the city he once ruled as an emperor. As epic biopics go, it is easier to watch than *Gandhi* which, for all Ben Kingsley's fine work in the title role, was, as David Thomson said, "a soporific non-threatening tribute to non-violence which allegedly moved millions to tears."

LAWRENCE OF ARABIA 1962

Director David Lean Cast Peter O'Toole, Omar Sharif, Alec Guinness, Anthony Quinn, Claude Rains

Fortunately Katharine Hepburn persuaded producer Sam Spiegel that Albert Finney wasn't the man to play Lawrence and that an almost unknown Irishman was. O'Toole wanted the role with a manic intensity which matched his character's. He had surgery to straighten his nose and correct a squint and learned how to ride camels. They obviously respected him. When he was downed in a fight between the extras on set, the camels formed a protective circle around him to keep the mob at bay. Amazingly, he didn't watch the film himself until the 1980s. Lawrence remains almost as much of an enigma four hours later as he does at the start of the film, but it captures brilliantly the desert which seduced him and where this strange hero seemed most at home. O'Toole celebrated the end of the shoot by going on a year-long bender.

LUDWIG, REQUIEM FOR A VIRGIN KING 1972

Director Hans-Jurgen Syberberg Cast Harry Baer, Ingrid Caven

The fainthearted may prefer Visconti's *Ludwig*, released the

HITLER: THE MOVIES

Adolf Hitler's life, death and crimes have inspired a glut of good, bad and extremely ugly movie interpretations of how Der Führer goose-stepped his way to glory and oblivion.

One of the most famous cinematic Hitlers is to be found in Charlie Chaplin's playful spoof, *The Great Dictator* (1940). Chaplin plays Adenoid Hynkel, a World War I soldier with a toothbrush moustache who becomes the bumbling dictator of Toumania, a fictitious European country under the flag of the sinister "sign of the double cross". Chaplin also plays a barber, the little trampish hero of the (happy!) Jewish ghetto, who impersonates Hynkel and thus saves the day.

Far funnier is Dick Shawn's hippie Hitler in Mel Brooks' classic *The Producers*. Shawn

plays bohemian actor Lorenzo Saint DuBois (aka LSD), the flower-powered, finger-cymbal flexing Führer who unwittingly makes theatrical producers Max Bialystock (Zero Mostel) and Leo Bloom's (Gene Wilder) surefire get-rich-quick flop *Springtime For Hitler* into a Broadway smash. Before they find DuBois, Bialystock and Bloom audition a cowboy Hitler, an operatic tenor Hitler, and one (Rusty Blitz) whose sole contribution is a warbling Brooklyn rendition of *Beautiful Dreamer*.

The real Hitler's dream of world domination ended when he blew his brains out on April 30, 1945, deep in the bowels of his secret Führerbunker under Berlin. The 10 days which led up to his demise were acted

same year, starring Helmut Berger as the mad king of Bavaria and Trevor Howard as Richard Wagner. Even that lasts at least 173 minutes so be ready to lose an evening of your life. Syberberg's requiem for the same king is a challenging documentary, the first of a trilogy. The second (*The Confessions of Wilfred Wagner*) runs to 302 minutes in its original version. The final part, a 407-minute epic called *Hitler: A Film From Germany*, is the most contentious, his implication made clearer in the film's international title: *Our Hitler*. Often pretentious, often powerful (the juxtaposition of Peter Lorre's voice from *M* and Hitler's gives you a jolt), it is a perverse tour de force.

THE STORY OF MANKIND 1957

Director Irwin Allen *Cast* Ronald Colman, Vincent Price, Hedy Lamarr, Peter Lorre, Dennis Hopper

You might think that any film which purports to tell the story of mankind might be monstrously long but Allen zips through it in 100 minutes flat. The plot is as follows: mankind is on trial (for discovering the super-H-bomb 60 years early) with Price as the devil prosecutor and Colman defending mankind. Any film which casts Dennis Hopper as Napoleon and Harpo Marx as Sir Isaac Newton can't be all bad, although the enterprise has a certain predictability. When the marquis tells Marie Antoinette that the people have no bread, is there anybody alive who can't anticipate her next remark?

> **"OF COURSE, I'M THE MAN FOR THE JOB. WHAT IS THE JOB BY THE WAY?"**
> TE Lawrence, Lawrence Of Arabia

out to perfection by Alec Guinness in Ennio De Concini's historically accurate account *Hitler: The Last Ten Days* (1973), which captured the madness and desperation of Hitler's final hours. *Hitler* (1962), starring Richard Basehart as Adolf, is best remembered for the Hitler lookalike contest launched to promote it.

The fantasy of what may have happened had Hitler survived has long attracted moviemakers, especially those with bunker low budgets. One hideous example is David Bradley's Z-movie *They Saved Hitler's Brain* (1968), where Hitler's head (played by Bill Freed) is transplanted from his body by his followers, placed in a jar and stored on top of what looks like a swastika-emblazoned

tower hi-fi system. For pure Hitler kitsch, however, try Russ Meyer's *Up!* (1976), which opens with ageing, masochistic, Hitler lookalike Adolph Schwartz (Edward Schaff) being whipped by a stud resplendent in a pilgrim outfit. The pilgrim later makes up for what the 'Master Race' did to Poland by brutally invading Der Führer from the rear with his impressive knackwurst.

Who do you think you are kidding, Mr Guinness?

Losange/Group X, MGM/Wolfgang Reinhardt/Westfilm

HORROR

What's your favourite scary movie? (Probably not *Scary Movie*.) Everyone likes to be scared. Before film, people could read the works of Edgar Allen Poe, Mary Shelley and Bram Stoker to send a shiver down their spine, and before the written word people had the bejesus scared out of them as tales of werewolves, vampires and ghosts were circulated around the campfire. In those bygone days, you needed a vivid imagination to fully experience the fear factor. These days, all we need is a film director.

"IN FACT, CIVILIZATION AND SYPHILIZATION HAVE ADVANCED TOGETHER"
Professor Van Helsing, Bram Stoker's Dracula

With film, all your worst fears can be splashed across a 70mm screen in glorious technicolor. And they have been – to great effect. Some of the most memorable moments (and characters) in screen history have been from horror movies. Who can forget Linda Blair vomiting green stuff in *The Exorcist*? The eerie kids from *Village Of The Damned*? Bela Lugosi rising from the crypt in *Dracula*? The shark in *Jaws*? Norman Bates? Carrie? Hannibal? Pinhead?

Those gothic novels of Shelley, Stoker and Poe were the inspiration for many of the early horror films, which date back to the beginning of silent film. European and American film directors explored the art of chilling audiences to the bone with the legends of Frankenstein, Dracula (the inspiration for FW Murnau's *Nosferatu*) and the werewolf (first the subject of a horror movie back in 1919) and made household names of the actors who appeared in them: Lon Chaney, Bela Lugosi, Boris Karloff (British-born William Henry Pratt) in the 1930s, and Christopher Lee and Peter Cushing in the British Hammer film equivalents of the 1950s and 1960s.

But horror is also an excuse for filmmakers to come up with inventive ways to have us scurrying under the seat in front. Alfred Hitchcock, one of the masters of the genre, could turn the most ordinary situation into a moment of terror ("Always make the audience suffer as much as possible," said the master).

Once the censorship laws were relaxed (especially in the US: countries like Italy were already more relaxed about screen violence, giving free reign to artists like Dario Argento), moviemakers didn't only hint that there was something out there (usually with a bloody axe), but they made sure that we saw it, just to make sure that we were really, really too scared to go home alone (although that's a different sort of scary movie altogether).

In the more liberal 1960s and 1970s it was just another day on the soundstage when an actor gave birth to something creepy (*Rosemary's Baby*), was raped by a ghost (*The Entity*) or just became plain possessed (*The Exorcist*). By the 1980s – thanks to the success of *Friday 13th* and John Carpenter's seminal *Halloween* – the slasher movie had been born, and although some movies in the UK were banned ('video nasties' like Wes Craven's *Last House On The Left* and revenge flick *I Spit On Your Grave* that received vitriolic notices in the UK press, and later, *Henry: Portrait Of A Serial Killer*), buckets of blood still splashed across the screen everywhere from Spielberg's mainstream *Jaws* to cult favourites like *Salem's Lot* and *Hellraiser*.

Bette believed they were on a Christmas winner with the Baby Jane merchandising

Horror also became big business – *The Silence Of The Lambs* made over $130m in the US alone – while *The Sixth Sense* has surpassed $300m and *The Blair Witch Project* (which, let's face it, was all hype and about as scary as an evening with Mary Poppins) over $150m. Now that is frightening.

AN AMERICAN WEREWOLF IN LONDON 1981

Director John Landis *Cast* David Naughton, Jenny Agutter

It's hard to believe director Landis was just 19 when he wrote this imaginative horror comedy in 1969. It took another 12 years for his work to make it to the screen (after the success of *National Lampoon's Animal House*) but the timing was brilliant as audiences got to enjoy a more sinister side of London during the year of Charles and Diana's 'fairytale' wedding. Naughton and Griffin Dunne are the American tourists who, despite being told by the regulars of the Slaughtered Lamb not to, venture on to the Yorkshire Moors only to be bitten by a werewolf. Dunne isn't long for this earth (although he returns as a ghost), while Naughton realises he's half-wolf when he wakes up nude in the zoo. Packed with gruesomely funny scenes (Naughton meeting his gnawed victims in a cinema) and terrific casting (Agutter as the pretty nurse, Brian Glover as the grim pub patron), this also boasted great werewolf effects, which prompted Michael Jackson to hire Landis to direct his video epic, *Thriller*.

BLOOD FEAST 1963

Director Herschell Gordon Lewis *Cast* William Kerwin, Mal Arnold

Herschell Gordon Lewis has been justly dubbed The Godfather Of Gore for creating the celluloid equivalent of the French theatrical form *grand guignol*. *Blood Feast* is his most notable (and notorious) creation. A ludicrously OTT fable of sacrificial slaughter, cannibalism and violent death, it centres around the murderous mission of psychotic Egyptian caterer/high priest Fuad Ramses (Arnold). Hired to supply an exotic banquet, Ramses takes to hacking out the vital organs of young girls as an offering to his goddess (a shop-window mannequin) which he then serves up as an 'Egyptian Feast' to the unsuspecting diners. Ramses gets his just desserts, however, by falling into a garbage truck compacter where he is crushed to a pulp. A terrible end that mirrors his acting ability.

BRAM STOKER'S DRACULA 1992

Director Francis Ford Coppola *Cast* Gary Oldman, Winona Ryder, Anthony Hopkins

> "NOW GET THE HELL DOWN IN THE CELLAR. YOU CAN BE THE BOSS DOWN THERE. I'M THE BOSS UP HERE"
>
> Ben, Night of the Living Dead

More a love story than a horror movie, *Bram Stoker's Dracula* (the author's name was added because another studio had the rights to the name Dracula) nonetheless has some good bits of gore – most notably during the early flashback scenes of a bloody rampage through 15th-century Romania. Oldman is effective as Prince Vlad, who decides a young woman in Victorian England (Ryder) is the reincarnation of his dead wife. Hopkins provides some nice sarcasm as vampire-hunter Van Helsing (and Keanu Reeves a few sniggers as naïve lawyer Jonathan Harker), but it is Coppola's luscious direction that makes this stand out from scores of other Dracula pics. The stunning castle, Vlad's red cloak slithering across the stones, the brides of Dracula getting it on with Keanu – all are stunning set pieces that make this odd movie worthy of a second look.

THE CORPSE GRINDERS 1972

Director Ted V Mikels *Cast* Sean Kenney, Monika Kelly

"Turn bones and flesh into screaming, savage blood death!" yelped the publicity blurb for this outrageous horror comedy from legendary exploitation movie mogul Ted V Mikels. The plot rotates around the crippled owners of a failing cat-food company who, to spice up their product, employ a couple of grave-robbing maniacs to supply them with dead bodies which they then grind up and sell to cat-lovers. After a few cans the felines develop a craving for human flesh and start attacking their owners. This leads to a factory visit by veterinarian Dr Howard Glass (Kenney) and his nurse assistant Angie

Robinson (Kelly), whose covert investigation uncovers the entire ghastly scheme. The star of this movie is the prop of the title: a painted cardboard box which, every time a body is pushed through it, has hamburger meat dropping out of the other end into a bucket.

THE DEVIL-DOLL 1936

Director Tod Browning Cast Lionel Barrymore, Maureen O'Sullivan

Best known for *Freaks* and 1931's *Dracula*, director Browning's 20-year career also included this oddity. His last but one film before retirement, it was originally titled *The Witch Of Timbuctoo* but the title was changed when the script was altered because of censorship concerns. Co-written by actor/director Erich von Stroheim,

The Wicker Man: a great twist and a great way to recycle all of that 1970s furniture

the story follows a Devil's Island escapee (Barrymore) who hits upon the idea of shrinking humans to doll size for his own evil ends (can't think why no one's thought of it before). Undeniably silly, this bizarre film mixes horror, sci-fi, melodrama and revenge thriller all into one, and contains a plethora of ideas and images (Barrymore in drag being one of them) that were considered shocking in 1936.

EL BARON DEL TERROR 1962 THE BRAINIAC

Director Chano Urueta Cast Abel Salazar, Ariadna Welter

Probably the weirdest and most disturbing horror movie ever created. Made in Mexico on a shoestring budget, *El Barón Del Terror* tells the grisly tale of an evil baron (Salazar) from a few centuries back who is reincarnated and, riding on a meteor, returns from outer space as a brain-eating monster with an enormous forked tongue. He uses this gruesome appendage on his unsuspecting dinner-guest victims, first killing them with a campy kiss before scooping out their grey matter and gulping it down. What the creature can't manage in one sitting is saved in a secret cupboard for seconds. The hallucinatory feeling that one experiences while watching this movie is certainly hard to shake off. And here's a fascinating fact: cult rock musician Captain Beefheart (aka Don Van Vliet) paid lyrical homage to *El Barón Del Terror* in a song called *Debra Kadabra*, which he co-wrote with Frank Zappa for the *Bongo Fury* album (1975).

EVIL DEAD 1982

Director **Sam Raimi** *Cast* **Bruce Campbell, Ellen Sandweiss**

The *Evil Dead* had a budget of less than $100,000 and was essentially director Raimi, his brother Ted and a group of mates (including star Campbell and then-assistant film editor Joel Coen) making a jokey horror movie set in a woodland cabin. Despite the lack of cash, they produced some great effects as Campbell and pals accidentally unleash abominable demons. (Many of the crew returned five years later to do it all again as semi-remake *Evil Dead II* – budget $3m – with even more gore and humour. *Evil Dead III: Army Of Darkness* cost $30m.) Some have complained about the graphic gore (especially the raped-by-a-tree scene) but no-one can deny that all three are the funniest, most cleverly made horror movies around.

> "THE NAME'S HOMER. H-O-M-E-R. MISPRONOUNCE IT AND I WOULDN'T WANT TO BE YOU"
>
> Homer, Near Dark

THE EXORCIST 1973

Director **William Friedkin** *Cast* **Ellen Burstyn, Max von Sydow**

Regularly voted the scariest movie of all time, thanks to William Friedkin's taut direction, wonderful performances (especially from Jason Miller as Father Karras and Burstyn, who damaged her spine carrying out one effect) and the gripping source material by William Peter Blatty (who has a cameo as the producer of the film Burstyn is acting in). Many scenes have become the stuff of legend: possessed child Regan (Linda Blair) vomiting pea soup or getting a bit graphic on the bed with a crucifix – but the creeping horror of the movie remains embedded in your mind well after the credits have rolled. A director's cut version is available, featuring Regan's infamous 'spider walk' and an altered ending.

HALLOWEEN 1978

Director **John Carpenter** *Cast* **Jamie Lee Curtis, Donald Pleasence**

The daddy of all those 1980s slasher movies (including its own five sequels – *Part III, Season Of The Witch* doesn't count), this grips from the opening long single take that introduced the world to Michael Myers. Fifteen years after slashing his sister to death and being institutionalized, Myers returns to his hometown of Haddonfield for a knife-wielding reunion. Shot in only three weeks for just $300,000, *Halloween* marked the feature debut of 'scream queen' Jamie Lee Curtis (who also starred in Carpenter's *The Fog* and two of *Halloween*'s sequels) and became an incredibly influential horror movie. From the stalk-and-slash 'he's behind you' shocks that have been ripped off ad infinitum to Carpenter's unforgettable score and direction, this classic has caused whole generations to check what's behind the wardrobe door before going to bed.

HAXAN 1922

Director Benjamin Christensen
Cast Maren Pedersen,
Oscar Stribolt

Eighty years on, Christensen's
use of real life, animation and
dramatic sequences for his
disturbing documentary about
witchcraft through the ages has
lost none of its ability to shock.
His silent scenes of demonically
possessed nuns and friars – and
the tortures which they were
forced to suffer to extract sorcery
confessions – are made more
upsetting by the fear-filled
expressions of the actors.
Elsewhere, his re-enactment of
a witches' sabbat and the horrors

Old Leatherface, like Norman Bates and Jame Gumb in *Silence of the Lambs*, was inspired by real killer Ed Gein

surrounding it, gives you the uneasy feeling that the Danish
director could have been present at such events in real life.

NEAR DARK 1987

Director Kathryn Bigelow *Cast* Adrian Pasdar, Lance Henriksen

Director Bigelow borrowed half of then-husband James
Cameron's cast of *Aliens* (Lance Henriksen, Bill Paxton, Jenette
Goldstein) for this vampire horror-meets-western. Pasdar is the
simple farmhand who realises the love bite he got from cute
(but strangely pale) out-of-towner Jenny Wright has given him
a hunger for blood, while Paxton and Henriksen get all the
best lines as her fellow vamps who are are making monster
munchies of most of the townspeople of the Midwest. Oddly
romantic, this vagabond fang-gang tale works beautifully as
both a horror movie and a love story, and should have made a
star of pretty-boy Pasdar (who went on to star with Emily Lloyd
in the risible *Cookie* instead).

NIGHT OF THE LIVING DEAD 1968

Director George A Romero *Cast* Judith O'Dea, Duane Jones

Filmed on a shoestring budget of little more than $100,000,
George Romero's black-and-white zombie flick remains one of
the most unforgettable horror movies ever made. Shot in
Pittsburgh using local talent to keep costs down (one investor
was a butcher: he supplied the blood and guts), its premise is
simple. Seven people shut themselves inside a farmhouse as
zombies intent on death and destruction close in on them. It

was Romero's first film; he followed it 10 years later with the daft but enjoyable *Dawn Of The Dead* and 1985's *Day Of The Dead*, while Tom Savini used Romero's script to remake the first film with flashier effects in 1990.

NOSFERATU – EINE SYMPHONIE DES GRAUENS 1922

Director FW Murnau *Cast* Max Schreck, Alexander Granach

The fictional account of the making of *Nosferatu, The Shadow Of The Vampire* has added a new dimension to this already fascinating and shiversome version of Dracula. (Director Murnau changed the vampire's name hoping Bram Stoker's estate wouldn't recognise the tale; Mrs Stoker later sued and got the movie removed from cinemas.) Murnau was, by all accounts, dedicated to bringing the movie to the screen whatever the cost to the sanity of his cast and crew, and the casting of Max Schreck (making his debut) as the title character was a stroke of genius. Few creepier characters have appeared on screen (Schreck stayed in make-up and character all the time on set, unsettling his co-stars), and with Murnau's clever use of black-and-white photography (using the negative to create white trees against a black sky etc), no horror movie has remained as long in our collective memory. A classic.

> "THERE IS ONE OUTSIDE CHANCE OF A CURE... HAVE YOU EVER HEARD OF AN EXORCISM?"
>
> Dr Klein, The Exorcist

ROBOT MONSTER 1953

Director Phil Tucker *Cast* George Nader, George Barrows

Out-of-work actor George Barrows is Ro-Man in Phil Tucker's baffling 2-D sci-fi schlocker. Instructed by 'Great Guidance', an overweight man in a gorilla suit with a toy space helmet on his head plots world domination from inside a desert cave – by phoning home, using what turns out be a bubble machine. *Robot Monster* has, however, more going for it than the Golden Turkey Awards judiciary would have you believe. This is, albeit unintentionally, surrealist filmmaking at its finest: a veritable feast of shaky props, lizards made up to look like dinosaurs and an alien monster who pities his victims. This warped blend of near-Shakespearean pathos and *Ed Wood*-like insanity blasts *Robot Monster* into the realm of the remarkable. Incidentally, in John Carpenter's Lovecraftian *In The Mouth Of Madness* (1994), *Robot Monster* is the late-night movie playing on the TV in the motel room of protagonist John Trent (Sam Neill).

THE SHINING 1980

Director Stanley Kubrick *Cast* Jack Nicholson, Shelley Duvall

The best adaptation of a Stephen King book is actually a mini-series (*The Stand*), but *The Shining* is the most memorable movie based on one of his horror novels. Devoted fans were upset that the ending was changed, but director Kubrick brings his own charm and foibles – and that jaw-dropping tracking shot of the boy on the tricycle – to this psychological horror that is essentially a haunted house movie of the first degree. Nicholson chews up the scenery as Jack Torrance, who becomes caretaker of the remote Overlook Hotel during the winter months when it's closed and cut off from the rest of civilisation by snow drifts; Duvall is the wife who goes through hell when he begins to lose his marbles. Most impressive of all, however, is six-year-old Danny Lloyd as their son who has the gift of 'shining' (clairvoyance). Legend has it that Kubrick kept a careful eye on Lloyd so he didn't realise he was involved in the making of a horror movie until a few years later (Lloyd didn't get bitten by the acting bug: he is now a science teacher).

SHIVERS 1975

Director David Cronenberg *Cast* Paul Hampton, Joe Silver

Canadian director Cronenberg's early low-budget films remain his most effective. *Rabid*, *The Brood*, *Shivers* and *Scanners* deliver more yuckiness than his better-known movies like *The Fly*, *Naked Lunch* and *Crash* (although the gynaecological implements of *Dead Ringers* and James Woods' extra orifice in

HE'S BEHIND YOU!

TOP SEVEN SIGNS TO TELL IF YOU'RE IN A HORROR MOVIE

1 If you're a teenager and you have sex, you will be dead before the night is over.

2. Any character shouting: "Is anyone there?" will always discover that yes, someone is there, and they have a big axe/gun/knife and now know where to find you. Similarly, anyone who says: "I'll be right back" clearly won't.

3. The "he looks dead so I'll stop running and stand near him" ruse, where the killer is clearly just waiting before making the audience jump one last time. Surely no one should be surprised by this 'twist' any more?

4. At the end the killer really is dead – except there is one final scene hinting he may

nonetheless recover from multiple gunshot wounds and a beheading, just in case the film is a hit and someone subsequently decides to cash in with a sequel.

5. Young women with big breasts running away from the murderer will always stumble. (Is this a gravity thing?)

6. He's viciously stabbing, maiming and slaughtering people because his mother didn't love him.

7. If you've escaped the maniac, reached the car and found your car keys, rest assured the engine won't start first time. Or second time. But just as he reaches you and hacks through the soft-top, that dead battery/loose connection rights itself and you escape. But he's probably now in the back seat.

Videodrome deserve special mention for stomach-churning). *Shivers*' plot is based around parasitic creatures turning people in an apartment block into sex maniacs. But it's really an excuse for Cronenberg to pile on the grossness as the little buggers burrow into people's bodies or are transferred from body to body during snogging (watch out for the flying parasites which attach themselves to a victim's face – the one time in the movie you'll laugh instead of shiver).

A winning smile always guaranteed a lock-in down at Jack's local

SUSPIRIA 1976

Director **Dario Argento** *Cast* **Jessica Harper, Stefania Casini**

With *Suspiria*, director Argento proved that you don't need a complex plot to scare the bejesus out of people. Atmospheric direction, clever camera work and a creepy score will do the trick (though lashings of violence help too). An opera of death and suspense, the plot is simple: girl (Harper) turns up at a dance academy to find it's a witches' coven. Those who don't want to join in meet an ugly death. In the hands of Argento, this is anticipation to the point of torture, which he relieves by showing us the killings that come at close hand. Suspenseful, violent fare with music by cult Italian band Goblin.

THE TEXAS CHAINSAW MASSACRE 1974

Director **Tobe Hooper** *Cast* **Marilyn Burns, Gunnar Hansen**

Real-life killer Ed Gein was the inspiration for Jame Gumb in *Silence Of The Lambs*, Norman Bates in *Psycho*, and (here) Leatherface – a member of a strange family who slice and dice a group of travellers who make the mistake of coming near their Texan farm. Not as scary or gruesome now as it seemed at the time, this was nonetheless refused a certificate by the British Board of Film Classification and only allowed an uncut release in the UK in 2000. Perhaps the censors' problem with the film – apart from a long scene near the end when the surviving girl is chased, or perhaps the theme of cannibalism – is that there is no explanation for the attacks. A terrific exercise in terror, and one that should be played to all teenagers and young adults planning a road trip for their summer holidays.

"I WILL NOT BE THREATENED BY A WALKING MEATLOAF"
David Naughton,
An American Werewolf In London

VILLAGE OF THE DAMNED 1960
Director Wolf Rilla *Cast* George Sanders, Barbara Shelley

More than four decades after it was made in Letchmore Heath in England, this adaptation of John Wyndham's *The Midwich Cuckoos* remains astonishingly creepy. One day, everyone in an English village falls asleep during the middle of the afternoon; months later all the women capable of having children give birth to sinister blond tots with penetrating eyes and the ability to communicate telepathically. Brunette children were given blond wigs to get a striking contrast for black-and-white cinematographer Geoffrey Faithfull, and the young actors give skin-crawling performances as the little monsters with unblinking stares. Shun the 1963 sequel *Children Of The Damned* and John Carpenter's 1995 remake with Kirstie Alley.

WHAT EVER HAPPENED TO BABY JANE? 1962
Director Robert Aldrich *Cast* Bette Davis, Joan Crawford

There's a strange fascination to this film because even onscreen you sense its stars, as Aldrich said, "are circling each other like two Sherman tanks". The tale of two ageing sisters and showbiz has-beens plays off the real life Crawford-Davis feud so wonderfully it carries the film, one of the most stressful the

FANGS, FEAR, FUN AND FRANKENSTEIN

THE HISTORY OF HAMMER

"Hammer Horror, Won't leave me alone. The first time in my life, I keep the lights on, To ease my soul," sang Kate Bush, paying homage to the small British film production company founded in 1948. Hammer made more than 70 horror, sci-fi and thriller movies in two decades from 1957 when it released the first British gothic horror in colour, *The Curse Of Frankenstein*, starring Peter Cushing and Christopher Lee. Those two actors became forever linked with the studio and reteamed for kitsch classics like *Dracula* (and numerous spin-offs and sequels), *The Mummy* ("It snaps men's spines like matchsticks!") and *The Gorgon*. Twenty-two-year-old Oliver Reed was paid a princely £90 a week to star in 1961's *The Curse Of The Werewolf*, while Joanna Lumley

pops up as vampire-hunter Van Helsing's granddaughter in *The Satanic Rites Of Dracula* (1974). By the1970s, Hammer's horror movies were increasingly titillating (check out *Lust For A Vampire, Hands Of The Ripper*, and *Dr Jekyll And Sister Hyde*) to compete with the success of sex comedies of the time. But by 1975 the British film industry had ground to a virtual standstill, and future Hammer Horrors like *Vampirella* (described as an interstellar 007) were put on permanent hold.

Lee: handsome beast

Warner/Stanley Kubrick; Warner/Hammer

director had ever made. Crawford got through the film on Pepsi spiked with vodka, which she drank pretty much all day everyday. Davis survived the shooting on ego, watching in horror as (she claimed) her co-star strapped ever larger fake boobs to her chest as shooting progressed. Crawford got her revenge on her co-star for cutting her scalp by strapping weights to herself for a scene where Davis had to carry her. All of which was pretty much how you imagine their characters would have behaved – sometimes it really is all in the casting.

THE WICKER MAN 1973
Director **Robin Hardy** *Cast* **Edward Woodward, Britt Ekland**
A horror fantasy classic that plays on what we've always feared about people living on remote islands. Edward Woodward is the Christian policeman who's investigating the disappearance of a girl on the Scottish island of Summerisle. He arrives to find the islanders have strange rituals and different stories about what happened to the girl. Beautifully written by Anthony Shaffer ("You'll simply never understand the true nature of sacrifice") and tautly directed by Hardy, this has stood the test of time thanks to a terrific twist and fine performances from Woodward and Christopher Lee as the island's leader, Lord Summerisle. Atmospheric and unforgettable, although usually only available in an 85-minute version (the original was 105 minutes).

"NO CORPSES IN MY GARAGE"

SAY HELLO TO WES CRAVEN
A former humanities professor, director Wes Craven has been credited with revitalising the horror movie (which had become a seemingly endless stream of cheap stalk'n'slash movies like the *Friday The 13th* series) not once but twice. First, in 1984, with *A Nightmare On Elm Street* he took the low-budget slasher movie and turned it into a witty, special effects-heavy teen phenomenon, and then again in 1996 with *Scream* (and its two sequels), which spoofed the genre Craven had helped to create.

The Ohio-born filmmaker first tapped into what makes audiences squirm with the 1972 shocker *Last House On The Left*, which is infamous in the UK for being one of the government's video nasties of the mid-1980s. It's a distasteful film, and it was made to be

that, made to be ugly, Craven remembers. "It's not a film I go back to and enjoy watching, but it's still powerful, and definitely has a kick to it."

After directing the equally notorious *The Hills Have Eyes* (about a family of cannibals), Craven made *A Nightmare On Elm Street* and unleashed the metal-clawed Freddy Kreuger. "When the film came out," Craven notes, "I got a letter from a college which had screened the film, telling me that grown men were crying during it. I framed that one."

Quietly spoken, in person Craven does not have the sinister presence you expect. "People seem to think I should think violent thoughts, be wracked by nightmares or live in a cave," he smiles. "They think I watch horror films all the time and have bodies hanging in my garage. Neither of which are true, I assure you."

INDEPENDENT

Telling independent from Hollywood isn't easy these days as the distinctions between the two have become as blurred as a very blurred thing indeed. But none of the films that follow were made by major studios or even minor studios (which only remain minor because they haven't had enough hits to become major ones).

AMERICAN HISTORY X 1998

Director Tony Kaye *Cast* Edward Norton, Edward Furlong

Despite the moving, if violent quality of director Kaye's debut, the film was not what he had envisaged. According to Director's Guild of America rules, pseudonyms are only allowed to be used when no specific reason has been stated for the decision. Kaye, however, had made it very clear, in a *Variety* ad no less, that Norton's re-editing, rumoured to include more scenes of himself, was unacceptable and he wished the director credit to be Humpty Dumpty. Kaye's subsequent decision to sue New Line Cinema was not a great career move; this is his sole film to date. Norton gained a best actor Oscar nomination as Derek, one of two brothers who fall under the spell of a neo-Nazi activist, but who decides (after a brutal spell in prison) to break free. Told in flashback, with black-and-white shots for the past and colour for present events, this is a stirring if brutal film.

BOYS DON'T CRY 1999

Director Kimberley Peirce *Cast* Hilary Swank, Chloë Sevigny

Powerful and disturbing story based on the real life of Teena Brandon, a teenage girl who preferred to live life as a boy, Brandon Teena. As Brandon she meets and falls in love with Lana (Sevigny), who right up until the end has no clue that Brandon is not a man. While this is not a film about lesbianism, since Teena was more a transsexual, it is the bigotry and homophobia of the other characters, particularly Lana's brother, that leads to

The boys had to take extreme measures to cure Sara of her addiction to television

the tragic ending. Those with weak stomachs would best avoid the harrowing rape scene. Peirce fought for a long time to get this film made, and the critical approval it received, including a best actress Oscar for Swank, is testament to her tenacity.

ERASERHEAD 1977

Director **David Lynch** *Cast* **Jack Nance, Charlotte Stewart, Laurel Near, Allen Joseph**

Lynch's first major film tells the strange tale of Henry (Nance) and Mary X's (Stewart) bizarre relationship when, during a family dinner, they are informed that they are now the proud parents of a helpless, mewling, phallic-necked premature baby creature. Essentially about the horror of procreation, *Eraserhead* is full of subliminally sexual nightmare images of tiny bleeding chickens, exploding womb sacs and Henry's slowly plummeting severed head. *Eraserhead* has echoes of Buñuel and Dali's *Un Chien Andalou*, as though Lynch had allowed that film's dark dreams to mutate and fester anew through Henry, the hysterical Mary, the bandaged, fly-blown baby, and the putty-faced Radiator Lady who exists in Henry's imagination. Jack Fisk as the Man In The Planet is surrounded by the same aura that made Buñuel's moon-gazing eye-slasher so memorable.

> **"LIFE IS TOO SHORT TO BE PISSED ALL THE TIME"**
> Danny, American History X

FLAMING CREATURES 1963

Director **Jack Smith** *Cast* **Sheila Bick, Joel Markman, Marian Zazeela, Mario Montez**

Jack Smith (1932-1989) was a writer, photographer and filmmaker who soared to (underground) fame with this Baudelairean epic, made the same year that Warhol shot *Blow Job*. Like Warhol, Smith was surrounded by his own coterie of talent such as the astonishing Dolores Flores (aka Mario Montez), a transvestite who appears as a fandango dancer with a rose between his/her teeth. This eye blast of soft focus genitalia and transsexual frolicking – all of which leads up to the notorious 'earthquake orgy' section, where a group of Flaming Creatures grapple a scantily clad Delicious Dolores (Bick) to the ground and crawl all over her – has been hailed as high art by those enchanted by Smith's deliriously original vision, and an obscenity by the authorities. John Waters was obviously influenced by Smith's masterpiece when he assembled his own cast of social misfits (Divine, Edith Massey and Mink Stole) to make *Pink Flamingos* (1972).

FLIRTING 1991

Director **John Duigan** *Cast* **Noah Taylor, Thandie Newton**

This sequel to Duigan's *The Year My Voice Broke* – an excellent movie in its own right – is set in a boarding school in rural Australia in the 1960s. Bookworm Danny (Taylor) is persecuted by his classmates because he stutters, while across the lake at the girls school, Ugandan beauty Thandiwe (Newton) endures the same treatment because she is black. When the two meet she instantly recognises that he is infinitely superior to his lunkhead schoolmates (and indeed many of his bigoted teachers) and a clandestine romance between the two outcasts blossoms. This is an intelligently scripted, genuinely funny coming-of-age fable that avoids the usual gamut of crass cracks. Newton and Taylor's studied performances are far beyond their then years (19 and 21 respectively) and Duigan directs with a subtle sensitivity that never strays into schmaltz. Nicole Kidman has a minor role.

GO FISH 1994

Director Rose Troche *Cast* Guinevere Turner, VS Brodie

Low-budget, black-and-white film about a group of women conspiring to matchmake Turner, a young and pretty lesbian, with the older, plainer Brodie. Meanwhile, another friend, the unashamedly promiscuous Daria, is berated by her lesbian sisters for sleeping with a male friend. The film does suffer from the usual budget problems of stilted performances (using friends as actors and never having enough film to do more than two takes) and static cameras, but the film is so sweet and good-hearted that those things can be forgiven. At the Sundance screening, they gave out nailclippers to the audience: you'll have to watch the film to find out why.

HAPPINESS 1998

Director Todd Solondz *Cast* Jane Adams, Jon Lovitz, Philip Seymour Hoffman

Not an easy film to take. Writer/director Solondz here sees the cruelty of daily life as a given. Focusing on three middle-class New Jersey sisters and their families, it's full of eccentric grotesques, from the paedophile who is disturbingly honest with his son about his actions, to a telephone stalker whose target rings him back for more.

INDY SIGNS

WHAT IS AN INDEPENDENT MOVIE?

Independent is a pretty broad term but there are certain elements you can look out for to distinguish your *Sex, Lies & Videotape* from your secretly big-wig funded *Jackie Brown*.

STAR POWER

True independents are generally made up of a cast of nameless faces with one you do recognise, usually a star who's canvassed for the project since the start, such as Harvey Keitel in *Reservoir Dogs* or Danny De Vito for *Livin' Out Loud*. If the film is any good, the rest of the cast will have been snapped up by Warners before it's even released.

SOUNDTRACKS

We're not talking John Barry but usually a blend of classics from certainly the director's, and maybe your own, youth, combined with ones you're never heard. Alas, there will come a day when a director's youth involved heavy doses of S Club 7.

STEADYCAM SHOTS

You may not know the term but you've seen it a million times. Basically if your view is that of following a character around a scene, this is steadycam at its best. See Kevin Smith's *Clerks* and *Chasing Amy* and every Tarantino film to date.

A film which covers such topics as murder, child molesting and pornography shouldn't really manage to stir a titter. But it does.

THE LAST SEDUCTION 1994

Director John Dahl *Cast* Linda Fiorentino, Peter Berg, Bill Pullman

Bridget (Fiorentino) is one of those rare cinematic creations: a femme fatale for the 1990s who didn't turn into a camp send-up of Barbara Stanwyck. Bridget isn't happy with her current lot in life (she only has beauty, intelligence and a doctor husband). This is probably because, as events will reveal, underneath it all she is so evil that even Freddie Kreuger would steer clear. She and her husband start working for professional drug-dealers, which goes well until Bridget runs off with the loot. On the run, she persuades Pullman, another hapless suitor, that it's his job to get rid of her husband. Dahl set out to make a film where you didn't fall in love with the central character. He almost succeeded – but women who had been screwed over by men soon founded their own Last Seduction Club on the Internet.

MAD MAX 1979

> "I WANT KIDS THAT LOVE ME AS MUCH AS I HATED MY MOTHER"
> Helen, Happiness

Director George Miller *Cast* Mel Gibson, Joanne Samuel

The fresh-faced youth of his debut film, *Summer City*, was not the Gibson who turned up to audition for this. Miller was searching for someone beaten and rough-looking for the title role, and Gibson got his face cut in a bar fight the night before his audition. Set in the post-apocalyptic near-future, Gibson is one of the few cops left to maintain law and order, constantly battling with biker gangs. Made for $400,000 the film grossed $100m. The low budget was aided by Gibson being paid by the word in a film where atmosphere is almost everything.

REQUIEM FOR A DREAM 2000

Director Darren Aronofsky *Cast* Ellen Burstyn, Jared Leto

"Hi! Is this where the modern dysfunctional family lives?"

Based on the novel of the same name by Hubert Selby (the author behind the equally impressive *Last Exit To Brooklyn*), this is the story of dreams and addictions and how they affect our lives. Burstyn is Sara, whose addiction to television and sugar soon becomes an addiction to diet pills when she believes she is set to appear on her beloved television and just must fit into her favourite red dress. Her son, his girlfriend and best friend are all in turn addicted to heroin, their dream being to become major dealers. The psychological effects of each addiction are remarkably and realistically played out, possibly enhanced by the director's insistence that Leto and co-star Marlon Wayans give up sex and sugar for a month so they would understand their characters more. A remarkable movie.

SCORPIO RISING 1964

Director Kenneth Anger *Cast* Bruce Byron

Anger became involved with the movies as a child, when he played the (uncredited) part of the Changeling Prince in the 1935 MGM Max Reinhardt/William Dieterle version of *A Midsummer Night's Dream*. Anger, the author of *Hollywood Babylon*, also made his own films, many influenced by the magickal teachings of magician, poet and mountaineer Aleister Crowley. Anger's 'hymn to Thanatos [Greek for death]' is a magickal take on *The Wild One*, replete with a 1960s' pop soundtrack, Nazi memorabilia, a homo-erotic biker gang and scenes from a found black-and-white biblical movie which the director spliced into his own footage. The diabolical result is provocative, unsettling and yet strangely alluring, tinged throughout with devilish, sardonic humour.

SECRETS & LIES 1996

Director Mike Leigh *Cast* Timothy Spall, Brenda Blethyn, Marianne Jean-Baptiste

An unusual box office success for writer/director Leigh. Despite the potential minefield implied by the title, this is more about how each member of the impressive ensemble cast reacts to each other's secrets than any intrigue. These are ordinary people with ordinary secrets, and the usual fixtures of the modern dysfunctional family. Although Leigh can take credit for the essence of the film, he allowed the actors to develop the characters of their onscreen personas themselves, with much of the interaction being improvized. Blethyn and Jean-Baptiste had never met before their initial onscreen meeting as mother and long-lost daughter. A fine, bittersweet comedy.

TOTALLY F***ED UP 1993

Director Gregg Araki *Cast* James Duval, Roko Belic

Nihilist teen angst-fest documenting the lives and loves of a group of gay and lesbian Los Angeles teenagers who have been disowned by their parents and drift aimlessly from café to mall and from one sexual relationship to another. Despite being hailed as a breakthrough in youth movies, this is in fact actually not that far removed from more standard Hollywood fare dealing with coming of age and sexuality. Duval is excellent though, and went on to star in Araki's later, and better, movies, *The Doom Generation* and *Nowhere*.

Welcome to children's movies, a magical world where men wear tights, girls follow the yellow brick road and the best friend a child can have is a lonesome mountain lion. The very best of these films work on two levels: entertaining the audience while imparting some greater (but partially) hidden truth. If you do find the hidden meaning in *Santa Claus Conquers The Martians*, let us know.

ADVENTURES OF ROBIN HOOD 1938

Director **Michael Curtiz** *Cast* **Errol Flynn, Olivia de Havilland, Basil Rathbone**

Childhood isn't childhood unless you've watched at least one film where men run around in tights in a good and noble cause and where true love triumphs. And as men-in-tights movies go, this is probably the finest, with Flynn at his energetic best (before all those years living at a house called Cirrhosis-by-the-Sea had taken their toll) and Roy Rogers' steed Trigger turning in one of his more compelling performances as de Havilland's horse. For a pleasant variation on this theme try *Ivanhoe* (1952) starring two Taylors: Robert and a very beautiful Liz.

"YOU'LL NEVER GET AWAY WITH THIS, YOU MARTIAN!"
Billy, Santa Claus Conquers the Martians

AYSECIK VE SIHIRLI CUCELER RUYALAR ULKESINDE 1971

Director **Tunc Basaran** *Cast* **Zeynep Degirmencioglu, Cemal Konca**

The scarecrow is a closet homosexual, the tin man is almost clubbed to death and the munchkins are homicidal maniacs. Welcome to the film which is unofficially known as 'The Turkish Wizard Of Oz'. Dorothy is called Ayse (played by the voluptuous Degirmencioglu) and undergoes a similar, but twisted, version of the original odyssey. This film, which is not so much a remake as an inspired riff on the original, is packed with song and dance numbers by a cast who can't do either. But when the music stops, the picture gets darker or simply weirder. The scarecrow gets disembowelled, the munchkins fire cannon at dancing cavemen and stand around laughing at the ensuing carnage, and boulder-wielding soldiers almost kill the tin man. As for the wizard, he makes the briefest of appearances before riding into the sunset on a balloon to the tune of *Hot Time In The Old Town Tonight*. The only drawback with this weird trip to Oz is that the filmmaker's budget didn't stretch to a yellow brick road.

BACK TO THE FUTURE 1985

Director Robert Zemeckis *Cast* Michael J Fox, Christopher Lloyd
This is the pleasing time-travel caper that made Michael J Fox a movie star (he only got the part of Marty because original choice Eric Stoltz looked too old). Zemeckis keeps the action and the laughs coming fast enough to make light of its 113-minute length and there are lots of little movie in-jokes. When Marty returns to 1955, the movies on at the local cinema are *A Boy's Life* (the working title for *ET*) and *Watch The Skies* (the working title for *Close Encounters*). But probably the most ironic twist is that this utterly good natured and charming fantasy was filmed at a school in Whittier, California, whose most famous alumni was Richard Nixon.

CHARLIE, THE LONESOME COUGAR 1967

Director Winston Hibler *Cast* Ron Brown, Brian Russell, Linda Wallace
The best-remembered Disney true-life adventure is probably the Oscar-winning *The Living Desert*. But this, made 14 years later when the formula was no longer striking box-office gold, has many of the same virtues without the same desperate desire to trivialize in the name of entertainment. Some loggers adopt a mountain lion which begins to cause chaos as it grows older, and just at the point where junior's attention is beginning to wander, the film ends.

CHITTY CHITTY BANG BANG 1968

Director Ken Hughes *Cast* Dick Van Dyke, Sally Ann Howes, Lionel Jeffries
This could have kickstarted Phil Collins' acting career – he was one of the children who storm the evil baron's castle at the end – but he was edited out because he had a large bandage on his head to cover a cyst. Pity he wasn't wearing one in *Buster*. Anyway, this is a charming

"What do you see? You people looking at me? That's right, a stand in for Julie Andrews"

fantasy adventure from the pen of Ian Fleming, taking a rest from his more onerous duties writing 007 novels. The car is the star – which child, after seeing this film, has not pined for such a vehicle? Ann Howes is no Julie Andrews, ie she's not as irritatingly winsome but still sings beautifully. And Jeffries plays Van Dyke's dad brilliantly given that he's seven months younger than his screen son. The Kiddie Catcher is still scary today.

> "THEY DON'T
> UNDERSTAND YOU
> AT HOME. YOU
> WANT TO SEE
> OTHER LANDS,
> BIG CITIES, BIG
> MOUNTAINS,
> BIG OCEANS!"
>
> The Professor, The Wizard Of Oz

E.T. 1982

Director **Steven Spielberg** *Cast* **Drew Barrymore, Dee Wallace, Henry Thomas, Peter Coyote**

The cuddly alien is one of the cinema's many disguised Christ figures, the only difference being that God has stopped arranging for his only son to be crucified and now resorts to phoning and asking him to come home, a bit like any father with a lower case f. You can watch out for the clues (mmm, Elliot's mum is Mary!) if you're not captivated by the story. ET's face was based on an amalgam of those of Albert Einstein and American poet Carl Sandburg, and his voice was produced with the help of Debra Winger. Gee, thanks Debs.

THE NUTTY PROFESSOR 1963

Director **Jerry Lewis** *Cast* **Jerry Lewis, Stella Stevens**

After Lewis split with Dino, he seemed to devote an inordinate amount of effort to proving the dubious proposition that he was a singer as well as a comedian. Here, at least, his singing has

THE TRIVIA OF OZ

WIZARDLY FACTS

The Wizard Of Oz is the grassy knoll of movie trivia. Many of the wilder rumours can be blamed on the presence of so many munchkins. And those rumours of mass munchkin orgies are, film historians assure us, vastly exaggerated. Some critics say that Oz is really Hollywood (which is why it's in colour while dreary old Kansas is black and white) which, like the wizard, is in the business of making dreams come true. Anyway, here are seven true pieces of Oz trivia.

1 Two of the seven pairs of ruby slippers made for the film are still missing. Each pair are worth at least $1.5m.

2 WC Fields and Shirley Temple were also

tipped to play the wizard and Dorothy.

3 Buddy Ebsen stopped playing the tin man because the aluminium powder make-up was poisonous and he had an allergic reaction to it. His voice can still be heard in the song *We're Off To See The Wizard.*

4 The song *Over The Rainbow* was almost cut.

5 Oliver Hardy played the tin man in a silent 1925 version. In all there have been 17 film versions of the tale and four spin-offs.

6 *The Wizard Of Oz* made less at the box office ($3m) than Garland's other MGM picture, *Babes In Toyland* ($3.3m), released that year.

7 Margaret Hamilton (the wicked witch of the West) really did go up in a puff of smoke on set. And was badly burned in the process.

some point to it: he sings when he's chemically transformed into the fantastically named Buddy Love, the persona he uses to woo Stella Stevens. Some of the gags in here are worthy of the French master Jacques Tati. Ironically Lewis' own children were not allowed to see the film because his wife disapproved of the Buddy Love character. Make sure you pick up the original version – the remake starring Eddie Murphy can be found in the family section of video stores but brace yourself for questions like: "Dad, what's cunnilingus?"

Chocolate barons Joe, Charlie and Willy Wonka stand accused of exploiting the Oompa Loompas' cheap labour

SANTA CLAUS CONQUERS THE MARTIANS 1964
Director Nicholas Webster *Cast* John Call, Leonard Hicks

The Martians haven't got a Santa of their own so they kidnap ours. That's the plot, if that's the right word, of this cult classic often unofficially described as the worst Christmas movie of all time. This seems a tad harsh: for kids, it's a damn sight more fun than that Michael Keaton film *Jack Frost* where Dad's a crap musician, dies and comes back as a snowman. It's also hard to be too frosty about a film which stars Pia Zadora as a melancholy Martian moppet and which includes the immortal couplet: "He's fat, he's round but jumpin jiminey/He can climb down any chimney." Some have insisted this movie is an allegory about the dangers of technology with the Martians as hard-boiled scientists who have to be softened by Santa/Christ's good cheer. Others may choose to see some sinister significance in the fact that Santa's reindeer is called Nixon.

THE SECRET GARDEN 1993
Director Agnieszka Holland *Cast* Kate Maberly, Maggie Smith, John Lynch, Andrew Knott

Frances Hodgson Burnett's classic story has been filmed many times but this version stands out from a packed field. Holland's first American film, made under the aegis of Francis Ford Coppola, tells the story of a neglected girl who finds a key to a secret garden which she restores. Is it an allegory about sexual repression? Or a broader indictment of Victorian society? Both, neither or either, this still makes a wonderful film.

SEE SPOT RUN 2001

Director John Whitesell *Cast* David Arquette, Paul Sorvino, Michael Clarke Duncan, Leslie Bibb

This film about a dog which is taken into the witness protection programme was universally loathed by critics for its apparent obsession with jokes about faecal matter. There's nothing quite as pompous as a critic pontificating about what films kids ought to watch, especially when the film is held to be yet more damning evidence that things ain't what they used to be. Cue harking back to a golden age of family movies which is mysteriously always located in the critic's own golden childhood. This isn't the kind of children's comedy they made when you were knee-high to a grasshopper, a fact for which today's kids are probably pretty grateful. A future cult classic.

DINOMITE

DINOSAUR
Dull Disney retread of a story told better in *Land Before Time* series.

JURASSIC PARK
The first (and best) blockbuster. The FX were better in the sequels but you have to await *Jurassic 4* with trepidation. What's the twist this time? Are the dinosaurs armed? Or are the FX just better again?

ONE MILLION YEARS BC
While the youngsters can gawp at Ray Harryhausen's effects, grown ups can feast their eyes on John Richardson and Raquel Welch. Yet again, men get the better deal.

WILLY WONKA & THE CHOCOLATE FACTORY 1971

Director Mel Stuart *Cast* Gene Wilder, Jack Albertson, Peter Ostrum

Dahl's work has a streak of cruelty in it which children familiar with such fairy tales as Hansel and Gretel quickly latch on to. Most of the children who win a tour of a chocolate factory come to decidedly sticky ends. Wilder plays Wonka superbly, at times seeming firm but fair and at others downright perverse. Keep an eye out for the scene where the Paraguayan newsreader holds up the photo of the man whose chocolate bar contained a lucky ticket: the photo is of Nazi exile Martin Bormann.

THE WIZARD OF OZ 1939

Director Victor Fleming *Cast* Judy Garland, Frank Morgan, Ray Bolger, Jack Haley, Bert Lahr

A movie shrouded in showbiz gossip and then wrapped in several layers of myth. Its influence on popular culture is astounding (with everyone from Pink Floyd to Salman Rushdie paying homage), one possible explanation is the way the underlying story runs counter to the official narrative. When Dorothy returns to Kansas, it is not the usual MGM happy ending because we know, from those chilly black and white scenes at the start, that Dorothy is very lonely there, clutching her pet Toto. Kansas may be home but it is deadly dull and monochrome compared to the colourful land of Oz/Hollywood.

KITSCH

Kitsch is defined by the dictionary as "garish, tasteless or sentimental art". A definition which would, if taken literally, make it one of the fastest-growing genres in the movies. You can normally find at least two of those three qualities in any John Waters movie and in *Cecil B. DeMented* you can find all three. Here we trawl through the turgid, the trashy and the triumphant films which have made movie history of some kind or another.

ATTACK OF THE 50FT WOMAN 1958
Director Nathan Juran *Cast* Allison Hayes, William Hudson, Yvette Vickers

What a paranoid decade the 1950s were. Dominated by worries about Commies and bodysnatchers (or were they the same thing?), the end of the decade saw a plethora of B movies where the forces doing the attacking were giant leeches, crab monsters, killer tomatoes and, of course, a 50ft woman. You can see the plot, where a woman is enlarged after a meeting with aliens and takes revenge on her husband and her tormentors, as a proto-*Life And Loves Of A She Devil*. Only instead of Julie T Wallace we have the beauteous Hayes who, although she has the film stolen from her by Vickers, plays the loosest woman the filmmakers could get past the censors. Remade in 1998 (starring Daryl Hannah) with more money but less conviction.

ATTACK OF THE MUSHROOM PEOPLE 1963 MATANGO
Director Ishiro Honda *Cast* Akira Kubo, Yoshio Tsuchiya, Kumi Mizuno, Hiroshi Koizumi

Honda, who directed this movie, was not one of the Japanese directors who became a household name in the West but he worked as assistant director on Akira Kurosawa's late masterpiece *Ran* and the great man gave the eulogy at his funeral. This movie sums up why Honda gave up directing his own films. Having made *Godzilla* in 1956, he found himself increasingly confined to sci-fi and monster movies like this, a strange tale of a group of shipwreck survivors who get turned into mushrooms. The film contains one of the all-time great credits when it lists Eisei Amamoto as "skulking transitional

"WHO EXPECTS A PSYCHOLOGIST TO THINK? ESPECIALLY WHEN YOU ARE SO BUSY THINKING WHAT YOU THINK OTHER PEOPLE ARE THINKING"
Hans, Bedtime For Bonzo

Matango". It's great Saturday afternoon entertainment for kids, just not the kind of film you'd want to spend your life making.

ATTACK OF THE PUPPET PEOPLE 1958

Director Bert I Gordon *Cast* John Agar, John Hoyt, June Kenny

Mad scientist shrinks people – yes, it's Tod Browning's *Devil-Doll* revisited. The 1950s were a tough decade for Agar: if he wasn't wrestling with mole people, he was pitting his wits against a tarantula, trying to figure out if his wife (Dr Jekyll's daughter) was a crazed killer or, worst of all, having his body taken over by a brain from another planet. His monstrous over-acting in *The Brain From Planet Arous* has earned him a permanent place in cult movie fans' hearts. Here he's more restrained, assuming his normal manner of acting like someone who was trying out what it was like to be one of the living dead. This may well be the best-known picture that Gordon directed.

BEDTIME FOR BONZO 1951

Director Frederick de Cordova
Cast Ronald Reagan, Diana Lynn

Until Bonzo's co-star became President of the United States, this was just another Hollywood comedy, albeit one about a professor who treats a chimp as a child. It isn't even Reagan's worst performance as an actor. But after his 1980 election victory, the movie poster became a pin-up for those who disagreed with Reagan's politics and the vicious rumour was spread that he was out-acted in this film by a chimp. Nothing could be further from the truth. The fact is Bonzo just wasn't that great an actor.

BELA LUGOSI MEETS A BROOKLYN GORILLA 1952

Director William Beaudine *Cast* Bela Lugosi, Sammy Petrillo, Duke Mitchell

In the course of this curious movie, Lugosi (a mad scientist on – hey! – a jungle-covered Pacific island) injects a de-evolution serum into 'entertainer' Duke Mitchell, turning him into a singing gorilla. After watching 74 minutes of this film, the only rational conclusion is that

TITLE BOUT

Films where you feel more effort has gone into the title than anything else.

CAN HIERONYMUS MERKIN EVER FORGET MERCY HUMPPE AND FIND TRUE HAPPINESS? (1969)
What kind of fool am I? Anthony Newley asked. Does this answer the question?

I KILLED MY LESBIAN WIFE, HUNG HER ON A MEAT HOOK AND NOW HAVE A THREE-PICTURE DEAL AT DISNEY (1995)
To which the only appropriate response seems to be: "Bully for you".

FEUDIN', FIGHTIN'N'FUSSIN' (1968)
Not to be confused with *Feudin', Fussin' And A-Fightin'* (1949).

TEENAGE PSYCHO MEETS BLOODY MARY (1964)
Aka 'The Incredibly Strange Creatures Who Stopped Living And Became Mixed-Up Zombies'.

HOW BRIDGET SERVED THE SALAD UNDRESSED (1898)
Silent comedy of manners in which serving girl Bridget is told to serve the salad undressed and, you guessed it, takes her clothes off.

HOW MUCH WOOD WOULD A WOODCHUCK CHUCK (1976)
Werner Herzog's documentary about the world championship for cattle auctioneers. It's better than it sounds.

WHAT ARE THOSE STRANGE DROPS OF BLOOD DOING ON JENNIFER'S BODY? (1972)
Actually this Italian serial chiller isn't bad.

"Listen up, kids, this is your last chance to buy popcorn before the Pearl & Dean ads start"

a similar serum must have been used on Beaudine and scriptwriter Tim Ryan. Mitchell and Petrillo were the B movies' answer to Martin and Lewis who, in turn, were the less expensive version of Hope and Crosby. This movie's only purpose is to emphasise how far Lugosi had sunk since he personified Dracula for Universal in 1931. There was worse to come, including a chance comic encounter with Old Mother Riley later in the same year. By 1955, Lugosi had succumbed to drug addiction and died a year later. The final indignity came when Martin Landau won an Oscar as Lugosi in *Ed Wood* in 1994, an honour the Hungarian horror king had never won.

BLOODY MAMA 1970
Director Roger Corman *Cast* Shelley Winters, Bruce Dern, Robert De Niro, Don Stroud
Normally the words "based on a true story" make your heart sink. With Corman in charge what you have here is not the dogged, small-minded, pursuit of literal truth but a gorgeously OTT confection, symbolized by Winters' own melodramatics as the evil Ma Barker, sex-crazed mother of a violent, criminal gang. Dern and De Niro give able support in a trashy classic.

THE CARS THAT ATE PARIS 1974
Director Peter Weir *Cast* John Meillon, Terry Camilleri
It's hard to believe that it took three people (Weir, Keith Gow and Piers Davies) to write this 'horror' flick. That it was helmed by the man who made *Witness*, *Dead Poets Society* and *The Truman Show* may, however, explain its cult status. The,

> "I'M NOT INTERESTED IN SOME KIND OF MEAL YOU HAVE TO BEAT WITH A MALLET WHILE WEARING SOME STUPID LITTLE BIB, WHILE FAMILIES OF MUTANTS GAWK IN YOUR FACE"
> Honey Whitlock, Cecil B. Demented

erm, plot follows the plight of nice-but-dim Arthur Waldo (Camilleri) who wakes up in an Aussie outback hospital after his car crashes. It takes 91 minutes of wandering through a town full of blood-crazed youths driving spiked jalopies for Arthur to work out that the mental patients in the upstairs ward are all lobotomized accident victims and the contents of their contrived car-wrecks the local currency. There's a spurious sub-plot about Arthur learning to conquer his fear of driving and a brief appearance by Bruce Spence (the Gyro Captain in *Mad Max 2*) as the nuttiest of the fruitcakes, but that's about it. So why watch it? Because like Ed Wood's cult 'classic' *Planet 9 From Outer Space*, it's so bad it's hysterical.

Supercool Trouble Man, one good mother, complete with special bulletproof tie, ya dig that, dude?

CECIL B. DEMENTED 2000

Director John Waters *Cast* Melanie Griffith, Stephen Dorff, Alicia Witt, Ricki Lake, Patty Hearst

Griffith reminds everyone what a fine comic actress she can be in this affectionate satire about the movie business. She plays a star who is kidnapped by a cult leader (Dorff) to be used as part of his revolutionary assault on mainstream cinema. Griffith queens it as an egomaniac star who is made over to look more and more like Waters' departed muse Divine. The gags are fast, furious and usually funny (the cinema multiplex they attack is showing *Patch Adams: The Director's Cut* and *Gump Again*) and movie in-jokes abound. The scene where Griffiths rejects her limo because it's the wrong colour really happened (Ginger Rogers did the spurning). Thank God for John Waters.

DR GOLDFOOT AND THE BIKINI MACHINE 1965

Director Norman Taurog *Cast* Vincent Price, Frankie Avalon, Dwayne Hickman, Susan Hart

Price sends up his own image as the evil genius of the title whose mad plan it is to make lady robots to marry wealthy men and persuade them to sign away their assets. Avalon, having tired of an endless beach party, tries to foil him. The highlights are the Supremes singing the title song and the chase scene. This was successful enough to spawn an Italian-American sequel *Dr Goldfoot And The Girl Bombs* in which Avalon, having been summoned back to the beach by that jealous minx Annette Funicello, is replaced by Fabian. It's the same plot only this time the girls, as the slogan for the film says, have thermonuclear navels. Yes, it does sound a bit desperate.

EEGAH! 1962
Director Arch Hall Sr *Cast* Arch Hall Jr, Marilyn Manning, Richard Kiel

Arch Hall Jr didn't want to be in Dad's movie. "Gee Pop," he said, "I can't sing." But his father said that a lot of people who couldn't sing had done well in the movies. So *Eegah!* was born: an attempt to make an Elvis Presley movie without Elvis (but with the director's son), with fewer songs but with the added bonus of a prehistoric giant played by a chap called Richard Kiel, who was then a bouncer at a nightclub the director knew. The giant falls in love with Manning, fights with Tommy (Hall Jr) but Tommy, amazingly, wins. If this was *The Player* you could imagine one of the studio execs saying: "It's *King Kong* meets *Blue Hawaii*." Which is pretty much what it is.

I DISMEMBER MAMA 1974
Director Paul Leder *Cast* Zooey Hall, Geri Reischi, Joanne Moore Jordan

"May she rest in pieces," says the poster. But don't build your hopes up. The title is braver and more gruesome than the film itself, which is actually a rather dull study of sexual perversion with Hall turning in the kind of performance which would justly bring his career to a close. One of those movies that never lives up (or should that be down?) to its poster.

JESSE JAMES MEETS FRANKENSTEIN'S DAUGHTER 1966
Director William Beaudine *Cast* John Lupton, Narda Onyx, Cal Bolder

If Ed Wood hadn't existed, it would not have been necessary to invent him: the world could have lived happily in the knowledge that in William Beaudine we had the next best/worst thing. 'One Shot' Beaudine had developed a new micro-genre of B movie (some would call it a rut) where two major genres collided on screen. Not content with uniting Bela Lugosi and a singing gorilla, he would create a couple more screen partnerships unique in the history of cinema: Dracula and Billy the Kid and Frankenstein's daughter and Jesse James. This was Beaudine's 199th movie and, even though he never reshot a scene, you can sense exhaustion setting in. The fantastic comic/horror/western possibilities of a charismatic outlaw

"They'll cut that, won't they? Whoever told Donald Pleasence he could disco dance?"

coming into conflict with a girl whose birthright was a bolt through the back of her neck were never really explored. Bizarrely, Beaudine plays this one straight.

MYRA BRECKINRIDGE 1970

Director Michael Sarne *Cast* Mae West, John Huston, Raquel Welch

This film of Gore Vidal's sex-change novel was promoted with the slogan: "Everything you've heard about Myra Breckinridge is true." Which audiences took to mean that the critics were right and this really was the worst movie ever to grace a cinema screen. Any movie whose 'plot' involves Rex Reed becoming Raquel Welch is up against it from the start and the decision to cast the 78-year-old Mae West, still using her patented come-up-and-see-me-sometime routine (she wrote her own dialogue), lengthened the odds on this film succeeding even more. The rest of the actors don't seem to have been cast but rounded up from a nearby party and confined on set against their will for

BE VERY AFRAID

THE WILLIAM CASTLE STORY

The title of William Castle's memoirs says it all: *Step Right Up, I'm Gonna Scare The Pants Off America!* If you're still in any doubt, the titles of some of the films he directed might reinforce the point: *Let's Kill Uncle (Before Uncle Kills Us), Macabre, The Tingler.*

Born William Schloss (Schloss is German for castle hence the showbiz name) in New York in 1914, Castle spent most of his professional life in the backlots of studios like Columbia and Monogram producing low-budget thrillers. The films themselves weren't especially good or bad. *When Strangers Marry* is a classic, and the first major role for Robert Mitchum. Others, especially *The House On Haunted Hill*, have become cult favourites. While his films were seldom out of the ordinary, he had a fertile imagination for stunts with which to promote them. For *Macabre*, (1958), he took out insurance in case any

member of the audience died during it. For *Haunted Hill*, he invented a process he called Emergo, where he wired up plastic skeletons to fly over audiences' heads. And for *The Tingler*, he literally shocked cinemagoers by giving them an electric shock from their seats.

Castle's last film as a director, *Shanks* (1974), was not a chiller inspired by the career of the late great football manager but a strange movie, with minimal dialogue, starring Marcel Marceau as a persecuted deaf mute who brings his mentor back to life.

It was Castle's fate to direct movies where the promotional budget was usually as big as the budget for making the film. Having scared America's pants off with his memoirs in 1976, he died a year later from a heart attack.

John Goodman played the William Castle character to near perfection in *Matinee* (1993) which is where the popcorn selling alien at the cinema (on p245) comes in.

the duration of shooting. Welch (as the man-hating Myra who enrols in acting school to get into Hollywood to destroy the American male – yes, it's that weak) struggles valiantly to stop the movie from sinking but fails. A moustache-less Tom Selleck plays a stud and Farrah Fawcett plays a dumb blonde. The movie might have been a bit funnier if they'd been cast the other way around.

SERGEANT PEPPER'S LONELY HEARTS CLUB BAND 1978

Director Michael Schultz
Cast The Bee Gees, Peter Frampton, Frankie Howerd, Donald Pleasence

If the Queen ever sees this film and realises that Sir George Martin is listed as musical director, she'll ask for the knighthood back. In Sir George's defence, however, full criminal responsibility for this movie should fall on Robert Stigwood, the Bee Gees and director Schultz. The plot (local band made good – the Gibbs plus Frampton – battle it out with music industry and bad band – Aerosmith, after Kiss pulled out) is terminally average. The decision to only have spoken dialogue from the narrator (George Burns) is a brave one but what really lifts this into a class of its own is the use of the Beatles songs which provide the only possible excuse for this movie's existence. The sight of Donald Pleasence disco dancing, however unnerving you may find it, somehow fails to prepare you for the full horror of seeing Frankie Howerd singing *When I'm 64* to a young woman called Strawberry Fields he's hoping to seduce.

TROUBLE MAN 1972

Director Ivan Dixon *Cast* Robert Hooks, Paul Wonfield, Ralph Waite

"So man if you don't dig this super cool black… stay away from the box office you motherf–." That, at least, was how one critic greeted the arrival of Mr T – not the *A-Team* star, but the hero of this blaxploitation film. Another reviewer obviously felt threatened by Hooks' bullet-proof private eye (who can close pool halls with a stern glance), complaining that the character looked "so cool as to make one suspect it isn't Coke he is constantly drinking but antifreeze". The soundtrack is by Marvin Gaye and it's a pity he didn't write the script. It's a pity somebody didn't write the script.

MYRA OH MY

With dialogue like this, it's really hard to understand why Gore Vidal disowned *Myra Breckinridge*, the film of his novel.

Surgeon: We're going to have to blow up your tits with silicon.
Myron: I thought they used paraffin.

Letitia Van Allen: Don't forget to remind me about the policeman's balls – I mean the policeman's ball.

Surgeon: You realise once we cut it off it won't come back?
Myron: Do you think I am an idiot?

Myra: How should a man act?
Student: He should ball chicks.

LAS VEGAS

Jesus had to starve in a desert for 40 days to be tempted, Americans just have to fly (or drive) across a desert to Las Vegas where (as a recent movie suggested) very bad things can happen. 'Bad things' can mean anything from becoming addicted to gambling, dying of alcoholism or seeing 34 flying Elvises. Maybe one reason Hollywood likes setting movies in Vegas so much is that in both places appearances are a) deceptive, b) everything.

BUGSY 1991

Director **Barry Levinson** *Cast* **Warren Beatty, Annette Bening, Harvey Keitel**

For the last quarter of a century Beatty has been mostly playing romantic loners. Sometimes they join revolutions (*Reds*), sometimes they stand for re-election to the Senate (*Bulworth*) and sometimes (as here) they create Las Vegas. Beatty relies less on the mannerisms that got him through *Reds* and *Dick Tracy* and really gets inside the part of the doomed gangster too much in love with a leggy starlet (Bening) and his vision for Vegas to notice his paymasters getting restive. The film never really explains the dichotomy between the ruthless gangster and the romantic dreamer, but Beatty may yet star in and/or direct the best Vegas movie if he ever gets round to doing a similar job on the city's sinister *eminence grise*, Howard Hughes.

> "IF YOU WANT A SIMPLE YES OR NO, YOU'RE GONNA HAVE TO FINISH THE QUESTION"
>
> Virginia Hill, Bugsy

CASINO 1995

Director **Martin Scorsese** *Cast* **Robert De Niro, Sharon Stone, Joe Pesci, James Woods**

Brian Le Baron plays the valet parker. In a striking coincidence, he reappears three years later as a car park attendant in Terry Gilliam's *Fear And Loathing.... Casino* encourages such lacuna because, even if it is the third part of Scorsese's mafia trilogy (after *Mean Streets* and *Goodfellas*), it is three hours long. During the first hour the detail about how the mafia ran casinos in Vegas is so intense it's like watching a documentary about the mob's business practices. De Niro plays the casino owner who falls in love with and marries a hooker (Stone) who then has a fling with hubby's hitman (Pesci). This triggers the mafia's undignified exit from Vegas. In a strong cast, Stone carries the film, without uncrossing her legs. An intriguing exercise in one of Scorsese's favourite sports, historical revisionism: while the world cheers the sanitising of Vegas, Scorsese sounds a note of quiet regret that an outlaw's paradise has become another Disneyland.

FEAR AND LOATHING IN LAS VEGAS
1997
Director Terry Gilliam *Cast* Johnny Depp, Benicio Del Toro

Too weird to win over the masses, too rare to sink without trace, Gilliam's *Fear And Loathing…* is a healthily bizarre curio. Devotees of writer Hunter S Thompson's account of his drug-fuelled voyage around Vegas with his Samoan attorney will love this, even though it can't quite capture the laugh-out-loud quality of the book. But if you don't like Thompson and like films to have a plot, this will impress you about as much as the drunk who tries to engage you in conversation when you're walking home. All that said, we wouldn't have missed it for the world.

Taken by a mad doctor, developed by Boots: another snap for Hunter's album

HONEYMOON IN VEGAS 1992
Director Andrew Bergman
Cast James Caan, Nicolas Cage, Sarah Jessica Parker

Cage plays a man who vowed on his mother's deathbed that he'd never marry, but must now choose either to break that vow or lose his girlfriend (Parker). They come to Vegas to find an instant wedding chapel but then he gets cold feet. To say more is to a) give the game away and b) reduce the plot to something which sounds like it's from a sitcom. The weird thing is, it is a daft kind of sitcom plot but Bergman makes it believable and funny while packing it with incidental stuff which takes the film into a strange realm of its own – a realm not unlike the popular vision of Vegas as a place where normal rules are suspended.

THE LADY GAMBLES 1949
Director Michael Gordon *Cast* Barbara Stanwyck, Robert Preston

Las Vegas hadn't long stopped being a chicken run when this film – about a woman who accompanies her husband to Vegas and becomes addicted to gambling – was made. Gordon would later direct two Doris Day comedies but here he shines a pretty remorseless light on the ugly seam already running through

Vegas life. The scene where Stanwyck gets beaten up by thugs in an alley is remarkable for what is, for all its noir trappings, a star vehicle. Look out for Tony Curtis as a bellboy and for the film crew reflected in the window of the bus Stanwyck is on.

LEAVING LAS VEGAS 1995

Director **Mike Figgis** *Cast* **Nicolas Cage, Elisabeth Shue**

Cage is a failed writer who loses his soul but finds a beautiful hooker (Shue) in a film which should have done for tourism in Las Vegas what Titanic (the ship, not the movie) did for luxury cruises. It's not Vegas' fault exactly – Cage arrives there with the express intention of drinking himself to death – but it is the venue for scenes of embarrassment and horror. The opening scene where a drunken Cage is trying to borrow money to get even more drunk is enough to make viewers who haven't signed the pledge, cringe with pained recognition.

> **"YOU JUMPED OUT OF A PLANE FOR ME!"**
> Betsy, Honeymoon In Vegas

OCEAN'S ELEVEN 1960

Director **Lewis Milestone** *Cast* **Frank Sinatra, Dean Martin, Sammy Davis Jr, Angie Dickinson**

Eleven men try to rob five Vegas casinos at once in this film which brings together the entire Rat Pack to little effect. Dino sings *Ain't That A Kick In The Head* a lot, Sammy Davis Jr sings a bit and Ol' Blue Eyes sings nothing at all. The female characters are slight (although at least they're not just playing themselves). Dino says at one point: "Take the vote away from women – make slaves of them," and you begin to feel like you're watching a Rat Pack home movie. Whether we get anything out of it seems incidental. If you want to watch a Rat Pack movie, *Robin And The Seven Hoods* is more genuine fun, thanks partly to the addition of Bing Crosby and Peter Falk.

VIVA LAS VEGAS 1964

Director **George Sidney** *Cast* **Elvis Presley, Ann-Margret**

Elvis' biggest-grossing movie has his best female co-star and some of his best tunes (the title track, *C'mon Everybody*, the beautifully phrased ballad *I Need Somebody To Lean On*). Margret and Elvis fell in love on set (marriage was discussed) and their chemistry helps make this the best of three films in which he plays a professional racing driver. The duet *The Lady Loves Me*, while amusing, isn't really up to the stars' combined talents. Pity the best duet, a slinky revamp of the old blues number *You're The Boss*, was cut because the Colonel was worried Margret was getting too many close ups.

"And I'm just a devil with love to spare – viva!, viva Las Vegas!"

MARTIAL ARTS

By the time Bruce Lee burst onto western movie screens in the early 1970s, martial arts movies had enjoyed almost a decade of supremacy in cinemas across Asia. The rush of new moviemaking was inspired by imported samurai films from Japan, supported by developing superpower China and paid for by a newly flourishing Hong Kong.

ee was the first pan-Asian superstar and the first real martial arts movie legend. In the 1960s he developed Jeet Kune Do – a street-fighting system inspired by all martial arts. Lee wanted to turn his back on the supernatural 'Monkey King' style and he inspired a generation of followers, including *Once Upon a Time in China* star Jet Li and Jackie Chan, who first came to prominence as a stuntman on Lee's *Fist Of Fury*.

Kung fu's successful sortie west cleared the way for other martial arts styles. Jean-Claude Van Damme kicked his way to stardom in the 1980s with *Kickboxer* and *Bloodsport*. *Karate Kid* (1984) was a smash while *Teenage Mutant Ninja Turtles* and *Mighty Morphin Power Rangers* catered for kids. Ironic that Lee, the tough guy who started it all, died of an allergy to aspirin.

CROUCHING TIGER, HIDDEN DRAGON 2000
Director Ang Lee *Cast* Chow Yun-Fat, Michelle Yeoh
Chow Yun-Fat's first martial arts movie is a breathtaking mix of fighting, choreography and filmmaking. Okay, so the story wouldn't win any Oscars, but it does focus on love, honour, duty and good versus evil as much as it opens the way for young co-star Zhang Ziyi to display her impressive acting and fighting. The special effects in this film were minimal. Harnesses and cables, edited out in post-production, rather than computers, were used to help the stars skate walls and leap rooftops.

DRUNKEN MASTER 1978 ZUI QUAN
Director Yuen Woo-Ping *Cast* Jackie Chan, Siu Tien Yuen
Jackie Chan's finest film. The kung fu is phenomenal, the verbal and physical jokes are laugh-out-loud funny and the action never stops. Chan plays the talented but ill-disciplined son of

> "USE HEAD FOR SOMETHING OTHER THAN TARGET"
> Mr Miyagi, The Karate Kid

Bruce took his mirror fight too seriously, having to be dissuaded from killing his opponent

a local master, sent for a year of training by his infamous uncle, Beggar Su. Su, aka Drunken Master, is a red-nosed, wine-sloshing kung fu genius with his own unique style. By the end of the movie Chan has learned the secrets of the Eight Drunken Gods – including his own version of the God Miss Ho, the drunken goddess flaunting her body (as you'd expect Chan makes the most of it) – and fought to match a bounty hunter out to capture the price on his father's head.

ENTER THE DRAGON 1973

Director Robert Clouse *Cast* Bruce Lee, John Saxon, Kien Shih

The first Hong Kong/US movie production and the film Lee hoped would make him a Hollywood star. Lee goes undercover to a martial arts contest on the island of a Hong Kong millionaire recluse. The mirror room finale is one of the most memorable fight sequences ever. According to director Clouse, the fight between Lee and Bob Wall became real, extras convincing Lee that to save face he'd have to kill his rival. Luckily Clouse persuaded Lee that Wall was needed in post-production. The movie was an instant hit but, alas, Lee did not live to see the final cut. Steer clear of Lee's *Way of the Dragon* unless you're in thrall to gratuitous shots of Italian breasts.

THE KARATE KID 1984
Director John G Avildsen *Cast* Ralph Macchio, Pat Morita

"Wipe on. Wipe off." Perhaps the most famous martial arts movie line in the West from this, the cheesiest of Hollywood fight blockbusters. Daniel is the new kid in town (although Macchio was actually a very young looking 23-year-old at the time). Everything goes well until stick-thin Daniel chats up the school's karate star's girlfriend. But wait – the ageing Japanese maintenance man turns out to be a crack karate expert, all too willing to help! Many crane stances on windswept beaches and much waxing of cars later, and our weedy hero is ready to take on the champ. Guess who wins. No, go on, guess.

KICKBOXER 1989
Director Mark DiSalle *Cast* Jean-Claude Van Damme, Tong Po

When Jean-Claude Van Damme's mullet-haired brother is paralyzed in a Bangkok kickboxing contest, Kurt (Van Damme) swears vengeance against the mighty Tong Po. With the aid of a fast-talking Vietnam vet he finds help in the sort of retired forest-living master who tends to frequent martial arts movies. The training sequences – including Kurt felling palm trees with his bare shins – are spectacular. The dancing is not. But when, finally, he heads back to the city to take on Tong Po with his hands traditionally strapped, waxed and dipped in shards of glass, the blood really starts to flow.

LEGEND OF A FIGHTER 1982 HUO YUAN-JIA
Director Woo-Ping Yuen *Cast* Ka-Yan Leung, Yasuaki Kurata

The best of the movies of the life of Chinese hero, Huo Yuen Chia. Set during Japanese occupation, Yuen Chia fights not only the Japanese but also the idea that kung fu should be reserved for a minority. This is minimalist kung fu with breathtaking fight sequences. There is also a real storyline and top-quality acting. A brilliant antidote to the farce and bluster of too many poor quality martial arts 'hits'.

> "WHY DOESN'T SOMEBODY PULL OUT A 45 AND, BANG, SETTLE IT?"
> Lee, Enter the Dragon

THE NEW ONE-ARMED SWORDSMAN 1971
Director Chang Cheh *Cast* David Chiang, Ti Lung , Cheng Lei

An inauspicious opening, complete with cardboard prop swords, a *Star Trek*-style set and plenty of overdubbed steel-on-steel sounds leads to an ultimately impressive tale of honour, friendship and sword-fighting. Young knight Lei Li fulfils a pledge to cut off his right arm after losing a fight with an older, dishonourable master and is forced to retire. But everything changes with the arrival of a sword-bearing love interest, and Feng Junjie (Ti Lung), a young knight after Lei's own heart. Atmospheric shots of fights on deserted bridges, bloodstained sleeves and truly spectacular sword action ensues.

ONCE UPON A TIME IN CHINA 1991 WONG FEI HUNG

Director Tsui Hark *Cast* Jet Li, Yuen Biao, Rosamund Kwan

Jet Li shows off his supreme versatility playing Wong Fei Hung, a 19th century legendary Chinese kung fu fighter and healer. Li's mastery of the wu shu style of fighting makes for thrilling viewing and the final fight sequences are incredible. But then, by the time this movie was released Li had been in intensive training for years. China's national Wu Shu champion aged 11, his first US starring role was in the same year on the White House lawn before President Nixon. In this film he shows off his phenomenal acrobatic ability. After a fallow period, *Once Upon A Time In China* shot Li back to the big time.

PANTYHOSE HERO 1990

Director Sammo Hung *Cast* Sammo Hung, Alan Tam, James Tien

Surreal kung-fu action 'comedy' in which larger than life *Martial Law* star Sammo Hung and his partner go undercover as a gay couple to investigate a murder. Cue a tightly curled brilliantined hairdo for Sammo and a mincing walk, pouts and prances for Alan – nicknamed Gaykey. The acting is as gruesome as the blood-spurting chainsaw close-ups that earned the 18 rating, but the showdown at a well-equipped but handily deserted construction site is worth the wait.

THE BRUCE LEE MYSTERY

When it comes to staging a memorable movie death, the martial arts genre rarely lets you down. Neatly rolled umbrellas, underwear, even twirling moustaches – all have been used as lethal or near-lethal weapons. So when a real life martial arts hero dies, it shouldn't be that surprising that the fans can't swallow a straightforward explanation.

Bruce Lee died in his sleep, aged only 32, on a hot Hong Kong day in 1973. According to the coroner's report, he suffered a hyperallergic response to an aspirin. But the Hong Kong press was having none of it. According to which edition of the papers you read, Lee had been murdered by triads, given an untraceable Oriental poison, killed by a psychic, faked his own death to escape gangsters, been the victim of a martial arts 'death touch' or been slain by seriously bad feng shui. The fact that Lee had predicted that he would live to only half the age of his father – who died at 64 – only served to fuel the speculation.

THE QUEST 1996

Director Jean-Claude Van Damme

Cast Jean-Claude Van Damme, Roger Moore

The Quest is an often excruciating film starring Van Damme as a 1920s American gangster who finds himself abandoned and learning kickboxing on Thailand's Mutai Island. However it has two redeeming features. First, Roger Moore as Lord Edgar Dobbs, an amoral pirate seeking to make a fast buck out of Van Damme's bad luck. Second, the rather inevitable martial arts competition between champions from the "four corners of the world". Cue a Scottish competitor with red hair and a kilt, a Brazilian shouting "Ole! Ole!", a Spaniard with a touch of flamenco about his fighting and a rather good finale.

MEDIA

Whether you're a war correspondent, a newsreader or just a guy on the radio, in movies you're only ever a few blunders away from death, or worse, starring in a 24-hour TV series against your will.

ACE IN THE HOLE 1951

Director Billy Wilder *Cast* Kirk Douglas, Jan Sterling

Wilder's most savagely sardonic and cynical film was a controversial flop when released but has come to be regarded as a darkly prophetic, increasingly relevant indictment of media sensationalism (and much imitated, most blatantly in Costa-Gavras' vehicle for Dustin Hoffman and John Travolta, *Mad City*). Douglas, never better, is washed-up reporter Charles Tatum. When he finds a man trapped in a cavern he exploits the situation relentlessly to restore his career and creates a media and merchandising circus. Paramount re-released this as *The Big Carnival* but failed to attract audiences to an all too truthful human interest story. Wilder's wife Audrey suggested the most famous line, where Tatum tells the trapped man's tough cookie wife (Sterling) to go to church and she retorts: "I don't pray. Kneeling bags my nylons."

"Press one to hold the front page, press two to free a condemned man"

A FACE IN THE CROWD 1957

Director Elia Kazan *Cast* Andy Griffith, Patricia Neal

Sam Goldwyn wasn't always wrong. His suggestion that messages were best left to Western Union makes sense when you see this film, underrated because its makers stuffed more messages into it than it could bear. It stars future TV king Griffith as a hillbilly singer who makes his start on Memphis TV and becomes a national icon. Yes, it's the story of Johnny Burnette. Anyway, the singer becomes a political monster – instead of just meeting Nixon, Elvis becomes Nixon. Look out for Lee Remick, on her debut, and enjoy this prescient satire.

ALL THE PRESIDENT'S MEN 1976

Director Alan J Pakula *Cast* Robert Redford, Dustin Hoffman

Redford just wanted to produce this movie but no studio would

"NOTHING'S RIDING ON THIS EXCEPT FREEDOM OF THE PRESS, AND MAYBE THE FUTURE OF THE COUNTRY. NOT THAT ANY OF THAT MATTERS, BUT IF YOU GUYS FUCK UP AGAIN, I'M GOING TO GET MAD"

Ben Bradlee, All The President's Men

take it on unless he starred in it. Just as well because he and Hoffman are a perfect double act. The account of the *Washington Post*'s investigation into Watergate is superbly cast and full of classic one-liners, mostly delivered by Jason Robards who plays editor Ben Bradlee to such perfection it's a wonder the real Bradlee didn't ring him up and ask him to make the impersonation permanent. One of the film's many virtues is the way it takes us back to the time when the very idea that a president would be involved in a third-rate burglary seemed like ludicrous nonsense. You see Redford and Hoffman piecing it together, not quite believing it themselves. The last word belongs to Bradlee/Robards: "We are about to accuse Haldeman, who only happens to be the second most powerful man in this country, of conducting a criminal conspiracy from inside the White House. It would be nice if we were right."

CITIZEN KANE 1941

Director **Orson Welles** *Cast* **Orson Welles, Joseph Cotten**

One of the many remarkable achievements of this all-time great is to define the way we see media moguls. Not just William Randolph Hearst, whose life partly inspired this, but also Murdoch and Maxwell; all are seen through the refracting lens of Welles' fictional creation. Yet Welles (and writer Herman Mankiewicz) also smuggled details of the star's biography into the film and this movie has as much to say about Welles as about its apparent subject (this is especially true of its portrayal of

Kane's relationship with his parents). Pop it in the video again and see if you can remember which scene comes next – one of the film's great gambits is the way it defies the chronology of time, relying on its emotional chronology to tell the story.

DISPAREN A MATAR 1992

Director **Carlos Azpurua** *Cast* **Amalia Pérez Diaz, Jean Carlo Simancas, Daniel Alvarado (II)**

Azpurua has made two brave films about Venezuelan politics. In 1998 he made *Almanecio de Golpe* about the 1992 military coup, but he is probably more famous for this piece, aka *Shoot To Kill*, about a woman who (having seen her husband killed by the dictatorship 30 years ago) persuades a reporter to investigate the beating to death of her son. Like Costa-Gavras' more famous *Missing*, the film uses the techniques of a thriller to tell the story as the reporter comes into conflict with his editor and the state.

Marcello often forgot to use his Head & Shoulders before a big date

LA DOLCE VITA 1960

Director Federico Fellini *Cast* Marcello Mastroianni, Anita Ekberg, Anouk Aimee

A film inspired by the media (the events that Mastroianni's gossip columnist covers come from actual newspaper stories) which would influence the media in ways that Fellini couldn't have foreseen. The character of Paparazzo, the photographer, would coin a new word. And the phrase "La dolce vita" became part of a drive for tourism in Rome and Italy. When this was released in America cinemas were asked to persuade local shops to sell "dolce vita" goods such as chocolate and Italian products. The tale of Mastroianni's descent into decadence was slammed by the Catholic church, Fellini's old mentor Roberto Rossellini and by film critic Pauline Kael, who called it the "come-dressed-as-the-sick-soul-of-Europe party". Fellini didn't approve of the "dolce vita" set, hence his refusal to cast Paul Newman in the Mastroianni role. He didn't want the Hollywood brand of star charisma to blind us to the story and saw the Italian actor as more of an everyman figure.

> **"I'VE MET A LOT OF HARD-BOILED EGGS IN MY TIME BUT YOU, YOU'RE 20 MINUTES"**
> Lorraine, Ace In The Hole

NETWORK 1976

Director Sidney Lumet *Cast* Peter Finch, Faye Dunaway, William Holden

This gripping satire looked overcooked on release. But all TV producer Dunaway really, really wants is her own brand of reality TV – only instead of inmates in a house having or not having sex, she wants terrorism on prime time TV ("Joseph Stalin and his merry band of Bolsheviks"). Her newscaster Howard Beale (Finch) is doing his bit by threatening to kill himself on air, an event which as Holden, the cynical but ethical old hand, says "will guarantee a 50 share". After the initial thrill of Finch's divine madness the film loses its way a bit but picks up when Holden becomes an Old Testament prophet, telling his lover Dunaway that she and TV destroy everything they touch.

QUIZ SHOW 1994

Director Robert Redford *Cast* John Turturro, Rob Morrow, Ralph Fiennes

The key here is the casting. We share in the guilt. We would rather see a crooked Fiennes (as cheating, quiz show guest Charles van Doren) answer the $64,000 question than sweaty, ugly Turturro (a cracking performance from an actor who is synonymous with the Coen brothers' films). Fiennes also makes us understand how easily we might succumb to the same temptation. Redford sees this scandal as the loss of American innocence, although if that means that Americans stopped

And the $64,000 question is... wouldn't you cheat if you were offered fame and fortune?

believing that Geritol would heal "tired blood" this may not have been a bad thing. The film subtly suggests that when the Congressional investigator Goodwin (Morrow) tries to keep his friend Van Doren out of the hearings into the scandal, he's making the same kind of casting decision as the networks and the sponsors.

SHOCK CORRIDOR 1963
Director Samuel Fuller *Cast* Peter Breck, Constance Towers

The dialogue in this film sounds like it's been plucked from a tabloid front page and the plot (about a newspaper reporter, Breck, who fakes madness to gain entry to an asylum to win a Pulitzer Prize but really goes mad) is taken to its illogical extreme. The whole film is a shock corridor: at one point six nymphomaniacs devour Breck. Elsewhere a black patient who thinks he's a white supremacist shouts: "Burn that freedom bus!" The asylum's inmates are so animated you almost expect them to launch into a high-stepping version of *Anything Goes*. You may not like this but, as is usually the case with Fuller, you won't forget it.

> **"YOU WANT TO BE WORSHIPPED? GO TO INDIA AND MOO"**
> Herbie Stempel, Quiz Show

TALK RADIO 1988
Director Oliver Stone *Cast* Eric Bogosian, Alec Baldwin

This is the film about the talk radio show host who gets murdered. So it's not to be confused with the film about the DJ whose comments inspire murder (*The Fisher King*), the film about the pirate radio show host whose wisecracks lead to suicide (*Pump Up the Volume*), the film about the pirate radio station that interferes with passing planes (*Big Swinger*) or the film about the talk radio host who looks like Dolly Parton (*Straight Talk*), all of which were released between 1988 and 1992. The Bogosian/Stone effort is easily the best thanks to Bogosian's intensity as the talk radio host (he had written and starred in the Broadway play) and to Stone's subtle camera work which lets you feel the interplay between host and caller.

TO DIE FOR 1995
Director Gus Van Sant *Cast* Nicole Kidman, Matt Dillon

"You know Mr Gorbachev, the guy that ran Russia for so long? I am a firm believer that he would still be in power today if he had had that ugly purple thing taken off his head." The wisdom of Suzanne Stone Maretto (Kidman), TV weathergirl, knows no beginning. One thing she does know, though, is that she wants hubby (Dillon) out of the way because he is generally being a drag on her relentless progress to the top. Kidman plays a woman who doesn't know what to say if she hasn't got a teleprompter with scary conviction.

TODOS SOMOS ESTRELLAS 1994 WE'RE ALL STARS
Director Felipe Degregori *Cast* Milena Alva, Mariella Balbi
Peruvian satire about a family whose application to appear on the TV game show they all watch is accidentally put at the top of the pile even though they are so not the kind of family to appear on the show. The satire loses some of its sting (though not, perhaps, as fast as *Broadcast News* does) but the film is engaging, humorous with moments of genuine emotion.

HOLD THE FRONT PAGES

Seldom can a Broadway play have been so often filmed as Ben Hecht and Charles MacArthur's *The Front Page* about a news editor (usually Walter Burns) trying to stop a reporter (usually Hildy Johnson) from marrying and giving up journalism. Burns always tries to tempt Johnson with a story about a condemned man. But are they all worth watching?

THE FRONT PAGE 1931
Directed by Lewis Milestone, starring Adolphe Menjou and Pat O'Brien, this amusing original version suffers from poor sound. Menjou took over as Burns after Louis Wolfheim died.

HIS GIRL FRIDAY 1934
For most fans, the definitive version and Rosalind Russell's finest hour. Director Howard Hawks is said to have made Hildy Johnson's character female after his secretary read the script. He also turned what had been a wisecracking crime story into a screwball comedy played at a breakneck pace, inserting a few in-jokes, most memorably when Grant/Burns says that a character "looks like Ralph Bellamy". He is, in fact, played by Ralph Bellamy

THE FRONT PAGE 1974
Only Billy Wilder would have the nerve to rewrite 60 per cent of the dialogue in the Hecht-MacArthur original. Worse was his decision to get rid of any overlapping dialogue, so that, despite the artistry of Walter Matthau and Jack Lemmon (as Hildy), the film dragged. Wilder was also sufficiently unsure of what audiences wanted by the 1970s to make the dialogue cruder, thinking this would appeal. Not bad, but not what Wilder would have done in his prime.

SWITCHING CHANNELS 1988
The Front Page in a satellite TV channel with the twosome becoming a threesome as Christopher Reeves' part as the fiancé (mostly off-screen in the other films) is expanded. Burt Reynolds and Kathleen Turner do their best but the script reads like it's been written by someone who honed his dialogue writing skills in Coca-Cola commercials and guess what? It has.

TOUT VA BIEN 1972

Director **Jean-Luc Godard** *Cast* **Jane Fonda, Yves Montand**

Fonda has spent so long playing news reporters it came as no surprise when she married a media mogul (Ted Turner). This is a must-see because it's the kind of film (Godard's first after four years of self-imposed exile) you can debate into the night. Is it a Marxist film? A Mao-nihilist film (whatever that might be)? A parody of a Marxist movie? Or an anti-Marxist movie? The plot is easier to describe: Fonda and Montand are reporter and TV producer whose commitment to each other, and the revolution, is called into question by the workers occupying a factory.

> **"NO, NO, KEEP THE ROOSTER STORY, THAT'S HUMAN INTEREST!"**
>
> Walter Burns, His Girl Friday

THE TRUMAN SHOW 1998

Director **Peter Weir** *Cast* **Jim Carrey, Ed Harris, Laura Linney**

Whatever else this movie is, it's proof of the old adage that the only people who are nostalgic for the American small town are those who never lived in one. The best of three movies made on a very similar theme at a very similar time (the others being *EDtv* and the very funny *Pleasantville*) has Carrey as the unwitting star of a 24-hour TV show whose world is just one big special effect. At one point, the show's producer Harris even says: "Cue the sun." The logic of film suggests that Carrey has to try to break out of this trap. Scripted by Andrew Niccol, who wrote and directed *Gattaca*, this is an eerie, memorable film with a fine (and subdued) performance by Carrey at its centre.

UNDER FIRE 1983

Director **Roger Spottiswoode** *Cast* **Nick Nolte, Gene Hackman, Joanna Cassidy**

Some directors' entire oeuvres are a cult. Other workhorses are lucky to conjure one special movie. Spottiswoode, formerly an editor for Sam Peckinpah, outdid himself with this electrifying political thriller that skillfully treats real-life events and mature romantic drama with suspense, and is superior to the more famous *Salvador*. Three front-line newshounds – TV man Hackman, correspondent Cassidy, and photographer Nolte – move with the pack from one hotspot to another with the ethic of Nolte's often quoted line: "I don't take sides, I take pictures." In Nicaragua, Nolte and Cassidy are drawn together and to the revolutionary Sandinistas, exposing themselves to professional ruin and mortal danger. Savoury elements include Ed Harris in an early, eye-catching turn as gung-ho soldier of fortune, and Jerry Goldsmith's urgent, thrilling score.

Faye has a message for anyone who doesn't like her network

MUSICALS

When people think of musicals, they usually think of the big American films, often screen versions of Broadway hits, always colourful, sometimes laughable, but definitely gaudy, good-natured and happy. While it is true that the musical, in the strictest sense of the word, is a creation that started out and achieved its pinnacle in Hollywood, there are also musical films where a significant amount of music is provided by onscreen characters. And then, in a cinematic world of its own, there is *Spice World*.

As long as there have been moving pictures, there have been musicals. Before sound, singers would lip-synch live to onscreen stars, and every musical tradition – opera, vaudeville, jazz, even Jewish canticles – made it to the screen. It was a musical, *The Jazz Singer* (1927), that ushered in the era of talkies, when Al Jolson broke off from singing to ad lib a few fragments of speech, and in the years that followed, musicals were found contributing to almost every film genre.

The sci-fi musical comedy, *Just Imagine* (1930), set in a hypothetical 1980s New York and chronicling a mission to Mars with a Swedish comedian as a stowaway, was one of the more offbeat attempts to bring music to the big screen. In the early years, musicals were a great way to show off innovations in sound, and in colour film, often used just for musical numbers in an otherwise black and white movie.

As the Great Depression took hold, the waning interest in musicals was revived by all-singing, all-dancing extravaganzas like those made by innovative choreographer, Busby Berkeley, who had started out working for the great Broadway showman, Florence Ziegfield. Berkeley's numbers, spoofed a thousand times over in the years since, featured rafts of dancers, always arranged in some perfect pattern and often filmed through an emergency hole cut in the studio roof. Also in the mid-1930s, the extraordinarily successful partnership of Fred Astaire and Ginger Rogers took over the world's screens, and the accepted musical format of a narrative linked by song and dance numbers was firmly established.

"A one, a two, a three" Not a cue for music but counting up all Gideon's women

In the 40s and 50s the classic Hollywood musicals that litter Sunday afternoon TV schedules were being churned out by the dozen. Stars like Gene Kelly, Debbie Reynolds, Howard Keel, Kathryn Grayson, Mario Lanza, Gordon MacRae and Jane Powell found their talents in great demand. Numbers got longer and more complicated (*June is Bustin' Out All Over* from *Carousel* is a case in point), and the costumes more spectacular (Howard Keel's fetching pink turban in *Kismet*, please step forward).

The music, however, rose above all its trappings with some of the best composers and lyricists – George and Ira Gershwin, Cole Porter, Jerome Kern and Irving Berlin – contributing songs and incidental music. The best and most enduring musicals of this time were made by MGM, especially by Arthur Freed's production unit with such classics as *Meet Me in St Louis*, *Brigadoon* and *Gigi*, along with forgotten offerings like the gloriously titled *Panama Hattie* starring Lena Horne.

Gradually the number of musicals declined, shored up by the beach blanket musicals starring teen heart-throbs like Elvis and Frankie Avalon. Only a few Broadway transfers such as *My Fair Lady*, or children's films like *Mary Poppins* made it to the big screen with the same detail as the earlier musicals. Despite a slight resurgence in original material in the late 1970s, with *Grease*, *Saturday Night Fever* and even *Nashville* providing a modern reworking of the genre, hardly any musicals, except for those animated by Disney, have made it to the cinema in recent years. Fans of musicals are currently pinning their hopes on Australian director Baz Luhrmann, director of such OTT treats as *Strictly Ballroom*, *Romeo and Juliet* and *Moulin Rouge*, to lead a resurgence in the popularity of onscreen song and dance.

The musical's fall from grace is often blamed on the sophistication of today's audiences (although anyone attending a screening of *Scary Movie II* may dispute that assertion). People have a problem taking a story seriously when its characters keep bursting into song. However, those who say they hate musicals because they are unbelievable are missing the point entirely. Musicals are about escapism, with the numbers a respite, a fantasy, or simply a glorious blurring of the distinctions between reality and dreamland.

"IF I DIE, I'M SORRY FOR ALL THE BAD THINGS I DID TO YOU. AND IF I LIVE, I'M SORRY FOR ALL THE BAD THINGS I'M GONNA DO TO YOU"

Joe, All That Jazz

ABSOLUTE BEGINNERS 1986
Director Julien Temple *Cast* Patsy Kensit, Eddie O'Connell

A musical with the Notting Hill race riots of the late 1950s as a finale sounds pretty bad doesn't it? And it is, in parts. However, Temple's attempt to create a musical out of Colin MacInnes' novel is brave and often visually stunning, with pop art sets and neon-soaked musical numbers featuring artists like David Bowie and Sade. The film was slated when it came out, partly due to the overly self-conscious performances from the two leads and a script that in places sank to its knees in embarrassment, but also because film fans were simply not interested in musicals in 1986. Despite its flaws, this has great music from Ray Davies and Slim Gaillard. Worth a second look.

ALL THAT JAZZ 1979
Director Bob Fosse
Cast Roy Scheider, Jessica Lange

Fosse tells his own life story as a womanizing, pill-popping Broadway choreographer in this stunning film packed with fantastic music from standard Broadway dance routines to flight-of-fancy, rock opera-type numbers. Scheider plays Joe Gideon who has an ex-wife, a current girlfriend, any number of mistresses, as well as a daughter just reaching puberty. He drinks heavily, is addicted to speed and ignores the warnings of his body. He also has a show to produce. Throughout the film he has dreamlike dialogues with death (Lange) discussing his fascination with the subject and his shortcomings as a man. The final number is an extraordinary fantasy with Ben Vereen (Chicken George in *Roots*) If you've only seen Scheider in *Jaws* and the only musical you've seen is *The Sound of Music,* this will blow you away.

AN AMERICAN IN PARIS 1951
Director Vincente Minnelli
Cast Gene Kelly, Leslie Caron

Possibly the perfect Hollywood musical. A struggling painter is discovered by an heiress interested in more than just his talent, while he is in love with a dancer who is engaged to someone else. The screwball plot is played out against some of George Gershwin's loveliest songs like *I Got Rhythm* and *It's Very Clear*, and the final ballet is

THE TALENTED MRS NIXON

GHOST WITH THE MOST
Hollywood being Hollywood, they never let a thing like vocal ability get in the way of casting a singing role. Which is why three of the all-time classic musicals feature non-singing actresses in the lead roles.
Audrey Hepburn in *My Fair Lady*, Deborah Kerr in *The King and I*, and Natalie Wood in *West Side Story*, were all dubbed for their films by the same ghost voice, the amazingly talented Marni Nixon. The classically trained Nixon was somehow able to adapt her singing voice to reflect the tone and patterns of the actresses' speaking voices, so ensuring a seamless transition between speech and song. In *West Side Story*, apart from her efforts with Wood, she also dubbed one number for Rita Moreno, effectively singing a duet with herself. (Leonard Bernstein was so impressed he gave her a quarter of a percent of his royalties from the film.) Nixon, who still tours with a one-woman show, was also the voices of the angels in Ingrid Bergman's *Joan of Arc*, and appears, onscreen for once, as a nun in *The Sound of Music* – obviously Julie Andrews needed no dubbing whatsoever.

a masterpiece of Kelly's deceptively easy-going choreography. To persuade MGM that a dance musical could succeed, Kelly screened *The Red Shoes* (see p94) for studio executives.

THE BAND WAGON 1953

Director Vincente Minnelli Cast Fred Astaire, Cyd Charisse

Minnelli's eye for colour and form lifts this pedestrian musical. Astaire plays a film star down on his luck who is asked to star in a small show two old friends have devised. Chaos ensues when an avant-garde theatre director turns up and proceeds to create his own idea of a modern day Faust. Only worth watching for the hilarious sequences of the pretentious on-stage numbers, a couple of the comedy routines, especially *Triplets*, and of course, the rallying cry of all musical lovers, *That's Entertainment!*

BLUE HAWAII 1961

Director Norman Taurog Cast Elvis Presley, Joan Blackman

The ultimate beach musical which set the standard for most of the subsequent Elvis movies. Not a lot of plot (Chad, just back from the army, is torn between his parents' ambition for him and his desire to have a good time) but who cares? It's Elvis, surrounded by bathing beauties and singing classics like *Can't Help Falling In Love* and *Rock-a-Hula, Baby*. A young Angela Lansbury plays Elvis' mum, despite being only 10 years older than him. Cliff's *Summer Holiday* (1963) is in similar vein.

> "WE'RE NOT FIGHTING! WE'RE IN COMPLETE AGREEMENT! WE HATE EACH OTHER!"
>
> Lily, The Bandwagon

THE BOY FRIEND 1971

Director Ken Russell Cast Twiggy, Christopher Gable

Fans of the director's gothic offerings might be surprised to discover what seems a mundane piece of musical fluff about a finishing school on the French riviera in the 1920s. But this is vintage Russell. He takes Sandy Wilson's pedestrian show, sets it in a rundown regional theatre where the cast outnumbers the audience, and while the musical is being performed onstage, the lives and loves of the company are played out behind the scenes. Add to this the fact that there is a talent scout in the audience and it's a recipe for glorious backstabbing farce. Entertaining and offbeat with some wonderfully OTT numbers (the nymphs and satyrs scene is a must-see) and great performances from a relatively unknown cast. Look out for the brief uncredited cameo from Glenda Jackson.

CABARET 1972

Director Bob Fosse Cast Liza Minnelli, Michael York

Deservedly swept the boards at the 1973 Oscars winning eight, including best director, best actress and best supporting actor for Joel Grey, the sinister and brilliant MC of the Kit Kat Club. Based on the play *I Am A Camera* (itself based on Christopher Isherwood's memoirs *Goodbye to Berlin*), *Cabaret* tells the story of a Bohemian romance, set against the rising tide of Nazism in 1930s Germany. Fosse's outstanding direction, his use of mirrors and odd angles to distort and frame the characters, gives the film a dark edge that sets it apart from so many screen musicals. Most of the numbers are set in the seedy gloom of the club but the most chilling of all, *Tomorrow Belongs to Me*, showing the

On the run from the law and in fine voice – the once and future Foggy Bottom Boys

Germans' growing devotion to Hitler, is set in the dappled sunshine of a country afternoon. An absolute film masterpiece.

CABIN IN THE SKY 1943

Director Vincente Minnelli Cast Ethel Waters, Eddie "Rochester" Anderson

Rarely seen now, due to its stereotypical characters and underlying racism, this musical curiosity was one of the first large-scale all-black musicals. The story is a simple fantasy – when Joe is nearly killed in a bar-room brawl, the fight for his soul between the God and the Devil is played out in dream sequence, as the fight for his body goes on between his faithful wife, Petunia, and the alluring Georgia. Notable mainly for the prodigious talent of the cast (Louis Armstrong also features) and Lena Horne's big number, *Honey in the Honeycomb*.

THE COMMITMENTS 1991

Director Alan Parker Cast Robert Arkins, Andrew Strong

Parker's amazing adaptation of Roddy Doyle's energetic novel follows Jimmy Rabitte as he tries to form a band to bring soul music to the streets and dance halls of Dublin. Although it's in the tradition of the classic "let's put on a show" musicals of Hollywood's heyday, this couldn't be further from a glossy song and dance extravaganza. Vicious arguments, shattered home lives and rundown estates are the background for all the characters, and Jimmy has got his work cut out to keep total chaos at bay. Beyond it all, however, the music is wonderful, with Andrew Strong's astounding voice making the most of the soul classics. The audition sequence is utterly hilarious (look out for Andrea Corr as Jimmy's younger sister). At the audition someone sings a song from *Fame*, Parker's other great musical, which launched a thousand legwarmers and fuelled kids'

The hat may be a bit *Clockwork Orange* but Liza Minnelli's performance is sheer gold

fantasies of dancing on top of New York taxis. The 1970s musical is a brilliantly composed film that feels like a slice of reality – with the noise and energy of a big performing arts school throughout – but it's also a glorious fantasy about coming of age in a place where anyone could break into song at any moment. They keep pianos in the canteen, just in case. Pretentious, angsty, but absolute bliss, it also has one of the best title tracks of all time.

THE COTTON CLUB 1984
Director Francis Coppola Cast Richard Gere, Diane Lane, Gregory Hines
Vastly underrated piece of musical cinema, which suffered at the box office because of negative publicity about production difficulties and the imminent collapse of Coppola's Zoetrope Studios. It's a great shame, as this is a truly wonderful film, set in the gangster-owned Cotton Club of the 1920s, and the fantastic jazz numbers are woven in brilliantly (check out the scene of Gregory Hines' tap dancing intercut with machine gun fire from a mob hit). Gere gives one of his very best performances and Bob Hoskins, Laurence Fishburne, Nicholas Cage and Fred Gwynne are all perfect in their supporting roles. What really makes it work is that there is no stylistic difference between the singing and dancing stars and the straight actors – it also helped that Gere, a talented cornet player, was able to play all his own solos.

DANCER IN THE DARK 2000
Director Lars von Trier Cast Björk, Catherine Deneuve
Odd, if compelling, story of a young Czech-born mother (Björk) working in a US factory during the 1960s. She is trying to save money to cure her son from an inherited eye condition, which is causing her own blindness, and escapes from the tedium and stress of her life by pretending she is in a musical. Fans of Björk's yowling vocal style are most likely to enjoy the numbers, but even those unfamiliar with her music will be entranced by the way von Trier weaves the sounds of the machinery she works with, as well as the local railway engines, into the score. Despite the bleak premise there are some hilarious moments, especially when the local drama group casts

Selma as Maria in *The Sound Of Music*. Despite some reports of on-set tensions and a mixed reception, the film won a Palme D'Or and a best actress award for Björk at Cannes.

HAIR 1979

Director Milos Forman *Cast* John Savage, Treat Williams

A young Oklahoman on his way to enlist for Vietnam falls in with the flower power set. This was one of the biggest stage hits of the late 1960s, and while the film version is a vibrant and brave adaptation, with gorgeous cinematography of Central Park, the fact that it came out many years after flower power had waned and Vietnam was over gives it a self-conscious edge. By 1979 disco fever had taken over and *Hair's* ersatz hippies seem lost. Still, the musical numbers are worth watching, especially for modern dance guru Twyla Tharp's choreography.

LITTLE SHOP OF HORRORS 1986

Director Frank Oz *Cast* Rick Moranis, Ellen Greene

This musical remake of the 1960 Roger Corman/Jack Nicholson classic tells the story of a nerdy florist's assistant who tends a giant man-eating plant in return for magical intervention in his lacklustre love life. Every song is a jewel, especially those sung by Levi Stubbs as the voice of the plant, and the film is packed with hilarious cameos like Steve Martin and Bill Murray playing, respectively, a sadistic dentist and his masochistic patient in a hysterically sickening sequence. The Greek chorus of Motown-style backing singers (called Crystal, Chiffon and Ronette as a tribute to the girl bands of the 1960s) pulls the whole thing together into a riotous delight.

LOVE ME OR LEAVE ME 1955

Director Charles Vidor *Cast* Doris Day, James Cagney

Surprisingly hard-hitting offering from Doris Day, playing real-life torch singer Ruth Etting whose successful career was aided, (and frustrated) by the interference of her gangster boyfriend, Marty Snyder (Cagney). Day's distinctive voice is a gift to ballads like *I'll Never Stop Loving You* and the wonderful *Ten Cents A Dance*, and the Oscar-winning script keeps the drama high throughout. Day was the first actress in more than 30 years to get top billing over Cagney; when you compare her passionate performance here with later sugary offerings like *Pillow Talk*, it's hard not to wonder what might have been.

THE MUSIC MAN 1962

Director Morton da Costa *Cast* Robert Preston, Shirley Jones

Robert Preston didn't make enough films. Or rather, he didn't

> **"I THRILL WHEN I DRILL A BICUSPID/ IT'S SWELL THOUGH THEY TELL ME I'M MAL-AD-JUST-ED"**
> Orin, Little Shop of Horrors

make enough good ones, being mostly relegated to the anonymity of B pictures, which is an extraordinary shame as *The Music Man* shows just how charismatic his screen persona could be. What's more he only got the role (despite winning a Tony for it on Broadway), after Cary Grant had turned it down. The story of a confidence trickster persuading a small town to form a boys' marching band, trips along at a lively pace, with Jones giving one of her best performances as the local madame librarian Marian who stops Preston in his tracks.

O BROTHER, WHERE ART THOU? 2000

Director Joel Coen *Cast* George Clooney, John Goodman, John Turturro, Tim Blake Nelson, Holly Hunter

> **"IT'S A FOOL WHO LOOKS FOR LOGIC IN THE CHAMBERS OF THE HUMAN HEART"**
> Ulysses, O Brother, Where Art Thou?

It's as if the Coen brothers (Ethan wrote it) set themselves a theoretical challenge of making a film which could spin off Homer's Odyssey, encompass Baby Face Nelson and the Ku Klux Klan and throw in their favourite folk band singing *He's In The Jailhouse Now*. All that and Clooney, Turturro and Nelson on the top of their form as prison escapees fleeing across the south. The scene where Nelson thinks Turturro has been turned into a toad is both spooky and hilarious. Goodman, as usual, is charismatic, flamboyant and deceitful.

OH WHAT A LOVELY WAR 1969

Director Richard Attenborough *Cast* Malcolm McFee, Colin Farrell

A vicious surreal satire on World War I, with musical numbers, many based on soldiers' marching songs, linking representations of some of the more terrible events of the war, including a friendly-fire massacre of Irish soldiers taking a ridge and the extraordinary ineptitude of the generals in charge. Some of the sequences sag under their own weight, particularly the long explanatory opening section, and in places the original stage show is followed so closely it doesn't quite work on celluloid. But the film remains incredibly innovative and absorbing and the cast reads like a who's who of British theatre and film. Worth viewing if only for the stunning final scene.

ON THE TOWN 1949

Director Stanley Donen, Gene Kelly *Cast* Gene Kelly, Frank Sinatra

Three sailors on shore leave have just 24 hours in which to experience the delights of New York. A classic Kelly film, with wonderfully energetic musical numbers and terrific choreography – although the ballet towards the end makes the whole thing droop a little. What really makes this one noteworthy, however, is the use of real locations. Up until then musicals, and most films, were filmed solely on studio sets or constructed backlots. Donen and Kelly managed to persuade Arthur Freed to let them film in New York, up the Empire State Building and down in the subway. The result is not only a great musical but a wonderful chance to see what New York really looked like in its prime.

THE ROCKY HORROR PICTURE SHOW 1975
Director Jim Sharman *Cast* Tim Curry, Susan Sarandon

You look at photos like this and you can't help asking, what happened to Tim Curry?

A newly engaged couple break down on a lonely road and find themselves at the mercy of local weirdo, Dr Frank-N-Furter. The cult musical to end all cult musicals is still packing them in at late-night showings, complete with a costumed audience and alternative script to be shouted at the screen at the right moment. Curry has never been better as the louche transvestite, and knowing the kind of dramatic, worthy projects that Sarandon has chosen since, it's a hoot seeing her running around in her underwear. Great songs, great cameos, Koo Stark in an uncredited role as a bridesmaid and a truly bizarre final number.

SEVEN BRIDES FOR SEVEN BROTHERS 1954
Director Stanley Donen *Cast* Howard Keel, Jane Powell

Seven backwoods brothers kidnap seven local girls, hoping to persuade them to be their wives, and create another musical based on unlikely source material – the ancient story of *The Rape of the Sabine Women* (worked into the story in the song *Sobbin' Women*, one of Hollywood's better puns). With such a huge cast, the film makes the most of its sumptuous widescreen photography, especially in the famous barn-raising scene. Tommy Rall, who played Frank, was borrowed from the New York City Ballet to add finesse to the dance sequences. The film got a deserved nomination for a best picture Oscar, but lost out to the rather less shiny *On The Waterfront*.

SINGIN' IN THE RAIN 1952
Directors Stanley Donen, Gene Kelly *Cast* Gene Kelly, Debbie Reynolds

Where to begin? Well how about posing the question, what is it that puts *Singin' In The Rain* repeatedly in people's Top 10 film lists? It seems that Kelly's funny and innovative story about the fates of two silent screen stars during the transition to talkies just strikes a chord with almost everyone who sees it. It helps that the supporting cast is so strong: Donald O'Connor's *Make 'em Laugh* is one of the greatest numbers in musical history, and the inspired Jean Hagan as Lina Lamont, the actress whose voice is like salt in a wound, gained a cult following. Whatever it is – the music, the dancing, the romance, that makes *Singin' in the Rain* such a joy – we should just be thankful.

THE SOUND OF MUSIC 1965

Director Robert Wise *Cast* Julie Andrews, Christopher Plummer

If you happen to pass a certain London cinema on Sunday afternoons, you may be treated to the sight of various Fraulein Marias, several Von Trapp children and a gaggle of nuns queuing to get into a screening of *Sing-a-long Sound Of Music*, a high camp afternoon of singing along with helpful subtitles, waving pieces of curtain fabric and plastic Edelweiss, and booing whenever the Baroness or Rolf come on screen – a good-natured tribute to one of the best-loved musical films of all time. The other bonus about going to something like this (the show occasionally tours regional cinemas) is that you get to see the whole film, nearly three hours of it, including the stunning cinematography so often removed for the TV version.

SWEET CHARITY 1969

Director Bob Fosse *Cast* Shirley MacLaine, John McMartin

Fosse gets to every last bit of MacLaine's offbeat talent in this psychedelic groove-fest about a downtrodden dancer for hire who hopes for better things when she meets a rich young man about town. Based on Fellini's *Nights Of Cabiria*, but with the

ending radically altered, *Sweet Charity* is a warm-up for Fosse's later directing work, with his trademark choreography, zooming cameras, spaced out supporting cast and terrifyingly hip settings (Ricardo Montalban's apartment has to be seen to be believed). Despite the patchy quality and wandering storyline, it's worth seeing for the numbers, especially Sammy Davis Jr's fabulous *Rhythm Of Life*.

TARS AND SPARS 1945

Director Alfred E Green *Cast* Janet Blair, Sid Caesar

Hardly ever seen now, this small, endearing musical tells the story of the coastguard's wartime concert party and their onstage and offstage complications. It has some very funny numbers but it's most notable for the talent of its cast, particularly Caesar, who went on to become one of America's biggest entertainers, and co-star Janet Blair who was a regular on his show.

They're never short of a few umbrellas in sunny Cherbourg

TOP HAT 1935

Director **Mark Sandrich** *Cast* **Fred Astaire, Ginger Rogers**

The plot, a lighthearted mistaken identity farce, is merely an excuse for Astaire and Rogers to dance the night away in various different settings, including a recognisable London and a wholly unbelievable Venice (where they went to the extreme lengths of dying the set's Grand Canal black to contrast with the all white set. The best and most memorable number is *Cheek to Cheek*, but *It's a Lovely Day* is great too. At one point the dancing duo had a string of films that all were number one at the box office, a testament to the extraordinary chemistry that they generated. As one person put it: "She gave him sex, he gave her class."

THE UMBRELLAS OF CHERBOURG 1964
LES PARAPLUIES DE CHERBOURG

Director **Jacques Demy** *Cast* **Catherine Deneuve, Nino Castelnuovo**

This odd but satisfying French operetta, with every piece of dialogue sung throughout, tells the story of Geneviève, whose widowed mother owns an umbrella shop. When her lover goes into the army, a pregnant Geneviève marries a rich older man. Demy pays huge attention to the look of the film, its spectacular richness and fantastic use of colour will take your breath away, as well as getting truly heartfelt performances out of his entire cast. All this French chic, coupled with one of the most wonderfully romantic screen endings, give this film huge appeal for musical fans.

WEST SIDE STORY 1961

Director **Jerome Robbins, Robert Wise**
Cast **Natalie Wood, Richard Beymer**

Souped-up reworking of Romeo and Juliet set in the slums of New York, featuring dazzling dancing and an incomparable score from Leonard Bernstein with lyrics by Stephen Sondheim. While this is rightfully considered a classic, that's probably not because of the lead actors. Neither Wood nor Beymer exhibit much of a range here and it is the outstanding supporting cast, especially Rita Moreno as Anita, George Chakiris as Bernardo and Russ Tamblyn as Riff, who steal the show and make the film what it is. To date this is still the only film to share a best director Oscar between two collaborators.

FACING THE MUSIC

NO GRAND FINALES

Stars of the great movie musicals seem to have an unnatural affinity for personal tragedy, as if the colour, glamour and happy endings of their onscreen lives were reversed in real life, and without a script and song to hand, they were completely lost.

This is not always true but for every Gene Kelly, retiring gracefully, there is a Judy Garland, dying of an accidental overdose of barbiturates in a Chelsea hotel. For every Fred Astaire giving crowd-pleasing cameos in films like *The Towering Inferno*, there is a Mario Lanza, a manic depressive dying mysteriously in Rome at the age of 38 or Dorothy Dandridge, committing suicide after losing all her money in an oil scam.

Less final but almost as tragic are the fates of Shirley Jones (forced into a humiliating life of appearing in *The Partridge Family*) and Howard Keel, reincarnated as Miss Ellie's main squeeze in *Dallas*. Jones has been spotted advertising incontinence supplies. Presumably hitting all those high notes must have taken its toll.

RKO, Col/TCF; Buena Vista/Touchstone/Universal; ABC Pictures/Allied Artists; TCF; Parc/Madeleine/Beta

Movies with a paranoid mindset became mainstream with film noir and Alfred Hitchcock. But the threat of nuclear apocalypse and the assassination of two Kennedys and one King would encourage full-blown raving paranoia among filmmakers. From *Dr Strangelove* onwards, in a certain kind of film the hero knew only two things: yes, he was paranoid, and yes, they were plotting against him.

CONSPIRACY THEORY 1997

Director Richard Donner Cast Mel Gibson, Julia Roberts

"Serial killers have only two names. But lone gunmen assassins have three names: John Wilkes Booth, Lee Harvey Oswald, Mark David Chapman." So says Gibson as the conspiracy obsessed newsletter writer and taxi driver. He is just a lone nut himself until one of his theories proves to be accurate. Don't think we're giving much away if we tell you one of the theories that isn't proved right is: "The Vietnam war was over a bet that Howard Hughes lost to Aristotle Onassis." Mind you, Gibson claims Stone is a "disinformation junkie" for the powers-that-be: "The fact that he's alive says it all." *Lethal Weapon* meets *Pretty Woman* meets *JFK* yet somehow it still works.

THE CONVERSATION 1974

Director Francis Coppola Cast Gene Hackman, Robert Duvall

Hackman has seldom bettered his performance as the surveillance expert desperate to prevent a murder he overhears being planned (though he gets excellent support from Duvall and, in a small part, a young Harrison Ford). With its muffled soundtrack the film can confuse but keep an eye on the taped words which run throughout the film. Works as a statement about American society in the 1970s (Coppola began working on it two years before release when Nixon's tapes were still a White House secret) and as a psychological thriller.

"HIS BRAIN HAS NOT ONLY BEEN WASHED IT'S BEEN, AS THEY SAY, DRY CLEANED!"
Dr Yen Lo, The Manchurian Candidate

DR STRANGELOVE 1964

Director Stanley Kubrick Cast Peter Sellers, Sterling Hayden, George C Scott

Like all of Kubrick's movies, this repays repeated viewing. You might not, for instance, notice on the first run through that General Buck Turgidson (Scott) is clutching a book entitled *World Targets In Megadeaths*. Hayden's General Jack D Ripper seems like a purely satirical figure until you recall that General Curtis Le May, after the Russians began to take their missiles out of Cuba, turned to JFK and said: "Why don't we go in anyway?" It's not too far from there to Ripper shooting himself rather than reveal the codes which will bring the missiles back. A very funny film about a very chilling subject with Sellers even more effective as the prissy president than as the Nazi Dr Strangelove who only comes to life when someone mentions the word "slaughter". Kubrick once wanted to end the war room scene with a pie fight. Thankfully he didn't. The only thing that mars this movie is a certain coldness about the outcome, as if part of Kubrick thinks this is actually what we all deserve.

DREAMSCAPE 1984
Director **Joseph Ruben** *Cast* **Dennis Quaid, Max von Sydow**
Dennis Quaid can see into people's minds (pity he couldn't see into Russell Crowe's mind but that's another story) as part of a government-funded experiment which is designed to create a breed of dream assassins. (The theory is that if these guys can make you die in your dreams, you'll never wake up again.) The FX were state-of-the-art but now look wobblier than the walls at the Crossroads motel used to. Still, this sci-fi thriller is based on a cracking idea even if the script never quite delivers.

EXECUTIVE ACTION 1973
Director **David Miller** *Cast* **Burt Lancaster, Robert Ryan**
Chilling, entirely plausible, 'how the plot was done' film about a conspiracy to kill JFK because he's gone soft on commies and blacks and hard on tax concessions for oilmen. Unlike Stone, Miller (and scriptwriter Dalton Trumbo) lay out their story clearly and plausibly, focusing more on the core of the plot and less on the bizarre detail. Ryan and Lancaster are superbly sinister as leaders of the right-wing conspiracy and the decision to intersperse clippings of JFK's own speeches is an effective reminder of why so many Americans still care about what really happened in Dallas.

THE HITCHER 1986
Director **Robert Harmon** *Cast* **Rutger Hauer, C Thomas Howell**
The film which did for hitch-hiking what *The Omen* had done for having kids called Damien and what *Single*

"Did somebody mention the word slaughter?"

Burt in Executive Action says the new Dealey Plaza one-way system won't work

White Female would (six years later) do for flatmates. As if we've not got enough to worry about, Hollywood scares the hell out of us with stuff like this and we, suckers that we are, love 'em for it. Hauer is strangely credible as the killer without wheels even if the film lapses first into self-parody, then into a state which needs a critic with more imagination than this reviewer to invent a word you can put in the dictionary which means "beyond self-parody". The finger in the french fries scene has launched a thousand urban myths.

JFK 1991

Director **Oliver Stone** *Cast* **Kevin Costner, Sissy Spacek, Joe Pesci**

This deeply controversial movie is usually assailed for playing fast and loose with the facts, especially by those who insist that Kennedy was killed by a lone gunman. It's a claim that provokes two thoughts: 1) it is a movie, not a historical document; and 2) it's probably more accurate than the Warren Commission's report on the assassination. Kennedy was, in Stone's eyes, killed by the military-industrial complex (the mob is hardly mentioned, but then Stone's hero Jim Garrison would come under suspicion for making the same omission). The question of veracity doesn't change the fact that this is a very good film which plays to the audience's sense that since JFK's death, something has gone wrong with America.

THE MANCHURIAN CANDIDATE 1962

Director **John Frankenheimer** *Cast* **Laurence Harvey, Frank Sinatra**

The second film about political assassination in which Sinatra starred (see *Suddenly* below), this is one of the best political thrillers of the 1960s. A mordant, funny, but tense film which puts Harvey's woodenness to good use as an assassin brainwashed by the North Koreans and sent back to America to do some unspecified evil. The brainwashing sequences at the start of the movie are unforgettable and Angela Lansbury plays to perfection the part of the mother who smothers Harvey. You'll have to discover the rest on your own. One final oddity: seven members of the platoon in Korea are named after the cast and creator of *The Phil Silvers Show*.

MEMENTO 2000

Director **Christopher Nolan** *Cast* **Guy Pearce, Carrie-Anne Moss**

Nolan is nothing if not confident: the British director raised money for this film by showing its predecessor at a Hong Kong film festival and asking the audience to cough up. Here he asks the audience to concentrate as we follow Pearce's quest to find his wife's killer, a quest complicated by the fact that her death has so traumatised him that he can only remember things for a few minutes. To conquer what, for an amateur sleuth, seems an insuperable obstacle, he stores information on polaroids and tattoos all over his body. Confused? The big question most viewers ask about this film is if Pearce has no long-term memory since the death of his wife, how can he remember his own memory loss? To save you rummaging through a pile of psychological textbooks, the simple answer is: because it says so in the script. The set-up of a man without memory trying to solve a crime in which he may be implicated is at least as old as film noir but after 60 years Nolan has given it a neat new twist.

JFK AT THE MOVIES

JFK was fascinated by Hollywood in life. In death, Hollywood has returned the compliment. It isn't just Oliver Stone, JFK's life and death affected films soon after trigger(s) was (were) pulled in Dealey Plaza in 1963.

Arthur Penn's *The Chase*, released in 1966, was set in a town in Texas (no coincidence). It stars Marlon Brando and Robert Redford as the liberal sheriff and the angelic escaped convict killed as mob rule breaks out.

Lilian Helman's script is often seen as a comment on the national mood after Kennedy was shot. But the beating dished out to Brando's sheriff and Redford's murder (he dies, as Brando biographer Richard Schickel says, "like the president, for no good reason other than that he stirs inchoate anxiety and, perhaps, happens to be in Texas") make the film seem more like an accusation. The charge is similar to that in the Stones' song *Sympathy For The Devil*: "I shouted out 'who killed the Kennedys?' but after all it was you and me".

In the 1970s, filmmakers referred to the assassination more explicitly in *Executive Action* and *The Parallax View*. The level of inquiry dropped in the Reagan years only to be upped dramatically by Stone's meld of fact,

rumour and supposition, *JFK*. A year later, John MacKenzie's *Ruby* was released with David Duchovny as the police officer allegedly shot by Oswald (surely the greatest X-File ever). Danny Aiello is impressive as the man who definitely shot the man who may have shot JFK.

More remarkable, and tangential, was the same year's *Love Field*, starring Michelle Pfeiffer as a blonde obsessed by Jackie Kennedy who leaves her husband to go the president's funeral. In 1993 Clint Eastwood was a guilt-ridden secret service agent who'd failed to stop the bullet(s) which killed JFK in Wolfgang Petersen's *In The Line Of Fire* and Kennedy's charisma is compared to the uninspiring incumbent Eastwood has to save.

This year Kennedy's presidency returned to the screen in *Thirteen Days*. This didn't do boffo business – it was, after all, just a film in which a bunch of white guys stood around talking, even if they were talking about the end of the world. Bruce Greenwood's *JFK* is a performance which, though less showy, stands comparison with Hopkins' *Nixon*. Kennedy may have died 38 years ago this November but Hollywood clearly hasn't finished with him yet. Or the grassy knoll.

MISSING 1981

Director Costas-Gavras *Cast* Jack Lemmon, Sissy Spacek

This politically charged movie works because it tweaks the old thriller device of an innocent on the run. Lemmon is the innocently conservative dad who is slowly immersed in the nightmare of what happened to his liberal son when the Allende government was overthrown by a coup. Lemmon is exactly the right person to play this role, by turns baffled and appalled as he sinks into the nightmare. The State Department didn't like this movie, which is as good a recommendation as you can get.

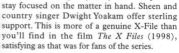

> "GENTLEMAN, YOU CAN'T FIGHT HERE, THIS IS THE WAR ROOM"
>
> President Mervin Muffley, Dr Strangelove

THE PARALLAX VIEW 1974

Director Alan J Pakula *Cast* Warren Beatty, Paula Prentiss

This film isn't out to help anybody solve any particular assassination but it does give you a horribly plausible account of how such things happen. Beatty is the reporter whose smug pursuit of the Pulitzer Prize takes him in too deep as people around him start dying and the shooting of a senator develops more connections to a mysterious corporation called Parallax. If you're not already paranoid, this could tip you over the edge. In a scenario which could have been lifted from the film, Pakula suspected Paramount were refusing to promote the film, becoming so enraged that he broke his umbrella against the wall in a hotel room row with Paramount boss Robert Evans.

ROSWELL 1994

Director Jeremy Paul Kagan *Cast* Kyle MacLachlan, Martin Sheen

Good, single-minded, drama about the day the remains of something (a flying saucer or a secret Air Force balloon) were found in the New Mexico desert. MacLachlan is impressive as the military intelligence officer who becomes the fall guy when the powers that be order a cover up and this meticulously researched film eschews the obligatory Hollywood sub-plots to stay focused on the matter in hand. Sheen and country singer Dwight Yoakam offer sterling support. This is more of a genuine X-File than you'll find in the film *The X Files* (1998), satisfying as that was for fans of the series.

Suddenly, hitching up with Doris Day again doesn't seem such a bad idea

SECONDS 1966

Director John Frankenheimer *Cast* Rock Hudson, Salome Jens, John Randolph

Make sure you're in a good mood when you watch this. Frankenheimer took a risk using Rock Hudson (more usually teamed with Doris Day) in this paranoid sci-fi fantasy and, in box office terms, the risk didn't pay off. Hudson fans weren't going to see him in this doom-laden scenario, made more alien by the black and white format and cameraman James Wong Howe's risky camera work. Noirer than the darkest noir, this stars Randolph as a banker who gets a chance of a new life from a mysterious company and re-emerges as a bohemian artist. The final scene is probably one of the most terrifying ever. Suffice to say there's a drill and a head involved.

SUDDENLY 1954

Director **Lewis Allen** *Cast* **Frank Sinatra, Sterling Hayden**

Sinatra leads a trio of assassins who arrive in a small town just in time to shoot the president. It's a compelling premise, well-performed and well directed, but you probably haven't heard of it for one simple reason: Lee Harvey Oswald was rumoured to have been watching this on the evening of 21 November 1963. Sinatra heard the rumour years later and pulled the film, horrified at the thought that this movie might have had anything to do with the plot to kill his old friend.

WINTER KILLS 1979

Director **William Richert** *Cast* **Jeff Bridges, John Huston**

A much mutilated (by the original distributors) and misunderstood comedy about the Kennedy assassination based on the Richard Condon novel. Bridges is the Bobby Kennedy figure investigating his brother's murder who unearths enough red herrings to keep Billingsgate fish market supplied for an eternity. Condon's satire is wide-ranging, sending up assassination buffs, lone gunman theorists and the Kennedy family. The stellar cast (which also includes Anthony Perkins, Eli Wallach and Liz Taylor as a madame) plays it straight and because Richert doesn't really camp it up until right at the end, it offended many who expected a serious Oliver Stone-like investigation into that day in Dallas. But it's very dark and very funny with Huston unforgettable as the randy old patriarch in red boxer shorts, possibly as close as any movie has yet got to portraying the real Joe Kennedy Sr.

HELLO JOHN

CONSPIRACY THEORIST

Forget Oliver Stone for the moment, the real pioneer of the paranoid conspiracy thriller in American movies is John Frankenheimer. Frankenheimer came late to movies but in the 1960s he made a trio of films (*The Manchurian Candidate, Seven Days In May* and *Seconds*) which formed a powerful critique of American society.

The first film was made in the face of studio resistance with JFK himself intervening to make sure it got made. If you've ever wondered what Janet Leigh is doing in that film, consider the possibility that she was actually Sinatra's controller, that the 'hero' had been brainwashed too. Frankenheimer's films often betrayed inside political knowledge and he campaigned hard for Bobby Kennedy, driving him to the Ambassador Hotel in Los Angeles on 5 June 1968, the day RFK was shot. Booze took its toll on Frankenheimer in the 1970s and 1980s and his form has been inconsistent since. *The Fourth War* (1990) was a return to form, a quietly convincing film about how one crazy US officer might sabotage *détente*. In *Ronin* (1994), a film decked out with all the usual accoutrements of an action thriller, he imbues it with a sense of realpolitik missing from the run-of-the-mill efforts in the genre.

POLITICS

Politics and movies don't mix well. Yet they have much in common: the tyranny of focus groups, the incessant clash of egos and a suspicion that the rest of the world doesn't take them seriously

ADVISE AND CONSENT 1962

Director **Otto Preminger** *Cast* **Henry Fonda, Charles Laughton**

The use of homosexuality as a plot device was doubly daring: the 1960s had yet to swing and Laughton had spent most of his career as a screen actor concealing his own sexuality. Franchot Tone, the former Mr Joan Crawford, is the ill president who wants to promote Fonda but is opposed by southern senatorial demagogue Laughton. Based on the novel of the same name by Allen Drury, this gains Washington cred by having president Kennedy's brother-in-law Peter Lawford in a supporting role.

THE ASSASSINATION OF TROTSKY 1972

Director **Joseph Losey** *Cast* **Richard Burton, Alain Delon**

Losey's name is listed as director but a combination of drink and personal crises meant he was so out of it that Burton occasionally had to jump in and correct errors of continuity. This is a great shame as there were enough similarities between character and actor (the sense of promise unfulfilled, of exile, of being hounded, to name just three) to spark Burton's interest. But there's too much talk and not enough action and you get a sense of what it must have been like to go out on the razz with Burton and listen to him tell the same stories over and over again. Not smooth or well-made enough to be really boring.

> **"IF IT WASN'T FOR GRAFT, YOU'D GET A VERY LOW TYPE OF PEOPLE IN POLITICS, MEN WITHOUT AMBITION, JELLYFISH"**
> The Politician, The Great McGinty

THE BEST MAN 1964

Director **Franklin Schaffner** *Cast* **Henry Fonda, Cliff Robertson**

Gore Vidal has never quite recovered from the realisation that he was not, after all, going to be President of the United States. The second blow to his ego came when his friend, JFK, did just that. So he has been amusingly condescending about American politics (and his assassinated pal) ever since, once rejecting the idea of Ronald Reagan as president purely on the grounds that it was an error of casting. Here he scripts a fine tale about presidential hopefuls (Fonda and Robertson) with dark secrets.

As you would expect from Vidal, the film zings with one-liners – this is the film where one character said of another: "He has every characteristic of a dog save loyalty."

BOB ROBERTS 1992

Director Tim Robbins Cast Tim Robbins, Giancarlo Esposito

This documentary-style satire uses a senatorial campaign to indict American society for the greed-is-good decade. Written, directed and starring Robbins this is an uncompromising movie which sees the down-home fascism of Roberts (Robbins) triumph over the irrelevant liberalism of his opponent (Gore Vidal) and a reporter with some dirt on the candidate. The film eventually veers off into a very implausible sub-plot in which the journalist is set up and framed, but for most of the time it's a merciless dissection of a system and a society where money doesn't just talk, it swears. Warren Beatty's *Bulworth* (1998) covers similar terrain and, at times, more audaciously before losing its way, a brave picture overpraised by those who (like this reviewer) sympathize with Beatty's message.

BURN 1968

Director Gillo Pontecorvo
Cast Marlon Brando, Evaristo Marquez

Making *Queimada*, as it's known to most of the world (the Portuguese word for 'burnt') was never going to be easy. Supposed to be a 'film of ideas' and an Errol Flynn-style adventure it disappointed fans of both. Coming as it did in Brando's fallow period of the late 1960s, it has been largely ignored since. The film tells the story of an agent provocateur (Brando) sent by the British to stir up revolution in the Antilles, who is then called upon to suppress the very uprising he helped inspire. Pontecorvo took the brave decision to cast a cane cutter, who had never acted in his life, as the leader of the revolutionaries. While his acting is better than one might fear, it didn't help the film as the director often had to kick him (just below camera level) to get him to move. Brando, initially patience

Bill McKay decided the best way to decide the California Senate seat was to play gridiron for it

> ## "NICE THING ABOUT YOU JOE IS THAT YOU CAN SOUND LIKE A LIBERAL BUT AT HEART YOU'RE AN AMERICAN"
> TT Claypoole, The Best Man

personified, soon got bored and fled. He was tempted back to finish his scenes but later vowed that if he ever saw Pontecorvo again he would kill him.

THE CANDIDATE 1972
Director Michael Ritchie *Cast* Robert Redford, Peter Boyle

Jeremy Larner wrote the script and the film is full of the inside info he picked up as a speechwriter for Democratic presidential aspirant Eugene McCarthy. It's all here: the hollowness of the candidates' debate, the vacuous marketing ('The better way with Bill McKay'), a decent liberal man who gains office and loses his beliefs, and the fixer, subtly played by Boyle. In the back of the limo, Redford mixes all his clichés together ("Think of it, the biggest most powerful nation on earth cannot house its houseless, cannot feed its foodless") and concludes with the thought: "And on election day vote once, vote twice, for Bill McKay, you middle class honkies." The only problem is that Redford is too likeable for the satire – you still want him to win, meaningless as the victory is. And the speeches Larner writes for his candidate, supposed to be satirical, are more stirring than the hornswoggle we get from politicians today. Ironic footnote: Labour used 'The better way' slogan in 1979.

CAPITAES DE ABRIL 2000
Director Maria de Medeiros *Cast* Stefano Accorsi, Maria de Medeiros

The most expensive film ever made by the Portuguese film industry and thankfully one of the best. You probably remember de Medeiros best as Bruce Willis' girlfriend in *Pulp Fiction* but here, in her directorial debut, she mixes fiction and fact in this finely drawn account of the Portuguese revolution of 25 April 1974. The film is true in spirit to the history of the revolution – the rebels' tanks really did stop at red traffic lights – although it doesn't dwell on the rumour that the country's entry in the Eurovision Song Contest was a signal to the plotters. Well made, easy to watch and just a few minutes too long.

DEFENCE OF THE REALM 1985
Director David Drury *Cast* Gabriel Byrne, Greta Scacchi, Denholm Elliott

British political thrillers of the 1980s were often more effective on the small screen (*Edge Of Darkness*) but this holds its own, as a kind of bleaker spin on *All The President's Men*. Here there is no real victory for Byrne as the newspaper reporter who begins to wonder if the scoop he wrote about an MP and a call girl was a frame up. Elliott is wonderful as an older reporter who raises Byrne's doubts and then dies. And the very thing the frame up protects, American nuclear weapons based in the UK, remain in place so no Bernstein and Woodward cheer here.

DIE BLEIERNE ZEIT 1981

Director Margarethe von Trotta *Cast* Jutta Lampe, Barbara Sukowa

Called *Marianne and Juliane* in the UK after the sisters who are at the heart of the movie. Both sisters want to change society but Juliane (Lampe), an editor, wants to do so within the system, Marianne (Sakowa) tries to do so as a terrorist but is soon caught. It was a theme von Trotta had already touched on with her first film as a director, *The Lost Honour of Katherine Blum* (which she co-directed with future husband Volker Schlondorff) but returns to it with great effect here.

THE GREAT McGINTY 1940

Director Preston Sturges

Cast Brian Donlevy, Muriel Angelus

The only way Sturges could persuade Paramount to let him direct his story about a bum who becomes governor was to sell the screenplay to the studio for a dollar. And he had to make the film for $325,000 and use Brian Donlevy, not the best actor in the world, as lead. Sturges did all that and, though he didn't know one end of a viewfinder from the other when shooting started, made a fantastic film which, like so many of his great works, is almost impossible to describe. Donlevy's potential is recognized early on by The Boss (Akim Tamiroff) who is impressed by the way Donlevy votes 37 times for the same mayor because he gets two bucks for each vote. Not quite Sturges' best but the satire goes further than most other directors would dare.

MEDIUM COOL 1969

Director Haskell Wexler

Cast Robert Forster, Verna Bloom

Forster is a TV news cameraman caught up in such events as the Democratic Party convention in Chicago, scene of the world's most famous police riot, who

THE GREAT DICTATORS

(AND THEIR MOVIES)

Whenever Adolf Hitler was suffering from insomnia, his staff would screen *Mazurka*, a tear-jerker starring Pola Negri. This must have been his favourite film (he watched it at least twice a week) although he was also fond of a film of a famous actress stripping, which he showed to guests in his own cinema at Berchtesgaden over Christmas 1937. Hitler's taste in porn was shared by Leonid Brehznev, a fan of *Emmanuelle* but also of *Dirty Harry*. Stalin loved cowboy films which, said his successor Nikita Khruschev, he would "give the proper ideological evaluation" before ordering more. But the Ceaucescus were never happier than when watching Robert Redford in *The Great Gatsby*. Here at last were people living in the style to which they planned to become accustomed.

Dirty Harry: Dirty Leonid was a big fan

Silkwood were an underrated early 1980s rock band, the thinking man's Reo Speedwagon

is also trying to keep his private life from disintegrating. An odd, influential movie whose cast includes Mariana Hill, an escapee from Elvis' *Paradise Hawaiian Style* (1966). The director was one of the greatest cinematographers of his day and, after the apathy with which this effort was received, he virtually gave up direction.

MOONLIGHTING 1982

Director Jerzy Skolimowski
Cast Jeremy Irons, Eugene Lipinski

Tradesmen do not make conventional movie heroes but this engrossing film centres on the tribulations of a group of Polish workers (led by Irons) who smuggle themselves into England to renovate an apartment. With no work permits, they have to do their work in secret while, at the same time, Irons (who is the only one who speaks English) hears that martial law has been declared in Poland. Skolimowski wrote the script in a day and the film used three Polish emigrants who were living (legally) in his home. Irons is incredible. A home-made gem.

NIXON 1995

Director Oliver Stone Cast Anthony Hopkins, Joan Allen, JT Walsh, James Woods, David Hyde Pierce

In the middle of a harangue by Kissinger, Nixon gets up and offers his hand to a dog which yelps and flees. "Aw fuck it," says Nixon, "he doesn't like me." A small scene. Telling only when you compare it to the shot in the credit montage for *JFK* where a dog is shown eating out of Kennedy's hand. Or when you remember that a dog (Checkers) famously starred in Nixon's first great political crisis, when he was almost deselected as vice president in a scandal over campaign funds. Stone's film is full of such incidental delights (especially the performances by Woods, Walsh and Allen as people closest to, and suffering most from, Nixon) but is dominated by Hopkins' Nixon. Once you get past the lack of physical resemblance you find the charmless, awkward, incomplete personality that is the real Richard Milhous. Altman's *Secret Honor* (1984) is a one man show by Philip Baker Hall and almost as telling as Stone's film.

> "MY GOD, THAT WAS TOO BIG EVEN FOR JESUS CHRIST. DON'T YOU KNOW, HE GOT HIMSELF CRUCIFIED"
>
> Henry Miller, Reds

REDS 1981

Director Warren Beatty Cast Warren Beatty, Diane Keaton, Jack Nicholson

You have to respect Beatty's dogged determination, in Reagan's

America, to get this made at all. A movie which used the Russian revolution as a heroic backdrop for a love story between a left-wing activist and a famous American Communist and journalist would always be a hard sell. The studio tried (and failed) to sell it as *Dr Zhivago*, only this time Yuri and Lara are Americans! Good as it is, the film (Beatty's attempt to prove he was a serious filmmaker) does drag. You begin to pine for Nicholson to appear as Eugene O'Neill.

SALT OF THE EARTH 1954

Director **Herbert J Biberman** *Cast* **Rosaura Revueltas, Juan Chacon**

A miraculous event in what was still (when this was made) the McCarthy era – a left-wing film to come out of Hollywood. American films of this period, if they dared to criticize the status quo at all, normally blamed whatever social ill they were confronting on an individual rotten apple. This film, about a successful strike at a tin mine in New Mexico, makes no such

JOHN DOES VS THE SYSTEM

IT'S CAPRA-ESQUE!

Frank Capra's trilogy of social conscience comedies (*Mr Deeds Goes To Town, Mr. Smith Goes To Washington* and *Meet John Doe*) founded the humorous, sympathetic and warm Capra-esque mythos which idealizes small town Americana, scorns big city cynicism and celebrates the goodness of common people. Reluctant heroes, suicide attempts, fickle mobs and Christmas regularly feature.

The pictures all affirm democracy while expressing disillusionment with its failings, raising up messianic innocents to denounce the corruption, greed and selfishness of politicians, journalists and lawyers (Mr Deeds says of an attorney: "Even his hands are oily"). *Deeds* and *Smith* were hits. Darker and bleaker, *Doe* was not. Rediscovered in the 1970s when they became a bargain package TV syndication, Capra's message movies were embraced for their charming passion for traditional values.

KNOW YOUR CAPRA EVERYMEN

Mr Deeds Goes To Town (1936)

Hard-nosed reporter Jean Arthur mocks naïve poet and tuba player Coop, who inherits a fortune and is beset by grasping city slickers. His decision to give away his millions sees him in a court battle to decide his sanity, but goodness, empathy for the needy and love win out. Released to acclaim in the Soviet Union retitled *Grip Of The Dollar*.

Mr Smith Goes To Washington (1939)

Hard-nosed secretary Jean Arthur mocks naïve new Senator James Stewart who is framed for misconduct by a corrupt political machine, but goodness, democracy, a lost cause and love win out. Capra's and Stewart's favourite film although they were conservatives and it was (brilliantly) scripted by active Communist Party member Sidney Buchman.

Meet John Doe (1941)

Hard-nosed reporter Barbara Stanwyck invents a fictitious 'everyman' and hires naïve Coop to impersonate him. The national movement his philosophy inspires is manipulated by a fascist, but goodness, the little man and love win out. Capra filmed several endings, and after audience tests, decided against the hero's suicide for a blatantly phoney happy ending.

concessions. The writer and the director were blacklisted and because it was, as one Congressman announced, "Communist-made", it only played in 13 cinemas in the US.

SEVEN DAYS IN MAY 1964
Director John Frankenheimer *Cast* Burt Lancaster, Kirk Douglas, Fredric March

The movie's central premise, that a military conspiracy should try to topple the President for signing a nuclear disarmament treaty, sounds like a paranoid fantasy by Oliver Stone. But John F Kennedy found this horribly plausible, saying that if his presidency had had another Bay of Pigs fiasco, he could imagine the generals trying to take over. Frankenheimer was always good for political gossip and he slips in a disguised version of the rumour that Truman stopped Eisenhower from running in 1952 with some stolen love letters.

SILKWOOD 1983
Director Mike Nichols *Cast* Meryl Streep, Kurt Russell, Cher

This film catches Streep just before her accent-hopping progress around the globe. She stars as the titular character, a worker at a nuclear power plant who is on her way to reveal wrongdoing to the press when she dies conveniently in a road accident. Streep doesn't try to charm the viewer, having the guts to portray her character as she really was. But director Nichols always seems happiest when he's not dealing with the broader implications of the story and focusing on the heroine's love interest. A brave failure.

THE RACE CARD

BIGOTRY IN THE MOVIES

Hollywood's record on racism is inconsistent: occasional flashes of bravery and integrity followed by shifty evasiveness: ie much the same as most other industries. The stain of DW Griffith's Klan-friendly *Birth Of A Nation* began to show itself when Will Rogers made *Judge Priest* in 1934 about a liberal judge who prevents a black man from being lynched. The effect was muted somewhat when the scene was cut in southern cinemas.

Mark Robson's *Home Is The Brave* (1949) challenged the official myth of the multi-racial but all-American platoon in World War 2. *Pinky* (1949) is almost as good although it stars Jeanne Crain as a light-skinned black woman who has been passing herself off as a white woman whereas the actress is actually white, passing herself off as a light-skinned black woman who's passing herself off…

Hollywood's Jewish moguls had always been nervous about confronting anti-semitism but finally did so in the late 1940s with *Crossfire* and *Gentleman's Agreement*. In the latter, Gregory Peck stars as a reporter who pretends to be a Jew to see how people treat him. In the light of what had just happened to Jews in Europe, his own suffering (being insulted at a golf club) seems tame. Writer Ring Lardner Junior summed up the film when he said: "The moral is never be mean to a Jew because he might turn out to be a Gentile."

SPARTACUS 1960
Director Stanley Kubrick
Cast Kirk Douglas, Laurence Olivier, Jean Simmons, Peter Ustinov, Charles Laughton, Tony Curtis

This ancient political epic tells the tale of a slave, Spartacus (Douglas) and his revolt against the Roman Empire. As much as audiences of the 1960s were enamoured by ancient epics (see also *Ben-Hur* and *El Cid*) the politics behind the scenes were equally as fascinating. Donning his producer's hat, Douglas hired Hollywood Ten blacklisted screenwriter Dalton Trumbo, insisting he be officially credited rather than under a pseudonym. He also hired blacklisted actor Peter Brocco in the supporting role of Ramon. Star and director didn't see eye to eye with Douglas describing Kubrick as a "talented shit" who tried to claim he was the auteur

Z is the end of the alphabet and the beginning of Costa-Gavras' fame

of the film. On its release the film also caused controversy with a scene involving the seduction by Marcus Licinius (Olivier) of slave Antoninus (Curtis). The scene was cut but restored in 1991. Douglas said he spent longer making the film of Spartacus' rebellion than the slave had originally spent rebelling.

VIVA ZAPATA! 1952
Director Elia Kazan *Cast* Marlon Brando, Jean Peters, Anthony Quinn

Novelist John Steinbeck won an Oscar for his script but the auteur of this film is really Kazan who saw parallels between his account of the Mexican revolutionary Zapata's rise to (and renunciation of) power and the fate of many of the more idealistic leaders of the Russian revolution. The studio wanted Kazan to cast Tyrone Power as the revolutionary leader, figuring that at least that way the crowds that had loved him in *Mark Of Zorro* would turn out. Kazan wasn't keen and they settled on Brando. Quinn won an Oscar too, for his portrayal of Zapata's brother, but the key actor is Joseph Wiseman, who plays the Stalin figure Fernando. Brando may have thought he starred in a film celebrating Mexico's revolution but *Zapata* is really a film that attacks the Stalinist inheritors of the Russian revolution.

Z 1968
Director Costa-Gavras *Cast* Yves Montand, Jean-Louis Trintignant

A sensational film which stars Trintignant as the judge probing into the death of Montand who begins to uncover proof that the government has blood on its hands, and faces pressure to stop the investigation. This made Costa-Gavras' reputation, using thriller techniques to expose corruption in a government which is a flimsily disguised version of Greece from 1973 to 1973 under a dictatorial regime. Worth seeing in tandem with the slightly less successful *State Of Siege* (1972) which again stars Montand as the leader of a guerrilla movement which resembles Uruguay's Tupamaros.

> **"A GOOD BODY WITH A DULL BRAIN IS AS CHEAP AS LIFE ITSELF"**
> Batiatus, Spartacus

PRISON

Okay, so prisons aren't meant to be a holiday camp but you wouldn't send your worst enemy to a movie clink, which generally consist of sado-masochistic wardens, ritual beatings and rapes. Even more worryingly, most prison dramas are based on true stories, so if you are tempted by a life of crime just hope you get Tom Hanks as your warden, not Patrick McGoohan.

BIRDMAN OF ALCATRAZ 1962

Director **John Frankenheimer** *Cast* **Burt Lancaster, Karl Malden**

An atypical prison movie, *Birdman's* appeal lies in its powerful conviction that even the most reprehensible life has redemptive value. Lancaster's sensitive portrayal of Robert Stroud, a murderer who became a world famous authority on birds while in the pen (in Leavenworth; he was not allowed to keep birds on the Rock) led to a campaign for Stroud's release before his death in 1963. The film doesn't stress that Stroud was a violent psycho who killed two people in prison, stabbed an orderly and was in solitary for the safety of his fellow inmates but as Joe E Brown says in *Some Like It Hot*: "Nobody's perfect."

> "MAKE THE BEST OF WHAT WE OFFER YOU AND YOU WILL SUFFER LESS THAN YOU DESERVE"
>
> Camp commandant, Papillon

BRUBAKER 1980

Director **Stuart Rosenberg** *Cast* **Robert Redford, Yaphet Kotto, Jane Alexander**

Blond-haired, blue-eyed sweetness and light Redford was perfectly cast as the righteous Brubaker, a prison warden on a mission to ensure even criminals receive justice. By posing as an inmate, he discovers the scale of the corruption and violence but as the reform warden finds himself opposed by the local community, the system and by homicidal guards. Replacement director Rosenberg, (Bob Rafelson was set to direct, however was fired by Redford for hitting a producer) turns in a downbeat, slightly portentous film, with an early notable performance by an almost unrecognisable Morgan Freeman.

COOL HAND LUKE 1967

Director **Stuart Rosenberg** *Cast* **Paul Newman, George Kennedy**

Rosenberg's classic anti-hero prison drama, with Newman

(second choice after Telly Savalas refused to fly back from Europe) as the irrepressible, non-conformist Luke. Released at a time when any sign of rebellion against the establishment was revered, audiences lapped up classic scenes such as the opening destruction of parking meters (particularly popular today no doubt), but Newman's egg-eating feat remains the pinnacle of his cool. The only downer is Rosenberg's use of religious symbolism with Newman as a Christ figure. Look out for early performances by Dennis Hopper and Harry Dean Stanton.

It was tough being a rebel in the 1960s. You had to eat 50 eggs, behave like Christ and die

THE CRIMINAL CODE 1931

Director Howard Hawks Cast Walter Huston, Boris Karloff

Originally a stage play, Huston is a DA turned prison warden who is assigned to the jail where he previously sent a young kid, (Philip Holmes) down for 20 years for a crime which was essentially self defence. Realizing Holmes is close to the edge, he makes him his driver. The relationship comes to a crisis when Holmes sees his cell-mate committing a murder and must decide where his loyalties lie. Hawks' direction is slightly dated, but the film is a good gritty examination of prison life and it's a pleasant change to see Karloff without a bolt through his neck.

ESCAPE FROM ALCATRAZ 1979

Director Don Siegel *Cast* Clint Eastwood, Patrick McGoohan

Deserves praise just for not having a role for Clint's then-girlfriend Sondra Locke, Eastwood is Frank Lee Morris, a real life convict, who along with co-escapees John and Clarence Anglin, became legendary for their successful escape from the supposedly impregnable Alcatraz. Despite director Siegel and Eastwood initially falling out over who would produce, Siegel brought the best out of Eastwood as an actor. A prison caper movie and a detailed examination of the boredom and repetitiveness of prison life where time is a convict's only asset (but very useful when your escape involves tunnelling out using a pair of nail clippers). Siegel's 1954 prison drama *Riot in Cell Block 11* is more realistic, almost documentary-like.

THE GREEN MILE 1999

Director Frank Darabont *Cast* Tom Hanks, David Morse, Michael Clarke Duncan

The second collaboration from the director and writer behind *The Shawshank Redemption* and named after the green floor of Death Row, is an unusual slant on the classic prison drama. For a start, the prison wardens are (with one exception, a political appointee who likes watching convicts fry) good-natured men, just trying to cope with their job of sending men to their death. Hanks is chief warden, with a urinary infection, who narrates the tale in flashback explaining how the arrival of the 8ft tall, gentle Duncan changed their lives forever. Not from the realist school of prison drama, this is a powerful, at times scary fantasy.

I AM A FUGITIVE FROM A CHAIN GANG 1932

Director Mervyn LeRoy *Cast* Paul Muni, Glenda Farrell

The granddaddy of prison movies was in its time a shocking

exposé of penal practices and, with its titanic performance from the great Muni, the best of the hard-hitting social-protest dramas Warner Bros specialized in during the 1930s. Based on an autobiographical story by Robert E Burns, it vividly depicts an innocent man criminalized by the justice system as a down-on-his-luck war veteran is railroaded into shackles and hard labour. Rock splitting, torture by sadistic guards, escapes (including the seminal pursuit by baying bloodhounds through a swamp), solitary – the vocabulary of the genre was laid down here. Worth seeing just to appreciate how often it has been referenced in other films

"I can't believe you haven't seen that bit where he eats all the eggs, it's amazing"

(most recently in the Coens' *O Brother, Where Art Thou?*), it is dated but still powerfully disturbing right down to the unforgettable, haunting last line. As Muni's fugitive Jim slips off into the night his lover plaintively asks: "How do you live?" From the darkness comes the tragically ironic whisper: "I steal."

KISS OF THE SPIDER WOMAN 1985

Director Hector Babenco *Cast* William Hurt, Raul Julia, Sonia Braga

Babenco produces a rare, intimate film from Manuel Puig's novel. Hurt is perfectly cast as the homosexual Luis (Burt Lancaster was originally set to star), imprisoned for corrupting a minor. His cellmate is the aggressively straight political revolutionary Valentin (Julia). The pair begin as enemies, Valentin opposed to Luis' sexuality and politics, but slowly begin to respect one another. The Spider Woman of the title refers to an old movie plot, which Luis recounts to Valentin. This is just one of many, however; the film is interspersed with moments of fantasy and classic film noir images, Luis using the films to escape from prison life. Braga, here making her English-language debut, takes on three roles, including the role of Valentin's lover and the Spider Woman.

> **"WHAT KIND OF CAUSE IS THAT? ONE THAT DOESN'T LET YOU EAT AVOCADO?"**
> Luis Molina, Kiss Of The Spider Woman

MIDNIGHT EXPRESS 1978

Director Alan Parker *Cast* Brad Davis, John Hurt

An unusual choice of follow-up to *Bugsy Malone*. Parker turns in probably his best and most gut-wrenching film. Davis keeps your sympathy, just, as Billy Hayes, caught trying to smuggle drugs out of Turkey and sentenced to life in a Turkish prison to "make an example". Enduring physical and psychological abuse, filmed in all its violent, gritty glory (although thankfully the rape is only hinted at), Hayes realizes his only chance of survival is escape. Scripted by Oliver Stone from Hayes' book, the film would have us believe that it is closer to the truth than it actually is and Hayes himself doesn't come across as the most pleasant character. The meathook scene is, of course, legendary.

ONE DAY IN THE LIFE OF IVAN DENISOVICH 1970

Director Casper Wrede *Cast* Tom Courtenay, Espen Skjonberg

This Anglo-Norwegian production focuses on one day in the life of Solzhenitsyn's hero Ivan (Courtenay), a prisoner in a Siberian gulag. Wrede and cinematographer Sven Nykvist (an Ingmar Bergman favourite) successfully capture the bleakness of the camp's surroundings and the quiet desperation of each day of Ivan's 10-year sentence. Shot on location in Norway, the film is stark in appearance, atmosphere and subject matter with none of the clichés of an American prison film. Bleak, yet intriguing. The best line: when Denisovich is told that the Communist Party has decreed the sun will now reach its zenith at 1pm: "Can they even tell the sun what to do?"

PAPILLON 1973
Director Franklin J Schaffner *Cast* Steve McQueen, Dustin Hoffman

Treacherous nuns, gracious lepers, nubile native maidens and an inventive use for coconuts that would make a spiffing *Blue Peter* project are among the colourful elements that open up the imprisonment ordeal of lengthy solitary stints eating bugs in one of McQueen's hard-nosed rebel performances. Based on the autobiography of French criminal Henri 'The Butterfly' Charriere (dubbed after his tattoo), this account of his captivity in the penal colony in French Guyana, his escapes, sufferings and exile (with poignant, puny comrade Hoffman) is harrowing and exciting by turns. That this bad hat should be so resoundingly rooted for is a testimonial to our affection for a man who defies all the odds and refuses to be denied his liberty. It was the last screenplay from blacklist survivor Dalton Trumbo, who appears as prison commandante.

> **"SOME BIRDS AREN'T MEANT TO BE CAGED. THEIR FEATHERS ARE JUST TOO BRIGHT"**
> Red, The Shawshank Redemption

SCUM 1979
Director Alan Clarke *Cast* Ray Winstone, Mick Ford

Originally made as a BBC play and banned for brutality before it was ever screened, this was remade as a film. Winstone starred again as Carlin, in a stunning debut. Within a budget that wouldn't stretch to shoestrings, Clarke uses a documentary style, making the scenes of violence and abuse in a British borstal all the more disturbing. A strong stomach and good hearing (for the occasionally unintelligible dialogue) are needed.

THE SHAWSHANK REDEMPTION 1994
Director Frank Darabont *Cast* Tim Robbins, Morgan Freeman

A beautifully crafted, superior adaptation of a Stephen King story (*Rita Hayworth And The Shawshank Redemption*, and from the same volume, *Four Seasons*, which yielded *Stand By Me* and *Apt Pupil*), Shawshank is that unlikely thing, a feel-good prison movie. Cultured banker Robbins is convicted for murder despite his protestations of innocence and, with the friendship of philosophical lifer Freeman, endures dehumanisation and brutality, wins the hearts of fellow inmates and serves up canny comeuppances to tormentors in an astonishing climactic coup. Although it did disappointing business on release – so unfashionable had the prison picture become – multiple Oscar nominations, video and word of mouth saw it grow into one of the most fiercely-loved, uplifting male weepies of modern times.

PRISONER OF WAR

Not exactly a dead genre, as complete world peace remains just a concept in John Lennon's *Imagine*, the prisoner of war movie peaked in the early 1960s, rather like Harold Macmillan. But the genre has made an unlikely comeback in, of all places, Chechnya.

THE BRIDGE ON THE RIVER KWAI 1957

Director David Lean *Cast* William Holden, Alec Guinness, Jack Hawkins

David Lean's epic tale of British soldiers imprisoned in a Burmese POW camp and recruited to build a bridge over the river Kwai, could have been very different if Charles Laughton and Cary Grant had been available to play the Guinness and Holden roles respectively. Laughton was said to be daunted by the prospect of the heat in Ceylon, not to mention the ants. The film won seven Oscars but it wasn't until 1984 that co-writers Michael Wilson and Carl Foreman were honoured for their work, having been ignored because they were blacklisted. Wilson didn't live to see his name honoured and Foreman died the day after. Kwai is unusual for a war film because it doesn't obviously depict war as hell or glory and Lean still gives the film the small human touches which had marked his fine *Great Expectations*.

THE CAPTIVE HEART 1946

Director Basil Dearden *Cast* Michael Redgrave, Basil Radford, Gordon Jackson

To stand out from a glut of British POW films, director Dearden bravely decided to avoid the usual melodrama and highlight, in quasi-documentary style, the frustration and claustrophobia of the camps. Redgrave, in his final film before Hollywood discovered him, plays a Czech officer who assumes the identity of a dead British officer. To avoid

"Chuck us the other glove will ya?"

exposure, he has to write love letters to the dead man's wife. The film, which features early performances by Jackson and Rachael Kempson (Redgrave's wife) obviously inspired some scenes in Billy Wilder's *Stalag 17*.

THE GREAT ESCAPE 1963

Director **John Sturges** *Cast* **Steve McQueen, James Garner, Richard Attenborough**

Based on real Allied prisoners plotting a mass breakout from a German POW camp, Sturges conducts a smashing ensemble (some of whom, including Donald Pleasence, had been POWs) through their ingenious, comic, nail-biting paces outwitting the Krauts in an ever-popular affirmation that war is really a grand, ballsy adventure. After he crashed his motorcycle (an anachronistic 1960s British Triumph 650) at the border fence, McQueen had to let mate Bud Elkins double him (still, he did the stunt of the German cyclist hitting the wire himself), but the image of him on the Triumph is an enduring icon of defiant, freewheeling cool. His exploits as Cooler King Hilts, along with Garner's scavenging and Elmer Bernstein's jaunty theme, are so entertaining they obscure tragic reality. The handful of survivors rued the tone since, one later insisted, they would never have tried to escape if they had foreseen the executions in reprisal. There were no Americans in the camp when the escape occurred but, heck, facts never got in the way of a great yarn. This has been paid loving homage in *The Simpsons*, while the hilarity of *Chicken Run*'s poultry farm breakout relies almost entirely on familiarity with *The Great Escape*.

> "ALWAYS REMEMBER, JUST BECAUSE THE KRAUTS ARE DUMB THAT DOESN'T MEAN THEY'RE STUPID"
>
> Mail carrier, Stalag 17

LA GRANDE ILLUSION 1937

Director **Jean Renoir** *Cast* **Jean Gabin, Erich von Stroheim**

Deemed one of the greatest cinematic achievements of all time and the ultimate anti-war film, Renoir's examination of a German POW camp during the First World War became a slice of history when it was decreed: "Cinematic Public Enemy No 1" by Nazi propaganda meister, Joseph Goebbels. The original print was smuggled across borders, rumoured at one point to be destroyed, only to be finally discovered after Renoir's death in Toulouse. Although depicting World War 1 camps, the film was a timely warning of horror to come. The story opens with a pair of French fliers shot down by ace German (Austrian actually) flier, von Stroheim. They are sent to a POW camp with barracks filled with officers from every country, working together to escape. The scenes of the men tunnelling influenced Sturges in *The Great Escape*, right down to the detail of how the men got rid of excess soil. But unlike the famous caper film, Renoir's focus is the relationship of upper and lower classes, and how Stroheim's character still lived by a gentleman's code of honour. When the prisoners say they will not try to escape, he believes them. The sap.

THE MCKENZIE BREAK 1970
Director Lamont Johnson *Cast* Brian Keith, Helmut Griem
An unusual take on the standard POW drama, staunch Nazi Griem is chief prisoner at a German camp in Scotland who leads an escape bid. No-nonsense Irish intelligence officer Keith has to foil the plot, pitting his wits against Griem who will sacrifice anyone and anything for the glory of his Fatherland. A refreshing change to the formula with Johnson focusing on the war from the other side of the fence and the relationship between prisoner and captors.

MERRY CHRISTMAS MR LAWRENCE 1983
Director Nagisa Oshima *Cast* David Bowie, Tom Conti, Ryuichi Sakamoto
Funny, brutal and just mystifying, this is a horse designed by an Anglo-Japanese committee, working from a blueprint supplied by Sir Laurens van der Post's novel. Bowie is the masochistic soldier, racked by guilt over his childhood betrayal of his brother; Conti is Mr Lawrence, the POW camp conscience, and Sakamoto is the Japanese officer unlikely to fulfil his ambition (in Conti's words) to become a "superhuman God", as opposed to a human God. Jack Thompson is effective as the British officer uneasily aware of his own inadequacy while Sakamoto's score is better than his acting. Uneven, but not uninteresting.

PARADISE ROAD 1997
Director Bruce Beresford *Cast* Glenn Close, Frances McDormand
In another chance for Close to show off her singing, here she is one of a group of women imprisoned in a Japanese POW camp in Sumatra during World War 2. They form a symphonic chorus, filling the screen with beautiful melodies in the face of adversity. As cheesy as it may sound, the film is based on a true story, although Beresford does lay on the sentimentality in places. Try to ignore the groomed appearances of the women prisoners and focus on the ensemble cast's performances.

PRISONER OF THE MOUNTAINS 1996
Director Sergei Bodrov *Cast* Oleg Menshikov, Sergei Bodrov Jr
Based on Leo Tolstoy's short story *The Cossacks* but equally applicable to recent times. Chechen rebels capture two Russian soldiers and imprison them for a future trade off. Bodrov, who

"Don't tell anyone but Billy's stolen several scenes from *The Captive Heart*"

used his own son to play the younger prisoner, focuses on the distinction between individuals and 'the enemy', with the chief captor reluctant to kill the men despite the pleas of his own people. Filming, which took place 20 miles from real battles between Russian and Chechen forces, stopped briefly when amateur actress Susanna Mekhraliyeva was taken prisoner after guerrillas discovered that she was being paid in US dollars.

STALAG 17 1953

Director Billy Wilder Cast William Holden, Otto Preminger

Seamless comedy-drama with realistic squalor and squabbling in the daddy of World War 2 prison camp movies. Mischievous wit Wilder subverted the genre with a bitter, cynical anti-hero (Holden, who won the Oscar as Sefton, who is closest, of all Wilder's characters, to his alter ego), a lone wolf whose racketeering and self-interest target him for suspicion and brutal retaliation when the captives realize there is a Nazi informant among them. Wilder adapted the play brilliantly (with original cast members Robert Strauss and Harvey Lembeck reprising their hilarious double act as the goofs obsessed with Betty Grable) and coaxed fellow Viennese Jew Preminger into a rare turn as the caustic Prussian commandant. Wilder threatened to stop filming when studio execs complained that he was making prisoners too dirty and ignoble, and got the last laugh with Sefton's parting shot: "If I ever run into any of you bums on a street corner, let's just pretend we never met before." This is one of Wilder's own favourites.

THREE CAME HOME 1950

Director Jean Negulesco Cast Claudette Colbert, Patric Knowles, Sessue Hayakawa

Not one of Colbert's most famous performances but possibly her best as the real-life authoress held in a Japanese POW camp. Separated from her husband and left to bring up her son in the camp, she has to deal with the unpleasant reality of POW life and the unsolicited attention of camp officer Hayakawa. The violence of the unpredictable officers is tame by recent standards (after all this is still a Claudette Colbert movie) but it's notable for what was, at the time, an unusually sympathetic view of what the Japanese themselves suffered in the bombing of Tokyo and Hiroshima.

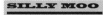

SILLY MOO

HOW NOW?

For such an unassuming creature the cow has played a prominent place in prisoner of war films. In *La Grande Illusion*, after Gabin's character has escaped, we find him pondering his fate with a cow: "You're a poor cow and I'm a poor soldier. We each do our best, eh?" Twenty years later, we find a cow in pride of place in director Henri Verneuil's *La Vache et la Prisonnier*. Here the hero, Fernandel, escapes a POW camp, managing to sneak through Germany disguised as a farmer, complete with milking pail and, of course, a cow. Despite his star status, the cow didn't get a mention in the credits.

United Artists/Mirisch/Alpha, Paramount

PRIVATE DETECTIVES

Private eyes are the definitive heroes of the latter half of the 20th century. They work alone, their heroism constantly reaffirmed by the risks they take, the beatings they endure. They owe no allegiance to any group or power structure – only to a code of morality which they (and we) fear will soon be out of date. Their affairs are ephemeral, like their apartments and offices. What endures is the quality of their repartee: they give good wisecrack.

There are two types of private detectives: those who solve crimes and those for whom crime solving is merely an alibi (for us and them). This section will focus mainly on the latter and less on detectives who, like Philo Vance, spend their films walking around picking up invisible jigsaw pieces and then, with the cunning of a magician, recreate the puzzle for us (and their peers) to gasp at as if they had sawn a woman in half.

Private detectives on the big screen are, primarily, an Anglo-American phenomenon. (There are glaring exceptions, two of which are cited below, and *Peril At End House*, a 1989 Russian movie starring Anatoli Ravikovich as Hercule Poirot, omitted mainly because we couldn't track down a copy.) And they flourish in such times of moral uncertainty as the late 1940s and the mid-1970s, periods of disillusioned hangover after times of immense idealism. Today they are almost as rare on film as cowboys, with aficionados asking: "Where have all the private eyes gone?" The only logical conclusion to be drawn from their habitual consumption of tobacco (in memory Bogart always has a cigarette) and alcohol (think of old Nick Charles, downing six martinis, a feat his wife felt obliged to match) is that they have smoked or drunk themselves to death.

"HOW MUCH BETTER CAN YOU EAT? WHAT CAN YOU BUY THAT YOU CAN'T ALREADY AFFORD?"
Jake Gittes, Chinatown

ALPHAVILLE 1965
Director Jean-Luc Godard *Cast* Eddie Constantine, Anna Karina
Private eye films are famed for their dialogue but this futuristic

thriller, with Constantine as a detective called Lemmy Caution sent to rescue a scientist from a city run by an electronic brain, has some of the most extraordinary dialogue in the genre. As the electronic brain says: "Sometimes reality is too complex for oral communication. But legend embodies it in a form which enables all over the world." Top that Philip Marlowe. Beautiful to look at, hard to follow, this is fascinating, irritating viewing. If you're bored just spot the influences on Philip K Dick's *Do Androids Dream Of Electric Sheep?*, the source for *Blade Runner*.

> "A MAN ONCE TOLD ME THAT YOU STEP OUT OF YOUR DOOR IN THE MORNING AND YOU ARE ALREADY IN TROUBLE. THE ONLY QUESTION IS ARE YOU ON TOP OF THAT TROUBLE OR NOT"
>
> Easy Rawlins, Devil In A Blue Dress

ANGEL HEART 1987

Director *Alan Parker* Cast *Mickey Rourke, Robert De Niro, Lisa Bonet*
Some films come pre-packaged as cult films and this is one of them. There are the characters' names (Rourke is private eye Harry Angel, hired to find a man called Johnny Favourite, and De Niro is devilish Louis Cyphre), the gore (watch out for the sudden switch to open heart surgery) and generous helpings of occultism. And it works, partly because Rourke has seldom looked so rancid and *Cosby Show* kid Bonet has seldom looked more beautiful. Charlotte Rampling is intriguing as a voodoo debutante and De Niro overacts as Satan, but doesn't everybody?

THE BIG FIX 1978

Director *Jeremy Paul Kagan* Cast *Richard Dreyfuss, Susan Anspach, Bonne Bedelia*
Dreyfuss is the former radical turned private eye who has to track down a missing revolutionary (F Murray Abraham) in this well made mystery which ends with the dreams of a generation exposed as a fraud. Look out for future small-screen stars Mandy Patinkin and John Lithgow.

"Jack, how can I ever repay you for giving me that urine sample to throw into the director's face?"

THE BIG SLEEP 1946

Director *Howard Hawks*
Cast *Humphrey Bogart, Lauren Bacall*
What movie, apart from *Casablanca*, has been as mythologized as this version of *The Big Sleep*? Ironically, the film based on the work of two fine writers (Raymond Chandler wrote the novel and William Faulkner helped write the script) started life as a sequel to *To Have And Have Not*. Warners didn't really care what the film was about as long as it starred Bacall and Bogart. (Indeed, after the first version was completed, the

studio would insert extra scenes with its stars before it was released in 1946.) The plot was changed dramatically because Chandler's original plot didn't hang together (one of the bigger loose ends being who killed the Sternwood family's chauffeur) and because the censors wanted somebody punished: if not the decadent Sternwood family then the gangsters. Hawks didn't mind, the censors' ending was more violent than his and less complicated than the one Chandler suggested. Chandler's hero didn't like women much, not a point of view the usually broad-minded Hawks had much time for, so he made the women in the film as available as he could, without having them actually walking the street. Out of these conflicting priorities and commercial considerations emerged a masterpiece. But for the depressed alcoholic Faulkner, it was the film which finally persuaded him to give up screenwriting.

CHINATOWN 1974

Director Roman Polanski *Cast* Jack Nicholson, Faye Dunaway, John Huston

Polanski won the big argument: that a film called *Chinatown* had to have at least one scene set in a real chinatown. The overruled writer, Robert Towne, insisted it was just a metaphor. The director, whose first reaction to the script was to say: "I should have stayed in Poland," spent much of the film rowing with Towne, photographing topless teenyboppers jumping off the diving board and telling Faye Dunaway, whenever she queried her motivation: "Just say the fucking lines – your salary is the motivation." Nicholson charmed enough people to get the film made without too much violence breaking out, although he may have provided the urine in the cup Dunaway threw in Polanski's face. What ended up onscreen is a real noir classic, worthy of the greats of the 1940s, right down to the downbeat, cynical ending. In memory, it is often reduced to a procession of scenes: the nose slitting (performed by Polanski), the joke about the Chinaman having sex, the horror of the closing scene. The long-postponed sequel *The Two Jakes* has its good moments but is mainly for completists.

DEVIL IN A BLUE DRESS 1995

Director Carl Franklin *Cast* Denzel Washington, Tom Sizemore, Jennifer Beals

This is so good you want to write to Washington (Denzel not DC), Walter Mosley (who wrote the book) and Terry Wogan on

HELLO GIRLS

WOMEN WHO SOLVE CRIMES
If they're not called Miss Marple, they're often amateurs. With one terrible exception.

JANE
Joe Briggs is in the brig for a murder he didn't do and it's all down to Jane's boyfriend. Can Jane catch the real murderer? This is *Stranger On The Third Floor* (1940) and we think you know the answer.

KANSAS
A secretary every man would die for. It's down to Ella Raines to get her innocent boss out of the clink in *Phantom Lady* (1944). Pity the plot has her turn to mush at the end.

MARY GIBSON
Kim Hunter is the orphan who ends up in Manhattan searching for her sister in above average mystery *The 7th Victim* (1943).

VI WARSHAWSKI
The private eye whose surname sounds like a simultaneous cough and a sneeze sank despite Kathleen Turner's sass. But it was scripted by dumb, dumber and dumber still.

Points Of View to demand that the same team films the other three novels (*A Red Death*, *White Butterfly* and *Black Betty*) which star Mosley's black private eye, Easy Rawlins. Here he investigates the murder of his lover Coretta and is paid by a thug to ask questions about Beal, a white woman who likes "the company of Negroes". Washington gives Rawlings a character and a conscience in this entertaining tour of the jazz clubs and back streets of 1940s LA.

FAREWELL MY LOVELY 1976
Director Dick Richards *Cast* Robert Mitchum, Charlotte Rampling

If Mitchum's Marlowe has time on his hands, he could do worse than investigate the mysterious disappearance of the director of this film. The former magazine photographer directed six films (although he was uncredited on his last, Burt Reynolds' *Heat*) of which this is easily the best, a brooding, tense movie based on the Raymond Chandler mystery. Richards has a real feel for this material and makes up for the disadvantage of colour (in a noir film) by visualing Marlowe's world in orange hues. Mitchum is Marlowe in a way that Dick Powell and, possibly even Bogart, never quite were. The world weary cynicism he brings to lines like: "It's July now and things are worse than they were in spring," sounds completely authentic. Marlowe's attempts to find Velma takes him into his usual milieu of lies and double-crosses. Pulp crime author Jim Thompson has a minor, but key, role as a dying millionaire. Steer clear of Winner's follow up *The Big Sleep* which is the exact opposite of the director's surname.

HARPER 1966
Director Jack Smight *Cast* Paul Newman, Robert Wagner, Lauren Bacall, Shelley Winters

Sinatra turned down the chance to play Lew Archer, the hero of the Ross Macdonald private eye novels, and then regretted it when he saw the box office takings. (Instead, the Chairman made two films as Tony Rome of which the first, simply called *Tony Rome*, is easily the best.) Archer became Harper because the star

> "I USED TO BE A SHERIFF TILL I PASSED THE LITERACY TEST"
> Lew Harper, Harper

superstitiously felt he did better with movie titles which began with H (it worked for *Hud* and *The Hustler* but not later for *Hombre*). Newman picked up the role and, after telling tyro screenwriter William Goldman that the script was a "piece of shit," led a strong ensemble cast in a fast moving mystery. In the vital confrontation between Newman's hero and Wagner's villain, Wagner began to cry real tears; a fact which so excited the method actor in Newman that he fluffed all his lines.

THE KENNEL MURDER CASE 1933
Director Michael Curtiz *Cast* William Powell, Mary Astor

Powell is Philo Vance, a dapper detective who takes cases only because they amuse him and certainly for no reason as sordid as because they pay the rent. Powell toned down some of the hero's foppishness from the books but his ever-present gloves are a sign that this sleuth isn't going to get his hands dirty. This is the archetypal whodunnit, certainly more absorbing on film than any of the subsequent adventures of Hercule Poirot.

KISS ME DEADLY 1955
Director Robert Aldrich *Cast* Ralph Meeker, Albert Dekker

Watch this and feel Hammer's pain. He's driven over a cliff, given a needle, knocked out by a blackjack, strapped to a bed and worked over by heavies and finally shot. Not since Rasputin has one man taken so much punishment and lived. Of course, the mad monk was finally thrown into a river with weights attached, one of the few kinds of violence not seen in this flashy, brutal, movie. (The highlight, or lowlight for the squeamish, is when a woman gets tortured almost to death with a pair of pliers.) Hammer's only mistake is to give a lift to a woman he finds running along the road. And some mistakes you never stop paying for. But then Hammer, played here by movie heavy Meeker, is not a character we are encouraged to like. Just as well because most of the sympathetic characters get killed in Aldrich's vision of an America run by con men, fascists and gangsters. Probably the biggest single influence on the French Wave, this is a thoroughly nasty gem.

THE LONG GOODBYE 1973
Director Robert Altman *Cast* Elliott Gould, Nina Van Pallandt, Sterling Hayden

Marlowe's most controversial screen incarnation yet is

also one his most satisfying. The film is now chiefly famous for the final scene where Gould shoots his duplicitous old friend Terry Lennox, something critics insist the old Philip Marlowe would never have done. Yet anybody reading Chandler's prose would have to conclude that rage, of the kind which leads Gould to pull the trigger, is always present in Marlowe's character. Cinematographer Vilmos Zsigmond's work adds to the uncertainty – he's always either zooming in or out of the characters or arcing around or tracking across them. The film has a nightmarish, haunting, quality and Gould conspires with Altman to strip away the invisible suit of armour which always protected Bogart's Marlowe. A brave, well made film, possibly saved by the fact that Dan Blocker, Hoss in *Bonanza*, died before he could play the key role of writer Roger Wade.

> "I'M TIRED. MY
> JAW HURTS AND
> MY RIBS ACHE.
> I KILLED A MAN
> BACK THERE AND
> I HAD TO STAND
> BY WHILE A
> HARMLESS LITTLE
> GUY WAS KILLED"
>
> Philip Marlowe, The Big Sleep

THE MALTESE FALCON 1941
Director John Huston *Cast* Humphrey Bogart, Mary Astor, Peter Lorre, Sydney Greenstreet

This is Hollywood's third attempt to capture Hammett's novel on the big screen. The first two, *The Maltese Falcon* with Ricardo Cortez as Sam Spade and *Satan Met A Lady* (starring Bette Davis) bombed, but this one made Huston and Bogart, who only got the part because George Raft had a clause in his contract which meant he didn't have to appear in remakes. Bogart is substantially different to Hammett's depiction of his hero in the book (Spade is, at one point, compared to a "blond

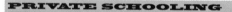

PRIVATE SCHOOLING

So you wannabe a private eye? Get ready to be vulnerable on three counts.

1 Physical You get your nose slit like Jake Gittes in *Chinatown*, drugged like Marlowe in *Murder My Sweet*, beaten up twice like Marlowe in *The Big Sleep* or six times like Mike Hammer in *Kiss Me Deadly*. Them's the perks.

2 Emotional Is there something phallic about a private dick with a gun? Why do four women flirt with Bogart in the first 15 minutes of *The Big Sleep*? Some of us go entire lifetimes without that much flirting. But then you have to fall for the heroine who probably isn't a heroine (Brigid in *The Maltese Falcon*) or if she is, like Evelyn Cross, she's probably deeply mad albeit with good reason. You may end up with the

dame as the credits roll but we all know it's not permanent. The girl is normally trouble with a capital T and that rhymes with P and that stands for Prison.

3 Moral You can resist anything except temptation and that might come in the form of that strumpet Carmen or because you've deluded yourself that Terry Lennox is your mate so you'll cover for him until the only way to clear up the mess is to go to Mexico and shoot him. Remember, the cops are mostly crooked or stupid, the judges are drunk or bribed and the DA is keener on winning votes than winning convictions, so if there's to be any kind of justice in this world, you'll just have to dispense it yourself.

Satan") but this version had the courage to pursue Hammett's original ending where Spade hands over Brigid, the femme fatale (Astor), to the cops. The film's dark cinematography anticipates film noir although it disguised the paucity of the sets at Warners, a studio known then as "San Quentin" for the luxurious facilities provided for cast and crew. Spade isn't as moral as Marlowe (he admits he might not have turned Brigid in if the falcon had been real) but in his refusal to "play the sap" he sums up the creed of many of his successors.

Paramount/Long Road, United Artists/Lions Gate

THE MOST TERRIBLE TIME IN MY LIFE 1993

Director Kaizo Hayashi Cast Masatoshi Nagase, Shiro Sano

From the hero's name Maiku "Mike" Hama (it is, the character insists, his real name) you might assume that this is a kitsch comic homage like *Austin Powers*. The director's love of B movies can be seen from the fact that Hama is one of the few big screen private eyes whose office is also a projection booth (his clients are forced to buy tickets to see the films by the clerk who grumbles ominously: "If you don't see movies, you're finished"). But Hayashi took the detective business seriously enough to try to become one (the film, unusually, comes with a recommendation by the Japan Association of Detective Agencies) and the homage here is deep and affectionate with Hama (played by arthouse icon Nagase, best known as the Japanese tourist in *Mystery Train*) hired to find a Taiwanese waiter's lost brother. Underneath all the fun there's a point too about Japan's xenophobia. A little gem.

Spot the PI: the crumpled, slept-in suit among the cotton-wearing tourists is a bit of a give-away, Elliott

NIGHT MOVES 1975

Director Arthur Penn Cast Gene Hackman, Jennifer Warren, Melanie Griffith

One of the keys to this film is an apparently innocuous exchange when Hackman (as private eye Harry Moseby) is watching American football on TV and his wife asks him who's winning. "Nobody," he says, "one side's just losing slower than the other." Hackman's Moseby is no Marlowe and the deconstruction of the private eye hero went too far even for audiences in the 1970s, so this bombed and has been underrated ever since. Moyes is in pursuit of Griffith, a young girl who is so liberated that one of the characters says: "When we're all as liberated as her, there'll be fighting in the streets."

SECOND SIGHT 1989
Director Joel Zwick *Cast* John Larroquette, Bronson Pinchot, Bess Armstrong
The tagline "He's in the detective biz with a psychic whizz" is fair warning of what is to come. Larroquette is the ex-cop turned private eye and Pinchot is the psychic helping him find a missing girl. Not satisfied with this premise, the filmmakers also threw in a nun as love interest, a wardrobe full of check jackets so loud that it's hard to hear Larroquette's dialogue over them and a lot of mind-reading jokes of the kind which remind you of the old line from Chandler on *Friends*: "That's funny. That's painfully funny. No wait, it's just painful." One of those rare films which actually prompted people to walk out of the cinema before it ended. In these days of soaring ticket prices, that is not an achievement to be sniffed at.

SHAMUS 1973
Director Buzz Kulik *Cast* Burt Reynolds, Dyan Cannon
Aka *Passion For Danger* which aptly describes the interests of director and star. There's a certain shamelessness in a movie about a shamus which calls itself Shamus and that extends to the plot which doesn't so much thicken as solidify. Just watch it for the action and to see Reynolds get beaten up. Repeatedly.

THE THIN MAN 1934
Director WS Van Dyke *Cast* William Powell, Myrna Loy
Some films are best watched with the sound off (try the *Quick And The Dead* that way, it makes far more sense), but with *The Thin Man* you could almost watch from behind the sofa because nothing in this brilliantly executed work quite matches the dialogue. Dashiel Hammett's detective Nick Charles (Powell) is reviewing his reviews in the papers: "I'm a hero, I got shot twice in the *Tribune*." Nora (Loy) points out that it was five times in the tabloids to which hubby replies: "It's not true. He didn't come anywhere near my tabloids." The case he's working on is well-plotted (missing man is accused of murdering his mistress) but finally incidental, probably not as important as the case of scotch he's working on.

PROPAGANDA

The power of movies to move the masses (that's everyone except you and us) was bizarrely recognized by the *Daily Express* in the 1930s when it complained Hollywood was making "temporary Americans" of millions of Brits. Tyrants as diverse as Adolf Hitler, Erich von Stroheim and the late L Ron Hubbard have used the power for their own nefarious ends. And much good did it do them.

Battleship Potemkin was "a marvellous film without equal in the cinema... anyone who had no firm political conviction would become a Bolshevik after seeing the film". This is the kind of reaction every director hopes to inspire in a reviewer. Even if the director happens to be Sergei Eisenstein and the reviewer happens to be one Josef Goebbels.

The use of movies for propaganda was almost as inevitable as their use for pornography. During World War I, Erich von Stroheim played a succession of sinister German officers often with a surname which began with 'von' (as close as any of these films came to realism). In *The Unbeliever*, he rips a boy's hair out by the roots and in *Heart Of Humanity* he rapes a nurse and throws a baby out of the window on the grounds, presumably, that it'll save him from having to pull the child's hair out later. In the summer of 1918, with peace near, officials in Washington DC wrote to producers telling them not to be beastly to the Hun.

By the time hostilities recommenced in 1939, governments were more actively involved in the making and commissioning of these films, the power of which had been proved by filmmakers like Leni Riefenstahl. Famous directors like Frank Capra and John Ford enlisted to make films of the 'Why We Fight' variety. Some efforts rebounded on the makers. MGM's *Song Of Russia* (1943), greeted by Bosley Crowther at the *New York Times* as "very close to being the best film about Russia in the Hollywood popular idiom" was later pored over by US Congressman as if it were *Das Kapital*. Ayn Rand, right-wing author of *The Fountainhead*, testified that the film was propaganda because nobody smiled in Russia any more.

Far more sinister than *Song Of Russia* were films like Walt Disney's *Cleanliness Brings Health* (1945), which contrasts two families to suggest that cleanliness is next to godliness, the implication being that only Commies leave their washing up in

"IT IS OUR WISH AND WILL THAT THIS REICH AND STATE SHALL STAND FOR A THOUSAND YEARS TO COME!"
Adolf Hitler, Triumph of the Will

the sink overnight. The propaganda film, like the western, has declined as a genre. This is a shame because as John Travolta's pseudo-Scientological *Battlefield Earth* shows, really bad propaganda provides some of the cinema's funniest moments.

BATTLESHIP POTEMKIN 1925

Director **Sergei Eisenstein** *Cast* **Alexander Antonov, Vladimir Barsky**

Inspired by American pioneer DW Griffith, the Red Army veteran, champion of the masses and creative genius Eisenstein greatly enlarged the vocabulary of cinema with his development of montage, visual metaphor and rhythmic editing and his experiments in colour and sound. His most remarkable film was an assignment from the state Central Committee and shot by a film collective, with Eisenstein focusing not on individual characters but class types. The resulting drama of a battleship mutiny, which commemorates the aborted 1905 revolution, is a cornerstone of film studies, while its immortal sequence on the Odessa Steps (mother loses grip on baby carriage, camera follows its inexorable descent and infant's crushing under stampeding feet of fleeing mob) may be the best known, most imitated scene in the history of motion pictures.

THIS IS THE ARMY 1943

Director **Michael Curtiz** *Cast* **George Murphy, Joan Leslie, Ronald Reagan**

The most profitable movie to come out of Hollywood between 1940 and 1945. Move over *Casablanca*, make way for the all-singing, all-dancing US Army. The film, starring a future president and a heavyweight champion (Joe Louis), has been vilified for trivializing the reality of war. But this is an Irving Berlin musical which has as much to do with war as it does with existentialist philosophy and exists to mobilize the American public for a noble, undefined, cause. And make Warner Bros richer. For a complete contrast see John Huston's *Let There Be Light*, a documentary made with the aid of the US Army but banned for 35 years because of the harrowing scenes of returning GIs' emotional suffering.

TRIUMPH OF THE WILL 1935

Director **Leni Riefenstahl**

Hitler asked dancer, actress and filmmaker Riefenstahl to film the sixth Nazi Party Congress held in September, 1934 at Nuremberg – the medieval Bavarian showplace where, with deliberate irony, an Allied court convened in 1945 to judge war criminals. With 30 cameras and 120

technicians Riefenstahl fulfilled her brief – to glorify the might
of the Nazi state and tighten its grip on the hearts and minds of
Germany — with breathtaking imagery on a spectacularly
sinister, epic scale, creating an infamous masterpiece. The
Fuhrer's acclamation by saluting multitudes, young men
disporting, torchlit swastika-brandishing ritual, militaristic
display, stirring anthems, thousands of disciplined children
pledging themselves to the movement, an endless parade: it's a
fascinating, chilling testament to the power of film to impose a
false, spiritual aesthetic on the overtly political. After the war
Riefenstahl was jailed for four years for her propaganda work.
Repeated bids to revive her career were unsuccessful.

The Battleship
Potemkin, preferable
to Battlefield Earth
both as a movie
and as a work of
propaganda

YOU NATZY SPY! 1940

Director Jules White *Cast* Curly Howard, Larry Fine, Moe Howard
The Three Stooges send up Hitler in this spoof set in the
fictional land of Moronia (any resemblance purely coincidental
etc) which, if you believe the *Weekly World News,* so enraged the
Führer that he formed a hit squad to get Curly, Larry and Moe.
Understandable perhaps as the film is very funny indeed.

PSYCHIATRY

Psychiatrists have always appealed to filmmakers, ever since Sam Goldwyn offered Sigmund Freud $100,000 to help him create the ultimate love story. (Freud, alas, passed.) They have an eternal appeal as a plot device for genres as diverse as thrillers and comedy. In *Analyze This*, Billy Crystal's shrink enables De Niro to spoof his own movie myth. In Woody Allen films, where Freudian analysis often takes over the script, therapists are peripheral figures, fashion accessories or sounding boards. When they do take centre stage, it's either because they're the villain, about to perform a miracle cure or, as happens in one in ten films in which a shrink appears, they're mattress-surfing with their patient.

ANGEL BABY 1995

Director Michael Rymer Cast John Lynch, Jacqueline McKenzie

"THERE IS NO
OUT OF HERE.
YOU'VE BEEN
KILLED, DON'T
YOU REMEMBER?"

Evil doctor, Jacob's Ladder

A love story with a difference about two schizophrenics who meet in a drug therapy session. Overshadowed by *Shine*, another Australian film about a character struggling with mental illness, this is more low key and downbeat. A truly realistic film about schizophrenics falling in love would be almost unwatchable but this manages to convey some of the tragedy. *I Never Promised You A Rose Garden* (1977) is an intelligent take on the same condition.

BIRDY 1984

Director Alan Parker Cast Matthew Modine, Nicolas Cage

Parker passed on this when he saw proofs of William Wharton's novel in 1978 but returned to it five years later. Modine is the ex-soldier whose ambition to become a bird man has nothing to do with Alcatraz but everything to do with his service in Vietnam. Or maybe his determination to fly without aircraft is just the result of too many Dan Air flights. With a muted score by Peter Gabriel and fine performances from Modine and Cage as his buddy, the film makes you sympathize with Birdy although Parker spoils it all with a rather dodgy ending.

FACE TO FACE 1976 ANSIKTE MOT ANSIKTE

Director Ingmar Bergman Cast Liv Ullmann, Erland Josephson

This near definitive slice of Nordic misery from the gloommeister marked Bergman's return to form and the exorcising of his own personal demons. The film tells the story of the breakdown of a psychiatrist (Ullmann) overwhelmed by memories of her past when she returns to her family home. Watch it and it'll infiltrate your own memories. This was a 200 minute TV series but had 65 minutes cut for cinemas and it's so harrowing, some might see that as an act of mercy.

FAMILY LIFE 1972

Director Ken Loach Cast Sandy Ratcliff, Bill Dean, Grace Cave

Grim docudrama that portrays the psychiatric profession as a tool of state oppression. Subtlety has never been one of Loach's long suits, especially when he has a point to make, and he makes a good case against the state's definition of mental health. The electric shock treatments are especially horrific. The controversial US documentary *Titicut Follies* was banned for 25 years in America, possibly because the authorities saw the title and thought it was a Russ Meyer sexploitation movie. It's actually a chronicle of the mistreatment of mental patients in Massachusetts and makes an even more powerful case than Loach's.

JACOB'S LADDER 1990

Director Adrian Lyne Cast Tim Robbins, Elizabeth Peña, Danny Aiello

PSD or not PSD, that is the question? Robbins does well in the tough role of Vietnam vet Jacob Singer trying to hold onto reality while haunted by memories of war and his dead son (yes, that is Macaulay Culkin in that sequence). Films about post-traumatic stress disorder don't usually set the box office alight and this, sadly, was no exception. Pity, because Lyne is better served by this than stuff like *Fatal Attraction*.

Tim Robbins is haunted by war and the thought that his dead son was that kid in *Home Alone*

LA SEPTIEME CIEL 1997 SEVENTH HEAVEN

Director Benoît Jacquot Cast Sandrine Kiberlain, Vincent Lindon, François Berléand

An intriguing oddity. A serious, ambiguous film about therapy and marriage where the patient is warned: "If you continue sleeping to the southeast, be prepared to suffer the consequences". Yes, Freud has been superseded by feng shui

309

> THEY WAS GIVING ME TEN THOUSAND WATTS A DAY, YOU KNOW, AND I'M HOT TO TROT: THE NEXT WOMAN TAKES ME ON'S GONNA LIGHT UP LIKE A PINBALL MACHINE AND PAY OFF IN SILVER DOLLARS!
>
> Randle Patrick McMurphy, One Flew Over The Cuckoo's Nest

and hypnotism in the treatment of Kiberlain, who happens to be a compulsive shoplifter and painter. Her therapist's cures begin to threaten her marriage as hubby becomes jealous. Nothing is resolved but watching Jacquot leave things hanging is better than watching most directors tie up every loose end.

THE MADNESS OF KING GEORGE 1994
Director Nicholas Hytner *Cast* Nigel Hawthorne, Helen Mirren
The royal stools were much examined to decide whether King George III really was mad although one doctor admits: "One may produce a copious regular evacuation and still be a stranger to reason." Quite so. Hawthorne's performance as the King is so in key with both the lightness and the asperity of Alan Bennett's script that he is a joy to watch. (Mirren impresses too in a tough role as the Queen) For a contemporary film making a similar point, albeit about a patient of lower rank, try *Girl, Interrupted* with Winona Ryder and Angelina Jolie.

ONE FLEW OVER THE CUCKOO'S NEST 1975
Director Milos Forman *Cast* Jack Nicholson, Louise Fletcher
James Caan turned down Nicholson's role because there'd be "too many white walls", a fact for which we and Jack should be eternally grateful. Nicholson and his character Randle McMurphy seem to merge in this harrowing tale of life and rebellion in an asylum. Many of the group therapy scenes were refilmed with actors adding detail and nuance as they went along. Danny DeVito has a small role and Anjelica Huston is a member of the crowd on the pier when McMurphy and the boys go fishing. Ken Kesey, who wrote the book, says he'll never watch it. It's his loss. Nicholson would return to similar territory with *As Good As It Gets* (1997) which isn't as good as Jack gets but is one of the few Hollywood films where a patient is seen getting effective medical treatment.

DR SEX

In Mike Figgis' 1993 film *Mr Jones*, Lena Olin plays a therapist who has an affair with a patient. Understandable in that her patient is Richard Gere. But if you ever have a therapist who looks like Olin, don't get your hopes up. Okay, in 29 films the female therapist sleeps with her patient compared to just 17 in which the male therapist sleeps with his patient. But in this, as so often, movies have inverted reality: in sexual misconduct cases, male psychiatrists outnumber their female colleagues ten to one.

SHOCK 1946
Director Alfred L Werker *Cast* Vincent Price, Lynne Bari
The ultimate expression of the psychiatrist as Dr Evil. Woman sees a murder, goes into shock and is handed over to a shrink, who just happens to be the killer. Funnily enough, psychiatrists found this view of their profession less than flattering and Hollywood, eager to make amends, proceeded to make a string of films where the psychiatrist was the hero.

SPECIAL TREATMENT 1980 POSEBAN TRETMAN

Director Goran Paskaljevic *Cast* Ljuba Tadic, Dusica Zegarac

Fanatic doctor (Tadic) decides to take the group of alcoholics he's been curing and/or terrorising to a brewery to show off his healing powers. Jokes about piss-ups in breweries soon give way to Paskaljevic's broader purpose, focusing on the nature of fascism. But the director keeps a firm grip and humour is never too far away.

SPELLBOUND 1945

Director Alfred Hitchcock *Cast* Gregory Peck, Ingrid Bergman

Hitch almost disowned this picture in an interview with Francois Truffaut. Maybe because he never felt it was his: the title was provided by one of David O Selznick's secretaries, Dali's dream sequence is stranger than anything else in the movie and the director even complained about the score. He had wanted to make the first proper movie about psychoanalysis and some of that ambition survives on screen as Bergman tries to help Peck prove his innocence. It's just a pity that some of Dali's work, especially a scene where Bergman is turned into a Greek statue that explodes, didn't make it.

THE THREE FACES OF EVE 1957

Director Nunnally Johnson *Cast* David Wayne, Joanne Woodward, Lee J Cobb

In American films of the 1950s, the 'expert' was almost always right. Whereas the heroes of the 1930s and 1940s were cops and soldiers, in the 1950s they were usually professional experts, often doctors and psychiatrists. There are few better examples of this trend than this film, based on a true story, in which Joanne Woodward overcomes a poor script and lack of direction to give a performance that dominates the film and won her an Oscar. Unfortunately, like many films of this ilk, it offers a "magic bullet" cure.

MIND GAMES

CARRY ON SCREAMING!

There are three types of shrink in films: Dr Wonderful, Dr Evil and Dr Dippy, as they are known to the psychiatric profession.

DR WONDERFUL Robin Williams as therapist Sean McGuire in *Good Will Hunting*; Barbra Streisand as Susan Lowenstein in *The Prince Of Tides* helping Nick Nolte face the past; Adam Williams as Dr Brown who leads Jimmy Piersall out of mental illness and back to baseball in *Fear Strikes Out* (1957).

DR EVIL Hannibal Lecter in the *Silence Of The Lambs*; Herbert Grimwood as Dr Ulrich Metz who tries to drive Douglas Fairbanks to suicide; the anonymous psychiatrists who will 'cure' the young woman Karin in Bergman's *Through A Glass Darkly* (1961).

DR DIPPY Peter Sellers as Dr Fassbender trying to cure a woman-chasing Peter O'Toole in *What's New Pussycat*; Dr Dippy in *Dr Dippy's Sanitarium* (1906); Diane Keaton's shrink in *Manhattan* who is even more screwed up than Keaton's or Woody Allen's character; Tom Cruise and Nicole Kidman are deeply dippy in *Eyes Wide Shut*.

"Look Doc, if you want my advice, don't do the Norwegian flag gag"

RELIGION

God was always going to be big in the movies. As far back as 1910, a film of the Oberammergau passion play was selling out theatres in New Jersey. And in an industry where the biggest studio claimed it had more stars than in heaven, heaven's biggest star has remained a perennial attraction. But the era of Biblical epics has been superseded by films which give both *The Bible* (and the church) a bit of a bashing.

THE BIBLE 1966
Director John Huston Cast Michael Parks, Ulla Bergryd, Richard Harris, George C Scott, Ava Gardner

There are 39 books in the Old Testament. This takes 174 minutes to tell half of the first – at that rate, if Huston had filmed the rest, the resulting movie would have been over nine days long. God, of course, created the world in seven but then he didn't have Dino de Laurentis as a producer. Huston also stars as Noah and his performance (and that of George C Scott as Abraham) shames the rest of the cast. For a more successful (and much more original) Italian take on the good book try *The Gospel According To St Matthew* (directed by Pier Paolo Pasolini in 1964) which portrays Jesus as a Marxist revolutionary.

> "NOAH WAS A DRUNK. LOOK WHAT HE ACCOMPLISHED. AND NO ONE'S EVEN ASKING YOU TO BUILD AN ARK"
> Metatron, Dogma

BLACK NARCISSUS 1947
Director Michael Powell, Emeric Pressburger Cast Deborah Kerr, Jean Simmons, Flora Robson

When Martin Scorsese saw this film for the first time, he said he wasn't sure if it was the best film he'd ever seen but he knew he'd seen something revolutionary. Outwardly, this is a relatively straightforward story about nuns who try to start a school and hospital in the Himalayas and go almost mad in the attempt. It is a rare treat to see nuns that don't want to sing or dance but serve God, just as it is a rare feat for the Archers (as Powell/Pressburger called themselves) to produce a subtly erotic film about nuns. The Himalayan scenery is especially remarkable because it sets the mood of the film perfectly and was all created on a sound stage at Pinewood.

DOGMA 1999
Director **Kevin Smith** *Cast* **Ben Affleck, Matt Damon, Linda Fiorentino**

A comedy about two fallen angels who spot a loophole that would enable them to get back into heaven although to do so they would have to destroy humanity. There were the usual howls of outrage when this was released but you know what to expect from the moment the cardinal/church PR man unveils the new 'buddy Jesus' who smiles, winks and gives the thumbs up and is, therefore, a much better brand than the depressing old crucified Jesus. Smith fans will note the obligatory hockey reference but underneath the laughs is a serious message that Christianity would be a lot better off without so much, well, dogma really.

THE FLOWERS OF ST FRANCIS 1950
Director **Roberto Rossellini** *Cast* **Brother Nazario Gerardi**

Scripted by Fellini and directed by Rossellini, this film is really about what monks do, day in, day out than about St Francis (Gerardi) himself. For a film which focuses on Francis more, try Zeffirelli's 1973 *Brother Sun Sister Moon*. In terms of dramatic power, this movie lacks the punch of *Il Miracolo* (1948), another religious themed film written and directed by the same team, but repays viewing.

THE GREATEST STORY EVER TOLD 1965
Director **George Stevens** *Cast* **Max von Sydow, Carroll Baker, Charlton Heston**

The nuns in *Black Narcissus* had a hard time figuring out where exactly in the Himalayas Pinewood was

And the greatest cast he may ever have assembled (also starring are Sidney Poitier, Angela Lansbury, José Ferrer and, of course, John Wayne) but not, sadly, the greatest movie Stevens ever directed – that honour must go to *Shane*. This film is chiefly remembered for the perverse decision to suggest, with the casting of John Wayne, that one of the Roman centurions who stood guard that fateful day must have come from somewhere near Dodge City. At three hours and 20 minutes (in the edited British version) for all of Stevens' craft, this will inevitably test the patience of a saint from time to time.

JESUS OF MONTREAL 1989

Director Denys Arcand *Cast* Lothaire Bluteau, Catherine Wilkening

A group of young actors revamp the traditional Passion Play and then – guess what? – they start behaving like Jesus and his disciples. Sounds trite, particularly as most of the scenes have parallels in the New Testament (eg the scene where the actor playing Jesus runs riot on the set of a TV commercial). But if you're not allergic to allegory this is worth the effort, especially for Bluteau's intense performance as Danile/Christ. Bluteau is equally impressive as a Jesuit priest on a spiritual voyage of discovery in *Black Robe* (1991). As celluloid Jesuits go, Bluteau probably just shades it over Jeremy Irons in *The Mission*.

> **"I FIND IT DIFFICULT TO BELIEVE GOD WOULD HAVE INTRODUCED SUCH A FOUL BEING INTO CREATION WITHOUT ENDOWING HER WITH SOME VIRTUES, HMMM?"**
>
> William De Baskerville, Name Of The Rose

JOAN OF ARC 1948

Director Victor Fleming *Cast* Ingrid Bergman, José Ferrer

A big budget ($4m) and a big role for Bergman who, although occasionally lapsing into a rather whiny singsong, convinces as the most famous Joan (guided by divine voices and burnt at the stake trying to save France from English dictatorship) in the history of the world. Her devotion to the Dauphin does, though, seem increasingly inexplicable the more ineffectual he becomes in Ferrer's portrayal. This is vastly preferable to Luc Besson's 1999 remake starring Milla Jovovich, who is fine as a 15th century Lara Croft but is out of her depth when she has to wrestle with theology. The finest version, for those who find the story intriguing enough to watch 336 minutes of it, is probably the 1994 two-part *Jeanne La Pucelle*.

KING OF KINGS 1961

Director Nicholas Ray
Cast Jeffrey Hunter, Siobhan McKenna, Robert Ryan

Ray's surprisingly subtle and moving take on the great book makes the average Hollywood biblical epic look about as complex as a religious calendar. It doesn't quite do for the biblical genre what Ray's *Johnny Guitar* did for the western and it lacks the focus on a few characters which marks his best work but this is mercifully free of the doggerel which passes for dialogue in many of these epics. A welcome change.

"Your disguise is complete 007, your mission: to infiltrate this monastery and find the villain stroking a white cat"

THE LAST TEMPTATION OF CHRIST 1988

Director Martin Scorsese *Cast* Willem Dafoe, Harvey Keitel, Barbara Hershey

Let's be quite clear about this: if you're watching this for the sex scene, you'll be deeply disappointed. This is actually a very serious movie about Christ, based on the Nikos Kazantzakis novel, which Scorsese had been wanting to make since 1972. The director pored over old Hollywood epics, art from the *Biblical Archaeology Review* and the paintings of Hieronymus Bosch in his quest to make this film look and feel absolutely right. He had one slice of luck: David Bowie refused to play Pontius Pilate with a Scottish accent, despite Sean Connery's suggestion that that was where the man responsible for the most famous act of hand washing in history was born. This is an imperfect but serious film about the central paradox of Christianity: how could Christ be God and man at the same time?

THE NAME OF THE ROSE 1986

Director Jean-Jacques Annaud *Cast* Sean Connery, Christian Slater, F Murray Abraham

Some critics were a bit sniffy about this little marvel starring Sean Connery as a Franciscan Sherlock Holmes, William De Baskerville, who is attempting, with the help of novice Adso von Melk (Slater), to solve a series of savage murders in a monastery while simultaneously fending off the Holy Inquisition. The plot is not immune to the usual absurdities but any film in which characters get to argue such complex theological issues as whether laughter is a sin against God (and, for that matter, whether Christ himself laughed) is alright by us. The monks are such a fantastic array of grotesques you fear they must imminently return to the Bosch painting from whence they came.

NAZARIN 1958

Director Luis Buñuel *Cast* Francisco Rabal, Marga López, Rita Macedo

Religion and death, Buñuel famously said, had marked him for life. They certainly left an indelible imprint on his film work. In *Viridiana* (1961), he was attacked for sending up *The Last Supper* and in *Simon Del Desierto* (1965) he tells a bizarre tale of a 4th century man who is so desperate to get closer to God he climbs up a column whereupon, for reasons which need not detain us here,

GOD SPEAKS

God has a reputation, largely deserved, for being a bit deep. But when he speaks in the movies, as you can see below, this isn't always the case.

Jesus: What is your name my friend?
James: James. Little James. They call me Little because I'm the youngest. What's yours?
Jesus: Jesus.
James: Ah, that's a good name. Thank you.
THE GREATEST STORY EVER TOLD, 1965

Jesus: My name is Jesus. I come from Nazareth.
Guard: Nazareth? I've not been there for many years. Yet your face is familiar.
Jesus: You once came to our house and spoke to my mother.
Guard: The house of the carpenter – oh yes.
KING OF KINGS, 1961

Jesus: Did I ever tell you I used to read feet?
Jeffrey: You used to... what?
Jesus: Some people read palms or tea leaves. I read feet.
GODSPELL, 1973

Jesus: Tomorrow is my birthday, yet all is not right.
Stan: Your birthday is on Christmas? That sucks, dude!
THE SPIRIT OF CHRISTMAS, 1995

he is whisked to modern New York by the devil. In *Nazarín*, Buñuel's purpose is clearer: to point out how difficult it is for the lapsed priest to live by the laws of Christ. Not as witty as his later masterpieces, this is still a credible work from a director in geographic, political and (almost) professional exile.

THE RAPTURE 1991

Director Michael Tolkin *Cast* Mimi Rogers, Patrick Bauchau, David Duchovny

That rarest of modern American movies: a film that takes the fundamentalist view of the apocalypse seriously. Sharon (Rogers) is a bored phone operator who uses group sex to liven up her routine. And then one night, for reasons that Tolkin makes believable, she calls out in the night to God and is born again. Ensuring the viewer understands that God is definitely out there – it's hard to say much more without giving too much away – the film ends with an apocalypse and Tolkin has the nerve to press things to the only logical conclusion.

THE INFAMOUS FIVE

Towering infernal

They say the devil has the best tunes. Just as well really because he also has the worst movies. Most devilish characters are called Nick or have suggestive names (like Louis Cyphre in *Angel Heart*,

geddit?). Others have a Satanic barnet which isn't a Kevin Keegan perm but hairs sticking up like horns. Our five top screen devils are (in ascending order of demonic energy):

5 JOHN MILTON THE DEVIL'S ADVOCATE

Eye-popping, teeth-flashing, sinister-laughing Pacino is a lawyer who, you guessed it, proves to be the devil.

4 LOUIS CYPHRE ANGEL HEART

De Niro uses a black beard, slicked hair and lighting to make himself look like his favourite

director, Scorsese. A wonderful homage when you consider he's playing Old Nick.

3 DARYL VAN HORNE THE WITCHES OF EASTWICK

Jack Nicholson's satanic charisma completely unbalanced this movie of the John Updike novel. Jack took this role seriously enough to read *St Thomas Aquinas* and pore over Gustave Doré's illustrations for *Dante's Inferno*.

2 GEORGE SPIGGOTT BEDAZZLED (1967)

While Liz Hurley was curvaceously tempting in the remake, there is something delightfully un-Hollywood about Peter Cook's portrayal of the devil as a seedy nightclub owner called George.

1 NICK LEWIS THE PRIVATE LIVES OF ADAM AND EVE

How can you resist a film in which former Andy Hardy actor, Mickey Rooney plays a devil in a snakeskin suit and gives the kind of performance which defines that underrated genre of acting known as 'scenery chewing'.

THE ROBE 1953

Director Henry Koster Cast Richard Burton, Jean Simmons, Victor Mature

Richard Burton's breakthrough film took 10 years (and $4.5m) to make but somehow one of the characters was still permitted to say (of Jesus Christ): "We gotta find out where he holes out at night." Shot in Cinemascope, in Hollywood's vain bid to fight off the threat of television, this film only intrigues because of Burton's performance as the centurion who is converted through the cloak of Christ. Second unit director Henry Klune, who plays Christ, had to eat in his dressing room because he stayed in costume all day and Fox thought it inappropriate to have Jesus eating in the canteen.

"What change is there in me? Egyptian or Hebrew I am still Moses." Uh, not really, Charlton

THE SINGING NUN 1965

Director Henry Koster Cast Debbie Reynolds, Ricardo Montalban

The Catholic church gave its blessing to this disguised biopic of a Belgian nun who rode motor scooters and made hit records; the Pope, being infallible, can't have been consulted. Debbie Reynolds plays the nun (no longer Belgian) and Ricardo Montalban looks as if he's already rehearsing to be the host of *Fantasy Island*. Supposed to be spiritually uplifting, this film's only uplifting effect was to persuade audiences to rise from their seats and run for the exits. It's a miracle that Katharine Ross's performance as a Belgian tramp didn't end her acting career. Nuns also appear to better effect in *The Nun's Story* (with Audrey Hepburn, 1961) and *Two Mules For Sister Sara* (starring Shirley MacLaine). For those whose devotion to women of the cloth knows no bounds there's also *Change Of Habit* (Elvis, Mary Tyler Moore) and *Space Nuns* (1995) about, yes, a nun who's always wanted to fly in space.

"YOU HAVE A RAT'S EARS AND A FERRET'S NOSE!"
Rameses, The Ten Commandments

SOLOMON AND SHEBA 1959

Director King Vidor Cast Yul Brynner, Gina Lollobrigida, George Sanders

Tyrone Power died 60 per cent of the way through this movie to be replaced by the actor formerly known as the King of Siam. (You can still see Power in some long shots.) The film only went ahead because the studio collected $1.1m on the insurance for

Power's death, one of the rare instances when the world would have been better served if the insurer had refused to pay out. He was a wise king, she was, as they said in the markets of old Palestine, no better than she ought to be so they were destined, according to Hollywood rules, to fall in love. Made in Super Technirama-70 by one of Hollywood's legendary directors, it wouldn't have made sense in any format, although the free interactive bible kits used to promote the film in schools were pretty decent. Presumably they didn't dwell on the fact that, as the ads said: "In her [Sheba's] navel is a crescent-shaped ruby which gleams and glitters while she performs the orgiastic dance which ends in her seduction of Solomon." The famous orgy scene cost $100,000 to make but then it did help the film rake in $15m at the box office.

OH FATHER

Ingmar Bergman's dad was a chaplain to the Swedish royal family and a forbidding personality who was incapable of expressing any emotion. You can find the two traits combined in the frightening figure of Bishop Edvard Vergerus in the autobiographical *Fanny And Alexander.* Where a man of the cloth is presented more sympathetically, such as the pastor in *Winter Light (*1957), it is often because they've lost or are losing their faith. Belief in God, it is strongly held, may be equated with personality disorder (Katrin, the schizophrenic at the heart of *Through A Glass Darkly,* comes to believe God is visiting her). And critics complain that hanging over many of his films is the 'Nordic gloom' – the belief that there is little mercy in the world and even littler hope of salvation.

Warner/Guber Peters/Kennedy Miller; Paramount/Cecil B. DeMille

THE TEN COMMANDMENTS 1956

Director Cecil B DeMille Cast Charlton Heston, Yul Brynner, Anne Baxter

You have to have the confidence of the Almighty to take seriously a film in which Nefertiti says to Moses: "Oh Moses, Moses, you stubborn, splendid, adorable fool". Fortunately, DeMille had that confidence and the self-conscious showmanship to make this tale work. That said, even his efforts might have been in vain if his original choice for Moses, William Boyd (Hopalong Cassidy) had accepted the part. Instead, Heston, once described as "the only American who looks good in a toga" plays the first of many authority figures which would include El Cid, King Henry VIII, General Gordon and a colonel who didn't like apes touching him. Robert Vaughn makes his big screen debut (uncredited) as a spearman. Among the other DeMille biblical movies, *Samson And Delilah* is worth watching for the scene where a stunt man stands in for Victor Mature who, strangely, refused to wrestle a toothless lion.

WISE BLOOD 1979

Director John Huston Cast Brad Dourif, Harry Dean Stanton, John Huston

Hazel Motes (Dourif) is a war veteran who returns to the deep south to found the Church Without Christ. Asa Hawks (Stanton) is a blind preacher whom Motes meets and Huston plays Dourif's grandfather preacher in flashbacks. A grim but compelling slice of southern gothic. Motes plays the philosopher king with lines like: "A man don't need justification if he's got a good car."

REMAKES

The phrase "There is nothing new under the sun" is particularly true in movies. Filmmakers continually raid other work for inspiration, ideas, storylines and plot twists. They like to call it paying tribute to films of the past. You could also call it stealing. The original is usually more intriguing than its remake, especially when an offbeat European film gets the Hollywood treatment to overcome the American public's pathological phobia of subtitles.

The movies that emerge from this process have usually been robbed of all their individuality, dumbed down, and often feature a mainstream Hollywood star who thinks they are being artistically daring by doing a project based on a foreign film. However, there are cases where talented directors have taken a dull, recycled story and turn it into something quirky, changing the film's characters, or plot devices, or even genre to make it their own. Some directors even remake their own work, when social or technical advances allow them to make a film more in tune with their original concept.

Since it would be unfair to look only at original movies, and equally so to concentrate on remakes alone, the films below are a mixture, depending on which is the more interesting.

> **"TWO THINGS ARE IMPORTANT IN LIFE: FOR MEN, WOMEN; FOR WOMEN, MONEY"**
> Parvulesco, A Bout Du Souffle

A BOUT DE SOUFFLE 1960

Director Jean-Luc Godard Cast Jean-Paul Belmondo, Jean Seberg
This hugely influential film about a car thief (Belmondo) on the run with his American girlfriend (Seberg) was at the vanguard of the French New Wave, a movement spearheaded by François Truffaut (who conceived the story, even though Goddard wrote the script) and the critics of the Cahiers du Cinéma. Much looser than earlier formulaic, studio-led films, and the subject matter more daring for its day. What is interesting is Belmondo's character's admiration for Humphrey Bogart, down to his imitation of Bogart's nervous lip-wiping, emphasising the idea that the film is a new take on classic Hollywood genres. It was remade as *Breathless* in 1983, with Richard Gere and Valérie Kaprisky, but with the frisson of anti-establishment naughtiness gone. It deservedly sunk without trace.

LA CAGE AUX FOLLES 1978

Director **Edouard Molinaro** *Cast* **Michel Serrault, Ugo Tognazzi**

This perfectly-timed farce about an ageing gay couple, Renato and Albin, forced to conceal their lifestyle when Renato's son announces he is marrying the daughter of a right-wing politician, went Hollywood in 1996 (*The Birdcage*) with Mike Nichols directing and Robin Williams and Nathan Lane in the leading roles. The remake was nearly saved by Lane's brilliant performance and the character of the hopeless Latino house boy (Hank Azaria), but the plot was just too dated by then to really succeed. The original may have done nothing to dispel gay stereotypes but it still stands up as one of the funniest French comedies ever.

THE CHAMP 1931

Director **King Vidor** *Cast* **Wallace Beery, Jackie Cooper**

One of the all-time great weepies about a young boy's relationship with his father, a down-on-his-luck ex-prizefighter who gambles and drinks, but would do anything for his son. When his ex-wife appears back on the scene the stage is set for family drama, Hollywood-style. Beery, despite looking hopelessly out of shape in his comeback fight, won an Oscar (he shared it with Fredric March for *Dr Jekyll And Mr Hyde*) for this role, and Cooper, here at the height of his prolific child star career, made excellent use of his ability to weep buckets on demand. The film was remade in 1979 by Franco Zeffirelli with Jon Voight and Ricky Schroder, with Faye Dunaway as the mother. Despite being stunning visually, the newer version trips self-consciously on the transplanted 1930s sentimentality, and never reaches the tissue-soaking heights of the original.

MILLER'S CROSSING 1990

Director **Joel Coen** *Cast* **Gabriel Byrne, Marcia Gay Harden**

The Coen brothers' terrific tribute to film noir features one of their trademark complex plots about a scheming young political advisor caught in the shifting loyalties between two crime bosses when a war erupts over a bookie who has been cheating one of them. Its plot was inspired by the 1942 film *The Glass Key*, based on a Dashiell Hammett story and starring Alan Ladd, Veronica Lake and Brian Donlevy (an even earlier version featured George Raft and Claire Dodd). The Coens' version is much harsher with Gabriel Byrne as the utterly callous manipulator, running rings around the other characters, even though he doesn't really gain anything from it himself. There are flashes of the blackest humour like the scene where a gang is being ripped to shreds by machine gun fire to the strains of

Danny Boy. The stalwart Coen supporting cast of Steve Buscemi and Jon Turturro add their own offbeat dimension to the film.

OSSESSIONE 1942

Director Luchino Visconti *Cast* Clara Calamai, Massimo Girotti

James M Cain's novel, *The Postman Always Rings Twice*, has had two versions made in America, the 1946 film noir with Lana Turner and John Garfield and the 1981 Bob Rafelson version with Jessica Lange and Jack Nicholson. In this rarely-seen

Gabriel Byrne makes a living "intimidating helpless women". Someone's got to do it...

version, the tale of a drifter who falls for a discontented wife and helps murder her husband, gets the Italian treatment, and becomes a compelling and powerful sexual melodrama. Elio Marcuzzo is perfect as Giovanna's fat older husband, and Visconti is at his best in his big scene, the opera singing contest, a masterpiece of filmmaking. *Ossessione* is also credited with starting the Italian neo-realism movement, whose films were a reaction to the fascist era and dealt with modern subjects and a desire for social change, and in fact the negative of this film was destroyed by Mussolini's police. Visconti managed to save a single print, which is why the movie is still occasionally seen today.

OUTLAND 1981

Director Peter Hyams *Cast* Sean Connery, Frances Sternhagen

You can almost hear the pitch meeting – "It's *High Noon*, only in space" – and you might think, when you'd finished cringing, that such an idea could never reach the big screen. Well, amazingly it did, and even more amazingly, it's a really tight, entertaining sci-fi thriller, with excellent performances and a great atmosphere. Fred Zinneman's classic western about a sheriff abandoned by his townspeople when crooks call in to take revenge, becomes a story of a space mining colony run by a grasping boss who encourages his men to take performance-enhancing drugs so they can produce more. Eventually the drugs send them mad (as with the miner who walks out of an airlock without his space suit on, yuck) and the boss hires assassins to kill the new marshal (Connery) when he says he'll stop the practice. There are lots of clever nods to the film's origins, including the saloon-style swinging doors on the space station bar, and the macho, isolated world of the miners mirrors the other frontier perfectly.

> "ALL IN ALL NOT A BAD GUY – IF LOOKS, BRAINS AND PERSONALITY DON'T COUNT"
>
> Tom Reagan, Miller's Crossing

SABRINA 1954

Director Billy Wilder *Cast* Audrey Hepburn, Humphrey Bogart, William Holden

A classic case of Hollywood raiding its own back catalogue badly was the 1995 remake of Billy Wilder's romantic classic, with Harrison Ford and Julia Ormond. A chauffeur's daughter is in love with a rich playboy, but is persuaded to fall for his older brother. As hard as the new film tries to get round the fact that the story relies heavily on the social set up of the 1950s, it just doesn't work. The original remains a joy. Bogart overcomes miscasting and his famed antipathy to Hepburn (he wanted wife Lauren Bacall to play the role), to be surprisingly convincing as a romantic comedy lead. The script sparkles and Hepburn floats around in various glorious Givenchy creations.

THE SEVEN SAMURAI 1954

Director Akira Kurosawa *Cast* Takashi Shimura, Toshiro Mifune

A rare example of a story where the remake and the original are equally good, if for quite different reasons. Kurosawa's brilliant tale of a good-hearted samurai who recruits six others to help defend a small town under constant attack from bandits, was transplanted to America where it became John Sturges's *The Magnificent Seven*. The US version is a hugely entertaining, about a bunch of men who come together to protect the weak and helpless. (Let's just pretend that *Return of the Magnificent Seven* never existed.) The Japanese original is less sure of its message and more interested in its characters. It's an absorbing and violent drama where the samurai fight to regain their honour, and the deal between them and the townspeople is complicated by class distinction. Kurosawa also explores filmmaking as an art, with vivid imagery, making it an emotional and visual masterpiece.

TROIS HOMMES ET UN COUFFIN 1985
THREE MEN AND A CRADLE

Director Coline Serreau *Cast* Roland Giraud, Michel Boujenah, André Dussollier

The American remake of this immaculate French farce, *Three Men And A Baby* (the three men being Steve Guttenberg, Ted Danson and Tom Selleck or, wait, was one of them the baby?) was likeable and genuinely funny, unlike its woeful sequel *Three Men And A Little Lady*. The French original is quieter and more touching, especially as these men are not well off (in the US version you can't

"OK, the remake has some striking imagery but Wim's composition is breathtaking"

help thinking the rich bachelors should just hire a nanny), and must care for the baby themselves. The drug sub-plot gives the film pace and it is worth seeing for the hysterical first half alone.

WINGS OF DESIRE 1987 DER HIMMEL UBER BERLIN
Director Wim Wenders *Cast* Bruno Ganz, Solveig Dommartin, Peter Falk

Wenders's masterpiece about an angel who loves a mortal and wishes to become human, was remade 11 years later as *City of Angels*, with Nicolas Cage and Meg Ryan. The original, with Ganz's Damiel wandering around Berlin comforting unhappy souls until he sees a trapeze artist and falls in love, is not a linear story with a build up and payoff, more an incredibly moving exploration of what it means to be human, to experience physical life, to suffer and to know joy. Falk has a pivotal role as a fallen angel, but it is Ganz's gentle melancholy that makes the film. The well made American version has striking imagery, but it simply can't compete with Wenders's breathtaking composition and Henri Alekan's sumptuous photography.

DEJA VU ALL OVER AGAIN
A TALE OF TWO PSYCHOS

In 1998 Gus Van Sant released a new version of Alfred Hitchcock's classic thriller *Psycho*. Van Sant's film stars Ann Heche as the doomed Marion Crane with Vince Vaughn as Norman Bates, as well as William H Macey and Julianne Moore in supporting roles. This rendition (Van Sant actively opposes calling it a remake) is a shot by shot copy, sorry, homage, to the original. Why, you may ask?

Van Sant even has a walk-on part, talking to a Hitchcock lookalike in the scene outside Marion's office where Hitch himself appeared in the original. Surely the point of remakes is to do something more interesting or relevant for the time with the original premise?

Actually, many film fans support this type of experiment as they feel that remaking a classic is a way to study and pay tribute to the work of the original filmmaker, as well as providing a better understanding of the original by having something with which to compare it. Certainly elements of Van Sant's film shed interesting light on the original, but

these are mainly where he diverges from it. In the scene where Norman is spying on Marion, there is now a sound effect of Vaughn masturbating, adding to the tension and changing Norman's sexuality.

The main problem the new version faces is that the actors are not the same. Vaughn is gifted but hamstrung by Van Sant reproducing camera angles that were designed to make the most of Anthony Perkins' odd looks. This is most obvious in the scene where the detective checks the register. Perkins was shot from below for part of the scene, emphasising the movement of his very prominent adam's apple as he swallows nervously. Vaughn is a much stockier actor (which also begs the question of how he fits into his mum's dresses), without such a skinny neck, so that camera angle is wasted on him. The new version of *Psycho* is not bad by any means, but while watching it, you might find yourself wondering what, exactly, the point was.

ROAD

The road trip is very much an American rite of passage. Whether it's strangers sharing a ride like *Boys On The Side* (1995), a family escaping poverty as in *The Grapes Of Wrath* (1940), or a couple on the run from the law as in Nicholas Ray's story of doomed love, *They Live By Night* (1948), packing up the car and heading out of town is always the start of something. A road movie can feature any of the above, although the classic is a couple at odds with society who embrace life on the road for the freedom it allows them. Or, as in *Easy Rider*, because they like to drive very fast.

The road movie appeals to filmmakers for the same reason: the chance to make full use of the camera, from intense, claustrophobic exchanges inside the vehicle to vast panoramas of stunning landscapes. Characters' journeys can be funny – think of the late, great John Candy playing with the car seat controls in *Planes, Trains And Automobiles* (1987); violent – in Sam Peckinpah's *Bring Me The Head Of Alfredo Garcia*, the splatter escalates with every mile covered; dull – *Stranger Than Paradise*, with Jim Jarmusch's long, longshots of people driving to Florida or just plain weird – Kathryn Bigelow's vampire bus movie, *Near Dark* (1987) but the road remains a constant companion, almost, you could say, a character in itself.

Road movies are essentially a post-war phenomenon because World War II caused America to build the interstate motorways that have played host to film fantasies ever since. Not all great road movies are American but America does them best, with huge, boat-like convertibles sailing down endless highways to who knows where. And don't forget, that in a true road movie, you never reach your destination, if you ever had one in the first place. Easy, rider.

In *Easy Rider*, they've all gone to look for America, oblivious to the fact that Paul Simon's got it

200 MOTELS 1971

Director Tony Palmer, Frank Zappa *Cast* Frank Zappa

Crazy, wandering tale of a rock group on tour, interspersed with music performances and based on the experiences of The Mothers of Invention·and their overwhelming desire to get laid and paid. There's rather more movie than road in this, as it's basically a series of random scenes taking place as the group tours the country. Persevering with all the weirdness (trippy camerawork and bizarre imagery) will reward you with hilarious cameos from Ringo Starr, Keith Moon and Theodore Bickel.

THE ADVENTURES OF PRISCILLA, QUEEN OF THE DESERT 1996

Director Stephan Elliott *Cast* Hugo Weaving, Guy Pearce, Terence Stamp

Three drag queens, or rather two and a transsexual, hired to perform at a resort in Alice Springs, buy a bus, the eponymous Priscilla, and drive themselves across the country, encountering Aborigines and gay bashers along the way. Unashamedly camp, with more rhinestones and feathers than a Danny La Rue retrospective, the three friends sing, dance and bitch their way through Australia's stunning outback, astounding the locals wherever they go. Along the way, they meet a Thai exotic dancer whose striptease, which includes a gimmick that only a real woman could perform, is one of the film's funniest moments.

> "BEING A MAN ONE DAY AND A WOMAN THE NEXT IS NOT AN EASY THING"
> Bernadette, The Adventures Of Priscilla, Queen Of The Desert

THE CANNONBALL RUN 1981

Director Hal Needham *Cast* Burt Reynolds, Roger Moore

Comedy caper movie with an all-star cast about an illegal cross-country car race. Reynolds and Moore are joined by Farrah Fawcett, Dom DeLuise, Peter Fonda and even Jackie Chan as all these eccentrics proceed to speed, cheat and backstab their way through the wide-open spaces of America. Stupid but fun, and even if you hate it, you can always play the 'count the stars who still have careers' game. Shouldn't take you long.

THE DOOM GENERATION 1995

Director Gregg Araki *Cast* James Duval, Rose McGowan

Araki's favourite theme of troubled teens. Jordan White and Amy Blue pick up a drifter, Xavier Red, and together they embark on a crime spree and sexual triangle. What humour there is, is of the blackest kind, so much so that it sometimes misses the mark, but no one can deny the impact of the film with its gore, out-there dialogue and tortured characters. Self-consciously trashy, fast-paced, violent and sexy, this is one for viewers who like to concentrate and also have a strong stomach.

DUEL 1971

Director **Steven Spielberg** *Cast* **Dennis Weaver**

Spielberg's brilliant TV movie put him on the map in terms of filmmaking, and deservedly so. This is a road trip gone horribly wrong, with Weaver's businessman being harassed by the malevolent driver of a tanker after he tries to pass him on a stretch of open highway. The tension created by one man (we never see the face of the truck driver) and two vehicles is astounding and will have you on the edge of your seat throughout. If you think any of your own encounters with road rage are scary, watch this and think again.

FALLING DOWN 1993

Director **Joel Schumacher** *Cast* **Michael Douglas, Robert Duvall**

On a blistering LA morning, Douglas abandons his car in the middle of a traffic jam, and begins to walk from one side of the city to the other, trying to reach his ex-wife and their daughter on her birthday. He carries a briefcase, containing nothing but the sandwiches his mother has made for him, having been made redundant some time earlier. Michael Douglas is brilliant, that's right, Michael Douglas is brilliant as the disenfranchised loner on his violent odyssey, and Duvall plays the about-to-retire policeman who tries to track him down. The scene in the burger bar is worth watching the whole film for, although the gun dealer who thinks Douglas is doing a great job as a vigilante, makes you suspect that this is a scarily accurate portrait of America's dark side.

Columbia/Pando/Raybert; Paramount; Channel Four Films

"Is it true that the length of a man's pipe is directly proportional to the length of his...? "Sadly, Dorothy no"

GET ON THE BUS 1996

Director **Spike Lee**
Cast **Richard Belzer, De'aundre Bonds**

Lee's film follows a ragged busload of African American men travelling from Los Angeles to Washington for the 1996 million man march, pledging to be better husbands and fathers. A mixed bunch, there is the father (whose son is shackled to him as a condition of his parole) who hopes this will improve their relationship, the callous salesman, the actor, the policeman and so on. All these men have different hopes for the march, and different stories to tell. Beautifully observed, paced and acted.

THE GODS MUST BE CRAZY 1980
Director Jamie Uys *Cast* N!Xau, Marius Weyers, Sandra Prinsloo
A Kalahari bushman, Xixo, finds a Coca-Cola bottle and brings it to his tribe where they believe it has been sent by the gods. When the tribes-people start squabbling over it, Xixo decides to return it to the gods by throwing it off the end of the world. On his journey, he encounters modern life for the first time, including a school-teacher, a socially inept scientist and a tyrannical despot. The movie pokes fun at modern society as seen through the eyes of a more innocent person. Xixo's travels go from broad slapstick to savage satire in moments.

KINGS OF THE ROAD 1976 IM LAUF DER ZEIT
Director Wim Wenders *Cast* Rüdiger Vogler, Hanns Zischler
The last, and best, of Wenders's road trilogy (the others being *Alice In The Cities* and *Wrong Move*) tells the story of Bruno and Robert, two friends who travel the often deserted roads of the border between East and West Germany, repairing old cinema projectors. The shadow of post-war American cultural imperialism looms large over the whole film, both in the 'border country' setting and the stretches of open highway, as well as in the theme of the decline of the German film industry (symbolized by broken projectors), trampled on by Hollywood. Deliberately slow and introspective, the characters don't get anywhere, but somehow it's still both absorbing and moving.

"THIS SNAKE-SKIN JACKET SYMBOLIZES MY INDIVIDUALITY AND BELIEF IN PERSONAL FREEDOM"
Sailor, Wild At Heart

ROAD TO UTOPIA 1946
Director Hal Walker *Cast* Bing Crosby, Bob Hope, Dorothy Lamour
It was only after producer Harlan Thompson saw Crosby and Hope fooling around on the Paramount lot he decided they would be perfect to replace Fred MacMurray and George Burns in his *Road To...* movies. Dorothy Lamour was added as the love interest and the series eventually spanned seven movies, (although Lamour, to her annoyance, was replaced by Joan Collins in the final film). The *Road To Utopia* and the *Road To Morocco* are the best of the lot. Forced to swap their usual exotic sunny climate for arctic temperatures in Alaska, Crosby and Hope play Chester and Duke, out (as usual) to seek their fortune. Luckily discovering a treasure map, they disguise themselves as thugs to blend in to Alaskan society, but find themselves in farcical peril. Unadulterated fun, the film boasts Hope's classic line: "I'll have a lemonade. In a dirty glass."

THE STRAIGHT STORY 1999

Director David Lynch *Cast* Richard Farnsworth, Sissy Spacek

Gentle and sweet film, based on a true story about an old man who drove for six weeks on a ride-on lawnmower in order to visit his sick brother. Farnsworth plays Alvin Straight, a man who cannot be dissuaded from his journey, no matter how many offers of help he gets from people along the way. Fans of Lynch who expect the lawnmower to burst into flames, or Alvin to suddenly develop a healthy sexual perversion or a bizarre hairstyle, will be disappointed. This is the director at his lyrical, thoughtful best – still concerned with people's underlying quirks, their individuality and personal stories, and Middle America in general, but leaving his more twisted territory alone for a while. Farnsworth, an ex-stuntman who used to double for Roy Rogers and Gary Cooper, is a joy as Alvin and deserved his Oscar nomination for the role. Sadly he committed suicide last year after receiving a diagnosis of terminal cancer.

THELMA AND LOUISE 1991

Director Ridley Scott *Cast* Geena Davis, Susan Sarandon

"LOOK, YOU SHOOT OFF A GUY'S HEAD WITH HIS PANTS DOWN, BELIEVE ME, TEXAS IS NOT THE PLACE YOU WANT TO BE"

Louise Sawyer , Thelma And Louise

Groundbreaking feminist buddy movie, or exploitative piece of cinematic styling? Whatever your take on Scott's lavish production about two women on the run in southwest America after one of them kills an attempted rapist when a weekend away goes horribly wrong, it's impossible to deny that it's a stunning film, beautifully acted, with an Oscar-winning script from Callie Khouri that subtly conveys everything you need to know about these women – their backgrounds, hopes and disappointments – without beating the audience over the head with it all. Delicious scenes include Thelma's boorish husband (Christopher McDonald) trying to be nice to her on the phone, and Harvey Keitel verbally beating up Brad Pitt for seriously escalating the women's problems after his night of passion with Thelma. All this, along with the breathtaking cinematography, makes for a truly wonderful movie.

TWO FOR THE ROAD 1967

Director Stanley Donen *Cast* Albert Finney, Audrey Hepburn

Finney and Hepburn travel from London to the South of France three times – once as poor students falling in love, once as newlyweds, accompanied by an obnoxious pair of friends and their spoilt child, and once as an older couple, bored with each other and their marriage. What makes the film especially interesting, apart from Frederic Raphael's sparkling script, is that these three journeys are all intercut with each other, so, for example, when the older couple's smart car passes two hitchhikers, they are quickly revealed to be the younger versions of themselves, trying to flag a lift. The shifting time frame is done simply by changing hairstyles, cars and the expressions on the faces of the leads, and as the French landscape rolls by, so do the 12 years of marriage that have brought them to this make or break point. Like life, it is sometimes funny, sometimes cynical, but usually entertaining.

TWO LANE BLACKTOP
1971
Director Monte Hellman
Cast James Taylor, Warren Oates

Suffering from tremendous hype when released, *Blacktop* disappointed critics who were expecting an offbeat, but still mainstream, masterpiece along the lines of *Easy Rider*. It soon sank without a trace, but not before gathering a small band of enthusiastic fans who still hail it as the road movie that puts all the others in the shade. It deals with a cross-country race between an alienated driver with his silent mechanic (Dennis Wilson, drummer for the Beach Boys) and GTO, a character of the road, that gets disrupted by The Girl, a hippie hitchhiker. The winner of the race is supposed to get the other's car but the race is about more than winning, in this existential study of life on the road and what it means to the men, the woman and society at large. Hellman makes extraordinary use of his camera, with mesmerising down shots of the road markings flashing by, and experimental elements like the melting celluloid at the end.

Who would have thought that David Lynch could direct a story as straight as this? You keep waiting for a woman to appear nursing a log for no apparent reason or an owl called Bob...

WILD AT HEART 1990
Director David Lynch Cast Nicholas Cage, Laura Dern

Before Cage became a mainstream Hollywood lead, he was the darling of independent filmmakers, and *Wild At Heart* marked the peak of his alternative career. He plays Sailor, in love with Lula (Dern), but hated by her crazed mother (Diane Ladd, Dern's real-life mother in a gift of a role). Lula and Sailor take off in his convertible on a journey that could be in hell, or along the Yellow Brick Road, peppered with car wrecks, ex-lovers and the usual bunch of Lynch crazies and dropouts. Spiced with plenty of black humour, explicit gore and the dirtiest kind of sex, the film teeters on the edge of parody - of the road movie, of all 'outsider' films, and of Lynch's own work. When Lula says it's all "wild at heart and weird on top", she's not wrong.

ROCK

It's a toss up as to which has been the most insignificant: rock music's contribution to the movies or the movies' contribution to rock music. For every *Stop Making Sense* there's been a *Can't Stop The Music*. Most baffling of all: the number of directors who felt their films just weren't complete without Herman's Hermits.

A HARD DAY'S NIGHT 1964

Director **Richard Lester** *Cast* **The Beatles, Wilfrid Brambell**

Painful as it is to admit, for those of us who grew up with rock music, you can count the number of truly great movies with rock musicians in on the fingers of one hand – if you've lost three of your fingers. Yes, this is it. Part of the charm is that Lester has the guts to make a movie in the Beatles' own image The fab four were given one-liners in the screenplay but they often used their own. Shot on $500,000, half the money spent on Elvis' *Kissin Cousins*, released the same year, this is a marvellous record of springtime for the Beatles, (if it's winter you're after, try *Let It Be*) and very funny.

CAN'T STOP THE MUSIC 1980

Director **Nancy Walker** *Cast* **The Village People, Valerie Perrine, Steve Guttenberg**

Never let anyone kid you that *Saturday Night Fever* is the quintessential disco movie. The quintessential disco movie doesn't worry about such things as plot, character, narrative (all of which *Fever* has - plus the Bee Gees!) but focuses on disco music. Such a film is *Can't Stop The Music*, directed by the woman who played Rhoda's mum on TV. The film's 'true story' of the Village People would be, well, true if it dared to admit they were gay. For all its many flaws, this film is not without genuinely scary moments, especially the scene in the record shop where people are queuing up to buy an ELO album.

THE DECLINE OF WESTERN CIVILISATION PART II: THE METAL YEARS 1988

Director **Penelope Spheeris** *Cast* **Aerosmith, Kiss**

In 1992 Spheeris gave us *Wayne's World*. Four years before, she made this, the second (neglected) part of what became a "Decline-Of" documentary trilogy. Spheeris sticks the camera in the face of heavy metal and comes up giggling as such lipstick metallers as Poison and Megadeth's Dave Mustaine strut and pout as though *Spinal Tap* hadn't been invented in 1984. Ozzy Osbourne, in full 1980s excess mode, provides a commentary, clad in what looks like the wife's best dressing gown, in his kitchen, with his eyeliner running. His laconic remarks on the young guitar poodle generation are spot-on.

GENGHIS BLUES 1999

Director Roko Belic

Paul Peña, a blind blues musician, makes a pilgrimage to Tuva, in Mongolia, to attend the annual throat-singing contest. This may sound like a missing *Ripping Yarns* episode, but it's actually a lovely, warm and moving film. Throat-singing, if you don't know, is a technique whereby singers isolate their vocal chords and sing harmony with themselves, so it sounds as though more than one person is singing. After hearing a Russian broadcast of it on his shortwave radio, Peña decides to learn all about it himself. His fascinating journey culminates with him being taught the technique. The culture clash between Kyzyl (Tuva's capital) and San Francisco makes for some very funny moments along the way, and the singing is astounding.

HARDER THEY COME 1973

Director Perry Henzell Cast Jimmy Cliff, Janet Bartley,

Cliff plays Ivan Martin a small-town boy who heads to Kingston seeking fame and fortune as a singer. Rejected for refusing to sign his rights away, he turns to a life of crime, but when he kills a police officer, he becomes a hero to the masses. Marketed as a blaxploitation film, this was too original to score with those who wanted another *Shaft*. Even without the reggae score, it would be a good film. With songs from Cliff, Desmond Dekker and the Melodians this becomes a classic.

HEAD 1968

Director Bob Rafelson Cast The Monkees, Victor Mature,

Plotless collaboration between the prefab four, Rafelson and Jack Nicholson, which took in a grand $16,000 at the US box office. From the moment Mickey Dolenz tries to jump off a bridge, the movie jumps, hither and thither, while the Monkees happily sign their own death warrant as teen idols. The dialogue, the weird cameos (from Victor Mature to Sonny Liston) and the music are all groovy. Ironically, for a band that began as a Beatles rip-off, this is the drug-fuelled, free-form

> "HE'S VERY FUSSY ABOUT HIS DRUMS YOU KNOW, THEY LOOM LARGE IN HIS LEGEND"
>
> George, A Hard Day's Night

MGM

Elvis can't find a partner or a wooden chair but still seems to be enjoying himself in the days before he was obliged to sing *Queenie Wahine's Papaya* to make an honest crust

film the real Fab Four never got to make. That said, it is also very hard to watch all the way through unless you're using the same chemicals as the people who were making it.

HEARTS OF FIRE 1987

Director Richard Marquand *Cast* Bob Dylan, Fiona, Rupert Everett
Proof that Dylan could make a film as bad as any of Elvis's. Something's happenin' here but neither we or the cast have a clue what. Fiona is a pop star who gets advice from Everett and Dylan, who has become a chicken farmer in Pennsylvania so profound is his disgust with the business. Fans would be better served by *Renaldo And Clara*, although His Bobness does recommend that you only watch it when stoned.

JAILHOUSE ROCK 1958

Director Richard Thorpe *Cast* Elvis Presley, Judy Tyler
Gene Kelly was in the wings applauding as they filmed the title number. This (and its successor *King Creole*) were as close as Elvis got to film noir in 30 musicals. The King comes good at the end but for most of the film, after he's sent down for killing a man while defending a woman's honour, he's the perfect heel. His cellmate is played by Mickey Shaughnessy, an odd choice as he had made a living with a nightclub act taking Presley apart. As Elvis' manager, he gets the star to sign away 50 per

cent of his earnings, the same percentage the real Elvis would later give Colonel Parker on some of his income.

LENINGRAD COWBOYS GO AMERICA 1989

Director Aki Kaurismäki Cast Matti Pellonpää, Kari Väänänen

Hopelessly crazed and hilarious film about a Finnish rock band that travel to America in search of fame and fortune and aiming to reach Mexico. Resplendent in huge quiffs and clown-like winklepickers, they are possibly the most pathetic rock band ever to tour the States, lurching from one mishap to another, whether it's the village idiot who has followed them from Finland hoping to join the band, their failed revolt against their overbearing Russian manager who refuses them any money to buy food, or having the engine stolen out of their Cadillac (sold to them by Jim Jarmusch). The Leningrad Cowboys discover an America that is a stream of run-down gasworks, seedy strip malls and devoid of any charm whatsoever.

RADIO ON 1979

Director Christopher Petit Cast David Beames, Lisa Kreuzer

The film all good wearers of long, grey overcoats had to see or face social exclusion. On paper, it looks utterly pretentious – a picaresque black-and-white drift through sullied, late 1970s/early 1980s England in the company of a (reasonably) hip young gunslinger (Beames) who sets off in search of what sounds like a very dodgy brother after he receives a parcel of music tapes from said sibling, last seen in the Bristol area. But it isn't. From the music (Kraftwerk, Lene Lovich, Robert Fripp) to the architecture (the Temple Meads flyover! The quarry that looks like the one where they used to film *Dr Who!*) and the cars (Sting is good as an Eddie Cochran-obsessed garage attendant), it glows.

SID AND NANCY 1986

Director Alex Cox Cast Gary Oldman, Chloe Webb

This is the "Peter Pan version" of the lives of Sid Vicious and Nancy Spungen according to Johnny Rotten. Which makes you wonder which version of Peter Pan Mr Rotten Snr regaled the Rotten household with. Cox now feels the ending (where the couple's ghosts take a taxi ride into the sunset) was too romantic but almost everything else in this film stacks up as the punk paramours descend into heroin hell. Courtney Love has a small part as one of Nancy's friends. Julien Temple's *The Great Rock 'N' Roll Swindle* is also worth a look but Cox's film is a work of brilliance and rare compassion.

STARDUST 1974

Director Michael Apted *Cast* David Essex, Adam Faith

In the early 1970s, Essex appeared in two films about fictional rock star Jim Maclaine (this is the second) which, dated as they sometimes seem now, still have moments of real power and humour. Maclaine's rise, isolation and fall become the archetypal rock story in music journalist Ray Connolly's script. And Essex makes Maclaine so charming and likeable he retains our sympathy even when his life vanishes into a pile of drugs. After this, Essex retired from acting to make films like *Silver Dream Racer* which, on this evidence, was a small pity.

STOP MAKING SENSE 1984

Director Jonathan Demme *Cast* Talking Heads

One of the many interesting things about this rockumentary is how critics invariably compare Talking Heads presiding genius David Byrne to a different dancer from Hollywood's golden age (Fred Astaire and Donald O' Connor are most often cited), as if dancing on the walls and ceiling was a Talking Heads stunt before the Heads were invented. Demme avoids most of the devices which slow similar efforts (tedious crowd reaction shots and meaningless band interviews) focusing on the music and the geeky quirkiness of Byrne. Compulsory viewing in its time, compelling viewing today. Scorsese's *The Last Waltz* comes close to this but Byrne is more charismatic than Robbie Robertson.

> "I'LL NEVER LOOK LIKE BARBIE. BARBIE DOESN'T HAVE BRUISES"
>
> Nancy Spungen, Sid And Nancy

WHEN THE BOYS MEET THE GIRLS 1965

Director Alvin Ganzer *Cast* Connie Francis, Harve Presnell

Probably the best movie ever made to star Connie Francis, Liberace, Louis Armstrong and Herman's Hermits. Francis and her pa open a nightclub which, thin as it is, is all the excuse this film needs to showcase the musical talents of Liberace, Satchmo and the Hermits. Francis and Presnell duet on *I Got Rhythm*, but the exercise serves to prove only that they haven't.

WOODSTOCK 1970

Director Michael Wadleigh

The film was made on a hunch. Wadleigh felt Woodstock might be more than a run-of-the-mill rock concert so he cobbled together a production team at the last minute and headed to upstate New York. The director's cut is, for once, a genuine bonus with more footage of Janis Joplin and of Jimi Hendrix's famous version of *The Star Spangled Banner*. This is a historical snapshot of an age when people thought music could change society and when the musicians didn't change their act for the cameras. Watch it and find yourself making the peace sign.

ROMANCE

Most films have a love story buried somewhere within them, whether they are westerns, horror movies or sci-fi. It seems we just really like stories that end with people getting together. It's cinematic wish-fulfilment at its most obvious and lucrative.

The first close-up screen kiss was featured in *The Widow Jones* (1896), a two-minute short recreating the final scene of a popular stage musical. A journal of the day branded the film "absolutely disgusting", but it was still the Edison Company's most popular release of the year. From then on, romance was big box office and films like *The Sheik* (1921), starring Rudolph Valentino, packed women into the cinemas – women who went on to make huge stars out of romantic leading men like Clark Gable, Ronald Colman, Errol Flynn, Cary Grant and Rock Hudson.

The golden age of Hollywood was also the golden age of romantic drama, with melodramatic films of love and loss, like those from director Douglas Sirk, made to satisfy a hungry, eager audience. But as the 1960s wore on, audiences stopped believing a wedding ring was the answer to all their problems, and romantic films became more troubled, depicting relationships that were far from straightforward in films like *The Graduate*.

Today, a romantic film is most likely to be a comedy, and if it came out of Hollywood, most likely to star Meg Ryan. *When Harry Met Sally* is the perfect example of a sassy modern film with an unashamedly slushy ending. Although British love stories like *Notting Hill* have made a mark, European filmmakers can't believe in romance anymore, as even that was finished with American money. Still, if it's a love affair you're after – traditional and comforting and chock-full of grand gestures, or offbeat and modern with none of the trappings of conventional love – you will find it at the movies.

Buena Vista/Cecchi Gori/Tiger/Pentafilm/Mediterraneo/Blue Dahlia/Canal

"I thought this was a dystopian sci-fi film called *The Postman* with Kevin Costner"

A MATTER OF LIFE AND DEATH 1946

Directors Michael Powell, Emeric Pressburger Cast David Niven, Kim Hunter, Raymond Massey

A young British fighter pilot, Peter, talks to a female radio operator, June, as his burning plane heads towards the English Channel. Miraculously, he is washed up alive, but it turns out his escape is a mistake when Heavenly Conductor 71, played deliciously by Marius Goring, shows up to escort him to heaven. So begins a debate about heaven and earth, life and death, and the power of love to overcome fate. Not only is the story truly original and hugely entertaining but the technical brilliance of the film is breathtaking. Heaven is shot in black and white, with earth in saturated technicolour, and whenever Goring appears, all the earthbound characters and movement, bar Peter, freeze, even a mid-air ping pong ball. Such stunning effects don't look ropey, even today. A profound influence on Scorsese (the restored version carries the words: "Presented by Martin Scorsese") and simply one of the best films of all time.

BRIEF ENCOUNTER 1945

Director David Lean Cast Celia Johnson, Trevor Howard

A happily married housewife meets a handsome stranger, also married, on a station platform. Over the course of a few more weekly meetings, they fall desperately in love, even though they know nothing can happen between them. Although this is a romance from another era, it has lost none of its poignancy and both Johnson and Howard are so sincere in their performances that the slightly dated dialogue hardly registers. It's an expanded version of a Noel Coward one-act play, and as with so many of his stories, is imbued with a certain kind of British clipped restraint, all the while hinting at the repressed passion lurking within the middle class English soul. You'll never look at a station waiting room the same way again.

> "I USED TO BREAK INTO PET SHOPS TO LIBERATE THE CANARIES BUT I DECIDED THAT WAS AN IDEA WAY BEFORE ITS TIME. ZOOS ARE FULL, PRISON IS OVERFLOWING... OH MY, HOW THE WORLD STILL DEARLY LOVES A CAGE"
>
> Maude, Harold And Maude

CYRANO DE BERGERAC 1990

Director Jean-Paul Rappeneau Cast Gérard Depardieu, Anne Brochet, Vincent Perez

This is based on one of the all-time great love stories, which inspired several film adaptations as well as a number of movies that lifted the plot and gave it a new set of characters (*Roxanne* and *The Truth About Cats And Dogs*, to name just two). This luscious adaptation of Rostand's play is the definitive version, with Depardieu in the performance

Just an everyday love story, a blind artist and a punk who wants to star in a circus

of his career as the hulking, big-nosed rabble-rouser with the soul of a poet (his final scene is a tour-de-force of astounding power), and Brochet and Perez perfectly cast as the prettier, shallower couple, whose love Brochet stage manages despite being in love with Brochet himself. Beautifully shot and acted, and infused with unexpected humour, heartbreaking passion and, of course, old-fashioned Gallic panache.

GONE WITH THE WIND 1939

Director **Victor Fleming** *Cast* **Vivien Leigh, Clark Gable**

David O Selznick's stunning adaptation of Margaret Mitchell's Civil War novel is among the highest box office earners of all time, confirming that audiences still hope Scarlett's romance with Rhett will eventually run smooth. A technical triumph in its day, with ambitious use of colour, lavish scenes of luxury and wartime tragedy (the famous scene of the wounded soldiers at the railway yard remains hugely impressive), it's also a ripping, romantic yarn of the first order, as it would have to be to keep an audience happy for over three and a half hours. George Cukor was the original director, but was replaced by Fleming when leading man Gable complained he was paying too much attention to the female stars. The film has come under attack for its portrayal of the black characters and its attitude to slavery, so if you're interested in filmmaking but uncomfortable with the racial issues, watch the film and then read Alice Randall's brilliant parody, *The Wind Done Gone*.

HAROLD AND MAUDE 1972

Director **Hal Ashby** *Cast* **Ruth Gordon, Bud Cort**

Strange and wonderful black comedy about a young man who repeatedly stages his own suicide before falling in love with a 79-year-old woman, who is so in love with life that his nihilistic angst seems petty in comparison. Maude lives in a railway carriage, steals cars for fun, and expresses a desire to become a sunflower, while all the time encouraging Harold to see his life as

---

NUPTIAL GIGS

HERE COMES THE BRIDE!
Filmmakers love a really romantic wedding. Or a truly disastrous one.

BETSY'S WEDDING (1990)
Alan Alda and Joe Pesci's competitive fathers ruin their children's wedding day. If it can go wrong, it does, and more besides.

FIDDLER ON THE ROOF (1971)
When Chava marries Motel and the whole village sings *Sunrise Sunset*, you'll be blubbing before they finish the first line.

GOODBYE, COLUMBUS (1969)
Proof that money does not buy taste in this over-the-top society wedding that degenerates into a drunken debacle.

THE SOUND OF MUSIC (1965)
Fraulein Maria's wedding scene is often cut on TV. Pity, as she walks down the aisle to the tune of 100 nuns singing a nicely restrained version of *What Are We Going To Do About Maria?* Nice frock, too.

CHICKS IN WHITE SATIN (1993)
A documentary which proves that even a lesbian wedding cannot escape warring relatives and angst-ridden discussions about commitment and cakes.

Miramax, Gaumont/FR3/SFPC/Bioskop/Films du Lozange

more than just a boring charade among people he despises. The shocking opening scene is worth seeing the movie for alone, and the ending fits exactly with the lovers' unexpected passion. After an understandably bemused initial reception, the film has gained a loyal following among fans of unusual love stories.

IL POSTINO 1994

Director **Michael Radford** *Cast* **Massimo Troisi, Maria Grazia Cucinotta, Phillipe Noiret**

Famous poet Pablo Neruda is exiled to a small Italian island where the locals have to draft in a new postman just to deliver his fan mail. Gradually, Mario's daily visits give him an understanding of poetry, and the advice of the writer comes in handy when Mario tries to woo a fiery local beauty. A gentle, lyrical film about finding poetry in every area of life, and finding love even when you think it has passed you by. Tragically, Troisi, who plays Mario with such tentative charm, died of heart failure just 12 hours after the filming finished.

LES AMANTS DU PONT NEUF 1991

Director **Leos Carax** *Cast* **Juliette Binoche, Denis Lavant**

> **"HOW OFTEN DID YOU DECIDE YOU WERE NEVER GOING TO SEE ME AGAIN?"**
> Alec Harvey, Brief Encounter

A compelling, often overwhelming, story of a relationship between a vagrant would-be circus performer, Alex, (Lavant) and a homeless artist, Michele (Binoche), who is slowly going blind. While Alex's love for Michele borders on obsession, it is still a stunning film about the power of feeling and the strength of two people together, even in the most degraded of circumstances. At the time it came out it was the most expensive film ever made in France, and you can see why with its extraordinary visuals, bordering on the surreal, especially the scenes of the bicentennial celebrations which fill the screen with amazing colour and light.

MARTY 1955

Director **Delbert Mann** *Cast* **Ernest Borgnine, Betsy Blair**

For obvious reasons, Borgnine rarely played romantic leads, but his performance here as the ungainly butcher who has given up on finding love until he meets the equally plain Clara at a dance is so tender and genuine that it's easy to forget he usually played heavies in westerns or gangster films. Paddy Chayefsky's beautifully understated script captures in heartbreaking detail how lonely both Marty and Clara have been, and how tentative they are at first, scared of yet more rejection. Marty's friendship with Angie (Joe Mantell), an infantile pretender who rubbishes Clara for her lack of sex appeal, is another joy, especially their repeated exchanges of: "What do you wanna do tonight?"

SPLENDOR IN THE GRASS 1961
Director Elia Kazan Cast Warren Beatty, Natalie Wood

Young love is at its most intense in this powerful study of high school infatuation, set in the 1920s. Wood and Beatty play a couple, deeply in love, whose parents think they are far too young to marry. Frustrated by Wood's self-restraint, he turns to a local floozy for relief and, when she finds out, Wood ends up in an asylum.

Melodramatic? Yes, but it is saved from parody by the genuinely moving performance of both leads (who did, of course, become an item during filming), the outstanding supporting cast, including Pat Hingle's appallingly authoritative father, and the beautifully bittersweet ending. Meg Ryan's favourite film.

Jeremy Irons in one his more animated moments as Proust's hero, Swann. For a long time he slept early and for an even longer time his friends couldn't tell if he was awake or not

SWANN IN LOVE 1984 UN AMOUR DE SWANN
Director Volker Schlöndorff Cast Jeremy Irons, Ornella Muti

Gorgeously photographed, rather erotic, tale of love between Marcel Proust's hero and Odette, the femme from the wrong side of *le track*s. Muti and (in a supporting role) Alain Delon are simply superb, which is just as well because Irons, apart from one love scene, plays Swann as if he was doing his famous impersonation of a piece of cardboard. It's a shame because this is a worthy attempt to film one of literature's most complex and haunting love stories which may make you nostalgic for the novel, even if you haven't read it.

WHITE PALACE 1990
Director Luis Mandoki Cast Susan Sarandon, James Spader

Hollywood has churned out hundreds of love stories where one of the couple is from the wrong side of the tracks, but this film is set apart from the rest of the pack because not only is Sarandon's Nora a waitress in a seedy burger joint, she is also 17 years older than Max, a widower with a career in advertising. Their relationship is initially one of sexual attraction, but it gradually becomes more than that, even as the objections to it from their friends and family keep mounting. Spader's line to a yuppie party hostess: "There's no dust in your dustbuster," sums up his disillusionment with the repressed, tidy world he inhabits, even though he can't bring himself to treat Nora the way he would a more socially acceptable girlfriend. A deeply untypical love story, this is a brilliant and moving study about whether or not it's important to find an "appropriate" partner.

SCHOOL

School days, good old golden rule days... alas, tearjerking tributes to "sir" are out of fashion, schools are more violent, the pupils meet up after the bell to study drugs, not maths. But you can still find the occasional classroom dominated by a teacher with the inspirational gifts of Sidney Poitier, Robin Williams or Michelle Pfeiffer.

THE BELLES OF ST TRINIAN'S 1954
Director Frank Launder Cast Alastair Sim, Joyce Grenfell
An American movie about a school full of crazy girls, with a dotty headmistress whose brother is a spiv would have been plotted to death or dullness with gags underlined with a giant invisible Biro. But the writing team of Launder and Gilliat, well served by Sim in drag as the headmistress, make this fast, painless and almost as funny as the Ronald Searle cartoons it is based on. George Cole's spiv, Flash Harry, is probably the most compelling character, a dry run for Arthur Daley.

BLACKBOARDS 2000 TAKHTE SIAH
Director Samira Makhmalbaf Cast Saïd Mohamadi, Bahman Ghobadi, Behnaz Jafari
Somewhere in Iranian Kurdistan, near the Iraqi border, a group of teachers who have no school wander around with blackboards on their backs looking for pupils to teach in exchange for food... This is about as far away from Hollywood's conception of the school movie as it's possible to get. Makhmalbaf's second film is not for those who worry about the plot being resolved or like an inspiring upbeat message but it has breathtaking moments (especially the opening scene) and the sense of suffering and hardship is painfully real.

DEAD POETS SOCIETY 1989
Director Peter Weir Cast Robin Williams, Robert Sean Leonard
Ancient formula about good kids vs authoritarian oldsters. Williams is the inspirational teacher who comes into inevitable conflict after inspiring the boys in his English class. (In the original script, Williams was supposed to die of leukaemia but

Weir changed the plot so the film focused more on the boys.) The final scene will either have you complaining you've got something in your eye or clutching your stomach. Those in search of something subtler in similar territory may prefer Maggie Smith in *The Prime Of Miss Jean Brodie* (1969).

GOODBYE, MR CHIPS 1939

Director Sam Wood *Cast* Robert Donat, Greer Garson

From the moment the train whistle blows, you know exactly what you're in for in this sentimental nonsense which is so expertly done that for the 114 minutes it runs you'll be half convinced that your own school days were the best days of your life. Donat nicked the best actor Oscar off Clark Gable (who'd only played a bloke called Rhett Butler that year) and really did use it as a doorstop for the toilet. Donat could play the slightly befuddled but deeply charming Englishman better even than Leslie Howard and seemed more at home in the medium than the young Olivier. Avoid the 1969 musical remake unless you're a Petula Clark fan. No, especially if you're a Petula Clark fan.

ROCK 'N' ROLL HIGH SCHOOL 1979

Director Allan Arkush *Cast* PJ Soles, Vincent Van Patten, Clint Howard, the Ramones

Deeply silly, obviously low-budget and utterly enchanting. Essentially an updated 1950s teen movie (and produced under the aegis of Roger Corman) in which a teenager, Soles, tries to liberate her school from the principal, attend a Ramones concert and sell her song to them. In the concert scenes, the patron saints of punk perform such classics as *Teenage Lobotomy* ("I'm gonna have to tell 'em/That I've got no cerebellum"). The stunts go further than in the 1950s (adults are thrown out of windows but only when absolutely essential to the plot) and there are some neat running gags (the constantly evolving photo of coach Lombardi). Just thank the cinematic gods that Arkush persuaded Corman not to make this a disco high school movie.

TOM BROWN'S SCHOOLDAYS 1951

Director Gordon Parry *Cast* John Howard Davies, Robert Newton, Hermione Baddeley

Young hero vs school bully is the other great conflict of this genre and nowhere is it described better than in the novel this film is based on. This British version (which features a young Max Bygraves as a coach guard) is slightly easier on the sense of irony than the 1940 Freddie Barthomolew version. Davies, who had already played Oliver Twist, gave up playing schoolboys and urchins and, in 1969, directed *Monty Python's Flying Circus*.

> **"THE ONLY THING I'LL EVER LAY IS A RUG!"**
> Tom, Rock 'n' Roll High School

SCI-FI

The future's so bright you gotta wear shades. Or not. Science fiction can never decide. Mind you, the entire genre oscillates between high art and high camp, between asking basic questions about the way we live and scaring us with mutant walking catfish. But that's what makes science fiction so different, so appealing.

To infinity and beyond has been the cry for many filmmakers ever since Georges Méliès made a 14-minute short called *A Trip To The Moon* in 1902. Those filmmakers had so many subjects to consider: aliens, monsters, space exploration, time travel, mad scientists, dystopian futures, other worlds, robots, post-apocalyptic worlds, superheroes and space battles, to name just a few (Fritz Lang, one of the first true sci-fi film directors, managed to cram the mad scientist, robots and dystopian future into 1925's *Metropolis*).

Early silent sci-fi films explored the possibility of space travel (1924's animated *A Trip To Mars*) but by the 1930s directors were making up new planets for actors to visit, so American cinemagoers could travel to exciting new worlds and forget about the Depression. In this decade the movie-going world first met *Flash Gordon* (1936) and *Buck Rogers In The 25th Century* (1934), while *Superman* debuted onscreen in 1941.

Trust the British to be full of doom and gloom while the Yanks were all thigh-slapping entertainment and fun. The paranoia of the sci-fi future that truly kicked in the 1950s was already there in the British film *Things To Come* (1936), which predicts decades-long wars, plague and general grumpiness in the future and not a superhero in sight. Cheery, huh?

The 1950s were a mix of the paranoid 'oh-god-we're-all-going to-die' invasion films with titles like *The Day The Earth Stood Still*, *The Thing From Another World*, *When Worlds Collide*, *War Of The Worlds* and the campy kitsch of cheap, silly sci-fi laden with big-breasted babes like *Queen Of Outer Space* ("Mankind's first fantastic flight to Venus – the female planet!") and *Attack Of The 50ft Woman*. Creature features were a staple in the 1950s and 1960s. Japan (almost equalling the US in sci-fi output) gave us *Godzilla*, America discovered *The Creature From*

> **"MAKE LOVE? BUT NO ONE'S DONE THAT FOR HUNDREDS OF CENTURIES!"**
> Barbarella

The Black Lagoon and a score of films were released with 'Creature' or 'Monster' in the title, featuring a being swollen to enormous size after nuclear experiments (not that Americans were worried by those 'controlled' testing explosions taking place somewhere in Nevada, oh no).

It took Stanley Kubrick, with *2001: A Space Odyssey*, to turn sci-fi from high camp (with the exception of occasional doom-laden films like *Fahrenheit 451*) to high art. Sci-fi was cool again, and the late 1960s and 1970s saw some of the finest sci-fi films (*A Clockwork Orange*, *The Man Who Fell To Earth*, *Close Encounters Of The Third Kind* and *Star Wars*). George Lucas turned sci-fi into space opera with *Star Wars*, revolutionized special effects with his firm Industrial Light and Magic and changed the movie-going experience with the sound system THX, while Steven Spielberg made the impressive *Close Encounters*, the yucky *ET* and recently *AI: Artificial Intelligence*, once a pet project for Kubrick. Many other

"Look, Roger, I know you like me to dress up, but this is going too far"

directors have advanced sci-fi's cause: Ridley Scott (with *Blade Runner* and *Alien*), James Cameron (*Aliens*, and ground-breaking use of CGI in *The Abyss* and *Terminator 2*), John Carpenter (who combined horror and sci-fi so successfully in *The Thing*), Terry Gilliam (with *12 Monkeys* and *Brazil*), and Larry and Andy Wachowski for *The Matrix*, which took special effects to new heights. Méliès would have been dead chuffed.

BARBARELLA 1968

Director Roger Vadim *Cast* Jane Fonda, John Phillip Law

Vadim got the idea for this film, according to *Life* magazine, when he saw his wife walking around their villa topless. This, he decided, was something the world should see. Titillation commences as the opening credits roll, with the famous sequence in which Fonda strips. Somewhere in here is a devastating satire of the 1960s written by Terry Southern but with seven other writers involved that soon vanished. So what we get is kitsch sci-fi with Fonda/Barbarella searching for the missing mad scientist Durand Durand and his, er, weapon, the Positronic Ray. It's a lot of fun even if Vadim, for all his eye for talent, couldn't direct to save his life.

BLADE RUNNER 1982

Director Ridley Scott *Cast* Harrison Ford, Rutger Hauer, Sean Young

Like so many films in this book, this was a critical and box office failure on release: costing $27m to make, it took less than $15m in the US. But its reputation has been soaring ever since especially with the release of the director's cut, showing the full subtlety of Scott's vision. Visually stunning, this tale of a weary cop (Ford) who in the LA of 2019 has to track down four android replicants draws on film noir (the femme fatale, the alienated hero) and westerns like *High Noon* to produce something unique. One of the most influential films of the genre, even if the human story never lives up to the visual feast.

THE DAY THE EARTH STOOD STILL 1951

Director Robert Wise *Cast* Michael Rennie, Patricia Neal

A UFO lands in Washington DC and alien Klaatu (Rennie) jumps out, only to be shot at. Luckily he's brought his robot Gort (played by Lock Martin, spotted for the movie while working as a doorman at Grauman's Chinese Theater) who decides to turn the world to toast unless someone can pass on Klaatu's dying message (the unforgettable "Klaatu barada nikto") before it's too late. It has been debated whether this is a Jesus allegory (Klaatu poses as Mr Carpenter, his arrival on Earth with a message of peace, the fire next time). Watch one of the best sci-fi films ever (effective special effects, seriously great performances, Leo Tover's atmospheric cinematography) and decide for yourself.

"I am a replicant and whatever Ridley says, Harrison and I agree that Deckard wasn't"

DUNE 1984

Director David Lynch *Cast* Kyle MacLachlan, Francesca Annis, Sting

David Lynch turned down the chance to direct *Return Of The Jedi* (what a different film that would have been) to devote more than three years to filming Frank Herbert's doorstop of a novel. For all the flaws, there are moments of pure Lynchian genius, from jaw-dropping sci-fi sets to the intriguing casting of actors like Annis, Jürgen Prochnow, Max von Sydow and Sting (whose barking performance in a leather nappy makes *Dune* so bad it's addictive). A rambling oddity that has to be seen to be believed.

EDWARD SCISSORHANDS 1990

Director Tim Burton *Cast* Johnny Depp, Winona Ryder, Dianne Wiest,

Burton's left-of-field follow-up to his

hugely successful *Batman*. Edward (Depp) is an incomplete man-made boy whose inventor father (Vincent Price) died before he had time to replace his scissor hands with human ones. Peg Boggs (Wiest) takes him under her wing, ingratiating him into society through his topiary and hairdressing skills. The idea for this fable, a kind of updated Frankenstein, came to Burton as a child. Scissorhands may also be another Christ figure although he never says: "Klaatu barada nikto".

THE EMPIRE STRIKES BACK 1980
Director Irvin Kershner *Cast* Mark Hamill, Harrison Ford, Carrie Fisher

Arguably the best – and definitely the coolest – of the original *Star Wars* trilogy, *The Empire Strikes Back* has little of the cute cuddly stuff (no Ewoks, just Yoda) of *Return Of The Jedi*, nor the geeky 'boy tries to save the good guys' naivety of *Star Wars*. Luke Skywalker is tougher (Hamill had survived a car crash that left him facially scarred, explained away by the movie's wampa attack) yet conflicted. Cocky Hans and icy Princess Leia are now proper characters (he's not so cocky and she's not as strong as she pretends to be), and the ending leaves you hanging as Darth Vader gets the carbonite machine out. Dark, delicious stuff from Lucas.

THE FIFTH ELEMENT 1997
Director Luc Besson *Cast* Bruce Willis, Milla Jovovich, Gary Oldman

Futuristic fashion by Jean Paul Gaultier, a cast and crew of hundreds and a $90m budget all hinted that director Luc Besson wasn't going to make just any old sci-fi adventure. Visually rich, from the *Blade Runner*-like scenes of New York complete with flying cars to the floating Titanic-like resort and the gothic alien creatures, this is also a rollickingly good adventure. Cynical (isn't it always?) cab driver Bruce Willis finds himself reluctantly helping to save the world (and unusual gal Jovovich) from evil dude Oldman (expanding on his nutty bad guy in Besson's *Leon*). Lavish in the extreme

Marianne/Dino DeLaurentis; Warner/Ladd/Blade Runner Partnership

---

NO BUDGET

PITCH BLACK
A $23m budget for a sci-fi movie is bargain-basement today, and this proves that dark shadows and a gruff villain (Vin Diesel) can be more effective than flashy special effects

MAD MAX 2: THE ROAD WARRIOR
A post-apocalyptic world that cost just $4m to create with director George Miller's vision and Mel Gibson's monosyllabic hero.

THE TERMINATOR
The sequel was flashier, but Arnold Schwarzenegger got the role of a lifetime as the robot from the future sent to kill.

THE BLOB
Steve McQueen had his first leading role in this sci-fi horror that cost little more than $200,000 to make.

THX 1138
A pre-*Star Wars* George Lucas explores a dystopian future similar to Orwell's *1984*, on a shoestring budget.

THINGS TO COME
£300,000 was spent adapting HG Wells' *The Shape Of Things To Come* for the screen, in this 1933 British alternative to *Metropolis*.

THE HIDDEN
Classic alien organism-on-the-rampage flick with Michael Nouri and Kyle MacLachlan among the low-budget stars.

and populated by eccentric characters, this is an outlandish fable which still contains surprises after the 10th viewing.

THE FORBIN PROJECT 1969

Director **Joseph Sargent** *Cast* **Eric Braeden, Susan Clark**

Also known as *Colossus*, the name of the computer that gets a bit too clever for man in this precursor to the similarly-themed (but not as effectively executed) *Demon Seed*. Colossus controls the American defence systems, but once the machine detects that it has a Russian counterpart (Guardian), the two machines merge to become one super-computer hell-bent on telling man what to do, under threat of nuclear war. This works best in the scenes where the machine's creator, Forbin (Braeden) is forced to go about his daily business knowing his every move is watched by the machine he created, and in the uncompromising, non-Hollywood ending (which studio executives disliked so much they caused the film to be shelved for a year, until they saw the success of *2001*).

INVASION OF THE BODY SNATCHERS 1956

Director **Don Siegel** *Cast* **Kevin McCarthy, Dana Wynter**

The best of the three movie versions of Jack Finney's novel (though Philip Kaufman's 1978 remake isn't half-bad), partly because the paranoia running through the film sits particularly well with its McCarthy era setting. A doctor in a small town notices that a lot of his patients are worried their families aren't acting like themselves, but doesn't realise until too late that pods from outer space are replicating and replacing humans all around him. Watch out for a cameo from Sam Peckinpah (said to have helped with the script). In the Kaufman version, Kevin McCarthy – the hero in Siegel's original – turns up as a raving lunatic and Siegel has a brief cameo as a cab driver.

> **"STOP TRYING TO RATIONALIZE EVERYTHING, WILL YA? LET'S FACE IT, WE HAVE A MYSTERY ON OUR HANDS!"**
>
> Jack, Invasion Of The Body Snatchers

LOGAN'S RUN 1976

Director **Michael Anderson** *Cast* **Michael York, Richard Jordan**

A movie ripe for remaking (there were rumours, sadly unfounded, of a 2000 version with Leonardo DiCaprio as the star), mainly because the costumes, sets and Michael York's performance belong firmly in the mid-1970s. It's the 23rd century and man lives in a bubble-encased city where all the inhabitants are under the age of 30. This is because, once you get to the big three-oh, you participate in 'carousel' (which basically means being sucked up into mid-air while everyone cheers, and then exploding). York's job is to hunt down anyone who tries to escape this fate (which isn't that many, as most believe they have the chance of being reborn, the fools) but once he gets outside the world he has known and gets horizontal with Jenny Agutter, he realises that living past 30 might not be a bad idea after all. Silly but gripping.

MARS ATTACKS! 1996

Director Tim Burton *Cast* Michael J Fox, Pierce Brosnan, Jack Nicholson, Glenn Close

Burton's homage to the kitsch sci-fi trading cards of the 1950s was unjustly ignored on theatrical release, but is a favourite with those who get the director's skewed sense of humour and delight in watching Jack Nicholson playing not one but two over-the-top characters as Martians land on earth and crisp up a few cows as a calling card. Burton took a cast of revered actors and gave them their nuttiest roles ever: Nicholson as the president under fire, Close as the prim

first lady, Annette Bening as the New Ager who wants to greet the Martians, Sarah Jessica Parker as the vacuous TV presenter who has her head grafted on a dog's body by the aliens, Brosnan as a vain scientist and Tom Jones as, well, Tom Jones. Very silly, packed with kitschy sets and daft humour – check out the reassuring credit at the end: 'No living animals were barbecued during the production of this film.' Good to know.

METROPOLIS 1926

Director Fritz Lang *Cast* Alfred Abel, Gustav Fröhlich

The original dystopia movie, described by HG Wells as the silliest film he had seen (possibly because the screenwriter had borrowed some of the author's ideas). Lang's most famous film took a year and a half to make and was not regarded as a classic until almost 60 years after it was released, when it was restored to something close to the director's original vision (it had been edited and reworked over the years). While the plot is muddled, Lang's spectacular set pieces (from the futuristic scenery to dazzling scenes like the burning of the robot) have made this a classic, much-copied, piece of art. (You can find references in *Blade Runner*, *Dr Strangelove*, and *Bride Of Frankenstein*.) Turn the sound off on Giorgio Moroder's restored 1984 version and avoid the Pat Benatar/Freddie Mercury soft-rock soundtrack.

THE OMEGA MAN 1971

Director Boris Sagal *Cast* Charlton Heston, Anthony Zerbe

Richard Matheson's 1953 novel *I Am Legend* (which Ridley

HG Wells called *Metropolis* the silliest film he'd ever seen. Probably a good job he died before he saw Marlon Brando and Val Kilmer in *The Island Of Dr Moreau*

UFA, Wade Williams Productions

UNSPEAKABLE
HORRORS FROM
OUTER SPACE
PARALYZE
THE LIVING
AND RESURRECT
THE DEAD!

PLAN 9 FROM OUTER SPACE

WITH
BELA LUGOSI
VAMPIRA
LYLE TALBOT

A J. Edward Reynolds Production

Produced and Directed by
Edward D. Wood, Jr.

Cool poster, OK cast, shame about the story, the director, the hub caps posing as UFOs

Scott later wanted to adapt with Arnold Schwarzenegger) was the inspiration for *The Last Man On Earth* and Romero's *Night Of The Living Dead,* as well as this 1970s look at what the world (well, LA) would be like after most of humanity is wiped out by a plague. The few survivors are homicidal albinos. Only walking monolith Heston is immune (he had injected himself with an experimental vaccine), allowing him to roam the city looting for supplies by day, and hide from the mutants in an abandoned apartment by night. Thought-provoking stuff (would being the only person left on earth, able to do what the hell you want, really be that great?) and pretty violent for its time.

PANIC IN THE YEAR ZERO 1962
Director Ray Milland *Cast* Ray Milland, Jean Hagen, Frankie Avalon,

LA gets it again, courtesy of a Russian nuclear device, while Milland's family are out on a fishing trip. The family head for a remote cave but find their way blocked by anarchy, highways with ever-changing numbers of lanes which have become car-parks, and fiends who want to rape Milland's daughter. This is Milland's only film as a director and it's hard not to feel that this time it's personal. And if this is how he sees the post-apocalyptic world you begin to understand why he looks so miserable in so many of his movies. Dystopia has seldom seemed so dyspeptic or so ugly. On the plus side, this film may offer proof that Frankie Avalon could act.

PLAN 9 FROM OUTER SPACE 1956
Director Ed Wood *Cast* Gregory Walcott, Bela Lugosi

Director Wood got a boost of cool when Johnny Depp portrayed him (complete with his love of directing while wearing women's clothing) in Burton's quirky biopic, but his cheap sci-fi flick is widely regarded as the worst film ever made. The plot is hilarious (aliens whose first eight plans have failed to get mankind's attention try re-animating a few corpses) and the effects are risible (hub caps as UFOs). In truth it's the stories of how Wood got it made that make this movie such a fascinating piece of history: funding from the local Baptist church led to the cast and crew being baptized; Wood mixed footage from another film he'd begun with Bela Lugosi with scenes played by a much taller man disguising his face with a cape; cardboard gravestones wobbling in the wind... a classic.

PLANET OF THE APES 1967
Director *Franklin J Schaffner* Cast *Charlton Heston, Roddy McDowall*

Astronauts land on a planet to discover it is populated by mute humans ruled by apes in this almost perfect sci-fi film that spawned four so-so sequels, a dreadful TV series, a hilarious spoof (*Planet Of The Apes: The Musical!*) on *The Simpsons* and a disappointing Tim Burton remake. Muscular Heston (who spends most of the movie in little more than a leather handkerchief) was at his gruff, powerful best as the astronaut caught on this godforsaken planet. McDowall never quite escaped the shadow of his superb, sarcastic portrayal of simian Cornelius, who helps the human survive and discover what planet he is on. Despite a limited budget (only $50,000 allocated to ape make-up) this is powerful stuff with a humorous script and one of the best endings in movie history.

THE PHANTOM EMPIRE 1935
Directors *Otto Brower, B. Reeves Eason* Cast *Gene Autry, Dorothy Christy*

Not to be confused with *The Phantom Empire* (1986), a witless horror about a cave creature who owns a pile of uncut diamonds that would bankrupt DeBeers if sold on the world market. This is a 12 episode serial starring singing cowboy Autry who finds a civilisation at the bottom of a mine. The people of Murani have TV, ray guns and radium which attracts some unscrupulous humans. Autry, oscillating between his Radio Ranch and Murania, can't stop the Muranians being killed by a death ray. But he consoles us by singing *Silver Haired Daddy Of Mine*. Why weren't there more sci-fi/musical/Western serials?

SOYLENT GREEN 1973
Director *Richard Fleischer* Cast *Charlton Heston, Edward G Robinson*

Based on Harry Harrison's sci-fi novel *Make Room! Make Room!*, this is a depressing but thoroughly gripping view of the near-future. Cop Heston roams the overpopulated streets of 2022 New York, where real food is so scarce that people queue for days for a ration of manufactured nourishment – soylent green – and the ultimate in luxury for the super-rich is a jar of jam. Heston's discovery of the origins of soylent green is the

> **"I THINK WE SHOULD HAVE HAD SEX, BUT THERE WEREN'T ENOUGH PEOPLE"**
> Luna, Sleeper

film's major body blow, but the scene featuring Robinson (in his final role) watching scenes of the 20th century prior to his euthanasia remains the film's most powerful sequence.

STARSHIP TROOPERS 1997

Director Paul Verhoeven *Cast* Casper Van Dien, Dina Meyer

Robert A Heinlein's fascistic 1959 sci-fi novel seems unusual source material for the director who gave us *Showgirls*, but a naked mixed-sex shower scene early on dispels thoughts that it could have been anyone else behind the (steamed-up) camera. Some time in the future, young adults are signed up to fight against giant bug thingies from the planet Klendathu, even though they (and we) know that most of them will end up skewered. As you'd expect from the director of *Total Recall*, the effects are superb, but what makes this a cult classic isn't what's good but what's bad – the hammy acting from a cast of wooden TV actors (Van Dien, Neil Patrick Harris), ridiculous dialogue ("I'm from Buenos Aires, and I say kill 'em all!") and the jingoism that one suspects is Verhoeven's muddled attempt at satire. There are some great deaths-by-arachnid, though.

> "PAIN CAN BE CONTROLLED, YOU JUST DISCONNECT IT"
>
> Kyle, The Terminator

THE TERMINATOR 1984

Director James Cameron *Cast* Arnold Schwarzenegger, Michael Biehn, Linda Hamilton

Lance Henriksen was director Cameron's original choice for the role of the robot who travels back to our present to kill the future mother of a resistance leader (so that the leader will never be born), but the producers wanted a famous name. Then-mildly-hot Schwarzenegger was hired and the rest, as they say, is blockbuster history. (Henriksen settled for the supporting role of cop Vuckovich). While the careers of Linda Hamilton (the machine's target) and Michael Biehn (the man sent from the future to help her and, er, father the future resistance leader) didn't exactly soar after this film was released, this simple yet effective movie turned Arnie from the struggling-to-speak-English muscular Austrian oak joke of the *Conan* movies into the coolest guy on the screen (Cameron, wisely, didn't give him that much dialogue).

THEM! 1954

Director Gordon Douglas *Cast* James Whitmore, Edmund Gwenn

Sci-fi horror trying to combine biblical prophecies of the end of the world with an anti-nuclear message using mutant 20ft ants (the result of radiation from atomic bomb tests). The giant ants wreak havoc in south-west America, killing indiscriminately and stealing sugar, before taking up residence in LA's sewers. Two little boys getting trapped at the final hour provide some action after a tedious stretch, and helped make this Warner's most successful film of the year. Look out for Leonard Nimoy tapping away on a coding machine and also for the aquaducts which hosted the famous *Grease* drag races 24 years later.

THE THING 1982

Director John Carpenter *Starring* Kurt Russell, Wilford Brimley

Based on the 1938 story *Who Goes There?* (the source material for 1951's *The Thing From Another World*), *The Thing* was released in the same year as that other alien movie, *ET*, and provided a welcome antidote to Spielberg's cuddly creation. This alien definitely does not pop up at an isolated Antarctic research station to eat sweets and get adorably drunk on beer – this creature hides by changing shape and bursts from his unfortunate host in a bloody heap. Carpenter favourite Kurt Russell (who also starred in Carpenter's *Escape From New York* and *Big Trouble In Little China*) is the gruff hero, while Richard Dysart, Wilford Brimley and Donald Moffat are among the classy supporting cast in a suspenseful (and deliciously gory) movie that boasts a teeth-gnashingly good ending.

NO ONE CAN HEAR YOU...

The Nostromo. Sigourney Weaver battling the alien in her vest and pants. The chestburster. There are so many memorable moments in Ridley Scott's *Alien* and, for that matter, the first sequel, James Cameron's more action-adventure-style *Aliens* ("Get away from her you bitch!"), it is impossible to pick a favourite.

But one thing remains constant in all of the *Alien* movies, including David Fincher's claustrophobic but confusing *Alien3* and Jean-Pierre Jeunet's rambling *Alien: Resurrection* – HR Giger's metallic, skeletal, flesh-crawlingly sinister alien (and, in the first film, the glimpses of the organic ship it had inhabited).

A Swiss illustrator fascinated with all things skeletal after his pharmacist father brought home a human skull when he was a child, Giger was hired by Ridley Scott as a creature designer in 1978 after Scott had seen his art book *Necronomicon*, but Giger also became involved in the film's sets and the sculpture of the alien environment.

While he didn't work on Cameron's *Aliens* (although his earlier designs were used) and the work he did for *Alien3* didn't appear in the final film, his biomechanical creatures have set the standard for special effects artists when they are creating beings from another world (Giger also designed the Sil alien for *Species*).

An Oscar-winner for his work on *Alien*, Giger's sculptures now have their own museum in Switzerland, while his unique style has been used for such diverse projects as Debbie Harry's *KooKoo* album cover (the one with nails going through her face) and a special microphone stand designed for the lead singer of Korn.

TIME MACHINE 1960

Director **George Pal** *Cast* **Rod Taylor, Alan Young, Yvette Mimieux**

Special effects maestro George Pal was the ideal candidate to tackle HG Wells' classic tale of time travel. Aussie brawn Taylor is Wells, heading into the future to the year 802,701, where he finds damsel in distress Weena (Mimieux) at the mercy of the evil Morlocks. Although the Morlocks can resemble dudes with their shaggy blonde manes, Pal himself designed the look of the beasts. While Wells' complex novel is here scaled down to its barest bones, the film is an enjoyable piece of easy entertainment. Pal went on to co-write the sequel, the imaginatively titled *Time Machine 2*, with Jo Morhaim. The film also stars Alan Young, better known as the voice of Wilbur the talking horse in the television series *Mr Ed*, a versatile bugger who provided the voices of many characters in *Duck Tales*.

2001: A SPACE ODYSSEY 1968

Director **Stanley Kubrick** *Starring* **Keir Dullea, Gary Lockwood**

Many believe Kubrick's space opera can only be completely understood if watched under the influence of acid, but the director himself hinted that his intention was to make something that people would puzzle over for years to come, doped or sober. Any film that causes such heated debates – Is it about man's relationship with technology? Human aspirations? What the bloody hell does the end mean? – is worthy of respect, and Kubrick's attention to detail (he had tons of sand imported, washed and painted for the moon's surface), the superb set pieces (most notably the docking of the spaceship in time to *The Blue Danube*) and, of course, HAL, make this one the sci-fi movie against which others are still measured. It wasn't just Kubrick: Arthur C Clarke, who wrote the story, said that if you understood it, he had failed.

WESTWORLD 1973

Director **Michael Crichton** *Cast* **Yul Brynner, Richard Benjamin**

Crichton, who also wrote *The Andromeda Strain*, *Coma* and *Jurassic Park*, is clearly trying to tell us not to mess with things we don't understand. His other films may have applied this to nature or disease, but here it's machines that are going to get everyone into trouble. In the future, rich holidaymakers can go to a resort and live out their fantasies with the help of robots. Richard Benjamin and pal James Brolin sign up to experience the Western town on offer, only to be stalked by determined robot Brynner (a possible forerunner of *The Terminator*?) when the machines begin to malfunction. Gripping stuff from Crichton, but avoid the useless sequel *Futureworld*.

SEA

The sea used to be the setting for the windblown heroics of Errol Flynn, Tony Curtis or Gregory Peck in *Captain Horatio Hornblower*. Since the decline of that genre (from which we recommend *The Sea Hawk* and *The Black Swan*), the sea has become an eternal wreaker of havoc and mayhem. So don't let the *Perfect Storm* kid you, the movie business is now dominated by landlubbers.

THE ABYSS 1989

Director James Cameron *Cast* Michael Biehn, Ed Harris, Mary Elizabeth Mastrantonio

Life's abyss and then you die. That, at least, was how the cast and crew felt along with some critics who insisted the director had made a waterlulu. Yet this peculiar hybrid of underwater adventure and *Close Encounters*-style sci-fi, about an oil rig crew sent to rescue a nuclear sub, still works. Cameron is nothing if not audacious and his decision to shoot this in a half-completed nuclear reactor which he filled with seven million gallons of water pays off. The cast had to become certified divers, the crew spent long enough under water to need decompression, and the director watched many of the dailies through a window, while decompressing and hanging upside down because his shoulders couldn't cope with the weight of his helmet. And it's this pathological obsession for authenticity which carries the film.

THE ENEMY BELOW 1957

Director Dick Powell *Cast* Robert Mitchum, Curt Jürgens

A classy, above-average movie about the contest between two very skilled captains: Mitchum, on a US destroyer, and Jürgens, on a German sub. Concentrating on the tactical and psychological duel between the captains, this eschews the usual black-and-white morality of most war movies of this era. The viewer is even invited to feel some sympathy for Jürgens, who is portrayed as loving his country and hating the Nazis. Former film star Powell directs with assurance, with one fantastic vertical panning shot that follows a fishing line into the water and down to the submarine on the ocean bed.

> **"IT'S ALWAYS TOO COLD OR TOO HOT, WHEREVER THERE'S A WAR ON"**
> Captain Murrell, The Enemy Below

MOBY DICK 1956

Director John Huston *Cast* Gregory Peck, Richard Basehart, James Robertson Justice, Orson Welles

Look closely at the sky as Starbuck plans to shoot obsessed Captain Ahab and you might see the vapour trail of a jet plane. Even Huston, who invented a new process to make this film look like the old aquatint whaling prints, couldn't have legislated for that. He could, though, have saved himself and his film a lot of grief by not casting Peck as Ahab, the skipper seduced by the gods of vengeance to go in pursuit of the notorious whale. Peck always said Huston himself should have played Ahab. Perhaps a better choice might have been Welles, whose stirring speech as Father Mapple won him a standing ovation from the crew. The other obvious choice (Charles Laughton) was too firmly equated with another berserk skipper. Peck tries hard but doesn't quite have the range (though he later impressed as Mapple in a TV remake). Unfortunately his performance was more than enough reason for critics to turn on a film which, because the fake white whale kept getting damaged and having to be rebuilt, ended up costing more than $5m.

> "TO BE ENRAGED WITH A DUMB BRUTE THAT ACTED OUT OF BLIND INSTINCT IS BLASPHEMOUS"
>
> Starbuck, Moby Dick

THE OLD MAN AND THE SEA 1999

Director Aleksandr Petrov *Cast* Gordon Pinsent, Kevin Delaye

If you believe that Ernest Hemingway was quite as important as he thought he was (or you just like watching Spencer Tracy doing his stuff) you'll prefer the 1958 John Sturges film of the same name. But this Russian, Oscar-winning animated version, made with Japanese partners, reduces the tale to a decent length (40 minutes) and should take your breath away. Petrov painted 29,000 images with pastel oils on sheets of glass to tell this story. It was worth the effort. If you want to see Ernie himself, get the Sturges film; the author has an uncredited bit part.

THE PERFECT STORM 2000

Director Wolfgang Petersen *Cast* George Clooney, Mark Wahlberg, Mary Elizabeth Mastrantonio

This is a near-perfect film about a storm. Or three great storms which met in the mid-Atlantic in 1991 and of two boats, one a fishing vessel called the Andrea Gail captained by Clooney and one a luxury sailboat, trying to escape what seems an increasingly inevitable fate. If you haven't heard the true story on which this film is based, you might be tempted to play 'disaster movie Russian roulette', and try to guess which characters will survive. Don't bother, just sit back and prepare for your stomach to start churning.

THE SEA HAWK 1940

Director Michael Curtiz Cast Errol Flynn, Brenda Marshall, Claude Rains

Errol Flynn is Rafael Sabatini's English buccaneer out to cause havoc on the high seas, this time against the Spanish. Although lacking in the colourful splendour of Robin Hood or the Private Lives of Elizabeth and Essex, the rousing score by Wolfgang Korngold keeps the excitement alive, and Errol is as dashing and heroic as ever. British actress Flora Robson plays Queen Elizabeth, here in her third performance as the virgin queen. Rains excels as de Cordoba, with Errol's sidekick support, on and off screen, provided once again by Alan Hale.

TREASURE ISLAND 1950

Director Byron Haskin Cast Bobby Driscoll, Robert Newton, Basil Sydney

Newton, as Long John Silver, really will shiver your timbers in this Disney classic, giving the definitive interpretation of the one-legged parrot perch. (Orson Welles' 1972 impersonation of Silver belongs to that period where he described his job as bringing a touch of class to films which were foredoomed to fail.) Newton would soon climb inside a bottle to return, occasionally, for cameo roles in films like *Around The World In 80 Days*. He died in 1956 at the age of 51, leaving this film as the main evidence of the talent the film world had lost.

20,000 LEAGUES UNDER THE SEA 1954

Director Richard Fleischer Cast James Mason, Kirk Douglas, Peter Lorre

We'll let Mason himself review this one: "Unlike most of my films, it has made mountains of money. Every four or five years it is exposed to a new bunch of kids who think the world of it. I saw it once dubbed in German and it became better than ever. Not only did they give me a marvellous deep gravelly voice but they fitted one to Kirk which matched his teethplay." It still works, even in the original English.

FANTASY ISLANDS

Shipwrecks have long been a good substitute for a plot. As the film opens, with the sailor prostrate on the shore, the waves crashing around him, it is a fair bet that this refuge will not prove to be the tropical paradise it appears.

The best a sailor can hope for is that the island is home to man Friday or populated by Marlon Brando and a bunch of actors dressed up in British naval uniforms wasting millions of dollars of MGM's money.

At worst, though, you could have landed in a place ruled by Dr Moreau, a multi-headed mad scientist who might resemble Brando, Charles Laughton or Burt Lancaster. Still even that would be better than landing on…*Blood Island.*

You've not heard of *Blood Island*? Obviously you're not familiar with the Philippines' contribution to the horror genre. *Blood Island* is actually derived from HG Wells' story about the mad doctor and christened Isla de Sangre. This provided the setting for *Terror Is A Man* (1959) where the shipwreck victim has to cope with a panther man, *Bride Of Blood Island* (1968) where a monster took on the onerous chore of scaring the locals and three other films in the same series. So popular were these at American drive-ins, that an American film *Brain Of Blood* (1972) was made in the Philippines to capitalise on demand. Meanwhile Filipino cinema moved on, as directors realized that you could have blood without *Blood Island.*

SERIAL KILLERS

American Psycho's Patrick Bateman is "into murders and executions". But let's face it darling, who isn't these days? We're no longer shocked by acts of cannibalism (*Silence Of The Lambs*), seeing a woman torn apart between two trucks (*The Hitcher*) or just motiveless murderous mayhem (that's you, Bateman). But then even psychos have their reasons. Their mum, usually.

AMERICAN PSYCHO 2000
Director Mary Harron Cast Christian Bale, Willem Dafoe, Jared Leto

Fans of Bret Easton Ellis' third novel must have counted their blessings when the title role went to Bale instead of Leonardo DiCaprio (although it would have been interesting to see what Oliver Stone, once lined up to direct, might have made of it). The most chilling thing about Bale's character may be that he admires the "professionalism" of Huey Lewis and the News. Gore is kept to a minimum, (aside from a grotesque chainsaw scene) so as not to detract from the film's satirical take on the 1980s and its central character. The only trouble is that after a while the film, like the novel, suffers from what can only be described (with pun intended) as overkill.

THE BOSTON STRANGLER 1967
Director Richard Fleischer Cast Tony Curtis, Henry Fonda

Detectives believed the killings of 11 women between 1962 and 1964 were random, not the work of one serial killer. But as the split-screen direction shows us, the public did not. Presumably Fleischer wanted to get as far away from his last film, the talk-to-the-animals flop *Dr Dolittle*, as he could. Curtis underplays as Albert da Salvo, at that time probably the most famous serial killer in the US. He did manage to terrify wife Janet Leigh with his comment: "There's a bit of the Boston Strangler in all of us." The split screen works less well than the recurring motif of mirrors to stress the duality of Curtis and his interrogator.

HENRY: PORTRAIT OF A SERIAL KILLER 1986

Director John McNaughton *Cast* Michael Rooker, Tracy Arnold, Tom Towles

Loosely based on the real-life killings of Henry Lee Lucas, this film takes us through one graphic killing after another. Although the real Henry was caught and convicted, here he remains free, as the film focuses on a disturbingly realistic examination of killing. The use of unknown actors, coupled with debut director McNaughton's gritty visual approach, has you feeling at times like a voyeur. Some scenes proved too much even for the actors, with one actress going into shock after her scene as a victim. Pop it on the video next time your gran comes around – but only if you want to finish her off.

> **"WARS, CONFLICT. IT'S ALL BUSINESS. ONE MURDER, A VILLAIN; MILLIONS, A HERO. NUMBERS SANCTIFY"**
>
> Henri Verdoux, Monsieur Verdoux

MONSIEUR VERDOUX 1947

Director Charles Chaplin *Cast* Charles Chaplin, Martha Raye

"How could this man so methodically take these women out and cut them up and burn them in his incinerator, and then tend his flowers with the black smoke coming out of the chimney?" It was the question Chaplin asked his son as he finished the script for his black comedy (based on a real story) about a serial lady killer. After a bloody conflict with the censor (who objected to the fact that Verdoux called a priest "good man" and not "father") the film was made and then lost in the political storm over whether its maker was a Communist or not. It is a sour, cruel "comedy of murder", as Chaplin called it, and it was his last film before he was forced into Swiss exile.

THE ROLE MODELS

Most actors go to a lot of trouble to get into character. But if you're playing a serial killer, where do you go to get your creative juices flowing?

ANTHONY HOPKINS AKA HANNIBAL LECTER

According to the star Lecter is based on comic genius Tommy Cooper. For the voice Sir Anthony drew on Truman Capote and Katharine Hepburn.

JACK NICHOLSON AKA JACK TORRANCE

Nicholson's performance in *The Shining* as the crazed caretaker with a severe case of cabin fever, was, critics insisted, just a little OTT. The actor may have found this a tad ironic as he had partially based his portrayal on real-life killer Charles Manson.

For a Hannibal Lecter take a Welsh knight...

... and add one comic magician. Just like that

MGM/Universal/Dino DeLaurentis

PROFUNDO CARMESI 1996 DEEP CRIMSON

Director Arturo Ripstein *Cast* Regina Orozco,
Daniel Giménez Cacho

Set in Mexico in the 1940s, *Profundo* retells the story of the
infamous 'Lonely Hearts Killers', a grotesque couple who
preyed on lonely, affluent widows before killing them. In
glossier serial thrillers, you may develop an unnatural
attachment to the killer in question (see *Silence Of The Lambs*),
but neither obese nurse Coral (Orozco) or her lover Nicholas
(Cacho) display any redeeming qualities – Coral has abandoned
her children in pursuit of gigolo/con-man Nicholas. Director
Ripstein began his career as assistant to Buñuel and is
now Mexico's most acclaimed director. Although often
compared to *Bonnie & Clyde*, the killers are never romanticized.

SE7EN 1995

Director David Fincher *Cast* Morgan Freeman, Brad Pitt,
Gwyneth Paltrow, Kevin Spacey

Director Fincher lulls us into thinking this is just another film
about a mismatched pair of cops on the trail of a madman. But
Se7en manages to break all the conventions of the serial killer
movie. This killer doesn't kill his victims the same way each
time, and although *Se7en* is possibly one of the most disturbing
commercial films of all time, you never see any of the killings
take place. The bleak conclusion leaves you feeling that
this can't be the end, this just doesn't happen in the movies.
Indeed, the studio tried to change it but Pitt (good on him)
refused to do the film unless they stuck to the script.

SILENCE OF THE LAMBS 1991

Director Jonathan Demme *Cast* Anthony Hopkins, Jodie Foster

"A census taker once tried to test me. I ate his liver with some
fava beans and a nice chianti." Surely one of the most quoted
lines from the movies, and as in *Manhunter* (1986), the horror
stems from the insight into the killer's mind. Clarice Starling
(Foster) is an ambitious FBI agent, Hannibal Lecter (Hopkins)
is her subject, the pair uniting to trap another killer, Buffalo
Bill. Lecter is thankfully fictional but Buffalo Bill is an
amalgamation of real serial killers: Ed Gein (skinned his
victims), Ted Bundy (used a cast on his hand to lure women to
help him) and Gary Heidnick (kept women hostage in a
basement). Michael Mann's *Manhunter*, with Brian Cox as
Lecter, is very slick visually, has some classic moments (the girl
screaming on the plane at the grisly photos which have dropped
out of the hero's case) and a killer's eye-view opening sequence,
the basis for a famous scene in *Henry: Portrait Of A Serial Killer*.

> "DO YOU KNOW
> HOW YOU
> CAUGHT ME,
> WILL? WE'RE
> JUST ALIKE.
> YOU WANT
> THE SCENT,
> SMELL
> YOURSELF"
>
> Hannibal Lecter, Manhunter

SHORTS

Who says a film has to be an hour and a half long and tell a story? One of the greatest films ever made *Un Chien Andalou* lasts for 16 minutes whereas *Raise The Titanic* (at 115 minutes) seemed to take longer than it would have done to drain the Atlantic.

CAPTAIN EO 1986
Director Francis Ford Coppola *Cast* Michael Jackson, Anjelica Huston

Jacko's film career has so far been even less artistically significant than his ex-father-in-law's. This short space odyssey comes to you courtesy of Coppola (hey, he's paying the rent), Jackson and Disney. Jacko is the aforementioned captain who has to deliver a gift to a queen who lives in a desolate world (no, it's not Liz Taylor) and just at the point where the plot begins to sag, the FX start flying and the skipper starts dancing. Actually, the 3-D stuff is veddy well done. Only the very strong or the very stupid can sit in the front row and watch without ducking.

THE CASE OF THE MUKKINESE BATTLE HORN 1956
Writer Spike Milligan *Cast* Spike Milligan, Dick Emery, Peter Sellers

This historic curio was released as a support feature in the early 1970s in British cinemas. When it was made Milligan and Sellers were 66.7 per cent of the Goons and this is a more extravagant version of that brand of humour. As Superintendent Quilt of the Yard, Sellers (as ever) is in a semi-autonomous comic republic of his own while Milligan does his usual shtick, trying to squeeze in as many really corny jokes as possible while laying out a comic conspiracy involving a vicious international ring of mukkinese battle horn smugglers.

THE DAY OF THE FIGHT 1951
Director Stanley Kubrick *Cast* Douglas Edwards (narrator)

It cost the young Kubrick $3,900 to make this film, based on his own photoshoot of a boxing match for *Look* magazine. This three-part story focusing on the boxer Walter Cartier is rarely seen now. This is a shame because it has a distinctly noirish tone and there are some lovely moments, particularly the scene where the boxer confronts his face in the mirror before the

SHORT CUTS

The Yellow Rolls Royce is not one of the greatest movies of the 1960s. It wasn't even one of the 10 best films in 1965, the year it was released. But it is a good example of a cinematic sub-species which never goes completely out of fashion: the portmanteau.

The only constant in the smooth stellar confection, scripted by Terence Rattigan, is the car of the title, shown in three separate stories (one for each new owner).

In the 1970s, Robert Altman would make films like *Nashville* which enabled him to bring in a vast range of characters, not for box-office plunder but because the mosaic effect suited his style. He would return to the same device triumphantly with *Short Cuts*, a series of overlapping stories about LA life which, as David Thomson says, "caught the hazy, slippery looseness, the casual violence and childishness" of the city of angels.

More direct descendants of the *Yellow Rolls Royce* include two Neil Simon films: *California Suite* (the trials of four sets of guests at the Beverley Hills Hotel) and *Plaza Suite* in which Walter Matthau plays the male lead in three different stories set in the same hotel room. *New York Stories* tried a similar trick with three discrete shorts from Coppola, Scorsese and Woody Allen (Allen's is easily the best). But the most ambitious film in this vein has to be *Aria*, in which 10 different directors interpret 10 different arias, an opera film for people with the attention span of an MTV video.

fight. Kubrick made a $100 profit on the film, selling it to RKO, which incorporated it into a triptych called *This Is America*. The narration is, at times, a bit sub-Hemingway but this is still a cracking debut

LA JETEE 1962

Director *Chris Marker* Cast *Jean Négroni, Hélène Chatelain, Davos Hanich*

It would take longer to read the synopsis of this 28-minute short than to watch it. *12 Monkeys* buffs will find it awfully familiar: it is filmmaker Marker's vision of a post-nuclear Earth where the survivors have to travel back in time to find food. (His real name is Christian Bouche-Villeneuve, he chose the Marker surname after the Magic Marker pens). The film, Marker's only foray into fiction, is almost completely made up of still frames (one scene contains some movement) but the effect is startling.

VINCENT 1982

Director *Tim Burton* Cast *Vincent Price*

Burton based this on a poem he'd written about a boy who wants to grow up to be just like Vincent Price (who narrates this). And, as Burton's subsequent work shows, he was being completely serious. Interesting as one of the first uses of the claymation technique, the film's real charm is provided by Burton's vivid, sometimes gruesome, imagination.

WHAT'S OPERA DOC? 1957

Director *Chuck Jones* Cast *Mel Blanc, Arthur Q Bryan*

Richard Wagner meets Bugs Bunny and, as usual Bugs wins, humiliating Elmer Fudd in the process. The wascally wabbit was actually a hare between 1936 and 1938. He was named after a Warner Brothers' artist Ben 'Bugs' Hardaway, who drew the character and wrote "Bugs' bunny" on the sketches. The rabbit has appeared in 158 films but won his only Oscar for *Knightly Knight Bugs* in 1958. As so often happens, he got the right award for the wrong film: Bugs never topped this fusion of opera and cynical humour and Wagner would never seem quite this slick and hip again.

SHOWBIZ

There's no business like show business… well, it's certainly true for movie-makers. Almost everything about it is appealing to film folk for whom the roar of the greasepaint, the smell of the crowd, the tragic lives of stars and the ennui of the director are the stuff of inspiration. Or, as in the case of the wannabe TV movie *Gable And Lombard*, the stuff of Mr Streisand's nightmares.

The movie industry is justly famous for its ability to spend long hours inspecting its own navel fluff. Mind you, it is one of the rare businesses that can repackage that fluff and sell it to the waiting millions for a fat profit. But then the old triumphant style of no business/show business biopic, as summed up by the lyrics of that Irving Berlin song in *Annie Get Your Gun*, was already out of fashion by 1950 when that picture was released. *All About Eve* had filled several limos with Oscars by suggesting the line "there's no people like show people" better be taken ironically. But *Eve* looked innocent compared to *Sunset Boulevard*, a film noir, monster movie and merciless dissection of showbiz all rolled into one (for a review turn to the film noir section on p180). If you like your showbiz films in a minor key, try Woody Allen's gentle *Radio Days* and his wistful B*roadway Danny Rose*. Like Tim Burton's affectionate *Ed Wood*, *Danny Rose* is a reminder that failure can make for a more satisfying movie than success.

THE BAD AND THE BEAUTIFUL 1952
Director Vincente Minnelli Cast Lana Turner, Kirk Douglas, Walter Pidgeon

"Don't worry. Some of the best movies are made by people who hate each other's guts." So says Douglas's movie mogul in this film. In which case, cast and crew of this movie ought to have been at each other's throats. They weren't, although things might have kicked off if Turner's boyfriend hadn't positioned himself permanently on set to 'protect' her from Douglas. Michael's old man is beautifully bad as the manipulative movie

Olivier: happier addressing a music hall audience than poor Yorick

tycoon whose rise and fall are told from the point of view of a director, a writer and an actress (Turner). The film began life as a story in, of all places, the *Ladies Home Journal*, about a "bad" Broadway producer. 'Beautiful' was added to the title when Turner was cast, to make sure her fans knew she was in the film.

BARTON FINK 1991

Director John Turturro, John Goodman, Judy Davis, John Mahoney

> **"I'LL SHOW YOU THE LIFE OF THE MIND!"**
> Karl Mundt, Barton Fink

This Coen brothers film works as a very sharply observed black comedy complete with their favourite vignette of a leader with a Hitler complex: a tyrant standing behind a desk at the other end of the room from the viewer and the central character. Goodman is a joy to behold in the kind of role (the smooth-talking, unreasonably affable psycho) he would reprise in their later work *O Brother, Where Art Thou?* And in the title role Turturro does, as one critic who seriously disliked the film said, offer the most "fanatically detailed caricature of a nerd since the heyday of Jerry Lewis". But for all that it is very funny indeed. Fink is loosely based on Clifford Odets, a playwright whose dream of theatre for the common man evaporated in the swimming pools of Beverly Hills, but this is not an attack on Odets or anyone else. You could even argue that it's a warning by the Coens to themselves not to lose their own individuality in the smooth path to hell that Hollywood can be.

BOOGIE NIGHTS 1997

Director Paul Thomas Anderson *Cast* Mark Wahlberg, Burt Reynolds, Julianne Moore

Wahlberg is the porn star (Dirk Diggler) who is so blessed by nature that if he hung around Newmarket when a race was going off he'd be dragged into a paddock. After a prolonged build up, we finally get see the organ known as Mr Torpedo Area at the end of this dazzling memoir of the 1970s porn business. Reynolds is excellent as a sleazy but sincere porn baron. Anderson shows off with the camera to good effect, especially in the scene around Reynolds' swimming pool which is worthy of Altman. Sadly, by the end of the movie, Diggler is shouting: "I'm ready to shoot my scene right now!" A reminder that those who live by Mr Torpedo Area, may die by it too.

BROADWAY DANNY ROSE 1984

Director Woody Allen *Cast* Woody Allen, Mia Farrow

Casting aside arty Manhattan, Allen travels to the swamps of New Jersey (not far in a car but quite a distance for Allen as a filmmaker, even if the film does soon return to New York) for this bittersweet tale of a theatrical manager who specializes in such novelty acts as blind xylophone players and finds his big chance for the big time with a crooner, only for the mob to try and muscle in on the action. This is both touching and funny, with Allen's snappy one-liners replaced by a sadder humour which emerges more often from the characters. Some critics reckoned this was Allen Lite; don't believe them.

DAY FOR NIGHT 1973
Director Francois Truffaut *Cast* Jacqueline Bisset,
Jean-Pierre Aumont

"Shooting a movie is like a stagecoach trip. At first you hope for a nice ride. Then you just hope to reach your destination." So says the narrator in Truffaut's movie about movies and, in particular, about a director

about to make what is obviously going to be a seriously awful film called *Meet Pamela*. Not that the director is kidding anybody: this is a man who, when he wasn't interviewing Alfred Hitchcock, made 25 films in 25 years. And made them for the simple reason that he never felt as good doing anything else. This is deeply enjoyable fluff with the in-joke of a cameo by Graham Greene appearing as an insurance company salesman.

Jacqueline has just realized that the old bloke who has broken the 'no visitors on set' rule is Graham Greene

ED WOOD 1994
Director Tim Burton *Cast* Johnny Depp, Martin Landau,
Sarah Jessica Parker

Two cheers for Burton for not making this a camp classic but instead an affectionately amusing piece about the man who has posthumously been dubbed the worst film director in the world. It would have been easy to camp it up: Wood (Depp) was a director, after all, who claimed to have gone to war wearing panties and bra underneath his uniform. A director whose cast, as girlfriend Parker says in this film, consists of "the usual gang of misfits and dope addicts". Burton gets one more cheer for giving the film some emotional depth, with its depiction of Wood's relationship with Lugosi (brilliantly played by Landau) who is his co-star, friend and patient. A very funny, affectionate movie. Bill Condon's *Gods And Monsters* (1998), with Ian

McKellen as the openly gay horror movie director James Whale, may also appeal if you enjoyed this.

8½ 1963

Director Federico Fellini *Cast* Marcello Mastroianni, Anouk Aimée

Boring, self-indulgent, a parade (to use a Fellini-esque word) of images and not ideas – as a film, this pleads guilty to all of these. But it is also, as the American critic Roger Ebert says, a film "about artistic bankruptcy... richer in invention than almost anything else around". Mastroianni is, as usual, Fellini's surrogate, a director bored with the sci-fi epic he is about to direct and with his complex love life. Any film which takes its title from the number of films the director had made up to that point is never going to escape a charge of self-indulgence but this is more than worth the effort if only to see the seductive form of Claudia Cardinale. Look out for two of the director's many trademarks: the rocket tower going to nowhere (on the film set) and the circus-style parade at the end of the film.

THE ENTERTAINER 1960

Director Tony Richardson *Cast* Laurence Olivier, Brenda de Banzie, Roger Livesey

Usually billed as Olivier's greatest performance but people who saw the John Osborne play would disagree. The film's attempt to disguise its stage roots, in the eyes of film writer Richard Schickel, interrupts the arc of Olivier's performance. Those of us too young to have seen Olivier live aren't burdened by such memories and can just enjoy this for what is still a fantastic turn full of self-loathing, bravado and doubt as the music hall comedian Archie Rice, who destroys everyone's life around him but is too blind to realize it. Olivier said, while making this, that he'd never been Hamlet but he'd always been Archie Rice at heart. Certainly he never looked more at home on the screen.

FRANCES 1982

Director Graeme Clifford *Cast* Jessica Lange, Sam Shepard

Even the makers of this film don't seem to know why actress Frances Farmer, the 'heroine' of this movie, self-destructed. The documentary *Committed* focuses more heavily on her radical political views but in this film the emphasis is more on the personal, especially on her relationship with the mother who allowed her to be declared insane (some kids do 'ave 'em). Lange is very moving as Frances but the script lets her and Shepard down somewhat. If you want to see the subject in her own best film, look out for *Come And Get It* (1936), in which she plays a dual role of saloon singer and daughter. Six years after that (and after Paramount had dropped her) she was arrested for drink driving and the hell (including 11 years in assorted asylums and a partial lobotomy) would begin.

SULLIVAN'S TRAVELS 1941
Director **Preston Sturges** *Cast* **Joel McCrea, Veronica Lake**
Sullivan (McCrea) is a director for whom things go from bad to worse. His relationship with Lake founders as do his plans to make a "picture of dignity, a true canvas of the suffering of humanity" (which he wants to call *O Brother Where Art Thou?*) and he ends up, for reasons that you need to see the film to understand, losing his freedom and identity and finishing up in a prison camp where he finally discovers the uplifting power of a Disney cartoon. Yes, this is pretty strong stuff for 1941 and it's a celluloid miracle that he ever got to make this film in the way he wanted. Sturges' movie was interpreted as suggesting that directors should stick to entertainment, which wasn't quite what he meant, but the irony is that his own career as a director would begin a Sullivan-like slide a few years later.

TONIGHT, MATTHEW...

STARS WHO PLAYED OTHER STARS
THE GOOD
Bette Davies as Joan Crawford
Her relationship with Joan Crawford was dubbed Hollywood's "divine feud" so imagine Bette's delight when she realized she could play the role of an Oscar-winning actress who refuses to admit that her career was over as if she was Joanie! The character's name changed but this was a better Crawford impersonation than Faye Dunaway's in *Mommie Dearest*.
Rudolph Nureyev as Valentino
When you're playing the greatest screen lover ever, you need charisma above all and Nureyev, in his first real film role, has it in spades even if his technique sometimes lets him down.
THE BAD
James Brolin as Clark Gable
Jimmy must have a certain something because he has wed diva of divas, Barbra Streisand. But whatever 'it' is, is not apparent in this 1976 biopic where he plays the King of Hollywood. But it was a stretch for an actor best known as

a guest on *Marcus Welby MD*. Not that the script helped. As he inspects the wreckage of the plane in which his wife Carole Lombard had died, what does the King of Hollywood say? "I told her she should have taken the train." That's pathos. Or bathos.
Guy Pearce as Errol Flynn
When Pearce was still mainly known as wimpy teacher on *Neighbours*, he appeared in the biopic *Flynn*. If Errol had been alive when this was made it wouldn't have been called a biopic, it would have been called libellous.
THE UGLY
Misty Rowe as Marilyn Monroe
Hollywood has been saying goodbye to Marilyn for 39 years now but never quite as nastily as in this sexploitation account of her rise. Six rapes later (and memorable dialogue like "I am somebody, I really am somebody") she has passed her first screen test. Rowe allegedly has a daughter called Dreama Jane but that may be just something her enemies have put around to discredit her.

BL/Bryanston/Woodfall/Holly, Films du Carrosse/PECF/PIC

Silent movies spoke to nobody and everybody. DW Griffith's masterpiece *Birth Of A Nation* caused riots when it was released (even if the reports were exaggerated for publicity purposes) and movies have had the attention of most of the world ever since. The universal language of silents died out in the 1930s leaving us only with the universal language of Esperanto. Even today the silent era exerts a fascination which can't quite be explained by jerky black and white films of actors making the kind of hand gestures for which you can get arrested in the world's more repressive regimes.

"I MUST KNOW EVERYTHING. I MUST PENETRATE TO THE HEART OF HIS SECRET. I MUST BECOME CALIGARI"

Dr Caligari, Das Kabinett Des Doktor Caligari

Pity the poor residents of Hollywood in the 1910s. Cowboys would ride whooping across their manicured lawns, Keystone Cops' kiddy-wagons would skid across their street, and one day in 1917, when Cecil B DeMille was directing the shooting of *Nan Of Music Mountain*, a blizzard of asbestos snow blew all the way down the street from the studio and along the whole of Hollywood Boulevard.

By then, though, the residents would probably have sussed that it was pointless to complain. Fuelled by the government's apparently insatiable demand for propaganda pictures to spur the war effort, Hollywood was already on its way to becoming the movie capital of the world. With hindsight, such domination seems inevitable but it didn't look like that at the time. The invention of moving pictures was the subject of as many claims and counterclaims as the location of the Holy Grail had been in 13th-century Europe. America and France had the best claims, Germany's were pressed only when the Nazis came to power. And westerns, that quintessentially American celluloid phenomenon, were being filmed in the French mountain region of Camargue as far back as 1907.

World War I tipped the balance, just as its sequel would elevate America to superpowerdom. European film industries were shut down as governments, slow to realize the power of propaganda, mobilized the chemicals used in film for the war effort. By the time the war was over, Hollywood had become the largest manufacturer of escapist entertainment in the world. Throughout the 1920s, while the Germans were experimenting with expressionism, Hollywood was making the pictures which, although most of them weren't considered pioneering or experimental, made the most money. A pattern had been established.

To be fair, some of Hollywood's silents were exceptional (as you will see from the selection of films here) and this peculiar part of California was never quite as crass as the rest of the world would like to believe. To take one spectacularly pointless example of Hollywood's loftier artistic ambitions: by 1924, the American film industry had made 32 different films based on the works of William Shakespeare, including *Indian Romeo And Juliet* and *Daring Youth*, based on *The Taming Of The Shrew* which, as it was directed by William 'one shot' Beaudine, may be the worst movie of the Bard's work ever. Two versions of *Macbeth* were made without the actor being given the chance to orate: "Tomorrow and tomorrow and tomorrow", but the first filmmakers did at least have the sense to leave *Hamlet* and all that "to be or not to be" stuff until the coming of sound.

What follows is a potpourri of silent films chosen because they have some merit, technical significance or were, in the opinion of the reviewers, good to watch.

DAS KABINETT DES DOKTOR CALIGARI 1920

Director **Robert Wiene** *Cast* **Werner Krauss, Conrad Veidt**
The best way to describe this film is to use the words of the opening title. It is, the writers Hans Jonaowitz and Carl Mayer insist, "a modern representation of an 11th-century myth in which a mountebank monk bears a strange and mysterious influence over a somnambulist". Except, of course, the 11th-Century myth is a 20th-Century invention. Full of zombies, mad scientists and just the plain mad, Caligari may be the movie which invented the horror genre. And like the truly great horror films, argument rages over what it all means: is the sleepwalking zombie who's controlled by an evil man an allegory of World War I? The film's point of view, a man in an asylum telling a story which may or may not be true, also seems years ahead of its time.

FLESH AND THE DEVIL 1926

Director **Clarence Brown** *Cast* **Greta Garbo, John Gilbert**
The 1920s may have been the decade which put the sin

THE HELPLESS ELF
Almost every comedian suffers from Charles Chaplin syndrome. Even Charlie Chaplin himself. Put simply, it is a comic's natural urge to prove they are not just a funny face. So Charlie the clown becomes Charles the social satirist. Chaplin had the art to make the switch. Rival silent clown Harry Langdon didn't. Nursed by Frank Capra, Langdon was one of the funniest stars of the 1920s with a naïve charm which made him the equal of Chaplin, Keaton and Lloyd. Then he sacked Capra, took control and made duff films. By the time he realized his error, sound had made him obsolete. He ended up making films on Poverty Row but his classic *Long Pants* is still one of the golden silents.

Harry Langdon, comic champ and a legend in his own mind, was lovely in *Long Pants*

into syncopation but the star was not happy with her image. After reading the script, Garbo told MGM boss Louis B Mayer that she could not see the sense in getting dressed up and tempting men in her pictures: "They said: 'That's just too bad. Go on and get your clothes on and get ready.'" When she tried to pick the less vampish costumes she was threatened with suspension. None of this mattered because Garbo, who had recently separated from her mentor Maurice Stiller, fell in love with her co-star. In one famous scene she turns around the communion cup to the exact place her lover had drunk from, turning a holy rite into a sensual act but did so with such suffering that the censor could not possibly object. Buoyed by the publicity surrounding their affair, the film was a box office smash and the pattern was set: Garbo would play vamps almost as often as John Wayne would play a cowboy.

"HERE THE STORY SHOULD REALLY END, FOR, IN REAL LIFE, THE FORLORN OLD MAN WOULD HAVE NOTHING TO LOOK FORWARD TO BUT DEATH"

Title card, The Last Laugh

THE GENERAL 1927

Directors Clyde Bruckman, Buster Keaton Cast Buster Keaton, Marion Mack, Glen Cavender

The first cannonball shot didn't go to well so to make sure the ball shot into the cab correctly, Keaton counted out the grains of gunpowder with a pair of tweezers. Amazingly, when the film was released, you could have almost picked up its box-office takings with the same tweezers. This comic retelling of a Civil War railroad raid would have to wait a while before achieving classic status. One critic called it a "mild Civil War comedy". But Keaton refused to mug for the camera in a way which even such gifted rivals as Chaplin and Harold Lloyd would do, one reason why his films are so easy to watch today. He was rediscovered in the 1960s and fans should try and get hold of Buster Keaton Rides Again (1965), a 'making of' documentary about the same year's The Railroder which includes clips from The General and shows Keaton at work, devising gags.

GREED 1925

Director Erich von Stroheim Cast Gibson Gowland, Zasu Pitts

You might find this 140-minute classic hard going. But not as hard as von Stroheim did. His quest for realism, in this tale of an innocent dentist driven to double murder, was so intense that he filmed the final Death Valley scene in Death Valley. The crew mutinied, von Stroheim slept with a pistol under his pillow and during one scene, where the actors weren't fighting with enough venom, he shouted: "Fight! Fight! Try to hate each other as you hate me!" When the film was finally finished, it was nine hours long. First six, then seven hours were cut for release. Stroheim told MGM boss Louis B Mayer he was less than rabble, a remark which Mayer greeted with a punch which sent the director spinning through the office door and onto the floor, still clutching his cane and gloves. Was the film worth it? God yes, if for no other reason than the last scene where the hero frees his pet canary in the desert which then flutters a little and dies. It's hard to watch that image and not chuckle at the horror and rage with which Mayer must have reacted when he saw it.

THE LAST LAUGH 1924

Director FW Murnau Cast Emil Jannings, Maly Delschaft

Wilhelm Plumpe wanted to be an actor but his red hair and the fact that he was nearly six-and-a-half feet tall counted against him. As FW Murnau he would become one of the three greatest German directors of the 1920s (alongside Fritz Lang and Ernst Lubitsch). In this simple tale of a hotel doorman (Jannings) who is demoted and humiliated, Murnau pioneered the use of the tracking camera while making an almost perfect silent film. The flow of the camerawork was emphasized by the fact that the film only had one title card and that was inserted partly because the studio didn't like the end. Writer Carl Mayer, forced to add a happy ending, had his revenge by inserting a title which pointed out the ensuring twist was "quite improbable". It was a shame because there is something

Louise Brooks, the first actress to become synonymous with a hairstyle and a fetching range of jim jams

WHAT HAS DW DONE FOR US?

DW Griffith is the most famous name of the silent era. Those of us who aren't film buffs may know that he directed *Birth Of A Nation* which, a bit like the year 1066 in British history, sounds important. At least with 1066 we know there was a Battle of Hastings. With Griffiths' epic its importance (like his) is elusive. So what, apart from starting a fashion among film moguls for the use of initials (they stand for David Wark by the way) did he ever do for us? Here is a list in the order they sprang to mind.
1 He discovered Lillian Gish, Mary Pickford and Mack Sennett.
2 He discovered (with cameraman Billy Blitzer) how to shoot scenes towards the light.
3 He changed the way actors acted. Director Allan Dwan (most famous for *The Sands Of Iwo Jima*) recalled: "His girls never made the wide, sweeping old-fashioned theatrical movements such as we'd get from the old

hams. We all imitated him."
4 He "virtually invented the profession of film director," say the Association of US Film Critics. Certainly he created a stereotype of how directors behave. He was quoted, by Josef von Sternberg, as telling an assistant: "Move these 10,000 horses a trifle to the right, and that mob out there three feet forward."
5 He did more than anyone else to overcome the middle class' distrust of film by making epics on 'important' subjects like the reconstruction of the South, the American Revolution and the importance of tolerance.
6 He founded United Artists studio with Chaplin, Pickford, and Fairbanks.
7 He revived the Ku Klux Klan. His epic *Birth Of A Nation* was pro-Klan and led to an immediate boost in recruitment: 25,000 members in costume walked through Atlanta to celebrate the film's première in 1915.

peculiarly German about the doorman's tragedy – and his pride in position and uniform seem to anticipate the rise of the Nazis.

PANDORA'S BOX 1929 DIE BUCHSE DER PANDORA

Director GW Pabst Cast Louise Brooks, Fritz Kortner

"Every actor has a natural animosity toward every other actor, present or absent, living or dead." So said Brooks in her amusing account of the making of this psycho-sexual melodrama. Kortner hated her so much that after every scene he would run to his dressing room and beat the walls with his fists. The director, Brooks decided, was filled with "sexual hate" towards her. Some of this oddness infuses the story of Lulu, a woman who doesn't start out as a prostitute, she just behaves like one and has the fatal lack of taste to give Jack the Ripper a free one. Brooks' Lulu is one of the most enigmatic, erotic, presences ever conjured up on celluloid but there's something more... it's the look on her face as a lover gets accidentally shot, as if she is a spectator, watching her own life and his death.

THE PASSION DE JEANNE D'ARC 1928

Director Carl Theodor Dreyer Cast Maria Falconetti, Eugene Silvain

The only surviving print of this film ended up in a mental institution in Oslo. Luckily, it was rescued. Danish director Dreyer threw away the screenplay he had been given and went back to the transcript of the trial. He cast an actress, Falconetti, who never made another movie, and shot the film in close-ups and medium shots. The University of Wisconsin's David Bordwell, who analysed the film, found that: "Of the film's 1500 cuts, less than 20 carried a figure or object over from one to another." The effect is to strip away the normal frippery of historical drama and force us to focus on the relationship between Joan and her inquisitors. Jean Cocteau famously said the film is like "an historical document from an era in which the cinema didn't exist". Robert Bresson's *The Trial Of Joan Of Arc* (1962) is the only other version which stands comparison.

THE THIEF OF BAGHDAD 1924

Director Raoul Walsh Cast Douglas Fairbanks, Julanne Johnston

Walsh has always been vastly underrated. His name was not mentioned in glowing reviews of Fairbank's most extravagant fable, not even by the critic who said it had learnt from the errors of DW Griffith's *Intolerance*. The marvel is that the Arabian nights settings and the stunts still seem fresh today, possibly because the director and star employed William Cameron Menzies, who would later design *Gone With The Film*.

SOUNDTRACKS

Movies have always had music, even the silent ones. And let's be honest, who has not watched a film and thought there was something to be said for the local part-time pianist? Music and film have not always had an easy marriage. When David Selznick wanted a love theme for his 1947 epic romance *Duel In The Sun*, he told composer Dimitri Tiomkin his score lacked passion. "That's just not an orgasm," he shouted. "It's too beautiful. It's not shtump. It's not the way I fuck." To which Tiomkin famously replied: "Mr Selznick, you fuck your way, I fuck my way. To me, that is fucking music!" For once, the composer won the argument.

A STREETCAR NAMED DESIRE 1951
Director Elia Kazan Music Alex North

When Maurice Jarre's score for *Ghost* was nominated for an Oscar, many felt North should have shared that citation as it was his song, *Unchained Melody*, written for a movie called *Unchained* in 1955, which set the musical mood for the film. For *Streetcar*, North introduced jazz to the Hollywood score and did away with the traditional symphony orchestra with which every scene or emotion had hitherto been underlined. He got his first Academy Award nomination for having the gall to introduce blues and jazz to the movie score but, as with the other 13 nominations, he didn't win. Pity really, because critics will tell you this is the most important score in the history of American film. And they're only exaggerating very slightly.

BREWSTER MCCLOUD 1971
Director Robert Altman Music Gene Page

Gene Page was the evil genius behind many of Barry White's biggest hits but it isn't his score that makes this soundtrack so special, it's the input of the late John Phillips, singer/songwriter and creative guru for The Mamas And The Papas. Of the eight songs, four are written by Phillips (*White Weather Wings*, *Promise Not To Tell*, *Last Of The Unnatural Acts* and *The First And Last Thing To Do*). He sings all but *White Weather Wings*. These are the tracks which really stand out on the soundtrack album (apologies Mr Page) and while they don't match the glory of

> "MY BROTHER MADE MUSIC WITH HIS FISTS SO THAT I MIGHT MAKE A GENTLER MUSIC"
>
> Eddie Kenny, City For Conquest

Monday Monday or *California Dreamin'* they are a classy bunch. Oh, and the film, about a boy who dreams of flying in the Houston Astrodome, isn't bad either.

CLOSE ENCOUNTERS OF THE THIRD KIND 1977

Director **Steven Spielberg** *Music* **John Williams**

"IT WAS A BIT FROM THE GLORIOUS NINTH BY LUDWIG VAN
Alex, A Clockwork Orange

The famous five-note alien message motif in this sci-fi epic was Spielberg's idea. Williams had wanted a longer motif but they noticed that even adding just one or two notes began to create a tune. So he stuck to five notes and created 350 combinations, all of which were played on the piano with Spielberg to decide which was the most haunting. It later emerged that Williams, who began thinking about the score two years before the deal was finalized, often wrote music for Spielberg to put scenes to. The two collaborated to more serious effect on *Schindler's List*.

ESCAPE FROM NEW YORK 1981

Director **John Carpenter** *Music* **John Carpenter**

SUPERFLY

THE FLYING SCORE

Superfly has the rare distinction of being the only movie to be outgrossed by its own soundtrack, which sold four million copies. This so-so, 1972 blaxploitation flick about a cocaine dealer who wants to get out of the business was supposed to star Ron O'Neal but really stars Curtis Mayfield, whose soundtrack is far, far cooler than O'Neal and the movie put together. And, apart from Marvin Gaye's *What Goes On*, can lay claim to being the best soul album of the 1970s. Mayfield's live performance of *Pusherman* in the club may just be the best thing in the movie. The only downside about his work is that it encouraged the producers to make a sequel the year after (adding TNT to the original title in a vain attempt to ignite some box-office dynamite).

Carpenter comes from the 'If you want something doing, do it yourself' school of film music, having scored 16 of his 19 films. But then his dad was head of music at Western Kentucky University. He likes to cast musicians like Alice Cooper and Isaac Hayes in his films. His scores, though, don't have much in common with Cooper or Hayes; they are normally electronic soundscapes which appal hardcore movie music fans. The melody in this film, one buff said, sounds like one of Casio's digital watches. That said, Carpenter always sticks close to the original aim of film music: to make the film more effective.

THE FABULOUS BAKER BOYS 1989

Director **Steve Kloves** *Music* **Dave Grusin**

Dave Grusin earned his second Oscar nomination in a row for this score even though when you mention the music in this film, most of us think of Michelle Pfeiffer making whoopee on a piano. Grusin started out accompanying Andy Williams and it sounds trite to say that as a composer he's emulated the Emperor of Easy but he's often subtle and seldom showy. At its worst, his music for this film sounds like a better than average theme for a hit cop series on US TV. At its best, it contributes beautifully to the bitter-sweet mood of the film. Pfeiffer's character sings several other standards to great effect as well as memorably observing that the world would not be a vastly poorer

SOUNDTRACKS

place if nobody ever sang Morris Albert Kaisermann's *Feelings* in public again. That said, when she says that *Feelings* is like parsley, you can't help feeling that parsley should be able to sue.

GOLDFINGER 1964

Director Guy Hamilton Music John Barry

This was the score which defined the Bond sound. Take one gorgeously OTT ballad (preferably sung by Shirley Bassey or, failing that, someone with as powerful a pair of lungs, like Sheena Easton), work the theme throughout the film and pump in some serious brass and percussion action. All that and make sure there's a dodgy rhyme in the theme song (William McGonagall would be proud of goldfinger/coldfinger). It's such a perfect mix here that the soundtrack album knocked The Beatles off the number one spot. Barry would score nine Bond movies in total but he would never really top this.

THE LONG GOODBYE 1973

Director Robert Altman Music John Williams

John Williams is justly famous for his music for megahits like *Star Wars* but his contribution to Altman's oblique take on Philip Marlowe is finer still. He was set an incredibly difficult brief by his director, as the soundtrack consists of endless variations of one song (with the lyrical refrain "The long goodbye, it happens every day" written by Johnny Mercer) rearranged, with voices and as an instrumental, throughout the film. It's risky but it works. The unusual effect undoubtedly adds to the movie's haunting, melancholic mood while ensuring that the film would have no spin-off soundtrack album. Which may explain why Williams' work on this film has never really had the credit it deserved.

THE MOON IN THE GUTTER 1983

Director Jean-Jacques Beineix Music Gabriel Yared

Yared is best known for his Oscar-winning music for Anthony Minghella's *The English Patient* (even if cynics accused him of merely trying to be a John Barry clone after he composed it) but 13 years before that he contributed this sumptuous score to Beineix's moody, mesmerising tale of rape, guilt, class and love set in some mysterious, menacing docks. Indeed there are times when the cinematography by Phillipe Roussellot and Yared's surging, rather grand, music completely take over the film and Gérard Depardieu and Natassja Kinski seem like figures walking in someone else's dream.

RY SPRY

Ry Cooder's long movie career is in danger of being summed up in two films: *Paris, Texas* and *Buena Vista Social Club*. The 1983 Wim Wenders road movie starring Harry Dean Stanton was in the cinematic territory which seemed to suit Cooder best – he always seems more at home making music for movies set in the American south and west. Cooder himself says: "Everyone seems to like *Paris, Texas*. Even the Tuvans thought it was great and they're pretty dour and rock hard. As far as they're concerned, 20th-century life is a crock of shit but they liked *Paris, Texas*, even though I don't think they saw the film."

373

ONCE UPON A TIME IN THE WEST 1968

Director **Sergio Leone** *Music* **Ennio Morricone**

Leone and Morricone were almost as established a movie double act as Laurel and Hardy. Like any partnership, it had its odd moments. Leone recalls sitting with Morricone in the viewing theatre while the composer roared with helpless laughter as his *Dollars* films were shown – and not just at the bits that were supposed to be funny. For this film, Morricone had composed the music before the cameras started rolling. Leone recalls: "Throughout the shooting schedule we listened to the recordings, followed its rhythm and suffered its aggravating qualities which grind the nerves." Henry Fonda, Jason Robards and Claudia Cardinale all have their own signatures. Morricone has never matched his work here, except possibly on *The Mission*.

PULP FICTION 1994

Director **Quentin Tarantino** *Music supervisor* **Karyn Rachtman**

Purists often complain that the noble art of film music has been corrupted by the arrival of a greatest hits-style soundtrack designed to keep MTV viewers tuned in. Many films are now better to listen to than to watch and understand, but Tarantino devised an eclectic, but apt, selection of songs for *Pulp*. These vary from the apparently innocent but sinister sounding *Flowers On The Wall* by the Statler Brothers to Urge Overkill's true to the spirit cover of Neil Diamond's *Girl You'll Be A Woman Soon*. In a similar vein, the soundtrack to *The Blues Brothers* is light years ahead of the usual greatest hits package with Aretha Franklin singing *Think* while Jake and Elwood (and Joe Walsh) do that rarest of musical beasts, a decent cover of *Jailhouse Rock*.

OLD MASTER

Miklos Rosza "never went near the studio unless absolutely necessary". He had good reason: the Hungarian composer deemed his score for *Spellbound* his finest work until Hitchcock, stupidly, told him he didn't like it because it got in the way of the film. Rosza didn't arrive in Hollywood until 1940, imported at the behest of Alexander Korda. It's just as well he came because film noir wouldn't have been as noir without Rosza's eerie scores, which is why Steve Martin asked him to work on his private eye spoof *Dead Men Don't Wear Plaid*. Between 1940 and 1995 he scored almost every kind of film (winning an Oscar for *Ben-Hur*) and, for *The Killers*, invented the "dum de dum dum" theme used for *Dragnet*... all that and *Spellbound*.

THE SEA HAWK 1940

Director **Michael Curtiz** *Music* **Erich Wolfgang Korngold**

You can meet students of film music who will tell you Erich Wolfgang Korngold is the finest composer of the 20th century. To which the only response is to smile quietly and head for the nearest exit. He was called Wolfgang, he was born in the old Austrian empire and he was a child prodigy, but there the resemblance to Mozart ends. But if anybody can be held to have invented orchestral film music, it's probably Korngold. *Kings Row* is often held to be his finest film score but there's an adolescent grandeur to his music for this seafaring adventure yarn which nobody has yet surpassed.

SPACE

There are people alive today who think "Houston we have a problem" was originally said by Tom Hanks. Nasa may have trouble getting funds for the space race but the odyssey, at least as far as the world's filmmakers are concerned, is far from over.

APOLLO 13 1995

Director **Ron Howard** *Cast* **Tom Hanks, Bill Paxton, Kevin Bacon, Gary Sinise, Ed Harris, Kathleen Quinlan**

Director Howard sensibly opted to make *Apollo 13* – the story of the mission in which Nasa nearly lost its astronauts– a virtual docu-drama. Sticking closely to mission member Jim Lovell's book *The Lost Moon*, he focuses on the technical details of the shuttle and the period details of the 1970s, with the tension and suspense stemming from the relationships of the crew members and the Nasa team back on Earth. The world's lack of initial interest in the mission is cleverly underlined. Hanks, who mercifully replaced original choice Kevin Costner, gives a measured performance as the experienced Lovell, allowing his co-crew, particularly Bacon, to shine. Harris is good as the kind of solid, reliable, executive you wish really was running Nasa.

ARMAGEDDON 1998

Director **Michael Bay** *Cast* **Bruce Willis, Ben Affleck, Liv Tyler**

"The fate of the planet is in the hands of a bunch of retards I wouldn't trust with a potato gun." A pretty fair summation of our heroes in this tale of deep-core drillers asked to save the world by planting nuclear bombs in an asteroid hurtling towards Earth. Although an all-out action fest, the scenes of our band of heroes drilling an asteroid while trying to prevent themselves shooting into the void are some of the most exciting space scenes yet filmed. Billy Bob Thornton also gives excellent support as the obligatory man on the ground guiding the crew.

CAPRICORN ONE 1977

Director **Peter Hyams** *Cast* **Elliott Gould, James Brolin**

The premise of this sci-fi thriller more than makes up for the film's failings. Three astronauts are asked to fake a Nasa mission to Mars in a studio when their ship is found to be

> **"I KNOW I'VE MADE SOME VERY POOR DECISIONS RECENTLY, BUT I CAN GIVE YOU MY COMPLETE ASSURANCE THAT MY WORK WILL BE BACK TO NORMAL"**
> HAL, 2001: Space Odyssey

Warner/Ladd

"The next person to ask me if I've got the right stuff gets it"

defective, but they learn part of the plot is that they die in 'outer space' so that the big secret never gets out. Hyams (who also directed the kitschy *Outland*, *2010* and *Timecop*) keeps the pace up, and while some of the dialogue is dreadful (and co-star OJ Simpson's delivery even worse) this is a hugely entertaining guilty pleasure. The film stars both Barbra Streisand's first husband (Gould) and her current one, Brolin.

COUNTDOWN 1968
Director **Robert Altman** *Cast* **James Caan, Joanna Moore, Robert Duvall, Barbara Baxley**
Overshadowed by *2001*, which was released the same year, *Countdown* captured brilliantly the race between the Americans and the Russians to land the first man on the moon. Caan stars in an early performance as Stegler, who is chosen over Chiz (Duvall) to lead the US mission but has only three weeks to train before he is sent into space in the old-generation Gemini craft. The Russians, however, take off first. Altman focuses on the emotional crises affecting the men and their families, a relief from space movies' customary reliance on technical features.

THE DISH 2000
Director **Rob Sitch** *Cast* **Sam Neill, Kevin Harrington, Tom Long**
This Australian comedy (from the director of the equally funny *The Castle*) is based on a true story and offers a unique take on the 1969 Neil Armstrong moon landing. A satellite system on

a small sheep farm in Parkes, deep in the heart of Australia, is chosen as Nasa's back-up dish for transmitting pictures of this historic event to the world. Comedy comes from the array of peculiar characters in Parkes, including the pipe-smoking scientist Cliff (Neill) and his team of semi-professionals, and the possibilities of things going wrong – starting with the dish being in the middle of a sheep farm in the first place. A slight comedy of the underdog shining through.

FOR ALL MANKIND 1989
Director Al Reinert

Talented as Hollywood is, you can't beat actual footage of man's travels in space for sheer exhilaration. On all 24 space missions between 1968 and 1972, a camera was placed on board, recording every moment of these historic outings. Splicing together excerpts from more than six million reams of film, director Reinert captures the beauty of the mission and the Brian Eno/Daniel Lanois soundtrack is incredibly haunting.

OCTOBER SKY 1999
Director Joe Johnston Cast Jake Gyllenhaal, Chris Cooper, Laura Dern

Focusing on what was every boy's dream during the height of the 1950s space race, this is based on Homer Hickman's best-selling novel *The Rocket Boys*. (The film title is an anagram of the novel's title, a compromise between writer and studio.) Gyllenhaal lives in the mining town of Coalwood. When Sputnik goes into orbit, he and his friends decide they'll try to build rockets, alienating their families and the townsfolk in the process. Only a teacher (Dern), supports them, entering them in the National Science competition. Although the film sounds like a TV movie, it is exhilarating entertainment and a reminder that the nothing-is-impossible spirit that the space race was founded on didn't always sit well in American society.

> "THAT'S BULLSHIT. YOU JUST BULLSHITTED NASA!"
> Ross 'Mitch' Mitchell, The Dish

THE RIGHT STUFF 1983
Director Philip Kaufman Cast Sam Shepard, Scott Glen, Ed Harris, Dennis Quaid

If you didn't know the events were true, Kaufman's adaptation of Tom Wolfe's book would seem ludicrous. The film opens with Chuck Yeager (Shepard) breaking the sound barrier and starting the space race. Although more than three hours long, it's an enthralling piece of cinema with Kaufman focusing on each of America's first astronauts. Most of the actors met their real-life counterparts – only Scott Glen chose not to meet Alan Shepherd until after the film was done, preferring to observe footage and talk to friends. Mainly a character piece, but it does feature the first realistic shots of a spacecraft re-entering Earth's atmosphere, using small models of the Mercury capsule ignited. Watch out for a cameo by the real Yeager as a bartender.

SEX MISSION 1984 SEKSMISJA

Director Juliusz Machulski Cast Ryszarda Hanin, Elzbieta Jasinska
For this Polish filmmaker, the future is full of nudity and sex. Two scientists are chosen as guinea pigs for a test in human hibernation, only to wake up 50 years later to find that they are the only living men on an earth inhabited solely by women. You can probably guess where the film goes from there.

SOLARIS 1971

Director Andrei Tarkovsky Cast Natalya Bondarchuk, Donatas Banionis
Nearly three hours long, *Solaris* (loosely based on Stanislaw Lem's novel of the same name) was Tarkovsky's response to *2001*, an often meandering, metaphysical tale of a psychiatrist investigating strange events on Solaris, a planet which conjures up spirits (including that of his wife who committed suicide years before). More a piece of poetry than a movie, this won the grand jury prize at Cannes although it is said to be one of the director's least favourite of his own movies.

SPACECAMP 1986

Director Harry Winer Cast Kate Capshaw, Lea Thompson, Kelly Preston, Tom Skerritt
Meant to be a light-hearted adventure (about a group of kids and instructors from a space camp accidentally getting hands-on experience of life in space), this was all set for release when the real-life Challenger disaster struck. Eerily, the cause of the Challenger disaster was similar to the malfunction in the movie, which was put on hold. It's a cool film for the kids, however, with Skerritt very plausible as a spaceman.

THE WOMAN IN THE MOON 1929

Director Fritz Lang Cast Fritz Rasp, Gerda Maurus, Willy Fritsch
Lang's last silent film still managed to stir controversy and make its own mark in history. On finding there's gold on the moon Pohl joins with ambitious engineer Fritsch to journey there. Too many cooks spoil the broth, however, and trouble brews between the pair and their crew. The film does contain the first ever countdown launch – Lang's most ingenious dramatic invention – and Lang's vision of a rocket turned out to be a little too close to the mark: the Nazis withdrew the film in a bid to preserve the secrecy of their own rocket.

SPOOFS

What other kind of film can you stick on when you get in from the pub, whether you want to roll around laughing with your mates or prefer to intellectually dissect the essential ingredients of the Hollywood blockbuster with reference to the self referential subplot and singing nuns? As relentless as a sequel, there will always be a spoof following hard on the heels of any successful film. Parodies can take on specific films (*Airplane!*), entire genres (*Blazing Saddles*) or just be an excuse for gags about bodily functions.

AIRPLANE! 1980

Director Jerry Zucker, Jim Abrahams, David Zucker
Cast Leslie Nielsen, Robert Hays

Probably the best known spoof movie, based on the events and characters from the *Airport* trilogy and other disaster movies, though it doesn't lose a jot of its humour if you've never seen them. Keep your eyes peeled for the full 90 minutes because there is a constant hammering of jokes going on – other than the one you are currently laughing at – and nearly all the gags have aged well. Robert Hays, who stars in both *Airplane* movies, is perfectly cast as dull Ted Striker the hapless hero, who has to overcome his fears and step into the pilot seat when a plane's crew falls victim to food poisoning. The sequel however, is not directed by the same Zucker/Abrahams/Zucker trio, and suffers quite a bit as a result.

Blazing Saddles had its sound censored on TV but not, thank god, the scene where the sheriff sings *I Get A Kick Out Of You*

BLAZING SADDLES 1974

Director Mel Brooks Cast Gene Wilder, Cleavon Little

Brooks' first hit movie is a western spoof, which almost 30 years on is still hugely popular – last year ranking sixth in the American Film Institute's funniest US films of all time. It's offensive, sexist and rude and one of the few films to have had sound censored. The TV version cut the flatulence of the campfire scene and replaced it with belching. Coincidentally, the name of the character Brooks plays (Governor William J

"THESE ARE PEOPLE OF THE LAND. COMMON CLAY OF THE NEW WEST – YOU KNOW, MORONS"
The Waco Kid, Blazing Saddles

"Yeah Captain I have seen a grown man naked. It was in a Turkish prison. There was this fat guy on a meathook"

Petomane) is taken from the stage name of a popular French performer whose speciality was telling stories punctuated with bottom burps. Class act or what?

THE DISCREET CHARM OF THE BOURGEOISIE 1972

Director Luis Bunuel
Cast Fernando Rey, Delphine Seyrig, Stéphane Audran, Michel Piccoli

To call this a spoof is a bit like calling *As You Like It* a sitcom. Bunuel's satire is a very funny attack on a certain way of life but it is also a send-up of our own need for movies that take themselves seriously, ask us to take them seriously and generally make some kind of narrative sense. The director was 72 when he made this, probably his most internationally renowned film, and there's a sense of him doing what he feels like: dreams unfold within other character's dreams. In *That Obscure Object Of Desire* he would have two actresses play the same role, just because he wanted to. Here the bourgeoisie find their attempts to have dinner frustrated by inconvenient corpses and military manoeuvres. Very funny and very unsettling to boot.

DEAD MEN DON'T WEAR PLAID 1982

Director Carl Reiner *Cast* Steve Martin, Rachel Ward

"LET'S GO OUT DANCING! YOU PUT ON YOUR BLACK DRESS AND I'LL GO SHAVE MY TONGUE"
Rigby Reardon, Dead Men Don't Wear Plaid

Parody of a 1940s thriller with Steve Martin playing detective Rigby Reardon, who has to uncover the truth behind the mysterious death of a scientist. Characters and scenes from film noir footage are pasted into the action. Martin's assistant is none other than Humphrey Bogart in his role as Philip Marlowe. (One of Ward's lines is "If you need me, you know how to dial don't you?" an echo of Bacall's famous line to Bogie.) The clips also show legendary designer Edith Head's early work, *Dead Men Don't Wear Plaid* was the final film she worked on.

GALAXY QUEST 1999

Director Dean Parisot *Cast* Tim Allen, Sigourney Weaver

Washed up sci-fi actors find themselves transported into space with the arrival of aliens who have taken their TV show as a documentary, building their entire culture around it. It's obviously *Star Trek* (with a bit of *Alien* thrown in), but you don't have to be a diehard Trekkie to get the gags, although some of them may pass you by if you're not. In fact if you are a Trekkie, be prepared for a good bit of ribbing. As in all good sci-fi movies there has to be an evil warlord and this one is named Sarris, after film critic Andrew Sarris who slated producer Mark Johnson's *The Natural*. Serves him right.

THE GREAT DICTATOR 1940

Director Charlie Chaplin Cast Charlie Chaplin, Jack Oakie

In Chaplin's first full-length talkie, he plays both the part of the dictator Hynkel, who is persecuting the Jews, and the poor Jewish barber who is mistaken for the megalomaniacal leader. If you're thinking that Chaplin would make a great Hitler send-up just on looks alone, you'd be right: it was a friend of his that suggested the similarity which gave Chaplin the idea. Work on the film began in 1937, years before the true extent of Hitler's atrocities came to light. Chaplin later said that he would never have made fun of Hitler's "homicidal insanity" if he had known the full facts. The Führer himself banned the film from all occupied countries. He eventually had a copy brought in to Germany through Portugal which he screened twice out of curiosity, though no record was ever made of his thoughts on it.

HIGH ANXIETY 1977

Director Mel Brooks Cast Mel Brooks, Madeline Khan

Comedy thriller inspired by you know who, and includes scenes from *The Birds* (with the tastiest bird droppings ever – spinach and mayonnaise), *Psycho* and *Vertigo*. Brooks plays a psychiatrist who has just been promoted to head of the Psychoneurotic Institute for the Very Very Nervous after his predecessor dies mysteriously. Death and mayhem ensue. Rudy De Luca (director of spoof horror *Transylvania 6-5000* – see below) appears as a killer and Albert Whitlock, Hitchcock's special effects man, has a cameo.

HOT SHOTS 1986

Director Jim Abrahams Cast Charlie Sheen, Cary Elwes

Primarily a spoof on war films, but with Sheen credited as Rocky, Rhett Butler and Superman along with his fighter pilot role, there's more to this movie than you might

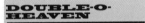

DOUBLE-O-HEAVEN

"I'm going to place him in an easily escapable situation involving an overly elaborate and exotic death"
Austin Powers: International Man of Mystery

It's inevitable and all too easy – which probably explains why the first James Bond spoof appeared only three years after the original *Dr No*. More recently, Mike Myers has starred as goofy time-travelling secret agent Austin Powers. His humour doesn't restrict itself to just Bond, launching off all the 1960s spy movies, although Dr Evil is Blofeld revisited, while his sidekick Random Task and the sinister Alotta Fagina have more than a dictionary definition in common with Oddjob and Pussy Galore. Anoraks may notice that Myers also manages to allude to *Our Man Flint*, using the same distinctive telephone ring for Austin Power's phone.

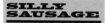

SILLY SAUSAGE

Die Kronung (1999) is a movie short, spoofing detective film noir, mostly parodying Raymond Chandler's Philip Marlowe (*The Big Sleep, The Long Goodbye*...). For just $1 an hour, two private detectives are hired to investigate the case of the Hamburg Bratwurst Queen who has lost her crown and her will to live. Oh, and it's all seen through the eyes of a bulldog of course.

first imagine. Sheen plays ambitious ace pilot Topper, ("Playing to lose is like sleeping with your sister. Sure she's a great piece of tail with a blouse full of goodies, but it's just illegal") who's obsessed with living down his father's disastrous reputation. *Platoon* and *Top Gun* are the obvious victims, though keep your eyes open for spoofs of *Dances With Wolves* and *9 1/2 Weeks* too. Like most popular spoof movies, there was a sequel sending up *Rambo*, a doubly redundant exercise.

MONTY PYTHON AND THE HOLY GRAIL 1975

Director Terry Gilliam, Terry Jones *Cast* John Cleese, Eric Idle, Graham Chapman

The second Python feature failed to impress the original investors (which incidentally included Led Zeppelin, Pink Floyd, Tim Rice and Andrew Lloyd Webber). So much so that the scene which asks whether the audience are enjoying themselves was almost cut for tempting fate. However, the mix of English slapstick wit, phoney sets, chivalric spoofs and speculation about the coconut carrying habits of African swallows saved the day. If you've seen it and find the ending a bit weak, bear in mind it's not the original scripted version – which was to wrap up with King Arthur and his Knights' search ending in Harrods. If you've not yet seen it, watch it now and never be bored in the pub again. Altogether now, "We are the knights who say 'Ni!'"...

> "SO IT'S A KIND
> OF PSYCHIC
> POLITICAL
> THRILLER COMEDY
> WITH A HEART"
> Griffin Mill, The Player

THE NAKED GUN 1988

Director Jerry Zucker, Jim Abrahams, David Zucker *Cast* Leslie Nielsen, Priscilla Presley

The feature-length film of the very short-lived 1982 TV series *Police Squad!* (six episodes shot, four aired but it was officially cancelled after just one) transfers brilliantly to the silver screen and Nielsen continues his fantastic role as incompetent cop Lt Frank Drebin. In this, the first and best *Naked Gun*, he's trying to prevent the assassination of Elizabeth II while falling in love ("Jane, since I've met you I've noticed things I never knew were there before; birds singing, dew glistening on a newly formed leaf, stoplights"). Even if you've never seen it, you've probably heard the best lines already.

THE PLAYER 1992

Director Robert Altman *Cast* Tim Robbins, Greta Scacchi, Fred Ward, Whoopi Goldberg

Apart from *Short Cuts* (1993) this is probably Altman's only really good film of the last decade. A knowing, detailed satire of all things Hollywood, the film stars Robbins as a studio executive who is being pursued by a writer and finally, almost accidentally, takes the law into his own hands. The film is mostly famous for its cast of celebrity cameos (65 of them!) and the opening tracking shot (variously timed at six-and-a-half to eight minutes). The satire, funny as it is, is at the expense of some easy targets but the people you really have to feel sorry for are Tim Curry, Jeff Daniels, Franco Nero and Patrick Swayze. Sixty-five cameos in this film and they are the four poor buggers whose cameos end up on the cutting room floor.

SCHLOCK 1971

Director John Landis *Cast* John Landis, Saul Kahan

'Due to the horrifying nature of this film, no one will be admitted to the theatre', is one of the taglines to Landis' first production, closely followed by: 'The first musical monster movie in years', which gives you some idea of what you are about to encounter. The premise? A monster falling in love with a blind girl. You start to get the picture... Listen out for the line "See you next Wednesday" which became a trademark of Landis' films. It's a line from *2001: A Space Odyssey*, and is the title for a film idea Landis had when he was 15. Whenever he finds himself using ideas from this film in his later work, Landis puts in the phrase as a reference to it.

TAKE THE MONEY AND RUN 1969

Director Woody Allen *Cast* Woody Allen, Janet Margolin

Woody Allen's directorial debut is a mockumentary with himself cast as incompetent crook Virgil. Everything gets in his way – from his handwriting, which hampers his attempts at a hold-up ("that looks like 'gub' – it doesn't look like 'gun'") to using guns made of soap – and getting caught in the rain. Not least of his problems is falling in love with his intended victims – "I was so touched by her that, I don't know, after 15 minutes I wanted to marry her... and after a half-hour I had completely given up the idea of snatching her purse." Eventually, he pulls off a bank heist and is locked up, which is where this film begins, interviewing his family and friends who try to shed light on Virgil's dismal past.

Tim is about to realize every Hollywood executive's favourite fantasy: he's going to murder a writer

THEATRE OF BLOOD 1973

Director Douglas Hickox *Cast* Vincent Price, Diana Rigg

Price does such a good job playing a not very good classical actor that you almost wonder… no, stop that. Here, aided by his luscious daughter (Rigg), he takes revenge on his critics by killing them in appropriate ways, selected from the works of the Bard. Yes, one of the ends is taken from *Titus Andronicus*. Robert Morley gets to eat a meal so unpalatable that even your local landlord wouldn't use it as a pensioners' special. With many spoofs you sense them winding down as if the makers are running out of gags. That never happens here. You can see Price's eyes gleaming with merriment as he tells a victim: "I'll kill you when I'm ready – next week, next month, next year."

TOP SECRET! 1984

Director Jerry Zucker, Jim Abrahams, David Zucker
Cast Val Kilmer, Lucy Gutteridge

"I'm not the first guy who fell in love with a woman that he met at a restaurant who turned out to be the daughter of a kidnapped scientist only to lose her to her childhood lover whom she last saw on a deserted island who then turned out 15 years later to be the leader of the French." So sums up Kilmer,

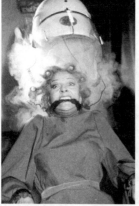

Warner/Crossbow ; Paramount/Howard W. Koch; Guild/Avenue, United Artists/Cinemm

Hair today, gone later on today: A critic dies by the Bard in... *Theatre of Blood*

in his first big screen lead, as an American popstar invited to Nazi Germany as a propaganda stunt in this oft-forgotten spoof classic. Fantastically stupid fun that becomes even funnier if you know German (the officer replies to his orders "I love you, my treasure").

TRANSYLVANIA 6-5000 1985

Director Rudy De Luca *Cast* Jeff Goldblum, Joseph Bologna

Great title. Frankenstein has re-appeared and two reporters go to Transylvania to investigate. You'll either love Goldblum in his deadpan role, or hate the cheap lines. You might prefer Mel Brooks' *Young Frankenstein* for a parody of the monster horror genre, featuring Gene Wilder as Frankenstein and Marty Feldman as Igor. It was shot in the same castle (with the same props) as *Frankenstein* (1931). The reason the horses neigh whenever Frau Blucher's name is mentioned? Possibly because she shares her name with the mad Prussian general who rode to Wellington's rescue at Waterloo. Presumably the sound stirs the horses' ancestral memory.

SPORTS

Only in a sports film could an actor utter the words "win just one more for the Gipper" and be taken seriously. Sports films have always been about the suspension of disbelief, and if two tonnes of disbelief are hanging from the ceiling by the time the credits roll, all the better. That did change after kitchen-sink realism when sport became a metaphor for society's ills. But there has been a backlash against the backlash with a certain kind of baseball movie harking back, albeit wistfully, to the simplicities of yore.

BODY AND SOUL 1947

Director **Robert Rossen** *Cast* **John Garfield, Lilli Palmer**

Body And Soul is both a film noir and a classic sports film. There is a flawed protagonist faced with a terrible moral dilemma, in this case young boxer Charlie Davis who has to decide between throwing a fight for mob money or winning it for himself. And for an additional noir-ish twist this is allied to Davis' choice between his loyal girlfriend and the suspect charms of a femme fatale straight from the pages of Raymond Chandler. Shot with newsreel realism, *Body And Soul* won a place in the canon of sports movies in its own right, but it will also be remembered as the film that helped launch a genre.

THE CREATOR'S GAME 1999

Director **Bruce Troxell** *Cast* **Dakota House, Al Harrington**

It's more than just field hockey with bags on sticks – *The Creator's Game* is easily the best film about lacrosse. (For obvious reasons.) The plot concerns Daniel Cloud, an Iroquois who aspires to coach American football at university. As luck has it, the only coaching vacancy left open is for the lacrosse side, a game Daniel plays rather well. Lacrosse was invented by native Americans, and with a big game coming up, it's up to Daniel to draw on his Iroquois heritage for inspiration.

DOWNHILL RACER 1969

Director **Michael Ritchie** *Cast* **Robert Redford, Gene Hackman**

Directed by the Ritchie who isn't Guy (and sadly isn't alive

"FAT MAN, YOU SHOOT A GREAT GAME OF POOL"
Eddie Felson, The Hustler

anymore either), this film wilfully, laudably, refuses to obey sports movie conventions. A film about skiing with a central character who is entirely unlikeable, this is a brave movie, not least because the loatheable lead is played by all-American hero Redford. As such, this is probably the most honest look at the mindset of the successful professional athlete. Redford's character ignores the advice of his coach (Hackman) and even eschews the traditional moment of father/son bonding. He's trying to win a place in the Olympic skiing team, a poor boy from a small town surrounded by rich kids, but that's about as far as our sympathy for him extends. To Ritchie's credit, he doesn't explicitly rebuke his 'hero' either. The credo, as Redford said at the time, is: "Who cares about the good guy who comes second? It's the creep who wins we tolerate."

THE FINAL TEST 1953

Director *Anthony Asquith* Cast *Jack Warner, Robert Morley*

The greatest cricket movie ever made? Well, almost the only serious cricket movie ever made. Scripted by Terence Rattigan, this stars Jack (*Dixon Of Dock Green*) Warner as an ageing Test cricketer whose son is a budding poet. Will the son watch his

THE MASKED WRESTLER

Years before the Rock made the short jump from WWF to TV movies, a masked wrestler was enthralling cinema audiences in Mexico with epic life-and-death victories over such opponents as the *Brain of Evil*, the *Infernal Man*, the *King of Crime* and an entire hotel in the imaginatively entitled *Hotel of Evil*.

The man was El Santo, and for over 20 years, he and his companions perfected the Mexican wrestling movie. Wrestling had travelled to Mexico from the US in the 1930s and became lucha libre, literally "free fighting", a Mexican version of professional wrestling.

An American wrestler sporting a mask briefly captured fans' imagination as El Enmascarado (the masked one). He didn't stick around, but with the rise of superhero comics in America, Mexico soon grew its own heroes, who fast migrated to the silver screen. Made quickly and cheaply in Miami and Cuba, the films were faithful to the spirit of the original

wrestling matches, with the *rudo*, a thug who used brute force opposed to the masked hero, and the *técnico*, who used skill and technique.

The *rudo* became increasingly elaborate, but with a blue and silver mask, Santo was the undisputed star. He made his film debut in 1958 fighting the *Brain of Evil*, which loses something in translation from the Mexican *Cerebro de Mal*. He went on to meet the *Diabolical Brain* (any relation?) in a 25-year career that pitted him against Frankenstein, zombies and organized criminals. His biggest challenge was perhaps *Santo the Silver-Masked One vs the Martian Invasion*. Try fitting that onto a single poster.

Santo never removed his mask in films, or in public. Legend has it that when he went to Miami, he flew on a separate plane so cast and crew would not see him reveal his true self to customs officers. He finally unmasked himself on TV in 1984, dying weeks later aged 67.

dad's final Test or accept an invitation to visit his idol, an eccentric writer (Morley)? The film is really about the father-and-son relationship but the cast includes real Test cricketers Denis Compton, Len Hutton and Jim Laker. Compton appeared in the less well known film *The Small Town Story* the same year. He also had an Oscar publicly dedicated to him by Tim Rice.

THE HUSTLER 1961
Director Robert Rossen Cast Paul Newman, Jackie Gleason

With the easy charm of Travis Bickle and the inarticulacy of mumbling Terry Malloy, Jake just had to be a boxer

It's hard to think of a more equivocal hero than Newman's Fast Eddie Felson. Determined to beat pool legend Minnesota Fats (Gleason), Fast Eddie loses the game and his self-belief, only to find redemption in the love of alcoholic misfit Sarah Packard, a towering performance by Piper Laurie. Just as the couple seem to have found salvation, Fast Eddie risks it all by selling out to George C Scott's pool hustler Bert Gordon for another shot at Minnesota Fats. *The Hustler* has generated its own mythology, and Fast Eddie's alliance with Bert Gordon is said to parallel Rossen's own decision to name names in the McCarthy era. True or not, there's no doubt surrounding the film's most famous cameo – Jake 'Raging Bull' LaMotta plays the bartender. Martin Scorsese's *The Color Of Money* (1986), which teamed up Cruise and Newman, is a case of same bloke, different hat, although it let the Academy give Newman the Oscar it should have given him for the first film.

> **"YOU HAD ME AT 'HELLO'"**
> Jerry Maguire, Jerry Maguire

JERRY MAGUIRE 1996
Director Cameron Crowe Cast Tom Cruise, Renée Zellweger

It's a sports version of *A Christmas Carol*. As near as damn it. Tom Cruise is the world's most diminutive sports agent, with all the personal warmth his profession requires. But Cruise is, y'know, a bit different. He's a sports agent who surprises himself with the need for something more than success, and sets out to get it. Armed with his new, soundbite-friendly, pop-psychology view of the world, Cruise becomes a sports agent with, y'know, a heart, and he's like, y'know, still successful. It's a film you'd like to hate and roll your eyes at –

SPORTS

In Paul Newman's ice-hockey team, helmets are only for wimps

"look kids, being successful doesn't mean not having principles" – but you can't. You find yourself cheering Jerry to the rafters, wanting him to find love with ditzy Zellweger and wanting his naff new ethics to be validated. What next? Cruise as the estate agent we love to, er, love?

LE MANS 1971
Director Lee H Katzin Cast Steve McQueen, Siegfried Rauch
The motor-racing movie for fans who don't worry about plot or dialogue and who don't mind watching the star run through the whole gamut of emotions from A to A-. This is a bit like watching the sport on TV only done better. Most motor racing movies end up substituting race for plot but if you want more human drama, try *Grand Prix*.

THE LONELINESS OF THE LONG DISTANCE RUNNER 1962
Director Tony Richardson Cast Tom Courtenay, Michael Redgrave
In the eight years between Redgrave appearing in *The Dambusters* and making this, a sea of change had taken place in British cinema. In *Loneliness*, Redgrave is the earnest but flawed governor of a borstal charged with taming working-class rebel Colin Smith, played by Tom Courtenay. Redgrave may preside over a barbaric regime but believes in the redemptive power of sport. He turns Courtenay from a delinquent into a promising runner, and at the climactic moment, Courtenay rejects Redgrave's ideology, and the banality of working-class life, by throwing a race against the local public school. Like many kitchen-sink dramas of the time, *Loneliness* can be heavy-handed. It stereotypes the north (grim) and the working class (ee bah gum), but both Courtenay and Redgrave give strong performances as victims of conflicting emotions.

THE MEAN MACHINE 1974 THE LONGEST YARD
Director Robert Aldrich Cast Burt Reynolds, Eddie Albert
You can bank on Burt, he's as reliable and manly as Brut. Or is he? As fallen American football idol Paul Crue, he's a washed-up hero, fallen from grace for throwing a game and imprisoned for stealing his ex-girlfriend's car and punching out a police officer while suffering from the delusion that he was in *Smokey And The Bandit*. Told to build a prison team to challenge the guards, Burt builds them into the Mean Machine; when the governor offers Crue the chance for an early release he can redeem his honour, or sell out his buddies one more time.

There's a distinct post-Watergate disaffection to Albert's corrupt prison governor, and Reynolds' equivocal hero, making this film more complicated than the trot through prison movie clichés it might seem. Look out for the brawny transvestite cheerleaders who cheer on the Mean Machine like the Supremes with testosterone.

THE NATURAL 1984

Director Barry Levinson *Cast* Robert Redford, Robert Duvall, Kim Basinger

Unless you've never seen a film before, you know what's going to happen in *The Natural* before Redford has spoken a word. He's a washed-up baseball player. He joins a team of no-hopers. Guess what happens next. Yet of all the characters in the zero-to-hero genre, Redford's character Roy Hobbs is one of the most likeable, and Levinson uses baseball to retell the Arthurian legend of the search for the Holy Grail. With a team called the Knights and a bat cut from a tree struck by lightning, *The Natural* manages to dwell in the realm of fantasy without churning stomachs. Word of warning: don't watch it if you like the Bernard Malamud novel this is 'based' on. Like *Field Of Dreams*, this film has been known to make grown men cry, especially the scene where Red tells Hobbs: "You're the best goddamn hitter of the ball I've ever seen."

PLAYERS 1979

Director Anthony Harvey *Cast* Ali MacGraw, Dean-Paul Martin

Up-and-coming tennis pro falls for kept woman. Yes, it's *Room At The Top* with a tennis backdrop (and a cast of tennis greats including John McEnroe, Ilie Nastase and Dan Maskell) but without any of the original's narrative drive or redeeming cynicism. This is utter bilge which ended Nastase's movie career and helped kickstart Steve Guttenberg's.

RAGING BULL 1980

Director Martin Scorsese *Cast* Robert De Niro, Joe Pesci

Raging Bull is about boxing in the same way that *Battleship Potemkin* is about a boat. Like all the best sports films, the sport itself is a vehicle for exploring more complex themes, not least the relationship between masculinity and violence. *Raging Bull* shows its subject Jake LaMotta, warts and all, as a figure whose capacity for violence in the ring is indivisible from his capacity for violence outside it. De Niro, in arguably his finest performance, went into full-on Method mode and gained several stone to provide the film's most arresting image as the young winner becomes a fat loser. The juxtaposition of soaring

"YOU COULD HAVE ROBBED BANKS, STOLE DOPE OR STOLE YOUR GRANDMOTHER'S PENSION BUT SHAVING POINTS OFF A FOOTBALL GAME. MAN THAT'S UNAMERICAN"

Caretaker, The Mean Machine

strings above scenes of brutality would be done again – Barber's *Adagio For Strings* in *Platoon*, for instance – but seldom have beauty and savagery been allied to such devastating effect.

SLAP SHOT 1977

Director **George Roy Hill** *Cast* **Paul Newman, Michael Ontkean**

Slap Shot is a difficult film, alternately funny, profane and violent. Despite the humour it is the darkness that prevails. Newman takes over a struggling ice-hockey team based in an industrial town suffering from a similar reversal of fortune and recruits three violent players to bludgeon the opposition into submission. The decision enables the film to raise questions about the morality of the win-at-all-costs mentality, as well as deploring the violence that ensues. It never quite answers them convincingly, but the action and the anarchic humour of the dressing room make up for its faults, and the scene where the leading scorer circles the ice naked lives long in the memory.

> "I'M YOUNG, I'M HANDSOME, I'M FAST, I'M PRETTY AND CAN'T POSSIBLY BE BEAT"
> Muhammad Ali, When We Were Kings

THIS SPORTING LIFE 1963

Director **Lindsay Anderson** *Cast* **Richard Harris, Rachel Roberts**

Grey rainy streets, mean trapped lives. It's a wonder anybody who lived in the north of England in the 1950s bothered to get up, let alone spend 12 hours down t'pit just to earn tuppence. But Frank Machin not only has the energy to get up, but also to use his skills at rugby league as a way out of all the above. Because *This Sporting Life* is a thick lardy slab of kitchen-sink realism, Frank, superbly played by Richard Harris, is in for a bitter disappointment. He's trapped by his own attitudes as much as circumstance, and just as exploited in his new profession as he would have been as a miner. *This Sporting Life* might not be the film you reach for when you're feeling ill-used by life, but it's incredibly powerful.

United Artists/Chartoff-Winkler;

"You're going downhill fast. That's your life from now on mate"

WHEN WE WERE KINGS 1996

Director **Leon Gast** *Cast* **Muhammad Ali, George Foreman**

By 1974, Ali's star seemed to be descending. His refusal to be drafted cost him his title and the ensuing ban cost him the best years of his career. His decision to challenge champion George Foreman for the heavyweight title at the age of 32 seemed suicidal. Foreman was rumoured to be the hardest hitter in boxing history. But in the soaring temperatures and the clamour of Kinshasa… heck, you can guess the rest. The Greatest in the greatest sports documentary.

SPY MOVIES

The trouble with being a spy is that you never know how the villains are going to take over the world. They might nuke Florida, send a crack squad of Stepford-wife nannies to infiltrate the West or just decide to take control of the weather. And all you have to fight the multifarious nefarious forces of evil is yourself, your raised eyebrows and a few fancy gizmos, untried and untested. But don't lose heart – the future of the free world depends on you.

Spying may be the second-oldest profession but it's the duplicity and ambiguity of modern warfare which has made the spy thriller an entertainment genre. Spies used to be amateurs like Richard Hannay, hero of John Buchan's *The Thirty Nine Steps* (filmed three times: definitively by Hitchcock in 1935; with Kenneth More as Hannay-lite in 1959; and with Robert Powell as a surprisingly effective Hannay in 1978).

The Cold War changed all that. At first, in films such as *Notorious*, the spies were still FBI agents, and even in 1956, when *The Man Who Never Was* came out, most spy movies harked back to an earlier, easier conflict. But then Ian Fleming invented James Bond, a laconic, iconic superhero. At a time when the real spy war was becoming an increasingly bureaucratic and corporate affair with the agencies fighting for market share, Bond struck a chord, especially when JFK listed an 007 novel as one of his all-time favourite reads. (This was dismissed as a PR stunt but it wasn't: Kennedy was impressed by Fleming, some of whose dafter ideas the CIA used in its war against Castro.)

In 1962 James Bond became flesh in the person of Sean Connery in *Dr No*. Success bred repetition, imitation and parody, so the 1960s saw a glut of ludicrous spy films full of post-modern irony before the term had even been invented. None has proved as durable as Bond, but Michael Caine's Harry Palmer in *The Ipcress File* (1965) was an entertaining antidote.

For a while, every filmmaking nation wanted its own Bond: Japan, Italy (played by Neil Connery), Sweden (his name, Carl Hamilton) and Greece. The Greek spoof, alas, only lasted for one film although fans insist it's "funnier than Austin Powers". But if you're going to have spy comedy, let it be of the class of *Our Man in Havana*, starring Alec Guinness as the vacuum cleaner salesman 'hero' of Graham Greene's novel.

There have been many thoughtful contributions to the genre, often based on the works of John Le Carré and Greene. The 1958 version of Greene's *The Quiet American* is unjustly ignored, possibly because Audie Murphy is cast as the lead. Wait, we haven't even mentioned Tom Clancy. Funny that.

CHARADE 1963

Director **Stanley Donen** *Cast* **Cary Grant, Audrey Hepburn**

In the 1960s there were three kinds of spy movies: 007 & Co, spoofs, and movies like this which had a foot in both camps. (The other famous example is the Gregory Peck-Sophia Loren collaboration *Arabesque*, which is only superior if you're in thrall – as this reviewer is – to the young Loren.) Hepburn plays a recently bereaved woman pursued by several strangers (Grant among them) after her old hubby's fortune, and unsure who to trust. Grant loved making this, saying: "All I want for Christmas is to make another film with Audrey Hepburn." A strong supporting cast (including Walter Matthau, George Kennedy and the future Derek Flint, James Coburn) is outclassed by the leads. Grant got the script changed so Hepburn would be pursuing him, less risk (he felt) of being seen as a dirty old man. The best moment? Probably when Hepburn tells him: "Do you know what's wrong with you? Nothing!"

> "I LIKE A GIRL IN A BIKINI – NO CONCEALED WEAPONS"
> Francisco Scaramanga
> The Man With The Golden Gun

DANGER: DIABOLIK 1968

Director **Mario Bava**

Cast **John Phillip Law, Marissa Mell**

Yet another James Bond spoof which is "funnier than Austin Powers". *Diabolik* is an Italian-French production starring John Phillip Law in the title role as a super thief who has a fine old time stealing gold and murdering innocent people. (After all, where's the fun in murdering guilty people?) Catherine Deneuve should have had a lead role but the director, as an Italian schlock artist, found her acting wanting. (Or he was scared she'd find the rest of the cast's acting wanting.) Cheesy fun badly acted (especially by Law).

Alicia and Dev had popped into a garage on their way to dinner to buy some cheap glasses

DAY OF THE JACKAL 1973

Director Fred Zinnemann *Cast* Edward Fox, Alan Badel

The 1997 remake has more stars but fewer real actors, so stick with this first version of Frederick Forsyth's best novel. There's a rather unpleasant wit about Zinnemann's film (as when the police stenographer complains he can't understand one of the confessions because the witness is screaming too much under torture) and a laudable refusal not to 'explain' Fox's assassin. So we are spared the flashbacks about his relationship with his mum (according to filmmakers, the main reason good boys go bad). A subtle film given the subject: the most violent image is a burst watermelon. For a stylish French variation on this theme, try *La Femme Nikita*, which takes *Pygmalion* from the drawing room and transplants it to a school for assassins. Cool hand Luc Besson directs.

> **"I DON'T THINK I WANT TO KNOW YOU VERY WELL. I DON'T THINK YOU'RE GOING TO LIVE MUCH LONGER"**
>
> Kathy Hale, Three Days Of The Condor

FATHOM 1967

Director Leslie Martinson *Cast* Raquel Welch, Tony Franciosa

How did Fathom Harvill get her name? As Welch explains in one of the film's best running gags, it's because she's deep. The same can't quite be said of the movie, but Welch is actually very funny as the sky-diving dental assistant who gets embroiled in

AN IMPERFECT SPY

Many of us still recall the Cold War. And the places where it got hottest: Berlin, Vietnam, Cuba and the Middle East. And where, you might ask, was the West's greatest spy, James Bond, while all these crises were going on?

While the eyes of the world were focused on Checkpoint Charlie, the Ho Chi Minh trail, the Bay of Pigs and the Golan Heights, 007 was on 'duty' in Jamaica, Istanbul, Venice, Switzerland, Amsterdam and Las Vegas. Okay, he saved the world from a series of villains but why was he buggering about with clowns such as Katanga and Blofeld when he could have been zapping the Vietcong or nobbling the warheads that Khruschev smuggled into Cuba?

In espionage, as in football, you have to judge a man partly on the quality of

his opposition, and the only opposition 007 should have cared about was the KGB. The real Soviet spymasters infiltrated MI5, taught the Bulgarians how to kill people with umbrellas and helped to destabilise Africa and Asia. 007, meanwhile, was practising re-entry with some bimbo in a capsule near Sardinia, changing his mind about his favourite vintage of Dom Perignon (1953 in *Dr No*, 1957 in *On Her Majesty's Secret Service* and 1962 in *The Man With The Golden Gun*) or wrestling with some metal-toothed giant.

Either this is a flagrant misuse of one of the free world's most valuable human resources or 007 is scared that he won't cut the mustard against the serious players. C'mon, M – sort it out.

A scaredy cat and two chicks?

intrigue. It doesn't hurt either that she's wearing a succession of spectacular bikinis. Clive Revill is wonderful too as a dotty billionaire allergic to bad weather. Sadly unavailable on video.

> "I HAVE A VERY LOW THRESHOLD OF DEATH"
>
> Jimmy Bond, Casino Royale

THE IPCRESS FILE 1965

Director Sidney J Furie *Cast* Michael Caine, Nigel Green

The first problem Furie, Caine and producer Harry Saltzman had when filming Len Deighton's novel was that the spy in it didn't have a name. They wanted a really boring name and Caine finally said Harry was the most boring name he could think of. There was a stunned silence while Saltzman's acolytes waited to see if the boss would take umbrage. But he laughed and just said: "Harry it is. My real name's Herschel." Saltzman said the most boring man he'd ever met was called Palmer and so Harry Palmer was born. Saltzman also suggested Caine wear glasses, which he did in real life, because the producer was sick of seeing actors who didn't wear glasses in real life mishandle them in movies. They did have one difference of opinion: Saltzman was worried a scene where Palmer pushed his own supermarket trolley would be taken to mean the spy was gay. (They solved this by making him use the trolley as a weapon.) It's a toss up between this and *The Spy Who Came In From The Cold* for the best spy movie of the 1960s.

THE FORCES OF EVIL

How do we all sleep at night knowing this little lot are hatching evil plans faster than battery hens lay eggs?

Big O Not to be confused with Roy Orbison, this nefarious organisation wants to take over the world but only after it's set an atom bomb off over New Mexico (*The Silencers*)

Smersh They want to take over the world by smuggling female spies disguised as nannies into the West (*Casino Royale*)

Spectre They want to take over the world but only when they've killed James Bond first (*From Russia With Love*)

Thanatos They want to take over the world using a magnetic wave generator (*Operation Kid Brother*)

Thrush They want to take over the world but at the moment they're having more fun sending a fake Napoleon Solo to infiltrate the UN (*The Spy With My Face*)

IVANOVO DETSTVO 1962

Director Andrei Tarkovsky *Cast* Nikolai Burlyayev, Yevgeni Zharikov

This, Tarkovsky's first feature, was made in the Khruschev era. (He would not be so lucky with his second – *Andrei Rublev* – of which the Brehznev drones disapproved and only allowed to be screened at 4am on the last day of the Cannes festival.) Here, the spy is a 12-year-old boy called Ivan (a fantastic performance by Burlyayev), prematurely aged by the Great Patriotic War. His inner life (especially his dreams, beautifully shot by the director) is more important to the film than what he does, although we see him growing into his spy role to the point where he starts ordering the men around. A wonderful, difficult film.

LIVE AND LET DIE 1973

Director Guy Hamilton *Cast* Roger Moore, Jane Seymour

New Bond, new bloke writing the theme tune

(some chap the tabloids call Macca) and new Bond girl (the future Dr Quinn, medicine woman). It was too much change for some Bond diehards, who also missed Q and his gadgets, but this remains an entertaining caper. Bond has to escape a few hungry crocodiles, deal with a different kind of villain (Kotto as a drug baron) and there are some neat touches too (Tee-Hee and his mechanical arm). Oh, and the best Bond theme. Sorry, Mr Barry. *Goldfinger* may be the best Connery Bond, but Moore was always closer to Ian Fleming's ideal. *On Her Majesty's Secret Service* needs reappraising – George Lazenby is so unsure in the role that, for once, Bond seems like a human being.

How to be a spy, part 1: Look slightly dishevelled and turn your collar up...

MATA HARI 1931

Director George Fitzmaurice Cast Greta Garbo, Ramon Novarro

Garbo vamps it up and camps it up in this cracking slice of historical nonsense. The life and crimes of the world's most famous woman spy, Mata Hari, were really just an excuse for Garbo to play the fallen woman and suffer moral retribution (although she is 'purified' by being escorted to her execution by a squad of nuns). Bizarrely, this got into trouble over a scene which showed Novarro peering at the Virgin Mary and then turning to Garbo. Cue cries of blasphemy! But Garbo pays for her sins. As her colleague tells her: "The only way to resign from our profession is to die."

THE MILLION EYES OF DR SUMURU 1967

Director Lindsay Shonteff Cast Shirley Eaton, Frankie Avalon

If you haven't already met Su-Muru (Eaton), it's time you were formally introduced. She is a diabolical, sadistic, man-hating Amazonian goddess. The film, which also stars Frankie Avalon, isn't as good as *Grease* but not as painful as *How To Stuff A Wild Bikini*. Take the worst dialogue from the Bonds, the stupidest stunts from that era's Hong Kong kung fu films, and the daftest plot this side of a Matt Helm spoof, and you have *Sumuru*.

NOTORIOUS 1946

Director Alfred Hitchcock Cast Cary Grant, Ingrid Bergman, Claude Rains

How to choose just one of the master's spy movies? This has a great back story. The script was turned down by Warners because they didn't believe the plot, which mentioned uranium. The FBI liked the script so much that they spied on Hitchcock for months. The director always said the uranium (hidden in a wine bottle, evidence of a plot by Rains' Nazis) was incidental:

How to be a spy, part 2: Hang around the Berlin Wall in the rain until your hair is all over the place

this was really a film about a man (Grant) in love with a girl (Bergman) who had to marry another man (Rains) as part of her job. The film is partly so unsettling because Rains, whom Bergman betrays, seems to love her more than Grant's Devlin. Grant was also the object of FBI interest. His *None But The Lonely Heart* was cited as Communist propaganda by the FBI's LA office for the line: "You're not going to get me to work 'ere and squeeze pennies out of little people poorer than I am." You wonder how that affected his ambiguous portrayal of an FBI agent in the film.

OPERATION KID BROTHER 1967
Director Alberto De Martino *Cast* Neil Connery, Lois Maxwell

That's Neil Connery (as in Sean's brother) playing the "brother of a British secret agent". Bernard Lee plays a man who does a job rather like M in a certain spy movie series, Lois Maxwell plays a secretary and Daniela Bianchi is a Connery girl, not the Bond girl she played in *From Russia With Love*. But is the film any good? Well, the ads proclaimed "*Operation Kid Brother* too much for one mother!" (hey, it rhymes) and Neil plays a hypnotist, plastic surgeon and lip reader. That'll be a "no" then.

THE PRESIDENT'S ANALYST 1967
Director Theodore J Flicker *Cast* James Coburn, Severn Darden

Coburn starred in a couple of spy semi-spoofs as Derek Flint but they were the kind of films (the 1960s were full of them) that obviously assumed they were wittier than they were. Then again, can you have an international superspy called Derek? But in *The President's Analyst*, Coburn casts off the smugness in a very funny satire, as a shrink who (because of the identity of his new client) is soon pursued by every spy on Earth. Most original character? An armed and dangerous Canadian agent who hates Americans. Maybe that's why Americans have all those guns: you just never know when Canada might invade.

THE SILENCERS 1966
Director Phil Karlson *Cast* Dean Martin, Stella Stevens

Call us old fashioned but we always get a tad worried when

a film's cast list is longer than its script. This Matt Helm caper (the first) is fun (partly due to Stella Stevens' comic gifts). The tagline invites us to follow Dino from bedroom to bedlam. In the sequels, the transition was from bedlam to boredom.

SPIONE 1928

Director Fritz Lang *Cast* Willy Fritsch, Rudolf Klein-Rogge

Spy number 326 (Fritsch) can't close down a spy ring because he's in love with Sonja, much to the chagrin of the ring-master (Klein-Rogge) who seeks to neutralise 326. This is the German granddaddy of Bond and probably the most distinguished silent spy movie. This was a genre to which Lang would return (most notably with *Man Hunt*). To watch this is to see many of the genre's clichés on screen for the first time, even the daft bits – the banker/spymaster has a part-time job as a clown.

THE SPY WHO CAME IN FROM THE COLD 1965

Director Martin Ritt *Cast* Richard Burton, Claire Bloom

John Le Carré didn't want Burton to play his spy, Alec Leamas. He preferred Trevor Howard, whom he thought had a more lived-in look. There was a further complication: Burton's co-star Claire Bloom had been the other woman in Burton's marriage before Liz Taylor came along. And finally, Burton didn't like the director's ideas about his character. Ritt wanted to flatten him out, denying Burton most of the opportunities for the kind of magnetic flamboyance which was his trademark. But for all that, the film works brilliantly. Burton was drunk and miserable for much of the filming and when Le Carré first saw the film he realized that he'd been wrong: Burton was perfect.

THREE DAYS OF THE CONDOR 1975

Director Sydney Pollack *Cast* Robert Redford, Faye Dunaway, Cliff Robertson

After Nixon quit, almost every movie made in America was described as showing what was invariably referred to as "post-Watergate disillusionment". Well, this one really does. Redford plays a CIA researcher who goes out for lunch and returns to find his co-workers all dead. For a movie star of his magnitude, Redford was refreshingly willing to play characters who were just slightly out of their depth, and in this film his character's only unqualified victory is to be still alive when the film finishes. Dunaway (as the stranger with whom he seeks refuge), Robertson (as a CIA boss) and Max von Sydow (as an assassin) give good support. And the anti-climactic ending, where Redford doesn't

> **"MY NEIGHBOURS, THEY'RE SO CONSERVATIVE. THEY OUGHT TO BE GASSED"**
> Wynn Quantrill
> The President's Analyst

007 TOP GADGETS

001 Infra-red glasses for cheating at cards
002 The atomic bomb pill
003 Radioactive lint
004 Rocket-firing cigarettes
005 Harpoon-firing scuba tank
006 Hovering metal tea tray to slice someone's head off
007 Gas-spraying parking meters

even have the satisfaction of knowing he's blown the whistle, is a bonus. An underrated gem.

TRUE LIES 1994

Director **James Cameron** *Cast* **Arnold Schwarzenegger, Jamie Lee Curtis**

Arnie sells computers, or so his wife thinks. Presumably Jamie Lee thinks he got those pecs from lugging all those bulky monitors around. He's often late home because he is America's top secret agent, so secret that even his missus can't be trusted. But then Arnie finds she can't be trusted because, in flagrant breach of Hollywood's star system, she appears to be doing the dirty deed with a salesman. This is joyous nonsense, with nifty set pieces (such as the scene where he fires a missile, with a terrorist on the end, at a chopper full of terrorists) and the director has the foresight to nuke part of Florida.

WHAT'S UP TIGER LILY? 1966

Director **Woody Allen** *Cast* **Tatsuya Mihashi, Woody Allen (narrator)**

As early as 1964, the James Bond formula had inspired a Japanese spoof entitled *Kokusai Himitsu Keisatsu: Kagi No Kagi* (its literal English title was *International Secret Police: Key Of Keys*) which was successful enough to inspire sequels. Woody Allen bought the rights to the movie, and dubbed a completely new narration so that the plot now centred on the fight to control a top secret recipe for egg salad. Funnily enough, two of the actresses in the original movie became Bond girls.

ROYALE JELLY

Casablanca was a triumph of human creativity over chaos. In *Casino Royale*, on the other hand, chaos won hands down.

The rights to Fleming's novel *Casino Royale* were bought by Charles K Feldman long before the commercial potential of James Bond became apparent. Feldman then sat on *Royale* until Cubby Broccoli's 007 films made a mint, whereupon he decided to make a spoof.

David Niven was signed fairly early on, a good move as he was Fleming's first choice to play Bond in *Dr No*. Peter Sellers was also hired, a bad move as he kept disappearing and didn't finish his scenes as his contract was up.

Miraculously he did film the sequence where he faces Orson Welles across the gaming table. Sellers and Welles hated each other, presumably because as wayward artistic geniuses and famed ladies' men they couldn't stand the competition. So the scene was shot on two separate days with doubles standing in for one of the stars.

The first director, Joe McGrath, quit. Other directors were called in to film pages as they were written by (among others) Woody Allen, Ben Hecht, Joseph Heller and Terry Southern. This line-up may explain why, for all the film's gaping flaws, there are still some decent jokes.

Niven found it all so painful he ignored the film in his memoirs. Still, he did get to deliver lines like: "I remember your chap Lenin very well. First class organiser. Second class mind."

STRAIGHT TO VIDEO

If you think of some of the guff you see on the big screen, it's amazing any films are deemed bad (or uncommercial) enough to go "straight to video". But there's something wrong with the quality control system, because lurking on the shelves of your local video shop you'll find a lost Coen brother movie, a film that closes the file on the JFK case and the inevitable Alan Smithee flick.

BURN HOLLYWOOD BURN 1997

Directors Alan Smithee, Arthur Hiller *Cast* Ryan O'Neal, Eric Idle, Sandra Bernhard, Cherie Lunghi

This film's full title is *An Alan Smithee Film: Burn Hollywood Burn*, which is far more deliciously ironic than anything you will find in the film itself, brought to you from the pen of Joe *Showgirls* Eszterhas. The film was supposed to be about a director called Alan Smithee (Idle) who wants his name removed from a movie because it's so bad. The trouble is, his real name is the pseudonym that directors use whenever they don't want their real name attached to a film. So far so satirical, but wait – the real director of this film, Arthur Hiller, disliked the studio's cut of it so much he asked for, you guessed it, Alan Smithee's name to be listed as director. That is the funniest thing about this Hollywood comedy. That and watching Sly Stallone try to play himself and failing.

> **"THIS FILM IS WORSE THAN SHOWGIRLS"**
> Alan Smithee, Burn Hollywood Burn

CAPTAIN AMERICA 1992

Director Albert Pyun *Cast* Matt Salinger, Ronny Cox, Ned Beatty

You can see why this 1990s version of *Captain America* became a straight-to-video release when it boasts such insightful lines as: "Gee whizz, Mr President." For those unfamiliar with this stirring tale, Captain America (Salinger, and yes he is JD's son) was a simple American soldier before he underwent experiments to become a super-soldier. Freed from the ice, Cap arrives in the 1990s to face his old adversary Red Skull. A former Nazi, Skull is so incredibly evil that he is to blame for the deaths of men such as Martin Luther King and John F Kennedy, a theory nobody (not even Oliver Stone) saw coming.

> **"HOW DO YOU LIKE YOUR EGGS IN THE MORNING, SCRAMBLED OR FERTILIZED?"**
>
> Bartender, 200 Cigarettes

8 HEADS IN A DUFFEL BAG 1997

Director Tom Schulman *Cast* Joe Pesci, Andy Comeau, Kristy Swanson

When a mafia hitman's luggage (containing proof of his latest contract) gets switched with a medical student's, all kinds of complications, especially of a black comedy kind, ensue. Sadly, Schulman, whose first effort this is, doesn't quite have the timing to make the premise work. At its best, it almost reaches the inspired heights of screwball comedy but its best, sadly, doesn't happen frequently enough.

FLICKS 1987

Director Peter Winograd, Kirk Henderson *Cast* Pamela Sue Martin, Joan Hackett, Martin Mull

Nine years after the release of *Movie Movie* came *Flicks*, a doubly doomed attempt to resurrect the spoof/parody movie. Doomed once because this most 1970s of genres had died of its own volition since the parodies had given way to self-parody, and doomed again because this was just the kind of witless rubbish which had killed the audience's appetite for this guff. This space series spoof ('starring' the original Fallon Carrington Colby) features such whimsical notions as Starship President Nixon, while Bogart is sent up in *Philip Alien Space Detective* in which a four-armed caterpillar wears shades and a trenchcoat and solves the case of a missing caterpillar.

JENNIFER 8 1992

Director Bruce Robinson *Cast* Andy Garcia, Uma Thurman, Lance Henriksen, John Malkovich

Big city cop (Garcia) moves to small town, finds himself investigating a murder and attracted to a blind woman (Thurman). This thriller, directed by the man who gave the world *How To Get Ahead In Advertising* and adapted *Withnail And I* for the screen, does eventually get lost in its own plot and the bad weather which, in what presumably is a tribute to noir, seems to permeate so many scenes, but it's a half-decent effort.

THE NAKED MAN 1998

Director J Todd Anderson *Cast* Michael Rapaport, Rachael Leigh Cook, John Slattery

If you've ever thought that they don't make enough

THE LOST McQUEEN

Steve McQueen's last but one film, a version of Henrik Ibsen's *An Enemy Of The People*, wasn't so much released by First Artists as allowed to escape. It didn't quite go straight to video (it's not available on video today) but was pulled after audiences reacted badly to the idea of their hero in a beard and specs. In the UK its release was slightly wider.

Today, though, it is McQueen's forgotten movie, even though it is probably one of his best in the final years. Apparently he only suggested making it because he had one picture on his contract with First Artist and could choose any project he liked. So he picked Ibsen's play as an act of adolescent revenge.

But when he started making it, he began to fall in love with the film, saying he thought it was the best work he'd done. It isn't that good, but it's easily good enough to merit a wider viewing.

movies which explore the interface between chiropractors and comedy, this one's for you. And if you've ever thought you'd like to see a film where a cripple with machine-gun crutches and a peanut-butter-and-bacon-chewing Elvis impersonator go around killing people for no apparent reason, this is especially for you. Written by Ethan Coen and directed not by Joel but by their storyboards artist Anderson, this isn't a real Coen movie because the hero's battle against the drug-dealers who try to muscle in on Dad's small-town pharmacy store is played strictly for laughs. But it's nowhere near as dull as some of the stuff which does make it into British cinemas.

THE NEWTON BOYS 1998
Director Richard Linklater *Cast* Matthew McConaughey, Ethan Hawke, Skeet Ulrich, Julianna Margulies
The Newton Boys robbed more banks in the 1920s than either John Dillinger or Bonnie and Clyde but they've never had the same box-office appeal, probably because they weren't that fond of killing people. Despite a decent cast with McConaughey and *ER's* Margulies as lurve interests, this did nothing to change that pattern, making it straight to video in the UK even though it's actually quite enjoyable in its own quiet way. Maybe someone should remake it and turn the Newton boys into mass murderers. Or maybe people didn't want to see a movie they assumed was about Sir Isaac Newton's offspring.

200 CIGARETTES 1999
Director Risa Bramon Garcia *Cast* Ben Affleck, Christina Ricci, Courtney Love

This above average indie comedy set in New York on New Year's Eve 1981 has a talented cast (Kate Hudson makes her debut), lots of cigarette-smoking and a soundtrack bursting with vintage Elvis Costello tunes (little Elvis even gets to make a cameo appearance). None of which was enough to earn it a UK cinema release. Pity, because this is a pleasant, quirky, light romantic comedy. The possibility of romance between Lucy (Courtney Love) and Kevin (Paul Rudd), the only people in their circle of friends with no date on this most crucial of nights, is wittily explored and Garcia, casting director on many of the biggest movies in recent Hollywood history, picks the right bunch here. Jay Mohr is particularly good as the guy who complains women keep falling in love with him: "It's like a curse, it never ends."

"It's at moments like this that I wish actors could have a pseudonym like Alan Smithee"

SUPERHEROES

What does and doesn't constitute a superhero? Fan conventions across the globe are still debating this question. Do super gadgets (like Batman's car and cave) make you a superhero, or are you just a great inventor? Is Flash a superhero or just a sci-fi star? Other key questions spring to mind: like, why are we discussing this? We're talking superheroes. Like, hello, they're not real.

Okay, superheroes usually fit a certain mould. The obvious requirement is super powers: be it super-strength, the power to fly, or see through women's clothing. A sure-fire way to become a superhero is to volunteer for weird government experiments. Many superheroes have a dual identity: you can't have Batman without Bruce Wayne. Other traits? Well, they spend an inordinate amount of time in caves and ~~one~~ boxes and they're just so damn good. Super powers are ~~...~~, super even, but you have to use them for good, not evil. There's also a giveaway in the very term "superhero": they're ~~...~~ men. How many super-heroines can you name? Wonder Woman may have been a super chick on the small screen but she didn't cut the mustard in celluloid heaven.

THE ADVENTURES OF BUCKAROO BANZAI ACROSS THE 8TH DIMENSION 1984
Director WD Richter Cast Peter Weller, John Lithgow, Ellen Barkin, Jeff Goldblum, Christopher Lloyd
In his first crack at saving the world (Weller went on to play Robocop), Buckaroo Banzai is a superhero/rock star/brain surgeon/Samurai warrior who must fight evil creatures from the eighth dimension. Able to travel through solid matter (making him indestructible if he were ever in a cartoon), he can call on a band of Hong Kong cavaliers, including a cowboy-brain surgeon and a 6ft ET rasta. All the baddies are called John, with John Lithgow as evil boss Lord John Whorfin stealing scenes.

BATMAN 1989
Director Tim Burton Cast Michael Keaton, Jack Nicholson, Kim Basinger, Michael Gough
Batman doesn't have superpowers as such but he's still a superhero with his costumes, alter ego and mission to rid

Flash! Saviour of the universe! Useful for cleaning kitchen floors!

Gotham City at least, of crime and peril. Burton's visually stunning intro to the bat legend sees Keaton, personally approved by creator Bob Kane, as our brooding hero and brings in the best adversary of the series, The Joker (Nicholson). Nicholson's expressions, particularly the terrifying fixed grin, were based on the main character Gwynplaine in *The Man Who Laughs* (1928) who had a grin carved permanently onto his face by the king in revenge for his father's treachery. Nicholson's line to Vicki Vale: "Have you ever danced with the Devil in the pale moonlight?", is said to be the lothario's own chat-up line.

> **"HAVE YOU EVER DANCED WITH THE DEVIL IN THE PALE MOONLIGHT?"**
> The Joker, Batman

FLASH GORDON 1936

Director Frederick Stephani *Cast* Buster Crabbe, Jean Rogers, Charles Middleton

It may look dated, but this 1936 print of the adventures of Flash, Dale and Dr Zarkov against the merciless Emperor Ming wipes the 1980s remake off the screen. This is the opening, and still the best, Flash adventure. Star Crabbe was an Olympic swimming champion who entered Hollywood as the obvious rival for Johnny Weissmuller's (another Olympic star) crown. Starring first as Tarzan, Crabbe carved a niche in such sci-fi adventure flicks as Flash and Buck Rogers. He later played Billy the Kid.

HAK HAP 1996

Director Daniel Lee *Cast* Jet Li, Ching Wan Lau, Karen Mok

The old formula: man undergoes scientific tests and becomes superhuman. Former martial arts champ Jet Li is Michael, the newly created superhuman who must give up life as a librarian (Mum was right: you really do have to watch the quiet ones) and fight the forces of evil, aka his old comrades. As he can't let his former allies see him turn traitor, he becomes the Black Mask. Where *Hak Hap* differs from most in this genre is in its violence: the martial arts scenes were strong enough to warrant an R rating.

MYSTERY MEN 1999

Director Kinka Usher *Cast* Hank Azaria, Janeane Garofalo, William H Macy, Ben Stiller, Greg Kinnear, Eddie Izzard, Geoffrey Rush

The Shoveler, one of the band of merry

SUPER WHO?

THE FORGOTTEN & NEVER HEARD OF SUPERHEROES

"The Superhero Who Streaks To The Rescue." This is the unlikely tagline for *Kekkō Kamen* and a superhero with the power to streak (yes, that does mean go naked, not incredibly fast). She's just one of many ridiculous superheroes eager to take over the mantle of Batman, Superman and Howard The Duck.

BLANKMAN (1994)
Fights crime in his bullet-proof pants.
CONDORMAN (1981)
Frank Spencer as a superhero. Has to be seen to be believed.
FLASH II: REVENGE OF THE TRICKSTER (1991)
Flash has the power of speed. Plausible so far, but wait for it, his evil nemesis is Mark Hamill, aka 'The Trickster'. Evil? Come on, this is Luke Skywalker.
GENTLEMAN (1997)
Fights crime in a designer tux rather than his granny's tights.
STEEL (1997)
Steel's (Shaquille O'Neal) fantastic power is that he can create anything out of, well, steel. So we have a 7ft tall hero dressed as a walking junkyard. They still weep at DC Comics if you mention this.

amateur superheroes assembled in *Mystery Men*, has one power: "God's given me a gift. I shovel well. I shovel very well." As the movie's tagline enthuses, these are not your classic heroes, these are the other guys. Aside from the standard 'superhero saves the day' plot, your saviours here are The Blue Raja (hurls forks and spoons, complete with English accent), The Spleen (uses his flatulence to bring down evil), The Bowler (complete with golden bowling ball encasing her dead father's head), Mr Furious (a time bomb of fury) and a host of new recruits. This amiable spoof basically has one joke – these guys are crap – but the one-liners are so weird they're like jokes with random words edited out of them (Mr Furious: "Don't mess with the volcano, my man, 'cause I will go Pompeii on your butt").

THE PHANTOM 1943

Director B Reeves Eason *Cast* Tom Tyler, Jeanne Bates, Kenneth MacDonald

Although the 1996 remake of Lee Falk's masked superhero *The Phantom* scored zero for credibility (a cast of Billy Zane, Kristy Swanson and Catherine Zeta-Jones says it all), 'the ghost who walks' was never as popular as Batman or Flash anyway. Having a hero in purple tights wandering around the jungle was certainly different, but the original 15 serials had all the other essential elements of superherodom. Having Tom Tyler as Geoffrey Prescot/The Phantom probably helped as he was already accustomed to the man-in-tights-saves-the-world role, having played Captain Marvel in 1941.

SUPERMAN 1948

Director Spencer Gordon Bennet, Thomas Carr *Cast* Kirk Alyn, Noel Neill, Carol Forman

Superman must be the superhero of all superheroes. This alien (which most people forget that he is) can fly, has superhuman strength, can freeze things just by blowing on them and he has X-ray vision. We've all seen the 1978 Christopher Reeve *Superman*, but the 1948 serial remains one of the best. Obviously the effects are limited – you may notice the odd wire suspending Superman in the sky and Clark's glasses are dated to say the least, but if you're a Superman fan it's a must-see. Stars Kirk Alyn and Noel Neill had cameo roles in the 1978 film as young Lois' mother and father. The 1941 animated version by Max and Dave Fleischer is a knockout too.

SUPERMEN

THE MIGHT HAVE BEENS

Christopher Reeves' career prior to *Superman* consisted of a TV movie and 16th billing on a poor Navy drama, *Gray Lady Down*. No surprise therefore that he wasn't the producer's first choice. Fortunately, their first choices weren't available.

WARREN BEATTY
Could have become Superman vs the Republican party.

ROBERT REDFORD
No one would ever have believed that the all-American hero was an alien from outerspace.

NICK NOLTE
Maybe if this were the R-rated version, or maybe if the Kryptonite was down and out in Beverly Hills.

ARNOLD SCHWARZENEGGER
Too many lines for the Austrian oak to cope with this early in his career.

EMI/Famous/Starling

TEEN MOVIES

"Dear Mr Vernon, we accept the fact that we had to sacrifice a whole Saturday in detention for whatever it is we did wrong, but we think you're crazy for making us write an essay telling you who we think we are. You see us as you want to see us, in the simplest terms, in the most convenient definitions. But what we found out is that each one of us is a brain, and an athlete, and a basketcase, a princess, and a criminal. Does that answer your question? Sincerely yours, The Breakfast Club."

AMERICAN GRAFFITI 1973
Director George Lucas Cast Richard Dreyfuss, Ron Howard, Charles Martin Smith, Cindy Williams, Paul LeMat
This highly entertaining 'coming of age' tale is notable as the film which launched a thousand Hollywood careers (yes, we have this film to thank for launching the straight-to-video acting skills of Suzanne Somers). This nostalgic view of how a group of friends in 1962 spend their last night together before going their separate ways into adult life is a funny, charming piece of cinema which filmmakers have been playing homage to ever since (see *Dazed & Confused* for the 1990s retread). *American Graffiti* was one of the first mainstream films to use music as such a fundamental part of the action, and the rock 'n' roll slots perfectly into this story of adolescents taking their first tentative steps into sex, booze, music and cars. The really astonishing thing about this film is that Lucas hardly spoke to the actors (he didn't know what to say to them, so he hired a drama coach). It was partly blind luck that the cast included such actors as Dreyfuss and Harrison Ford who could make their lines work.

THE BREAKFAST CLUB 1985
Director John Hughes Cast Emilio Estevez, Anthony Michael Hall, Ally Sheedy, Molly Ringwald, Judd Nelson
If the 1980s were your years of teenage kicks, *The Breakfast Club* was your signature film, capturing the highs and lows, not to mention the fashion for fingerless gloves. Written and directed by John Hughes, this is his second, and best, foray into teen cinema (it began to go awry when he met the Culkin boy),

> **"IF YOU WERE HAPPY EVERY DAY OF YOUR LIFE, YOU WOULDN'T BE A HUMAN BEING, YOU'D BE A GAME SHOW HOST"**
> Veronica Sawyer, Heathers

and showcases a wealth of great young talent, not many of whom have enjoyed great careers. Despite the clichés, notably the premise of putting a stereotype jock, princess, criminal, basket case and brain in the same room and watching them react, the film plays well on teenagers' instinctive belief that the world is against them. The script contains a few classic one-liners ("Does Barry Manilow know you raid his wardrobe?") and funny moments (Anthony Michael Hall becoming Mr Cool after smoking dope for the first time), showing teens doing what they do best – experimenting. See *St Elmo's Fire* for what happens when you leave school.

COM LICENCA, EU VOU A LUTA 1986
Director Lui Farias *Cast* Fernanda Torres, Marieta Severo

Teen angst in Brazil as seen through the eyes of a 15-year-old girl and her suburban family. One of the more realistic tales of its ilk, it shows Elaine trying to cope with the usual trials and tribulations and the unnatural animosity shown by her mum (Severo). Torres, the 21-year-old actress playing Elaine, was on top form when the film was made, going on to win best actress at Cannes for her role in *Eu Sei Que Vou Te Amar*. The soundtrack also boasts a rather fine selection of Brazilian pop.

EMPIRE RECORDS 1995
Director Allan Moyle *Cast* Anthony LaPaglia, Liv Tyler, Renée Zellweger

Much more upbeat than director Allan Moyle's 1990 view of teen angst *Pump Up The Volume*, *Empire Records* sees the teenage staff of the titular record store fighting to save the shop's independence. Although no teenager ever really had a job this good, the film, aided by a hip soundtrack, pans to shots of the employees and punters looking like wannabe hosts on MTV. In true teen torment format, each employee has their own cross to bear: nightmare parents, drug-dependency, unrequited love, suicidal tendencies, general low self-esteem...

FERRIS BUELLER'S DAY OFF 1986
Director John Hughes *Cast* Matthew Broderick, Alan Ruck, Mia Sara

To be blunt, Ferris is a pain in the butt. We're talking about a guy whose biggest gripe is he got a computer instead of a car from his parents, but John Hughes (yes, him again) makes him a loveable rogue. Ferris convinces his parents, yet again, that he is sick and skives school, dragging his girlfriend (Mia Sara) and best mate (the superbly dry, not to say neurotic Alan Ruck) around Chicago. Most kids would be happy to veg in front of the telly but Ferris bombs around town in a vintage Ferrari, takes a carnival party by storm, and eats at the most expensive restaurant in town, without paying. Our hero's philosophy on life? "Life moves pretty fast. If you don't stop and look around you might miss it." Despite his dubious, very 1980s line of sweater-vests, you can't help liking this smug little bastard.

Heathers: A tragic tale of an actor realising he's not Jack Nicholson

GREGORY'S GIRL 1981

Director Bill Forsyth *Cast* John Gordon Sinclair, Dee Hepburn, Jake D'Arcy, Claire Grogan

Painfully true to life, Gregory is a lanky teenager whose personal sea of troubles includes acne, peer pressure, ginger hair and his relegation to goalie after a girl (Dee Hepburn as Dorothy) joins the footie team. The presence of a girl on the boys team never becomes an issue (mostly because she's so good) so the focus is on the three central characters – the third being Susan, the girl Gregory ends up with after falling out of love with Dorothy. Like much of Forsyth's best work, this has the feel of being a slightly more whimsical version of real life.

HEATHERS 1989

Director Michael Lehmann *Cast* Winona Ryder, Christian Slater

From the opening shot of Ryder's head being used as a human peg in a game of croquet, you know you're in for a surreal ride. High school student Ryder is forced to become a lowly member of the elite Heather's clique. But new arrival Slater leads her into a plot to teach the Heathers a lesson by murdering one of them and faking it to look like suicide. Daniel Water's sharp script ridicules every other teen drama. One hippy teacher lectures the students on committing suicide the correct way as "there's only one chance to get it right", and the principal deems a cheerleader's death worth a half-day's mourning. Producers New World insisted Lehmann tweak the end (no mass suicide and school bombings, thanks) but *Heathers* is still one of the quirkiest takes on teen life. You might end up quoting its slang for ever: "Lick it up baby. Lick it up."

HIGH SCHOOL CONFIDENTIAL 1958

Director Jack Arnold *Cast* Russ Tamblyn, Mamie Van Doren

Undercover cop Tamblyn tries to crack down on high school

drug use. He ought to be worried by the presence of bourbon-swillin' Jerry Lee Lewis, who married his own 13-year-old cousin. Then there's Mamie Van Doren, whose chest looks more menacing than Tamblyn's switchblade. Stirring, innocent stuff.

THE OUTSIDERS 1983

Director Francis Ford Coppola *Cast* C Thomas Howell, Rob Lowe, Patrick Swayze, Matt Dillon, Ralph Macchio

This was probably the first and last taste that actors (in the loosest sense of the word) like Patrick Swayze had of method acting. To create a suitably hostile atmosphere between those playing the 'socs' and those playing the 'greasers', Coppola gave the socs leather-bound scripts and put them up in swanky hotels, with the greasers making do with paperback scripts and cheap digs. The scheme worked and we are left with an engaging tale of youths from both sides of the tracks clashing in 1960s Oklahoma. Famous faces abound, most notably Tom Cruise and Nicholas Coppola, aka Nicolas Cage.

> **"IF YOU FLAKE AROUND WITH THE WEED, YOU'LL END UP USING THE HARDER STUFF"**
> Tony Baker, High School Confidential

REBEL WITHOUT A CAUSE 1955

Director Nicholas Ray *Cast* James Dean, Natalie Wood, Sal Mineo

This, the seminal teen-angst movie, deals with the barriers between adults and teens, peer pressure, friendships and a taste for reckless pursuits – car-racing in this case. Ray put his heart and soul into the piece, riding around with notorious LA gangs and hiring former gang member Frank Mazzola as Crunch, who taught Dean how to fight with real switchblade knives. No American actor has been able to play a misunderstood teen since without being aware of Dean's performance.

VIRGIN SUICIDES 2001

Director Sofia Coppola *Cast* Kirsten Dunst, Kathleen Turner, James Woods, Josh Hartnett

An extreme look at the power of the emotional uncertainty of adolescence. This directorial debut from the youngest of the Coppola clan (Sofia was previously critically panned for her acting in dad's *Godfather III*) sees the Lisbon family struggle to cope with their youngest daughter's attempted suicide. The film focuses on each daughter's reaction to their oppressively strict Catholic upbringing (no boys, no parties, not even cinema) as the girls become legendary for their promiscuous behaviour. Despite the film's dark subject, Coppola uses rich hues of yellow, orange and red coupled with a haunting soundtrack from French band Air to symbolise the emotional intensity throughout the film, and a morbid sense of humour flows throughout. One of the more unusual views of teen angst.

3-D

In the 1950s, the movie industry's shrewd response to the threat of the small screen was to make the big screen bigger and then, with the kind of genius which is never in short supply in Hollywood, to make it three-dimensional! All you needed was an extra projector in the cinema and the kind of glasses which obviously made a deep impression on the psyche of young Reg Dwight in Pinner.

THE CHARGE AT FEATHER RIVER 1953
Director Gordon Douglas Cast Guy Madison, Vera Miles
Of the many Westerns which exploited 3-D by chucking bows and arrows out of the screen at a constantly ducking audience, this is probably the best. The yarn is standard western fare (settlers try to cross territory owned by Cheyenne Indians and become embroiled in the inevitable dispute) but features the voice of American quiz-show tycoon Merv Griffin and the underrated Vera Miles. Cult schlock director William Castle had a stab at the 3-D western in *Fort Ti* (1953), which starts with the title being shot out of a cannon at the audience, later a character spews whisky out of the screen.

HOUSE OF WAX 1953
Director André De Toth Cast Vincent Price, Frank Lovejoy
One-eyed director De Toth was a brave choice by Warner Bros to usher in the 3-D revolution. Yet the fact that he only had a theoretical idea about how this film might look in this new fangled process doesn't seem to have affected his work. This is a cult classic (which still works in 2-D) with Price trying to replace the wax figures in his showplace with human beings and generally camping things up to such effect that he would spend the next 15 years in roles like these. Charles Bronson (billed as Charles Buchinsky) has a small part as a deaf-mute.

JAWS 3-D 1983
Director Joe Alves Cast Dennis Quaid, Bess Armstrong
Not to be confused with *Jaws*, and not to be confused with a real movie either. The great white shark heads to a Sea World

park in Florida to find a more exciting menu. There's the usual wailing of human victims and gnashing of shark's teeth, this time shown (very slowly) in 3-D. The only reward for the patient is the scene where the shark blows up in 3-D. The rest is just proof that as far as Hollywood was concerned, 3-D effects were a great excuse to get away with 1-D characters. You'll get more thrills from *The Treasure Of Four Crowns* (1982).

KISS ME KATE 1953

Director George Sidney Cast Howard Keel, Kathryn Grayson

If you've ever watched this musical and wondered why people keep throwing stuff (or themselves) directly at the viewer, it's because it was originally filmed in 3-D. Not just 3-D but as the studio ad campaign proclaimed: "In 3-D on our Panoramic Screen with MIRACULOUS STEREOPHONIC SOUND! COLOR, too!" (punctuation and grammar as original). But don't be deceived: this is an above-average musical (Bob Fosse is in the cast), which didn't need all the gimmicks to entertain.

LUMBER JACK RABBIT 1954

Director Chuck Jones Cast Mel Blanc

Warners were so keen on 3-D that they enlisted Bugs Bunny in the cause. To celebrate the world's first 3-D animation, Warner even allowed their logo to crash into the screen. The enthusiasm didn't last though: *Baby Buggy Bunny* (released later the same year) reverted to plain old 2-D.

PARASITE 1982

Director Charles Band Cast Demi Moore, Robert Glaudini

In the early 1980s, movie-makers flirted with 3-D again for no obvious reason. The only apparent advantage for filmmakers like Band was that when viewers left the theatre they couldn't decide if their headache was due to wearing those funny glasses or because they'd watched a truly bad film. For the young Moore, this film about a man with a deadly parasite attached to his stomach was a definite step down from her debut *Choices*.

THE POWER OF LOVE 1922

Director Nat G Deverich Cast Elliott Sparling, Barbara Bedford

The very first 3-D movie, using Henry H Fairall's anaglyphic process, was a tale of a young sea captain who plied his trade off the Californian coast in the 1840s. *Radio Mania*, directed by Roy William Neill who would later take charge of the Basil Rathbone-Sherlock Holmes series, was released around the same time and told an unusual tale involving Martian flappers. After this initial spurt, interest in 3-D subsided until the 1950s.

THRILLERS

Ian Fleming, who knew a thing or two about thrillers, said his books were aimed "somewhere between the solar plexus and, well, the upper thigh". The only defining characteristic of a thriller is that it should offer (or attempt to offer) thrills. That principle can be applied to the serial *The Perils Of Pauline* in the 1910s, the best work of Alfred Hitchcock or a movie where a one-armed man walks into a western town on a mysterious errand.

C ritics have spent years analysing, categorising and theorising thrillers and devised no theory of the genre more satisfying than Fleming's desire to affect our solar plexus. How filmmakers do that differs but a few themes recur.

The hero and the conspiracy movie. The ultimate example is *JFK* which, whatever else it is, is the thrilling story of one man's unsuccessful bid to expose a vast conspiracy.

The transformation of the ordinary. The moment when mundane reality suddenly takes an unexpected left into a nightmare. It's the instant in *Spoorloos* (*The Vanishing*) when the wife goes back to the petrol station to buy some drinks for the journey – and disappears.

The innocent on the run. As in Cary Grant in *North By Northwest*, an advertising executive who is treated as if he is a mysterious person known as Kaplan. Sometimes the innocents won't be on the run but, like the children in Charles Laughton's *Night Of The Hunter*, are at the apparent mercy of evil.

The moral hero. In the days when our views on morality were even more black and white than the movies, the hero of a thriller had to be morally virtuous – that's why we rooted for him (and it usually was a him). Film noir qualified that: from Philip Marlowe on, the hero could just be the person in the film we most approved of – the least bad character. Other directors pushed that further still: Hitchcock took great delight in inserting scenes which force us to root, even temporarily, for the villain, as when Barry Foster tries to free his tie-pin from a victim's cold dead grasp in *Frenzy*.

> "THE GREATEST TRICK THE DEVIL EVER PULLED WAS CONVINCING THE WORLD HE DIDN'T EXIST"
>
> Verbal, The Usual Suspects

The thrill is the point. Those who like to believe that there was a golden age against which the present is found wanting insist that thrillers have become mechanical devices for extracting the maximum amount of shock from us. For once, it is not the movie industry which has lost the plot. The fact is thrillers have always tried to thrill the audience above and beyond anything else they want to do. The crop-duster and the Mount Rushmore chase in *North By Northwest* don't spring from the plot – they're set pieces and many thrillers always have built towards these set pieces, rather than focus on the plot. The quality and, perhaps, quantity of the set pieces may change but they've always been there.

> **"I CAN'T WORK OUT IF YOU'RE A DETECTIVE OR A PERVERT"**
> Sandy Williams, Blue Velvet

Ultimately, deciding what is and isn't a thriller can be about as satisfying as trying to decide whether there really is a Third Way in politics (don't ask us). What follows is a selection of films which do roughly what Fleming said, although solar plexuses being the unpredictable beasts they are, we offer no guarantee that yours will react in the same way.

BAD DAY AT BLACK ROCK 1954

Director John Sturges *Cast* Spencer Tracy, Robert Ryan

Proof that you don't have to have a fiendishly intricate plot to make a great thriller. Proof also that a modern Western can have the same level of intrigue as a thriller, even if it still ends in the traditional shoot out. The story may be familiar: a one-armed stranger (Tracy) arrives in town on a mysterious mission to find the townfolk mostly hostile and hiding, as they are, a dirty little secret. (It's a secret all of America shares: their treatment of the Nisei, American citizens of Japanese descent in World War II; this was the first major film to allude to it.) It's a highly charged film into which people have read many messages (is it an another allegory about McCarthyism?). Tracy and Ryan are wondrous; Ryan (one of Hollywood's most liberal actors) plays a snarling, defensive reactionary to perfection. The moment that lifts the film from being merely very good is when Tracy decides the odds are stacked against him and does what most of us would do: he tries to escape.

DIE JAMES!

As the screen's smoothest baddy, James Mason died many deaths. This list is a tribute to his fatal versatility.

Chopped up, put in sack, and dragged (*Genghis Khan*)
Hoisted to masthead and struck by lightning (*Frankenstein*)
Killed by a cannon loaded with gold (*Lord Jim*)
Shot by a slave (*Mandingo*)
Shot while dancing (*The Marseille Contract*)
Suicide by poison (*Rommel*)
Suicide leap from cliff (*The Upturned Glass*)
Suicide pact by drowning (*Pandora And The Flying Dutchman*)
Sunk by Italian submarine (*Torpedo Bay*)
Walked into the sea (*A Star Is Born*)

BLOW OUT 1981

Director Brian De Palma *Cast* John Travolta, Nancy Allen

Quentin Tarantino cites this as his favourite John Travolta film (presumably he really means second favourite). You can see why: Travolta is still trying to escape from teen films and stars as a sound recordist who picks up a noise he realises is the clue to an assassination. Tarantino might also like this because there's some serious homage going on. De Palma pays tribute to *Blow Up*, *Psycho* (as usual) and *The Conversation* which, in places, he almost copies scene for scene. But in *Blow Out* he's at both his flashiest and his darkest.

BLUE VELVET 1986
Director David Lynch *Cast* Isabella Rossellini, Kyle MacLachlan, Dennis Hopper

Repellent, fascinating, surreal – this is the kind of film for which critics ransack their entire vocabulary of adjectives. Never comfortable viewing, with the tone set from the opening shot of impossibly blue skies and white fences contrasted with wet, dark beetles. MacLachlan plays Jeffrey Beaumont, a character with certain similarities to the director (echoes which the actor played up by dressing and buttoning his

Rochefort protects the family jewels as he attempts to blend in with the range in *Wild Target*

shirt like Lynch) who finds a human ear and is embroiled in a horrific small-town mystery. Underneath all of Lynch's trickery, this is a very personal film. Many scenes (including the controversial scene where Hopper rapes and degrades Rossellini) have some link to the director's childhood memories. That may be why, for all the violence, this story always has a weird logic which propels it relentlessly forward.

DEAD CALM 1988
Director Philip Noyce *Cast* Sam Neill, Nicole Kidman, Billy Zane

Noyce's ocean-going thriller was based on a Charles Williams novel which Orson Welles had also tried to film (see Unreleased Movies, p426). But it's hard to imagine Welles doing it better than Noyce. The shot of two ships in an otherwise deserted ocean is critical: we know these three characters (with Billy Zane excellent as the killer) must resolve this themselves. You'll go a long way to find a better example of the movie cliché known as the 'undead dead' but this keeps your attention because the story is so simple and the performances are so strong. This movie launched a veritable sub-genre with films like *Circuit Breaker* (1997), described as "*Dead Calm* in space", but this is easily the best.

> "DON'T FEEL BAD ABOUT LOSING YOUR VIRTUE. I SORT OF KNEW YOU WOULD"
>
> Bree Daniels, Klute

DIVA 1981

Director Jean-Jacques Beineix
Cast Wilhelmenia Wiggins Fernandez, Frédéric Andrei

Beineix's debut inspired a thousand reviewers to pick the same adjective: stylish. Still, that's what you get if you insert an opera singer into a Hitchcockian thriller. (That's one up on Hitch himself who made do with Doris Day.) Andrei is a postman who tapes Fernandez's diva (who won't record any of her performances) but gets his tape mixed up with one which is vital evidence in a crime. After that all kinds of shenanigans ensue, all beautifully shot by Beineix who has struggled to match this mix of high culture and low thrills in his subsequent work. The chase along the Paris Metro is worth the price of admission (or rental) alone.

DON'T LOOK NOW 1973

Director Nicolas Roeg *Cast* Julie Christie, Donald Sutherland

The phrase "All is not what it seems" can simply mean that the viewer is about to be cheated by a meretricious director with a bag of tricks. But in Roeg's film the menace, the tension and the mystery emanate from the characters and the Venetian setting. Sutherland and Christie are in Venice to overcome their grief at their daughter's death but Christie is warned that

her husband will die if he does not leave and the city is racked by a series of murders. In Roeg's skilled hands the viewer gets a shocking denouement (watch out for the recurring motifs) and something deeper, an emotionally rich film about love and loss.

"You know what a love letter is – it's a bullet." Frank Booth's quaint romantic notions always amused her

KLUTE 1971

Director Alan J Pakula
Cast Jane Fonda, Donald Sutherland

There's an intensity to this film which isn't quite explained by Pakula's accomplished, noirish direction. There's a famous scene where Fonda unzips her dress, a scene Sutherland remembers well because as he said later in an interview: "I guess we'd made love an hour before we shot that." Fonda deserved her Oscar for her performance as the prostitute who is being stalked by one of her old clients and Sutherland, as the private eye who initially suspects her but feels obliged to protect her, matches her power.

LEON 1994

Director Luc Besson *Cast* Jean Reno,
Gary Oldman, Natalie Portman

This was one of many movie sets where a thief is supposed to have seen the actors dressed as police and surrendered. Besson's American debut troubled some by offering yet another revision of *Pygmalion*: this time Eliza Doolittle is a 12-year-old girl who wants to be a hitman like her neighbour Leon (Reno). Both are pursued by Oldman as a crooked drug cop in a performance which some saw as gutsy and others as carpet-chewing. Either way, he's a good contrast to the minimalist Reno.

LE SALAIRE DE LA PEUR 1953

Director Henri-Georges Clouzot
Cast Yves Montand, Charles Vanel

Four men stranded in Latin America embark on a suicidal mission to drive a couple of truckloads of nitroglycerin without proper safety equipment for hundreds of miles over roads where a sudden jolt might mean certain death. The premise is beautifully simple and Clouzot doesn't ease up. (But then this is the same director who made the great *Diabolique*.) There's a strange scene where his wife Vera, who often acts in his films, gets slapped for no reason to do with the plot but hey, who can really tell what goes on inside anyone else's marriage? Otherwise, Clouzot doesn't put a foot wrong.

MAN HUNT 1941

Director Fritz Lang *Cast* Walter Pidgeon,
Joan Bennett

Lang based this film about a big game hunter

THE PLANE TRUTH

Cary trying not to come a cropper

The classic crop-duster scene in *North By Northwest* was far from the first variation that Alfred Hitchcock and his scriptwriter Ernest Lehman came up with for the film. These are just some of the ideas they discussed and their fate.
a) Dolly shot takes viewer down **car assembly line** and when the car comes off the line complete, the door is opened and a **dead body falls** out. Nixed because Lehman told the director, "it does me no good."
b) At a religious retreat a **12-year-old girl** takes **a gun out** of her baby carriage and shoots someone. Nixed. Lehman said it didn't do him any good either.
c) Eventually Hitch says he wants to shoot a man who is **totally alone**. And then the villains try to kill him. Lehman wanted to know how. The director suggested a **tornado**. Lehman wondered how the villains could create a tornado to kill the hero at that moment. After a long silence, Lehman finally mumbles: "Maybe a plane, a crop-duster plane."

trying to kill Hitler on the Geoffrey Household novel *Rogue Male*. It's hard not to see a certain wish fulfilment in the choice of subject: he had fled Nazi Germany leaving behind a wife who had divorced him partly because of the authorities' disapproval. He adds an anti-fascist message to the film which, though typical for Hollywood films of the period, wasn't in the book. Lang creates an effective air of menace throughout and there is some neat, unobtrusive symbolism. Keep your eyes on the direction the arrows are pointing in.

MARATHON MAN 1976

Director **John Schlesinger** *Cast* **Dustin Hoffman, Laurence Olivier**

Yes, this is the film where Olivier advized Hoffman to try acting. Less famously, it's also the film where Hoffman told the greatest living actor to try improvising. Olivier wasn't very good at it, partly because he just didn't do that kind of thing (he liked his lines written down) and partly because he was in such excruciating pain he could hardly stand. All of which almost overshadows what you see on screen, especially after the filmmakers had been forced to cut the torture scene back because preview audiences were sick.

MS. 45 1981

Director **Abel Ferrara** *Cast* **Zoë Tamerlis, Bogey**

Ferrara has directed a lot of movies of which most of the world has never heard. A pity really because this film, about a mute woman who gets raped twice and seeks revenge – a kind of feminist *Death Wish* if you will, is well made. The poetry of the streets can be a bit overrated but garbage has rarely looked quite as good as it does here, clogging up the streets of New York. And Tamerlis makes a pleasant change from Charles Bronson as the avenger.

NORTH BY NORTHWEST 1958

Director **Alfred Hitchcock** *Cast* **Cary Grant, Eva Marie Saint, James Mason**

One day on set, Hitchcock and Mason were discussing the director's films and in particular his use of his favourite stars. "He told me that Jimmy Stewart was worth a million dollars more at the box office than Cary Grant," Mason recalled. Hitch valued Stewart for his appeal to middle America and used that folksiness to subversive effect in *Rear Window* and *Vertigo*. For this, of course, he used Grant, the only actor (according to Mason) who

RAY'S LAW

Raymond Chandler had one problem with his script for *The Blue Dahlia*, the Alan Ladd-Veronica Lake thriller. He didn't have an ending. To write one, his boss John Houseman had to provide him with:

1. Two Cadillac limos on call day and night outside the house to fetch the doctor, deliver script pages, take the maid to market and other emergencies
2. Six secretaries (in three relays of two) to be available at all times for dictation, typing and emergencies
3. A direct line open at all times to his office by day and the studio switchboard at night
4. A doctor to give him injections of glucose twice a day. (He refused to eat, living for seven days on glucose and bourbon.)

MGM. Buena Vista/Gaumont/Dauphin; Galaxie/Greenwich/Antenne 2;

showed the same grace and timing in his acting as Fred Astaire did in his dancing. Apart from *Charade*, this was probably Grant's last first-class role and he is perfectly cast as Roger O Thornton, the advertising executive who's a victim of mistaken identity. ("What does the O stand for?" "It stands for nothing." That exchange was a dig at Hitch's old partner David O Selznick, who used to say that, although the O did in fact stand for Oliver.) Mason is the epitome of evil urbanity in a film which packs in a surprising number of laughs for a Hitchcock thriller. Thornhill/Grant normally appears on the left side of the screen. No, we don't know what it signifies either.

Even George Bernard Shaw could never have anticipated just how Jean Luc Besson would update his Pygmalion story in Leon. Still, he might have preferred it to the My Fair Lady remake

PLAY MISTY FOR ME 1971
Director Clint Eastwood *Cast* Eastwood, Jessica Walter

One of only two Clint films scripted by a woman (Jo Heims, although Dean Reisner did rewrites), this isn't quite Hitchcock but it's more than half-decent. Walter is superb as the psychotic jealous lover, and her sudden, expletive-filled bursts of outrage are still shocking today. Eastwood benefits from the fact that, for once, he appears powerless as this madwoman takes over control of his life. The film is not without flaws: *The First Time*

Ever I Saw Your Face romantic interlude seems like an out-take from *Love Story*. But it is genuinely chilling and seems, though neither the crime nor the name are mentioned, to reflect the paranoia in California in general (and Hollywood in particular) after the Charles Manson case.

PROFONDO ROSSO 1975

Director Dario Argento *Cast* David Hemmings, Dario Nicolodi

Good to see Hemmings resurfacing in *Gladiator* after years in the wilderness as a guest actor in *Airwolf* and *Beverly Hills Cowgirl Blues*. When Hemmings made this, he was coming to the end of a glorious decade kicked off by his role as the photographer in *Blow Up*. This isn't in quite that class but it has its moments. Hitchcock liked it possibly because he recognized his influence in this tale of a jazz pianist (Hemmings) who is entangled in a series of brutal murders, tries to investigate them with Nicolodi, becomes a suspect and, finally, a target. The necklace beheading is a treat but the film does sag in parts.

PSYCHO 1960

Director **Alfred Hitchcock** *Cast* Anthony Perkins, Vera Miles

'Wimpy', as this production was known during filming, is both typically Hitchcockian and something of a departure for the director. He made it for just $800,000, using the crew for his TV show, in a deliberate (and successful) attempt to recreate the feel of the exploitation thrillers which were developing a cult audience. He was quite shameless about the effect his film had, telling Truffaut he played the audience like an organ. As usual, there is a lot else going on. The way the audience is led to believe that the real story is what happens to Janet Leigh's character is clever. There are squillions of references to birds (a plug for his next film?) and, of course, there's Norman Bates and his mother. For Perkins, this role was a breakthrough and a trap: he would usually play Bates (in name or in character) from now on. By the way, the slashing noise you hear in the shower is the sound of a knife slashing into a melon.

REPULSION 1965

Director **Roman Polanski** *Cast* Catherine Deneuve, Ian Hendry

Polanski must have had some seriously bad experiences in a city apartment. This, *Rosemary's Baby* and *La Locataire* form a loose trilogy about the perils of urban life. In *Repulsion*, his first English language film, a sexually repressed girl is left alone in her sister's apartment and has horrific hallucinations about rape and murder. Light it isn't, even if Polanski does play the spoons on screen. The scene where Deneuve beats a suitor with

"YOU'RE NOT
ONLY WRONG,
YOU'RE WRONG
AT THE TOP OF
YOUR VOICE"
John J McCreedy, Bad Day At Black Rock

a candlestick had to be reshot because Polanski wasn't happy. He baited Deneuve until she swung the candlestick at him, which is what you see in the final film.

RONIN 1998

Director John Frankenheimer
Cast Robert De Niro, Jean Réno

Aside from providing us with indelible proof that Sean Bean really cannot act, *Ronin* is an enigmatic, moody film which also includes a car chase to make the one in *Bullitt* look like a school run. Ronin, the

A thrilling opera singer in an operatic thriller

Japanese name for Samurai without a master, are seen here as a select group of ex-service experts: De Niro as leader and former CIA honcho, Reno, the equipment specialist, and Stellan Skarsgard, the technical expert. With their loyalty based solely on money, they are enlisted to retrieve an important briefcase before it is sold on. Manipulating and murdering them is Jonathan Pryce, suitably nasty as the IRA villain. Director Frankenheimer gives the film some of the visual quality of his best film *The Manchurian Candidate*. David Mamet was brought in as script doctor to snap up the dialogue, but felt his role was so minimal that he is credited under the pseudonym Richard Weisz.

SPOORLOOS 1988

Director George Sluizer Cast Johanna Ter Stegge, Gene Bervoets, Bernard-Pierre Donnadieu

A very unusual thriller. Unlike the abandoned husband in this film, you soon know who may be responsible for the wife's disappearance. Yet you can't stop watching. Sluizer directed this from his own screenplay (based on the novel *The Golden Egg* by Tim Krabbé, Jeroen's bro) and remade it as *The Vanishing* with Jeff Bridges and Kiefer Sutherland, but this is better: a tense, psychological jigsaw puzzle unfolding to a horrendous climax.

TAXI DRIVER 1976

Director Martin Scorsese Cast Robert De Niro, Jodie Foster

Scorsese edited this while on a diet of Dom Perignon and Quaaludes, and at one point threatened to shoot the studio boss who wanted to change the ending. Scorsese won the argument. His Vietnam vet Travis Bickle is one of film's great loners. Scriptwriter Paul Schrader always claimed he was inspired to write this by watching John Wayne's *The Searchers*, another film where the hero becomes obsessed with rescuing women. He

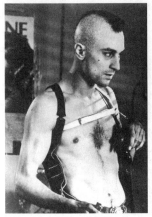

All together now: "You talking to me! You talking to me! You talking to me!"

was also inspired by diaries of the man who shot George Wallace: a fact which seemed doubly pertinent when John Hinckley would try to assassinate Ronald Reagan in part to impress Jodie Foster. The astonishing thing about the film is, even though we can all do Travis Bickle impersonations, how fresh it still seems. Bickle's aloneness is convincingly drawn. Not to be confused with *Confessions Of A Taxi Driver*, released the same year.

TIREZ SUR LE PIANISTE 1960
Director François Truffaut
Cast Charles Aznavour, Marie Dubois
Charles Aznavour may be most famous outside France as the singer who sounds as if his throat muscles had gone into agonising spasm but he is subtle and charming here as the piano player in Truffaut's second feature, an entertaining combo of thriller, gangster movie and comedy. His character used to be a virtuoso but instead of trying to revive his career, he sinks into his brothers' gangster world. A witty nod to the budget thrillers Truffaut liked, with a deeper meaning for those who need one.

THE USUAL SUSPECTS 1995
Director Bryan Singer Cast Stephen Baldwin, Gabriel Byrne, Kevin Spacey, Benicio Del Toro, Kevin Pollak

"THANK GOD FOR THE RAIN TO WASH THE TRASH OFF THE SIDEWALK"
Travis Bickle, Taxi Driver

The budget for this entire movie was smaller, said *Rolling Stone*, "than the cost of equipping Kevin Costner's mariner with gills that look like vaginas" in that summer's *Waterworld*. With no budget, no track record and no real stars (Byrne was then fading and Spacey almost unknown). Singer and writer Christopher McQuarrie delivered a pleasing, teasing tale of a cop who investigates an explosion which killed 27 people and rounds up five criminals, hence the title. Funnily enough, the title came from a magazine article (for all its obvious echoes of *Casablanca*) and the film was a poster before it became a script.

WILD TARGET 1993 CIBLE EMOUVANTE
Director Pierre Salvadori Cast Jean Rochefort, Marie Trintignant
Solitary, anal retentive, mother-dominated Victor Meynard (Rochefort) could make a living doing Hitler impersonations, so acute is the physical resemblance, but here he's a hitman. A hitman whose knack is deserting him. Otherwise why would

he spare a witness and decide to turn this naive innocent into his assistant and, for reasons that seem convincing as you watch, end up protecting the very woman he's supposed to kill? Salvadori keeps the twists and the jokes coming in this thriller-cum-black comedy. And, just at the point where its spell is starting to weaken, it stops. Wish more films would do that.

THE YEAR OF LIVING DANGEROUSLY 1982

Director **Peter Weir** *Cast* **Mel Gibson, Linda Hunt, Sigourney Weaver**
Set in Indonesia in 1965 (but shot in a Muslim ghetto in Manila), Weir's film tells two stories – one a choreographed account of the ouster of tyrannical President Sukarno – the other the relationship between an ambitious Australian reporter (Gibson) and his diminutive photographer (Hunt). Weaver is underused as an embassy attaché – her role is to provide love interest and perpetuate Gibson's eventual act of betrayal (the local art of shadow puppetry represents the disparity in ethics between Gibson and Hunt). Weir's concern is with people, not political morality, so don't expect a history lesson. While Gibson shines, Hunt steals the show. Her superbly nuanced portrayal of the enigmatic, passionate Chinese-Australian 'dwarf' is one of the few turns in recent years which really deserved its Oscar.

THE MALEVOLENT WASP

CHRISTOPHER WALKEN

Two men were brave enough to assault Walken in New York in 1980. (He'd asked them to turn the music down in their car.) Most of us, seeing his portrayals of a type he calls "the malevolent WASP" wouldn't dare risk a funny glance in his direction.

Ten years ago, when filming *The Comfort Of Strangers*, Walken famously observed: "I don't need make-up to look evil, I can do that on my own." He's been doing that since we first really noticed him as the Russian roulette fanatic in *The Deer Hunter*.

Director Mike Figgis tried to hire him once. He asked Walken if he'd read the script. Walken asked Figgis if he liked his face. The director said he did. "That's fucking great," said Walken, "because if you don't, get De Niro. Fuck you, I'm out of here." With that Walken was gone. Conversation over.

Mel Gibson says in real life, Walken doesn't walk, he glides like a vampire. They met at a party. "I just started talking about the Middle Ages. He's a very smart guy and began to talk tortures. And he was getting scary. I turned around to avoid his gaze and I saw a huge building with an illuminated '666' sign on top, in red. He started smiling and I thought: "Oh no – Chris Walken is the Antichrist."

"I don't need make-up to look evil"

TURKEYS

Bad movies are great. After all, we wouldn't know what good movies looked like unless we had bad ones to compare them with. Awful films inspire an essentially harmless kind of schadenfreude. There's nothing quite like watching Warren Beatty and Dustin Hoffman being out-acted by a blind camel to make us feel grateful that we're not film stars.

Films become turkeys for many reasons, not always because they are as bad as, say, *Howard the Duck*. Often a young director has had a huge hit, and, eager to cash in, a studio gives them free rein and unlimited funds to another. Then make there are films stymied by rumours from the set, stories of 'creative differences', which give a movie a bad rap before anyone has seen an inch of film. That's why publicists are now hired before shooting starts to make sure the production basks in the glow of positive comments throughout.

The big guys make their share of turkeys too – think of Terry Gilliam watching the budget spiral on *The Adventures Of Baron Munchausen*. As budgets are fuelled by special effects and star salaries, films will continue to fail to recoup their costs. But on the strength of the films listed below producers could improve their odds by not casting Warren Beatty or Nastassja Kinski.

THE ADVENTURES OF BARON MUNCHAUSEN 1988
Director Terry Gilliam Cast John Neville, Eric Idle, Sarah Polley
What impresses about Gilliam's film, which is ostensibly about the Baron's impossible adventures (but is really, the director insists, about old age), is the casual extravagance with which he spent the $46m he extracted from Columbia to make it. If you didn't put up the money then you might think it's been well spent on stunts like the one where the Baron and a pal climb

down from the moon on the same two lengths of rope over and over again. It's a cliché to say of big budget films that more could have been spent on the script but here it is, partly, true. (More could have been spent in the cutting room too.) But even in its present form, it's worth persevering with for the spectacle and the playful, inventive, humour. Asked by the sultan if he has any famous last words, Munchausen says: "Not yet," to which his interrogator replies: "'Not yet'. Is that famous?"

THE BIG TRAIL 1930
Director Raoul Walsh Cast John Wayne, Marguerite Churchill
Breck Coleman, a young trail scout leads a group of pioneers through Indian country on their way to settle in the West. One of the very early talkie westerns, the sound and performances appear creaky today but it's worth viewing mainly for Walsh's incredible composition and use of Grandeur, an early 70mm widescreen format which beautifully captures the scope of the old West. This was due to be Wayne's big break (although who he thought was going to take him seriously in those embroidered shirts, we're not sure). Unfortunately, audiences of the time were in love with comedies and musicals and the film flopped, consigning him to B movies for nine years until John Ford cast him in *Stagecoach* and the legend really began.

HEAVEN'S GATE 1980
Director Michael Cimino Cast Kris Kristofferson, Christopher Walken
Cimino's notorious western, a brave attempt to demystify the genre by adding gritty realism to a tale of immigrant farmers in Wyoming being hounded out by wealthy cattle owners, is now a cautionary tale for filmmakers across the world. Riding high on the success of *The Deer Hunter*, Cimino tried to make another 'important' film but was plagued with production problems and rows between the cast. And when it finally reached the cinemas (219 minutes long at first showing), the critics ran for their vitriol. Cimino returned to the cutting room to make the film a more acceptable length, but he could do nothing to clarify the muddled storyline and even stunning photography and extraordinary attention to period detail couldn't save it.

KING DAVID 1985
Director Bruce Beresford Cast Richard Gere, Edward Woodward
A foolhardy bid to revive the Biblical epic in the middle of the oh so forward-looking 1980s sees Gere struggling with a very weighty script. The film screamed "Look! We're doing the Bible" rather than telling what could have been a dramatic and bloodthirsty story. It recouped just $2.5m of its $22m budget.

> **"EITHER SHOOT ME OR LOWER YOUR VOICE"**
> Chuck Clarke, Ishtar

HELL'S ANGELS 1930

Director Howard Hughes *Cast* Ben Lyon, James Hall, Jean Harlow

Extraordinary aerial action sequences, way ahead of their time, and the discovery of Harlow make this slight story about a pair of brothers who enlist in the RAF during World War 1 worth a viewing. But it's also a story of filmic excess on a fantastically grand scale. Hughes spent a whopping $3.8m on it, shooting 249 feet of film for every foot used in the final cut, and insisted that every print was hand-tinted before it went out to theatres. Three pilots died during filming. Hughes insisted on doing some stunts and even crashed his own plane.

HUDSON HAWK 1991

Director Michael Lehmann *Cast* Bruce Willis, Andie MacDowell

Willis' misguided vanity flick, a reward for the success of *Die Hard*, features his own script about a cat burglar blackmailed into a series of daring heists, including one on the Vatican. It cost $56m to make and sold just over $17m worth of tickets. Supporting cast member Richard E Grant described the filming as a shambles of location changes and reshoots, which sent costs skyrocketing. It's a shame because it's actually a lot of fun, a hugely over the top comedy with some great action sequences and a superb supporting cast in Grant, Danny Aiello, James Coburn and David Caruso, although Sandra Bernhard gets a bit tiresome after a while.

> **"I WANT TO DO COMMUNITY SERVICE. I WANT TO TEACH THE HANDICAPPED HOW TO YODEL"**
>
> Hudson Hawk, Hudson Hawk

ISHTAR 1987

Director Elaine May *Cast* Dustin Hoffman, Warren Beatty

A comedy so lame it should have been shot as a mercy to us all. You know it's going to be dire when it emerges Hoffman and Beatty are singers; granted they're supposed to be bad, but still, it's terrible casting. The duo are on their way to play the Ishtar Hilton and as the plot gets more and more complicated, involving the CIA and a group of rebels, the flock of vultures and a blind camel are the best things in the film. Thankfully Hoffman survived the fact that it took only $14.4m against its $40m budget and made *Rain Man* the following year.

ONE FROM THE HEART 1982

Director Francis Ford Coppola *Cast* Teri Garr, Frederic Forrest

There were so many column inches written about this film during production, it's no wonder it buckled under the weight of expectation. Coppola spent much of the budget on state-of-the-art electronics so he could play back his scenes immediately after they were shot. This involved him spending hours huddled in a video van, rather than talking to the actors. And it shows.

The film, supposed to be about an unhappy couple finding love in Las Vegas with interesting strangers (Nastassja Kinski and Raul Julia), sacrificed all substance (and human interest) to the demands of technical style. Video playback is now the norm, and Coppola can say he was breaking new ground, but as one industry insider put it: "He took an $8m project and used the latest advances in video to bring it in for $23m."

Columbia/Delphi V; Prominent Features/Laura Film/Columbia TriStar

REVOLUTION 1985

Director **Hugh Hudson**
Cast **Al Pacino, Nastassja Kinski**

Burial at sea: Baron Munchausen and Sally Salt can only watch as their film's budget descends into a watery grave

It's hard to pinpoint just what makes this wannabe epic about an ordinary man caught up in the American Revolutionary War so bad. Is it that Pacino's Glasgow accent is so obviously forged in the Bronx? Or that Kinski weeps so much you feel she might die, despite surviving the weight of her ludicrous hairstyle at the start of the film? Or that the script makes you want to clap your hands over your ears? There are good points, such as Hudson's vivid camerawork and Donald Sutherland's sadistic officer. Other delights include spotting Sid Owen (Ricky in *EastEnders*) as Pacino's son, or being mesmerized by Sutherland's hairy facial mole, which practically becomes a character in its own right.

WATERWORLD 1995

Director **Kevin Reynolds** *Cast* **Kevin Costner, Jeanne Tripplehorn**

"Beyond the horizon lies the secret to a new beginning..." ran the tagline. Bet they couldn't wait to see the end though. If it hadn't cost $200m and not been dogged by so many disasters, such as the main set sinking in a storm and the difficulties of shooting entirely on water (in one scene the ocean and sky change colour with every cut), *Waterworld* might have been an entertaining, futuristic film with impressive action sequences and some nice one-liners. Costner's monosyllabic performance aside, the acting is fine, with Dennis Hopper having a whale of a time as the chief smoker (only in California could the tobacco industry be so despised that they base an entire evil cult around it) and the surprisingly non-irritating Tina Majorino doing a great job as the obligatory child who holds a key to the future.

UNRELEASED

It's extremely rare for a company (especially a Hollywood studio) to make a film and then simply not bother to release it. And the bad news for conspiracy theorists is that when this happens it's not usually because these films are a threat to the powers that be but because they are truly, badly, deeply so appalling that the studio can't foresee the peculiar combination of circumstances in which anybody would want to watch them. There are a few distinguished exceptions, as you'll discover if you read on…

THE DAY THE CLOWN CRIED 1972
Director Jerry Lewis Cast Lewis, Sven Lindberg, Anton Diffring
You might think this film has never seen the light of day because even the most cynical film executive recoiled from its plot about a Nazi clown who entertains children in a concentration camp before leading them to be gassed. If you thought that then you would, of course, be wrong: the film is the subject of a legal dispute so complex that only two men in the world know what's really behind it and neither of them is Jerry Lewis. Dino's former partner called this his "first serious movie". But if you're going to make a movie in that trickiest of genres you might call 'Holocaust comedy', it has to be sensitively directed and performed (as, say, Roberto Benigni's *Life Is Beautiful* was) but this wasn't. Lewis' own take on the film may explain why: "It is he [the clown] who is assigned to try to keep the kids in the camp happy – and it is he, in the end, who is expected to lead the children – into the ovens." Thanks for that Jerry.

> "THE GREAT 18-FOOT GRIZZLY HAS RETURNED TO KILL AGAIN!"
>
> Poster, Grizzly II: The Predator

DIANA & ME 1997
Director David Parker Cast Toni Collette, Dominic West
A gentle, romantic comedy about an Australian woman called Diana Spencer, who travels to London to meet her namesake and becomes involved with a member of the paparazzi pursuing the Princess, might have seemed a good idea at the time – until the real Princess of Wales was killed fleeing the paparazzi. Now you can begin to understand why hardly anybody has seen this movie or for that matter even heard of it. David Parker hasn't attempted to direct another film since. Poor sod.

GRIZZLY II: THE PREDATOR 1987

Writer David Sheldon *Cast* Charlie Sheen, George Clooney

Gorgeous George at least has some excuse for being involved in this ill-fated follow up to the 1976 film *Grizzly*: he needed the work. Quite what persuaded Charlie Sheen though, riding high after a recent triumphant appearance in *Wall Street*, to appear as Ron in this tale about a vicious bear who has to be hunted down remains a mystery. The film was marketed under the slogan "The great 18-foot grizzly has returned to kill again!" which, sadly, failed to impress a public who couldn't remember the homicidal creature's first appearance.

QUEEN KELLY 1929

Director Erich von Stroheim *Cast* Gloria Swanson, Walter Byron, Seena Owen

Hard to imagine how even Eric von Stroheim thought he was going to get away with filming a movie that called for the heroine (Swanson) to be whipped by her true love's fiancee (this was in 1929, remember) and ends with Swanson being crowned queen of her own east African brothel (hence the title). The film never even reached completion because Swanson, whose production company was partly involved in its financing, halted production early on. It was consequently 'finished' using stills and subtitles but von Stroheim wouldn't let this bastardized version be released. Ironically, the first the world saw of the footage was in *Sunset Boulevard* when Swanson, appearing as the mad, ageing Norma Desmond, has one of her own films screened to impress her young, cynical lover. Von Stroheim finally gave permission for a very limited theatrical release in which Swanson throws herself into the river and dies. But footage discovered in the 1960s shows our heroine fleeing to east Africa only to marry a loathsome lech who, for reasons best known to von Stroheim and his analyst, resembles a giant white spider with a body decaying from the inside.

ALL WELLES

The original wayward genius probably left more unfinished work behind him than an absconding cowboy builder. Here's some of the work he could have killed time with instead of being the voice of Domecq sherry.

THE DEEP 1967

Twenty-two years before Nicole Kidman made a splash in *Dead Calm*, Welles began filming this yacht-based thriller based on the same novel. The cast was headed by Laurence Harvey, Jeanne Moreau, Welles and his latest discovery, Hungarian actress Oja Kodar. Indeed, his biographer David Thomson suggests the film may have been a cover for his affair with Kodar.

IT'S ALL TRUE 1942

Welles' travelogue on Rio began filming before a line of dialogue had been written. However, that didn't stop him shooting thousands of feet of film with a crew from his studio, RKO. The original four-part plan for the film didn't even mention Rio. In the end, with the crew rebelling as scenes were endlessly re-shot, the film was aborted. Some clips surfaced in a documentary.

UNTITLED

A script about a man destroying himself in pursuit of "the wrong woman" may yet see the light of day. Could be good. After all, pursuing the wronged woman could have been Welles' specialist subject on *Mastermind*.

QUE VIVA MEXICO 1933

Director **Sergei Eisenstein** *Cast* **Felix Balderas, Martin Hernandez**

One of those works, the mere mention of which, can have cinema buffs gibbering incoherent sentences containing the words "missing" and "masterpiece". The famed Russian director had originally come over to film Theodore Dreiser's *American Tragedy* but for various reasons (including the fact that some bright spark at Paramount realised that a book with a title like that might have had an unhappy ending) it was never made. After a campaign of hate mail, Paramount ended Eisenstein's contract. Upton Sinclair, screenwriter and future Socialist candidate for the governorship of California, paid for the world's most famous film director to go to Mexico to make a documentary. After a row over budgets, Eisenstein stopped filming and his footage was sent back to Hollywood where it was edited without any reference to the director himself who soon fled back to the USSR. The original plan had called for a four-part film but his footage was edited into various pieces. Obviously, Eisenstein's vision of this film is beyond recovery, but the best version available is probably the 1979 *Que Viva Mexico,* cut for video by one of his associates.

SOMETHING'S GOT TO GIVE 1962

Director **George Cukor** *Cast* **Marilyn Monroe, Dean Martin**

The title of this planned remake of *My Favourite Wife* was sadly prophetic as Marilyn's life gave out before this film was finished. Some 37 minutes of the remaining footage were shown on a US cable channel's tribute on 1 June 2001, which would have been her 75th birthday. The film was also due to star Dean Martin, Wally Cox and Cyd Charisse alongside Monroe who had already been fired once from the set – allegedly for showing up for only 13 days of actual shooting – and then later re-hired. The remaining footage is rather eerie in places because it shows Monroe in surprisingly good shape (psychologically) given what was happening in the rest of her life. After her mysterious death in August 1962, *My Favourite Wife*, with its plot of a missing, presumed dead, wife suddenly reappearing very much alive, was remade by Doris Day as *Move Over Darling*. The contrast could not have been starker: the sauciest part of Day's movie was her singing of the theme tune. With Monroe starring it might have been a completely different kind of sex comedy (ie one which had some sex in it).

Marilyn in *Something's Got To Give*. The 'something' was her

WAR

War – what is it good for? Clearly, Bruce Springsteen hasn't been to the movies very often as almost the only thing war is good for (apart from sorting out the occasional evil dictator) is inspiring movies like *Apocalypse Now, Talvisota* and *Paths Of Glory*.

ar films, like Allied troops on Normandy beaches, come in waves. The market is usually boosted by real war so in 1944, in the midst of the tragic sequel to World War I, 32 war films were released. But after both world wars, demand evaporated almost as fast as you could say "armistice". Only after a decent interval (12 years in the case of Lewis Milestone's anti-war classic *All Quiet On The Western Front* and for Kubrick's *Paths Of Glory*) that filmmakers returned profitably to the field of conflict.

The obvious exception to this is the Vietnam War, which never inspired many propaganda films (apart from John Wayne's risible *The Green Berets*) but has been the conflict of choice for many directors (notably Coppola, Kubrick and Stone) with ambitions going beyond the 'blood and thunder' epics.

Vietnam so affected the American zeitgeist that its traces can be found in films like Spielberg's *Jurassic Park*, often cited as a Vietnam allegory, an updated Frankenstein's monster fable warning about the seduction of the kind of technology America used in south east Asia. George Lucas' *Star Wars* has some obvious parallels, with its small but brave band of rebels in continuous combat with a technologically sophisticated but evil empire, whose death star presumably, is a metaphor for napalm or just the fire unleashed on Vietnam from the air. And there are echoes of mood and tone between action scenes in *Star Wars* and the *Ride of the Valkyries* sequence in *Apocalypse Now*.

The essential choice facing any director who sets out to make a war film remains pretty much what it was when Milestone made his, er, milestone. Is war hell (*All Quiet On The Western Front, Apocalypse Now, Gallipoli*), glory (*In Which We Serve, Patton, Sands Of Iwo Jima, Zulu*), hell and glory with the glory of the cause just tipping the balance (*Saving Private Ryan*), absurd (*Oh What A Lovely War*), a sham (*Breaker Morant*) or a different backdrop for adultery (John Schlesinger's *Yanks*)?

"WHAT HE DID TO SHAKESPEARE WE ARE DOING TO POLAND"
Colonel Ehrhardt, To Be Or Not To Be

A filmmaker's choice of hell or war normally signifies another preference: for order or chaos. The organised wars of old, where the battlefield is a diagram and watches are eternally synchronised, have given away to the deadly chaos of *Apocalypse Now* or *Talvisota*. In part, this is due to an increased respect for historical accuracy, the effect of which can be seen if you watch Tony Richardson's *The Charge Of The Light Brigade* (1968) and compare it to the Michael Curtiz/Errol Flynn 1936 version.

War is, alas, something most countries have experienced in the last century, none more so than Russia which has made some of the finest war films (*Alexander Nevsky*, *Come And See*, *The Cranes Are Flying*). We also recommend *Dark Blue World*, the film about Czech pilots who fought in the RAF in World War II. Made on a budget only 50 per cent larger than the cost of the premiere party for *Pearl Harbor*, the film uses retouched footage from *The Battle Of Britain* (1969) and is the best Czech contribution to the genre since *Closely Observed Trains* (1966).

One of the finest statements of the nature of war comes in a film, *Breaker Morant*, where this is almost no action. The officer defending Morant and his colleagues, accused of war crimes, says: "The barbarities of war are seldom committed by abnormal men. The tragedy of war is that these horrors are committed by normal men in abnormal situations."

Francois Truffaut famously said no-one could make a truly anti-war film because movies can't help making combat like fun. That hard fact undercuts the message even in a dark anti-war masterpiece like *Apocalypse Now*. *Breaker Morant* scores by refusing its viewers that titillating distraction.

> **"YOU UNDERSTAND, CAPTAIN, THAT THIS MISSION DOES NOT EXIST, NOR WILL IT EVER EXIST!"**
> Colonel Lucas, Apocalypse Now

ALL QUIET ON THE WESTERN FRONT 1930

Director **Lewis Milestone** *Cast* **Lew Ayres, Louis Wolheim**

This, still the greatest anti-war film, was a big-budget venture for the time ($1.25m), made in Hollywood, yet based on the novel by German author Erich Maria Remarque. The film opens with a group of schoolboys persuaded to enlist by their teacher and, gradually throughout the film, death picks each one off. Initially filmed as a silent film, making some of the acting look a little OTT, it is the performances of the lead actors, particularly Ayres, which help carry the film through slow moments of observation. After Milestone sent out a request for authentic German uniforms for the shooting, he ended up casting a number of real-life German soldiers as officers as there were so many living in Los Angeles at the time. Future Hollywood luminaries working in the background included George (*Philadelphia Story*) Cukor as dialogue director and Fred (*High Noon*) Zinnemann as an extra.

BATTLE OF ALGIERS 1965

Director Gillo Pontecorvo *Cast* Yacef Saadi, Jean Martin,
Brahim Haggiag

An unusual war film which made Pontecorvo's reputation, shot
in a black and white semi-documentary style which leaves
moral judgements aside to focus on a thrilling reconstruction of
the civil war, balancing the French army's use of torture with
the terrorists' habit of setting off bombs in shops.

THE CRANES ARE FLYING 1957

Director Mikhail Kalatozov *Cast* Tatyana Samoilova, Alexei Batalov,
Vasily Merkuryev

Taking advantage of the thaw that followed Stalin's death
in 1953, Kalatazov dares to replace the idealized Socialist
androids (which usually represented the masses in Soviet
cinema) with individuals who fall in love, go off to war, get
seduced and die. It isn't giving too much away, given the
time and the fact that this is an anti-war movie, to say that
the love story between Batalov and Samoilova is tragic. The
scene where the dying soldier sees not his past but
the future which might have been is especially haunting.

CROSS OF IRON 1977

Director Sam Peckinpah *Cast* James Coburn, Maximilian
Schell, James Mason

Peckinpah's only war movie but then the body count in
his westerns was so high he hardly needed the excuse of a
world war to commence bloodletting. Coburn is the
German sergeant sick of war in the eastern front and of
the duplicity of officers like Schell who can't see past his
own need to win the Iron Cross. Slammed by critics,
praised by Orson Welles as the "greatest war film I
ever saw", this is a bittersweet drama whose funereal
photography perfectly brings home the claustrophobia
and fearful monotony of war. Robert Aldrich's *Attack* has
a similar feel and is similarly unjustly neglected.

DAS BOOT 1981

Director Wolfgang Petersen *Cast* Jürgen Prochnow,
Herbert Grönemeyer, Klaus Wennemann

Jonathan Mostow's *U-571* (2000) was praised for its
gripping sequences of a hunted submarine, silently diving
below a safe depth to escape depth charges, its rivets and
bulkheads creaking under the strain, but *Das Boot* had
done all this and more 20 years earlier. Petersen's classic
is the archetypal sub film, setting the style not just for

SHELL SHOCKED

Johnny Got His Gun is one of
the few war films to appeal to
Francois Truffaut and
Metallica. Truffaut cited the
1974 drama as a personal
favourite. In it, Timothy
Bottoms plays a young
American soldier who is hit by
a shell on the last day of WWI.
The explosion blows off his
arms, legs, nose, eyes, ears
and mouth and leaves him a
bed-bound invalid swathed in
bandages and with a bag over
his face. This unpromising
premise sets up some
imaginatively filmed fantasy
sequences including an
encounter between Bottoms
and a long-haired Jesus Christ
(Donald Sutherland).
Emerging from his visions,
Bottoms wants to be put on
show in a carnival as a
demonstration of the horrors
of war – all of which sounds
rather depressing, but inspired
Metallica to write a song called
One, the video for which
included footage from the film.

Mark and Mel's first trip to Europe was not a great success. The travel agent had been wrong about Gallipoli

U-571 but for other sweaty, claustrophobic underwater thrillers like *The Hunt For Red October*. Petersen shows that tension and suspense are more important to a good thriller than action and explosions, turning the constraints to his advantage with meticulous camerawork and an intense, cynical script that highlights the sailors' contempt for the Nazis. A 1997 re-release includes an hour of extra footage, but if you still want more, take a look at Petersen's 1997 thriller *Air Force One*, which milks the tensions of a confined space with similar skill.

THE DEER HUNTER 1978
Director **Michael Cimino** *Cast* **Robert De Niro, John Savage, Christopher Walken, Meryl Streep, John Cazale**
An epic stunner about the effects of the Vietnam War on the lives of the people from a small industrial town in Pennsylvania, especially two young steelworkers who enlist in the US army and find themselves caught up in a brutality they had never bargained for. The film is long (three hours) and slow in places, but this is a deliberate and effective ploy to make sure the audience is totally involved in the lives of those on screen, and is shattered as events both during and after the war change the men's lives forever. The Russian roulette scene with De Niro and Walken will have your heart in your mouth as well as serving as a powerful metaphor for the whole business of going to war. The scene where the plane gets snagged on the bridge was accidental, a member of the crew actually frees it and Cimino just kept the cameras rolling.

FLESH & BLOOD 1985
Director **Paul Verhoeven** *Cast* **Rutger Hauer, Jennifer Jason Leigh**
Verhoeven's first American, English-language film sees Hauer as a 16th Century mercenary, who kidnaps the betrothed princess of a noble's son in recompense for the nobleman cutting him, and his men out of their deserved loot. Despite being kidnapped and raped by Hauer, the princess (Leigh) seemingly falls in love with her captor, or does she? Hauer and his men await battle, holed up in a castle (the same as that featured in

El Cid) waiting for the nobleman's army and impending war, the princess' true feelings consistently ambiguous. The title perfectly sums up the film, violent and certainly bloody, but the skills of cinematographer Jan de Bont (of future *Speed* fame) shine through, ensuring an electrifying pace to the proceedings.

GALLIPOLI 1981
Director Peter Weir *Cast* Mel Gibson, Mark Lee, Bill Hunter

Though primarily about the Anzac's disastrous campaign to wrestle the Dardanelles from the Ottoman Empire, Weir was careful not to turn his large canvas production into an action film. Through the relationship between Frank (Gibson) and Archie (Lee), two young 'runners' on the road to adventure and an appointment with destiny, several important 'Australian' issues are examined, such as conscription, conflicting attitudes towards the Empire, sport and competitiveness, and the concept of 'mateship'. Particularly symbolic is the cinematography – Archie and Frank's carefree lifestyle under the big sky in Australia is brilliantly juxtaposed against the cloying claustrophobia of the trenches where the spirited young men become nothing more than cannon-fodder. And as the ANZACs launch their doomed offensive there's an underwater sequence that's as affecting (though considerably less graphic) as Spielberg's opening footage in *Saving Private Ryan*. But unlike that flag-waving epic, Weir's is a far more powerful examination of the utter futility of war.

> **"YOU WRITE 'BORN TO KILL' ON YOUR HELMET AND YOU WEAR A PEACE BUTTON"**
> Pogue Colonel, Full Metal Jacket

THE GREEN BERETS 1968
Directors Ray Kellogg, John Wayne *Cast* John Wayne, David Janssen

Wayne's Vietnam western tries to apply the simplicities of the American west to a new war in the east and gets hopelessly confused. The symbolic confirmation of this confusion is the final scene where the sun sets, triumphantly, in the east. This is Wayne's attempt, first mooted in a letter to president Lyndon Johnson, to help the Vietnamese war effort. The Pentagon ordered the script be rewritten, so what you see on screen is a straight good vs evil clash with marauding Indians replaced by massacring Vietcong. The Berets' base camp is even called Dodge City. This made a mint at the box office but failed in its main objective, to make America feel any better about Vietnam.

HAIL THE CONQUERING HERO 1944
Director Preston Sturges *Cast* Eddie Bracken, Ella Raines

Like most young lads enlisting for World War II, as a soldier, you want two things: to come back alive, and as a hero. Bracken plays Woodrow Truesmith, a small-town lad with exactly these aspirations, which are only to be dashed when he is invalided out. Too ashamed to go home he hides out, working in a shipyard while his family send letters to him all over the world. When some marines hear his pitiful story they drag him back home where he is mistaken for a returning hero, and runs for mayor. Great performances from Sturges regulars William Demarest and Frank Pangborn light up this film, the only anti-war satire made during World War II by a major studio.

> "DO NOT SPEAK
> TO ME OF RULES.
> THIS IS WAR. THIS
> IS NOT A GAME
> OF CRICKET"
> Colonel Saito, Bridge On The River Kwai

KELLY'S HEROES 1970
Director Brian G Hutton *Cast* Clint Eastwood, Telly Savalas, Donald Sutherland, Don Rickles, Harry Dean Stanton
This is the *Italian Job* of war movies – an enjoyable caper with a cracking ensemble cast, and written, like *The Italian Job*, by Troy Kennedy Martin. This time out, the gold that our ill-assorted crooks plan to steal is not in football-mad Turin but behind enemy lines in France during World War 2. The film re-imagines the war as a playground for drop-outs, rebels and misfits, notably Donald Sutherland's grinning, lazy-eyed Oddball, whose hippy turns of phrase ("Crazy! I mean like with so many positive waves maybe we can't lose!") define the film's anachronistic vibe. The trippy drum riff that runs through the soundtrack would fuel a generation of Manchester indie bands.

THE KILLING FIELDS 1984
Director Roland Joffé *Cast* Sam Waterston, Haing S Ngor
The saddest thing about this movie is that Ngor, after suffering trauma far worse than the filmmakers could bring themselves to show us in Pol Pot's Cambodia, came to America and was murdered in LA. This should be watched as a double bill with *The Green Berets* because few films better expose that picture's wilful absurdity. The reporter (Waterston) in Joffé's film is outraged, as are most of his colleagues, by the violence wreaked on Cambodia and with his stringer (Ngor) aims to show the world what is happening. There's only one laugh in this movie, when Richard Nixon appears on newsreel to announce that: "Cambodia is the Nixon doctrine in its purest form."

Charlie on a secret mission to find his dad, last seen in Cambodia with Marlon Brando

THE LIFE & DEATH OF COLONEL BLIMP 1943
Director Michael Powell *Cast* Roger Livesey, Deborah Kerr, Anton Walbrook
Michael Powell and Emeric Pressburger

took the 1940s caricature of the bluff old war-horse (as satirised in David Low's *Colonel Blimp* cartoon strip), and fleshed it out with a rich, touching life story that shows how a very British buffer evolved from a dashing young officer of the 1890s. Roger Livesey's portrayal of the decent, cheery Clive Wynne-Candy, lucky in friendship but unlucky in love, is sad, subtle and full of human contradictions. Deborah Kerr, meanwhile, is at her very best playing the three different women in his life. When Churchill railed against the film, Anton Walbrook (who plays Candy's German officer friend) told him "No people in the world other than the English would have had the courage, in the midst of war, to tell the people such unvarnished truth."

OPEN CITY 1946 ROMA CITTA APERTA

Director **Roberto Rossellini** *Cast* **Aldo Fabrizi, Anna Magnani, Marcello Pagliero**

Fellini wrote the script in a week in his kitchen – the only room in his house in Rome which had heat. Rossellini filmed this in bits, shooting on silent film stock, dubbing in the sound and dialogue at the last. This simple story about a resistance leader (Pagliero) on the run made a star of Magnani and so impressed the young Ingrid Bergman when she saw it in an art cinema in LA that she fell in love with (and later married) the director. Italian audiences hated its squalid realism, coming around only when it was acclaimed as a masterpiece in France and America.

PATHS OF GLORY 1957

Director **Stanley Kubrick** *Cast* **Kirk Douglas, George Macready, Ralph Meeker**

The film that made Kubrick even though it was never a box office or critical smash. Which is ironic because, according to Douglas, Kubrick's first contribution to the film was to rewrite the script, badly, and give it a happy ending. The actor, a fan of the director's talent but not his personality, also noted that Kubrick seemed unduly concerned about sticking signs up all over the set saying "Kubrick-Harris" (James Harris was the producer). Kubrick returned the compliment saying that Douglas was just an employee on the film. Based on a true story, the film highlights the difference between those fighting the war and those leading the charge from the back. Douglas is suitably indignant as the Lieutenant leading a suicidal charge, whose men are subsequently court-

CROSSING A GULF

JULIE CHRISTIE ON THREE KINGS

On the surface *Three Kings* fulfils the action-packed self-glorifying format of a war film but there is a subversive agent at work: the script. When a bullet enters a body we see a shot of its interior as the bullet wreaks its havoc. Reality, biology, enters the equation. Most unformulaic. The script gives the enemy a voice. Not the sentimental voice that is the stamp of the liberal war film, but a voice of utmost scorn for the obscenity of precision bombing.

When an American soldier tries to bridge the gap with his captor by evoking their shared parenthood, we flash to scenes of these two families: a view of the kindly, clean world of the American family where no bombs will fall and of the (no doubt) kindly clean Iraqi family living and dying under unrelenting attack. Perhaps unsurprisingly it wasn't a great commercial success. Could it be because it makes an invisible people almost visible?

marshalled for failing in an impossible task. The film was banned in France for its unflattering portrayal of the French World War I army, and by the Swiss army for containing "very much warfare know-how" but Winston Churchill liked it.

PLATOON 1986
Director Oliver Stone *Cast* Tom Berenger, Willem Dafoe, Charlie Sheen

The first in Stone's labour of love Vietnam trilogy is still the best of the bunch. The script took Stone a decade to write, possibly because Sheen's character is based on Stone himself, a veteran of Vietnam and winner of the Bronze Star and Purple Heart. This is war through the eyes of one misplaced youth and his memory of what it seemed like. We are never fed details of the war in general, and nor are we given a clear view of the enemy, allowing Stone to skilfully convey the over-wrought fear of so many young, naïve men sent into a surreal, deadly, hell.

RAN 1985
Director Akira Kurosawa *Cast* Tatsuya Nakadai, Mieko Harada, Satoshi Terao, Jinpachi Nezu, Daisuke Ryu

Kurosawa's re-imagining of *King Lear* shifts the story to medieval Japan, where an elderly warlord distributes his kingdom between his three sons. The result is civil war, brought to life by Kurosawa in moving, majestic battle scenes said to have influenced how Spielberg filmed the opening sequence of *Saving Private Ryan*. 'Ran' means chaos in Japanese and the film is at its best conveying the confusion of war in measured camerawork that somehow turns the bloody clashes into operatic tragedy. Some of the non-battle scenes drag a little and the portentous dialogue often seems like a poor précis of Shakespeare, but it's worth it for the final scenes of the hero facing his end in a burning castle, the sounds of battle muted from the soundtrack leaving only Toru Takemitsu's music.

SAVING PRIVATE RYAN 1998
Director Steven Spielberg *Cast* Tom Hanks, Tom Sizemore, Edward Burns, Barry Pepper, Adam Goldberg, Matt Damon

Spielberg's World War II film never regains momentum after the shock of the opening sequence, a brutally realistic exposition of the chaotic landing on Omaha beach (fine work by cinematographer Janusz Kaminski). Stephen Ambrose, the writer whose work inspired the film, had to stop his screening after 20 minutes, overcome by the authenticity of the scene. The story follows the army's attempts to bring home Private Ryan from enemy lines as his three other brothers have all died in the

> "I THINK YOU'RE SOME KIND OF DEVIATED PREVERT. I THINK GENERAL RIPPER FOUND OUT ABOUT YOUR PREVERSION, AND THAT YOU WERE ORGANIZING SOME KIND OF MUTINY OF PREVERTS."
>
> Colonel "Bat" Guano, Dr Strangelove

fighting. Spielberg insisted the leads had army training, with Hanks known as "Turd Number One". Robert Mitchum's *The Story Of GI Joe* (1945) is worth seeing in its own right and as an influence on this film.

These three kings find gold; the originals brought it with them. Kings ain't what they used to be

SCHINDLER'S LIST 1993

Director **Steven Spielberg** *Cast* **Liam Neeson, Ben Kingsley, Ralph Fiennes**
Martin Scorsese commissioned a script of Thomas Keneally's novel *Schindler's Ark*, but finally bailed out in 1991 feeling a Jewish director would do a better job. But it is Spielberg's skill at bringing serious subjects to the masses which is his greatest gift here. Neeson is breathtaking as a manipulative, womanising con man (Spielberg told the actor to base his portrayal on Time Warner chairman Steven Ross, to whom the film is partially dedicated) who initially sees the plight of the Jewish as his chance to get cheap, slave labour, yet ruins his businesses to save over a thousand Jews from certain death. Kingsley is equally impressive as Neeson's accountant

WAR MOVIES ARE HELL

Apocalypse Now may have been as close to hell as you could get without going to war.

Francis Ford Coppola had failed to convince his first director George Lucas who preferred to do something of his own called *Star Wars*, even though Coppola told Lucas his script was poor. Reluctantly, Coppola decided to direct.

Brando threatened to quit the film and keep his $1m advance. When Coppola insisted he was happy to get Redford (who had already turned him down), Brando turned up 40kg overweight, drunk, having not read the script or the *Heart of Darkness* story it was based on.

Coppola, eager to placate his star, allowed Brando time off with his family. This so upset Harvey Keitel that he walked out and Martin Sheen was drafted in. Sheen then had a heart attack and had to rest for two months. His heart may not have been helped by a two-day bender – he was still drunk when the opening

scenes in the hotel room were shot and smashed the mirror accidentally, suggesting he was the new king of method acting.

Smashing the mirror obviously gave Coppola seven years of bad luck, seven years which began when Hurricane Olga destroyed the sets of the fishing village, a Buddhist temple and a Saigon street built for the film.

Coppola struggled to get a coherent performance from Brando, who insisted that he be constantly shot in shadow and worked to an improvised script.

But it was Coppola's ego that almost killed the film. Asking his mentor Roger Corman's advice, he was told: "Don't go [to the Philippines for shooting]. You'll be in the middle of the rainy season." Coppola replied: "It will be a rainy picture." Cast and crew would come to regret that boast when they were desperately in need in a desperate land.

Ran is Lear set in medieval Japan. And no, it's not that boring

who helps construct the infamous list. Fiennes' fanatical Nazi officer, though superbly played, is coarsely drawn, it might have been more interesting if the villain of the piece had not been such an out and out monster.

633 SQUADRON
1964
Director Walter E Grauman
Cast Cliff Robertson, George Chakiris

For men who have an emotional age of nine (ie all of them), this film wrote the book about duty, courage, sacrifice and the importance of having a very hummable theme tune. The ill-fated squadron's mission is to destroy a Nazi munitions factory even if it means the squadron is destroyed in the process. When another squadron leader asks if the mission was worthwhile as the squadron is probably all dead, he is told: "You can't kill a squadron." Heroic stuff with Robertson impassively impressive and some beautiful shots of the Mosquito aircraft, the real stars of the film.

THE STEEL HELMET 1951
Director Samuel Fuller *Cast* Gene Evans, Robert Hutton, Richard Loo

Fuller's second most famous opening image, of a steel helmet which looks like a piece of debris but turns out to have a man under it, opens this cracking film set in the Korean War as a patrol wanders through the fog not in pursuit of a noble cause but in pursuit of some reason for actually being there. Fuller, often portrayed as an idiot savant, here directs a telling film about war which doesn't draw any easy moral lessons.

> "I APOLOGISE FOR NOT TELLING YOU SOONER THAT YOU'RE A DEGENERATE, SADISTIC OLD MAN"
>
> Colonel Dax, Paths Of Glory

TALVISOTA 1989
Director Pekka Parikka *Cast* Taneli Makela, Vesa Vierikko

War is a cold hell in this grim film (the most expensive ever made in Finland) about a group of Finns conscripted into the trenches to be bombarded by Soviet artillery and aircraft. Death is indiscriminate, messy and omnipresent in Parikka's film. Watch it and you'll also find out, if you don't already know, why the Molotov cocktail is really named after Molotov.

THE WAR GAME 1965
Director Peter Watkins *Cast* Michael Aspel, Dick Graham

Commissioned by the BBC as an hour long documentary for prime time viewing, the powers that be deemed Watkins's work too horrifying for a mass audience. Shelved, it was eventually released in the cinema, winning best documentary at the 1966 Oscars. This is the nightmarish vision of an English city in the terrifying throws of a nuclear catastrophe. Part interviews, part acting, the film is stunningly realistic. Michael Aspel narrates some of the most chilling lines of his career, almost as chilling, in fact, as when he said: "Vinnie Jones... this is your life."

ZULU 1964
Director Cy Endfield *Cast* Stanley Baker, Jack Hawkins,
Ulla Jacobsson, Michael Caine

The film that introduced two new stars to the world: Caine and Mangosuthu Buthelezi (the future leader of the Zulu nation, seen here playing his great-grandad Warrior Chief Cetewayo in the re-enactment of the battle of Rourkes Drift). The Zulus on set hadn't seen a movie before so the crew put on special screenings of Roy Rogers films. Like the rest of the world, the Zulus couldn't understand why this cowboy kept stopping his horse to burst into song. Caine was pleased with the reaction to his role as the lieutenant who doesn't like having spears thrown at him until Joe Levine, who ran the company which made the film, told him: "I know you're not but you look queer on screen." *Zulu Dawn* (1979) is not as stirring as the original but it usefully explains how the British got into that mess.

THE ALL-AMERICAN HERO

AUDIE MURPHY

Unlike, say, John Wayne – who avoided military service thanks to an ear infection – Audie Murphy knew what real action was like. The orphaned son of Texas share-croppers, his heroism on the battlefields of Europe led to him receiving every decoration for valour the US army could give. Yet strangely, it's his youth and innocence that shine through in John Huston's *The Red Badge of Courage*, in which Murphy plays a young Civil War soldier who runs away from the horrors of battle before overcoming his fear of death.

However authentic Murphy was, his limited acting smarts meant he was mostly confined to low-budget westerns. The glorious exception was a film of his autobiography *To Hell and Back* (1955), which was, until *Jaws*, the highest-grossing film ever. (He was also impressive as the innocent abroad in the film of Graham Greene's *The Quiet American*.)

Off-screen Murphy was a depressed insomniac, hooked on sleeping pills, which might today suggest post-traumatic stress disorder. After surviving bankruptcy (he was a heavy gambler) and a bar-room brawl that led to his trial for attempted murder, he died in a plane crash in 1971 when he was just 47.

WEEPIES

Great filmmaking is about inspiring strong emotions in the audience; be it excitement, terror, joy, disgust or any other reaction to characters or storylines. But the ultimate accolade for any movie must be that it moved its audience to tears (as long as they're not tears of derisive laughter) and boosted Kleenex sales.

In the years when women made up the majority of film audiences, loads of weepies were produced, the thinking being that women were more comfortable with a handful of tissues than men were. This was when classics like *Stella Dallas*, where Barbara Stanwyck gives up her daughter in order to give her a better life, or *Penny Serenade*, about a childless couple (Cary Grant and Irene Dunne) adopting an orphaned girl, were made to satisfy the demand for films that brought a lump to the throat. Not that all these films were great but they were single-minded in their intent to reduce the audience to snivelling wrecks. Modern weepies, like *Terms of Endearment*, are still mostly women's stories about self-sacrifice or doomed love.

It's important not to confuse a true weepy with the merely depressing. You may have cried buckets at *Nil By Mouth*, but it's not a classic weepy. If a weepy has a sad ending it should be gloriously, unashamedly heart-rending, revelling in its melancholy and inviting the audience to do the same. If it has a happy ending there should be buckets of schmaltz with no self-conscious apology for reaching into the audience's ribcage and giving their heartstrings a massive tug.

> **"I AM NOT AN ANIMAL! I AM A HUMAN BEING! I AM A MAN"**
> John Merrick, Elephant Man

A TIME TO LOVE AND A TIME TO DIE 1958

Director **Douglas Sirk** *Cast* **John Gavin, Liselotte Pulver**

Unusual World War II drama told from the German point of view about a young soldier finding brief happiness during a furlough from fighting on the Russian front. Sirk, who had fled the Nazis, made this intense, sweeping melodrama as a statement of his pacifism and an indictment of the barbarism and futility of sending young men to war. The novel by Erich Maria Remarque (who has a cameo in the film) was burned by Hitler's government and watching the film you realise how rarely the humanity of the German people during the war has been dealt with on screen. Added poignancy is created by the fact that Sirk's own son died during the same campaign.

THE BRIDGES OF MADISON COUNTY 1995

Director Clint Eastwood
Cast Meryl Streep, Eastwood

It's not often people cry at Clint Eastwood movies (well, only the very squeamish), but this is a superb modern weepy in the classic mould. It's about a photographer and a farmer's wife who

Elephant man is at the opera and scanning the stalls to see if his pal Lon Chaney has arrived

are both in late middle-age and, after meeting by accident, fall deeply and unexpectedly in love. The implication of the film is that if they had both chosen to follow their desires they would not deserve the feelings they have and so, as in so many sad films, they paradoxically sacrifice their future together so as to retain their love. Eastwood's camera acts like a voyeur, giving the audience glimpses of intensely private moments and creating an old-fashioned romance with a melancholy twist.

THE DRESSER 1983

Director Peter Yates *Cast* Albert Finney, Tom Courtenay

Backstage drama about an overbearing egomaniacal actor (Finney) always referred to as "Sir" and his devoted, put upon dresser, Norman (Courtenay). As Sir's troupe brings Shakespeare to the provinces he is in decline, drinking too much and unable to remember whether he is playing Lear or Othello. Without his dresser cajoling and massaging his ego the show most definitely would not go on. A beautiful story of a relationship between two men that's coming to the end of a long road, with incredibly moving performances from both leads as well as the supporting cast, especially Michael Gough as the old dodderer playing Lear's fool.

THE ELEPHANT MAN 1980

Director David Lynch *Cast* John Hurt, Anthony Hopkins

Based on the true story of the rehabilitation of John Merrick, horribly disfigured with Proteus Syndrome, rescued from being a sideshow freak by an eminent doctor of the time. Freddie Francis' black and white cinematography is stunning, capturing every detail and making Victorian London look absolutely authentic. Despite being encased in an extraordinary rubber mask (made using casts of the real Merrick's face), Hurt gives a beautiful performance as a man discovering his inner self and coming to realise that despite his honourable intentions he may have swapped one freak show for another. The desperately poignant ending, with Merrick rearranging his pillows, can melt the least sentimental heart.

THE HAIRDRESSER'S HUSBAND 1990 LE MARI DE LA COIFFEUSE

Director **Patrice Leconte** *Cast* **Jean Rochefort, Anna Galiena**

A young boy develops a crush on his hairdresser and years later marries an almost identical replica of his childhood fantasy, living an eccentric, happy life full of Arabic music and erotic haircuts while wife Mathilde wishes never to grow old. Leconte's gentle, absorbing and offbeat love story is one of the most evocative and saddest romances on film. Sensual, funny and beautifully made, it's a story about dreams coming true and whether they can stay fulfilled for ever.

HIROSHIMA, MON AMOUR 1959

Director **Alain Resnais** *Cast* **Emmanuelle Riva, Eiji Okada**

Haunting tale about a French actress who has a brief affair with a Japanese architect when she visits Hiroshima to make an anti-war film. He insists that despite visiting museums and trying to understand the bomb's effect she knows nothing of the true horrors, although she tells him of her appalling treatment by her family after she fell in love with a young German soldier. Even though the dialogue and performances are understated, the film is overwhelmingly moving as it sets one person's tragedy against the vast tragedy of Hiroshima, and the flashbacks set up a brilliant contrast between wartime France and post-war Japan. With lines like: "They make movies to sell soap, why not a movie to sell peace?", it's a classic of intellectual cinema that packs a huge emotional punch.

IMITATION OF LIFE 1959

Director **Douglas Sirk** *Cast* **Lana Turner, Juanita Moore, John Gavin, Robert Alda**

Ambitious mum (Turner) provides for her daughter financially while neglecting her emotionally and ignores the needs of her own heart at the same time. The eternally perky Sandra Dee plays the teenager whose coming-of-age sub-plot even involves her mother's long-lost

Phony Joanie, as her charming director called her, as melodramatic murdering mum Mildred

boyfriend. But it's the story of Annie Johnson (Moore), Turner's self-sacrificing housekeeper and her rebellious daughter that warrants inclusion here. Susan Kohner is brilliant as the fair-skinned Sarah Jane, rejected by local boys because she is black, who runs away in order to "pass" for white in the big city. The scene where Annie goes to find her daughter but doesn't give her away to her new friends despite urging her to be proud of her heritage perfectly captures the perversity of America's attitudes to race and their effect on individual's lives.

IT'S A WONDERFUL LIFE 1946
Director Frank Capra *Cast* James Stewart, Donna Reed
The all-time favourite family film about a man despairing of his future who is given the chance to see what his world would be like if he had never lived. Of course, it is a terrible place, controlled by a heartless despot where decent people are unable to be free and his wife is the local spinster librarian because he was not there to marry. No matter how many times you see this slushy, life-affirming parable of the worth of small-town life, it still brings a tear to the eye. Which makes it even more surprising that the film flopped at the box office, only becoming a perennial Christmas favourite after the copyright had expired. Poor Capra had hoped this would kick-start his career after the years spent making war documentaries.

JEZEBEL 1938
Director William Wyler *Cast* Bette Davis, Henry Fonda
Rushed out to beat *Gone with the Wind* to the big screen and effectively losing Davis a shot at the part of Scarlett O'Hara, *Jezebel* is a masterpiece of emotional storytelling. Davis is a true Southern belle, selfish and flirtatious, who flouts convention and loses her fiancé, Pres, by wearing the wrong dress to an important ball. When he returns years later she is prepared to beg to get him back but finds he has married a Yankee. As a yellow fever epidemic sweeps the state she is forced to learn about compassion and self-sacrifice, culminating in one of the great doomed-but-defiant movie endings. Davis won her second Oscar for the role and steals every scene here, making Pres' wife look even drabber by comparison. Incidentally, the famous red dress was actually green as it was deemed to photograph better in black and white.

MILDRED PIERCE 1945
Director Michael Curtiz *Cast* Joan Crawford, Jack Carson
An ambitious lower-class mother has an evil, selfish daughter who competes with her for the same man. Was this the story of

"I THINK ALLIGATORS HAVE THE RIGHT IDEA. THEY EAT THEIR YOUNG"
Ida, Mildred Pierce

Mildred Pierce or the story of Joan Crawford? Answer: either and both. This is superbly made melodramatic trash in which Crawford dominates, deserving her Oscar for best actress. Curtiz didn't want to cast her, calling her "Phony Joanie" to her face and once, enraged by her habit of glamming herself for the cameras, wiping her lipstick from her mouth with his fist. A film noir weepie even though after the movie was completed Crawford had to ask what film noir was, this gave its star a new career. Others in this vein include *Autumn Leaves* (1956) with excellent support from Cliff Robertson, but she wouldn't match this until *What Ever Happened to Baby Jane?* in 1962.

STEEL MAGNOLIAS 1989
Director Herbert Ross *Cast* Julia Roberts, Sally Field

With an ensemble cast to beat them all (Olympia Dukakis, Shirley MacLaine, Dolly Parton and Daryl Hannah also feature) and an unashamedly emotional storyline about love and loss in a Southern family, this is weepy filmmaking at its best. What sets it apart from the rest is the sparkling and, in places, hilariously funny script (for example, Dukakis' comment that an overweight wedding guest's outfit "looks like two pigs fighting under a blanket"). It's also elevated by the excellent performances from the whole cast, with Dukakis and MacLaine especially trying to act everyone else off screen.

ANIMAL TRAGIC

Now grand melodrama is out of fashion, let's hear it for the wildlife weepy. It seems that, especially in England, an abandoned puppy is enough to set us blubbing. We defy you to keep a dry eye through this little lot.

Born Free (1966)
Elsa the lioness steals the show in this gorgeous adaptation of Joy Adamson's books.

The Incredible Journey (1963 and 1993)
Whichever version you see (the later one has dialogue between the animals), when the old dog limps to his young master, it's a definitive weepy moment.

Kes (1969)
More than just an animal film, Ken Loach's extraordinary chronicle of a downtrodden boy who finds redemption in his relationship with a kestrel, is one of the most touching films ever.

Old Yeller (1957)
A Texas frontier family adopts a big, good-natured dog who is loyal, friendly and brave. Then he gets rabies.

Ring of Bright Water (1969)
This bittersweet tale of a semi-domesticated otter and his bemused human companion, is a real delight. Just watch out for the ending.

The Yearling (1946)
A young boy adopts a deer fawn, despite his mother's objections. Buy a very strong hankie if you plan to watch this one.

WESTERNS

Sadly the western is now as near as dammit dead. Every few years someone like Clint Eastwood will make one that the critics rate and there'll be a debate about whether this means the revival of the western, to which the short answer is always "no". Yet the western continues to be incredibly influential – just ask Steven Spielberg.

By 1969, word of the spaghetti western had still not reached John Ford. While talking to screenwriter Burt Kennedy, Ford remarked that if he had his choice, he would only make westerns. Kennedy asked him if he had seen any of the Italian or Spanish westerns, to which Ford replied: "You're kidding!" When Kennedy assured him these westerns were very popular, Ford asked what they were like. "No story, no scenes, just killing," said Kennedy.

Ford would die in 1973. By then the last rites had been read over the western. Deciding what killed it is like a Hollywood game of *Cluedo*: was it Sam Peckinpah with *The Wild Bunch* in the library? or Sergio Leone with *A Fistful Of Dollars* in the hall? Yet the genre is still influential. *The Searchers* is one of three films Spielberg watches before he starts a new movie.

The first movie cowboy ever to fire his pistol in anger did so in 1894. The first great western director was Raoul Walsh, who had ridden herds of cattle in his youth, starred in *Birth Of A Nation*, wore an eye patch (after losing an eye in a car crash) and discovered John Wayne, giving him the lead role in *The Big Trail* in 1930. Compare that to Ford who hadn't worked on a ranch (but said he had), insisted he'd played a Klansman in *Birth Of A Nation*, wore an eye patch for cosmetic reasons and discovered John Wayne, giving him a role in *Stagecoach* in 1939.

Until the late 1940s, one reason for the western's continuing appeal was its very predictability: the good guys always won, the 7th Cavalry always, as Gil Scott Heron said in *B Movie*, came to save the day at the last moment. But in the 1950s, influenced by film noir and McCarthyism's effect on Hollywood, the "adult western" was born. One wag famously defined the adult western as a western where the cowboy still kisses his horse at the end but feels guilty about it. But in the new West (in films like *The Gunfighter* and *Shane*), the gunfighters were eternally

"THIS STRETCH OF ROAD RUNS BETWEEN NOWHERE AND NOT MUCH ELSE"
Indian Shop Owner, Lone Star

weary, the populace likely to be more indifferent or cowardly (as in *High Noon*) than in earlier films and the moral resolution much less tidy. This sea change even began to affect the old masters like Ford, whose finest work in this decade (*She Wore A Yellow Ribbon*, *The Searchers*) had a moral and emotional complexity that belied his self-image as a "hard nosed director" for whom each film was "a job of work".

Ironically, the anti-heroism of films like *Lonely Are The Brave* (1962) may have paved the way for spaghetti westerns. At their worst, these were violent cartoons but at their best (in Leone's hands) they had a quirky momentum which Hollywood seemed to have lost. (Apart from William 'One Shot' Beaudine's heroic bid to meld western and horror with films like *Billy The Kid vs Dracula*.) Even the Duke had a fallow period (creatively) in the 1960s, spending most of his films living up to his writer Jimmy Grant's dictum that "All you need for a western is a hoity toity dame with big tits the Duke can put over his knee and spank".

Wayne had a late golden period from *True Grit* onwards but his death from cancer in 1976 marked the end of the traditional western. The new western, infused by Leone's ideas and techniques, could be seen in that year's *The Outlaw Josey Wales*, in Robert Altman's *McCabe And Mrs Miller* (1971) and the bizarre *El Topo* (1971), while the traditional formula was wittily deconstructed by Mel Brooks in *Blazing Saddles* (1974). The revisionist western – such as *Unforgiven* – still prospers with releases like *Tears Of The Black Tiger*, the Thai western whose gunfights top Peckinpah's. Even Sam never got around to having a baddie's teeth shower out of his mouth in fragments.

The western, like the poor, will always be with us. The old stock companies of cast and crew that supported great directors like Ford may have gone, but what we all share is a repertory company full of archetypes: the reluctant hero, the black-hatted villain, the whore with the heart of gold, the philosophising bartender. They remain in our memory, in a celluloid equivalent of indelible ink, for an actor or a director to use as they see fit. Yee-haw!

> **"ANY MAN FAILING TO REPORT FOR DUTY WILL BE PROMPTLY HANGED. AMEN"**
> Rev Rosenkrantz, Drums Along The Mohawk

DESTRY RIDES AGAIN 1939

Director **George Marshall** *Cast* **Marlene Dietrich, James Stewart**
A work of celluloid alchemy: Marshall's direction is dull, Stewart isn't quite at his best and Dietrich made this after a run of failures which led her to be labelled 'box office poison' by the dear folk who ran America's cinemas. Despite all that, this is gloriously funny, with Stewart as the lawman who helps a pal reform a crooked town and Dietrich as singer Frenchy, the source of Madeline Kahn's Lili von Schtupp in *Blazing Saddles*.

EL TOPO 1971

Director Alejandro Jodorowsky *Cast* Alejandro Jodorowsky,
Mara Lorenzio

This movie is too complex to be summed up in a review shorter than Tolstoy's *War And Peace,* but the tagline does as good a job as any: "See the naked young Franciscans whipped with cactus. See the bandit leader disembowelled. See the priest ride into the sunset with a midget and her newborn baby. What it all means isn't exactly clear, but you won't forget it." Even if you've got the long-term memory span of an absent-minded goldfish you're likely to find yourself haunted by this Mexican western which begins with El Topo (The Mole) riding on a horse with his naked son (Jodorowsky's own son) on his back and gets harder to fathom from thereon in.

FOUR FACES WEST 1948

Director Alfred E Green *Cast* Joel McCrea, Frances Dee,
Charles Bickford

The western beloved of trivia fans for being the only one where a shot isn't heard in the entire film. This is quite an achievement, since this budget picture follows Bickford (as Pat Garrett) chasing Joel McCrea's Billy The Kid. A film of rare, almost lyrical beauty, this is a real treat which, alas, didn't do the business at the box office. Good to watch after you've overdosed on the violence of *The Wild Bunch.*

If looks really could kill, the West would never have been 'won'. Eastwood's *Josey Wales* wasn't universally acclaimed: Benny Green said it would have been a fine film if the actors hadn't gotten in the way of the scenery

The Searchers was a great John Ford western, a great role for the Duke and a great 'making of' plugumentary

HELLER IN PINK TIGHTS 1960

Director *George Cukor* Cast *Sophia Loren, Anthony Quinn, Ramon Novarro*

Critically panned, especially by those who claimed that Cukor, as a director of women's pictures, gave far too much screen time to Loren as the blonde star of a theatrical troupe struggling to make ends meet in this comedy/romance/melodrama. But Louis L'Amour, from whose book this was made, ranks this alongside *Hondo* as his favourite version of one of his own works. Sit down and watch it without any preconceptions and you can see why. This film is also notable for the final screen performance of Ramon Novarro.

HUD 1963

Director *Martin Ritt* Cast *Paul Newman, Patricia Neal*

Alienated, cynical and unscrupulous, Hud is reprehensible, yet he famously exerts an almost irresistible fascination. This hard-hitting, adult, modern drama (adapted from the Larry McMurtry novel *Horseman, Pass By*) laments the deterioration of western moral values, as upright old-timer and cattle-rancher Melvyn Douglas fights his charismatic no-good son for the soul of his impressionable grandson. Neal won Best Actress as the blowsy housekeeper who resists Hud's easy charm and physical force ("I'll remember you, honey – you're the one that got away"). Veteran greats of old Hollywood, Douglas and cinematographer James Wong Howe, also won Oscars. Newman was one of Ritt's students when, to eke out a living after being blacklisted for Communist associations, he taught at the Actors Studio. They went on to make six films together.

JESSE JAMES 1939

Director *Henry King* Cast *Tyrone Power, Henry Fonda, Randolph Scott*

Neglected like its star, partly because this kind of biopic is out of favour, this is a much underrated telling of one of the West's most potent fairytales. Power, whose best performance as the conniving, womanizing circus-operator in *Nightmare Alley* was shunned by his fans, excels here as the most famous outlaw in the West and is ably supported by Fonda as his brother. King only directed three westerns (the other two are *The Gunfighter* and *The Bravados*), all of which are excellent. *The Long Riders* (1980), Walter Hill's take on the same legends, is worth watching because it's at the other end of the spectrum from this film – slick and fast-paced, but not necessarily more realistic.

LONE STAR 1996
Director John Sayle Cast Chris Cooper, Elizabeth Pena, Kris Kristofferson

The skeleton of a much-hated sheriff is found in the desert near a Texas town. The current sheriff suspects his own father may have committed the murder. While he's investigating the crime he does a favour for old flame Pilar, whom he might have wed if both families hadn't been so against an Anglo-Mexican marriage. The set up is marvellous and Sayle's execution more than lives up to its promise. Kristofferson is beautifully mean as the sheriff who deserved to die.

MCCABE AND MRS MILLER 1971
Director Robert Altman Cast Warren Beatty, Julie Christie

This is the anti-Ford Western – not to be watched if you are feeling suicidal, depressed or even not quite yourself. Beatty has never been better as McCabe, the braggart who tries to run a bordello with Mrs Miller (Christie). He is the doomed 'hero' of this film, which is not so much a western as an elegy to the

---

GOOD INJUNS

The first notable step forward in the presentation of native Americans on celluloid came in 1912 when director Thomas Ince filmed *The Indian Massacre*, unusually the massacre was of (not by) native Americans.

The 1950s improved matters with Jeff Chandler's portrayal of Cochise in *Broken Arrow* (1950) and Robert Aldrich's *Apache* (1954) which invited us to see the world through the eyes of its Apache hero, played by Burt Lancaster. You might wonder why Lancaster doesn't die, as is foreshadowed throughout the film. The simple answer was that United Artists wouldn't let him.

Six years later in *Flaming Star*, the half breed hero (Elvis Presley in a part written for Brando) does die, off-screen, partly because he despairs of racial peace on the frontier. The 'half-breeds must die' lesson was reinforced in Paul Newman's *Hombre*.

Tell Them Willie Boy Is Here (1969) focuses on the pursuit of the renegade Willie Boy but the reluctant sheriff Coop (Robert Redford) isn't too excited by his quest, telling a judge who's trying to give orders: "You ain't mayor yet judge, you're just running, like Willie."

Little Big Man (1970) starred Dustin Hoffman as a 100-year-old man who had been raised by Indians. Penn's theme of a white person raised by Indians would be used by Ralph Nelson in his bloody *Soldier Blue* which compared the Sand Creek massacre of 1864 to the My Lai atrocity in Vietnam. Kevin Costner's acclaimed *Dances With Wolves* (1991) took revisionism further and made $424m at the box office. Walter Hill's *Geronimo* (1993) further redressed the balance with its hero asking why there isn't enough land for everyone, a question to which the audience are invited to give the obvious answer.

WESTERN DISHES

Italy may have invented the spaghetti western but it wasn't the only country outside North America to make westerns. Here's a quick rundown of the best of the rest and the national dish they have been conveniently, and patronizingly, named after.

CHOP SUEY WESTERN

Hong Kong produced kung fu 'westerns' like *The Silent Flute*, inspired by Bruce Lee but with an international cast that included David Carradine (who has four parts), Eli Wallach and Christopher Lee.

MEXICAN WESTERNS

The most famous, if it is a western, is *El Topo* (1971), the strange tale of a Christ-like figure starring (and directed by) Alejandro Jodorowsky.

NOODLE WESTERN

Westerns in Chinese settings and made in Hong Kong were called 'noodle' westerns. The most famous were the *Once Upon A Time In China* series (no prizes for the title inspiration) which ran between 1991 and 1997.

PAELLA WESTERN

The spaghetti western was really born in Spain, where Joaquin Luis Romero Marchent made *El Coyote* (1954), one of the first Euro westerns. Two more (*Gunfight At High Noon*, 1963, and *Seven From Texas*, 1964) helped prove to Sergei Leone that you could make westerns in Europe.

SAUERKRAUT WESTERNS

Luis Trenker made *The Kaiser Of California* as far back as 1936 but the best-known German westerns were Harald Reinl's *Mannetou* series of the 1960s, which often starred ex-Tarzan Lex Barker as Old Shatterhand.

dead. The full misery of the movie is caught beautifully in the sudden pointless death of Keith Carradine and the occasional song on the soundtrack from 'Laughing' Leonard Cohen. Good as they are, neither *The Player* nor *Nashville* are Altman's masterpiece – this is.

THE MILAGRO BEANFIELD WAR 1988

Director Robert Redford *Cast* Ruben Blades, Sonia Braga, Chick Vennera

The pig is the catalyst in this whimsical tale pitting the Hispanic farmers of Milagro, New Mexico (population: 426) against each other, evil golf-playing land-developers and their henchman (Christopher Walken, underplaying for once as muscle-for-hire, who has the second-best line: "This posse couldn't find itself"). The beanfield in question is created by one farmer in anger and later devastated by the pig, leading to the final confrontation. Redford lapses into soft-focused liberal fantasy, but there are some fine moments including a gun stand-off between a truckload of octogenarians and a cop whose brains are all in his holster. Best line? Sheriff Montoya (Blades) explaining why he would have won by a landslide if Domingo and Gunther had been in town: "Those guys vote six, seven times apiece."

THE MISFITS 1961

Director John Huston *Cast* Clark Gable, Marilyn Monroe, Montgomery Clift

This very moving, but not as profound as it would like to think, movie was the last that Gable starred in, the last that Monroe completed and almost the last where anybody took any notice of Clift, who would die five years later in what one friend called the longest suicide in the history of Hollywood. Scripted by Monroe's husband Arthur Miller, the denouement was in doubt right up until the end was shot, with the playwright finally identifying with Gable and thus putting on film the hope that his marriage would end happily. The making of this film had more melodrama than the Christmas edition of most soaps but it is, at times, quite beautiful in a very melancholy way. Miller didn't really believe in the happy ending; nor do we.

THE NAKED SPUR 1953
Director Anthony Mann *Cast* James
Stewart, Janet Leigh, Robert Ryan
Another take on the old tale of a killer
and a girl, taken prisoner by bounty
hunters, who try to manipulate their
way out of captivity. The scenery is
spectacular, the Indians are a rarely
seen menace and the acting (especially
by the still underrated Ryan) is
magnificent. Stewart does well in one
of his darker roles as the bitter bounty
hunter. For a movie that sets its stall
out so clearly as a 'psychological
western' this never loses its tension.

When Lex Barker cast
off his loincloth he
enjoyed a successful
career as Old
Shatterhand, the
hero of sauerkraut
westerns

ONCE UPON A TIME IN THE WEST 1969
Director Sergio Leone *Cast* Henry Fonda, Charles Bronson,
Jason Robards, Claudia Cardinale
Bernardo Bertolucci wrote a script for Leone's magnificent
attempt to make the definitive western ("I had no lire and
I thought Leone was brilliant and vulgar"), borrowing from every
western the future director knew. In the film, the most obvious
quotes are from the iron-horse westerns, only this time the
railway is run by the villainous Fonda, brilliantly cast against
type, whose simple solution for anyone who stands in his way is
to have them executed. Bronson would make a fortune out of
the *Death Wish* movies but he is far more effective here as the
mysterious stranger who joins forces with a desperado to
protect a beautiful widow whose land the railway wants.

ONE-EYED JACKS 1961
Director Marlon Brando *Cast* Brando, Karl Malden, Katy Jurado
You can normally smell desperation in the tagline a studio gives
a movie. For Brando's sprawling, thoughtful western the best
Paramount could do was: "The motion picture that starts its
own tradition of greatness." Kubrick started directing but
eventually turned to Brando and said: "We've spent six months
on this film and I'm still not sure what the story's about." To
which Brando memorably replied: "It's about $350,000." On
one level, it's a straight revenge western with Brando as the
avengee and Malden as the sheriff who double-crossed him.
Rich in character and quite a bit too long, this is Brando's only
stint as a director (he took over after Kubrick quit in
frustration); its failure deepened his boredom and
disillusionment with movie-making.

"GET READY,
LITTLE LADY.
HELL IS COMING
TO BREAKFAST"
Lone Watie, The Outlaw Josey Wales

451

John Ford was stunned by John Wayne's performance in *Red River*, saying "I never knew the big son-of-a-bitch could act"

THE OUTLAW JOSEY WALES
1976
Director Clint Eastwood
Cast Clint Eastwood, Sondra Locke, Chief Dan George, John Vernon

When this was released, Benny Green said in *Punch*: "If only the actors hadn't gotten in the way of all this beautiful scenery it would have been a great film." This movie does have that effect on some of us. For the rest of us, this is an enjoyable romp with some of the sharpest dialogue you'll ever find in a western. Vernon, as the officer who believes the Union Army's offer of clemency after the Civil War and convinces his men to surrender, has many of the best lines. Told by a senator "There's an old saying: 'to the victor goes the spoils'", he replies: "There's another saying, Senator: 'Don't piss down my back and tell me it's raining.'" Wales escapes the massacre, and his subsequent flight and the way he accumulates the customary band of misfits makes for an entertaining tale.

RED RIVER 1948
Director Howard Hawks *Cast* John Wayne, Montgomery Clift

Hawks provided cutting-edge method actor Clift with his first screen role (and the hat given to Hawks by Gary Cooper), and The Duke with a turning point in his career, eliciting a revelatory performance as the Captain Bligh of the cattle trail. Frequently referred to as a 'western *Mutiny On The Bounty*', *Red River* also has the dimension of classical Greek tragedy (a son having to 'kill' his father to prove himself), with Wayne's tyrannical father figure Dunson – conflicted, proud, obsessive – provoking foster son Matthew to rebel on the pioneering drive of 9,000 head of cattle from Texas to Missouri on the Chisholm Trail. It's also notable as a mood piece of epic majesty, with a famous stampede and the much loved 'Yee haw' scene re-enacted in *City Slickers*. After seeing the movie, a startled John Ford told Hawks: "I never knew the big son-of-a-bitch could act!" and set Wayne more complex acting challenges in their own, legendary collaboration.

"MAN AND BEAST BOTH BLISSFULLY UNAWARE THAT THEIR REIGN IS OVER"

Intertitle, *Tumbleweeds*

THE SEARCHERS 1956
Director John Ford *Cast* John Wayne, Jeffrey Hunter

The Searchers is arguably Ford's masterpiece, referenced in films as diverse as *Taxi Driver, Star Wars* and *Close Encounters Of The Third Kind*. It was also one of the first films promoted with a 'making of' plugumentary. Wayne's towering performance as terse, tormented Ethan Edwards, driven by a relentless quest to find a niece (Natalie Wood) abducted by Indians, shows a complexity foreign to Ford's pre-World War 2 classic western heroes. In Ford's early mythos, cowboy and cavalry heroes built a nation over the dead bodies of savage Indians, but Ethan's racism is brought home to him with a shock in the sudden recognition of shared humanity. Among this emotive epic's stunning compositions is the immortal last shot of Wayne framed in the cabin's dark doorway, poised to walk away into the sun. Trivia hound's note: although Wayne and Wood run uphill in Ford Country (Utah's Monument Valley) in their climactic confrontation, the hill they scramble back down was 1,200 miles away in Los Angeles' Bronson Park.

THE SHOOTING 1967

Director Monte Hellman *Cast* Will Hutchins, Jack Nicholson, Millie Perkins, Warren Oates

This was the first existential western and one which comes to an extraordinary, genuinely unexpected, climax. Filmed (along with *Ride The Whirlwind*) for just $150,000 with a leading man (Hutchings) who'd just appeared in Elvis' *Clambake* and

THE WEIRDEST WESTERNS

7 JESSE JAMES MEETS FRANKENSTEIN'S DAUGHTER

On the run, Jesse hides out in a convenient castle where, despite the title, he meets Frankenstein's granddaughter.

6 BILLY THE KID MEETS DRACULA

"The West's greatest gunfighter! The world's most diabolical killer!" Billy gets married only to find that one of his in-laws doesn't get out much and refuses to get his teeth fixed.

5 TEXAS TO BATAAN

The two who rode together in this wartime western were Max Teerhune and his buddy Elmer (who was a wooden dummy). In this they defeat the Nazis and Japs and travel to the Philippines with 400 Texan horses.

4 HARD BOUNTY

Hard as in… well, this is the worst whore house in the West, starring Kelly Le Brock as the madam. Look out for the scene where

Le Brock pushes a villain and watch while the penny drops that he's supposed to fall down.

3 BLINDMAN

Subtle title for a subtle film about a blind gunslinger – trying to escort 40 mail-order brides – whose horse tells him where to shoot. With Ringo Starr as a villain, this played to packed houses in Karachi for six months.

2 THE TERROR OF TINY TOWN

"Ladies and gentlemen and children of all ages, we're going to present for your approval a novelty picture with an all-midget cast. I'm told it has everything that westerns have."

1 THE LITTLE COVERED WAGON

This Z western has all the usual stereotypes: the saloon singer, the disillusioned bartender, the villain with a black hat. So what's the twist? Well, they're played by chimps, their voices dubbed by (it sounds like) the same person, probably producer Sig Neufeld.

Nicholson, this is a mysterious fable about a motley crew in search, for reasons never spelt out, of a wanted man. Hellman, whose films are now regaining favour, may just be the missing link between Anthony Mann and Sam Peckinpah.

TUMBLEWEEDS 1925

Director *King Baggot* Cast *William S Hart, Barbara Bedford*

Hart was Hollywood's first cowboy star and this is his last, and finest, movie. He retired afterwards at the age of 61, fearing that audiences were more interested in pure action than the moral certainties of his earlier pictures. This is as good as silent westerns got, a spectacular account of the 1899 Oklahoma rush. Hart believed in it so much that he paid for a third of its production costs, but despite good reviews it lost money and Hart quit. Pity, because the theme (of homesteaders and cowboys fighting over the same land) was years ahead of its time and the land chase sequence is fantastic, far more stirring than either *Cimarron* film which covered the same event.

ULZANA'S RAID 1972

Director *Robert Aldrich* Cast *Burt Lancaster, Jorge Luke, Bruce Davison*

Aldrich had an unusual way with a western, as he first showed with *Apache*. The opening credits look much like any TV western but you are soon deep into allegorical territory (the allegory being drawn, as is so often the case in Hollywood westerns of this period, is with Vietnam). Lancaster is the cynical scout for a detachment of US cavalry tracking Ulzan's marauding Apaches. Sometimes the message in the dialogue between Lancaster as the been-there-done-that scout and Davison as the green lieutenant, gets too obvious, but this is well-made, gritty and very violent. Like a lot of Aldrich's films, this won't make you feel very good about the world.

> "NEXT TIME YOU BETTER PLAN YOUR MASSACRE MORE CAREFULLY OR I'LL START WITH YOU"
>
> Thornton, The Wild Bunch

UNFORGIVEN 1992

Director *Clint Eastwood* Cast *Clint Eastwood, Gene Hackman, Morgan Freeman, Richard Harris*

Eastwood received his belated due with Oscars for best picture and best direction for this, his 16th film as director – a saga of melancholy beauty and unflinching moral, physical and historical realism. It's a radical revision of his younger, iconic, supercool man with no name and few words, from a script that did the rounds for 20 years before Eastwood seized on it to play against his own myth. *Unforgiven* is an account of a reformed, retired killer in hard times (Eastwood as William Munny) who struggles to retain his humanity when he teams up with his former sidekick Ned (Freeman) to claim a bounty by avenging a knifed whore. Greying gunmen, oppressed women and the painful ugliness of death provide the dark matter; debunking western heroics and a dime novelist rewriting events he witnesses add sardonic humour. Hackman also won an Oscar for his portrayal of a sadistic sheriff, having turned down the script years before Eastwood bought it. The film is dedicated to 'Sergio and Don', Eastwood's directorial mentors Leone and Siegel.

United Artists/Kobal Coms./Up Road Movies/Arpos Universal

Sophia Loren in blonde wig in Cukor's romantic comedy western *Heller In Pink Tights*. Her pink tights are, alas, out of shot

THE WILD BUNCH 1969

Director Sam Peckinpah *Cast* William Holden, Ernest Borgnine, Robert Ryan

During the Nigerian civil war, the government showed this film to its troops, who were so excited by the work of a director who would be dubbed 'the Picasso of violence' that they fired a few rounds during and at the movie. The next day they marched off to battle shouting that they wanted to die like William Holden. Holden stars as the leader of a gang of ageing outlaws who rob one last bank to finance their retirement, but the heist goes wrong and they have to flee with Holden's reformed ex-partner (Ryan) hot on their heels. While most media attention focused on the 170 killings and the balletic violence, more striking now is Peckinpah's courage in casting his band of obsolete outlaws with actors who look so very nearly physically obsolete. It's hard, finally, not to equate the recurrence with which a bunch of wild, violently talented men are hired for a job which involves double-crossing, compromise and corruption in his films with Peckinpah's view of what it took to make a movie in Hollywood.

THE WIND 1928

Director Victor Sjostrom *Cast* Lillian Gish, Lars Hanson

The first 'adult' or psychological western. Gish is magnificent as a woman – driven mad by loneliness on a dusty plain in Texas – who murders her would-be seducer and then watches as the wind whips away the sand from the shallow grave in which she's buried her victim. Even MGM couldn't figure out how to tack a happy ending on this one, but star and director were rarely welcome on the studio lot again.

453

YIDDISH

To many people, Yiddish in the movies means a frantic Mel Brooks comedy, full of words like megillah, meshuggeneh and mishegoss. The films below were not made in the Yiddish language which explains why the classic Yiddel Mit'n Fiddle isn't mentioned.

CROSSING DELANCEY 1988

Director Joan Micklin Silver Cast Amy Irving, Peter Riegert

A sweet and thoughtful story about a young Jewish woman, Izzy, busy with her career and New York lifestyle, whose grandmother (Yiddish stage actress Reizl Bozyk) hires a matchmaker to find her a husband. When pickle-seller Sam expresses an interest, Izzy is mortified by the whole idea. The film is an underrated delight about the clash between the old way versus modern life, with an excellent supporting cast, particularly Jeroen Krabbé as the self-obsessed author who seduces Izzy, and Sylvia Miles as the over-enthusiastic marriage broker. Beautifully constructed, it deserves a wider audience.

FIDDLER ON THE ROOF 1971

Director Norman Jewison Cast Topol, Norma Crane

"AS THE GOOD BOOK SAYS, IF YOU SPIT IN THE AIR, IT LANDS IN YOUR FACE!"
Tevye, Fiddler on the Roof

Big-screen version of the hit musical based on the stories of Sholom Aleichem about a Jewish milkman trying to hold his family together during turbulent times in pre-revolutionary Russia. Pogroms may seem an unlikely subject to sing and dance about but this is a moving and beautifully made film. The music weaves in and out of the action perfectly as Tevye struggles to match the needs of his family with the demands of his traditions. Fans of *Starsky and Hutch* may be surprised to find Paul Michael Glaser in a musical role. Violinist Isaac Stern plays the fiddler's theme and solos with grace and clarity.

THE JAZZ SINGER 1927

Director Alan Crosland Cast Al Jolson, Warner Oland, May McAvoy

Chiefly famous for introducing sound to films, but its back story is as intriguing as what's on screen. When Harry Warner (of Warner Bros) bought the screen rights to the Broadway smash *The Jazz Singer*, he told the star George Jessel (who he also signed): "It would be a good picture to make in the name of racial tolerance." But Jessel didn't play the lead in the film, possibly because he was, says film historian Neal Gabler, "a strident professional Jew". The brothers Warner wanted a star as assimilated as they were, and cast Jolson as the singer who must choose between family and jazz. Odder still, his dad was played by Swedish actor Warner Oland, famous today for playing Charlie Chan. The film, in classic Hollywood fashion, fudges the choice. In the play, he takes his dad's

"Hang on a minute, didn't you used to be Fanny Brice?"

place in the synagogue. In the film, he sings *Kol Nidre* in the synagogue and then sings *Mammy* to a packed theatre.

UNCLE MOSES 1932
Directors Sidney M Goldin, Aubrey Scotto *Cast* Maurice Schwartz, Judith Abarbanel, Mark Schweid

Hugely overwrought melodrama about a wealthy Jewish sweatshop-owner who falls in love with the daughter of one of his staff, who in turn loves a young Marxist union organiser. About as subtle as a flying brick (Schwartz adapted Sholem Asch's novel, giving himself the meatiest emotional scenes), it's also a fascinating slice of life of Jewish immigrants on New York's Lower East Side, with the business owners ruling the community with their money and respectability.

YENTL 1983
Director Barbra Streisand *Cast* Barbra Streisand, Mandy Patinkin

Streisand's ultimate vanity picture, one that she campaigned for 10 years to make, is actually not as bad as you might expect from a film where a forty-something woman plays a 17-year-old boy. Yentl is a young Jewish girl who is keen to study, but is banned from doing so by the traditions of her society. Disguised as a boy, she gets a place with local scholars, falling in love with one of them (Patinkin) along the way. And it just gets more complicated from there. Saved from utter embarrassment by the genuine performances of the cast, some memorable music and deftly handled farcical situations, it is too long (12 whole solo numbers for Barbra? Please!) but still an interesting look at the restrictions that were often lifted when Jews emigrated from Europe to the relative freedom of America.

X-RATED

In the history of the cinema, X has marked the spot where a horror film became too horrific, a space movie alien became too grisly or sin a tad too obvious (or prolonged). All these films have been deemed (by various authorities) to be suitable for adults only.

A FISTFUL OF DOLLARS 1964

Director Sergio Leone *Cast* Clint Eastwood, Gian Marie Volonté, Marianne Koch

The debut of The Man With No Name (But Who Is Known To The Coffin Maker As Joe) was a brutal affair, mixing the traditional Western and Sicilian morality plays. Leone had, as Eastwood put it, "an interesting way with violence". Dissed by critics ("They simply made this out of 1,001 westerns they have seen and admired," complained one), this rejig of Kurosawa's *Yojimbo* still works, even after its sequels and imitators.

BEHIND THE GREEN DOOR 1972

Directors Jim, Art Mitchell *Cast* Marilyn Chambers

"DON'T BOGART THE JOINT"

Petronella Danforth, Beyond The Valley Of The Dolls

Overshadowed by *Deep Throat*, this slice of porno chic is well made and quite arty (although some of the 'artistic' scenes just seem amusing now). Chambers was famous in America as the "99.44 per cent pure" girl advertising a soap powder called Ivory Snow. Her purity percentage declines somewhat here as she is pleasured by nuns, a boxer and three trapeze artists.

THE BEST HOUSE IN LONDON 1969

Director Philip Saville *Cast* David Hemmings, Joanna Pettet, George Sanders

A Denis Norden-scripted comedy about government officials sponsoring a brothel, this was X-rated on its release. Norden packs his script with cracking jokes but no plot, but since John Cleese has a bit part and the cast also contains John Bird, Willie Rushton, Tessie O' Shea and dog food promoter Clement Freud, you can just sit back and wait for the next face or joke.

BEYOND THE VALLEY OF THE DOLLS 1970

Director Russ Meyer *Cast* Dolly Read, Cynthia Myers, Marcia McBroom, Strawberry Alarm Clock

Written by Meyer and movie critic Roger Ebert, this is the tale of a female rock trio who find that though successful, they can't rid their lives of such traumas as suicide, abortion, beheading and murder. Ebert says he and Meyer wrote the script in six weeks, laughing manically as they did so. Years later, Meyer and Ebert were hired to work on the Sex Pistols movie, *Who Killed Bambi?*. Johnny Rotten told them the thing he liked about *Beyond The Valley Of The Dolls* was that it was so true to life.

THE CURSE OF FRANKENSTEIN 1957
Director Terence Fisher *Cast* Peter Cushing, Christopher Lee
Horror in the 1950s was dominated by Commies disguised as aliens and ludicrous monsters until Hammer came up with this little gem which took the genre back to its roots and became, for many years, the most profitable film made in a British studio. One reason it made so much money is that they obviously didn't spend a mint on the Baron's castle. The film launched Cushing and Lee, partly because of the relish with which they and Fisher set out about the story's bloodletting.

DEEP THROAT 1972
Director Gerard Damiano *Cast* Linda Lovelace, Harry Reems
A film which reminds you the phrase 'adult movie' describes the genre, not how grown-up you have to be to watch it. Lovelace has since claimed that between 1971 and 1974 she was forced to commit various sex acts at gunpoint by her husband/manager Chuck Traynor (who, after Lovelace divorced him, married Marilyn Chambers, the second most famous US porn star). This movie was shot in six days but the only scenes where Damiano seems genuinely interested in the film are where Lovelace gives Coke a new image.

EMMANUELLE 1974
Director Just Jaeckin *Cast* Sylvie Kristel, Alain Cuny, Marika Green
The wonderfully named Jay Cocks, *Time* magazine's film reviewer when this came out, sneered: "Emmanuelle would have to go up against something like *The Greatest Story Ever Told* before it could be called titillating." Kristel is the innocent, yet sex-mad, title character who, for reasons convincing only the screenwriter, decides she wants to become a sexual animal.

FIRST MAN INTO SPACE 1959
Director Robert Day *Cast* Marshall Thompson, Marla Landi
Marshall Thompson, for once with no cross-eyed lions in sight, invents a rocket which his brother, disobeying orders, flies into space. But things go horribly wrong and he returns to Earth as a dust-covered, blood-crazed, axe-wielding monster – scary

enough to earn it an X. A few months after this was released, Yuri Gagarin lived up to the title for real.

GREETINGS 1968

Director **Brian De Palma** *Cast* **Jonathan Warden, Gerrit Graham**

De Palma made his name with two underground black comedies: this and the sequel *Hi Mom! Greetings* is a comedy which begins with president Johnson on TV and in front of the set is a book entitled *Six Seconds In Dallas*. Graham plays what is now an archetypal movie misfit: an assassination nut who draws the paths of the bullets on his girlfriend's sleeping body. This was the first film to receive an X rating and premiered in December 1968, six months after Bobby Kennedy was shot. Look out for De Niro as a filmmaker in his first credited role.

THE KILLING OF SISTER GEORGE 1968

Director **Robert Aldrich** *Cast* **Beryl Reid, Susannah York, Coral Browne**

A lesbian soap actress (Reid) worries that her character, Sister George, is to be killed off. Meanwhile, her younger lover (York) has caught the eye of a TV exec (Browne). Back in 1969, it wasn't the plot that upset anybody, not even the scene where a drunken Reid takes her frustration out on nuns in a taxi – it was the lesbian love scene that grabbed the headlines. This was proclaimed a first, although women snogging each other on screen could be traced back to the 1930 Marlene Dietrich movie, *Morocco*. The film holds up better than the fuss might suggest, although at 140 minutes it is a bit too long.

> **"GET YOUR HANDS OFF THAT STEAMING DOG TURD – IT'S MINE!"**
> Babs Johnson, Pink Flamingos

LOLITA 1962

Director **Stanley Kubrick** *Cast* **James Mason, Shelley Winters, Sue Lyon, Peter Sellers**

Vladimir Nabokov told Mason many years later that he rather liked this movie (Kubrick, he said, had added several things he'd have been pleased to have thought of) but wished it could be remade with a younger girl. It was a view some of the more left-field critics took when the film was released even though, as Mason points out, in the book Lolita ages from 12 to 18.

MIDNIGHT COWBOY 1969

Director **John Schlesinger** *Cast* **Dustin Hoffman, Jon Voight**

This is a touching movie (originally supposed to star Elvis as a gigolo) about a country boy who wants to become a (straight) male prostitute in New York, his descent into seediness and poverty, and his street-hustling pal's eventual death. Maybe it's the strong lead performances, or the way Schlesinger keeps it ticking along, or Nilsson's *Everybody Talkin'*, but this movie is far more enjoyable than it has any right to be from the synopsis.

PINK FLAMINGOS 1972
Director John Waters *Cast* Divine, David Lochary, Mink Stole

Divine proved that he would do anything for the sake of his art when he ate dog faeces in this, his breakthrough film. "I checked with the doctors and they said it really wouldn't hurt me. It was strictly done for shock value. I threw up afterward and then I used my mouthwash and brushed my teeth. There was no aftertaste or anything." The director promoted this as "the most disgusting movie of all time" which says it all really.

SATURDAY NIGHT SUNDAY MORNING 1960
Director Karel Reisz *Cast* Albert Finney, Shirley Anne Field, Rachel Roberts

Frank and often funny melodrama about a young factory worker (Finney) torn between conventional life and the pleasures offered by affairs, fighting, and generally thumbing his nose at authority. The film contains references to abortion, and some fairly graphic love scenes, which led to a ban on the film in Warwickshire after the production company refused to cut scenes that the County Council deemed too racy for the locals. The producer replied, "It is fortunate that Warwickshire's greatest and often bawdy son, William Shakespeare, was not subject in his day to the restrictions of prim and petty officialdom."

SATURDAY NIGHT FEVER 1977
Director John Badham *Cast* John Travolta, Karen Lynn Gorney, Barry Miller, Joseph Cali

"You can tell by the way I use my walk, I'm a woman's man, no time for talk." That one line, from the brothers Glibb, tells you almost all you need to know about the film that made Travolta, though *Airplane*'s parody of the white-suited dance scene may now be better known than the original. The film was X-rated because when the authorities could actually understand Travolta's dialogue they realized a lot of it rhymed with buck.

Hoffman and Voight find that somehow Midday Cowboy doesn't have quite the same ring to it

United Artists/Gerome Hellman

ZOMBIES

The zombie film is not just a celluloid curiosity. Seventy years after it was born, this genre, like the unfortunate creatures themselves, simply refuses to die, spreading like a virus from its spiritual home on the island of Haiti across the world to Hong Kong and Finland.

CARNIVAL OF SOULS 1962

Director **Herk Harvey** *Cast* **Candace Hilligoss, Frances Feist, Sidney Berger**

One of the few movies in this sub-genre not to have the word 'zombie' or 'dead' in the title, this is a stranger, subtler film than most movies about the undead. Mary (Hilligoss) appears to be the only survivor of a car crash, but if she did survive, why is she intermittently invisible and why does a ghostly white-faced man keep appearing? An intriguing, eerie (if at times over-acted) film which seems to anticipate directors like David Lynch.

CITY OF THE LIVING DEAD 1980

Director **Lucio Fulci** *Cast* **Christopher George, Janet Agren**

The second of three zombie films by Fulci, whose masterpiece is probably *Don't Torture The Duckling*. Anyone brought up on the cartoon violence of Elm Street might find this a little close to the bone, literally in the scene where a head and a drill come into sinister proximity. Fulci was inspired by George Romero (whose *Dawn Of The Dead* was released in 1979) and by the need for a hit after his earlier films (full of scenes driven by his violent hatred of the Catholic church) had led to him being almost blacklisted in the Italian film industry. This film, in which a clergyman's suicide prompts the dead to rise from their graves to fulfil an ancient curse, is typical of his second career when he reinvented himself as a slick dispenser of gory thrills.

> **"WE CAN'T BURY SHARYN. SHE'S OUR FRIEND"**
> Ash, The Evil Dead

I WALKED WITH A ZOMBIE 1943

Director **Jacques Tourneur** *Cast* **Frances Dee, Tom Conway**

Before this B movie, producer Val Lewton's biggest contribution to cinema was persuading Victor Fleming not to shoot a dinner scene in *Gone With The Wind* with two grapefruit in line with Vivien Leigh's breasts. But this film helped to rescue the horror movie from a clichéd world where monsters roared, heroines screamed and heroes rescued. Loosely based on *Jane Eyre*, it relied more on atmosphere and psychology than stunts. The plot centres on whether a plantation manager's wife is mad or, as people in Haiti fear, a zombie. Two things are worth noting: the use of black singer Sir Lancelot as a Greek chorus and that the hero of this (and most Lewton/Tourneur films) is a woman.

I WAS A ZOMBIE FOR THE FBI 1982

Director Marius Penczner *Cast* Larry Raspberry, John Gillick, James Raspberry

Not a no-holds-barred satire on the mental state required to be an efficient FBI agent these days but a tale of a pair of criminal siblings who survive a plane crash only to discover that aliens are plotting to rule the world by turning human beings into zombies. The FBI persuades the brothers to infiltrate the alien force. This black and white homage to the classic zombie films and the sci-fi flicks of the early 1950s, complete with overacting, is vastly superior to *I Was A Teenage Zombie* (1987) which marks the nadir of the 1980's boom in all things zomboid.

WHITE ZOMBIE 1932

Director Victor Halperin *Cast* Bela Lugosi, Madge Bellamy

Lugosi is in his prime here – this was released only a year after *Dracula*, although he still got paid a not-so-princely $500 for this part. (Co-star Bellamy got 10 times that for her role as the heroine who is turned into a zombie by a mind-controlling mill owner on – where else? – Haiti.) Just as *Dracula*'s success launched a cycle of spin-offs, zombies would regularly return to the screen in films which increasingly looked as if they were written, shot and directed by people in a trance. Lugosi himself would 'star' in *Zombies On Broadway* (1945).

ZOMBIE AND THE GHOST TRAIN 1991

Director Mika Kaurismaki *Cast* Silu Seppala

From the brother of Aki Kaurismaki (creator of *Leningrad Cowboys*) comes not a zombie movie as such but a reflection of the family passion for rock music. Zombie (it's his nickname) is a failure – even as a gurney-pusher in a morgue – whose strengths are playing bass guitar and swilling vodka. He gets his big chance with a group but keeps meeting a band of grim reapers called The Ghost Train which has "many gigs but nobody has ever heard it play." Probably the most entertaining movie ever about a depressed, unemployed alcoholic spending winter in Finland.

> "IT HAS BEEN ESTABLISHED THAT PERSONS WHO HAVE RECENTLY DIED HAVE BEEN RETURNING TO LIFE AND COMMITTING ACTS OF MURDER"
>
> Radio Announcer,
> Night Of The Living Dead

Charlotte Bronte didn't like what they had done to her script for *Jane Eyre*

Try as he might, even Elvis couldn't escape from his post-army movies of the 1960s

GUILTY PLEASURES

Like Doris Day, everybody harbours a secret love. Often this love is for a film we were foolish enough to like without realising that to do so was a major error of taste and judgement, akin to buying a Kajagoogoo box set. Here are seven of the editor's favourites, films that he cannot defend but still likes. If you e-mail him your own (on paul.simpson@haynet.com), he'll try to include them next time. Then again, you may decide discretion is the better part of valour.

1 WHAT DID YOU DO IN THE WAR DADDY? 1966

Director Blake Edwards *Cast* James Coburn, Dick Shawn

It's amazing how desperate you can get for a bit of good cheer on a wet Wednesday evening in the Midlands when you're 12. The film is essentially a farce in which the Italians and the Americans pretend to fight over a strategically important village to fool the planes doing reconnaissance. It isn't Oscar Wilde, it isn't even *Catch 22* but for the next decade or so in our family you only had to quote Coburn saying "And I'm the queen of the maid" for everyone to dissolve into laughter.

2 HAVANA 1990

Director Sydney Pollack *Cast* Robert Redford, Lena Olin, Alan Arkin

Okay, even I admit the film is an hour too long. The stars have less chemistry than in my O level exam (and I got a U). And the script veers into a falsely poetic mode where the fact that the hero doesn't have an iron is held to be symbolic of something. But none of that prevents me watching it over and over again. It's Redford's gambler Jack Weil who fascinates me. For most of this film (set in 1958 Cuba) he is very seedy indeed. When he propositions Olin (even though he knows she's married) she rebukes him. He shrugs and says: "Hey, I can be suave but

> "WOULD YOU STILL LOVE ME IF I HAD SMALL TITS AND WORKED IN A FISH HOUSE?"
> Blaze Starr, Blaze

I figure you know lots of suave guys. I got no edge that way. But how many crude guys do you know?" He is partially redeemed by his selfless love for Olin but we see him, at the end, peering into the sunset, saying that now he reads the papers for more than the odds. "Human interest. That's what I read. Identical twins meet after 30 years smoking the same brand of cigarettes and both married to someone called Shirley." I have only found one other person who liked this movie. Mind you, there's nothing quite as bonding in a friendship as sharing a fondness for a film that is universally (and probably rightly) despised.

> "YOU CAN'T LIVE IDEAS! MOST THINGS THAT ARE ALIVE DON'T EVEN HAVE IDEAS"
>
> Jack Weil, Havana

3 EL DORADO 1967

Director Howard Hawks *Cast* John Wayne, Robert Mitchum, James Caan

Mitchum isn't really a sheriff in this distinctly minor Hawks western. He is, as Wayne tells him, "a tin star with a drunk pinned on it." But for all that Hawks is playing this for laughs, the scenes of Mitchum's drunkenness and struggle towards sobriety are very real. This may be why, although *Blazing Saddles* is funnier, this is my favourite spoof western. Brooks gives you more belly laughs but there's a warmth and a good humour about *El Dorado* which seduces me every time.

4 BLAZE 1989

Director Ron Shelton *Cast* Paul Newman, Lolita Davidovich

Although critics rated it, this movie seemed to sink without trace when it was released in 1989. True, it was a film which focused on that traditional box office poison – politics – but as it dwells on the affair between a governor of Louisiana and a stripper, it seemed to have a better chance than most. Newman wanted the part because the scandal, based on the real life of Governor Earl Long, was the start of an era where the media assumed "what was in a man's pants was more important than what was in his head." It is also a reminder that there was more to the Lousiana Longs than you might have thought if you knew them only from Robert Rossen's Oscar-winning *All The King's Men*.

Ben Gazzara has lost the plot but found a beach full of sea gulls

5 HAREM HOLIDAY 1965

Director Gene Nelson *Cast* Elvis Presley, Mary Ann Mobley

In many ways this is the worst movie Presley ever made (no minor distinction). Elvis gets to play Johnny Tyrone, a rock 'n' roll singer who is kidnapped and ordered to murder the king of a fictitious Middle Eastern kingdom with his bare hands while singing "Shake that tambourine, that tambourine, that tambourine, that tambourine." (Actually his kidnappers don't order him to sing, he just does that to keep his spirits up.) There are two beautiful women, lots of silly songs (including a touching one where his reflection emerges from a pool to sing of the treasures of love), and a midget. None of which explains why, apart from the good ones, it's the Elvis video I watch most.

MGM; 23 Giugno/Ginis; UIP/Universal/Mirage

Never mind the movie being indefensible – what about Robert Redford's dress sense? 1958 Cuba is no excuse

6 WHISTLE DOWN THE WIND 1961

Director Bryan Forbes *Cast* Alan Bates, Hayley Mills, Bernard Lee

Sometimes, nothing can destroy your affection for a movie that caught you at the right time and in the right mood. Not even the fact that: a) the director's wife spent decades plugging washing-up liquid; b) 1980s throwback Nick Heyward sang a silly song which had the same title; c) Andrew Lloyd Webber made a musical out of it, and finally d) my wife's flesh creeps whenever she sees Alan Bates, so I can only watch this when it's on telly and she's out – two things which don't coincide very often. I'm not even sure why I like it. Unlike Paddy McAloon in Prefab Sprout, I'm not in love with Hayley Mills.

7 TALES OF ORDINARY MADNESS 1981

Director Marco Ferreri *Cast* Ben Gazzara, Ornella Muti, Susan Tyrell

I saw this in the early 1980s in what they still called, without any sense of irony, an art house cinema. As the film was based on American poet Charles Bukowski's *Erections, Ejaculations, Exhibitions And General Tales Of Ordinary Madness*, most of the crowd had come to see erections and ejaculations. But as we all found out, it wasn't that kind of film. The cinema was soon rippling with laughter as 'erotic' scenes passed by on the screen. My friend and I laughed, but guiltily. Although it's almost 20 years since I saw it, for that one and only time, I find scenes (not just the naughty ones) floating around in my memory like icebergs that have come loose. But then even dodgy films can leave you with memories you will never lose.

THE END

THE ROUGH GUIDE TO

CULT MOVIES

There are more than one hundred and fifty
Rough Guide travel, phrasebook and music titles,
covering destinations from Amsterdam to Zimbabwe,
languages from Czech to Vietnamese,
and musics from World to Opera and Jazz

www.roughguides.com

ROUGH
GUIDES

CREDITS

Text editor: Paul Simpson

Contributors: Helen Rodiss, Victoria Williams, Jo Berry, David Parkinson, Edwin Pouncey, Caroline Elliott, Angie Errigo, Michaela Dooley, Andrew Duffy, Richard Pendleton, Emma Young, David Butcher, Marianne Gray, Ann Oliver, Production: Caroline Hunt, Sue Weekes, Sarah H Carter, Ian Cranna, Michelle Corps, Nadia Damon, Aaron Brown. With help from Kath Stathers and Andy Hilliard
Picture editor: Dominique Bocaly

Images provided by: The Moviestore Collection

Thanks to: Julie Christie, Ray Winstone, Juliet Stevenson, Alison Steadman, Joan Collins, Edward Fox, Bert Kwouk, Simon Kanter, Mark Ellingham, Jonathan Buckley, Michelle Draycott, Geoff and Steve at Movie Store, Catherine Keen
From an original design by Tim Scott
Cover design by Peter Dyer

Layout: Dawn Hackett, Chris Taylor, Jon Butterworth.
Picture adjustment: Link Hall
Printed in Spain by Graphy Cems.
Dedicated to: Jack Simpson, Alex Hunt, Theo, Hugo Butler and Archibald Leach

PUBLISHING INFORMATION

This edition published October 2001 was prepared by
Haymarket Customer Publishing for Rough Guides Ltd,
62–70 Shorts Gardens, London WC2H 9AH

DISTRIBUTED BY THE PENGUIN GROUP

Penguin Books Ltd, 80 Strand, London WC2R 0RL
Penguin Putnam Inc., 375 Hudson Street, New York 10014, USA

A catalogue record for this book is available from the British Library.
ISBN 1-85828-960-2

Pic Cover, Spine and Back Cover: Paramount/Long Road; DeLaurentis; Buena Vista/Miramax/A Band Apart/Jersey; Riama/Pathé Consortium